BUSINESS ETHICS

Sunil G. Savur

BUSINESS ETHICS

The Sustainable & Responsible Way

1 Oliver's Yard
55 City Road
London EC1Y 1SP

2455 Teller Road
Thousand Oaks
California 91320

Unit No 323-333, Third Floor, F-Block
International Trade Tower
Nehru Place, New Delhi – 110 019

8 Marina View Suite 43-053
Asia Square Tower 1
Singapore 018960

© Sunil G. Savur 2024

Senior commissioning editor: Amy Minshull
Assistant editor: Charlotte Hegley
Production editor: Sarah Sewell
Copyeditor: Tom Bedford
Proofreader: Elaine Leek
Indexer: Elizabeth Ball
Marketing manager: Lucia Sweet
Cover design: Francis Kenney
Typeset by: C&M Digitals (P) Ltd, Chennai, India
Printed and bound by CPI Group (UK) Ltd, Croydon, CR0 4YY

Library of Congress Control Number: 2023940663

British Library Cataloguing in Publication data

A catalogue record for this book is available from the British Library

ISBN 978-1-5296-0445-0
ISBN 978-1-5296-0444-3 (pbk)

DEDICATION

To my parents, teachers, wife, son, and so many others who contributed to my ethical journey.

To all my students and colleagues. Thank you for making me a better teacher and writer.

CONTENTS

DETAILED CONTENTS

LIST OF BOXES

LIST OF TABLES

LIST OF FIGURES

LIST OF MAJOR CASES AT THE END OF EACH CHAPTER

ONLINE RESOURCES

This textbook is accompanied by online resources to aid teaching and support learning. To access these resources, visit: **https://study.sagepub.com/savur**.

A **Teaching Guide** providing practical guidance and support and additional materials for each chapter.

PowerPoint Slides that can be downloaded and adapted to suit individual teaching needs.

Sage Business Cases provide you with additional case studies linking to key themes in the book that you can use in tutorials.

ABOUT THE AUTHOR

Dr Sunil G. Savur is a business ethics researcher and lecturer at the University of South Australia Business Academic Unit.

He has a PhD in ethical decision-making, a master's degree in manufacturing management and a bachelor's degree in mechanical engineering. Prior to academia, since 1978, Dr Savur had a successful career of over 30 years in engineering, manufacturing, and general management, working at various levels with multinationals and SME organisations from India, the USA, Denmark, and Australia.

PREFACE

Business ethics is a field that has gained increased attention and importance in recent years. With rapid globalisation resulting in unprecedented growth in scale and complexity, businesses are expected to not only make a profit but also be responsible corporate citizens, contributing positively to society and the environment. The need for ethical decision-making has therefore become ever more critical.

This book aims to teach business students at undergraduate and postgraduate levels to appreciate and practise business ethics concepts, which will lead to the ultimate goal of generating a critical mass of ethical-minded businesspeople. This will be achieved by acquiring basic understanding and appreciation of ethics in general and business ethics in particular. The ability to recognise, make ethical judgements, take action, and develop practical competence in sustainability and responsibility will help make the world a better place in the future. The book can be used as a main textbook or as a supplementary or reference book.

The first ten chapters of this book are based mainly on and inform my current business ethics teaching courses at my university. The last two chapters are new in their concepts and contents.

Over the past couple of centuries, we only have to look at the industrial, social, and environmental disasters that the world has witnessed – Enron, the Global Financial Crisis, oil spills, the Rana Plaza collapse, the VW emissions scandal, child labour, and climate change, to name a few – to acknowledge that unethical and illegal activities abound. These shockingly large disasters result in enormous costs to stakeholders including employees, consumers, shareholders, communities, and the environment. Although business schools have endeavoured to teach business ethics as an essential course in most degree programmes, it seems reasonable to postulate that current ethical decision-making models, while useful, are insufficient to comprehend, analyse, and act on the ethical issues and dilemmas that we are facing now and will in the future.

This book goes beyond the existing 'off-the-shelf' techniques usually used in business ethics textbooks. Highlighting past and current cases, the book focuses on reflection, critical thinking, ethical decision-making, responsible leadership, environmental and social governance, and benefitting communities around us. Keeping in mind that today's students will be employed for several decades into the future, this book has sections on ethical issues in the fast-changing realms of technology and well-being. In addition, emerging concepts on the effects of spirituality in management and mindfulness on business are explored. A section on the nuances of the effect of cultural and religious beliefs on business ethics will enable diverse cohorts of readers worldwide to appreciate moral imagination.

With focused real-world examples, case studies drawn from a variety of industries and sectors, and online activities available at the end of each chapter, readers and users will benefit from a deep appreciation and practical application of ethical theories and concepts. This makes the textbook not only informative but also engaging and thought provoking. Students will see a change in themselves, in the ethical climate in their organisations, and beyond to make a positive change in their communities and society. This book can also be used by business practitioners who want to understand and resolve ethical challenges. Further, the user will be able to apply concepts from the book to answer the question 'how should we live?'

Some common obstacles that students and teachers of business ethics face are the broad disconnect between ethical theories and real-world events, motivating and improving moral reasoning (ethical decision-making), infusing strong ethical values in the face of self-interest and profitability, and integrating prescriptive (what should be) and descriptive (what it is) ethics.

The chapters and the contents therein have been thoughtfully designed and sequentially laid out to meet the challenges mentioned above. It begins with the 'root' of business ethics – the purpose of business – and segues into ethical concepts related to individuals and expanding outwards to organisations and society at large, and finally to the future challenges of business ethics. Most, if not all, chapters have special relevance to a diverse audience and the decolonisation of concepts. Incorporated within this are the unique pedagogical features for each chapter which will enable 'hands-on' experiences for students and teachers alike.

We hope this textbook is an invaluable resource for students, teachers, practitioners, and anyone who cares about the future of business and society. It will inspire people to become ethical leaders who can drive positive change in their organisations and society – with a larger goal to create a more just, sustainable, and equitable world for all.

The book has 12 chapters divided into three parts:

Part I – Introduction and theories

Chapter 1 begins with understanding and defining the terms 'ethics' and 'morality'. After the definition of 'business ethics', we will discuss the 'purpose' of business – what is it and why does it exist?

Considering the importance of stakeholders, Chapter 2 will explore the idea of contested values that exist between entities who are crucial to the success or failure of firms. A discussion on stakeholder theory will lead us to the practical processes of stakeholder management.

Managing business ethics requires a basic foundation of ethical theories. Chapter 3 will introduce well-known prescriptive approaches to ethical theories needed to understand ethical issues. These include utilitarianism, deontology, virtue ethics, ethics of care, justice, rights, discourse ethics, postmodern ethics, and ethical pluralism.

Chapter 4 will introduce, explore, and understand the application of an ethical decision-making model. Its various components include moral development, organisational factors, emotions, intuitions, reflection, exemplars, and moral imagination. This will develop an understanding of 'why good people sometimes do bad things'.

Part I ends with Chapter 5 that will enable us to appreciate and navigate through challenges posed by cultural diversity in domestic and international settings. This chapter will discuss business ethics as seen through the perspectives of dimensions of culture and the major religio-cultural traditions.

Part II – Ethical issues in business

Chapter 6 will identify and highlight typical ethical problems and issues facing managers and organisations. These include ethical issues such as bribery, corruption, conflicts of interest, diversity, equity, and inclusion, hiring, downsizing, and outsourcing.

Social and environmental sustainability will be the main theme in Chapter 7. Discussions on key concepts will lead us to explore sustainable business practices, the UN Sustainable Development Goals (SDG) and interactions between environmental, social, and governance (ESG) factors.

This will lead us in Chapter 8 into the positive aspects of business ethics – corporate social responsibility (CSR) and how a business can operate as agents of world benefit. This includes concepts such as the bottom of the pyramid, corporate social innovation, and social entrepreneurship.

With globalisation comes global strategies and managing ethics overseas can be challenging. Chapter 9 discusses ethical issues and responsibilities surrounding strategies such as knowledge management, liability of foreignness, modern slavery, international transfer pricing, and corporate governance.

Responsible leadership has been recognised as a key component of business ethics. Chapter 10 will explore why it matters, challenges facing leaders in a globalised world, what competencies are required, and types of roles demonstrated by responsible leaders.

Part III – New horizons

This part has two chapters. Chapter 11 introduces and explores spirituality in management and in the workplace as an alternative way forward for business ethics. It examines the balance between instrumental aspects (useful approach to ethics as a tool to realise some external goal) and intrinsic aspects (inner commitment that the good we want is good in and of itself).

In the final chapter, we discuss ethical issues emerging from new technologies and societal and environmental changes of the future. These include artificial intelligence, algorithmic bias, digital transformation, blockchain, smart farming, space travel, automation, and human–robot interactions. The chapter also introduces corporate digital responsibility.

Recommended readings will help in broadening your understanding of the concepts in each chapter. A list of videos, a set of quiz questions, and a self-assessment questionnaire are available for each chapter as online resources which can be administered by your instructor.

Each chapter begins with an opening case to set the stage for discussing key concepts of the chapter. Chapters also have several activities that can be done in classrooms to further appreciate certain specific concepts. Every chapter concludes with two major case studies to which the Case-Study Integrative Framework approach to ethical decision-making can be applied. Details of how this framework can be applied are elaborated below.

Case-Study Integrative Framework for ethical decision-making

For use at the completion of each chapter. Using the framework:

- For every chapter, the instructor uses the case studies from the chapter or introduces a different one to the class – a case which should have relevance to the concepts in the topic.
- There are two case studies at the end of every chapter. They are from different time periods (for example, one could be from the past, and one from the recent past) and/or different ethical settings (for example, one may have been unethical and one ethical).
- Individually or in groups, students go through the details of the cases (and do more research, if required), and engage in the following framework.
- Using the Case-Study Integrative Framework in Figure 0.1, discuss and compare the two cases on the following:

The key issues:

- Identify the ethical issues in the case study.
- How do you know that these are ethical issues? Justify your selections.

Inputs (reflections):

- Reflect on what would I have done intuitively.
- Reflect on why and who is/should be concerned and affected.
- Reflect on whether values and rights are created or violated.
- Reflect on the impact on business and society.

Processes:

- Concepts in this textbook segue from chapter to chapter. Each chapter builds on the concepts from the previous chapter. The concepts become more complex as we progress further into the book – so, ethical knowledge can be added on steadily. By the time we reach Chapter 12, we will have prior knowledge of concepts from Chapters 1 to 11 – so, all or some of them can be applied to the case studies in Chapter 12.
- Identify the concepts from the current chapter and previous chapters that can be applied to the issue.
- Apply these concepts to the issue by reflecting on the questions in the case study.

Processes that can be used/added for each successive chapter:

Chapter 1: Links between purpose, meaning, vision, strategy, and action

Chapter 2: Stakeholder management plus Chapter 1

Chapter 3: Ethical approaches and theories plus Chapters 1 and 2

Chapter 4: Ethical decision-making models plus Chapters 1 to 3

Chapter 5: Cultural differences plus Chapters 1 to 4

Chapter 6: Common ethical problems for managers plus Chapters 1 to 5

Chapter 7: Sustainability and ESG criteria plus Chapters 1 to 6

Chapter 8: CSR and world benefit plus Chapters 1 to 7

Chapter 9: Global business strategy plus Chapters 1 to 8

Chapter 10: Aspects of responsible leadership plus Chapters 1 to 9

Chapter 11: Spirituality in management plus Chapters 1 to 10

Chapter 12: Future issues and directions plus Chapters 1 to 11

Outcomes:

- What could have been done?
- What can be done now and in the future?
- What are the final outcomes likely to be?

Ethical issue:	Inputs (reflections):	Processes:	Outcomes:
• Identify the ethical issues in the case study. • How did you select these ethical issues?	• Reflect on what would I have done intuitively. • Reflect on why and who is/should be concerned and affected. • Reflect on whether values and rights are created or violated. • Reflect on the impact on business and society.	• Identify the concepts from this and previous topics that can be applied to the issue. • Apply these concepts to the issue.	• What could have been done? • What can be done now/in the future? • What are the final outcomes likely to be?

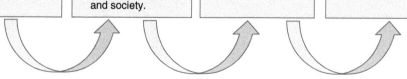

Figure 0.1   The Case-Study Integrative Framework for ethical decision-making

LIST OF ACRONYMS

ABA	Australian Banking Association
ABLIS	Australian Business Licence and Information Service
ACCC	Australian Competition and Consumer Commission
AGI	Artificial General Intelligence
AI	Artificial Intelligence
AIDS	Acquired Immunodeficiency Syndrome
ANI	Artificial Narrow Intelligence
ASIC	Australian Securities and Investments Commission
AUD	Australian Dollar
BAWB	Business as Agents of World Benefit
BCE	Before the Common Era
BoP	Bottom of the Pyramid
BP	British Petroleum
BPO	Business Process Outsourcing
BRT	Business Roundtable
CA	Capabilities Approach
CARL	Competency Assessment of Responsible Leadership
CBP	Customs and Border Protection
CDR	Corporate Digital Responsibility
CE	Common Era
CED	Committee for Economic Development
CEDM	Comprehensive Ethical Decision-Making (model)
CEO	Chief Executive Officer
CERN	The European Organization for Nuclear Research
CFP	Corporate Financial Performance
CG	Corporate Governance
CoI	Conflict of Interest
CI	Corporate Irresponsibility
CMD	Cognitive Moral Development

CNES	Centre National d'Etudes Spatiales (French space agency)
CPO	Chief Purpose Officer
CSI	Corporate Social Innovation
CSP	Corporate Social Performance
CSR	Corporate Social Responsibility
CV	Curriculum Vitae
DA	Delta Airlines
DDT	Dichlorodiphenyltrichloroethane (a chemical)
DEI	Diversity, Equity, and Inclusion
DfE	Design for the Environment
DMNE	Developed Country Multinational Enterprise
DoJ	Department of Justice, USA
EDM	Ethical Decision-Making
EEO	Equal Employment Opportunity
EF	Ecological Footprint
EGOS	European Group for Organizational Studies
EMNE	Emerging Country Multinational Enterprise
EMS	Environment Management System
EPA	Environmental Protection Agency
ERP	Enterprise Resource Planning
ESA	European Space Agency
ESG	Environment, Social, and Governance
ESI	Expressions of Spirituality Inventory
ESI-R	Expressions of Spirituality Inventory – Revised
EV	Electric Vehicles
EPS	Earnings per Share
ETL	Extra-Terrestrial Life
EY	Ernst & Young
FAA	Federal Aviation Administration, USA
FBI	Federal Bureau of Investigation, USA
FC	Four Component
FCEV	Fuel Cell Electric Vehicles
FCPA	Foreign Corrupt Practices Act
FDA	Food and Drug Administration, USA

FDI	Foreign Direct Investment
FoE	Firms of Endearment
FSC	Forest Stewardship Council
GB	Gigabyte
GBBI	Ghana Bamboo Bikes Initiative
GDP	Gross Domestic Product
GHG	Greenhouse Gases
GLOBE	Global Leadership and Organizational Behavior Effectiveness
GRI	Global Reporting Initiative
HBR	Harvard Business Review
HIV	Human Immunodeficiency Virus
HR	Human Resources
HRI	Human–Robot Interaction
HRM	Human Resource Management
HUL	Hindustan Lever
IBM	International Business Machines
ICAC	Independent Commission Against Corruption
ICEV	Internal Combustions Engine Vehicles
ICU	Intensive Care Unit
ILO	International Labour Organisation
IMF	International Monetary Fund
INR	Indian National Rupee
IoT	Internet of Things
IP	Intellectual Property
IPAT	Impact, Population, Affluence, Technology
IPCC	Intergovernmental Panel of Climate Change
IPO	Initial Public Offering (of shares)
ISRO	Indian Space Research Organisation
IT	Information Technology
ITP	International Transfer Pricing
LoF	Liability of Foreignness
JR	Jaipur Rugs
KM	Knowledge Management
KPMG	Klynveld Peat Marwick Goerdeler (the professional services firm)

LEED	Leadership in Energy and Environmental Design
LGBTQIA+	Lesbian, Gay, Bisexual, Transgender, Queer/Questioning, Intersex, Asexual, and Other
LIBOR	London Inter-Bank Offered Rate
M&A	Mergers and Acquisitions
MCAS	Manoeuvring Characteristics Augmentation System
MDMSB	Mann Deshi Mahila Sahakari Bank
MJ	Megajoules
MNC	Multinational Corporation
MNE	Multinational Enterprise
NASA	National Aeronautics and Space Administration
NBA	National Basketball Association
NGO	Non-Governmental Organisation
NSPE	National Society of Professional Engineers
NSW	New South Wales, Australia
OECD	Organisation for Economic Cooperation and Development
OHCHR	Office of the High Commissioner of Human Rights
OSI	Organisational Spirituality Identity
OST	Outer Space Treaty
PB	Planetary Boundaries
PCSR	Political Corporate Social Responsibility
PET	Polyethylene Terephthalate
PF	Philanthropic Foundations
Plc	Public Limited Company
PNG	Papua New Guinea
P–O	Person-Organisation
PoCA	Prevention of Corruption (Amendment) Act
PPE	Personal Protection Equipment
PRI	Principles of Responsible Investment
PwC	Price Waterhouse Cooper
R	Rand – South African currency
R&D	Research and Development
RBI	Reserve Bank of India
REE	Rare Earth Elements
RGE	Rapid Growth Economies

RL	Responsible Leadership
ROA	Return on Assets
ROE	Return on Equity
ROSCOSMOS	Russian Space Corporation
S&P 500	Standard & Poor 500 (a stock market index)
SDG	Sustainable Development Goals
SE	Social Entrepreneurship
SEB	State Electricity Board
SME	Small and Medium Enterprises
TBL	Triple Bottom Line
TED	Technology, Entertainment, and Design
TMT	Top Management Team
UA	United Airlines
UAE	United Arab Emirates
UDHR	Universal Declaration of Human Rights
UK	United Kingdom
UN	United Nations
UNCED	UN Conference of Environment and Development
UNEP	United Nations Environment Programme
UNEPFI	United Nations Environment Program Finance Initiative
UNGC	United Nations Global Compact
UNHRC	United Nations Human Rights Council
UNODC	United Nations Office of Drugs and Crime
UNOOSA	United Nations Office for Outer Space Affairs
US/USA	United States/United States of America
USD	United States Dollar
USEPA	US Environmental Protection Agency
VW	Volkswagen
WBCSD	World Business Council for Sustainable Development
WCED	World Commission on Environment and Development
WEF	World Economic Forum
WFH	Working from Home
WHO	World Health Organization
WPS	Workplace Spirituality
WTTC	World Travel & Tourism Council

ACKNOWLEDGEMENTS

Many people helped me create this book. Firstly, I am grateful for the assistance and support of many colleagues from my university, the University of South Australia (UniSA) in Adelaide. They helped me shape the book with their insights, suggestions, and ideas. They include Chris Provis and Howard Harris for insights into ethical theories and checking drafts of several chapters; Sukhbir Sandhu for insights into sustainability; Manjit Monga for social entrepreneurship; the UniSA business leadership team of Andrew Beer, You-il Lee, Ying Zhu, Peter Stevens, Lan Snell, and Cathie Brown for their suggestions and ideas; and Nicola Pless for inspiration on responsible leadership. I thank Thomas Maak (ex-University of South Australia), currently at the University of Queensland, for inspiration on various aspects of business ethics.

In addition, I acknowledge Prof. Edward Freeman, University of Virginia, for pointing me in the right direction and checking the draft chapter on stakeholder management; Prof. Laszlo Zsolnai, Corvinus University of Budapest, for checking the draft chapter on spirituality in management; and the head of the Vedanta Centre of Adelaide for clarifying spiritual concepts.

I am grateful to the reviewers of several chapters of this book for their invaluable comments and suggestions.

Special thanks to the Sage team – the commissioning editors Ruth Stitt and Amy Minshull, and their team members Charlotte Hegley and Jessica Moran – this book would not have been possible without their constant support and guidance. I would also like to thank Sarah Sewell, Lucia Sweet, Catherine Watts, Francis Kenney, Tom Bedford, Elaine Leek and Elizabeth Ball.

And finally, my wife, Suman, who not only was my anchor throughout this journey, but very patiently and diligently (being a librarian) proofread each and every one of the book's chapters.

PART I
INTRODUCTION AND THEORIES

1

INTRODUCTION, HISTORY, AND PURPOSE OF BUSINESS

─Learning objectives─

On completion of this chapter, you should be able to:

- Distinguish between morality and ethics
- Appreciate the origin of ethics and the history of ethical thought
- Understand how ethics are classified
- Define and understand business ethics and its evolution
- Explain the business case for business ethics
- Understand and explain the purpose of business
- Show how the purpose of a business can be implemented

─Key concepts─

- Ethics
- Morality
- The golden rule
- Descriptive, prescriptive, and metaethics
- Three levels of moral judgement
- Business ethics
- Globalisation
- Shareholder and stakeholder concepts
- Purpose of business

─Box 1.1 Opening case─

Morality changes over time

Over the past several centuries the world has seen monumental changes and reversals in societal and business attitudes. Consider the moral and legal acceptance of the trans-Atlantic slave trade between European nations, African populations, and American businesses; the anti-abortion laws; and the opposition to same-sex marriages that occurred in the past. These situations were subsequently changed to banning the slave trade, accepting abortion, and accepting same-sex marriages in some countries. In a similar vein, attitudes in business behaviour have also substantially changed over time – for example, from the appalling labour conditions during the **Industrial Revolution** period to modern-day conditions, the degradation of the environment to the new awareness of environmental sustainability. The purpose of business in the past seemed to have been based on maximising profit at any cost to satisfy investors and shareholders. Now, some businesses have decided they should align their business to a higher purpose such as social and environmental sustainability.

How did these changes happen? What are the factors that contributed to these changes? How does **morality** and purpose change over time? What do we mean by morality and what's its link to **ethics**? How do we define, create, and apply purpose in a business?

Ponder and reflect on these questions before moving on further in this chapter.

1.1 Morality and ethics

Moral dilemmas, in small and big ways, confront us all from time to time. We find ourselves faced with choices in which we need to decide a course of action, the consequences of which could be doing something that seems wrong to achieve good or doing the right thing to produce a bad outcome. Examples would be giving up our private information to access social media, prioritising ICU beds to patients with the best prognosis, to buy or not to buy fast fashion garments, restricting entry into countries to only those vaccinated for Covid-19 while vaccines remain globally scarce, editing children's genomes to achieve a desired characteristic, enabling supply of medicines without legitimate medical purpose, and raising prices of life-saving drugs exponentially when there's no justification for it.

Some questions that arise from the above examples are: (1) which is more important – doing the right thing or having a good result, (2) can the end justify the means, and (3) should we always do the right thing, regardless of the consequences? These questions hold relevance for individuals and communities in society, and also for businesses. In some situations, the relevant factors could be clear-cut enough to decide on a course of action. However, there are many more situations where the relevant factors will not be clear, and these create ethical or moral dilemmas.

The words 'morality' and 'ethics' are used in a variety of ways – 'sometimes ethics is synonymous with morality' (De George, 2010: 19); for example, a morally right action could also be called an ethical action and codes of moral conduct are also known as ethical codes. Definitions of morality and ethics are discussed below.

Morality

Morality is the term used to include those practices and activities that are considered importantly right and wrong; the rules that govern those activities; and the values that are embedded, fostered, or pursued by those activities and practices (De George, 2010: 12). This implies that morality is behavioural rules accepted by society (including institutions and governments) at a particular time in that society's history. So, as seen in our earlier examples, slavery was accepted, abortion and same-sex marriages were not. Subsequently, within the past century, the former was abolished and the latter two were accepted in most countries. Businesses such as Nike changed their business model from 'slave wages, forced overtime, and arbitrary abuse' to raised minimum wages, improved labour practices, and clean air in factories (Teather, 2005).

Ethics

Ethics is a systematic attempt to make sense of our individual and social moral experience, in such a way as to determine the rules that ought to govern human conduct (De George, 2010: 13). It involves judgements on good and bad, right and wrong, and what ought to be. Philosopher Epicurus defined ethics as dealing 'with things to be sought and things to be avoided, with ways of life and with the telos, the chief aim or end in life' (Hartman, 1998: 2). This implies that the role of ethics is to study morality using ethical theories, through observations and analysis, and if necessary, remedy any unjustifiable norms – as happened in the above-mentioned situations.

The link between morality and ethics now becomes clearer in Figure 1.1. We derive our understanding of what is good, bad, right, and wrong from a very early age mostly from adults with whom we live and interact. Thereafter, we gain more knowledge from family, schools, institutions, universities, friends, and colleagues. By the time we reach adulthood, we consider ourselves as having enough understanding of these concepts to be able to make judgements and take actions. These conceptions then transform into a set of values – which we call morality – which act as rules on how individuals, societies, governments, and organisations should behave. Individuals make friends, manage their families, and interact with others based on these sets of values. Societies proclaim and set standards of what are acceptable and unacceptable behaviours. Governments legislate laws and regulations, and organisations create their codes of ethics and conduct. Morality therefore prevails and operates in a particular period of time or era. In that period of time, if people are uncomfortable with that set of values, they will ask questions, gather data, analyse, and rationalise. Based on the outcome, they may propose and implement changes to the set of values – as evidenced by the examples given earlier. This process is facilitated by ethical concepts and theories which are used to 'test' the prevailing morality in societies. The following section will elaborate on ethical thought from around the world.

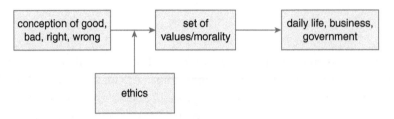

Figure 1.1 The link between morality and ethics

1.2 Origin of ethics, a short history of ethical thought, and how it is perceived around the world

The first ethical precepts must have been passed down by word of mouth from parents and elders. These were based on the need for reciprocity, survival, and kinship altruism but as societies learned to use the written word, they began to set down their ethical beliefs. These records constitute the first historical evidence of the origins of ethics. Subsequently, by attributing a divine origin to morality, the link between religion and morality was firmly entrenched. While this strong link implied that religion provides some answers to 'Why should I be moral? And how should we live?', as we will see below, there were several thoughts and philosophies that offered answers.

What follows are some major contributions to ethical thought through history. For more information see Singer (2021).

- Egypt 3000 BCE – how to live happily, ideals of conduct, how should rulers treat people justly, treating people with kindness – will lead to importance of a good name. Full of sound observations and practical wisdom but no notion of underlying principles.
- Code of Hammurabi (King of Babylon c. 1750 BCE) – an eye for an eye, a tooth for a tooth, but not consistently.
- The Ten Commandments, also known as the Decalogue mentioned in Exodus in the Hebrew Bible, were taught one for each finger so that they could be remembered easily.
- Indian ethics was philosophical from the beginning. It gave rise to several ethical systems – Hinduism, Jainism, Buddhism, and Sikhism. Hinduism derives its ethics from the *Vedas* written from about 1500 to 1200 BCE – essentially about how people ought to live, and how the ultimate truth of human existence is to understand what is right. Key concepts are *dharma* (righteousness or moral duty), and *karma* (action, work, or deed leading to cause and effect). Jainism was founded (from about 900 to 600 BCE) on the principle of non-violence as a guide to morality. Omitting to care for

an injured animal, telling a lie, and stealing are all forms of violence. Buddhism was founded by the Buddha around 500 BCE. It advocated a life devoted to universal compassion and brotherhood which might lead to the ultimate goal of *nirvana*, where all living things are free from pain and sorrow. Buddha propounded the middle path between extremes of sensual indulgence and self-mortification ideology. Sikhism originated in the 15th century CE, and it teaches living an active, creative, and practical life of truthfulness, fidelity, self-control, and purity.

• Ancient China had two great moral philosophers – Laozi and Confucius, both from the 6th century BCE. Laozi's *Dao* (Way) is based on not observing any set of duties or prohibitions but rather of living in a simple and honest manner, being true to oneself, and avoiding the distractions of ordinary living. The teaching of Confucius guides people to become a *junzi* (superior person), who is humane, thoughtful, and motivated to do what is good rather than for personal profit.

• Islamic ethics, originating from the teachings of the Prophet Muhammad from the 6th century CE, postulates that the purpose of human life is to achieve peace in this world and success in life by practising righteousness, piety, and worship. Islamic thinking in general is based on four fundamental principles, *usul*: the holy book the **Qur'an** that has 114 *suras* (chapters) – concerning mostly ethical and spiritual teachings; the **Sunnah** traditions – to denote common law; *ijma* (consensus) – to standardise legal theory and practice; and *ijtihad* (to endeavour) – to find legal or doctrinal solutions to a new problem (see the entry on Islam by Fazlur Rahman in *Britannica*).

• Western ethics can be traced back to the 5th and 4th century BCE Greek philosophers Socrates, Plato, and Aristotle, who claimed that goodness and justice are important, and are relative to the customs of each society, but they could be a disguise for the interests of the stronger. While Plato claimed that it is possible for one to know what goodness or justice is, the question or the challenge here is, why should one act justly if one could profit by doing the opposite? Plato and especially Aristotle, a proponent of virtue ethics, held that the life of virtue is rewarding for the virtuous as well as beneficial for the community. Aristotle applied an idea called the Golden Mean – a mean between two extremes such as deficiency of courage (cowardice) and excess of courage (foolhardiness). Other contributions of Aristotle were virtue ethics, *phronesis* (practical wisdom), and *eudaimonia* (condition of human flourishing or living well).

Ethics was also derived from the teachings of Jesus in the New Testament, which incorporated many moral injunctions. The first major influences to provide moral philosophy in Christianity came from St Augustine (354–430 CE) and St Thomas Aquinas (1225–1274) who blended Aristotle's teachings and Christianity. The Renaissance and the Reformation from the 15th century CE changed the focus to a new conception of human dignity and the importance of the individual. Prominent moral philosophers include Thomas Hobbes in the 17th century CE whose masterpiece **Leviathan** outlined the structure of society and government. The Enlightenment period in the 18th century CE focused on human happiness and the pursuit of knowledge obtained by means of reason. Later, David Hume postulated that reason cannot give rise to moral judgement, whereas intuition or moral sense can.

These led to two major approaches to ethical theories – utilitarianism, the idea that whatever increases the net surplus of pleasure over pain is right and whatever decreases it is wrong, propounded by Jeremy Bentham (late 18th century CE) and his successor John Stuart Mill (19th century CE) – and deontology, the idea that one's actions possess moral worth only when one does one's duty for its own sake, propounded by Immanuel Kant (18th century CE). There were others who followed and developed further on these ideas. These two approaches and virtue ethics are discussed in detail in Chapter 3.

One prominent ethical aspect understood commonly by most cultures around the world is the 'golden rule', the principle of treating others as one wants to be treated, found in the scriptures of most major religions of the world – Christianity, Judaism, Islam, Jainism, Hinduism, Confucianism, Buddhism, and other religions (Shaw and Barry, 2010: 12).

━━━━ Box 1.2 ━━━━

Understanding ethics and morality

Research how ethics and morality are defined and understood in your culture/community. Share and discuss your findings with another student/colleague. Your instructor can guide you with suggestions and examples.

Do you think ethics and morality have changed in countries that have transitioned from being colonised to becoming free? Discuss with examples.

1.3 Classification of ethics

Ethical theories have been classified into general ethics and special ethics. General ethical theory engages in developing and analysing moral issues in everyday life using easily understood language. Special ethical theory is involved in the specific problems of particular human endeavours. General ethics includes three related types of ethical study, commonly known as descriptive, prescriptive, and metaethics (De George, 2010: 13). The study and description of the morality of people, culture, or society is known as 'descriptive ethics'. The building and justification of a moral system based on the outcomes of descriptive ethics is known as 'prescriptive ethics'– also sometimes known as 'normative ethics'. Ethical theories such as utilitarianism, deontological, and virtue ethics are examples of normative ethics due to their attempt to explain and justify the morality of society in general (Boatright, 2003: 23; De George, 2010: 14). The third type of general ethics, known as 'metaethics' or 'analytical ethics', studies both descriptive and normative ethics by analysing the meaning of moral terms, studying the logic of moral reasoning, and analysing presuppositions of moral activities.

Special ethics involves the application of general ethics to solve particular problems in specialised fields such as business, medicine, engineering, accountancy, law, and information technology. Business ethics deals with business, which includes all 'economic transactions between individuals, between individuals and profit-making organisations, and between profit-making organisations and other organisations', and is involved in business activities such as producing, selling, and buying goods and services for profit (De George, 2010: 15–16). It encompasses geographical boundaries to include national, international, and global business.

Ethical theory is essential for a full understanding of the positions and arguments offered in business ethics. Most managers think of themselves as ethical people and may not see a need to have specialised knowledge or skills in ethics. However, more than three decades of research confirms that, in reality, most managers fall short of their self-perceptions of ethics. Research suggests that managers are prone to 'unintentional unethical decision-making' based on 'unconscious bias' (Banaji et al., 2003: 56). The sources of this unconscious bias have been identified as (1) implicit prejudice – bias that emerges from unconscious beliefs such as 'racism and sexism'; (2) in-group favouritism – bias that favours one's own group such as a friend, or a relative, or a colleague; (3) over-claiming self-credit – bias that favours oneself such as overrating one's own contribution leading to unfairly judging others; and (4) conflict of interest – bias that favours those who can benefit themselves such as when physicians accept payment for referring patients to clinical trials (2003: 58–61).

Ethical situations can arise in businesses that are not easily addressed by general ethical rules. This is because decision-making in business involves integration of three points of view: the economic, the legal, and the moral (Boatright, 2003: 7). The obligations of a role can appear to be in conflict with the obligations of ordinary morality such as a senior manager who is required to downsize the workforce of the organisation by deciding to outsource certain business activities. This role-act may not appear to be ethical to stakeholders such as employees but may be perfectly legal and a good economic decision for the good of the organisation. Thus, here the moral dilemma is 'should private, profit seeking organisations behave in a socially responsible and moral way, beyond the requirement of law, because it's the right thing to do or because it pays them to do so?' (Fisher and Lovell, 2009: 9). In other words, why should a business or people employed within the business behave ethically or be motivated to behave ethically beyond the legal requirement or beyond the profit-making goals of the business?

1.4 Making sense of ethics and morality

It has been suggested that individuals can have 'a number of legitimate concerns that may not be compatible with moral choice and lapses of ethical behaviour in business can be attributed to the low priority placed on the moral, even when the moral choice is very well understood' (Bebeau and Thoma, 1999: 345). What, then, is it that motivates moral behaviour and prioritises moral values over other concerns that people may have? Walker (2002) and Bebeau and Thoma (1999) contend that this is linked to the question of 'why be moral?'

The place of ethics and morality is in one way related to the consideration of consequences of what is considered as good. Why should one feel bothered about consequences to others? It can be argued that if I do not like a certain thing happening to me, I should also see that it does not happen to others. If I do not like other people telling me lies or hurting me, I should not do so to others. Another argument is to imagine a society in which there was no prohibition on murder – that is, people are free to kill other people at will. In such a society, no one will feel secure and everyone would have to be constantly on guard. Society would collapse as people wanting to survive would have to avoid other people as much as possible (Rachels, 1993: 26).

Although classical economists assume that all human behaviour is motivated by self-interest factors such as cost/benefit analysis, evidence such as helping strangers in distress, donating blood, and mailing back lost wallets to strangers indicate that people also act for altruistic or moral purpose. People are thus motivated by both economic and moral concerns (Treviño and Nelson, 2014: 23). Organisations may also be motivated to act ethically out of self-interest, for example avoiding criminal activities or gaining a bad reputation, or because it is the right thing to do. Martin (1998) suggests that there are four reasons that might persuade a business to act ethically: (1) legal – to avoid the risks of prosecution; (2) public image – to protect reputation and profitability; (3) pragmatic – the need for integrity in business transactions to maintain profitability; and (4) moral – to perform ethical actions simply because they are ethical. Reputation in particular, as mentioned by both Martin (1998) and Kaler (2000), has become an important motivation. Unethical behaviour by organisations can result in consumers boycotting their products and markets. As illustrated by Anderson (2005), damaged reputation can in turn lead to diminished sales, profits, employee retention, and ability to attract ethically motivated workers and customers. There have been several incidents and examples in recent decades to show that industries, senior executives, managers, employees, individuals, and society care about ethics for their own self-interests and for the reasons mentioned above (Treviño and Nelson, 2014). These will be more fully discussed in subsequent chapters.

However, even if there are good and sufficient reasons for individuals, groups, and businesses to behave ethically, finding and following the moral course is not always easy for individuals and may be particularly more difficult for people in business. Although the overall guide for good behaviour in business is the various laws concerning businesses, there are no clear moral guidelines when faced with a difficult decision such as downsizing and outsourcing or adapting someone else's ideas as one's own.

So, are there any moral principles or schemas that can be used to resolve conflicts and are there any means of showing that the rules of our morality are the right ones? What concepts do people in business use to make moral judgements?

1.5 Three levels of moral judgement processing

Researchers have proposed three levels of moral judgement processing: (1) abstract or general principles, (2) intermediate-level moral concepts, and (3) concrete rules or codes of ethics (Bebeau 2002; Bebeau and Thoma, 1999; Thoma, 2002; Walker, 2002).

Abstract or general principles

There are abstract or general principles that are described by philosophers and include principles such as 'greater good', 'utility', 'justice', 'beneficence', 'duty', 'moral rules', 'religious rules', 'the golden rule', and related principles such as 'equals must be treated equally'. The general or abstract level principles that can help guide individuals and businesses through ethical issues are generally known as ethical theories. Because these theories are general in nature, it is not obvious which theory should be applied to any particular circumstance, and they do not provide easy resolution (Fisher and Lovell, 2009: 101). However, they are useful because they (1) can explain why actions are right or wrong, (2) provide a decision procedure for resolving difficult situations, (3) make it possible for individuals who make moral decisions to explain and justify them to others, and (4) can be used to evaluate conventional morality. These theories include utilitarianism, deontological, virtue ethics, justice, and care encompassing Western and Eastern philosophies. Some of these general ethical theories are discussed in more depth in Chapter 3.

Intermediate-level concepts

These concepts include professional codes or policies developed for specific professionals in law, medicine, engineering, accountancy and finance, and insurance, among others. Examples are 'professional autonomy', 'competence', 'informed consent', 'confidentiality', 'due process', 'rule of law', 'whistle-blowing', and 'intellectual property'. Intermediate concepts thus apply to a range or class of situations and individuals are required to interpret and apply them in context. Examples include, among others, the NSPE Code of Ethics for Engineers, the International Code of Ethics for Professional Accountants, the Attorney's Code of Ethics, the Masters Builders Association Code of Ethics, and the Code of Medical Ethics.

The corporate and accounting scandals of companies such as Enron, Arthur Andersen, Tyco International, and WorldCom in 2000–2002 led to the Sarbanes-Oxley Act of 2002 which contains several governance and ethical initiatives for public companies. Similar legislated regulators exist in Australia such as the Australian Competition and Consumer Commission, and the Australian Securities and Investments Commission. International standards have been developed to provide guidelines and facilitate social, ethical, and environmental reporting. These include SA8000, a standardised code of conduct based on human rights and stakeholder theory (SA8000, 2022); the AA1000, a quality assurance standard for systems that can identify whether a company is acting unethically and suggest remedial actions (AA1000, 2022); the Global Reporting Initiative (GRI), which proposes guidelines and standards for reporting on the economic, social and environmental implications of business practices (GRI, 2022); the United Nations Global Compact, which provides the initiative for businesses to apply principles in areas of human rights, labour, the environment, and anti-corruption (UNGC, 2022a); and the Universal Declaration of Human Rights, which sets guidelines for human rights (UDHR, 2022).

Concrete-level concepts

These include codes of ethics and conduct at the organisational level and serve to direct individual behaviour in very clearly defined situations. These are essentially lists of specific prescriptions and prohibitions designed to serve as action guides in particular circumstances and seldom provide a rationale or explanation from moral theory. Codes at the concrete level derive their coherence from the intermediate-level concepts, and in turn the intermediate concepts may derive coherence from the more abstract and general principles such as justice or utility. Today most organisations have codes of conduct and/or ethics. A study by KPMG revealed that 76 per cent of the Fortune Global 200 of the world's largest corporations have business codes, 75 per cent of which address employee responsibilities towards confidential information, reporting of fraud, and dealing with gifts and entertainment (KPMG, 2014).

Research indicates that the intermediate- and concrete-level concepts that reflect the content of professional ethics are better guides to ethical action than abstract notions of morality.

═══ Box 1.3 ═══

Researching three levels of moral judgement processing

This activity will need some research. Individually or in groups, pick a business that you are familiar with. Download their code of ethics or conduct and determine whether the business applies:

1   Any abstract-level principles? Give examples and describe how they were applied.
2   Any intermediate-level concepts? Give examples and describe how they were applied.
3   Any concrete-level concepts? Give examples and describe how they were applied.

Do you think these levels are observable in emerging and less-developed countries? Reflect on this aspect for businesses in countries that had been colonised.

1.6 Business ethics

Reactions from people when they ask academics (who teach and research business ethics) what they teach or research are often 'isn't business ethics an oxymoron' or 'can it really be taught?' or 'it will be a very short course, won't it?' The implication here is similar to the notion that nothing can be 'bitter' and 'sweet' at the same time, and 'business' and 'ethics' cannot be combined to make sense. It further implies that businesses cannot be ethical. This reasoning has taken root due to the long list of business scandals that have been brought to people's attention in recent decades – such as hiding financials from stakeholders, irregularities in financial reporting, using corporate funds for personal investments, rushing to market unsafe products, environmental pollution, race and gender discrimination, and increasing CEO salaries after terminating employees. Of course, not all businesses exhibit such behaviour, because to be successful, businesses need values such as honesty, fairness, satisfying customers, and trust. So, when there's evidence of unethical behaviour, there's a need to understand and give an account of why does it happen, under what circumstances does it happen, what theories and principles can explain it, and more importantly what can be done to mitigate and manage it. This is the essence of business ethics.

While efforts to improve the ethical quality of business decisions have intensified over the past several decades (Ciulla, 2011; Ferrell et al., 1989; Goodpaster, 2010; Voegtlin et al., 2012), researchers have noted that lack of understanding, guidance, and application of ethical principles and moral philosophies (Ferrell et al., 1989; Treviño, 1986) could lead to ineffective ethical decision-making by business managers. Business ethics tries to remedy some of the problems by the application of general ethical concepts to solve particular problems in business.

The following section will outline the history of the development of business ethics as a field of study, research, and application. It will then discuss the business case for business ethics – 'should businesses behave in a socially responsible and moral way, beyond the requirement of law, because it is the right thing to do or because it pays for them to do so?' (Fisher and Lovell, 2009: 9).

History of the development of business ethics

With the advent of the industrial revolution and the exponential growth in innovation, production, labour, and population, the 19th century German philosopher Karl Marx (1818–1883) claimed that capitalism was built on the exploitation of labour and that the surplus between the value produced by the workers and the wages that they get paid amounts to the profit for the employer (Potts, 2011). This criticism has been 'adapted by many contemporary critics who claim that multinational corporations derive their profits from the exploitation of workers in less developed countries' (De George, 2015). In the 20th century, when communications and media technology and access to it grew exponentially, the idea of ethics in business continued and increased in people's minds. Examples of unethical or immoral activities by individuals and by businesses increased the criticism of multinational and domestic corporations that would engage in activities such as procuring manufactured items from sweat shops – for example Nike in the 1970s; securing contracts using kickbacks – for example the Australian Wheat Board, 1999–2001; product safety issues – for example the Ford Pinto, 1971–1980; corporate governance – for example, Enron, 2001; conflicts of interest – for example, when funding of research by pharmaceutical, tobacco, or chemical industry biases outcomes favourable to the sponsor (Bero, 2016); industrial accidents – for example the Bhopal gas tragedy in India in 1984, the BP oil spill in Mexico in 2010, or the Rana Plaza building collapse in Bangladesh in 2013; destroying heritage sites – for example, the Rio Tinto blasting of 46,000 year old Aboriginal sites in Australia in 2020; and environmental disasters – for example, decades of oil spills in Nigeria. In the minds of the general public, stories such as these and others emphasise the need for ethics in business.

As far back as 1961, Raymond Baumhart indicated that executives desired to raise the level of business ethics (Baumhart, 1961). Sixteen years later in 1977, Brenner and Molander conducted a similar study to compare the findings from 1961 and reported increased public awareness and concern over business ethics and even higher 'concern among those in business over their own values, norms, and conduct' (Brenner and Molander, 1977: 57). Business ethics, as an academic field, thus originated in the mid-1970s and its 'founders' were philosophers trained in ethical and political philosophy. Since the first academic business ethics conference held in 1974 at the University of Kansas and the first book on the subject in 1978–1979, the field of business ethics has evolved into an interdisciplinary area of research and scholarship – drawing from the strengths of philosophy, the social sciences, and from business itself (Arnold et al., 2010).

When unethical activities such as the ones mentioned above were made public by the media, activists such as Greenpeace International, founded in 1971 (Greenpeace, 2022), Rainforest Alliance, founded in 1987 (Rainforest, 2022), and others demanded change in business attitudes. This resulted in the development of the concept of social responsibility, more commonly known as corporate social responsibility (CSR; Boatright, 2003; Bolton et al., 2011; De George, 2015; Fisher and Lovell, 2009) discussed further in Chapter 8. The business courses on social responsibility that followed were slow to incorporate ethical theories and were primarily based on law and social issues (De George, 2015).

Business ethics became well established from the 1990s as an academic field with numerous textbooks, case studies, peer-reviewed journal articles and journals dedicated to business ethics issues such as the *Business Ethics Quarterly, Journal of Business Ethics, Business Ethics: A European Review, Asian Journal of Business Ethics, African Journal of Business Ethics, Research in Ethical Issues in Organizations, Journal of International Business Ethics*, and *Journal of Japan Society for Business Ethics Study*. It also sprouted the formation of associations such as the International Society for Business, Economics and Ethics. Today, business ethics, in academia and in practice, encompasses a large and wide body of applications – such as CSR, corporate social performance, corporate citizenship, social impact investment, sustainable business development, social marketing, responsible leadership, organisational ethics, and the Triple Bottom Line. The awareness and application of business ethics also spawned several pieces of legislations in the US, such as the Civil Rights Act, Occupational Health and Safety Act, Foreign Corrupt Practices Act, and Sarbanes-Oxley Act – which requires chief executives to certify the fairness and accuracy of corporate financial statements along with supplying a code of ethics for senior financial officers. Other countries have developed similar legislation (such as the Data Ethics Framework 2018 and Ethical Business Regulation 2016, both in the UK), and the United Nations developed the Global Compact which focuses on human rights, labour standards, and the protection of the environment.

Is business ethics getting better?

With the growth of business ethics as an academic field, the question to be asked is: is business ethics getting better? The answer does not seem to be straightforward. Carroll (2010), reviewing 20 years of the *Business Ethics Quarterly* journal, notes that top-level executive ethics eroded in the 2000s, evidenced by two business ethics eras – the Enron era from 2001 and the Wall Street financial scandal era from 2008 – and that 'the ethical problems seem to be systemic to the business system and the devastating financial impact has been worldwide' (2010: 717). Maitland (2010) suggested that the ethical business cycle is interconnected with the economic cycle of business – so, during an economic crisis or downturn, unethical behaviour decreases and vice versa. The Ethics Resource Centre's 2021 National Business Ethics Survey (NBES, 2022) found that on the one hand ethical culture strength remained high in workplaces, but on the other hand, pressure on employees to compromise standards is at an all-time high and retaliation has reached an alarming rate.

Thus, although business ethics and its various manifestations have become firmly entrenched, the concern for ethics in business continues. There may be two ways to make ethics in business more effective.

The first is to study the past. By incorporating the history of business and ethics into the study of business ethics, Ciulla (2011: 342) contends that 'it will compel us to think about the big questions concerning business and life', 'gain a richer insight into the values and motivations that shape the behaviour of people in business', and inculcate better leadership qualities in managers.

The second way is to look to the future. De George (2010) contends that since globalisation and the Information Age have changed the way business is being conducted and have also changed the ethical issues that businesses face, business ethics must change its focus accordingly. Globalisation is the process by which the economic and social systems of nations are connected together so that goods, services, capital, and knowledge move freely between nations. While there is a general agreement that globalisation is essential for reducing poverty through economic development and for achieving greater solidarity between nations, there is also evidence about ethical challenges resulting from the consequences of globalisation such as businesses closing down, increasing unemployment due to relocation and outsourcing, lowering of environmental standards, and flight of capital from nation to nation. These will be further discussed in Chapters 4, 7, 8, and 9.

Two case studies at the end of each chapter in this book have therefore been carefully selected to enable you to understand, appreciate, and analyse case studies in different periods of time. One other way of increasing the focus on ethics in business is to make a business case for business ethics.

Box 1.4

Business ethics in countries

Is business ethics getting any better? What's your opinion? Discuss using a past and a recent example as illustrations.

Reflect on whether business ethics has changed in countries before, during, and after colonisation. What has changed and why? Discuss with examples.

The business case for business ethics

In order to consider whether companies and organisations should act ethically and responsibly, we could ask: whose interests should companies and organisations exist to serve?

Should they serve the interests of particular groups within the company or society in general? There are two points of view that need to be discussed – the shareholder and stakeholder concepts.

The first view, called the shareholder concept, is based on the notion that corporations provide jobs and produce goods and services as a means to the end of increasing shareholder wealth. It considers the perceived shareholders' role of being speculative with no real interest in the long-term future of the company. According to this view, the task of a manager is to do their best to serve the interests of shareholders over and above all other interests (De George, 2010: 190).

The second view, called the stakeholder concept, is based on the notion that 'as different people may be affected differently by the same action then it is important to take these various impacts into account' (Fisher and Lovell, 2009: 17). The concept replaces the notion that managers have duties only to shareholders with the concept that managers bear a fiduciary relationship with stakeholder groups such as employees, suppliers, shareholders, customers, the local community, and management (Freeman, 2005).

If, however, the task of a manager is twofold – to serve the interests of the shareholders and also be fair to the other stakeholders, the question then is: do companies have to address the needs and values of all stakeholders? These issues will be discussed in further detail in Chapter 2.

Is ethics good for business?

On the question of whether ethics is good for business, Cohen (1996; 1999) points out that 'good ethics is good business', implying that ethical behaviour is of instrumental value only. Descriptive and empirical research on the link between ethics and return on investment (ROI) are available. A 1996 study on the perceptions of 892 students of business ethics indicated that ethical practices improve profit, ROI, the corporate culture, and public perception of the organisation (Stewart et al., 1996). There are two opposing views. One view emphasises that the ROI for ethics is problematic for business because it is difficult to justify that a company that acts ethically performs better than a company that does not. There is no empirical evidence to support that ethics pays, and because of the perception that ethics means that companies must always do the right thing, even if it is difficult and costly, it's hard to prove it brings a profit to the business. The second view emphasises that ROI for ethics has real value because ethics has an effect on expenses such as reduced expenses due to costs associated with unethical conduct, averting conduct, legal fees, insurance policies against loss, accidents, and fines incurred by acting unethically. It can have a positive impact on revenue from better business performance and reduced managerial misconduct. A 2019 analysis (see Figure 1.2) also shows ethical and stakeholder-focused companies yield much higher returns than the S&P 500 over a 20-year period – the S&P 500 doubled, ethical companies tripled, and stakeholder-focused companies quadrupled in value over 20 years (Torrey Project, 2019).

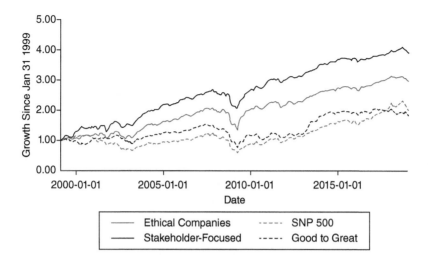

Figure 1.2 Ethical and stakeholder-focused companies outperform the S&P 500.

Source: 'Do company ethics and stakeholder focus equal greater long-run shareholder profits?'. Article published by The Torrey Project. October 25 2019. Reproduced with permission

This provides an indication that the bottom lines of companies are increasingly based not on revenue-producing assets but on the value of human and intellectual assets. This new form of equity is based on the return on relationships such as management of customers, employees, suppliers, strategic partners, and global brand reputation.

In summary, on one hand, there are several factors that can influence unethical business behaviour – competition, conflict of interest, nepotism, social pressures, power imbalance, diversity, globalisation, personal code of ethics, industry ethical climate, legislation, government rules and regulations, technology, culture, survival, and sustainability. On the other hand, there are several motivations for a business to be ethical – corporate reputation, media focus, effects of boycotts, stakeholders' satisfaction, employee recruitment and retention, and the effect of customer satisfaction on financial performance. Such motivations have resulted in businesses, senior executives, managers, employees, individuals, and society caring about ethics (Treviño and Nelson, 2014: 21–8). One indicator of businesses caring about ethics is the adoption and implementation of business codes which may consist of information such as mission and vision, responsibilities to stakeholders, and standards and rules. These factors will be elaborated on and discussed in the rest of the chapters in this book.

Businesses therefore can exist to benefit not just themselves but the community in which they operate, and indeed the world at large. Prominent examples are pharmaceutical giant Merck's decision to provide drugs to cure river blindness free of charge to millions of children in the Congo region, outdoor clothing company Patagonia's altering its entire supply chain to be environmentally friendly, Aravind Eye Clinic's model to perform cataract eye surgeries free of cost to the poor subsidised by paying patients, Hindustan Lever's Shakti project that enables rural women in villages across India to be entrepreneurs and become financially independent, and Sugru, the Irish company that promotes a culture of repair to help tackle the throwaway mindset of society. Such organisations have demonstrated their belief in a higher purpose than just making profits. The next section will define the concept of the purpose of business and discuss its relationship with the concept of business ethics.

1.7 Purpose of business

When people in classrooms and in businesses are asked what the purpose of business is, initial responses would be: making a profit, satisfying customers, designing and building products and services, and being competitive. These responses of course are not wrong, as they articulate what the business does and how. However, do they justify a business's existence in a society? These responses do not address fundamental questions such as why do businesses need to exist, what contributions do they want to make to society and the environment, and what do they want to be known for? Are businesses making the world a better place? (Mackey and Sisodia, 2014).

In essence, purpose can be said to be a definitive statement about the difference that a business makes. For this to happen, a purpose statement needs to have clarity, passion, be meaningful, and should make sense. See Box 1.7 for examples of purpose statements of businesses from around the globe.

A dataset for research on the 2019 World's Most Ethical Companies found a correlation between purpose, ethical leadership, and financial performance. The report provides the insight that to succeed at the highest level, companies must have a purpose, a 'why' for their actions, which must form the basis for ethical business conduct. PepsiCo's ex-chairperson Indra Nooyi devised the 'Performance with Purpose' strategy in which she defines purpose as a form of societal ethics (Erblich, 2019).

Many enterprises struggle or even fail to define their purpose. What is the reason for existing? What value is the business giving their employees, customers, suppliers, and the environment? And what is the business uniquely capable of providing? As Handy (2002) asks: whom and what is a business for? Perhaps the answer is not quite clear. There is a need to rethink our assumptions about the purpose of business. Many employees feel that they cannot clearly see their organisation's purpose. Most of them do not feel motivated or excited enough about their jobs. Solutions could be attracting the right people in the right roles, facilitating cross-functional collaboration, investing in the firm's purpose and ensuring leaders exemplify purpose through words and actions. Blount and Leinward (2019) suggest that a purpose statement needs to be implemented and executed.

In a similar way, brands also need to offer more than mere transactional satisfaction. They have to show a clear reason why they exist beyond profits. They need to clarify a clear purpose to attract job seekers, especially Millennials who prefer to work for companies that have a genuine purpose apart from profit. Why should job seekers choose to work for a brand, why should consumers buy a brand's product/services, and why should anyone invest in an organisation's brand? (Scales, 2020). In a TED talk about how great leaders inspire action, Simon Sinek asserts that 'People don't buy what you do, people buy why you do it' (Sinek, 2013).

A 2012 report on Good Purpose by Edelman Trust Barometer (Cone, 2012) indicated that when quality and price are equal, the most important factor influencing brand choice is purpose. There's a distinct competitive advantage when purpose is aligned with a company's brand, sometimes outpacing design, innovation, and brand loyalty. Consumers also like a brand that supports a good cause. New consumers in rapid growth economies (RGE) such as China, India, Indonesia, Malaysia, the UAE, and Brazil are showing more preferences for purpose compared to mature markets like the US and Western Europe. Consumers in the RGE markets are also more likely to pay a premium for products and services if the company supports a good cause (Cone, 2012).

So, is there a business case for identifying and implementing purpose? The EY Beacon Institute's study, in collaboration with HBR Analytic Services, surveyed global business executives on the business case for purpose. It reports that companies that are able to harness the power of purpose are most likely to have a distinct competitive advantage. They stress that the focus of 'purpose' is that meaning matters. Seventy-two per cent of the survey respondents indicated that one of the important elements of an organisation's purpose is to provide employees with a sense of meaning and fulfilment (Keller, 2015).

Leaders, therefore, need to think hard about how to make purpose central to their strategy. It has been suggested that leaders need to disseminate purpose throughout the organisation (Malnight et al., 2019), link it to meaning and connect the answers to 'why' questions to the mission and vision of the company. If there's a disconnect between the stated purpose and the answers to the 'why' questions, we need to go back and reflect.

In an interview, Hubert Joly, former chairman & CEO of Best Buy, asserted that 'business is fundamentally about purpose, people, and human relationships – not profit, at least not primarily. Companies are not soulless entities, but human organisations made of individuals who work together towards a common purpose' (Joly, 2021: 6). A noble purpose contributes to the common good, especially when an organisation's purpose aligns with an individual's own search for meaning. Business, therefore, does well by doing good (Leavy, 2021). Hubert also reiterates that business leaders should not only be clear about their own 'why', but also understand what drives people around them (Joly, 2021).

The importance of purpose has evolved from a concept to reality with businesses large and small actively pursuing the identification and implementation of the purpose of their businesses. In 2019, KPMG Australia created a new role and appointed Richard Boele as one of the first ever chief purpose officers (CPOs). Boele has stated that his tasks will include challenging the board on decisions that are not aligned with KPMG's purpose and values, sharing the stories of the firm's successes, and making the role of the CPO an integral part of the company to endure beyond his tenure (Consultancy, 2021; KPMG, 2022).

━━━━━━ **Box 1.5** ━━━━━━

Zappos

Founded in 1999 by Nick Swinmum, Tony Hsieh, and Alfred Lin, Zappos.com is an American online shoe and clothing retailer based in Las Vegas, Nevada. From 1999 to 2008, Zappos grew from USD 1.6 million to USD 1 billion in annual sales by expanding from shoes

(Continued)

to handbags, eyewear, clothing, watches, and kids merchandise. In 2009, Amazon acquired the company in a deal worth USD 1.2 billion. Zappos was consistently ranked high on the Fortune magazine's list of '100 Best Companies to Work For'.

The purpose at Zappos.com is: to live and deliver WOW. They say that they sell more than just shoes and other accessories. That 'more' is to provide the best customer service, customer experience, and company culture. They aim to inspire the world by showing that it is possible to simultaneously deliver happiness to customers, employees, vendors, shareholders, and the community in a long-term, sustainable way.

Zappos.com is known for its family spirit and fun workplace culture. Happiness is at the core of its culture – great culture leads to employee happiness; happy employees drive higher engagement and profitability, and low turnover of employees. Tony Hsieh, the ex-CEO, once proclaimed, 'We're willing to give up short-term profits or revenue growth to make sure we have the best culture'.

Zappos.com is driven by its ten core values:

1 Deliver WOW through service
2 Embrace and drive change
3 Create fun and a little weirdness
4 Be adventurous, creative, and open-minded
5 Pursue growth and learning
6 Build open and honest relationships with communication
7 Build a positive team and family spirit
8 Do more with less
9 Be passionate and determined
10 Be humble

Questions

- Do you think there's a link between the company's purpose and values to its growth in product range and sales?
- Do you think that Zappos's purpose would have remained the same or diminished after its acquisition by Amazon?
- Create a list of companies from other countries and cultures who have similar purposes.

Sources:
Zappos.com (2022)
Wiki (2022m)
Razzetti (2019)

From purpose to action

The process from purpose to action is represented in Figure 1.3. It has three blocks – why we exist (purpose and meaning), what we aim to achieve (mission and vision), and how we plan to achieve it (strategy and action). While there are some companies that have a combined purpose and mission statement, it is essential that purpose must come before formulating mission and vision statements. Purpose is the difference a business wants to make in the world, for example LEGO's 'the development of children's creativity through play and learning'. There's no mention that they want to be, for example, the number one toy company in the world. This statement should deliver clarity and be meaningful to its employees, customers, suppliers, and investors, among others. What does it mean to each of these entities? This can lead to a mission statement that establishes a meaning to fulfil that purpose. A vision articulates how the world would have changed after implementing the purpose. Strategy – such as product design, entering new markets, sales/marketing, financials, and logistics to name a few – comes next where the purpose, mission, and vision statements are cemented into proposing how to achieve them. This will finally result in actioning the strategic plans.

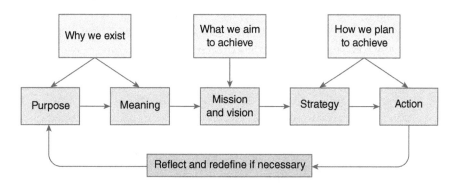

Figure 1.3 From purpose to action

Challenges

However, identifying and implementing the purpose of a business are not without challenges. Abhilash Mudaliar, Chief Portfolio Officer of Paul Ramsay Foundation and ex-Director of Research, Global Impact Investing Network, asserts that in the field of impact investing, the biggest change is the demand and desire to align purpose with business investing (Treadgold, 2022; Trinca, 2021a).

The story of the ousting of the purpose-driven CEO of Danone, Emmanuel Faber, by activist investors for being progressive, suggests what can happen if there's no right balance between shareholder value creation and a CEO's purpose of sustainability. It also indicates that leaders cannot affect systems changes on their own; they need to work together with all entities who are affected by these changes (Bris, 2021).

In a similar vein, Tim Orten, CEO of consulting firm Nous Group, observes that it can be hard for companies to embrace purpose due to existing business arrangements and pressures.

Purpose needs to be embedded throughout the organisation and that takes time – otherwise the purpose will remain just a statement with the organisation firmly focused only on profit (Trinca, 2021b).

The challenges of embedding purpose in an organisation and the need to work together with all entities leads us to the idea of contested values and stakeholder management to be discussed in Chapter 2.

═══════ **Box 1.6** ═══════

Purpose of business

Identify a business in and around where you live or work. Reflect on their stated purpose by asking yourself some of these questions:

What contributions do they want to make to society and environment, and what do they want to be known for? What is the reason for their existence? What value is the business giving to their employees, customers, suppliers, and the environment? Why should job seekers choose to work for this business? Why should consumers buy this business's products/services? Why should anyone invest in this organisation?

Has the business been able to implement their purpose into action? If yes, how do they do it? If not, what should they do? Should they change the purpose statement and/or align it to action?

═══════ **Box 1.7** ═══════

Examples of purpose statements from businesses around the world

IKEA, Sweden – to create a better everyday life for many people by offering a wide range of well-designed, functional home furnishing products at prices so low that as many people as possible will be able to afford them. https://ikea.jobs.cz/en/vision-culture-and-values/

AVON, UK – creating a better world for women which is a better world for all. https://avon.uk.com/pages/purpose

Google, USA – to organise the world's information and make it universally accessible and useful. www.google.com/search/howsearchworks/mission/

Green Monday, China – to construct a multifaceted global ecosystem of future food that combats climate change, food insecurity, public health crises, planetary devastation, and animal suffering. https://greenmonday.org/en/vision-and-mission/

Tata Group, India – stand the test of public scrutiny, what comes from people goes back to people, always promoting meritocracy, invest in people and build caring and collaborative relationships based on trust and mutual respect. www.tata.com/about-us/tata-values-purpose

VeggieVictory, Nigeria – bringing people a healthier and more sustainable lifestyle through plant-based meats and meals. https://veggievictory.com/

African Clean Energy, Netherlands – to eliminate the worst forms of poverty on a platform of clean energy and smartphone technology. https://africancleanenergy.com/

Natura, Brazil – to promote the harmonious relationship of the individual with oneself, with others and with nature. www.naturabrasil.com/pages/about-us

Summary

- The link between morality and ethics was highlighted – morality being the rules of the time or era under which society and business function, and ethics being the philosophy and theory which tests the morality and suggests changes to it if required. History of ethical thoughts was explored.
- Ethics is classified into descriptive ethics, the study and descriptions of the morality of people, culture, or society; prescriptive ethics, the building and justification of a moral system; and metaethics, analysing the meaning of moral terms and studying the logic of moral reasoning.
- We established that businesses could apply three levels of moral judgements – (1) abstract or general principles, (2) intermediate-level concepts which include professional codes or policies developed for specific professionals, and (3) concrete-level concepts which include codes of ethics and conduct at the organisational level.
- We defined, described, and explained 'business ethics'. We outlined the history of the development of business ethics as a field of study, research, and application.
- We engaged in the debates of 'Is business ethics getting better?', 'The business case for business ethics', and 'Is good ethics good for business?' To establish the business case, we introduced two views – the shareholder and stakeholder concepts.
- We theorised that the higher performances of ethical companies are the consequences of embedding the notion of a higher purpose of business – something beyond just making profits. We proposed a process on how a business can begin with defining their purpose, and finally implement concrete action plans to make it happen.

CASE STUDY 1.1
ENRON: THE RISE AND FALL – A CASE WHERE PURPOSE STATEMENT WAS NOT PUT INTO ACTION

Enron began its life in 1985 with the merger of two natural gas companies and was rebranded by its then Chair and CEO Kenneth Lay into an energy trader and supplier in 1986. Over the course of the next decade and a half, rapid growth transformed it into one the largest energy companies, and one of the most well-managed and admired companies in the US. It was named as America's most innovative company by Fortune for six consecutive years from 1996 to 2001. However, its downfall was equally

(Continued)

spectacular as its rise. Its share prices had zoomed to USD 90.75 per share in the middle of 2000 and dropped to less than USD 1 by the end of November 2001. The cause of its rapid downfall is well recorded in the business ethics, financial, and management literature. Top executives including the chair, the CEO, the chief financial officer, the head of Enron International, and others misrepresented earnings and modified balance sheets by the use of accounting loopholes, special-purpose entities, and poor financial reporting. They were able to hide billions of dollars in debt from failed deals and projects – assisted by one of the largest accounting firms at that time, Arthur Andersen (AA). On 15 August 2001, Sharron Watkins, Vice-President for Corporate Development at Enron, 'blew the whistle' about Enron's accounting practices. This finally resulted in Enron and AA's collapse, in one of the largest bankruptcies in US history affecting the livelihoods and savings of thousands of employees and investors. Sixteen people pleaded guilty. Eight executives testified against their bosses. The top executives responsible for this debacle were sentenced to several years in prison.

Surprisingly, Enron had well-developed codes of ethics and conduct. Its mission statement ('purpose' had not yet entered the business lexicon) stated:

> We treat others as we would like to be treated ourselves. We do not tolerate abusive or disrespectful treatment. Ruthlessness, callousness, and arrogance don't belong here. We work with customers and prospects openly, honestly, and sincerely. When we say we will do something, we will do it; when we say we cannot or will not do something, then we won't do it. We are satisfied with nothing less than the very best in everything we do. We will continue to raise the bar for everyone. The great fun here will be for all of us to discover just how good we can really be.

Questions

Using the Case-Study Integrative Framework in Figure 0.1, reflect on these questions:

Using the purpose to action process shown in Figure 1.3, reflect on the following:

- Purpose statement – do you think it was effective?
- What did it mean to employees, customers, suppliers, investors, and the environment?
- What kind of strategies do you think Enron developed from the mission statement?
- Find some examples/outcomes that resulted from these strategies.

Sources:
Cohan (2002)
Wiki (2022g)
Segal (2021)
Reference (2020)

CASE STUDY 1.2

LEGO: THE ICONIC TOY COMPANY – A CASE WHERE PURPOSE STATEMENT WAS PUT INTO ACTION

The name 'LEGO' is an abbreviation of two Danish words 'leg godt', meaning 'play well'. Founded in 1932 by a carpenter Ole Kirk Kristiansen, the meaning of LEGO has remained the company's ideal. His motto was 'only the best is good enough'. Passed on from fathers to sons, the company is now owned by Kjeld Kirk Kristiansen, the grandchild of the founder. The transformation of the company over its 90-year history has seen the journey from a small carpenter's workshop to a modern global enterprise – one of the world's largest toy manufacturers. Twice named the 'Toy of the Century', the LEGO brick as we know it today was launched in 1958 with its unique interlocking design offering unlimited building opportunities – for children and adults alike. Today, the company's expansion and diversification include theme parks, retail stores, business consultancy, video games, board games, films and TV, books and magazines, and clothing, including collaborations with Adidas and Levi's. In 2015, LEGO overtook Ferrari as the world's most powerful brand. As of 2021, LEGO operates 737 retail stores globally in 46 countries, positioning it as the world's number one toy maker.

LEGO is now investing USD 400 million to phase out single-use plastic bags from LEGO boxes, create more sustainable products, achieve zero waste, carbon neutral operations, and inspire children to learn about sustainability through play.

However, the journey to excellence was not without challenges. In the early 1990s LEGO suffered a dramatic downturn due to competition from toy retail discounters and a decline in the interest in playing with toys. To counter this, LEGO decided to diversify into new products such as childrenswear, books, movies, and TV ideas. The LEGO bricks themselves became increasingly complex with more unique components. Textbook strategies such as laying off people, globalising, and streamlining operations did not help.

A new CEO from outside of the family, Jørgen Knudstorp, was appointed to turn the company around. Jørgen soon realised the key strength of the company was being neglected – that customers loved LEGO and passed that sentiment to their children while still engaged with the toys themselves, that the company needed to re-engage with their community of loyal fans. He emphasised the need to promote LEGO's ideal of lifelong learning, teaching children the fundamentals of construction and creativity. His management style and ideals closely mirrored those of its founding fathers.

It is not clear when, but at some stage in the company's journey through these changes, while retaining the original motto of 'only the best is good enough', the company articulated its purpose statement to read as follows:

(Continued)

Inspire and develop the builders of tomorrow. Our ultimate purpose is to inspire and develop children to think creatively, reason systematically and release their potential to shape their own future – experiencing the endless human possibility.

Questions

Using the Case-Study Integrative Framework in Figure 0.1, reflect on these questions:

1   Where did LEGO go wrong when facing market challenges?
2   What motivated the new CEO Jørgen Knudstorp to change the direction of the company?
3   Do you think the original motto and subsequent purpose statement of the company helped revive the company? Why and how?
4   Using the purpose to action process shown in Figure 1.3, reflect on the following:

   • Purpose statement – do you think it reflects the motto?
   • What does it mean to employees, customers, suppliers, investors, and the environment?
   • Set specific mission and vision statements based on the purpose statement.
   • What kind of strategies do you think LEGO have developed from the above statements?
   • Find some examples/outcomes that resulted from these strategies.

Sources:

LEGO (n.d.b)
Wiki (n.d.b)
Brand Finance (2015)
LEGO (2022)
Comparably (n.d.)
LEGO (n.d.a)
Moss (2021)
Starvish (2013)

Compare and discuss

After completing the analyses for the above two cases, now compare the way Enron and LEGO went about articulating their 'purpose' and implementing it. Link it to the outcomes and consequences of their actions.

1   What did you learn and deduce from this comparison?
2   What would you recommend to both Enron and LEGO to do in the future?

── Recommended readings ──────────────────────

De George, R.T. (2015), A history of business ethics, (www.scu.edu/ethics/focus-areas/business-ethics/resources/a-history-of-business-ethics/).

An excellent account of what business ethics is, and its history from the 1970s to the present – a snapshot of the idea of ethics in business.

Handy, C. (2002), 'What's a business for?' *Harvard Business Review*, December: 49–55.

Handy explores why and how a few business leaders have been guilty of fraud (although they have been following rules) and asks what has gone wrong with business. The author suggests some answers and solutions by asking the fundamental question of 'what's a business for'.

Keller, V. (2015), 'The business case for purpose', *Harvard Business Review – Analytical Services Report*: 1–15.

This report from the Harvard Business Review is based on a global survey of 474 executives which found that while there's value of purpose in driving performance, only a few companies have embedded purpose in their strategies. Full of data, figures and graphs, this reading can support your understanding of the purpose of business.

Mackey, J. and Sisodia, R. (2014), *Conscious capitalism*, Boston, MA: Harvard Business School Publishing Corporation, p. 46.

These authors have reimagined capitalism – calling it conscious capitalism. Reading this will help you better understand the concept of 'higher purpose'. Very interesting and informative read with plenty of real-life examples.

Singer, P. (2021), Ethics philosophy, *Britannica*, www.britannica.com/topic/ethics-philosophy.

A very thorough insight into the history of ethical philosophy and thought complied by Peter Singer, who is one of the foremost thinkers in ethics. This will give you a good grounding and foundation for the origins and evolution of ethics from various cultures of the world.

2
CONTESTED VALUES AND STAKEHOLDER MANAGEMENT

-----Learning objectives-----

On completion of this chapter, you should be able to:

- Understand how businesses exist in an environment of contested values
- Distinguish between the concepts of ethics and law
- Appreciate why anyone should be ethical
- Describe and explain the stakeholder theory
- Apply the stakeholder management process
- Understand and reflect on the challenges of stakeholder management
- Consider alternative viewpoints such as the *Ubuntu* concepts

-----Key concepts-----

- Contested values
- Ethics and law
- Why be ethical
- Shareholders
- Stakeholders
- *Ubuntu*

—Box 2.1 Opening case—

The minibus-taxi industry of South Africa

Although the operations of the industry are informal and unregulated, the minibus-taxi industry is an integral part of the South African public transport sector and plays a critically important role in the country's economy. There are about 200,000 minibus-taxis in South Africa. The industry employs about 300,000 drivers and 100,000 taxi marshals. It also benefits 100,000 car washers and 150,000 vendors at taxi ranks. The industry accounts for 75 per cent of all daily transport – about 15 million commuter trips daily to work, schools and universities, to access healthcare or for leisure. Taxis are used by most commuters, even though they are more expensive than buses and trains, because they provide an efficient service, especially over shorter routes. They are also more widely available, reaching places that the buses and trains do not.

Given South Africa's high unemployment and poverty rates, the importance of the industry cannot be underestimated. Each taxi makes an estimated annual revenue of 450,000 Rand (R) (USD 25,200). On the route from Johannesburg to Durban (595 km), for example, the average profitability per taxi is R 37,000 (USD 2,072) a month. It is estimated that the industry generates R 90 billion (USD 5 billion) in revenue annually, and spends about R 39 billion (USD 2.1 billion) on fuel and about R 2 billion (USD 112 million) on vehicle insurance.

The outbreak of the Covid-19 pandemic resulted in hard lockdowns which hit the taxi industry particularly hard. In order to reduce the financial burden, they were subsequently allowed to operate at 70 per cent capacity. This encouraged illegal profiteering by drivers of truck and other private vehicles. Experiencing significant challenges from higher fuel prices, loss of fares, Covid-19 restrictions, insufficient personal protection equipment, and the difficulty in adhering to social distancing, the taxi industry voiced its grievances to the Ministry of Transport to ask for material and financial support. Hundreds of minibus-taxi operators in South Africa recently defied the government's Covid-19 restrictions prohibiting them from carrying full passenger loads. They complained that restricting them to a maximum 70 per cent load – to enable social distancing – made it impossible to make a profit and to earn a living. An estimated R 3.5 to 4 billion (USD 190–200 million) was required to provide relief to about 250,000 taxi owners. Drivers expected R 250 (USD 14) per day. Before the protest, the government allocated a one-off R 1.135 billion (USD 63.56 million) relief package to taxi operators. But the South African National Taxi Council rejected it as too little.

Some taxi operators have since increased fares by between 1 per cent and 25 per cent to make up the shortfall, hitting commuters. Some large organisations such as Nestle contracted private transport services to ensure safe travel for their employees. They also had compulsory sanitising protocols to support the private transports. The government eventually acceded to the industry's demand to be allowed to carry a full load of passengers – except for long distance travel.

However, overall, the industry received limited support – not everyone qualified for aid and some were not able to access financial relief due to lack of compliance with rules.

Finally, there was a call to all stakeholders in the taxi industry – food retailers, vehicle dealers, tyre companies, vehicle parts manufacturers, and the public – to contribute to the fund. Inter-governmental departments were also prepared to assist – the Competition Commission, Labour, Small Business, the Department of Trade and Industry, and the National Treasury and Transport.

Questions

- Identify the various entities affecting or affected by this situation.
- Identify the various values that are important to each of the entities involved in this situation.
- Do you think some of these values align with each other?
- Do you think some values are contesting with each other?
- What do you think the authorities should have done to prevent the situation escalating into a protest?

Sources: Adapted from Wakelin-Theron and Ukpere (2021) and Fobosi (2020)

2.1 Introduction

In Chapter 1, we asked: whose interests should companies and organisations exist to serve? It was suggested that there are two points of view – the shareholder and the stakeholder concepts. How can businesses serve the interests of shareholders and be fair to stakeholders? We also observed that stakeholder-focused companies yielded much higher returns than S&P 500 over 20 years. Further, we stressed that the challenges of embedding purpose in an organisation are linked to contested values and stakeholder management.

This chapter explores the idea of contested values that exist between entities who are crucial to the success or failure of organisations, followed by defining stakeholders, understanding stakeholder theory, its origin and current thinking, and ending with a practical process of stakeholder management.

2.2 Contested values

We begin with the idea that businesses operate in an environment of contested values. Consider a typical business – for example a clothing manufacturer. The entities that are involved and interested in this business, as shown in Figure 2.1, would be:

- Employees – they work to generate income for themselves and in the process create clothes valuable for the business.
- Suppliers – they supply materials such as cloth and machinery, and services such as power and maintenance to the business in order to generate profit for themselves.

- Customers – they buy the finished product such as fashion garments from the business.
- Investors/banks/shareholders – they provide the finance in the form of shares and working capital needed to run the business and also to receive income in the form of interest or dividends.

Figure 2.1 Clothing manufacturer and the four entities involved and interested in the business

There are many more entities, but we will restrict this discussion to these four. The values for these entities would be regular growth in income (for the employees), steady supply and increase in sales price (for the suppliers), steady supply with decrease in sales price (for the customers), and steady increase in dividends or interest payments (for the investors). Each of these entities would want to preserve and grow their value.

However, if the demand for higher wages by employees is agreed to by the business, the cost will likely be passed on to the customer by way of higher sales prices. Similarly, if the suppliers ask for higher prices for their materials, the customers may have to bear the increase in product prices. If the business absorbs these cost increases, then the profit margin will decrease, resulting in lower dividends or return-on-investment for the investors. This means that some entities will benefit, and some will not. So, in effect, the values of these entities are contesting against each other. Each one wants their demands and expectations to be met. In a similar way, there could be contested values between the business and the environment. A value for a business may be to maximise profits, but that may result in environmental value degradation such as deforestation or air and water pollution.

Business leaders and managers therefore have to ask: whose interest should companies exist to serve? Should they serve the interest of only some particular groups? Historically, there was a view based on the notion that corporations provide jobs and produce goods and services as a means to the end of increasing shareholder wealth. According to this view, the task of a manager is to do their best to serve the interests of shareholders over and above all other interests. The US organisation called the Business Roundtable (BRT) whose membership includes chairpersons, managing directors and CEOs of top companies, has periodically issued its Principles of Corporate Governance since 1978, which include language on the purpose of a corporation. Each version of that document states that corporations exist primarily to serve their shareholders. In 2019, the BRT issued a statement signed by CEOs of 243 top companies that they would aim to create value for all their stakeholders, whose long-term interests are inseparable, and to ensure more inclusive prosperity. Read the full statement in Box 2.2 (and for the names of the CEOs see BRT, 2019).

════ Box 2.2 ════

The BRT statement on the purpose of a corporation

Americans deserve an economy that allows each person to succeed through hard work and creativity and lead a life of meaning and dignity. We believe the free-market system is the best means of generating good jobs, a strong and sustainable economy, innovation, a healthy environment, and economic opportunity for all.

Businesses play a vital role in the economy by creating jobs, fostering innovation, and providing essential goods and services. Businesses make and sell consumer products; manufacture equipment and vehicles; support the national defence; grow and produce food; provide healthcare; generate and deliver energy; and offer financial, communications and other services that underpin economic growth.

While each of our individual companies serves its own corporate purpose, we share a fundamental commitment to all of our stakeholders. We commit to:

- Delivering value to our customers. We will further the tradition of American companies leading the way in meeting or exceeding customer expectations.
- Investing in our employees. This starts with compensating them fairly and providing important benefits. It also includes supporting them through training and education that help develop new skills for a rapidly changing world. We foster diversity and inclusion, dignity, and respect.
- Dealing fairly and ethically with our suppliers. We are dedicated to serving as good partners to the other companies, large, and small, that help us meet our missions.
- Supporting the communities in which we work. We respect the people in our communities and protect the environment by embracing sustainable practices across our businesses.

(Continued)

- Generating long-term value for shareholders, who provide the capital that allows companies to invest, grow, and innovate. We are committed to transparency and effective engagement with shareholders.

Each of our stakeholders is essential. We commit to deliver value to all of them, for the future success of our companies, our communities, and our country.

Signed on August 29, 2019, by CEOs of 243 large companies

Source: https://opportunity.businessroundtable.org/ourcommitment/

To understand the contexts that could have prompted the CEOs to issue such a statement, we only have to look at some of the well-known financial, environmental, and social issues over the past few decades. Major examples are:

- Financial: Enron 2001 US, Tyco 2002 US, the Global Financial Crisis 2008 US, the Bernie Madoff Ponzi scheme 2008 US, 2G Spectrum 2008 India, Satyam 2009 India, LIBOR scandal 2012 UK, 1MDB 2015 Malaysia, Choi Soon-sil 2016 South Korea, and Banking and financial services 2017 Australia.
- Environmental: Bhopal 1984 India, Chernobyl 1986 Soviet Union, Exxon Valdez 1989 US, Brent Spar 1995 UK, BP oil spill 2010 US, and VW emissions 2015 Germany.
- Social: Nike sweatshops 1990s US, fast fashion from 1990 onwards, and the Rana Plaza building collapse 2014 Bangladesh.

The rapid expansion of globalisation, and corresponding unprecedented economic growth, creates huge potential opportunities but also creates a series of 'divides' between the haves and have-nots, the educated and the illiterate, the wealthy and the poor, and so on. Sustain-Ability (2007) summarises ten such 'divides': demography, wealth, gender, nutritional, environment, health, educational, digital and information, security, and governance.

The key feature displayed by the entities or players in these and other similar examples is the idea of contested values. In each of these examples we can clearly see that such issues occur when the values of different entities compete against each other that can sometimes end in failures and disasters. When such instances happen with regularity, members of the public can become cynical, causing them to distrust businesses, governments, their leaders, and the overarching systems under which they operate. Evidence for the latest report from Edelman Trust Barometer (2022), surveying more than 36,000 respondents from 28 countries, indicates that:

- There is less trust in CEOs and government leaders compared to earlier years.
- More people in developed countries (compared to developing countries) lack economic optimism compared to earlier years.
- 58 per cent buy or advocate for brands, 60 per cent choose a place to work, and 64 per cent invest based on their beliefs and values.
- 81 per cent think CEOs should be personally visible when discussing public policy with external stakeholders or work their company has done to benefit society.

- Compared to earlier years, more respondents feel that businesses are not doing enough for societal issues such as climate change, economic inequality, workforce reskilling, access to healthcare, and systemic injustice.
- Trust in businesses in developing countries is higher than in developed countries. From 2021 to 2022, 11 out of 27 countries including China and the UAE gained trust in business, while it declined in 11 countries such as Germany, the US, and UK. Trust in governments fell in 17 countries, while NGOs showed increases in 16 countries.
- Trust in technology, education, healthcare, and manufacturing was high, neutral in fashion and financial services, and low in social media industries.
- Family-owned businesses were more trusted than privately held, publicly held, and state-owned businesses.

In Chapter 1, we defined ethical behaviour in business as behaviour that is consistent with the principles, norms, and standards of business practice that have been agreed upon by society. It has been seen that societies through their governments have often responded to unethical behaviour by introducing laws, acts, legislations, rules, regulations, and codes setting out what behaviours are expected of businesses, what behaviours are not acceptable, and what punitive measures can be enforced. One of the well-known laws from the US is commonly called the antitrust law which is a collection of federal laws that regulate the conduct of businesses with the intention to promote competition and prevent monopolies. The three main statutes are (1) the Sherman Act of 1890 which prohibits price fixing, the operation of cartels, and other collusive practices to prevent monopolisation; (2) the Clayton Act of 1914 that restricts mergers and acquisitions of organisations that may lessen competition and tend to create a monopoly; and (3) the Federal Trade Commission Act of 1914 that enable affected parties to bring civil actions in the courts to enforce the antitrust laws. An oft-cited case involving these laws is the Standard Oil Co., which by the end of the 19th century became the first and largest multinational corporation in the world. The founder and owner John D. Rockefeller became the richest person in modern history. However, in 1911 under the Sherman Act, the US Supreme Court ruled that it was an illegal monopoly and ordered its breakup into 34 companies – two of them became Exxon and Mobil which later merged into ExxonMobil, today one of the largest oil companies in the world. Similarly, the Sarbanes-Oxley Act of 2002 in the US mandates corporate and auditing accountability, responsibility, and transparency on all US public company boards of directors and public accounting firms – including avoiding the wilful destruction of evidence to impede a federal investigation. This law was enacted as a reaction to a number of scandals including Enron and WorldCom. Later, following the Global Financial Crisis of 2008, the US enacted the Dodd-Frank Wall Street Reform and Consumer Protection Act in 2010 which was designed to regulate the financial sector and protect consumers. In the UK, the Monopolies and Mergers Act was introduced in 1965. In India, the Monopolies and Restrictive Trade Practices Act was created in 1969, and the Competition Act in 2002. Australia has the Competition and Consumer Act 2010 which is enforced by the Australian Competition and Consumer Commission. China has the Anti-Monopoly Act of 2007, and in Africa, numerous countries including Botswana, Kenya, Ghana, Egypt, South Africa, and Mauritius have strengthened or introduced competition laws. Almost all of these laws are meant to prevent monopolistic tendencies and to protect the interests of consumers.

So, with so many laws in place, does it mean that if it is legal, it must be ethical? What is the relationship between ethics and law?

2.3 Ethics and law

As we saw in the previous section, new laws and regulations are introduced in response to crises in business ethics. These are expected to result in more ethical business behaviour. However, ethics and law can have contested values. The role of law, therefore, in business ethics issues needs to be understood and the connection between the two needs to be explored (Blodgett, 2011). There are two points of discussions here. The first one is the point of intersection of what *is* law and what it *should or ought* to be. Take the example of slavery. It *was* legal (in 1641 Massachusetts became the first colony to authorise slavery through enacted law), but what it *should or ought* to have been is different. The second one is to reflect on whether law is derived from ethics, or in other words, does ethics precede law, and can they be separated? Can there be morally bad laws? Can a rule that violates standards of morality become a rule of law, or conversely, can a rule be morally acceptable because it is law?

These ideas can be further expanded to reflect on whether every rule of law must satisfy a moral minimum in order to be law or whether a system of rules that fails to satisfy a moral minimum could indeed be legal. Laws are necessarily a set of 'commands' which need to be followed, and if violated, can result in some sort of punishment. Laws and regulations can also confer 'rights' to people to do certain specific things. However, rules which confer 'rights' may not be just or morally good rules – for example, the rights of a master over their slaves or the argument that World War II war criminals would have been punished had they not followed the rules. See Hart (1958), Paine (1994), and Dunfee (1996) for more arguments on the above.

The following literature also supports the close links between ethics and law:

> In the late 1980s and early 1990s, several US firms instituted foetal protection policies which excluded all fertile female employees from jobs which exposed them to hazardous substances. It was argued successfully in the US Supreme Court that these policies discriminated against women – an ethical issue (Sprotzer and Goldberg, 1992). Lopez Jimenez et al. (2020) further elaborate that creating advertising campaigns that meet ethical values need self-regulatory documents that include ethical standards that adhere to the law. The standards of behaviour should go beyond legal regulations to include ethical considerations. Conclusion from the analysis of four case studies – from the securities, automobile, pharmaceutical, and the mortgage banking industries – indicated that law is not necessarily determinative of corporate conduct, which will tend to be weak when the legal standards are vague (Di Lorenzo, 2007).

There could be four variations or combinations of this link between ethics and law. Please see details in Box 2.3 and do the activity mentioned in it.

━━━━━ **Box 2.3** ━━━━━

Ethics and law

There are four possible variations or combinations of the link between ethics and law:

1   Legal but unethical
2   Ethical but illegal
3   Illegal and unethical
4   Legal and ethical

Can you think of an example for each of these four variations? Reflect and justify your selections.

2.4 Why be ethical?

In Chapter 1, we asked and briefly explored the question 'why be moral'? in the context of personal and business reasons. We expand a bit further on this question in the context of contested values. When values are held so dearly and actively contested by various entities as discussed earlier in this chapter, does it make sense (for anyone linked to a business, for example) to be ethical as long as everyone operates within legal limits? In their book, Treviño and Nelson (2014) discuss that individuals, employees, managers, executive leaders, industries, and others in society (such as suppliers, customers, communities, and other stakeholders) do care about ethics and doing the right thing. Individuals care because people are motivated by economic and moral concerns – humans make decisions based on ethical and emotional considerations as well as rational economic self-interest. After all, why do people behave altruistically? There are examples of people helping strangers in distress such as fire, floods, pandemics, and even armed conflicts. Employees expect fairness in the workplace and that will determine the extent of employees' commitment to their employers. Employees are also more likely to 'blow the whistle' when they observe a problem (Weaver, 2004). Managers and executive leaders care about ethics because they may need to prevent, resolve, and manage unethical behaviours in their organisations, and because they are concerned about the image and reputation of their business in society. Industries care because even if one company within the industry gets bad publicity due to unethical behaviour, the entire industry can suffer – for example the financial and banking industry or the legal industry or even the second-hand car sales industry. Finally, the rest of the stakeholders in the society – shareholders, suppliers, customers, communities, the media, the government, activists, and others – also care about ethics as can be seen from product boycotts by customers, suppliers refusing to participate, governments introducing laws, media reporting unethical behaviour, and activists protesting against unethical (and maybe legal) actions of businesses. As we have seen in the opening case of the minibus-taxi industry of South Africa, when stakeholders of the industry realised not much was being done for the survival of the industry, they joined in a coalition to raise funds for those affected – because they care about doing the right thing.

2.5 Shareholder and stakeholder links to business viability

Considering that ethics is essential for business success and survival, and doing the right thing is always the right thing to do, the questions that then arise are how can we succeed and what is the 'right' thing in an environment of contested values? One of the ways these can be answered is through stakeholder management. In this section, we explore and discuss the origins, definitions, concepts, and management of stakeholders. We will discuss how the long-term sustainability of any business is dependent on the success of stakeholder management.

The shareholder link to business viability

For a long time, there have been discussions and arguments surrounding the key role that shareholders play in the running of a business and therefore whether the main and only responsibility and accountability of a business should be to satisfy shareholders (in terms of value creation through return on their investments). Shareholders after all provide the funds to finance a business's operations. The idea can be traced back to Adam Smith's 'Wealth of Nations' theory in 1776 that the 'invisible hand' of market forces and self-interest of owners of business will promote prosperity and welfare. Later, Milton Friedman proposed and popularised the notion that this can happen when appropriate laws are in place. In his seminal *New York Times* article, Friedman (1970: 120–22) says:

> In a free-enterprise, private-property system, a corporate executive is an employee of the owners of the business. He has direct responsibility to his employers. That responsibility is to conduct the business in accordance with their desires, which generally will be to make as much money as possible while conforming to the basic rules of the society, both those embodied in law and those embodied in ethical custom.

> In such a society [a free society], there is one and only one social responsibility of business – to use its resources and engage in activities designed to increase its profits so long as it stays within the rules of the game, which is to say, engages in open and free competition without deception or fraud.

Friedman thus endorses Adam Smith's theory that the invisible hand of market forces and self-interest of business owners will promote general welfare but thinks that 'self-interested actions tend to promote the general welfare only when appropriate laws are in place' and when businesses engage in competition without deception and fraud. Friedman questions: Why should corporations decide the charitable purposes that should be supported by the income of their stockholders? Why shouldn't each stockholder decide that? And why is the business community in general so insistent on supporting its own enemies?

The stakeholder link to business viability

While the term 'stakeholder' has been used since the 1960s, it was only in the 1980s that Edward Freeman proposed and popularised the idea that there are other entities (grouped together as stakeholders) who are equally, if not more, vital to the viability and success of a corporation than shareholders. Freeman contended that managers have a fiduciary relationship. A fiduciary is a person or organisation that acts on behalf of another person or persons, with a duty to preserve good faith. Being a fiduciary thus requires being bound both legally and ethically to act in the other's best interests. Freeman identified two categories of stakeholder groups (see Figure 2.2):

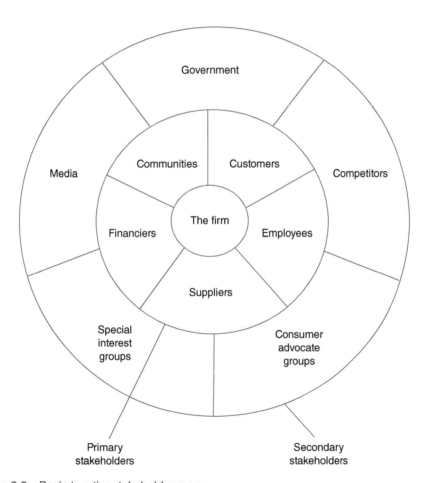

Figure 2.2 Basic two-tier stakeholder map

Source: Freeman et al. (2007), 'Chapter 3 - The basic framework'. In *Managing for stakeholders: Survival, reputation, and success*, New Haven: Yale University Press, pp.51. Reproduced with permission

1   Primary stakeholders: defined as those who are vital to the survival and success of the business such as employees, suppliers, shareholders, customers, the local community, and the management (Freeman, 2021; Freeman et al., 2007).

2   Secondary stakeholders: defined as those who can affect or are affected by the business, including entities such as competitors, the media, governments, activists, the wider community, and even the natural environment and terrorists (Phillips et al., 2003).

Although the 'stakeholder theory is a theory of organisational management and ethics', it is distinct from other management theories because 'it addresses morals and values explicitly as a central feature of managing organisations' (Phillips et al., 2003: 481). It is based on the principles of fairness and the subsequent obligations to the stakeholders. The principle of stakeholder fairness states (Phillips, 1997: 57; see also Phillips et al., 2003):

> Whenever persons or groups of persons voluntarily accept the benefits of a mutually beneficial scheme of co-operation requiring sacrifice or contribution on the part of the participants and there exists the possibility of free-riding, obligations of fairness are created among the participants in the co-operative scheme in proportion to the benefits accepted.

Researchers have so far explored stakeholders as resources leading to competitive advantage. Considering that the resource-based view is a leading contributor to the strategic management field, Freeman et al., (2021) argue that stakeholder theory can offer support to the resource-based view. The stakeholder approach requires a business to consider all of the obligations involved towards all entities that are vital to the business and those that are affected by the decisions and activities of the business. For instance, in the event of downsizing a business, where a substantial part of the workforce are required to be made redundant for reasons as varied as market downturn, financial crisis, and company relocation, instead of looking at the issue only from the profitability point of view, the stakeholder approach will require the business to assess and address the effect of downsizing on stakeholders such as employees, suppliers, consumers, the local community, and others. A further example would be product safety – should a company assess the safety of a product based on its effect on all stakeholders or should it rely only on a cost-benefit analysis and justify the consequences? For instance, Ford in the marketing of the Pinto placed 'profit over human lives (by not making an inexpensive modification), for being fully aware (based on crash tests and a cost-benefit analysis) that the defectively designed rear-end would result in human suffering, and for working all the while to delay and obstruct the National Highway Traffic Safety Administration (NHTSA) from developing and implementing safe standards' (Danley, 2005: 206).

From an ethical perspective, while it may conceptually be beneficial and desirable to balance the needs of multiple stakeholders, it is possible that 'doing so may compromise the ability to meet any stakeholder's needs by trying to meet all stakeholder needs at once' (Lepak and Colakoglu, 2006: 37). Stakeholders' needs are often diverse and diverge considerably; for example, employees' interests would be to secure better wages and working conditions which may increase the cost and price of goods and services, and this may not align with the interests of customers. One of the salient features, therefore, of the stakeholder theory is to understand and establish the relationships between the management of a company and stakeholders whose interests diverge from those of the firm and from each other (Jones et al., 2007). Since the relationships between management and shareholders and between management and stakeholders are different (Goodpaster, 1991), central to understanding these relationships are the three aspects of stakeholder theory set out by Donaldson and Preston (1995): (1) the descriptive aspect (describing what the company is and how it relates to its stakeholders), (2) the instrumental aspect (framework for examining the connections between stakeholder management practices and the achievement of corporate goals), and (3) the normative aspect (how should the company relate to its stakeholders?). Donaldson and Preston suggest that the normative aspect 'serves as the critical underpinning for the theory in all its forms' (1995: 66) and involves the acceptance of the ideas that stakeholders are identified by their interests in the company and that each group of stakeholders merits consideration for its own sake.

Freeman's thesis and work on the stakeholder theory inspired several articles and books to examine and argue for and against the theory. In one such book which supports Freeman's idea, Sisodia, Wolfe and Sheth (2014) propose the concept of Firms of Endearment (FoE), a list of companies that are motivated by and accountable for humanistic as well as economic performance. Such companies create emotional, spiritual, social, cultural, intellectual, ecological, and financial value for their stakeholders – customers, employees, suppliers, business partners, society, and investors (p. 3). According to them, 'a distinguishing core value of FoEs is service to all stakeholders without favouring one over the other' (p. 35). For their list of 72 FoEs (57 from the US and 15 from other countries), see pages 223–52 of their book *Firms of Endearment*. Freeman et al. (2020) take these ideas further by proposing an emerging business model built on five key principles:

- Prioritising purpose as well as profits
- Creating value for stakeholders as well as shareholders
- Seeing business as embedded in society as well as markets
- Recognising people's full humanity as well as economic interests
- Integrating business and ethics into a holistic model

The following sections discuss aspects of the stakeholder theory linked to globalisation, small and medium enterprises (SMEs), and ethical decision-making.

2.6 Globalisation and stakeholders

Three tasks can be identified for businesses to meet the ethical challenges linked to globalisation. The first task is for businesses to develop capacities to ensure effective delivery of their investments in CSR-related activities, and to foster genuine social development (Frynas, 2005: 597–8). The second task faced is related to the stakeholder theory. As shown earlier, stakeholder management is critical to the success of business. However, the idea of addressing the interests, demands and values of entities that affect or are affected by corporate decision-making needs to address the broader aspects of 'environmental and social challenges such as human rights, global warming, or deforestation' (Scherer and Palazzo, 2008: 19), and engage in activities that previously were the responsibilities of governments (Matten and Crane, 2005; Scherer et al., 2009).

The third task is that of incorporating business ethics concepts and approaches into business strategies to address the ethical issues arising out of globalisation. This is developed from the concept of corporate citizenship which has been described as the role of the corporation to administer aspects of citizenship, that is, social, civil, and political rights to stakeholders and other entities (see Matten and Crane, 2005). Administering citizenship to stakeholders is possible by pursuing socially acceptable goals in a socially acceptable manner (Palazzo and Scherer, 2006), and by applying the concepts and approaches of business ethics. This is relevant when it is argued that (1) the focus of business ethics should be on MNCs, being key players in the economic globalisation, and that they must be held accountable for their impact in society, and that SMEs have to follow them; (2) for SMEs the basic question is survival, not ethics; and (3) that SMEs in developing countries have limited access to information, education levels of employees and government subsidies (Enderle, 2004).

2.7 Small and medium enterprises and stakeholders

Fuller and Tian's study found that social interaction with stakeholders appears to shape responsible behaviour by SMEs and concludes that when one's business and life are inseparable, as often is the case in an owner-managed business, social relations of SMEs are powerful forces for ethical behaviour (Fuller and Tian, 2006). For example, Graafland et al. (2003) found that small firms rely, more than large firms, on dialogues with stakeholders. It has also indicated that in a small firm, business decisions cannot be separated from personal moral decisions (Dawson, 2001). Clarke (2006) suggests that 'SMEs [in Australia] are the forgotten stakeholders in the fair and efficient management of Australian corporate governance' mainly because corporate governance is associated with listed and other public companies. There is an assumption that the compliance, rules, norms, and best practice will 'trickle down' from the large companies to SMEs, but that rarely happens due to the characteristics and limitations of SMEs. However, research in several countries indicates that systematic corporate governance is largely associated with larger companies and the agency problem where there is a separation between ownership and control of a business.

2.8 Criticisms of the stakeholder theory

Some prominent theorists have criticised the stakeholder theory as proposed by Freeman et al. Criticisms came from scholars, students, and executives. In fact, the founders of the stakeholder theory (Freeman and associates) themselves were dissatisfied with the state of the theory – that the theory was undermined from distortions and misinterpretations. Phillips et al. (2003) assert that the stakeholder theory is not distorted as an excuse for management opportunism, that it cannot provide a specific objective function for the corporation, that it is primarily concerned with the distribution of financial outputs, and that all stakeholders must be treated equally.

Challenges for vulnerable stakeholders

There are instances where some stakeholders are quite powerless, do not have adequate legitimacy, and even when matters become serious and urgent, are helpless to do anything. In such situations, Barney (2003) suggests (1) a commitment to engage, (2) empathy to understand the needs and aspirations of stakeholders, and (3) the humility to respect the perspectives of stakeholders. In addition, honesty, transparency, and a willingness to acknowledge mistakes would also be beneficial. This might need assistance from an alternative viewpoint of the stakeholder theory – as discussed Box 2.4.

─────── **Box 2.4** ───────

Social complexities in stakeholder management

Barney (2003) highlights the relationships between businesses and vulnerable stakeholders in Odisha, one of the poorest states in India, with a very high percentage of the population at the bottom of socio-economic categories such as literacy, income, and well-being. The people in this region, belonging to tribes who have lived there for millennia, predominantly rely on agriculture and forest products. Understanding and engaging such stakeholders is challenging. Because of its rich deposits of minerals such as iron ore and bauxite, domestic and international mining companies have set up operations in these areas causing major displacements and disruptions to the local people's way of life. Insufficient consultations with the stakeholders led to a strong opposition to the proposed developments leading to a lack of trust and an unwillingness to take the businesses or the government at their word. The failure to consult was in the project cycle, inadequate assessment of affected people and failure to comply with the acts and laws to protect the rights of tribal people, and not articulating the benefits of the projects for all local people.

(Continued)

Question

Due to the social complexities in countries such as India and other developing nations, what management strategies other than the stakeholder management theory would you suggest in situations where vulnerable people who do not have power, legitimacy, or 'voice' are involved?

2.9 Prioritising stakeholders

So, since it is challenging to meet the needs of all stakeholders, there is a need to go beyond identifying stakeholders and placing managerial attention on them (Mitchell et al., 1997). How do we prioritise the needs of stakeholders? Mitchell, Agle and Wood's theory explains to whom and to what managers actually pay attention. They argue that the basis of 'stake' that decides 'what and who counts' as stakeholders, and for this we need to evaluate the stakeholder–manager relationships in terms of three attributes as shown in Figure 2.3: power, legitimacy, and/or urgency.

- Power in the stakeholder–manager relationship refers to when one can get the other to do something which the other would not have done otherwise. So, power can be coercive (force/threat), utilitarian (material/incentives), or normative (symbolic influences). A stakeholder or a manager can have latent power which can come into force depending on the situation.
- Legitimacy in the relationship refers to desirable actions of an entity based on norms, values, beliefs, and definitions at the individual, organisational, and societal levels.
- Urgency in this relationship refers to the degree to which stakeholders' claims call for immediate attention and action – for example when there's a managerial delay in attending to a claim made by a stakeholder.

The various combinations of these three attributes point us to the salience or importance of stakeholders:

- Low stakeholder salience: where only one out of the three attributes is perceived to be present – power (called Dormant Stakeholders), legitimacy (called Discretionary Stakeholders), or urgency (called Demanding Stakeholders)
- Moderate stakeholder salience: where two of the three attributes are perceived to be present – power and legitimacy (called Dominant Stakeholders), or legitimacy and urgency (Dependent Stakeholders), or power and urgency (called Dangerous Stakeholders)
- High stakeholder salience: where all three attributes are perceived to be present – power, legitimacy, and urgency (called Definitive Stakeholders)

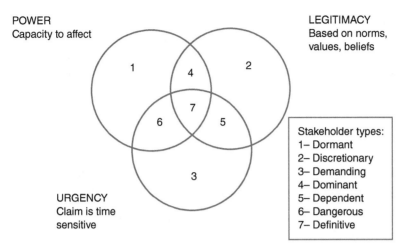

Figure 2.3 Attributes of stakeholder relationships – power, legitimacy, and urgency

Source: Adapted from Mitchell et al. (1997), 'Toward a theory of stakeholder identification and salience: Defining the principle of who and what really counts', *Academy of Management Review*, 22(4): 853–86

The implications are that stakeholders can exist with low salience and move into moderate and high salience if the situation demands it. Take for instance an example of employees' unmet needs of wage increases. At the initial stage, the employees (as stakeholders of the firm) could have low salience to the managers – there's no urgency, the matter has not yet acquired legitimacy, but they have the latent power (they could be part of a union). If the demands are unsatisfactorily discussed causing increased dissatisfaction among employees, they may acquire legitimacy by engaging support from society and the law, thereby moving them into the moderate salience territory. If there is no resolution for an unreasonable amount of time, the situation becomes urgent, and the stakeholders move into the high stakeholder salience area. At this point, the employees (and their union if they have one) could opt for drastic measures such as strikes, which will create major problems for managers in terms of loss of production, profits, and possible reputation. So, it implies that managers must know about stakeholders who hold power, and if power combines with urgency, must attend to it to serve the legal and moral interests of legitimate stakeholders. The management of stakeholders would thus initially involve identifying which stakeholders have the potential to move from low salience to moderate salience, and then from moderate to high salience. Once this mapping is done, the next steps would be to engage in discussions and consultations with relevant stakeholders in order to reduce the potential progression to 'Definitive Stakeholder' (high salience).

2.10 A suggested stakeholder management process

Considering the above discussions, a suggested process for stakeholder management would be:

Step 1: Identify the stakeholders of your organisation using Figure 2.3 Here at a generic level, select the primary and secondary entities that affect your organisation or can be affected by your organisation's decisions and actions.

Step 2: Segment the generic stakeholders identified in Step 1 into more detailed and meaningful segments – as shown in Figure 2.4. The dots in each stakeholder section represent the segments of that particular stakeholder. The length of the lines joining the dots to the firm (at the centre of the figure) in each stakeholder section could be used to signify how important that particular stakeholder is perceived to be to the firm. For example – in the 'customer' section, 'corporate customers' has a shorter line relative to 'singles' or 'families' or 'repeat customers' and are therefore perceived by this firm to be important and closer to the firm than other customers.

Step 3: Identify the salience or importance of each segmented stakeholder in terms of power, legitimacy, and urgency – as described in the discussions above.

Step 4: Incorporate the above data from Steps 1 to 3 in tabular form – as suggested in Table 2.1. You can of course create your own version of this table.

Step 5: Engage with all relevant stakeholders in discussions and consultations.

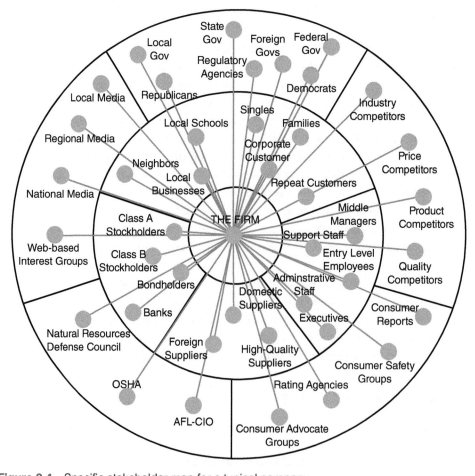

Figure 2.4 Specific stakeholder map for a typical company

Source: Freeman et al. (2007), 'Chapter 3 - The basic framework'. In *Managing for stakeholders: Survival, reputation, and success*, New Haven: Yale University Press, pp.62. Reproduced with permission

Table 2.1 Stakeholder mapping and prioritising – with example

Type	Stakeholder	Segment	Power	Legitimacy	Urgency	Total Ls	Total Ms	Total Hs	Actions required	When
					Salience					
	Employees	Entry level	L/**M**/H	L/**M**/H	L/M/**H**	0	1	2	Why are they leaving within a month of their appointment?	Next week
		Support staff	L/**M**/H	L/**M**/H	**L**/M/H	1	1	1		2 weeks from now
		Admin staff	L/**M**/H	**L**/M/H	L/**M**/H	2	1	0		3 weeks from now
		Middle managers	L/M/**H**	L/**M**/H	L/M/**H**	0	0	3	Start discussions to address their concerns	Now
Primary Stakeholders		Executives	L/M/**H**	L/M/**H**	L/M/**H**					
	Suppliers	Domestic	L/M/**H**	L/M/**H**	L/M/**H**					
		Foreign	L/M/**H**	L/M/**H**	L/M/**H**					
		High quality	L/M/**H**	L/M/**H**	L/M/**H**					

(Continued)

Table 2.1 (Continued)

Type	Stakeholder	Segment	Salience						Actions required	When
			Power	Legitimacy	Urgency	Total Ls	Total Ms	Total Hs		
	Government	Local	L/M/H	L/M/H	L/M/H					
		State	L/M/H	L/M/H	L/M/H					
		Federal	L/M/H	L/M/H	L/M/H					
		Regulators	L/M/H	L/M/H	L/M/H					
Secondary Stakeholders	Media	Local	L/M/H	L/M/H	L/M/H					
		Regional	L/M/H	L/M/H	L/M/H					
		National	L/M/H	L/M/H	L/M/H					
		Social	L/M/H	L/M/H	L/M/H					

Legend:

L = Low salience

M = Moderate salience

H = High salience

In this example:

1. Identify stakeholders at the generic level – employees, suppliers etc.
2. Identify segments for each generic stakeholder – entry level, support staff etc.
3. Select salience for each stakeholder segment – L/M/H (low or moderate or high) and highlight (bold) the selected ones
4. Total the Ls, Ms and Hs – for example: 0, 1, 2, or 3
5. Briefly write what actions are required and when

Note: Total salience of 3Hs will require immediate action and so on

Source: Author compilation

=== **Box 2.5** ===

Equinor's withdrawal

Equinor is a Norwegian state-owned multinational energy company, primarily engaged in petroleum with additional investments in renewable energy. In 2020, Equinor decided to abandon an AUD 200 million plan to drill for oil in the Great Australian Bight, an open bay of around 46,000 km^2 and one of the most pristine and untouched expanses of ocean. Equinor indicated it abandoned the project off the remote South Australian coast because it was not 'commercially competitive'. Equinor is the third major oil company to abandon plans to drill in the Bight, following BP and Chevron.

Equinor's proposal involved drilling 370 km off the coast in waters up to 2,500 metres deep. This brought extra technical complexity and made the proposal very expensive and environmentally risky. Equinor's environment plan also made overly optimistic assumptions and was inadequate in many ways, including the following:

Environmental risk

Equinor said it was committed to ecologically sustainable development and would adhere to relevant environment regulations. However, it is believed that the company did not comprehensively demonstrate how it would mitigate impacts on and restore populations of endangered species found within its well area, as is required under the Commonwealth Environment Act. In response to this criticism, Equinor said its environment plan 'was accepted by the independent regulator in December 2019'.

Public consultation

Equinor conducted only limited public consultation – within a 40 km radius of the well site. This excluded many relevant parties with a shared concern for the local environment. It was particularly egregious that Equinor failed to consult any Indigenous organisations despite numerous sea and land title claims that may have been affected by a spill.

Oil spill modelling

Equinor's modelling of the 'worst case discharge scenario' predicted a far lower oil flow rate than modelling by BP in 2016 for the same well location. But the scenarios Equinor developed would still have amounted to a catastrophic and unprecedented environmental event: a discharge of 42,387 barrels per day until the well was killed after 102 days, or 4,323,474 barrels of oil in total. This is a similar to the amount of oil estimated to have entered the Gulf of Mexico following the Deepwater Horizon disaster.

Why did Equinor abandon its plans?

Equinor says it abandoned its plans for commercial reasons – the same reason cited by BP and Chevron. However, firstly, the project failed to gain a social licence. Public surveys showed 68 per cent of people in South Australia opposed Equinor's plans. Secondly, it faced ongoing legal hurdles – The Wilderness Society's Federal Court challenge to the environmental approval. Thirdly, much of the world is now moving away from fossil fuels.

(Continued)

Questions

1 Identify the primary and secondary stakeholders in this case.
2 What are the contested values for each of these stakeholders?
3 Identify the salience (low, moderate, or high) in terms of power, legitimacy, and urgency for each of the stakeholders.
4 What do you think Equinor should have done right from the start of this project?
5 Do you think Equinor would have succeeded even if they had done proper consultation right from the start? Justify your answer.

Source: Adapted from Taylor and Soliman (2020)

2.11 Alternative viewpoints of the stakeholder theory

This section presents two alternative viewpoints: creating shared values, and an ethical tradition called *Ubuntu*.

Creating shared values

To reconcile the differing views of the shareholder and stakeholder views, Porter and Kramer (2011) proposed the concept of creating shared value. They build their proposition on the idea that the legitimacy of businesses has fallen to levels not seen in recent history. A major problem, they say, is that companies are trapped in an outdated approach of viewing value creation too narrowly (the Friedman approach) and overlooking the well-being of customers, natural resources, key suppliers, and communities (the Freeman approach). Acknowledging that 'business and society have been pitted against each other for too long' (2011: 64), they propose the concept of shared value which 'recognises that societal needs, not just economic needs, define markets' (2011: 65). The shared value concept is not about personal values nor about redistributing companies' profits, but it is about expanding the total pool of economic and social value. Examples are Fairtrade and improving suppliers' efficiencies which can benefit suppliers, customers, and companies.

Ubuntu

One of the common characteristics of the Sub-Saharan African region (the area south of the Sahara Desert in Africa) is an ethical tradition called *Ubuntu* which can be summarised as 'I am because you are' or 'a person is a person through others'. This forms the basis for a 'relationship theory' which can provide an alternative to and overcome the weaknesses identified with the stakeholder theory. In this view, it is argued that the three attributes of power, legitimacy, and urgency (discussed earlier in this chapter), become inadequate to view manager–stakeholder relationships as consensual and voluntary agreements. If for example certain stakeholder groups are unable to articulate their legitimate claims and have very little power over the organisation, it will be difficult or even impossible to hold organisations responsible for their actions (Woermann, 2011). Thus, the interests of the poor and needy stakeholders may not find salience with the firm and therefore contracts make it easy to dismiss the interests of such entities. Here, Woermann's claim is to shift the focus from stakes to harmonious relationships. The meaning of *Ubuntu* is 'a person is a person through other people' focusing on the rationality or interconnectedness of human existence.

Nussbaum (2001) indicates that *Ubuntu* is characterised by virtues of compassion, caring, sharing, and responsiveness to the community and Archbishop Tutu of South Africa (quoted in Woermann and Engelbrecht, 2019) suggests that an *Ubuntu* person is generous, hospitable, friendly, caring, and compassionate. The stakeholder in the *Ubuntu* context is 'relation-holder'. These characterisations of *Ubuntu* can frame a firm's relationship with others to foster harmonious, trusting relations via friendly means. So, the emphasis is centred on promoting harmonious relation with a relationholder rather than just ensuring that claims or stakes are met. If the firm is considered as a community rather than a nexus of contracts, it can treat employees, consumers, suppliers, and other entities linked to the firm in the *Ubuntu* way.

═══ Box 2.6 ═══

Applying the stakeholder management process

- Make groups and each group selects an organisation for this activity. Organisations could be MNEs or domestic or even a micro/family business.
- Within your groups, identify five generic stakeholders of the organisation that you have selected – use Figure 2.2 as a guide.
- Next, segment each stakeholder into further smaller entities – use Figure 2.4 as a guide. Next, create a table with your segmented stakeholders in the left-hand column and the attributes power, legitimacy, and urgency in the top row.
- Next for each stakeholder consider whether they have low, moderate, or high salience for each of the three attributes – power, legitimacy, and urgency.
- Are there any with low salience for all three saliences?
- Are there any with two moderate saliences?
- Are there any with one high salience?
- Reflect: under what conditions or situations do you think any of the stakeholders would move into the Definitive Stakeholder (high salience) area? What would you do about it?

======= **Summary** =======

- This chapter began with an opening case of the minibus-taxi industry of South Africa which highlighted the importance of contested values and the needs of different entities who have a stake in the success of individuals and organisations operating within this industry.
- The idea of contested values was developed – that businesses operate in such an environment where employees, customers, suppliers, and investors, among others, have certain values that they want to protect, enhance, and endure for a longer period of time. These values tend to contest between each other within the context of a business.
- We acknowledged that societies through their governments introduce laws and regulations to respond to the unethical behaviour of businesses. We outlined the relationship between law and ethics – with so many laws in place, does it mean that if it is legal, it must be ethical? We argued that law is not necessarily determinative of corporate conduct and that standards of behaviour should go beyond legal regulations to include ethical considerations.
- That brought us to discuss 'why be ethical and who cares?' We identified and provided reasons why individuals, employees, managers, executive leaders, industries, and society care about ethics.
- A major part of this chapter was devoted to the 'shareholder' and 'stakeholder' link and arguments for business viability. This included Milton Friedman's proposition that the only social responsibility of a business is to increase profits. In contrast, we presented Edward Freeman's proposition that primary and secondary stakeholders of a firm have more claims on a firm – they affect a business and can be affected by the decisions of a business.
- We showed the relationships between stakeholders and globalisation, SMEs, and ethical decision-making.
- The process of stakeholder management was discussed with the concept of prioritising stakeholders – to whom and to what should managers actually pay attention? This was evaluated using three attributes of stakeholders: power, legitimacy, and urgency. The salience of stakeholders was identified as low, moderate, and high, depending on the levels of the three attributes.
- A five-step process of stakeholder management was proposed using mapping and prioritising in a tabular format.
- Challenges for vulnerable stakeholders such as people at the bottom of socio-economic categories was highlighted – where they do not have any power or legitimacy to stake a claim on a business decision that affects them.
- An alternative viewpoint to the stakeholder theory called *Ubuntu* from Sub-Saharan Africa was introduced. The concept was summarised as a relationship theory which propounds 'I am because you are' or 'a person is a person through others'. If the firm is considered as a community rather than a nexus of contracts, it can treat employees, consumers, suppliers, and other entities linked to the firm in the *Ubuntu* way.

CASE STUDY 2.1
THE BRENT SPAR CASE

The Royal Dutch Shell Plc was formed in 1907 with the merger of the Royal Dutch Petroleum Company of the Netherlands and the Shell Transport and Trading Company of the UK. In January 2022, the firm was renamed to Shell Plc, a British multinational oil and gas company, headquartered in London. It is a public limited company and one of the largest companies in the world.

Shell's exploration and subsequent discovery of oil and gas in the North Sea resulted in rich oil fields such as the Brent fields. These were served by four large oil platforms – Alpha, Bravo, Charlie, and Delta. The Brent Spar commissioned in 1976 was a large oil tanker loading buoys for storing oil from Brent Alpha. After 15 years of operation, having reached the end of its productive period, Brent Spar was decommissioned and stopped operating in 1991.

Shell began decommissioning studies to assess options for Brent Spar's disposal. Initially, six options were proposed: horizontal dismantling and onshore disposal, vertical dismantling and onshore disposal, infield disposal, deep-sea disposal, refurbishment and reuse, and continued maintenance. These options were shortlisted, and feasibility studies were carried out only for the horizontal onshore dismantling and deep-sea disposal options – with the deep-sea disposal emerging as the winner with six times lower safety risks, four times less cost, and minimal environmental risks. An independent study by Aberdeen University endorsed the deep-sea proposal.

Following consultations with local governments, conservation bodies, and fishing interests, Shell applied to the UK government for approval, which was received in December 1994. Since no objections were raised within the normal time limit, Shell announced its deep-sea disposal plan in February 1995.

Greenpeace opposed this deep-sea disposal option. Greenpeace is an independent global campaigning network comprising of 26 national/regional organisations in over 55 countries. Founded in 1971 in Canada to create a GREEN and PEACEful world, it is known for its direct actions raising awareness and using public opinion to influence decision-making.

Greenpeace opposed the deep-sea disposal option for a number of reasons:

1   It would set a precedent for the 130 offshore Spars existing in the North Sea that would come up for disposal in the future.
2   The deep-sea disposal would damage the environment much more than Shell had indicated.
3   It was a matter of principle (such as 'the sea is not a dustbin') to not accept and allow deep-sea disposals.

When Greenpeace was not invited to the consultations between Shell and others, the British, Dutch, and German branches of Greenpeace decided to occupy the Brent Spar,

(Continued)

and in April 1995 protestors climbed to the top of the Spar platform to prevent Shell from towing it to the deep-sea disposal site. Greenpeace claimed (and later apologised for its inaccuracy) that the Spar contained 5000 tonnes of oil which would contaminate the sea if the deep-sea option was undertaken. Despite all of this, the UK government granted the disposal licence to Shell UK. However, the publicity generated by Greenpeace's occupation of the Brent Spar created waves of protests in continental Europe – these included consumers, politicians, and even governments. Protests came from German and other European ministers, and opposition parties in the UK. Then, in mid-1995, Greenpeace called for a Shell boycott and distributed leaflets to this effect in Germany. People stopped buying fuel from Shell petrol stations and some service stations were destroyed. A second occupation of the Brent Spar by Greenpeace began when protestors landed on the Spar by helicopter. There was now strong opposition from several European governments.

Finally, on 20 June 1995, Shell decided to abandon and halt its deep-sea disposal plans citing its position was untenable and no longer sustainable. The Norwegian government granted Shell permission to dock the Spar in a fjord until new disposal options were considered. After lengthy, prolonged, and detailed discussions with several companies interested in the onshore disposal option, the UK government in 1998 announced its approval of a solution. The project of onshore disposal was finally completed on 10 July 1999.

From the experiences of the Brent Spar and the lessons learnt from them, Shell improved and mastered the process of disengaging and lifting these giant structures from the ocean bed, transporting them to the shore, sometimes more than 700 km away, and finally dismantling and recycling up to 98 per cent of the structure.

Questions

Using the Case-Study Integrative Framework in Figure 0.1, reflect on these questions:

1 Identify the primary and secondary stakeholders in this case.
2 What were the key issues for these stakeholders?
3 Reflect on what values or rights were created or violated.
4 Reflect on the impact on business and society.
5 What were the contested values for these stakeholders? Why were they 'contested'?
6 Do you think the *Ubuntu* principles can be applied here? How?
7 What in your opinion would be the outcomes if stakeholder theory or the *Ubuntu* principles were applied?

Sources:
Weyler (2016)
Wiki (n.d.a)
Shell (2022)
There We Go – Lifting 25,000 tonnes in 9 seconds: Brent Bravo Lift (2019)
Zyglidopoulos (2002)

CASE STUDY 2.2
THE CIPLA AND GENERIC DRUGS CASE

Cipla Limited is an Indian multinational pharmaceutical company that develops and manufactures medicines to treat respiratory, cardiovascular disease, arthritis, diabetes, weight control, depression, and other medical conditions. Founded by Dr Khwaja Abdul Hamied in 1935 in Mumbai and inspired by **Mahatma Gandhi** for a vision of making India self-reliant and self-sufficient in healthcare, the company is now led by his son Yusuf Hamied. The company provides generic **AIDS** and other drugs to treat poor people in the developing world. It has 34 manufacturing units in eight locations and has a presence in over 170 countries.

The AIDS pandemic infected some 35 million Africans of whom about 15 million died – the majority of these deaths were in Sub-Saharan Africa. South Africa was the worst affected. Ten per cent of the population in the surrounding countries were also affected. Life expectancy for adults aged between 20 and 49 lowered dramatically by about 20 years.

However, people in these countries had no access to antiretroviral medication (to reduce the amount of virus in the body) and drugs to treat opportunistic infection (that occur more often or are more severe in people with weakened immune systems, including those with **HIV**). All such drugs were patented enabling (mostly) Western pharma corporations to charge prices which were out of reach of patients due to high costs. Pfizer for example sold drugs to avoid painful opportunistic infections from AIDS for USD 30 (typically USD 10,000 to 15,000 annually). A Médecins Sans Frontières team of doctors, nurses, pharmacists, scientists, and lawyers publicly challenged the high costs of HIV drugs.

This finally led to a confrontation between people dying of AIDS and big pharmaceutical companies, resulting in civil disobedience that included importing such drugs from Thailand where it was available for just US 5 cents.

In 2001, Cipla revolutionised HIV treatment by terming the situation as a humanitarian crisis and developed a drug called Triomune – a single tablet costing less than a dollar a day. A legal prohibition of patenting drugs in India ensured that the medicines including those for HIV could be produced much quicker and cheaper. India now produces about 92 per cent of all drugs sold in the world.

Dr Hamid, the founder of Cipla, has reportedly said that dividing people into those who can afford life-saving drugs and those who cannot amounts to people's right to life and health especially in the poorer sections of the world. There should be a deeper purpose (of healing human beings) than just making profits. Of course, global pharma companies were not happy about this.

(Continued)

Questions

Using the Case-Study Integrative Framework in Figure 0.1, reflect on these questions:

1　Identify the primary and secondary stakeholders in this case.
2　What were the key issues for these stakeholders?
3　Reflect on what values or rights were created or violated.
4　Reflect on the impact on business and society.
5　What were the contested values for these stakeholders? Why were they 'contested'?
6　Do you think the *Ubuntu* principles can be or have been applied here? How?
7　What in your opinion would be the outcomes if stakeholder theory or the *Ubuntu* principles were applied?

Sources:
Wiki (2022e)
Fire in the Blood – HIV AIDs drugs and big pharma (2020)
Fire in the Blood – trailer (2013)
Wiki (2022i)
Menghaney (2013)
Sisodia et al. (2014)

─Recommended readings─

Blodgett, M.S. (2011), 'Substantive ethics: Integrating law and ethics in corporate ethic programs', *Journal of Business Ethics*, 99(1): 39–48.

This article describes the integration of law and ethics as a mid-point between two polar views that define law and ethics either as having no relation or as being one and the same. It reveals that corporate ethics codes rarely express ethics and law as being integrated.

Donaldson, T. and Preston, L.E. (1995), 'The stakeholder theory of the corporation: Concepts, evidence, and implications', *Academy of Management Review*, 20(1): 65–91.

This article examines three aspects of the stakeholder theory – descriptive, instrumental, and normative. The authors conclude that these three aspects are mutually supportive and the normative aspect is fundamental.

Freeman, E.R., Harrison, J.S. and Wicks A.C. (2007), *Managing for stakeholders: survival, reputation, and success*, New Haven, CT: Yale University Press.

A definitive and seminal work by Freeman and colleagues on stakeholder theory. This book explains very clearly the practical aspects of the theory.

Friedman, M. (1970), 'The social responsibility of business is to increase profits', *The New York Times Magazine*, 13 September, (www.nytimes.com/1970/09/13/archives/a-friedman-doctrine-the-social-responsibility-of-business-is-to.html).

Another seminal work – arguments and explanations by Friedman on why he considers that businesses should restrict themselves to increasing profits rather than pursuing social responsibilities.

Mitchell, R.K., Agle, B.R. and Wood D.J. (1997), 'Towards a theory of stakeholder identification and salience: Defining the principle of who and what really counts', *Academy of Management Review*, 22(4): 853–86.

A must-read article on clarifying who really are stakeholders and the three factors of power, legitimacy, and urgency that can be applied to define and prioritise stakeholders.

Sisodia, R., Wolfe, D. and Sheth, J. (2014), *Firms of endearment*, 2nd edn, Upper Saddle River, NJ: Pearson Education, pp. 34–7.

This book reveals how remarkable and successful companies are generating more values that matter – emotional, experiential, social, and financial – not because they are politically correct, but because it's the only path to long-term competitive advantage.

Woermann, M. and Engelbrecht, S. (2019), 'The *Ubuntu* challenge to business: From stakeholders to relationships', *Journal of Business Ethics*, 157(1): 27–44.

This paper addresses to what extent the African ethic of *Ubuntu* can contribute to ethical thinking and provide an alternative to stakeholder theory. It suggests a 'relationship theory' that can overcome some of the weaknesses of stakeholder theory.

3

ETHICAL APPROACHES
UNDERSTANDING NORMATIVE ETHICAL THEORIES

─Learning objectives─

On completion of this chapter, you should be able to:

- Understand the concept of normative ethical theories
- Describe and critically examine different ethical theories and their implications for business
- Apply the theories to ethical issues in business and other organisations

─Key concepts─

- Normative or prescriptive ethical theory
- Ethical egoism
- Utilitarianism
- Deontological ethics and the Categorical Imperative
- Ethics of rights
- Ethics of justice
- Virtue ethics
- Ethics of care and feminist ethics
- Discourse ethics
- Postmodern ethics
- Ethical pluralism

─Box 3.1 Opening case─

The trolley problem

A thought experiment, the classic 'trolley problem', can help us focus on the complexities of ethics. There are many versions of this experiment. Imagine you are driving a heavy vehicle on a track and the brakes fail. If you proceed straight ahead, you will wipe out five construction workers. However, if you pull a lever, you can divert the vehicle onto another track where there's only one worker. All six workers are presumably unknown to you. You have two choices – do nothing, so the vehicle moves straight ahead and kills five people, or pull the lever and kill one person. Most people would opt for pulling the lever and thereby save the lives of five people. Now, there's new information come to you in your earphones – that the person working on the alternative track is your very close relative or friend. Would you change your mind now, that is – opt to kill five (unknown) people, and save your relative/friend? In the first situation, the answer seems to be quite straightforward. The second situation forces us to pause and think. Some people could still stick to the original decision of saving the five workers. Some others may do the opposite because of the changed situation. If you decide on saving that one person, was it because you felt it was your duty or a personal principle to do it? Should the driver take action to kill someone, or should the driver leave well alone and say, 'the brakes failed – I did no wrong'?

If you choose to save the lives of those five people, you have applied the 'utilitarianism' theory of ethics. It amounts to doing good for the greatest number of people. The end result was good even though the action was not the best. In the case where you decided to save your relative/friend, you have applied the 'deontology' theory. It indicates that it does not matter what the consequences are, so long as you consider the action is right. You have a chosen a duty or a rule (that could be a universal law) that says 'always protect your loved ones' (or something similar).

The trolley problem is being considered by companies like Google, Tesla, General Motors, Uber, and others when designing their algorithms for self-driving cars.

3.1 Introduction

As mentioned in Chapter 1, there are three related sections of ethical study – normative or prescriptive ethics, descriptive ethics, and metaethics. This chapter begins with ethical theories associated with prescriptive ethics that attempts to explain and justify the morality of society in general (e.g., how should we decide and behave). Chapter 4 discusses ethical concepts related to descriptive ethics that describes the morality of society including ethical decision-making (e.g., how do we actually decide and behave). Metaethics, which deals with the meaning of moral terms, such as what do 'good', 'bad', and other similar phrases mean, will be discussed very briefly – as it studies the logic of moral reasoning, it falls in the realms of philosophy and moral psychology which we need not concern ourselves with in this book. Concepts discussed in this chapter are based on the ancient Greek and the Judeo-Christian approaches to ethical study. Chapter 5 will focus on business ethics across cultures – including African, Confucian, Indo-centric, and Islamic cultures.

Philosophers have been contemplating the complexity of what in principle is right or wrong, and more importantly, what we ought to do in immediate circumstances. To arrive at morally correct answers to situations, philosophers therefore attempted and aspired to 'reduce ethics to a single, ultimate principle' (Nadler and Shapiro, 2021: 122).

There are several ethical theories that can help us navigate through complex ethical issues. The principles behind these theories may never change, but the moral landscape has changed since many of them were conceived and application in the 21st century will require flexibility, adaptability, and inventiveness. These changes constitute entirely new ethical issues – such as computer hacking, software protection from copying, protecting sea life from commercial activities, dumping used electronic goods on underdeveloped countries, storing nuclear waste in underground wastelands, human cloning, self-driven vehicles, and so on. The changes can also be attributed to increasing moral intensity – the increasing number of ethical issues that are pressing upon us for attention through the various forms of media and communication can cause 'compassion fatigue', when the ability to care gets numbed. Compassion can be defined as motivation to act by alleviating another's suffering or distress. This moral component of compassion is seen as a duty towards others and differentiates itself from empathy, sympathy, and pity that may not motivate one to act (Ledoux, 2015). Schur (2022: 147) introduces the term 'moral exhaustion', suggesting that trying to do the right thing all the time can be exhausting.

One logical approach to discern right and wrong would be to consider a spectrum with ethical absolutism and ethical relativism at either end. Ethical absolutism acknowledges the existence of moral principles, values, and rules as true. Regardless of culture and religion, moral principles are applicable eternally and universally. It implies that actions are intrinsically right or wrong. An example would be the 'golden rule' – that we should treat others as we would want to be treated – found in most moral and religious teachings. The other end of the spectrum would be ethical relativism, which states that moral principles are relative to the factors and circumstances in different contexts and there are not intrinsically right and wrong actions. It depends on local traditions, practices, beliefs, and convictions of those taking decisions so that it is not possible for one person to criticise the moral decisions of another person who may have different (but equally valued) beliefs and convictions. Ethical relativism holds that morality is relative to the norms of one's culture. For example, bribing in the form of gift-giving in business may be considered unethical in some parts of the world, but culturally acceptable in other parts. However, this should not be confused with differences of opinion (Jalsenjak, 2019). We may disagree with someone about the right thing to do or the better course of action. Ethical relativism involves judging whether an action is right or wrong depending on the moral norms of the society in which it is practised (Velasquez et al., 2022). Some call this 'when in Rome, do as the Romans do'. However, normative relativism suggests that no person or culture ought to judge the ethical codes of other cultures as being inferior, nor should any culture intervene in another culture to prevent it from carrying out the specifics of its ethical code (Rezkalla, 2022).

This chapter will discuss the following ethical theories associated with prescriptive ethics:

- Ethical egoism
- Consequence-based theory of utilitarianism
- Principle-based theory of deontology
- Ethics of rights
- Ethics of justice
- Virtue ethics
- Ethics of care
- Discourse ethics
- Postmodern ethics

3.2 Ethical egoism

From a psychology point of view, egoism holds that every person acts only from self-interest. The idea of ethical egoism in business has been associated with Adam Smith (1723–1790), the author of 'The Wealth of Nations' and 'The Theory of Moral Sentiments', who wrote: 'It is not from the benevolence of the butcher, the brewer, or the baker that we expect our dinner, but from their regard to their own interest' (Buchanan, 2002). Ethical egoism was further elaborated by the philosopher Henry Sidgwick in 1874. Comparing it to the philosophy of utilitarianism (discussed in a later section), Sidgwick contended that whereas utilitarianism sought to maximise overall pleasure, egoism focused only on maximising individual pleasure (Floridi and Craig, 1998). It is also important to distinguish egoism from selfishness. Self-interest emanating from egoism can be argued to benefit society, such as when people set up business for their own interest and thereby benefit society, through employment, the provision of goods and services, and even charity. A selfish person, on the other hand, is insensitive to the emotions and needs of others. However, arguments against the idea that self-interest is a requirement for businesses to prosper includes the observation that egoism can lead to uneven market competition, market failures and undesirable results. This is seen from the high inequality in the distribution of wealth – in the wealthiest nation on earth, the USA, between 1963 and 2016, the poorest ten per cent went from having on average zero assets to being USD 1000 in debt, while families in the top one per cent had more than seven times their prior wealth (Urban Institute, 2017). The wealth of the ten richest men doubled during the pandemic as 99 per cent of incomes dropped (Thorbecke, 2022).

3.3 Utilitarianism, also known as teleology or consequentialism

This ethical theory states that the rightness of an action can be judged only by its consequences. The word teleology is derived from the Greek 'teleos' meaning end, goal, or result. Since it relates to the production of good consequences and avoidance of bad consequences, the concept of goodness or utility becomes the fundamental feature of this theory. It supports actions that produce happiness or pleasure and opposes actions the cause harm or unhappiness. The development of utilitarianism is attributed to English philosopher Jeremy Bentham (1748–1832), although the word utilitarianism was coined by English philosopher John Stuart Mill (1806–1873) and in its simplest form holds that an action is right if it produces, or tends to produce, the greatest amount of good, such as welfare and happiness, for the greatest number of people affected by that action. Mill wrote 'The creed which accepts as the foundation of morals, Utility, or the Greatest Happiness Principle, holds that actions are right in proportion as they tend to promote happiness, wrong as they tend to produce the reverse of happiness' (Mill, 1863).

The most basic form of utilitarian analysis is the cost-benefit analysis, where the costs and benefits of a proposed action are compared and a decision that provides the greatest overall gain is taken. This utility approach is widely used in all areas of business and in moral reasoning as well – but often with a difference. In business, the cost-benefit utility approach is often used to compare and weigh the good and bad consequences of a proposed action in purely monetary terms – for example, in analysing the purchase of a computer, the cost of buying a computer would be weighed against the income that could be generated from the use of the computer and if the net income is positive or substantial, then a decision could be made to purchase the computer. Whereas in an ethical analysis, the comparison of the good and bad results of an action includes everyone affected by it – for example, when considering outsourcing of a business area such as manufacturing, the benefit of the outsourcing, which could be lower operational costs and the benefits to the local community at the new location, would be weighed against the loss of employment at the original manufacturing plant and the potential unhappiness in the local community as well as potential damage to the organisation's reputation.

Two forms of utilitarianism are *act* utilitarianism and *rule* utilitarianism.

- Act utilitarians believe that we should perform the action that will create the greatest net utility in any particular situation. In other words, do whatever will produce the best overall results on a case-by-case basis. For example: releasing an approved drug even with known side effects, because the drug can help more people compared to the negative issues with the side effects.
- Rule utilitarianism has two components – (1) a specific action is morally justified if it conforms to a justified moral rule; and (2) a moral rule is justified if it would create more utility than other possible rules. For example: when a company in times of market downturn, instead of downsizing, offers to retain employees on reduced wages.
- The key difference between act and rule utilitarianism is that the former applies to the evaluation of individual actions and the latter applies to the evaluation of moral rules and then evaluates individual actions based on those rules.

In the opening case 3.1 – the trolley problem, the action of sacrificing the life of one individual to save five lives would be an act utilitarian solution. Saving hundreds of lives by convicting one person and thereby preventing acts of terrorism can also be termed as act utilitarianism. In rule utilitarianism, based on the Hippocratic Oath (a rule) of 'do no harm', a medical doctor should never harvest organs of an unwitting healthy patient even if it can save five lives through transplants, because such actions can never conform to a moral rule (Nadler and Shapiro, 2021; Nathanson, 2022).

Utilitarian ethics in business

Utilitarianism is viewed as a strong theory because it suggests that business managers can carry out numerical analysis with considerable certainty about end results. It is also attractive because it seems easier to apply and is able to describe much of the decision-making process, and is therefore widely used in business and economics. For example, it may allow systematic and organised decision-making for practising managers by assisting them in accounting for their actions. However, it has some inherent weaknesses. One problem is that it may not be easy to evaluate the good or harm that may be done by an action. For example, what value to put on human life when evaluating a cost-benefit analysis – as shown in the Ford Pinto case (see Box 3.2). Similarly, how does one consider the value of the environment including animals and flora in the calculation? A second weakness is that the utilitarian approach, while agreeing on what to count as good or bad, says nothing about how the benefits and burdens ought to be distributed and doesn't seem to have a place for people's rights. In many cases, some individuals may get larger benefits or suffer greater harm than others. In the above outsourcing example, certain employee rights, such as the right to be treated fairly and the right to receive fair compensation due to loss of employment, may not be considered while conducting the cost-benefit analysis. A third weakness of utilitarianism is that the greatest number need not cover all people. Even if a majority may be covered, a minority may be left behind. One solution for this is John Rawls's distributive justice approach, which is discussed further later in this chapter. It holds that ethical acts or decisions are those that lead to an equitable distribution of goods and services.

━━━━━━ **Box 3.2** ━━━━━━

Has anything changed?

The Ford Pinto rear-end crash fire case and the Toyota sticky accelerator case

The Ford Pinto case 1971–1978

In the late 1960s the automobile market in the US was highly competitive with auto manufacturers from Japan and Germany vying for a larger share of the small-car auto market in the US. The Ford Motor Company in 1968 decided to produce the Pinto. This car was designed under the stipulations imposed by Ford boss Lee Iacocca that it should weigh no more than 2000 pounds and cost no more than USD 2000. To get it ready for a 1971 release, Ford decided to reduce the normal design-to-showroom time from three years to two. After several crash tests, Ford knew that the Pinto presented a serious fire hazard when struck from behind. Even at low speeds, collisions from behind would rupture the petrol tank resulting in dangerous leaks. Ford officials faced a dilemma. Should they go ahead with the existing design which would meet production deadlines but compromise consumer safety? Or should they redesign the petrol tank, delay production, and concede another year of dominance by foreign companies? Ford took the first option – they pushed ahead with the original design and stuck to it for the next six years. Between 1971 and 1978, the Pinto was responsible for several fire-related deaths due to rear-end collisions.

So, how did Ford reach the decision of not making the fuel tank safer? Ford's internal report revealed the cost-benefit reasoning to arrive at this decision. The estimated cost of improving the safety of the fuel tank was USD 11. With a total of 12.5 million cars and light trucks, the total cost would have been 12.5 million × USD 11 = USD 137.5 million. The number of incidents from potential crashes was estimated to be 180 deaths, 180 serious burn injuries, and 2,100 burned vehicles. The government had estimated the value of a human being killed in an auto accident at USD 200,000, injury at USD 67,000, and USD 700 per vehicle. The total benefits would therefore be: (180 × USD 200,000) + (180 × USD 67,000) + (2,100 × USD700) = USD 49.5 million. So, in effect, from these calculations, the cost of improving the safety was much higher than the benefits.

Sources: Adapted from Gioia (1992) and Matteson and Metivier (2023)

The Toyota case 2009–2014

In September 2009, a Highway Patrolman and three members of his family were killed when the accelerator in his Lexus had become stuck on the floor mat. Before the crash the driver was able to call 911 while his car was speeding over 160 kilometres per hour. Later, in 2009, reports emerged of several incidents where Toyota vehicles had safety issues caused by unintended acceleration. Initially, Toyota sought to assure its customers that the sudden acceleration was caused by floor mats or driver error. But more such incidents happened that had nothing to do with floor mats or with driver error. According to the FBI, Toyota put sales over safety and profit over principle, and the FBI further stated 'the disregard Toyota had for the safety of the public is outrageous. Not only did Toyota fail to recall cars with problem parts, but they also continued to manufacture new cars with the same parts they already knew were deadly. When media reports arose of Toyota hiding defects, they emphatically denied what they knew was true, assuring consumers that their cars were safe and reliable... More than speeding cars or a major fine, the ultimate tragedy has been the unwitting consumers who died behind the wheel of Toyota vehicles'. After media accusations, Toyota investigated the issue and announced massive recalls but concealed there was another cause of the sudden acceleration called 'sticky pedals' which refers to the accelerator getting stuck partially depressed.

Following a court case, Toyota admitted that it misled US consumers by concealing and making deceptive statements about the safety problems with unintended acceleration and agreed to pay USD 1.2 billion to avoid prosecution. The chief legal officer of Toyota asserted that they would put customers first, listen to customers' needs, and will take their responsibilities to them seriously.

Source: Adapted from Ross et al. (2014)

Questions

1 Reflect on the ethical issues in each of the two cases above. Did Ford and Toyota take the right decision considering the market and business conditions they were in?
2 Apply the relevant ethical theory and consider what you think they should have done.

(Continued)

3   In Ford's case, was the cost-benefit calculation inadequate? Is the calculation a moral question? What reasons are there for disagreeing with the government's numbers of death payouts?
4   In Toyota's case, what did Toyota expect to gain from 'misleading' consumers? What was Toyota trying to achieve by blaming the incidents on floor mats or driver error?
5   The incidents are almost 40 years apart, but it seems that lessons were not learnt. Why so?

3.4 Deontological ethics

The word deontological is derived from the Greek 'deon' meaning obligation or duty. This ethical theory states that the morality of action is not based on consequences but is a matter of doing one's duty, of doing what is right and for the right reason. The deontological approach suggests that ethical judgement should be based on what acts are like in themselves, by their intrinsic nature, rather than on their results. They do not depend on the production or failure to produce good. One's duty is to do what is morally right and to avoid the morally wrong, regardless of the consequences of doing so (De George, 2010: 77–8). Thus, from a deontological point of view, bribery, even if its consequences can bring the greatest happiness to the greatest number of people – for example, bribing to acquire a large contract to help sustain a business that employs a large number of people – is wrong, by its very nature, regardless of its consequences. The deontological approach has historical traditions dating back to the Ten Commandments and the golden rule ('treat others as you would like them to treat you'). An important version was formalised by the Enlightenment era philosopher Immanuel Kant (1724–1804). Kant bases his approach on the notion that human beings are rational and should follow and obey a version of moral law that he called the Categorical Imperative, which means that it is something to be done, absolutely and unconditionally, no matter what the circumstances or consequences. According to this view, for an action to be morally right, it must be possible for the person doing it to see it as something that everyone ought to do, and not just something for the person's own benefit. To that extent, it is seen as acting in accordance with a moral rule, and it can respect all rational beings as ends in themselves. An action is moral if it is carried out on that basis, not in expectation of a reward. Carrying out one's business honestly, for example, is praiseworthy, but what makes it moral is that a person can see honest behaviour as something everyone can do, and not just because it is the best policy to attract and stay in business and make more profit in the long run. Kant's Categorical Imperative has three maxims (Stanford, 2022a):

1   The Formula of the Universal Law of Nature – that we are to 'act only in accordance with that maxim through which you can at the same time will that it become a universal law'.
2   The Humanity Formulation – that 'we should never act in such a way that we treat humanity, whether in ourselves or in others, as a means only but always as an end in itself'.

3   The Kingdom of Ends Formula – that we must 'act in accordance with the maxims of a member giving universal laws for a merely possible kingdom of ends' – that is, all people should consider themselves never as means but always as ends.

Deontological ethics in business

One of the main strengths of deontological theory is that it makes sense of cases in which consequences don't seem to determine an ethical decision. For example – a manufacturer has an obligation to honour a warranty on a defective product even if the cost of doing so exceeds the benefit of satisfying the customer. Another strength is in evaluating motives of an action – for example, the motive for donating to charity may be genuine concern, or desire to impress friends, or to gain tax benefits. There are, however, several difficulties in applying the moral law of the Categorical Imperative. The first is that of generality. How do we determine the level of generality of the rule on which we are acting? For example, should a rule about bribing be 'bribe' or 'do not bribe' or 'bribe, if it is acceptable in another society or country', or 'bribe, only when necessary to sustain your business'? It is not always easy to categorically and accurately state the rule of an action, which may lead to a situation where we are tempted to fabricate a rule that will allow us to do what we wish, rather than stating the principle on which we want to act. A second difficulty in applying the moral law of the Categorical Imperative is when two moral laws, when needed to be applied to a proposed action, clash with each other. For example, should we be untruthful which might save someone or tell the truth when doing so will harm someone? Here, there are two moral laws – if we tell the truth, it will harm someone – violating one moral law. If we do not tell the truth, it will save someone – violating the other moral law.

3.5 Ethics of rights

When we consider the various ethical concepts discussed above – ethical absolutism, ethical relativism, utilitarianism, and deontological – the question that becomes most prominent is whether there are any rules that we should follow no matter what the consequences or what we desire, what our background is, where we come from or who we are? What could be the most basic and fundamental aspect for all sentient beings when considering ethical decision-making? One possibility that most traditions seem to accept is that all human beings have a fundamental human right to be treated with dignity and respect. Some traditions also extend such rights to all other sentient beings such as animals and birds. Philosopher John Locke wrote that all individuals are equal in the sense that they are born with certain 'inalienable' natural rights. Among these fundamental natural rights, Locke said, are 'life, liberty, and property' (Rogers, 2021). This idea was later incorporated in part in the US Declaration of Independence.

Donaldson (1991) developed a list of fundamental international human rights. These include three types of morally minimum mandatory duties that corporations, individuals, and governments must respect: (1) avoid depriving people, (2) help protect people from deprivation, and (3) aid the deprived people. The United Nations founded the United Nations Human Rights Council (UNHRC) to discuss all human rights issues and situations that require attention. Today almost every member state in the world has an Office of the High Commissioner of Human Rights (OHCHR, 2022; UNHRC, 2022). Further, recognising that the inherent dignity and equal rights of human beings is the foundation of freedom, justice, and peace, the General Assembly of United Nations in 1948 proclaimed the Universal Declaration of Human Rights. Consisting of 30 Articles, these are considered as a common standard of achievement for all peoples and all nations and today most countries have most of these articles incorporated into their constitution (UDHR, 2022). For example, there are six Fundamental Rights in the Indian Constitution: right to equality, right to freedom, right against exploitation, right to freedom of religion, cultural and educational rights, and right to constitutional remedies (MEA, 2022).

Applications of such rights can be seen in the objection to child labour because such practices violate a child's right to be treated with dignity, to be educated, to be respected, and not to be exploited. However, there can also be conflicts between ethical actions. The utilitarian telos (goal) where there could be the greatest good for the greatest number of people can affect an individual's right to own and retain property – such as when the authorities would want to acquire a person's land area for the purpose of constructing a rail line through the property. The rail line will of course ensure good or happiness to a great number of people but will also interfere with the individual's right to own the property and not move.

3.6 Ethics of justice

Dictionaries define justice as 'fairness in the way people are dealt with (Cambridge Dictionary), 'the quality of being just, impartial, or fair' (Merriam-Webster), and 'the fair treatment of people' (Oxford Learner's Dictionaries). 'In bioethics, justice is one of the basic principles, meaning fairness, impartiality, equity. It includes the concept of distributive justice, and application of affirmative action when this is desirable or necessary. In all aspects of law, including law relating to public health problems, justice means seeking the truth and basing judgements on evidence rather than on the eloquence of arguments for differing points of view' (Oxford Reference). Based on these definitions, we can now understand, in Western civilisation, almost every major work on ethics from Plato to John Rawls has held that justice is part of the central core of morality (Velasquez et al., 2022).

There are different kinds of justice – compensatory (compensating injustice), retributive (punishment for a law-breaker), procedural (fair decision procedures), commutative (in transactions), and distributive (distribution of benefits and burdens) – see De George (2010: 76–7).

Of these, commutative justice is important to business transactions, and distributive justice is central to both business and governmental actions. How can we hire people in a just and non-discriminatory manner? How do we ensure that allocating places in medical or management schools is fair to both mainstream and minority applicants? How do governments allocate funds to people in sudden distress (in times of floods, fire, or drought) versus ongoing needs of infrastructure or health? How is dignity to be restored to those who lose jobs through downsizing?

Decisions in business ethics can be influenced by cultural backgrounds (French and Weiss, 2000). Some cultures apply individualistic approaches to justice while others take a more community-focused approach. French and Weiss (2000) contend that ethics of justice can affect three perspectives: focusing on principles, purposes, and results. These perspectives align respectively with deontological and consequentialist ethics. An influential theory based on the Kantian deontological approach is John Rawls's theory of distributive justice, which attempts to answer questions such as those in the previous paragraph. These principles of distributive justice would thus be universal, respect all persons, and be rationally acceptable to all – the three main tenets of Kantian deontology. Rawls considers justice to be comparable only to truth and 'it is the first virtue of social institutions' (Höffe and den Haan, 2013). Rawls further contends that to ensure happiness of its people and to ensure liberty, the state uses principles of justice.

So, how can these principles of justice be structured and chosen? In his *Theory of Justice* Rawls argues that (1) each person is to have an equal right to the same basic liberties such as civil and political rights, and (2) social and economic inequalities have to benefit the least disadvantaged members of society – that is, 'while the distribution of wealth and income need not be equal, it must be to everyone's advantage' (Rawls, 1971: 51; 2001). Rawls further proposes the principles of justice would be chosen by free and rational persons in an initial position of equality, called the 'original position'. In it 'no one knows his place in society, his class position, or social status, nor does anyone know his fortune in the distribution of natural assets and abilities, his intelligence, strength, and the like... their conceptions of the good or their special psychological propensities' (Höffe and den Haan, 2013: 23). Rawls suggests we perform a thought experiment where decision-makers would be behind a 'veil of ignorance'. The decision-makers are rational and do not know the role they would be playing in the decision. So, they could be rich or poor, talented or untalented, handicapped or not, white or coloured, male or female, a senior executive or a worker, and so on. Rawls argues that our decisions will be relatively fair to all if we do not know which role we will be playing. This thus defends the idea that a society structured by principles of justice is more stable than other societies, as it can offer better guarantees (Westwood, 2020). From a position of total ignorance, we can then ask the question about what type of society we would like to live in with respect to issues such as political, social, gender, race, and religious equality or what should an organisation do with issues such as employment opportunities, outsourcing, downsizing, and child labour. Using the analogy of 'starting off with a clean slate', suppose a society gets an opportunity to choose the type of government they would like to have. From an 'original position' context and behind a veil of ignorance as described above, the choices could be democracy, feudal, dictatorship, or anarchy. In a similar vein, suppose an organisation intends to gain cost efficiencies by getting their products produced in a lost-cost country that engages child labour. Again, from an 'original position' context and behind a veil of ignorance, the organisation could think of ways of providing schooling and nutrition to the children who may be required to work to supplement their family income.

Rawls, however, concedes that there will be limits to what people can do – he calls this limit the 'strains of commitment'. It has been argued that we are not dependable enough to fulfil justice because facts such as regret, bias, and poor judgement are central to the human condition (Lebron, 2019). It follows that no one could foresee situations that could generate marginalisation, resentment, oppression, or give rise to hostility and protests from those in a socially disadvantaged position (Manzano, 2021: 128).

3.7 Virtue ethics

Virtue ethics can trace its origins to the ancient Greeks through Aristotle (382–322 BCE; see Aristotle, 350BCE/2000), the Chinese through Confucius (551–479 BCE), and the ancient Indians through the Bhagavad Gita (circa 5th century BCE). For contemporary readings see MacIntyre (2007), Lawrenz (2021), and Gupta (2006) respectively. Virtue ethics claims that the key to good ethics lies not in consequences or rules, rights, and responsibilities, but in the character of all people involved in the action. Both teleological and deontological ethics address the question, what actions are good or right? Virtue ethics asks: what kind of a person should we be and what character traits should we possess and exhibit? The answer is that a person should be virtuous, seeking to flourish and having the virtues needed for that. MacIntyre (2007: 44) contends that while Kant's moral philosophy argues that the rules of morality are binding on all rational beings, what is important is their will to carry them out.

The role of ethics, according to Aristotle, is to enable us to lead a 'good life', which is possible only for virtuous persons, that is people in possession of virtues. He described virtue as a character trait that manifests itself in habitual action in appropriate circumstances. Thus, courage as a virtue does not mean that it could be exhibited only once or twice – it should rather be a trait of a person who always exhibits courage when it is called for. Plato, Aristotle's teacher, had originally identified four virtues – wisdom, courage, self-control, and justice. Aristotle's concept of virtue was reflected in behaviours that represented a balance or a mean of the personal quality being considered (Provis, 2017c). Thus, courage is considered a virtue when it is the mean or the balance between cowardice, as the deficiency in behaviour towards danger, and rashness, as the excess in the behaviour. Other virtues are benevolence, compassion, courtesy, friendliness, honesty, loyalty, moderation, and tolerance. Virtue ethics postulates that a virtuous person in possession of virtues such as those above is motivated to do the right thing and cultivates the motivation in daily conduct. The theory further states that the virtuous person would know and do the right thing by exercising judgement, rather than by applying a universal set of rules, and that this is more generally reliable than trying to follow the rules.

Virtue ethics in business

By extending the notion that the virtues of a good businessperson should be the same as the virtues of a good person and considering that business is part of life and society, it is possible to suggest that virtue ethics could also be applied to businesses. Solomon (1992) posited that the two traditional approaches to business ethics, utilitarianism and Kantian ethics, are not the right kind of theories to provide the day-to-day understanding of business; rather virtue ethics with its emphasis on personal character is a more suitable theory. Boatright (1995: 358) further suggests that 'ethical problems are largely due to personal failings'. Some researchers have proposed that virtue ethics has the potential for leaders and managers 'to create and sustain "good" organisations and institutions' (Harris et al., 2013: 1). Since people spend most of their adult lives in business organisations, if they are to achieve happiness, they should be able to do so at work as well as in other spheres of their lives. However, considering that situations in business may be different from ordinary daily life, virtues of everyday life may not be applicable to business. Thus, the personal virtues of caring and honesty can be used in business, but their application in business could depend on the situation. Employees may be cared for but caring cannot be extended too much when downsizing the number of employees. This is consistent with the idea of virtue being not taken to an extreme. Similarly, complete honesty may not go far enough in certain aspects of business such as advertising, marketing, and negotiations. Regardless of the above discussion, it is important to determine character traits for businesspersons. De George (2010: 512) reiterates that 'we must have moral persons if we are to have moral businesses'. While the issue of the morality of management is 'problematic', Moore (2013: 28–30) has 're-imagined' the role of management to include good purpose, getting the right balance in the pursuit of external goods, character of the organisation, and an environment within which organisational virtue can flourish.

The main strengths of virtue ethics are:

- Based on the argument that although utilitarianism and Kantian ethics provide moral principles that can be applied to specific cases, people generally take decisions based on what they feel most comfortable with or what a person they admire would do.
- Characteristics, such as integrity and courage, of a professional may be a more effective guide than principles and rules.

Harris (2013: 68) contends that 'courage could be the most suitable exemplar for the wider consideration of the relevance of virtues in effective management'. On the other hand, a virtuous character can have limitations when dealing with some ethical dilemmas such as limits of rules and conflicts between rules. For example – will accepting a box of chocolates from a supplier be acceptable when compared to a holiday trip paid by a supplier, and is it acceptable to bribe an official to secure a contract to prevent the closure of one's business. This issue is addressed in the virtue ethics tradition by highlighting the need for phronesis which can be translated as practical wisdom (Aristotle, 350BCE/2000; Provis, 2017c). This means that there will be no easy answers to hard questions in ethics.

3.8 Ethics of care

Care is a major and important aspect of life. Sentient beings have been caring for each other from time immemorial. Animals, birds, and even insects care for their young and for others in their group. We care for people in need – such as those who are hungry, in pain, lonely, or needing any kind of help, as seen in recent disaster events such as bush/forest fires, floods, and pandemics. Care can also be a source of pleasure, making life meaningful and rewarding (Livnat and Villa Braslavsky, 2020). For human beings, ethics could be a derivative or an extension of care-giving. In business, ethics of care can influence decisions in terms of how they will affect people.

Simola (2003) notes the distinction between ethics of justice and ethics of care. Ethics of justice is oriented towards fairness, protection of individual rights, achieved through reciprocity, and using logic to evaluate conflicting rights and claims. It uses absolute standards of judgement based on impartial and bias-free considerations. Ethics of care, in contrast, is based on the creation and strengthening of relationships, and consideration of the feelings of others. Narrative and contextual complexities of relationships among people are applied to solve problems.

The approach to ethics of care can partly be traced to feminist ethics which focuses attention on power, privilege, or access to social goods. Borgerson (2007) contends that feminist ethics underpins business ethics and corporate social responsibility, and asserts that feminist ethics focuses on relationships, responsibility, and experience. The forerunner of feminist ethics, Carol Gilligan, suggested alternative ethical considerations to those postulated by another psychologist, Lawrence Kohlberg (whose concepts will be more fully explored later in Chapter 4), that included a voice of 'care' centred around values of care. Gilligan argued that when girls approach adolescence, their sense of morality diverges to a responsibility oriented towards caring for others, whereas male morality has a justice orientation respecting the rights of others (Welldon, 2012). Researchers however contend that it is not appropriate to characterise the ethics of care as specifically feminist (Borgerson, 2007: 485).

The notion of care in ethics, and leadership ethics in particular, includes empathy, relatedness, and cooperation, things often associated with femininity (Pullen and Vachhani, 2020). Borgerson (2018), however, expresses concern that caring characteristics when exhibited by women in work or everyday life appear to underestimate female potential thus blocking access to leadership opportunities and could undermine female leaders and their leadership styles. She contends that 'stereotypical masculine traits can be prominent in females and stereotypical feminine traits can be prominent in males'. In particular, reference is made to the ethics of care and power in the context of perceived male and female leadership styles, and the existence of a *glass cliff,* a phenomenon whereby women are promoted to leadership roles in organisations that are on the brink of failure (2018: 1–4).

Application of the ethics of care can be observed in everyday lives, professional practices, analysing social and public policies, international relations, and the design of physical environments (Barnes et al., 2015: 4). Stensota (2015) further developed the concept of public ethics of care in policy areas such as law enforcement, prison management, housing, infrastructure, and environmental policies. Employees performing public tasks needing to interpret and use rules can make judgements based on a care ethics perspective.

▬▬▬ Box **3.3** ▬▬▬

Applying ethical theories to the Ford and Toyota cases

Going back to the Ford and Toyota cases, discuss how can you apply some or all of the ethical theories discussed so far to them.

3.9 Discourse ethics

The theories discussed so far in this chapter are based on normative approaches to ethical theory – this means the theories are prescriptive in nature, telling us how we should resolve ethical issues. We have said earlier that ethics and morality are about good, happiness, utility, duty, obligations, care, rights, and justice. We claim that we 'ought to' and 'ought not to' do certain things. If we are governed by greater good or by Kantian universal norms and laws, can we claim that we actually know the truth and have the knowledge of these ideas? We cannot assume that everybody shares the same values to solve ethical issues in society and in business (Chen, 2021). For example, the issue of child labour across the world is addressed with different points of view and ethical ideas. This requires a different and new approach to resolving ethical issues. Discourse ethics seeks to do just that. It concentrates not on ethical principles or individual ethical decisions, but on procedures for resolving ethical disagreements, in the same way that virtue ethics concentrates on the character of the agent rather than on specific dilemmas.

The discourse approach is a normative approach that suggests a process of rational debate necessary to arrive at an ethical solution. It does not apply any ethical principles and does not distinguish between right and wrong; rather its approach is to seek the truth. Discourse ethics, while influenced by Kantian ethics, 'replaces the Kantian Categorical Imperative by a procedural moral argumentation' (Chen, 2021: 80). Habermas (1993) put forward the idea that the essence of discourse ethics is speech or in other words discourse using language. Ethical behaviour can be achieved not by applying ethical principles but through communication and arguments made for or against any proposition. For instance, a city may use an online forum to seek inputs from the public on budget priorities. Participants then seek understanding and consensus, and individuals make claims about what is 'right' or 'good' and offer reasons for those claims (Killian, 2021). Habermas (1993) posits that arguments are problem-solving procedures that generate convictions. By asking 'what should we do?', participants who are capable of understanding and judgement can justify or refute claims. In addition, the process of discourse can enable participants to learn from each other and adjust attitudes with meanings (Killian, 2021).

However, to ensure the right outcome, Habermas (1993) specifies that the core requirements in a discourse should allow everyone to take part, question anyone's assertions, introduce assertions themselves, express their attitudes, desires, and needs, and ensure that no one is prevented by internal or external coercion from exercising their rights. Chen (2021) summarises the core principles of discourse ethics as:

- Norms in a discourse should be acceptable to all participants.
- Norms should meet the consent of all participants who are affected.
- Consequences and side effects of norms on each individual should be accepted by all without coercion.

Referring back to the section on 'Challenges for vulnerable stakeholders' in Chapter 2, the principles and procedures of discourse ethics would have produced more positive and ethical outcomes for the disadvantaged people of Odisha by enabling them to voice their issues and problems.

3.10 Postmodern ethics

Modernism is a worldview associated with Western Enlightenment rationality dating back to the 17th to 19th century. Postmodernism, a late 20th century movement, is considered to be a reaction against the intellectual values of the 'modernism' period. In general terms, its principles can be described as denials of the philosophical viewpoints of the Enlightenment (Duignan, 2020).

Earlier in this chapter, we discussed two distinct positions of the approach to ethics in business – a utilitarian perspective and a deontological approach to ethics. Due to its basic cost-benefit structure, most managers follow a utilitarian approach evaluating behaviour in terms of consequences. However, questions arise – best consequences for whom and who decides who is to benefit from these consequences? The universalist deontological approach subscribes to the idea that ethical action is dependent on the intentions of the person taking the action and what one would want everyone else to do, not the consequences. An individual's decisions can be influenced by their level of cognitive moral development. There are shortcomings here too – applying moral principles universally and impartially to all individuals and leaving it to the individual to decide right and wrong by application of reason. Zygmunt Bauman in his seminal work on postmodern ethics addressed the shortcomings of business ethics theories by incorporating ethics in the way action is taken instead of as a set of abstract rules or positions (Kelemen and Peltonen, 2001). Bauman (1993: 3–4) suggests that 'the postmodern approach to ethics consists of first and foremost... in the rejections of the typically modern ways of going about its moral problems (that is responding to moral challenges with coercive normative regulation..., and the philosophical search for absolutes, universals and foundations in theory)'.

Gray (2010: 7) contends that 'the starting point of postmodern ethics is the recognition of the ever-present uncertainty when it comes to issues of morality, of the ongoing tensions in matters to do with values, ethics and morals'. Ways to deal with these tensions would be to be morally responsible for others and to care for others unselfishly in situations we might not understand and for which there are no knowable solutions. Bauman (1993) stressed that postmodern ethics is not about rational judgements, decisions, and choices. Rather than weighing all the factors involved, it is a responsive form of ethics prompted by what is needed and our responsibilities for others. It may not mean that we always respond and do the right thing. The next question would be 'How is right action determined?' Bauman (1998) further asserts that since human beings are 'morally ambivalent', no ethical code can fit the ambivalent nature of morality. This in effect means that moral conduct cannot be guaranteed, and we must rely on our conscience to instil moral responsibility.

Postmodern business ethics is still in its nascent stages of displaying its full potential. In 1993 Ronald M. Green was convinced that business ethics 'is profoundly a postmodern phenomenon' (Green, 1993: 219). Green contends that there are two aspects which indicate business ethics is postmodern. Firstly, postmodern business ethics rejects the idea that any single economic or ethical theory can address ongoing ethical problems of business. Secondly, business ethics addresses complex ethical issues by approaching and understanding such issues with a multiplicity of perspectives and views. This is further clarified by Gustafson (2000) who identified four characteristics of postmodern business ethics:

1　There should not be a separation of personal and professional ethical behaviour. Whether one acts as a self-interested private person or as a corporate agent, one is always a human being.

2　Postmodern business ethics rely on a narrative approach rather than attempting to attain an ethical position through abstract theory. In other words, it considers the entire worldview of a person, which is why virtue ethical theories that focus on character rather than rules are gaining credence.

3　Rather than a set of rules that is universally recognised, postmodern business ethics focuses on local rules that can work and be agreed to. The idea here is being aware of the uniqueness of situations and how a principle that works well in some situations may not apply as well in others.

4　Postmodern business ethics strives for ethics that makes more sense and can work better than other approaches tried so far.

3.11 Ethical pluralism

Ethical pluralism is the idea that there are several values which may be equally correct and fundamental, and yet conflict with each other. Philosopher and moralist Isaiah Berlin (1909–1997) explained ethical (or value) pluralism as 'When two or more values clash, it is not because one or another has been misunderstood; nor can it be said, a priori, that any one value is always more important than another' (Stanford, 2022b). There is a debate on whether ethical pluralism can be distinguished from ethical relativism. Berlin (and others) have clarified that relativism is a form of subjectivism – for example, these are our traditions which you do not understand, and yours are different which we do not understand. On the other hand, pluralism holds that understanding of moral views is possible among all people, and it can explain the possibility of moral communication – for example, accepting a basic 'core' of human values.

In this chapter, we have discussed several ethical theories and their values. Table 3.1 summarises the key differences in their concepts and the relevant questions for each theory. The idea here is that we can apply several or all of these questions to a particular ethical issue, to ascertain whether the decisions and actions taken or to be taken were or would be ethical.

Table 3.1　Summary of ethical theories with key differences

Ethical theory?	Key concept	Relevant questions
Ethical egoism	Focuses only on maximising individual pleasure, acting only from self-interest	Is this in the best interest of only the individual and/or the organisation?
Utilitarianism	An action is right if it produces the greatest amount of good, such as welfare and happiness, for the greatest number of people affected by that action	Will the consequences be positive for all concerned?

(Continued)

Table 3.1 (Continued)

Ethical theory?	Key concept	Relevant questions
Deontology	One's duty is to do what is morally right and to avoid the morally wrong, regardless of the consequences of doing so	What would happen if the decision was allowed to happen everywhere in the world?
Ethics of rights	All human beings have a fundamental human right to be treated with dignity and respect	Have human rights and dignity been considered?
Ethics of justice	Justice is the central core of morality – it means seeking truth and basing judgements on evidence rather than on the eloquence of arguments for differing points	Has everyone been treated fairly?
Virtue ethics	The key to good ethics lies not in consequences or rules, rights, and responsibilities, but in the character of all people involved in the action	What would a person of integrity and character do?
Ethics of care	Based on the creation and strengthening of relationships, empathy, cooperation, and consideration of the feelings of others	Is this based on strengthening relationships and consideration of the feelings of others?
Discourse ethics	Norms in a discourse should be acceptable to all participants, norms should meet the consent of all participants who are affected, and consequences and side effects of norms on each individual should be accepted by all without coercion	Is there open communication, involving appropriate people, and norms applied?
Postmodern ethics	Ways to deal with these tensions would be to be morally responsible for others and to care for others unselfishly in situations we might not understand and for which there are no knowable solutions	Is the decision based on what's needed and our responsibilities for others?

Summary

- This chapter has illustrated the wide array of ethical theories within the normative ethical approach to make ethical decisions. Starting with ethical egoism and ethical relativism, we discussed the concepts of greater good (utilitarianism), duty and obligations (deontological), integrity and character (virtue ethics), ethics of rights, care, and justice. Further, we showed discourse ethics as a process of rational debate to arrive at an ethical solution, ending with postmodern ethics as a responsive form of ethics based on what's needed.

- As would be quite clear from the various ethical approaches, it would be difficult to identify and specify any one or two ethical approaches to resolve ethical problems. Should some or all approaches be applied to an ethical issue? How do we select an ethical decision that would be 'best' suited to the situation at hand? Managers in business may feel comfortable with one or two approaches and use them to push through their judegement. Rather, it is suggested that ethical problems should be evaluated from a wide range of perspectives (also called 'ethical pluralism' by some researchers) such as the approaches discussed in this chapter.

- Some authors have suggested an ethical evaluation matrix consisting of the various ethical approaches, asking a key question for each theory, and responding with a simple positive (+) or a negative (–) answer for each approach. For example: take the B737 Max case. Ask relevant questions for each approach as shown in Table 3.1. There should be a direction to the resolution of the ethical problem, if for example there are more negative answers than positive ones.

CASE STUDY 3.1
BOEING B737 MAX CRASHES

This case study is based on the Boeing 737 Max crashes and the subsequent scandal that unfolded. There are numerous accounts, analysis, comments, and reporting that ensued from the crashes, available on the web.

The following text enumerates the situation briefly with key points. You will need to obtain further information from the resources mentioned at the end of this case study, and from your own research.

Following the 25 February 2009 crash near Amsterdam of a Turkish Airlines Boeing 737 NG (Next Generation), which was a predecessor of the Boeing 737 MAX model, it was determined that Boeing had not included vital information for the pilots about how to respond to sensor failures in the NG operations manual. The outcome of this investigation was not made public. Of the 128 on board the aircraft, nine people including the pilots died.

Nine years later, on 29 October 2018, a Lion Air B737 Max crashed into the Java Sea, 13 minutes after take-off from Jakarta, Indonesia; 187 people lost their lives.

Within five months, on 10 March 2019, an Ethiopian Airlines B737 Max crashed on take-off from Addis Ababa. All 157 people on board were killed.

Subsequent investigations revealed that Boeing's software called Manoeuvring Characteristics Augmentation System (MCAS) was faulty, allowing a sensor to push the aircraft's nose down after take-off. The circumstances that led to this situation included (but were not limited to) the following:

- Although Boeing knew about the problems with the MCAS system quite early, it chose to ignore the solution of providing two sensors instead of one.
- In a hurry to get the plane under operation, Boeing decided pilots did not need to be trained for this particular aircraft on a flight simulator.
- Boeing misled the Federal Aviation Administration (FAA) on this issue.
- There was a competitive rivalry between Boeing and Airbus, especially the B737 and A320 Neo respectively. Boeing was losing market share rapidly and had to 'do' something fairly quickly, not to mention addressing dwindling share prices and pressure from Wall Street investors.
- There were other factors which can be found in the resources below.

(Continued)

Finally, on 7 January 2021, the Department of Justice (DoJ) in the US, after their investigations, ruled that Boeing had to pay a total criminal fine amount of USD 2.5 billion. They said:

> The tragic crashes of Lion Air Flight 610 and Ethiopian Airlines Flight 302 exposed fraudulent and deceptive conduct by employees of one of the world's leading commercial airplane manufacturers. Boeing's employees chose the path of profit over candour by concealing material information from the FAA concerning the operation of its 737 Max airplane and engaging in an effort to cover up their deception. This resolution holds Boeing accountable for its employees' criminal misconduct, addresses the financial impact to Boeing's airline customers, and hopefully provides some measure of compensation to the crash-victims' families and beneficiaries.

Questions

Using the Case-Study Integrative Framework in Figure 0.1, reflect on these questions:

1. Boeing's mission and value statements are: 'People working together as a global enterprise for aerospace industry leadership. In everything we do and in all aspects of our business, we will make safety our top priority, strive for first-time quality, hold ourselves to the highest ethical standards, and continue to support a sustainable future.' Do you think Boeing has violated these statements? Justify your answer.
2. List Boeing's primary and secondary stakeholders. Based on the Mitchell, Agle & Wood (1997) article's concept of prioritising stakeholders, who would you consider Boeing's Definitive Stakeholder and why?
3. What were the ethical issues underlying the B737 Max disasters? Analyse with all applicable ethical approaches discussed in this chapter.
4. Based on your analysis above, identify and discuss the links between Boeing's strategic and ethical issues that led to the consequences. What actions do you think Boeing should have taken (a) before and (b) after the crashes? Support your recommendations with theories/concepts from this topic.

Sources:
Boeing (2022)
Gates (2020)
New York Times (2020)
Robison and Newkirk (2019)
US Department of Justice (2021)
Wall Street Journal video on B737 Max – what happened? (2020)

CASE STUDY 3.2

WHY THE TAJ MAHAL PALACE AND TOWER HOTEL EMPLOYEES RISKED THEIR LIVES

The Taj group is the largest Indian chain of hotels in South Asia and is a part of the Tata group of companies (established 1868) that includes industry sectors such as airlines, automotive, chemicals, defence, fast moving consumer goods, electric utility, finance, home appliances, hospitality, information technology, retail, e-commerce, real estate, salt, steel, cement, tea, and telecoms. With an estimated revenue of USD 103 billion in 2021, the Tata Group is one of the largest groups in India. Interestingly, the Tata family controls 66 per cent of the holding company, Tata Sons.

On 26 November 2008, terrorists simultaneously attacked about a dozen locations in Mumbai, India, killing 164 people. Nine of the gunmen were killed during the attacks, one survived.

The terrorists had travelled from Karachi, Pakistan, to Mumbai via boat. Along the way, they hijacked a fishing trawler and killed four crew members, throwing their bodies overboard.

The terrorists docked at the Mumbai waterfront near the Gateway of India monument. They hijacked cars, including a police van, and split into at least three groups to carry out the attacks, according to police. The attackers used automatic weapons and grenades.

For two nights and three days, they then held one of the most iconic buildings in the city, the Taj Mahal Palace and Tower Hotel ('the Taj') under siege. They took people hostage, killed others, and set fire to the famous dome of the hotel.

The siege of the Taj quickly became an international story. Lots of people covered it, including CNN's Fareed Zakaria, who grew up in Mumbai. In a report that aired the day after the attacks, Zakaria spoke eloquently about the horror of what had happened in Mumbai, and then pointed to a silver lining: the behaviour of the employees at the Taj.

Apparently, something extraordinary had happened during the siege. According to hotel managers, none of the Taj employees had fled the scene to protect themselves during the attack: they all stayed at the hotel to help the guests.

'I was told many stories of Taj hotel employees who made sure that every guest they could find was safely ferreted out of the hotel, at grave risk to their own lives', Zakaria said on his programme.

There was the story of the kitchen employees who formed a human shield to assist guests who were evacuating and lost their lives as a result. Of the telephone operators who, after being evacuated, chose to return to the hotel so they could call guests and

(Continued)

tell them what to do. The general manager of the Taj, who worked to save people even after his wife and two sons, who lived on the sixth floor of the hotel, died in the fire set by the terrorists.

During the crisis, dozens of workers – waiters and busboys, and room cleaners who knew back exits and paths through the hotel – chose to stay in a building under siege until their customers were safe. They were the very model of ethical, selfless behaviour.

What could possibly explain it?

Rohit Deshpande from the Harvard Business School conducted interviews with the hotel staff from managers to kitchen workers and reviewed the company's HR policies. His research revealed that it had something to do with how they recruit, train, and reward people.

For recruitment, the Taj avoids big cities and instead turns to small towns and semi-urban areas and develops relationships with local schools, asking the leaders of those schools to hand-select people who have the qualifications they want – not grades, but personal characteristics such as respect and empathy. This, he says, is also why recruiters avoid hiring managers for the hotel from the top business schools in India and deliberately go to second-tier business schools. In India, grades and attending a top-tier university are usually seen as extremely important by employers, so this approach was very unusual.

Everything about training in Taj involves rewards systems to encourage kindness. Rewards include gifts and job promotions.

Questions

Using the Case-Study Integrative Framework in Figure 0.1, reflect on these questions:

1   What do you think could be the business 'purpose' of the Taj Hotel?
2   Identify the ethical issues involved in this case.
3   Identify the primary and secondary stakeholders who were affected by this incident.
4   Analyse the incident and its associated ethical issues using these ethical theories – egoism, utilitarianism, deontology, virtue ethics, ethics of rights, justice, and care, and postmodern ethics.
5   Which ethical theories do you think can be used to explain the incident and its ethical issues?

Sources:
Deshpande (2012)
NPR (2011)
CNN (2021)
Stephens Balakrishnan (2011)

Recommended readings

De George, R.T. (2010), *Business ethics*, 7th edn, Upper Saddle River, NJ: Prentice Hall.

Written by one of the prioneers of business ethics education, this is an excellent book on the techniques and argumentation that are needed to analyse moral issies in business. Concepts, approaches, and theories are explained with examples from the business world.

French, W. and Weiss, A. (2000), 'An ethics of care or an ethics of justice', *Journal of Business Ethics*, 27(1/2): 125–36.

Investigates whether ethical decision-makers are motivated by ethics of justice or ethics of caring. It is a study of college graduates from six countries in predicating a justice or caring orientation.

Green, R.M. (1993), 'Business ethics as a postmodern phenomenon', *Business Ethics Quarterly*, 3(3): 219–25.

This paper contends that work in business ethics participates in two key aspects of the broad philosophical and aesthetic movement known as postmodernism.

Lawrenz, J. (2021), 'Confucius, Aristotle, and the Golden Mean: A diptych on ethical virtues', *The European Legacy*, 26(2): 149–69.

'How to live the good life' is a subject treated by Confucius and Aristotle in a manner that exhibits many surprising points of coincidence, not least in the colossal influence of both these philosophers on the social and political shape of their respective civilisations. This article correlates the relevant ideas which build a bridge between East and West on the perennial issues that affect all mankind in the context of a civil society.

Schur, M. (2022), *How to be perfect: The correct answer to every moral question*, London: Quercus Editions Ltd.

Accessible, humorous, and written in a clever style, this book draws on 2,500 years of deep thinking around the world. Schur starts off with easy ethical questions like 'Should I punch my friend in the face for no reason?' (no) and works his way up to the most complex moral issues we all face, like 'Can I still enjoy great art if it was created by terrible people?' and many more.

4

ETHICAL DECISION-MAKING UNDERSTANDING DESCRIPTIVE ETHICAL THEORIES

On completion of this chapter, you should be able to:

- Understand decision-making in management
- Understand ethical decision-making and explain the concepts using the Comprehensive Ethical Decision-Making (CEDM) model
- Critically evaluate the components, influencing factors, and processes in the CEDM model
- Apply the CEDM model to practical, real-life business issues

- The CEDM model
- Moral framing
- Four components of CEDM
- Moral intensity
- Cognitive moral development
- Internal and external organisational factors
- Emotions and intuitions
- Reflection
- Moral exemplars
- Moral rationalisation
- Moral imagination

─Box 4.1 Opening case─

Zinc plating of metal fittings

A manufacturer in Australia made thousands of metal fittings (used in construction and households, for example) – all reasonably priced for market sensitivity. These fittings were zinc plated for corrosion resistance. In the last 15 years environmental laws were tightened – so the zinc plating process became expensive because its filtration systems and the disposal of waste chemicals were expensive. However, customers who bought these products were being offered similar products from Asia – where zinc plating was done in backyards in unsafe conditions and used chemicals were poured into the ground. So, it was claimed that while the fittings were cheap, the process was detrimental for the environment. Rather than going out of business, the manufacturer started producing the same products in stainless steel which cost 4–5 times as much. They decided to come away from the market that buys zinc-plated products from overseas and now sell smaller quantities in stainless steel but still make a profit and remain in business. The business owner says, 'twenty years ago we did not face cheap imports from overseas, but we have now actually embraced in a hypocritical way that our society has demanded that we clean up our own environment and encourage the other countries to do the old environmentally unfriendly way'.

4.1 Introduction

The 'Zinc plating of metal fittings' opening case indicates that the organisation was confronted with an ethical issue and could have taken the decision of legally importing environmentally unsustainably produced products from overseas, but instead opted to manufacture the more expensive environmentally sustainable product locally. What was the decision-making process in this scenario? How and why did this organisation arrive at this decision?

While prescriptive or normative ethical theory as discussed in the previous chapter informs us what businesspeople should or ought to be doing, the descriptive ethical theory set out in this chapter describes how ethical decisions are actually made in business, and equally importantly it explains why people take those decisions. Explanations include factors that influence the process and outcomes of decisions. Descriptive ethics is a practical way of understanding how ethical theories from prescriptive ethics can be applied to business-related ethical issues. Thus, understanding and critically examining both types of ethical theories in conjunction can help us to be better prepared to make sound ethical judgements and actions. For example, when we examine what happened in the zinc-plating scenario (Box 4.1), we can describe the events by using a descriptive ethical decision-making model, analyse the factors and processes which led to the decision, explain why it happened by applying one or more of the prescriptive ethical theories, and finally come to a conclusion to recommend what should be done to manage similar occurrences.

So, what is decision-making and what are the processes employed in organisations? A wide range of approaches can be gleaned from various management areas.

The starting point is the fact that individuals in organisations make decisions. Decisions are made at different levels of the organisation, for example, top managers determine their organisation's goals, what products and services to offer or how best to organise the organisation; middle and lower-level managers typically determine production schedules, select new employees, and decide how pay rises are to be allocated. Non-managerial employees also make decisions that affect their work and the organisations they work for. Decision-making is thus an important part of the day-to-day activities of most individuals in an organisation.

Considering that decision-making occurs as a reaction to a problem, which exists when there is a discrepancy between the 'current' state of affairs and some 'desired' state requiring consideration of alternative courses of action, every decision requires interpretation and evaluation (Kinicki, 2021; Robbins et al., 2001). Several authors have noted the widespread use of the rational model of decision-making (Harrison, 1981: 53–7; Harrison, 1993; Johnson et al., 2005: 41–2).

However, there are conflicting views on the effectiveness of the rational decision-making model. It has been suggested that managerial decision-making is both a product of, and an influence on, the culture in which it exists. This resulted in a movement away from the traditional approaches to decision making such as the rational model which has its foundation in the quantitative disciplines of economics, mathematics, and statistics. The rational model assumes that all the significant variables in a given decision-making situation can be quantified to some degree. It also presupposes that there is one best outcome. This search for perfection is frequently a factor that delays making decisions. These models require a great deal of time and a great deal of information. As such, the rational model could be of limited use in most real-world managerial decisions involving high levels of uncertainty.

Alternative methods of decision-making in management decisions are often made by managers without necessarily following each step of the process. The full range of possible courses of action may not be considered or data may not be collected and used. Decisions may be dictated by the need to make quick decisions or may reflect the preferred style of decision-making of a certain manager.

It is therefore understandable when Kinicki (2021: 428) argues that non-rational models of decision-making explain how managers actually make decisions. These are based on the assumption that 'decision-makers do not possess complete information and that managers struggle to make optimal decisions'. Many decisions are characterised by complexity, relatively high uncertainty and goals and preferences that are neither clear nor consistent. Managers, therefore, frequently use methods alternative to the rational model for decision-making. Some of the alternative decision-making models are the 'satisfying' model, the 'implicit favourable' model, the 'intuitive' model, and the 'heuristics' process (see Savur, 2013 for details).

4.2 Introducing ethical decision-making

General theories of ethical decision-making include levels of decision-making consisting of the individual, the organisation, and the business system; factors involving ethical decision-making comprising the economic, legal, and moral; and approaches to ethical decision-making such as consequences (teleological theories), duties, obligations, and principles (deontological theories), and integrity (virtue ethics theories).

However, how does the manager know how to make decisions when faced with ethical dilemmas? Would they make a 'gut' decision; seek advice from peers; use a rule of thumb or some combination of these? Some answers found in studies conducted by Ferrell and Gresham (1985: 87) contend that 'ethical/unethical decisions are moderated by individual factors, significant others within the organisational setting, and opportunity for action'. Hunt and Vitell (1986) suggest that once an individual confronts a problem, they will perceive various possible actions. The individual may use some sort of a broad-based ethical judgement as a screening device and then apply an evaluation process.

Ferrell, Gresham and Fraedrich (1989) suggest that incorporating ethical principles into modern academic theories of decision-making has been slow. There could be several reasons for this. One reason may be that few scholars are interested in both ethics and decision-making because most ethical models have emerged from 'psychology-based disciplines, including organisational behaviour and marketing' (Jones, 1991: 367). Other reasons cited by Treviño (1986) are the delicate nature and complexity of this area and that 'managers are not likely to allow their "ethics" to be directly observed or measured', the lack of theory to guide investigation, and the notion that ethics is a branch of philosophy rather than social science – 'which may lead to the conclusion that business ethics is a "Sunday school" subject not worthy of serious discussion' (Treviño, 1986: 601).

In most situations ethical choices are clear enough for people to be able to decide what to do and for people in business to act accordingly. However, ethical decision-making becomes an issue when exceptions or novel situations occur and there is uncertainty about ethical obligations or when considerations of ethics come into conflict with the practical demands of business where multiple stakeholders, interests, and values are in conflict and laws are unclear (Treviño, 1986).

Several authors and researchers have contended that reason alone may not be sufficient to evoke a decision based on ethics. Rather, it could be dependent on intuition (Haidt, 2001; Narvaez and Lapsley, 2009; Pizarro and Bloom, 2003; Provis, 2017b), and heuristics (Hamilton, et al., 2009; Hayibor and Wasieleski, 2009). There are others who suggest that individual, organisational, and situational factors have significant impact on ethical decision-making. Individual factors may include the nature and personal characteristics of the decision-maker. Organisational factors may include the situation at issue, type of surrounding environment, and perceived organisational culture. Situational factors include referent groups, organisational factors, and industry factors. Referent groups include studies of peer groups, top management influences and the use of rewards and sanctions, all of which could be referred to as internal organisational factors. Industry factors include overall industry practices and business competitiveness, all of which could be referred to as external organisational factors.

4.3 Ethical decision-making models

Theoretical approaches to ethical decision-making (EDM) have transitioned to decision-making models. Over the last few decades, several EDM models have been proposed and integrated, and several business ethics researchers have turned to moral psychology for theory, constructs, and measures that could be applied to the business ethics domain.

A historical account of the development of EDM indicates that several authors have made attempts to ground ethical decision-making on some established theoretical approaches. Kitchener (1984) argued that both 'absolute thinking (dealing with rights and duties) and utilitarian thinking (doing the greatest good for the greatest number)' (p. 45) are involved in ethical decision-making, while Hare (1991) believed that the intuitive level is the main locus of everyday moral decisions. However, Hare aligned with Kitchener by contending that utilitarian thinking must be applied in situations where intuitions cannot 'settle the dispute' (p. 38). Lawrence Kohlberg in his cognitive moral development theory – discussed in greater detail later in this chapter – proposed that an individual's level of moral development strongly influences the person's decision regarding right and wrong and the rights, duties, and obligations involved in a particular ethical dilemma (Treviño, 1986).

EDM models could be categorised into ones that are rationalist-based and ones that are non-rationalist-based. The rationalist-based view led initially by Kohlberg (1981) and later by Rest (1984) assumes that moral reasoning leads to moral judgement and subsequent actions. The rationalist model was further developed by Ferrell and Gresham (1985) (social and cultural factors), Treviño (1986) (person–situation interaction), Jones (1991) (issue-contingent and moral intensity). The non-rationalist view assumes intuition and emotions influence moral judgement followed by explanations (reason) or justifications (rationalisations) (proponents led by Haidt (2001); Sonenshein (2007); Tsang (2002)). These concepts will be discussed further in this chapter.

Recently, attempts have been made to show that rationalist and non-rationalist approaches may not be mutually exclusive and may actually interact to achieve moral judgements. This integration, also known as 'dual-process' or 'two-systems', has been proposed by Greene et al. (2001) and Reynolds (2006), among others. Two recent models that illustrate such integrations are of particular interest to us: (1) the cognitive-intuitionist model proposed by Dedeke (2015) which consists of five stages – issue framing, pre-processing (automatic cognitions and emotions), moral judgement, moral reflection, and moral intent – and (2) the integrated ethical decision-making model proposed by Schwartz (2016) which consists of issue-norms, recognising ethical issues, mental processes of intuition-emotion-reason-rationalisation, judgement, intention, and action, influenced by situation, moral capacity, learning, and lack of awareness. Both models have their origins in and are based on James Rest's four-component model of ethical decision-making (Rest, 1984), widely acknowledged as the most significant rationalist-based model of EDM – see Lehnert et al. (2015) and Schwartz (2016) for more details.

While both integration models reflect the importance of reason and intuition in the moral judgement component of the EDMs, there is more to be said about moral judgement. Are there any moral principles that can be used to resolve ethical issues and dilemmas and are there any means of showing that the rules of our morality are the right ones? What concepts do people in business and society use to make moral judgements?

4.4 The Comprehensive Ethical Decision-Making model

As can be seen from the above discussions, ethical decision-making is a very complex process to understand and apply. In the rest of this chapter, we have condensed the contributions from various researchers and authors into a Comprehensive Ethical Decision-Making model (CEDM) that has the following features:

1   Components – consisting of moral framing, recognising ethical issues, making judegements, establishing moral intent, and taking action
2   Influencing factors – situational, organisational, and individual factors
3   Processes – emotions, intuitions, heuristics, exemplars, reflections, rationalising, moral imagination, and applying the three levels of moral judegements

The CEDM model depicted in Figure 4.1 represents the above three features with their individual sections. It should be noted that the figure is not a process flow diagram, rather it is designed to show how the various features of ethical decision-making can be configured around James Rest's most commonly used ethical decision-making model (Savur et al., 2018).

In Chapter 5 (Business Ethics Across Cultures), we will explore and discuss business ethics and ethical decision-making concepts in non-Western cultures.

Moral issue framing and norms

The process of the CEDM model begins at the point where individuals tend to perceive and process situations in different ways. There are two influencing factors at this stage – framing and norms. Framing occurs when individuals generate meaning from the external stimuli and could therefore perceive the situation either from a moral frame or a non-moral frame (Sonenshein, 2007; Tenbrunsel and Smith-Crowe, 2008). A non-moral frame would be a legal frame or business frame – for example, not considering the supply of expensive life-saving drugs at no-cost or subsidised cost to poorer countries – whereas a moral frame would consider ways to do it. The type of framing at this stage would dictate subsequent processes of the model. Individual decision-makers in business may apply either a business frame or an ethical frame. Applying business frames such as seeing an issue in financial terms related to profits or shareholder values inhibits ethical awareness and behaviours. Ethical aspects of the situation may get overlooked (Chen et al., 2020). Norms are standards or expectations of behaviour that are influenced by either normative conditions such as values, beliefs, and actions of external entities at national, cultural, and societal levels (Philippe and Durand, 2011), or by cognitive conditions such as internal taken-for-granted values and beliefs at work, group, and organisational levels (Hannah et al., 2011). An example of normative conditions would be bribery acceptable at the cultural or national level, and an example of cognitive conditions would be padding expense accounts being acceptable at the organisational level.

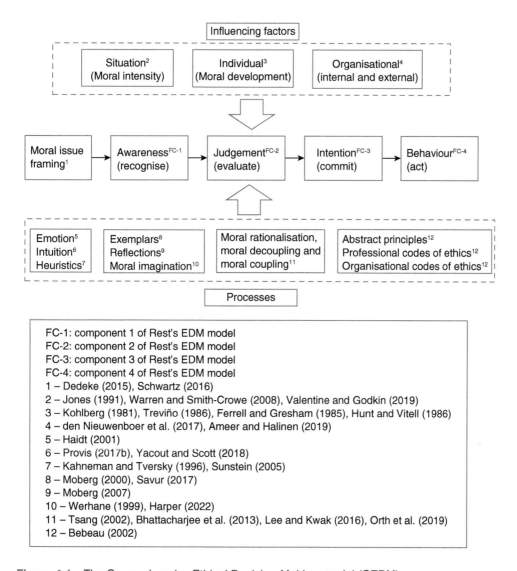

Figure 4.1   The Comprehensive Ethical Decision-Making model (CEDM)

—————— **Box 4.2** ——————

To sign or not to sign – that is the ethical dilemma

This is a true story. One of the responsibilities of working as a mid-level operations manager was signing off on sales invoices. The company was a start-up engaged in manufacturing engineering goods with the latest technology. One year, the company faced diminished working capital – the finance needed to purchase components and pay employees' salaries. The only way to access finance from the bank was to show evidence of inventory of materials and work-in-progress goods, or to show evidence of sales – based on which the bank could finance say up to 80 per cent of the value of the inventory or the sales invoices. Since neither of these two options was possible, the CEO approached the operations manager with a bunch of sales invoices and asked them to sign the documents, so that it could be presented to the bank to obtain finance for the badly needed working capital. The CEO rationalised this by arguing that this was only a temporary measure – that the finance received would enable the company to buy components, manufacture the final goods, collect money from customers, and return the finance back to the bank. All of this would take less than six months, nobody would know about it and the company would be able to survive for the future. The operations manager asked for time to go through the documents. Over the following night, the manager had time to reflect on the implications and consequences of signing off fictitious documents, and finally decided not to proceed with the CEO's request. When the manager informed the CEO of their decision, the CEO said, 'That's fine, don't worry. I will get it done by someone else'. The documents were signed off by some other manager, the company received the finance from the bank, and as predicted by the CEO, goods were manufactured and sold. Proceeds from the sales allowed the company to return the finance to the bank within six months. Unable to reconcile these events, the operations manager decided to resign from the company.

Questions

1   What role could moral framing have played in the decision-making that led to the CEO's actions?
2   What do you think the manager should have done?
3   Was the CEO's action acceptable considering that it saved the company?

Source: Adapted from the author's personal experiences.

Rest's Four Component model of ethical decision-making

Rest's Four Component model (FC) is based on individual ethical decision-making and behaviour, where a person faced with an ethical issue would recognise the moral issue, make a moral judgement, establish moral intent, and engage in moral behaviour (Rest, 1994; Rest, 1986: 3–5; Rest and Narvaez, 1994).

FC-1 – Moral awareness (recognising the moral issue) – involves interpreting the situation with sensitivity and involves imagining what courses of action are possible in a situation and tracing out the consequences of action in terms of how each action would affect each party involved (Rest, 1984; 1986). Subsequent components of the model do not come into play if the individual does not perceive some ethical content in a situation (Hunt and Vitell, 1986), or if a person at a lower stage of moral development (Blasi, 1990; Kohlberg, 1981; Rest, 1979) may not see a situation as an ethical issue (Ferrell et al., 1989). Recognition of an ethical issue can vary between persons because of the differences in a person's knowledge of the moral good (O'Boyle, 2002). Recognition of a moral issue can also depend on gender, nationality and culture, ethical experience, personal values and orientation, moral disengagement from the ethical aspects of a decision, factors such as job satisfaction, issue intensity (for example harming thousands of people is morally more intense than harming ten people), and organisational ethical climates generated by factors such as formal and informal systems (Tenbrunsel and Smith-Crowe, 2008). In the business context, Bebeau (2002) contends that recognising ethical issues can be influenced by knowledge of the regulations, codes, and norms of one's profession and recognising when they apply.

FC-2 – Make a moral judgement – involves determining what course of action would best fulfil a moral ideal, that is, what ought to be done in the situation (Rest, 1984; 1986: 8). From FC-1, a person is aware of the various possible courses of action, what the consequences would be to all parties involved, what principles are relevant and so on. In FC-2, a person needs to decide which of these courses of action is morally right, fair, or comes closest to a person's ideals. Making moral judgements has been suggested to depend on several factors: an individual's cognitive structure such as knowledge, values, beliefs, and attitudes; evaluation methods such as deontological and teleological; moral developmental stage; issue-dependency; and ability to think analytically.

FC-3 – Establish moral intent – involves resolving to place moral concerns ahead of other concerns by selecting among competing value outcomes the one to act upon, and deciding whether or not to fulfil one's moral ideal (Rest, 1984; 1986: 13). Having worked out what course of action would satisfy ethical requirements by applying one or several of the decision-making processes (FC-2), a person would now evaluate the moral decision with other competing values. Typically, moral values are not the only motives that people have and there is awareness of a number of possible outcomes based on different motives such as certain preferred consequences related to self-interest, for example advancement in careers, organisational pressures, desire to avoid aversive consequences, and internal stimuli such as emotions, feelings, and mood. Establishing moral intent is also dependent on social influence to guide behaviour, ego strength of conviction, locus of control (an individual's perception of how much control they exert over events in their lives), and the person's freedom to act.

FC-4 – Engage in moral behaviour (act) – involves executing and implementing a plan of action. It comprises figuring out a sequence of actions, working around difficulties, overcoming fatigue, resisting distractions, and not losing sight of the eventual goal (Rest, 1984; 1986: 15). Factors for engaging in moral behaviour include a combination of individual and organisational factors that can influence an individual's moral intention to take moral action and exhibit moral behaviour, opportunity to evaluate actual consequences, higher levels of moral development, organisational culture, the tendency of people to hold themselves less accountable for their behaviour than they would hold others in the same situation, and the courage to make behaviour conform to the good even when it is personally dangerous.

Returning to the opening case in Box 4.1 (on zinc plating of metal fittings), the ethical issue has been recognised (FC-1) as allowing imports of zinc-plated products at a lower cost and having strict environmental controls for the same process in Australia. The moral judgement (FC-2) made was that they will not import zinc products from overseas because of the utilitarian reasons of importing cheap products manufactured in unsafe and environmentally unsustainable conditions in order to make higher profits. Moral intent (FC-3) was established by not 'succumbing' to the pressure of achieving short-term high profits (by importing cheaper products). Moral behaviour (FC-4) was achieved by implementing the plan to manufacture stainless steel products at a higher cost but at the same time adhering to the environmental standards of Australia.

4.5 Influencing factors

Situational factors

Considerable research indicates that situational and organisational factors can influence ethical decision-making and have been included in various EDM models. The central aspect of the situational factor is moral intensity (Jones, 1991) – that the intensity of an issue will vary according to the following:

- The magnitude of consequences – for example: the consequence of an unfair dismissal from a job could be higher than when an employee is unjustly denied vacation.
- Social consequences – for example: bribing officials in your own country could have greater social consequences than bribing in other countries.
- Probability of effect – for example: businesses selling guns to known offenders has greater probability of harm (effect) than selling to a law-abiding citizen.
- Temporal immediacy – for example: releasing drugs that might have immediate side effects as compared to drugs that might have side effects after 30 years.
- Proximity – for example: layoffs in a person's work unit have greater moral proximity than layoffs in a remote work area.
- Proportionality or concentration of effects – for example: cheating an individual out of a given amount of money has a more concentrated effect than cheating an institutional entity for the same amount.

Moral intensity of an issue could increase when a situation requires breaking rules, codes, or laws. Higher levels of moral intensity would increase sensitivity to moral awareness (Schwartz, 2016). Other aspects related to situational factors are the importance of the issue – moral awareness can heighten based on how important the issue is to the individual – and issue complexity – for example an individual may not take ethical action if they feel that the whistle-blowing process is highly complex. In a study by Valentine and Godkin (2019), moral intensity has been shown to be positively related to ethical decision-making and whistle-blowing intentions. As perceptions of seriousness of consequences and proximity become stronger, recognition of an ethical issue, ethical judgement, and ethical intention will increase.

━━━━ **Box 4.3** ━━━━

Flights-to-nowhere: Ethical decision-making in tourism

Ethics in tourism has unique elements such as its cross-cultural settings, viewing tourism as a hedonistic activity, and environmental and social sustainability issues. Travel in the era of climate change has received some attention in both the academic literature and the mainstream news in the past decade as the existential crisis of climate change and air travel's contribution to it has grown in importance. It has been shown that air travel has consequences for the environment, predominantly in the form of greenhouse gas emissions, which contribute to climate change.

Studying ethics in tourism can help manage tourists' behaviour and these can be best informed by using specific scenarios and real-life examples. One such example is the flights-to-nowhere scenario. Most countries around the world imposed severe restrictions on international travel in early 2020. Towards the end of 2021, when restrictions started to ease in some parts of the world, potential tourists were eager to travel again. Given the need to satisfy tourism experiences and regenerate income, airlines offered 'flights-to-nowhere', sight-seeing flights that start and finish at the same airport, and do not arrive at a new destination. Flights were offered in Fiji, Hong Kong, Japan, Taiwan, and Australia, and the trips were booked out quickly. This happened at a time when there is a growing climate change emergency and during a global pandemic. Some say that it demonstrates how individuals address ethical dilemmas that involve individual and societal interests.

Several EDM model processes and factors, as discussed in this chapter, could be observed in the scenario.

Questions

Reflect on:

1   Why do you think passengers took flights-to-nowhere, given that these flights did not arrive at a new destination, but contributed to passengers' carbon footprint?
2   Analyse using Rest's Four Component model and situational factors. Where, do you think, the passengers digressed in their decision-making process?

Source: Adapted from Pratt and Tolkach (2022)

Individual factors

Researchers have integrated the influence of individual factors into most ethical decision-making models. These include factors such as cognitive stages of moral development (Kohlberg, 1981), individual values (Ferrell and Gresham, 1985), personal experiences (Hunt and Vitell, 1986), and locus of control (Treviño, 1986). All of these can be seen as parts of an individual's maturity and capacity to engage in recognising, judging, and acting on ethical issues. Locus of control describes how much personal responsibility we take for our own behaviour and its consequences. People with internal locus of control believe they control the events and are therefore responsible for the consequences, whereas people with external locus of control believe their behaviour is a product of circumstances beyond their control (Kinicki, 2021; Treviño and Nelson, 2014). Recent research has identified a variety of other factors such as 'moral character', 'moral conation' (the willpower or desire to act according to one's ethical principle), 'moral ownership' (feeling responsible for their and others' actions), and 'moral courage' (strength to resist pressure to act unethically) – see Hannah et al. (2011) for more details. There are other potential factors also that can affect EDM stages, such as demographic variables, personality variations, and ethical experience – see Craft (2013); Lehnert et al. (2015); O'Fallon and Butterfield (2005); and Weber and Elm (2018) for a list of individual and situational factors that influence ethical decision-making.

4.6 Cognitive moral development

Kohlberg's model (Kohlberg, 1981) lists three levels of development in moral reasoning and its transformations from childhood to adulthood, which include six separate stages. These stages are identified by the reasons an individual uses to justify a moral choice. The levels and stages are:

- Level 1: Pre-conventional morality (low cognitive moral development (CMD)
  At stages one (Obedience and punishment orientation) and two (Instrumental purpose and exchange), an individual is concerned about consequences, physical and serving one's own interests.
- Level 2: Conventional morality (moderate CMD)
  At stages three (Interpersonal accord, conformity, mutual expectations), and four (Social system and conscience maintenance), the individual conforms to avoid censure by legitimate authorities and to fulfilling social duties.
- Level 3: Post-conventional morality (high CMD)
  Stages five (Social contract and individual rights) and six (Universal ethical principles) are based on an individual's awareness of values and rights and defined by the decision of conscience in line with self-chosen ethical principles.

Recent studies on the effect of the levels of CMD on ethical decision-making have shown that people with high CMD working in the accounting profession act more ethically than people with moderate and low CMDs, people with moderate CMD are more ethical than people with low CMD (Habbe et al., 2020), and employees (in this case public sector auditors in Brazil) with shorter lengths of service will be at higher stages of moral development (Malagueno et al., 2020).

═══════ **Box 4.4** ═══════

Robert Kearns's intermittent wind-shield wiper

Robert Kearns was an American engineer who invented the **intermittent** windshield wiper systems that are now commonly used in all automobiles. His first patent for the invention was filed in 1964.

In November 1962, Kearns was driving his Ford Galaxie through the streets of Detroit when it started to rain lightly. In those days, even the most advanced wipers had just two settings, one for steady rain and one for heavy rain. His vision already impaired due to an earlier accident, Kearns was straining to see through the windshield, and there the idea for the intermittent windshield wiper entered his mind and he thought, 'Why can't a wiper work more like an eyelid? Why can't it blink?'

Having invented and patented the intermittent windshield wiper mechanism, which was useful in light rain or mist, Kearns decided that the time had come to demonstrate his invention to a car manufacturer. He chose Ford, because it had supplied him with some wiper motors to experiment on and because 'to me Ford was always the greatest'. Ford engineers waited for him in the parking lot, took turns running the wipers and even asked him how the wiper worked. Having received the go-ahead from Ford, Kearns successfully tested his intermittent wiper by putting it through three million cycles. He then called Ford with the good news, but Ford didn't seem overexcited. Rather, they said since wipers were a safety item, the law required disclosure of all the engineering before Ford could give Kearns a contract. This sounded reasonable to Kearns, so he explained to the Ford engineers exactly how his intermittent wiper worked. About five months later, Kearns was dismissed. He was told that Ford did not want his wiper system after all – that the other engineers had designed their own.

In 1969, Ford came out with a new, electronic intermittent windshield wiper, the first in the industry. It used a transistor, a resistor, and a capacitor in the same configuration that Kearns had designed. In 1974, General Motors began putting the intermittent wiper on its cars, and in 1977 it appeared on Chryslers. Saab, Honda, Volvo, Rolls-Royce, and Mercedes, among others, soon followed.

Kearns tried to get an explanation from Ford, but he soon discovered that like a 'diode, the information only went one way'. His lawyers wrote letters to Ford's legal department, informing it that Ford was infringing Kearns' patents. After lengthy delays, they received a letter back saying that Ford was not infringing Kearns' patents and that, in any case, Kearns' patents were invalid.

In 1978, Kearns filed a case against Ford for patent infringement. Eventually, he added other car companies to the suit. 'I just had an overwhelming feeling that what Ford had done was wrong,' Kearns said. 'It was unjust, and it was illegal'. In his case he asked for USD 350 million in lost profits, multiplied by three – the maximum penalty for wilful infringement – plus interest and costs, for a total of USD 1.6 billion.

The first trial lasted three weeks, and the jury found that Kearns' patents were valid, and that Ford had infringed them. Ford, concerned about the size of the award that a jury in Wayne County might give Kearns, offered an out-of-court settlement for USD 30 million. Kearns, against everyone's advice, turned the money down. 'To accept money from Ford would have been like admitting it was OK for them to do what they did,' he said.

So, there was a second trial, and the second trial awarded Kearns USD 5.2 million, or about thirty cents a wiper plus interest. Kearns wasn't there for the verdict, having left the proceedings in protest two weeks earlier. Finally, Kearns and Ford settled for USD 10.2 million. Further lawsuits against other car manufacturers resulted in further compensation in the millions of dollars for Kearns.

Questions

1   Analyse and identify Kohlberg's CMD level and stage that Robert Kearns can be linked to.
2   Explain how Kearns's CMD level and stage enabled him to arrive at his decisions using Rest's Four Component model.

Sources: Adapted from Flash of Genius (2010) and Seabrook (1993)

4.7 Organisational factors

Decision-making has been shown by several researchers to be influenced by organisational/ environmental factors. An ethical decision-making model proposed by Fritzsche (2000) portrayed the decision-maker with a set of personal values mediated by elements of the organisation's culture. It shows that the combination of personal values and organisational influences yields decisions which may be different from those based upon personal values alone. In attempting to answers the question of how and when people exercise moral judgements, two factors have been shown to be worthy of attention: the kind of problem or situation at issue and the nature of the person who chooses to address it.

Several empirical studies point to the relationship between organisational environment and ethical decision-making of individuals within an organisation:

- The perceived organisational environment is significantly related to the ethical decision of the respondent – from findings in a study with a sample size of 245 full-time employees, using a self-administered questionnaire in which variables such as perceived supervisor expectation, formal policies, and informal policies were assessed (Sims and Keon, 1999: 393).
- People are expected to comply with the law and professional standards over and above other considerations and everyone is expected to stick by company rules and procedures – from results from a study in which 285 managers from a high-technology firm were surveyed to examine the relationship between the different types of ethical 'climates' that exist in organisations and the ethical dimension of decisions (Fritzsche, 2000).
- While code of ethics content was found to lack sense, examples, and clarity, employee participation in code creation was linked to the probability that the code's content would be relevant and realistic – from a study conducted using 57 interviews at four large Canadian companies to examine employee perceptions regarding their companies' codes of ethics (Schwartz, 2004).
- Middle managers respond to upper management's directions by identifying and exploiting routines to generate and conceal deceptive performances – from den Nieuwenboer, da Cunha and Treviño's (2017) study to understand how middle managers induce their subordinates to engage in unethical behaviour.
- Factors affecting ethical decision-making in organisations are routinised activities of all relevant entities that are produced continuously in an organisation within a social context – from a study by Ameer and Halinen (2019). For example, a salesperson is connected to other entities through social relationships, such as members of the sales community or profession or customers and competitors with conflicting ethical interests. They contend that 'by socialising with these actors, salespersons develop their own patterns of behaviour and participate in unethical practice' (2019: 112).

Processes

Emotions and intuitions

Most early modern philosophers, including Descartes, Leibniz, Hume, and Kant (16th to 18th century), tried to construct a moral system entirely free of feelings using the argument that doing the right thing was a consequence of acting rationally (Lehrer, 2009: 172). It was only in the 20th century that much empirical research was done about the effects of emotion on ethical decision-making. The idea that emotions could have a role in moral decision-making was researched mainly in the 20th century. Researchers now suggest that emotions are linked to judgements and that our judgements or beliefs can determine our emotions (Nussbaum, 2001). The social-intuitionist model of ethical decision-making is based on the view that emotions dominate the fast intuitive process (Greene et al., 2004; Haidt, 2001). In some cases, emotion might be the initial response to an ethical situation or dilemma, followed by a moral reasoning process to justify the initial response (Haidt, 2001; 2012). Initial emotional responses such as anger or disgust can lead to intuitive moral judgements that a behaviour is unacceptable and needs to be addressed. Emotions can also lead to moral rationalisations (discussed later in this chapter), for example rejection for promotion could lead to rationalising the padding of an expense account (Dedeke, 2015).

Emotions and intuition play a significant role in the ethical decision-making process. Linehan and O'Brien (2017) provided evidence that emotions experienced during an interaction with employees influence understanding of ethical dilemmas. Other researchers observed that emotions such as anger and fear influenced ethical judgement (Singh et al., 2018), and fear, power, and excitement influenced ethical intentions (Yacout and Scott, 2018). Pride was shown as positively related to pro-environmental behaviours and guilt was shown as negatively related to behaviours such as reusing paper, recycling plastic, or saving water (Bissing-Olson et al., 2016). Another study that examined 603 ethical situations indicated that anticipating negative emotions because of carrying out an unethical behaviour influenced consumer ethical processes. Ethically favourable decisions emerge when consumers avoid feeling bad, rather than feeling good (Escadas et al., 2019).

While there's evidence that the initial 'gut' feeling of rightness or wrongness is typically followed by moral reasoning or rationalisation process (Dedeke, 2015; Haidt, 2001; Reynolds, 2006), there is an ongoing debate between rational-based and intuition-based decision-making. Psychologists have labelled the two modes of thinking as System 1, which operates 'automatically and quickly, with little or no effort and no sense of voluntary control', and System 2, which 'allocates attention to the effortful mental activities that demand it, including complex computations' (Kahneman, 2011: 20–1). System 1 includes skills such as recognising objects such as a table, orienting attention such as turning to a sound, and learned associations such as knowing the capital of France. System 2 includes the conscious reasoning self that makes choices, decides what to think about, and what to do. It requires attention and is disrupted when attention is drawn away, such as telling someone a phone number, parking in a narrow space, filling out a tax form, and checking the validity of a complex logical argument (Kahneman, 2011: 21–2). Most researchers contend that both processes are needed. Haidt (2010) contends that the duality can be framed into three types: one, where reasoning is a major partner – based on researchers such as Kohlberg and Rest; two, where reasoning and intuition are equally important – a view expressed by Narvaez; and three, where intuition is a major partner – the view expressed by Haidt and others.

- The first type in which reasoning is a major partner in the duality as expressed by Kohlberg and Rest has been discussed earlier in this chapter. Briefly, however, in the early and middle of the last century, some theorists considered judgement to be moral only if moral criteria were applied through deliberation, and over time this process would look like intuition (Narvaez, 2010). The reasoning approach derives its attributes from the cognitive moral development theory and the four-component ethical decision-making model.
- The second type where reasoning and intuition are equally important consists of 'ordinary moral sense' and 'facts of the situation'. Narvaez (2010) contends that good intuition and reasoning inform mature moral functioning, and while both processes can help in ethical decision-making, there are multiple systems for information processing. Provis (2017b: 12) has asserted that 'in areas like moral decision making our intuition and judgment may be improved by reflection on experience, and it is a combination of thought and experiences'. It has also been proposed that the form of presentation of the information has an influence on how people might process an ethical decision. For example, if information is presented in descriptive texts, recorded messages, or photographs, the decision-maker will tend to use intuitive processing. On the other hand, if information is presented with data points, measured quantities, or amounts, then decision-makers will be more inclined to use rational processing (Guzak and Hargrove, 2011).
- The third type where intuition is a major partner in the duality can be explained as follows. Haidt (2001: 814) constructs a social intuitionist model which contends that 'moral reasoning does not cause moral judgement; rather, moral reasoning is usually a post hoc construction, generated after a judgement has been reached'. In other words, 'intuitions come first, strategic reasoning second' (Haidt, 2012: xiv).

Empirical research on moral intuition has shown that much moral judgement is not well described by the application of rules and principles. Rather, that the adult mind is full of moral intuitions which are linked to the perception of a pattern in the social world and to moral emotion (Joseph and Haidt, 2007). Provis (2013: 55; 2017b) has argued that 'moral judgement involves the exercise of intuition that is developed by social interaction and feed-back', and that complex environments would need expertise developed through experience – personal and social interactions.

Heuristics

Findings by researchers show that heuristics are relied upon in uncertain decision-making situations where no certain answer is immediately obvious. A study of the decision-making processes among nurses reveals an essential component of clinical judgement to be intuition referred to by some as 'gut feelings' and by others as 'hunches or sixth-sense' (Cioffi, 1997: 203). Further, the study contends that nurses use heuristic strategies to arrive at intuitive judgements (see Klein, 2015).

Heuristics have been defined and described as probability judgements which are used to estimate the likelihood of reaching a decision. They include:

- Using similar examples as in individuals' memories (Cioffi, 1997).
- Reducing judgements to simpler ones when faced with difficult tasks (Tversky and Kahneman, 1973).
- Using mental shortcuts that reduce complex tasks to simpler judgemental operations (Dane and Pratt, 2007).
- Satisfying the constraints of time, knowledge, and computation by fast and frugal reasoning (Gigerenzer and Goldstein, 1996).

Shah and Oppenheimer (2008) while reiterating that heuristics serve the purpose of reducing the effort associated with a task, propose that the process is based on effort-reducing principles which underlie those heuristics. People use moral heuristics – moral shortcuts or rules of thumb – to make moral judgements (Sunstein, 2005). Examples are: do not knowingly cause a human death (with reference to cost-benefit analysis involving cost of safety precautions and cost of life saved); people should not be permitted to engage in moral wrongdoing for a fee (referring to payment of a fee or a tax to offset environmental harm like pollution); punish and do not reward betrayals of trust (implying that people do not like to be betrayed and a betrayal of trust will produce outrage); and do not tamper with natural processes for human reproduction (referring to human cloning).

One study by Hamilton, Knouse and Hill (2009) to identify methods for ethical decision-making in international contexts contends that despite the availability of theoretical frameworks, many managers have difficulty implementing them in daily practice. Managers in multinational enterprises, when confronted with a questionable practice, often rely on the moral consensus reflected in home country legal requirements or the laws and practices of the host country. Others apply general rules of thumb such as the 'Smell Test' – what would it smell like if we read about it in the press – or the past experiences of their firm to determine a plan of action.

However, while heuristics are often useful for making decisions in uncertain situations, they may also lead to errors. Kahneman and Tversky (1996) argue that judgemental heuristics which are mental operations leading to intuitive predictions and judgements are useful but can sometimes lead to errors and biases. Studies have suggested that individuals often choose to use heuristics even when they know they may deliver questionable outcomes. It has been argued that heuristics may lead to inaccurate intuitive judgements because they tend to be 'simple' (Dane and Pratt, 2007). Sunstein (2005) similarly argues that in particular cases, sensible rules of thumb lead to demonstrable errors in factual judgements, morality, politics, and law.

What then is the relationship between heuristic processing and intuitive thinking?

Gigerenzer (2008: 22) noted that people intuitively rely on heuristics. However, Kahneman (2011) contends that not all intuitive judgements under uncertainty are produced by heuristics. In particular, Kahneman suggests that intuitions of experts are 'better explained by the effects of prolonged practice than by heuristics and that skill and heuristics are alternative sources of intuitive judgements and choices' (Kahneman 2011: 11).

Moral exemplars

In general terms, an exemplar is defined as 'a person or thing to be copied'. Exemplars can include (1) persons who have their sense of moral commitment as a core part of their sense of self, take a principled personal stand (Huff and Frey, 2005), or (2) a role model (Moberg, 2000), or (3) an organisation committed to certain moral standards, or (4) other things such as case studies, anecdotes, and even fables and myths (deVries, 1986).

Exemplars play a far more central role in business ethics than do detailed rules. DeVries (1986) proposed four arguments for recognising the essential role of exemplars in business ethics:

1   Exemplars facilitate impartial agreement where agreement on moral rules eludes us.
2   Exemplars facilitate training and decision-making.
3   Use of exemplars cultivates personal judgement – making detailed moral rules only in exceptional cases.
4   Exemplars provide the flexibility necessary for making moral decisions.

According to DeVries, exemplars do not replace theory, but are necessary to make theories and principles work, and the essential role of exemplars in ethical decision-making has been ignored by most ethical theorists.

According to Moberg (2000: 675), while little is known about role modelling as a process, it is 'widely thought to be a principal vehicle for acquiring virtues'. However, a single role model may be insufficient as a guide to moral decision-making and Moberg (2000) suggests that different models may be used for different parts of the moral decision-making process, for example in Rest's Four Component model of moral recognition, moral judgement, moral intention, and moral behaviour. Among the various role models available, Ortega-Liston (2006) contends that public administrators are also well suited to serve as moral exemplars for other professions and for all citizens.

A study (Savur, 2017) to gain insights into understanding types of exemplars that have influenced ethical decision-making processes identified two types of exemplars – individual and organisational. Characteristics of individual exemplars included giving advice, working through issues, and virtues such as honesty and reliability. Organisational characteristics included moral commitment, business integrity, CSR activities, family-friendly policies, and culture. The study also indicated that due to limited resources of time, finance, and skilled employees, managers tend to rely on exemplars to guide their decision-making process.

Reflection

The word 'reflection' is derived from the Latin word *reflectere*, meaning to bend back. Its 'raw material' is an experience and the process 'involves "bending back" upon oneself to take stock, question, and assess an experience' (Moberg and Calkins, 2001). The tradition of reflection has shown it as a practice in the cultivation of wisdom and the contentions of 'know thyself' and 'the unexamined life is not worth living' which supports the suggestion that reflection is an essential process by which wisdom is acquired (Moberg, 2007). It is further contended that although it is very difficult to teach intuition, the process of reflective inquiry on practice can lead professionals to insights and ultimately improve on those practices (Shapiro and Reiff, 1993).

However, in spite of the acknowledgement of the importance of reflection, it has received little attention in business literature. Several suggestions to incorporate reflection in organisational decision-making have been offered by researchers. A starting point could be that business ethics courses can help improve students' ethics by teaching them about character in addition to mere principles, the application of which creates difficulties. This can be done in particular by helping students to consider their values and realise them in practice by a reflective process called dialectic – investigating or discussing contradictions and their solutions – attributed to Aristotle and Plato (Hartman, 2006).

Moral rationalisation, moral decoupling, and moral coupling

Moral reasoning involves a deliberative process leading to a particular moral judegement – such as reflecting upon the situation by considering stakeholder claims, or by applying certain ethical theories such as utilitarianism (greatest good for greatest number / cost-benefit analysis) and deontology (duty, obligations, intentions) (Saltzstein and Kasachkoff, 2004). However, certain business situations such as the impact of unethical behaviour of celebrities on brand endorsements can pose dilemmas for marketers as to whether they should continue or discontinue their relationship with the celebrities – for example, when Nike suspended Oscar Pistorius's contract after he was charged with the murder of his girlfriend in 2013 (Jurberg, 2020). Researchers have suggested three processes that can explain ethical decision-making in such situations – moral rationalisation, moral decoupling, and moral coupling.

- Moral rationalisation can be defined as the process of interpreting an issue so that immorality is justified, excused, or reduced, and when 'individuals convince themselves that their behavior does not violate their moral standards' (Tsang, 2002: 26).
- Moral decoupling is defined as a separation process by which individuals selectively dissociate judegements of performance from judegements of morality. By separating these judegements, moral decoupling allows individuals to support performance while simultaneously condemning unethical behaviour (Bhattacharjee et al., 2013). This can explain how people support public figures who behave immorally and how consumers continue to buy from firms which abuse suppliers or the natural environment (Orth et al., 2019). Bhattacharjee, Berman and Reed (2013) have further shown that moral decoupling is easier to justify and feels less wrong than moral rationalisation – probably because rationalising can be a deliberate process involving the risk of compromising one's moral standards (Tsang, 2002). For example, rationalising buying counterfeit products will require one to justify the act to themselves, or when not returning excess change received after purchasing an item. On the other hand, individuals would use the moral decoupling process to support

public figures who act immorally but deliver high performance – for example although a certain Australian prime minister from 1983 to 1991, who was an exceptional leader delivering several significant reforms, was often nasty, repellent, arrogant, and occasionally drunk, most members of the public considered him a giant in politics (Waterford, 2021).

- Further, in a recent study on consumers' moral reasoning choices, Lee and Kwak (2016) posited that consumers are not always motivated to separate judgements of performance from judgements of morality (moral decoupling) or simply excuse a wrongdoer (moral rationalisation), but also engage in moral coupling, defined as a process that integrates the evaluations of performance and morality. It can make it more difficult for individuals to separate moral judgements from performance judgements – specifically, when the immoral behaviour is directly relevant to performance (e.g., doping for an athlete).

Moral imagination

As discussed in the above sections, a variety of methods are available to SME managers for making moral judgements and enabling effective ethical decision-making. Reasoning processes and decision-making models can help resolve ethical issues where sufficient information is available. It was also indicated that when information is insufficient or when there are complex situations, people use other methods such as intuition, heuristics, exemplars, and reflection. In addition, moral imagination could be used as a process to counter organisational factors that corrupt ethical judgements (Moberg and Seabright, 2000; Werhane, 2002).

Moral imagination is defined as the ability in particular circumstances to imaginatively discern various possibilities which are not limited by any models or by a set of rules by envisioning the potential harm and help that are likely to result from a given action (Pardales, 2002; Vidaver-Cohen, 1997; Werhane, 1999). Werhane realised that ignorance of moral theory or lack of moral reasoning skills were not enough to explain questionable unethical activities engaged in by ordinary, decent, intelligent managers. Something else was involved and this was labelled by Werhane as 'moral imagination', which she argues is a necessary (but may not be sufficient) condition for managerial decision-making (Werhane, 1998; Harper, 2022). For a particular case or event, moral imagination begins with awareness of the event, awareness of the characteristics, the ethical dilemma of the issue, awareness of the context, its role in that context, and awareness of possible moral conflicts or dilemmas that might arise in that situation (Werhane, 1999: 103). Supplementing Pardales's (2002) argument that moral imagination will have greater ability to make moral judgements, Richard Rorty (quoted in Harper 2022: 169) contends that 'moral imagination moves morality forward because it helps leaders grasp novel solutions to customary questions that can then change the way we problematise people, places, and things in the present tense. In other words, the moral imagination can change with way we think about solutions by changing the way we think about problems'.

Moberg and Seabright (2000) describe the psychology of moral imagination as composed in the four components of Rest's model. They propose that:

1   Moral imagination enhances moral sensitivity (FC-1) by enlarging the set of possible actions and reflecting others' perspectives.

2   Moral judgement (FC-2) can be imaginative when decision-makers can be flexible between various ethical criteria such as rules, concepts, and relationships.

3   Moral imagination can shape moral intentions (FC-3) by involving the decision-maker's sense of personal or external standards (such as an exemplar) to evaluate the anticipated course of action.

4   Moral imagination can assist moral behaviour (FC-4) through the ability to adjust intentions to meet the practical necessities of the situation.

A study supported 'the hypothesis that individuals, who exercise moral imagination, including the ability for discerning moral issues and developing a range of possible outcomes during the decision-making process, are indeed more likely to generate a mutually beneficial outcome for a situation compared to those who do not exercise moral imagination' (Godwin, 2015: 254).

Three levels of moral judgement

Researchers of moral judgement have suggested that people in society and business alike utilise one or more of the following three levels of moral judgement: (1) abstract or general principles, (2) intermediate-level moral concepts, and (3) concrete rules or codes of ethics (Bebeau, 2002; Bebeau and Thoma, 1999; Thoma, 2002; Walker, 2002). These have been discussed in Chapter 1. To recap, abstract or general principles include ethical theories described by philosophers and include principles such as the greater good, utility, justice, beneficence, duty, moral rules, religious rules, the golden rule, and their related principles. Intermediate-level moral concepts include professional codes or policies developed for specific professionals in law, medicine, engineering, accountancy and finance, and insurance, among others. The concrete level includes codes of ethics and conduct at the organisational level and serves to direct individual behaviour in very clearly defined situations.

4.8 So, why do good leaders sometimes make unethical decisions?

Extensive examination, evaluation, and accounts of how ethical decisions should be made and how they are actually made are shown in Chapter 3 and this chapter. The majority of all employees including mid and senior managers do not intend to be unethical or run unethical organisations, yet we can see unethical business decisions. It is interesting to know why and how this can happen. Bazerman and Tenbrunsel (2011) have shed some light on this and conclude that there are five reasons why:

1   Ill-conceived goals – setting well-intentioned goals and incentives that can encourage negative behaviours.

2   Motivated blindness – overlooking the unethical behaviour of others when it's in our interest to remain ignorant.

3   Indirect blindness – when we hold others (for example, contractors and outsourcing) less accountable for unethical behaviour.
4   The slippery slope – when we are less able to see others' unethical behaviour when it develops gradually.
5   Overvaluing outcomes – when we allow unethical behaviour if the outcome is good.

4.9 Limitations of and reflections on ethical decision-making tools and models

It is to be noted that while several tools and models of ethical decision-making are available, such as the ones described and discussed in this chapter:

- There may not be 'right' answers to many dilemmas in business today. In many cases limited ethical guidelines are available to draw on to make ethical decisions.
- Tools, models, and frameworks can help us to understand and make informed arguments.
- Engagement with stakeholders can inform perspectives (as discussed in Chapter 2).
- We might also need to draw on other relevant frameworks such as industry regulations – for example, the Banking Code of Practice (ABA, 2021) or the Franchising Code of Practice (ABLIS, 2014) – and international codes of conduct – for example the OECD guidelines for MNEs (OECD, 2011) – to inform ethics decision-making.

═══════ **Box 4.5** ═══════

The Conzerv story: The need for speed… and the brakes

Conzerv Systems Pvt Ltd revolutionised the digital metering industry in India with its range of metering products. By pioneering the design and manufacture of digital meters and implementation of **energy management systems** for industrial applications, Conzerv grew into a 337 people power management hub and were the recognised market leader in energy efficiency in the Indian electricity market, serving industrial and commercial end-users.

In a bid to grow quickly as a start-up, the CEO gave in to the temptation of entering the fast-growing segment of **tariff meters** (that measures and records the amount of electricity used by a consumer) for the state-run electricity boards (SEBs) which were known for corruption. To manufacture these meters, the company set up a separate division and hired designers and salespeople. The first order received was from one of the SEBs of the largest state in India and a hundred times the size of their typical industrial orders. Very soon, the SEB official responsible for inspecting and approving the meters for dispatch started making demands for things such as free transport for his wife, college fees for their children, and so on. Because the company had a policy of not paying bribes, the demands were declined, and as a result the company faced obstacles at every step of the process. Payments, for example, were delayed by almost a year. In less than two years, the CEO decided to exit the tariff meters business, even though it was a lucrative market. They lost money in the process but absorbed all the employees from this division into the main business. One senior staff member was not happy with this decision. The head of manufacturing was upset they had shut down a 'money-spinning' business and accused the CEO of having no ambition, adding 'how will we grow if we are not willing to pay the price'. The CEO took the decision of letting the manufacturing head go. The only silver lining, as the CEO says, was 'the exercise had taught us what really matters to us as an organisation'. The sudden entry and quick exit from the tariff business did not go unnoticed. At a global trade fair overseas, the founder-chairman of one of the largest players in this business said to the CEO, 'Your company is the six sigma of values and ethics'. 'Six Sigma' is a set of techniques and tools for process improvements. As a result of being successful, Conzerv was acquired by Schneider Electric, a global specialist in energy management with operations in more than 100 countries.

Questions

1   Analyse using the CEDM model in Figure 4.1 the CEO's ethical decision-making. Which factors and processes were used by the CEO?
2   Can you think of any other way the CEO could have retained the tariff meters business while being ethical – that is, without paying bribes, withdrawing from the business, or sacking the head of manufacturing?

Sources: Adapted from Hattangady and Sen (2019) and Automation (2009)

══ Summary ══

- This chapter discussed the descriptive theoretical aspects of business ethics. Here, we strive to understand how people in business and society make ethical decisions. The Comprehensive Ethical Decision-Making (CEDM) model presented in this chapter condenses the contributions from various researchers and authors. The three features of the model (components, influencing factors, and processes) together contribute to an ethical decision outcome. Factors influence components – for example individual factors such as moral intensity and the CMD level can influence all five components. The wide variety of processes used in the CEDM indicates that a decision-maker has these processes available to them for ethical decision-making.
- We have discussed how 'moral framing', a frame of reference that can affect recognising ethical issues, is the key starting point of EDM.
- Thereafter, the ethical decision-making process involves Rest's four components, individual factors (such as Kohlberg's CMD), and organisational factors (such as ethical climate).
- We have shown that EDM is also influenced by our emotions and intuitions and our reflective capability.
- Other areas that are included in the EDM process are the application of moral exemplars, rationalisation, and imagination.
- Concepts from further chapters in this book can also influence ethical decision-making – for instance, culture (Chapter 5), sustainability (Chapter 7), corporate social responsibility (Chapter 8), responsible leadership (Chapter 10), and spirituality in management (Chapter 11).

CASE STUDY 4.1
MERCK: RIVER BLINDNESS

Onchocerciasis, also known as river blindness, is a disease caused by infection with the parasitic worm *Onchocerca volvulus*. Symptoms include severe itching, bumps under the skin, and blindness. It is the second-most common cause of blindness due to infection after trachoma.

The parasite worm is spread by the bites of a blackfly that breeds near fast-moving rivers, hence the common name of the disease. Once inside a person, the worms create larvae that make their way out to the skin. The parasite produces a threadlike microfilaria produced after it enters the skin of the victim through the bite of the female blackfly. The microfilariae migrate through the skin and cause blindness in humans by collecting in the eye. It affects about 20 million people: 99 per cent of these live in Africa, the remainder mostly in Latin America. In endemic areas, half become blind before they die and, at any one time, some half a million people with onchocerciasis are blind. Onchocerciasis has had a particularly devastating impact in Africa. All but the poorest of the poor have abandoned the endemic areas. In the worst affected villages, everyone is infected by the age of 14 or 15 years. People go blind in their 20s and 30s, just when these subsistence-farming families are raising children. A vaccine against the disease does not exist.

Merck scientists led by Dr William Campbell identified a potent substance called avermectin which proved to be very effective against a wide range of parasites in animals, including intestinal worms, mites, ticks, and insects. Merck's studies on avermectin led to the synthesis of ivermectin for the animal health market, which they introduced into several markets in 1981. By the second half of the 1980s, ivermectin became the largest selling animal health product in the world with annual sales around USD 1 billion, and by 1987, it was Merck's second largest selling product. It is a worldwide product used to treat heartworm in dogs, and a whole range of parasites in sheep, cattle, horses, pigs, and other animals.

After clinical testing on humans in Africa, Merck created Mectizan, developed from ivermectin, and applied for approval of the drug for use in humans. After the approval, Merck investigated several options for pricing and providing the drug, but realised that river blindness patients would not be able to afford to pay more than a negligible price for treatment. In October 1987, Vagelos, then CEO of Merck, announced that it would donate Mectizan free of charge 'to those who need it for as long as it was needed'.

Although Merck was selling huge amounts of ivermectin to treat animals, there were some 20 million people with onchocerciasis, and maybe 40 million who would need treatment. Treatment had to be continued for at least ten years. This was a huge commitment considering each pill was worth USD 3. However, Vagalos knew that if

Merck did not do something, this breakthrough treatment could never be afforded by the poorest of the poor. The direct cost to Merck of the ivermectin tablets donated during 2005–2011 was around USD 600 million.

Merck's contribution to the treatment and, in some areas, elimination of onchocerciasis was a significant contribution to human welfare and has been internationally praised as a prime example of corporate largesse in the public interest.

Merck's actions generated interest around the world when it became clear that a lot more money would be needed to distribute ivermectin in the 28 African endemic countries. The River Blindness Foundation, the Carter Center and other non-governmental organisations convinced the **World Bank** to start a special programme to distribute ivermectin in Africa, worth about USD 300 million. Another smaller programme was set up for the six endemic countries in Latin America. In 2002, nearly 50 million doses of ivermectin were given away free: over four million doses a month, treating about 100 people every minute. The commitment was to reach everyone who needs treatment and to eliminate onchocerciasis. Colombia was the first country in the world to be verified and declared free of onchocerciasis by the WHO. This was followed by Ecuador in September 2014, Mexico in July 2015, and Guatemala in July 2016. In Africa, Sudan, Uganda, and Ethiopia have reported near or complete elimination. The WHO expects 12 more countries to achieve elimination by 2030.

Questions

Using the Case-Study Integrative Framework in Figure 0.1, discuss the following:

1 What were the issues facing Merck and their CEO Roy Vegelos?
2 What do you think was the 'purpose' of Merck from the CEO's point of view?
3 dentify relevant stakeholders in this case. Who could be identified as 'definitive stakeholders'?
4 Analyse the case using as many ethical approaches (theories) as applicable. Which one (or more) of these approaches can be linked to Merck's (and its CEO's) behaviour and actions?
5 Apply the EDM process to this case – use as many situational, organisational and other factors that influenced or affected the behaviour and actions of Merck and its CEO.

Sources:
Hernando et al. (2016)
Lakwo et al. (2020)
Taylor (2003)
Walsh (1987)
WHO (2022)

CASE STUDY 4.2
MERCK: THE VIOXX CASE

Merck's Vioxx is a COX-2 selective non-steroidal anti-inflammatory drug, marketed to treat the signs and symptoms of arthritis, painful menstrual cycles, and acute pain in adults. In May 1999, after conducting clinical trials involving 5,400 patients, the US Food and Drug Administration (FDA) approved Vioxx, allowing the drug to be prescribed in the United States.

It was competing against Pfizer's Celebrex and Bextra in this billion-dollar market segment. While Vioxx was thought to be less harmful on the stomach, trials showed that Vioxx was in fact more damaging on the stomach than other classes of drugs. In early 2000, results of the initial trials showed evidence linking Vioxx to an increase in cardiovascular risks. Merck denied these claims and defended Vioxx, stating no conclusions could be drawn from the study. While the FDA felt the results were conclusive, Merck's executive management team decided to monitor current clinical trials and determine a plan of action after the results were available. Instead of taking the results of the initial trials seriously, Merck downplayed Vioxx's alleged risks for years, incorrectly stating that the patients were already at high risk for myocardial infarction and there was no significant link in lower risk groups. Records show that sales representatives were instructed to avoid questions from physicians regarding cardiovascular risks from Vioxx. The FDA did not request Vioxx to be withdrawn after the results, nor place a 'black-box' warning on Vioxx's label. Instead, it requested Merck to include information in the 'warnings' section of the product label. The Vioxx label was not adjusted until April 2002, two years after the results became public, and over one year after the FDA's request. In 2003 and 2004, clinical trials indicated that the drug increased cardiovascular risks in users by up to 120 per cent. In late 2004, the trial was halted, and after profiting by USD 10.5 billion, with over 20 million Vioxx patients, Merck voluntarily withdrew Vioxx from the market. The withdrawal was closely followed by investigations by the Securities and Exchange Commission, Department of Justice, United States Senate, and United States House of Representatives. In 2006, the *Lancet* journal estimated that 38,000 out of 88,000 Vioxx patients had heart attacks. In 2007, Merck paid out a settlement of USD 4.85 billion. Neither executives from Merck nor the FDA admitted fault. But so far, Merck has paid around USD 6 billion in litigation settlements and criminal fines over Vioxx, while the FDA continues to decide new drug approvals based on the 'benefits [that] outweigh its potential risks to patients'.

Merck denied that Vioxx caused cardiovascular events because it would reduce sales by billions if the drug was withdrawn. The FDA was under scrutiny for not addressing the concern of the increased risks in the trials of 2000. After four years of continued trials, the FDA finally issued a Public Health Advisory on Vioxx just two months after Merck voluntarily withdrew Vioxx. These and other incidents have impacted the reputation of the pharmaceutical industry.

Questions

Using the Case-Study Integrative Framework in Figure 0.1, discuss the following:

1   What were the issues facing Merck and their executives?
2   What do you think was the 'purpose' of Merck in this scenario?
3   Identify relevant stakeholders in this case. Who could be identified as 'definitive stakeholders?'
4   Analyse the case using as many ethical approaches (theories) as applicable. Which one (or more) of these approaches can be linked to Merck's behaviour and actions?
5   Apply the EDM process to this case – investigate the situational, organisational, and other factors that influenced or affected the behaviour and actions of Merck and its executives.

Sources:
Cavusgil (2007)
Compton (2021)
Cote (2021)
Grant (2009)
Wang and Wertheimer (2022)

Comparing Cases 4.1 and 4.2

The two cases are 15–20 years apart. The cases are about the same organisation but two different management teams.

1   Were the issues different in the two cases? In what way? Would the type of issue influence ethical decision-making? How so?
2   Do you think Merck's purpose in Case 4.1 was different from that in Case 4.2? If so, what was the difference and why did the purpose change over time?
3   Is the definitive stakeholder different in the two cases? Does the difference affect decision-making?
4   Can you distinguish the ethical approach(es) of Merck in Case 4.1 from Case 4.2? Reflect on this.
5   Compare the EDM process used by Merck in both cases. Reflect on the factors influencing the different decisions. Were these different?

——**Recommended readings**——————————————————

Habbe, A.H., Kusumawati, A., Alimuddin, Rura, Y. and Muda, I. (2020), 'Cognitive moral development, organizational situation and ethical decision making in business and accounting', *International Journal of Financial Research*, 11(5): 93–104.

This study examines the effect of the interaction between cognitive moral development (Kohlberg's three levels) and an organisational situation (agency and stewardship) in business ethical decision-making. It will take you deeper into the practical implications of the concepts.

Haidt, J. (2001), 'The emotional dog and its rational tail: A social intuitionalist approach to moral judgement', *Psychological Review*, 108(4): 814–34.
Haidt, J. (2012), *The righteous mind*, New York: Pantheon Books.

Both readings of Haidt (above) will provide you with a clear and comprehensive account of the importance of intuition in ethical decision-making. Haidt is well-known in this area.

Hilbig, B.E., Scholl, S.G. and Pohl, R.F. (2010), 'Think or blink – is the recognition heuristic an "intuitive" strategy?' *Judegement and Decision Making*, 5(4): 300–309.

This study showed that the use of the recognition heuristic was more likely when judegements were to be made deliberatively, rather than intuitively. It concludes that the potential application of heuristics is not necessarily a consequence of 'intuitive' processing; rather, their effort-reducing features are probably most beneficial when thinking more deliberatively.

Moberg, D.J. (2000), 'Role models and moral exemplars: How do employees acquire virtues by observing others?' *Business Ethics Quarterly*, 10(3): 675–96.

This paper shows how one person can find the actions of another person so inspirational that the person attempts to reproduce the behaviour in question.

Provis, C. (2017), 'Intuition, analysis and reflection in business ethics', *Journal of Business Ethics*, 140(1): 5–15.

This reading will give you a clear understanding of the relationships between intuition, reflection, and analysis in business ethics. Examples of business ethics problems are included to illustrate these processes.

Savur, S., Provis, C. and Harris, H. (2018). 'Ethical decision-making in Australian SMEs: A field study', *Small Enterprise Research*, 25(2): 114–36.

This paper provides evidence that organisations (SMEs in this study) apply all four components of Rest's model (and the CEDM in this chapter) in most of the ethical issues raised by managers.

5

BUSINESS ETHICS ACROSS CULTURES

──Learning objectives──

On completion of this chapter, you should be able to:

- Understand the history of globalisation and its links to cultural implications
- Appreciate that culture can be complex, sensitive, and difficult to define
- Understand Hofstede's five cultural dimensions and the GLOBE study
- Understand and critically review business ethics in four major non-Western culture-centres
- Examine research findings for cross-cultural effects on business ethics based on Hofstede's cultural dimensions
- Incorporate concepts from this chapter into the Comprehensive Ethical Decision-Making model (CEDM) that was introduced in Chapter 4

──Key concepts──

- Globalisation
- Hofstede's five cultural dimensions
- Concepts of business ethics in cultures such as:

  ○ African-centric (such as *Ubuntu, Kgotla, Indaba*)
  ○ Confucian-centric (such as *guanxi, ren, xin, li*)
  ○ Indo-centric (such as *Jugaad* (pronounced *joog-gaar*), *dharma, karma*)
  ○ Islamic-centric (such as *wasta, khuluq, 'adl, amanah*)

- Integrative Social Contracts Theory

—Box 5.1 Opening case—

The gig economy

Gig or freelance work is devoid of the binding obligations of typical full-time employment. In a **gig economy**, the **AI-enabled algorithmic management** enables a gig worker (e.g., an Uber driver) to work with autonomy and flexibility in areas of work hours, area and time of operation, and vehicle of choice, among others. However, it has been observed in Mumbai, India that such management enables round the clock surveillance by the parent organisation including constant performance evaluation with a rating system that grades the driver's performance on a ride-to-ride basis leading to fare rate determination, often leading to driver stress and burnout. The algorithm is designed such that the performance management (through ratings) is entirely determined by the customer. The app then makes decisions for the drivers based on these ratings. These decisions can affect workflow, payouts, and even their contracts. With car mortgages and other financial liabilities, drivers often have to work full time even on weekends, with limited or no exit options. Research shows that very soon workers tend to move away and disengage themselves from the organisation's projected realities and promises. At this point, they start looking for alternatives to break out of the app's control structures. One such alternative to improve an existing situation is *Jugaads* (as such processes are called in India) which are sometimes implemented without any second thought for the implications.

Drivers have been known to cut corners by switching between apps (one each in the morning and evening), asking passengers to cancel the trip midway and offering them a slightly lesser fare. Drivers justify this by saying that they do not feel anything for a company that does not value their 'sweat, blood, and time'. They feel it is better than paying the 'cut' to the company and do not feel any remorse because the app does not deliver any promises, so 'why should I be the only one playing by the rules?' The drivers have started to think of themselves as a collective and have formed a WhatsApp group where newcomers are informed of these methods and develop strategic alternatives to break out of the app's control. Strategies include sharing tips on where the rush sites are, where to avoid, best hotspots, current surge rates, and longest-lasting rate areas. If the trip is for a far suburb, they ask passengers to go for 'inter-city rides' as it is a better deal for both the driver and the passenger. To justify the *Jugaads*, drivers use the logic of day-to-day survival. After deducting car repayments, fuel, and maintenance, there's not enough left for rent and food. The 'only' alternative is to do some *Jugaad*. One driver summarised it by saying 'if they do not treat us well, why should we bother about them losing customers or revenue?' The *Jugaad* culture in India is examined further in the section 'Business ethics in the Indo-centric cultures'.

Questions

1   Do you think the drivers' *Jugaad* actions are justified?

2   If your answer is yes, what ethical theories (that you have learned from previous chapters) can you apply to support your assertion?

3   If your answer is no, what concepts (that you have learned from previous chapters) can you apply to support your assertion?

4   Discuss your reflections on the *Jugaad* culture in India and similar concepts in other cultures.

5   Do you think Western ethical concepts (that have been discussed in previous chapters) can be applied to explain *Jugaad*?

6   What would you recommend to people in such environments who use *Jugaad*?

Sources:

Ananthram and Chan (2021)

Jain (2022)

Jauregui (2014)

Prabhu and Jain (2015)

Shepherd et al. (2020)

Sivarajan et al. (2021)

5.1 Introduction

Globalisation can be explained as the ongoing integration of political, social, and economic interactions at the transnational level, regardless of physical proximity or distance. Thomas Friedman in his book *The World is Flat* (2007) contends that there have been three great eras of globalisation.

- Globalisation 1.0 – when countries and governments (mostly inspired by religion and imperialism) led the way to global interactions. Prior to the 15th century, most of the trade between countries was in the Asian and Middle East geographical areas. From the 15th to the 19th century, European nations opened up trade between the 'Old World' and the 'New World'.

- Globalisation 2.0 – roughly from 1800 to 2000, the advent of multinational corporations drove global integration by searching for markets and labour. This was powered by joint-stock companies, the Industrial Revolution, steam engines and railroads, and later telephones, the PC, satellites, fibre-optic cables, the introduction of the World Wide Web (the internet), and email. This era truly describes the definition of globalisation as we know it today.

- Globalisation 3.0 – from the year 2000 onwards, where individuals have the capacity to collaborate and compete globally, made possible by software applications and the high-speed global fibre-optic and satellite connectivity across the globe. Anyone can now conduct business from anywhere to everywhere, for example sitting in a café with just a laptop.

The spread of globalisation morphed into 'glocalisation' (a portmanteau of globalisation and localism). The word 'glocalisation' first appeared in a late 1980s *Harvard Business Review* publication. In the business sphere, the term is used to describe a product or service that is developed and distributed globally but adjusted to accommodate consumer needs in a local market. Examples would include location of the steering wheel in an automobile and cultural aspects such as global food chains offering location-specific menu items catering to local tastes. The ability to glocalise depends on local culture. 'The Indians, for instance, take the view that the Moguls come and go, the British come and go, [we] take the best and leave the rest – but [we] still eat curry, [our] women still wear saris and [we] still live in tightly bound extended family units' (Friedman, 2007: 325).

Landes (1998) argued that although climate, natural resources, and geography play vital roles in explaining why countries differ in terms of prosperity and progress, one of the key factors is a country's cultural endowments, particularly the degree to which it is open to change, new technology, and equality for women. Cultures that are willing to change seem to have a greater advantage. In many countries, a great-grandmother may be illiterate, the grandmother probably went to grade two, the mother may have gone to college, the sister has a master's degree, and a daughter could be at an overseas university – and all this in living memory!

While globalisation brings in integration and change through increasing overseas engage-ments as discussed above, it also causes organisations to be confronted with culture, law, and accountability. This is particularly relevant to business ethics due to the diverse and some-times contradictory ethical expectations in overseas markets. We don't have to look far to realise the attitudinal and cultural differences in various parts of the world in areas such as religious beliefs, racial and gender diversity, outsourcing, downsizing, hiring and firing employees, capital punishment, bribing, corruption, privacy, and even gun ownership. Business ethics takes place in a social and cultural environment governed by a variety of laws, rules and regulations, values and norms, and codes of conduct. Analysis of a dataset on ethical policies of 2,700 firms in 24 countries has reported significant differences among ethical policies of firms headquartered in different countries (Scholtens and Dam, 2007). For example, attitudes towards whistle-blowing vary significantly among different countries – group-oriented collectivist cultures may be more critical of illegal and immoral practices if these practices present threats to the group (Ermasova, 2021). In recent years, the influence of cross-cultural differences on the ethics perception has received great attention in the cur-rent empirical literature and a lot of these studies have used Hofstede's cultural dimensions' theory as a framework to describe the effect of a society's culture on the values of its members (pp. 98–9). Some studies (Beekun and Westerman, 2012; Robertson and Fadil, 1999) have proposed a culture-based ethical decision-making model where it was suggested that national culture affects Kohlberg's stages of moral development and that intention to behave ethically was significantly related to national culture.

Culture, therefore, plays a very important part in business ethics and ethical decision-making. However, before we embark to discuss the effects of culture on business ethics, we need to understand the concepts of culture and the research that has been done so far. In this chapter, beginning with the definition and kinds of culture, we will explore Hofstede's five cultural dimensions, geographic-locations based culture, and religion-based culture that influence business ethics and ethical decision-making outcomes.

Culture

Defining culture can be complex, problematic, sensitive, and difficult, because researchers from different disciplines focus their attention on several different aspects of culture. About 70 years ago, Kroeber and Kluckhohn (1952) organised 164 definitions of culture into broad categories that focused on content, social heritage, tradition, rules or ways of doing things, problem-solving, patterns and organisations, and product or artifact. Culture has also been defined based on the way people share goods, services, technology, ideas, knowledge, and rules of social behaviour and institutions. Researchers have agreed on certain characteristics of culture – (1) adaptive interactions between humans and their environments, (2) shared elements, and (3) transmitted across time periods and generations (Cohen, 2009). While there is a tendency to link culture with country, nationality, or ethnicity, there are other forms of culture such as religion, social class, and sub-groups within-country. People also equate the gay community, the Black community, or the Santhal community to culture. So, there are sub-cultures within cultures and sub-cultures within sub-cultures, and so on. We could now define culture as something to share (to some degree) values, roles, practices, norms, self-definitions, ideas, schemas, goals, and interactions with the environment (Cohen, 2010).

The complexity of defining and understanding cultures can be seen from several perspectives – one, that since culture affects how people structure their worlds, it can be difficult or impossible to understand meanings and practices from outside that culture, and second, that all cultures contain some similar ideas and meanings, but they emphasise more some ideas and values while de-emphasising others. A third perspective is multiculturalism where a person has a national origin, an ethnic origin, a religion (or lack of it), a socio-economic status, and a regional origin within a country. The complexity of defining culture can be further seen through the three types of cultural interactions that globalisation has contributed (Hassi and Storti, 2012):

1   Heterogenisation – where local cultures remain intact and largely unaffected even though they experience global factors and forces, resulting in a side-by-side coexistence of global and local cultures.
2   Homogenisation (also known as convergence) – where local cultures are shaped by other more powerful cultures, for example 'Americanisation' or 'McDonaldisation'.
3   Hybridisation (also known as 'glocalisation') – where there is a continuous process of mixing or blending cultures.

However, Hassi and Storti (2012) note that only peripheral elements such as cuisine, fashion, shopping habits, arts and crafts, and entertainment navigate across boundaries, whereas the deep-rooted underlying assumptions, values, and beliefs remain in their original cultural contexts.

Geert Hofstede in the 1980s developed one of the earliest and most popular frameworks of culture, measuring five cultural dimensions in a global perspective – power distance, individualism–collectivism, masculinity–femininity, uncertainty avoidance, and long-term vs short-term orientation. This framework was further explained by Hofstede, Hofstede and Minkow (2010) and extended by Robert House in 2004 with the Global Leadership and Organizational Behaviour Effectiveness (GLOBE) study of 62 societies on cultural, leadership, and organisational factors (House et al., 2004). Concepts from Hofstede and GLOBE are discussed below.

Hofstede's cultural dimensions

Hofstede (1980: 25) defined culture as 'the collective programming of the mind which distinguishes the members of one human group from another'. The 'programming' here refers to the mental programmes that exist within the social environment in which one grew up. It starts within the family, and continues within the neighbourhood, school, workplace, and community. It is 'collective' because it is at least partly shared with people who live or lived within the same environment (Hofstede et al., 2010). The framework was developed using data from over 116,000 surveys from around 88,000 employees from 72 countries in 20 languages at IBM. From the study, five cultural dimensions were identified to describe cross-cultural differences in behaviour:

- Power distance, defined as the extent to which a society accepts the fact that power in institutions and organisations is distributed unequally. It informs us about the dependence relationship in a country. In small-power-distance countries, there is limited dependence of subordinates on bosses – subordinates can easily approach and contradict their bosses. In large-power-distance countries, there is considerable dependence of subordinates on bosses – they will either prefer or reject such dependence.
- Individualism–collectivism: individualism describes the inclination of people to take care of themselves and of their immediate families ahead of any other stakeholders, while collectivism is characterised by a tight social framework in which people form strong and cohesive groups, and care for each other.
- Masculinity–femininity: masculinity is defined as the extent to which the dominant values in society are 'masculine' – that is, assertiveness, the acquisition of money and things, and not caring for others, quality of life, or people. Femininity refers to where the dominant values are 'feminine' – where people are supposed to be modest, tender, and concerned with quality of life.
- Uncertainty avoidance: defined as the extent to which a society feels threatened by uncertain and ambiguous situations and tries to avoid these situations by providing greater career stability, establishing more formal rules, and not tolerating deviant ideas and behaviours. There is a need for predictability, a need for written and unwritten rules.

- Long-term vs short-term orientation: long-term orientation refers to the fostering of virtues oriented towards future rewards such as persistence and thrift, whereas short-term orientation refers to the fostering of virtues related to past- and present-oriented values.

To compare the indices for each of these five dimensions for the 76 countries, go through the Hofstede website (www.hofstede-insights.com/fi/product/compare-countries) and Hofstede et al. (2010). Most of the research on the effects of culture on business ethics in various geographic locations has been done using Hofstede's cultural dimensions.

The GLOBE study

The GLOBE Research Program was conceived in 1991 by Robert J. House of the Wharton School of Business, University of Pennsylvania. The study expanded the five Hofstede dimensions to nine which included humane orientation, assertiveness, performance orientation, and gender egalitarianism. The study of 62 societies was based on results from about 17,300 middle managers from 951 organisations (Hofstede et al., 2010; House et al., 2004). The results enabled 60 countries to be placed into country clusters in which cultural similarities are greatest among societies in a cluster and cultural differences are greater the farther clusters are apart. For example, the Anglo cluster is most similar to the Germanic cluster and most dissimilar to the Middle Eastern cluster.

Further, the analysis generated 21 leadership scales ranked from most universally desirable to least universally desirable. The top three most desirable traits were being honest, inspirational, and visionary. The bottom three were autocratic, self-centred, and malevolent. Universal leader characteristics that contribute to an outstanding leader were identified as trustworthy, just, and honest, among others. Characteristics that inhibit an outstanding leader were identified as dictatorial, ruthless, egocentric, and irritable, among others. In addition, 35 culturally contingent leader characteristics were also identified. For a full list of these characteristics, refer to House et al. (2004).

5.2 Business ethics across cultures

As discussed in the introduction, Globalisation 2.0 and 3.0 have resulted in the development and expansion of enterprises, for-profit, not-for-profit, and state-owned, in many countries and this has exposed ethical issues, dilemmas, and social and environmental responsibilities of these enterprises. In particular, business strategies of multinational corporations include the social responsibility of the company for the host and home countries. One of the main problems that companies encounter, in both developed and developing nations, is the potential conflict between their own ethical standards and the customs, norms, and conditions of other cultures. Developing countries, due a lack of formal governance, in particular use informal networks that can facilitate business transactions and even protect property rights. Thus, today, a manager working in a multicultural environment will have to manage ethical issues about how to conduct business in different cultures and to provide the necessary guidance for employees to address ethical dilemmas.

Due to globalisation, cross-country migrations, and multicultural environments, delineating cultures based on geographic regions, or religion, or socio-economic status would be complex and confusing. For example, people who follow the Islamic culture are spread all over the world. Similarly, people who identify themselves with the Western culture can also be found in 'non-Western' countries. However, following House et al. (2004), we can differentiate major cultural attributes from around the world in the following manner:

1   Western-centric culture – typically identified with Judeo-Christian-Greek traditions. Countries within this segment would include the Anglo, Germanic, Latin European, Nordic, and some of the Latin American countries.
2   African-centric cultures – typically identified with *Ubuntu* and other traditions. Countries within this segment would include most of the countries in the African continent.
3   Confucian-centric culture – typically identified with Confucianism, Daoism, and Taoism traditions. Countries within this segment would include China, Singapore, Hong Kong, Taiwan, South Korea, Japan, and most South-East Asian countries.
4   Indo-centric culture – typically identified with Hinduism, Buddhism, Sikhism, and Jainism traditions. Countries within this segment would be India, Sri Lanka, Nepal, Bhutan, and some parts of South-East Asia.
5   Islamic-centric culture – typically identified with Islamic traditions. Countries within this segment would include Middle Eastern countries, Pakistan, Afghanistan, Bangladesh, Indonesia, North Africa, Central Asia, and some parts of South-East Asia.

So far in Chapters 1 to 4, the ethical theories and ethical decision-making processes were based predominantly on Western culture (the Judeo-Christian-Greek traditions). This chapter will focus on business ethics concepts and issues in (alphabetical order): African-centric, Confucian-centric, Indo-centric, and Islamic-centric cultures.

5.3 Business ethics in African-centric cultures

Countries from African-centric cultures include most of the African nations, and typically follow the traditions of *Ubuntu*. In this section, we will introduce and explore three aspects of business ethics in the African cultures: (1) the uniqueness of culture in these nations, (2) the concepts that underpin these cultures (such as *Ubuntu*, **Kgotla**, and **Indaba**), and (3) the evolution of business ethics in Africa.

African ethics has strong cultural roots. However, there exists in the minds of certain individuals in South Africa a victim and entitlement mentality, borne out of the Apartheid policy of previous regimes (Rossouw, 1997). This attitude is responsible for much of the unethical business practice which manifests itself in South African business circles

(Nicolaides, 2009) , where many business owners were previously disadvantaged by the Apartheid policy. Managers are eager to show that they have achieved success. Consequently, many seem to resort to shortcuts often leading to fraud.

African traditional and modern Western philosophy and culture are seen to be in direct conflict with each other. Western management advocates what is termed to be Eurocentricism, individualism, and modernity; African management thought, in contrast, stresses ethnocentrism, traditionalism, communalism, and cooperative teamwork, which are basically based on the philosophy of *Ubuntu* (Nicolaides, 2009). Nzelibe (1986) stresses that the adoption of a modern Eurocentric understanding of management, which is in essence incompatible with traditional African cultures, is responsible for the unethical management practices which exist in current African business practice.

A national ethics survey in South Africa, based on a sample of 166 respondents (UN Office on Drugs and Crime and SA Department of Public Service and Administration, 2003: 88–9), found that most organisations had a basic ethics infrastructure, including codes of conduct, in place. However, ethics training was too brief to be effective and did not focus on managers and new employees. Twenty-seven per cent of new employees were trained in applying codes of ethics, while only 13 per cent were taught ethical decision-making skills and 12 per cent of new employees were assisted in integrating ethics into their everyday activities. Further, many businesses had no senior manager assigned to handle ethics in the workplace, indicating that many businesses paid only lip service to ethics and were not really committed to it.

There is now growing interest and research in African indigenous philosophy and ethics that could be applied to business ethics, leadership, organisational behaviour, and cross-cultural management. Africa's unique social-cultural, institutional, and environmental realities could provide an alternative perspective to existing theories of the firm. In addition to the *Ubuntu* philosophy, concepts such as *Kgotla* and *Indaba* have alternative paradigms of social relationships (Adeleye et al., 2020; Newenham-Kahindi, 2009).

Ubuntu

As introduced in Chapter 2, the roots of African life, culture, and value systems are found in the philosophy of *Ubuntu*. The term *Ubuntu* is from the Nguni language in South Africa and has equivalents in many other African languages. While it can be translated into various words such as humanity, common sense, and generosity, most agree that it is basically a relational concept with interdependence and interconnectedness as the main features (Graness, 2018). It calls for caring for others and for upholding moral integrity. It is only through others that a person can be a person – '*Umuntu ngumuntu ngabantu*'. It is only through *imbizo* or participation that all people are treated inclusively and have their suggestions and ideas considered, and are treated with human dignity (Nicolaides, 2009). *Ubuntu* ethics is founded on the community and its welfare, where action is regarded as right if, and only if, it delivers community welfare. A recent study of a leading Nigerian pharmaceutical firm found a virtuous leadership model was underpinned by four primary African values – truthfulness, courage, humility, and humanity, within the context of the *Ubuntu* communitarianism (Adewale, 2019). However, according to Kayange (2018), this ethic has failed to deliver the expected results, with increasing numbers of immoral acts such as corruption, bribery, and nepotism taking place. Kayange argues that in addition to communitarian virtues, *Ubuntu* also includes some individual-based virtues, and suggests that in order to transform African organisations, there is a need to restore the importance of individual virtues alongside communitarian virtues.

Kgotla

A *Kgotla* (pronounced kootla) is a public meeting, community council, or traditional law court of Botswanan origin. It is usually headed by the village chief or headman, and community decisions are always arrived at by consensus. Headmen usually work as the advisers to the chief. No one may interrupt while another is having their say. Because of this tradition, Botswana claims to be one of the world's oldest democracies (see Wikipedia for more details). *Kgotla* can also refer to the place where such meetings are held. This can range from a few chairs under a shade canopy to a permanent ground with covered seating.

The *Kgotla* is led by the chief who is regarded as the custodian of the culture and responsible for upholding the moral and ethical standards of the community. Judgements seek to provide for coexistence between offenders and offended. Offenders also get advice on an accepted moral behaviour, and they continue to be integrated into the community. The principle behind this process is known as *botho*, meaning a person's humanity is relationally tied to those of others. Moumakwa (2011: 3–4) summarises this as follows:

> The *Kgotla* institution continues to play a vital role in modern Botswana in regard to addressing conflicts arising from within and between communities. Basic human values of sociability, respect, and inclusiveness are portrayed in a way which makes proceedings take social significance far exceeding that of the adjudication of petty individual cases. In theory, the *Kgotla* is inclusive, allowing both royals and commoners to participate equally in decision making at a local community level. Everyone has a space to dance, stomp, run and jump on it without hindrance. In other words, participation and attendances are open to all members of the community; therefore, anyone regardless of social stratification has a space to partake.

Indaba

An *Indaba* (pronounced in-da-ba) is an important conference usually held by the Zulu and Xhosa peoples of South Africa. 'The term *Indaba* refers to a traditional social structure of handling and resolving any debate or conflict that may arise in a group' (Newenham-Kahindi, 2009: 92). It implies experience and competence in leadership. Similar concepts are found in Tanzania in East Africa. The concept allows elders in the community to coerce groups into resolving issues collectively, rendering decision-making circular and inclusive. The concept is grounded in dignity and respect, where debates must be honoured and respected by all. Similar to *Ubuntu*, *Indaba* assumes that when stakeholders are treated well and their core needs are satisfied, there will be a reciprocal response from all. Employees will feel they are part of the firm's family leading to dedication to work, and high levels of trust. These concepts are reflected in a recent study of small and medium enterprises (SMEs) in South Africa that indicate SMEs view business ethics as behaviour and actions, with an emphasis on business relationships, and appear to be more value-driven than rule-driven (Van Wyk and Venter, 2022).

Naude (2019) raises the question of whether African ethics, especially *Ubuntu*, can provide an escape from coloniality and observes:

> Western knowledge traditions have become the norm for all knowledge; the methodologies underlying these traditions are seen as the only forms of true knowledge, which has led to a reduction in epistemic diversity; because of the institutional and epistemic power that Western traditions hold, they constitute the centre of knowledge so that other forms of knowledge are suppressed and are seen as inferior – a situation described as 'coloniality'. Decolonisation has specific relevance to Africa, as this continent finds itself in a postcolonial era, but its knowledge and university curricula still reflect the dominance of Western knowledge forms. (pp. 23–4)

Naude observes that there are efforts to develop an alternative moral theory via *Ubuntu* that qualifies as a decolonised form of Africa-centred knowledge. 'However, this project will be steeped in Western knowledge forms and rules of validation. The success of the project will depend on reconceptualising what is counted as moral "problems", moral "solutions", and ultimately moral "theory"' (Naude, 2019: 35).

================ **Box 5.2** ================

The case of a Nigerian pharma firm

Nigeria is Africa's biggest economy but also ranks low in the Corruption Perception Index – ranked 154 out of 180 countries (Transparency International, 2021). The pharmaceutical industry in particular has a long history of ethical issues including drug adulteration, illegal drug trials, bribery, and corruption. When under pressure to perform, employees of indigenous firms rely on their 'street smartness' technique to compete successfully against large foreign multinational corporations. To succeed, many cross moral boundaries, resorting to bribery, undercutting prices, and other unethical practices.

This case study, however, is about a Nigerian company that built on a positive and ethical reputation over two decades. It demonstrated the African tradition of community that refers to the ideal of how members of a group relate and interact, the notion that a community can have both an individual identity as well as acting in solidarity towards others for the common good.

This Nigerian pharmaceutical company, called PNP here (actual name withheld), a 26-year-old wholly Nigerian-owned firm employing over a thousand employees with an annual revenue of more than USD 40 million, has received several awards for excellence in leadership. Employees show a lot of admiration and respect for the leadership, particularly the

(Continued)

managing director / chief executive officer (MD/CEO). Employees feel PNP has a family-like environment and have even coined the term 'PNPian'. The MD/CEO make their moral values visible through character and conduct. The communitarian nature of the typical African society comes across through the leadership team's ingrained moral values. The top managers exhibited four African primary virtues:

* Truthfulness
* Courage (including owning up to wrongdoings and refusal to bribe)
* Humility
* Humanity

However, some employees have also expressed settings where the familial atmosphere of informality and familiarity impeded honesty in some instances, such as communicating facts is hindered by the fear of 'people not wanting to offend others'. In practice, an interesting pattern was observed. The four leaders' virtues were effective when dealing with external issues and matters concerning the wider society. But in handling domestic or internal issues, application of these virtues had shortcomings, especially with hierarchical privileges surpassing the 'common good'. This seems to mirror the functioning of traditional African families, in which members of families protect the dignity of their family names when dealing with external parties, but within the families, there will always be grievances, and heads of families run a patriarchal system with almost absolute power in presiding over matters.

Questions

1   How did PNP manage to distance itself from other typical Nigerian firms in terms of ethical behaviour?
2   Do you think the company's ethical climate will change if the MD/CEO is replaced?
3   Or are the African communitarian values embedded so much in the firm that the ethical climate will not change?
4.   Reflect on the problems that the firm is facing due to the functioning of traditional African families. What do you think can be done in this regard?

Source: Adapted from Adewale (2019)

5.4 Business ethics in Confucian-centric cultures

Countries from Confucian-centric cultures include Greater China, Singapore, Japan, and parts of South-East Asia, and typically follow the traditions of Confucianism, Daoism, and Taoism. In this section, we will introduce and explore three aspects of business ethics in the Confucian cultures: (1) the solution-seeking pragmatic guanxi culture, (2) the concepts that underpin these cultures (such as *ren, li, xinyong,* and *lijie*), and (3) the evolution of business ethics specifically in China.

Guanxi

The Chinese concept of *guanxi* has received considerable attention in recent times. The term *guanxi* is composed of two Chinese characters, *guan* meaning 'gate', and *xi* meaning 'connection' – literally meaning 'one must pass the gate to get connected to networks'. In other words, it is understood as referring to special interpersonal relationships between individuals which facilitate business activities and influence the behaviour of businesspeople. To establish business relationships, personal social networks and family background are more important than abilities and qualifications. While *guanxi* is not necessarily a must for all business transactions, it is considered as a foundation for building business relationships (Chen and Eweje, 2020).

Ulusemre and Fang's (2022) study of **expatriate** managers working and living in China found that the respondents found '*guanxi* ethically permissible when used to protect one's right to fair competition but found it immoral when used to violate one's right to fair competition' (p. 312). The findings indicated that their ethical judgements depended on the motivation behind *guanxi* and identified two forms of *guanxi* – a 'defensive' *guanxi* where they considered it ethical if used for market access and survival, and a 'competitive' *guanxi* if employed to gain unfair advantage over rivals. However, both forms of *guanxi* involved gift giving, banquets, and bribery. In a sense, this implies that defensive *guanxi's* purpose is to enter or stay in the game, while competitive *guanxi* aims to win the game.

A key component of *guanxi* is **renqing** which involves reciprocity by continuously exchanging favours with others. For example, when one person gives a favour, the other person must repay it and at times increase its value. This is termed as 'reciprocal' *guanxi* (Chen and Eweje, 2020). Managers may thus take advantage of this to gain individual benefits through *renqing*, often resulting in corruption and bribery which can have a detrimental impact on stakeholders, organisations, and society. It is therefore suggested that managers move from 'reciprocal' *guanxi* to 'ethical' *guanxi*.

Concepts that underpin business ethics in Confucian-centric cultures

Several studies have suggested that Confucian ethics can play an important role in establishing 'ethical' *guanxi*. Ko et al. (2017) assert that managers who behave like a *junzi* (an ideal Confucian person) tend to formulate 'ethical' *guanxi* with business partners. A *junzi* is defined as 'a noble person who attempts to actualise Confucian cardinal virtues in concrete human relationships at any cost' (Ahn, 2008: 103). It is possible to become a *junzi* by practising Confucian virtues such as *ren* (humanity), *xinyong* (trust), and *lijie* (empathy). Provis (2017a) contends that Confucianism shows similarities to Western virtue ethics but differs in highlighting the virtues of social life and attitude towards moral development which focuses on social harmony with special attention to ren (humanness), *li* (proper conduct or rituals), and filial piety (respect for parents and ancestors). Yuan et al. (2023) propose that an ideal Confucian leader prioritises self-cultivation (moral development) rather than status and material gain, and influences others by shaping an ethical culture through the process of rituals (*li*), and as Provis (2019) suggests, in business, everyday life is full of ritualistic behaviour such as our posture, gestures, language, mannerisms, and actions. A recent study (Beekun et al., 2019) of 360 executives and 190 MBA students in China found that Confucian values of *haoxue* (love of learning), *zin* (trustworthiness), *xin* (sincerity), *zhi* (wisdom), and *li* (ritual wisdom) influence ethical decision-making and resolving ethical dilemmas. Executives were more influenced by national culture and Confucian ideas than the younger MBS students. Further, the study demonstrated that Confucianism in China is still prevalent and key Confucian values and norms guide contemporary Chinese in dealing with ethical dilemmas.

Evolution of business ethics in China

The acceleration and the impact of globalisation has seen the gradual shift from central planning to a market system in China and this has affected Chinese values in what is called 'values evolution' (Lee et al., 2022). Robertson et al. (2012) suggested three perspectives of values evolution – global convergence, societal divergence, and multicultural crossvergence – that can describe how socio-cultural, economic, and political influences affect individuals' ethical judgements.

Global convergence suggests that industrialisation, technological development, political systems, and economic development will lead to a global convergence of values across societies, for example predicting that differences in ethical decision-making and associated moral philosophy between say China and the US would decrease significantly over time. Whereas advocates of the divergence concept perspective believe that socio-cultural influence will make individuals retain the specific value system of the culture over generations, and therefore differences in cross-cultural values will remain intact over time, predicting that individuals will retain the value systems of their national culture even if the country adopts new business ideologies. Crossvergence is described as the synergistic interaction of convergence (e.g., business ideologies) and divergence (e.g., socio-cultural influences) within a society, resulting in a unique value system, predicting that ethical decision-making and associated moral philosophy between China and the US may evolve in various ways depending on specific ethical problems over time (Lee et al., 2022). Their study and analysis of the experiences of Chinese and American managers from 1990 to 2000 suggest the following:

- Improvements in regulations could influence Chinese managers to make more ethical decisions related to problems such as overseas bribery, and environmental protection.
- Based on the strong correlation between managers' nationality and relationship with moral philosophies, MNCs desiring to devise a common code of ethics may need to consider cultural differences more carefully.
- Since managerial ethical decision-making may evolve over time, largely influenced by generational values evolution, policy-makers should adopt new norms and business leaders should adjust their codes of ethics in line with societal norms evolution.

Berger (2015: 116) identified the evolution of business ethics in China as shown in Table 5.1. Berger further suggests that the next stage in the transformation of Chinese ethics would include historically based elements grounded in Confucian principles such as caring for labour and workers' welfare, and Daoist teachings that emphasise flexibility and harmony.

Table 5.1 Evolution of business ethics in China

Stage period	Stage name	Characteristics
Up to 1949	Traditional Chinese Business Ethics	Business ethics based on Confucian and Daoism principles of keeping harmony and hierarchy
1949–1978	The Cultural Revolution	Denouncement of Confucian principles Loyalty only to the Communist Party
1978–1982	The Awakening	Socialist market culture with Chinese characteristics with an aim to get rich fast at any expense
1982–1994	Socialist Period	Formation of state capitalism and academic research on the best model for business ethics
1994–2001	The Emerging Period	A break from the 'Iron Rice Bowl' and a move to market competition through a revamp of the legal system
2001–present	State Capitalism	China is a part of the WTO, demanding its Western standards of laws, implementation, and business ethics

Source: Adapted from Berger (2015), 'The transformation of Chinese business ethics in line with its emergence as a global economic leader', *Journal of Chinese Economic and Foreign Trade Studies*, 8(2): 106–22

5.5 Business ethics in the Indo-centric cultures

Countries from Indo-centric cultures include India, Nepal, Sri Lanka, Bhutan, and some parts of South-East Asia, and typically follow the traditions of Hinduism, Buddhism, Sikhism, and Jainism. Cultures, according to Ramanujan (1989), have tendencies to think in terms of either the context-free or the context-sensitive kind of rules. He suggests 'actual behaviour may be more complex, though the rules they think with are crucial factors in guiding behaviour. In cultures like India's, the context-sensitive kind of rule is the preferred formulation' (p. 47). Marques (2010) contends that the rich traditions of Indo-origin cultures are focused on intuitive ethical decision-making as compared to the Western analytical approaches. In this section, we will introduce and explore three aspects of business ethics in the Indo-origin cultures: (1) the solution-seeking pragmatic *Jugaad* culture, (2) the concepts that underpin Indo-origin cultures (such as *dharma* and *karma*), and (3) the evolution of business ethics specifically in India.

The *Jugaad* culture in India

During the 20th century, most of the innovations that came from the more developed economies of North America, Western Europe, and Japan benefitted a relatively small number of people. These innovations were based on huge investments into research and development to develop premium-priced products targeted initially to consumers in developed countries and later to the rest of the world. This trend changed towards the end of the 20th century and more prominently in the 21st century with innovations emanating from large emerging economies such as Brazil, India, and China. A large proportion of such innovations are driven by local culture and ingeniously using existing resources, technologies, and improvisation with the intention of developing solutions for communities who were traditionally and historically denied access to such products and services. One such innovation culture is *Jugaad* (see the opening case of the chapter), which has existed in India for centuries and is now being recognised, researched, and written about extensively. Similar concepts in other countries include *gambiarra* or *jeitinho* in Brazil, *kanju* in some parts of Africa, *jua kali* in Kenya, *jiejian chuangxin* in China, Systeme D in France, and DIY (do-it-yourself) in the US, UK, and Australia.

Jugaad can be described as the 'Indian way' of innovation referring to 'workaround', 'creative improvisation', 'making things happen' in ways that are frugal (clever, sparing, and economical use of existing resources), flexible (adaptive, exploring options, view rules as pliable, and embrace ambiguity), and inclusive (solutions intended for communities and individuals typically not served by the formal sector). It is a product of the environment in which it operates – according to the Credit Suisse Global Wealth Report 2017 (Rohner, 2017), there are about 770 million Indians who earn less than USD 10,000 per annum and could be said to exist in the *Jugaad* culture environment. It therefore appears to be entrenched widely in the Indian culture and particularly among people who have grown up in these conditions. Reactions to the '*Jugaad* culture' can be observed as dichotomous. Research has shown that the concept of *Jugaad* on the one hand is celebrated as being successful in finding solutions for local issues through ethical means and can be a force for social good. Some examples of successful *Jugaads* at various organisational levels are:

- Social venture – MittiCool: a clay refrigerator that uses widely available materials like clay and water, highly affordable (a 50-litre unit is priced at INR 8,000 or USD 105) (https://mitticool.com/).
- SME venture – SELCO: solar lighting solution that rents solar charged batteries on a daily basis so it is as affordable as buying kerosene (https://selco-india.com/).
- Large MNC – General Electric: Mac 400 ECG machine that is portable and robust to enable doctors to carry the machines to rural clinics from cities (www.youtube.com/watch?v=TBjvCU9tdfQ).

On the other hand, *Jugaad* has also been criticised for bending the rules, blatant copying, and working the system that places them on shaky moral foundations. Some argue that it promotes dangerous practices (pushing equipment beyond its intended capacity), use of bribery, digital piracy, cheating, manipulation, and corruption to get things done. In a resource-poor environment, such 'creative' problem-solving reveals an attitude called 'assertive defiance', defined as an attitude of boldness, self-belief, and a disregard for traditions, conventions, rules, and regulations. This involves finding a way of ignoring or circumventing socially constructed constraints (Ananthram and Chan, 2021; Jain, 2022; Jauregui, 2014; Prabhu and Jain, 2015; Shepherd et al., 2020; Sivarajan et al., 2021).

Concepts that underpin business ethics in Indo-centric cultures

The philosophical foundations of the Indian culture could be traced back to the sacred scriptures called the **Vedas** originating in ancient India from 1500 BCE. The **Upanishads**, commonly referred to as *Vedanta*, were the last compositions of the *Vedas*, and are the foundations of Hindu thought and traditions. The cornerstones of Vedantic thought are the concepts of *dharma, karma, kama, artha*, and *moksha*, which influence business ethics and ethical decision-making in India.

Dharma is used to indicate a family of traditions originating in India and manifest in Hinduism, Buddhism, Jainism, and Sikhism (Malhotra, 2011: 3). It has multiple meanings depending on the context in which it is used. It is often translated as religion, path, law, ethics, conduct, duty, right, justice, virtue, and morality, thus making it hard to define. *Dharma* has the Sanskrit root word *dhri* meaning 'that which maintains the stability and harmony of the universe' or 'that which upholds'. Dharmic ethics are formulated in response to the situation and context of the problem. Ramanujan (1989) argues that cultures may be thought of as either context-free or context-sensitive. Since actual behaviour is complex, 'in cultures like India's, the context-sensitive kind of rule is the preferred formulation' (p. 47). While most Western conceptions and applications of ethics are independent of context (e.g. the Ten Commandments and Kant's Categorical Imperative), Dharmic traditions seek to balance universal truths and those acts that can be determined only in the context in which they occur (Malhotra, 2011: 193).

Dharmic context-sensitive ethics can be further illustrated by examining the six ethical views of *dharma* in terms of right and wrong behaviour: *asrama-dharma* (conduct that is right for one's stage of life, e.g. student, house-holder, retirement from work, and retirement from life), *varna-dharma* (occupational predispositions), *jati-dharma* (communal codes), *svabhava-dharma* (personal nature), *sva-dharma* (choice of path), and *apad-dharma* (conduct that is necessary in times of distress or emergency), and finally, there is *sadharan-dharma* (absolute/universal) which is the equivalent of 'last resort', i.e. a fall-back if no context can be found to apply (Malhotra, 2011; Ramanujan, 1989).

Thus, unburdened by the belief that there is only one right path, one has the freedom to choose a personal path to the ultimate truth. In most dharmic traditions, each individual has a unique personal dharma (*sva-dharma*). This is based on a person's character (*svabhava*) which is shaped by past *karma* (further elaborated in the next section) and on the context or circumstances of the person's life. The traditions mention that there are four main paths that one can follow, through one or in combination: acquired or intuitive knowledge (*jnana-yoga*), meditation (*dhyana-yoga*), devotion (*bhakti-yoga*), and perfection at work (*karma-yoga*).

Distinct ethical recommendations are also available based on various pursuits in life such as *artha* (pursuit of material wealth and prosperity by ethical means), *kama* (fulfilment of physical desires without compromising the ethics), and *moksha* (self-realisation and liberation). 'While *dharma*, *artha*, and *kama* are related to the goals of everyday life, *moksha* has to do with the ultimate goal of releasing oneself from the endless cycle of death and rebirth. It is believed that one who lives in accordance with *dharma* principles proceeds more quickly towards *moksha*' (Berger and Herstein, 2013: 1078–9). We can summarise that *dharma* is the ethical sense that helps regulate and discipline one's actions and was the earliest beginnings of ancient India's criminal and civil law. With the desire for *artha* (accumulation of wealth) coupled with economic liberation from 1995, Indians had to find a way to run businesses in a competitive business environment with a lack of resources – leading to *Jugaad* which is now recognised all over the world as an acceptable way of doing business in India (Berger and Herstein, 2013). However, instead of pursuing wealth through ethical means (the true meaning of *artha*), *Jugaad* seems to have diminished business ethics.

Evolution of business ethics in India

The evolution of business ethics in India is shown in Table 5.2. It traces the characteristics of business ethics in six stages from the ancient Vedantic era, through the British **colonisation** period, to the current period. The last two stages have been modified and added by the author.

Table 5.2 Evolution of business in India

Stage period	Stage name	Characteristics
Ancient	Vedantic era	Mechanisms based on Hinduism highlighted importance of applying ethical principles.
Up to 18th century	Panchayati Raj	Panchayati, a group of elders chosen and accepted by the local community to regulate the community. The core function was to create wealth for society through manufacturing, distribution, foreign trade, and financing, emphasising business ethics.
1858–1947	British Raj	Traditional business ethics practices were replaced by Anglo-Saxon and Greco-Roman practices, causing a collapse of the "old" system, and bringing a decline in ethical conduct. Indian businesspeople were absolved from the Vedantic-based moral and ethical responsibilities. Decline of Hinduism-based ethics seems to parallel stagnation and decline of economy – from one of the largest economies in the world (25 per cent of world economy in 1700) to one of the lowest (4 per cent at independence from Britain in 1947).

Stage period	Stage name	Characteristics
1947–1990	Licence or Permit Raj	Democratically elected leaders led India into a mixed economy combining state-controlled with free market economies. Opted for Western systems over Hindu Vedantic-based system. Growth was slow and over-reliance on state-controlled sectors led to inefficiency, corruption, and unethical behaviour.
1990–1995	Liberalisation of economy – phase I	Pressure from the IMF, WTO, and global markets resulted in privatisations with an emphasis on profits which has had the consequence of leaving business ethics behind. At the same, the liberalisation of the economy resulted in opportunities for entrepreneurial Indian firms.
1995–current	Liberalisation of economy – phase II	Accelerated growth propels India forward as world's fastest growing economy from 2013–2018, becoming the fifth largest economy in the world after the US, China, Japan, and Germany. Awareness of business ethics increases with globalisation and education.

Source: Adapted from Berger (2015), 'The transformation of Chinese business ethics in line with its emergence as a global economic leader', *Journal of Chinese economic and foreign trade studies*, 8(2): 106–22

5.6 Business ethics in Islamic-centric cultures

Countries from Islamic-centric cultures include Middle Eastern countries, Pakistan, Afghanistan, Bangladesh, Indonesia, North Africa, Central Asia, and some parts of South-East Asia, and these typically follow the traditions of Islam. In this section, we will introduce and explore three aspects of business ethics in the Islamic cultures: (1) the solution-seeking pragmatic *wasta* culture, (2) the concepts that underpin these cultures (such as *hadith*, *khuluq*, *tawhid*, *salihat*, etc.), and (3) the evolution of business ethics in Islamic cultures.

Within Islam, the term most closely related to ethics in the *Qur'an* (the holy book of Muslims) is *khuluq*, which means character, nature, and disposition (Beekun, 1996; Rahim, 2013). The *fiqh* (theory or philosophy of Islamic law) of whether an act is considered a virtue or a vice is determined in the primary sources of Islam – *Qur'an* and *Sunnah*, derived from the Prophet Muhammad's (pbuh) sayings and actions. In the Muslim world, when business people face ethical issues at work, they must adhere to the Islamic code of ethics. Their decisions are guided by faith, or *iman*, by following *shariah* law and engaging in what is *halal*, permitted, and avoiding what is *haram*, forbidden (Abuznaid, 2009). In Islam, ethics has two dimensions – first ethics towards Allah, the creator (e.g. by worshipping Him), and second ethics towards others (e.g. dealing ethically with others by maintaining good treatment and relationships). While the *Qur'an* uses a cluster of terms to denote the concept of moral or religious goodness, Rahim (2013) contends that the most critical challenge facing Muslims today is the lack of the ethical dimension in life, due to a lack of adherence to the code of ethics. Some of the factors that affect one's ethical behaviour include stages of moral development, personal values and morals, family influences and pressures, expectations of relatives and friends, peer influences and expectations resulting in *wasta* (nepotism which is unethical), previous personal experiences, and situational and societal factors. 'In the Arab world, *wasta* has effectively been used to override established laws and traditions which exist and are used in place of relevant regulations and standards' (Abuznaid, 2009: 282).

Wasta

Wasta is a social network, interpersonal connections rooted in a family, tribe, and extended relationships. It captures the dynamics of collectivism and communitarianism. It drives cooperation and obligation to others through an unwritten social contract. In addition to being useful for someone within a network, it can be used to help someone unknown if referred by someone with whom you have a *wasta* relationship (Alenezi et al., 2022; Zhang et al., 2021). The term *wasta* relates to the verb *yatawassat*, meaning to steer contradictory parties towards a mediation to obtain that which was otherwise expected to be unattainable. It can, for example, facilitate official paperwork and procedures, obtain benefits on behalf of a client, overcome obstacles from the authorities/government, and facilitate settlements of intergroup or interpersonal disputes (Algumzi, 2017). Further, individuals who ask for help have no obligation to offer reciprocal assistance. Alenezi et al. (2022) indicates that there are three components of *wasta*: *mohamala* (connection with family), *hamola* (to carry on something by people claiming descent from five to seven generations), and *somah* (relationships, mutual companionship, and teamwork).

A variation of *wasta* is a concept called *Et-Moone* which is also based on close and strong relationships that provide greater flexibility in business, and allows for unilateral decisions without causing any uneasiness or divisions between partners. The key drivers for *Et-Moone* are interpersonal liking, trust, and commitment in the relationships (Abosag, 2015). A study of 180 senior managers in Saudi Arabia confirmed the importance of *Et-Moone* in business-to-business relationships and its impact on cooperation (Abosag, 2015: 150). While *wasta* has a positive side that can be used to navigate bureaucracy and increased access to services, it can have a dark side as a source of nepotism, cronyism, and corruption (Zhang et al., 2021). A study by Alenezi et al. (2022) of 225 male and female employees from the private sector in Kuwait found that *mohamala* was the most influential factor between *wasta* and favouritism.

Several studies have found similarities between such concepts in other cultures. Zhang et al. (2021) compared *guanxi* (China), *yongo* (South Korea), and *wasta* (Arab countries). They found the same three underlying dimensions: reciprocity, affect, and trustworthiness. Velez-Calle et al. (2015) compared *guanxi* and *wasta* with the *compadrazgo* concept in Latin America's Hispanic cultures. *Compadrazgo* means a ritual kinship system that refers to ties developed outside the biological family, where through interpersonal relationships, members are bound to the same rights and obligations as parents and children, and reciprocity is expected. Smith, Torres et al. (2012) compared *guanxi* and *wasta* to *jeitinho*, a Brazilian characteristic of behaviour referring to creative ingenuity to rapidly achieve short-term solutions to problems; *svyazi*, a Russian system of informal interpersonal relationships; and 'pulling strings', a Western characteristic referring to obtaining favours through links with influential persons.

Concepts that underpin business ethics in Islamic-centric cultures

The main approaches to understanding Islamic business ethics have been based predominantly on the interpretations of the *Qur'an* and the *Sunnah*, and also to a lesser extent by the Western understanding of Islamic ethics. However, scholars have addressed the diversity of ethical positions in Islam by differentiating ethical thinking into (1) normative religious ethics, (2) ethical analysis in the religious tradition, and (3) ethical traditions by philosophers (Sidani and Al Ariss, 2015). Normative religious ethics relies on divine Muslim sources such as understanding what is lawful (*halal*), what is forbidden (*haram*), business practices related to justice (*'adl*), trusteeship (*amanah*), several criteria for business ethics relating to stakeholders, value-maximisation, production, consumption, sales, and distribution. Ethical analysis mainly involved the debate between traditionalists (who maintain that a judgement as to what is right and wrong should be based solely on the scriptures), and the rationalists (who assert that reason can be used independently of scripture to reach judgements about what is right) – see Sidani and Al Ariss (2015) for more details. The third position, ethical traditions of philosophers, relates to the role of Muslim philosophers (such as Al-Ghazali) played in progressing ethical theory. They were influenced by and made commentaries on Greek philosophies. For example Al-Ghazali (1058–1111) asserts that the ultimate goal is the pursuit of happiness which is the 'afterlife', and requires knowledge (*'ilm*) and actions (*'amal*). Four main themes emerge from his work: (1) knowledge before actions, (2) maximisation of profits is not a virtue, (3) justice and care for all stakeholders, and (4) *ihsan* (benevolence or doing good), an early reference to corporate social responsibility.

Trade, economic growth, and business were central to early Islamic thinking. Prophet Muhammad (pbuh) himself was a merchant and recognised the need and necessity of trade in the formation of social and political networks and in spreading his spiritual message to other regions. Trade was viewed 'as an instrument for realising religious, political, social and economic goals' (Ali and Al-Owaihan, 2008: 8). The Prophet preached that merchants should not only perform tasks that were morally required but also essential for the survival and flourishing of a society. Thus, Islamic business ethics (IBE) has been built on four primary concepts: effort, competition, transparency, and morally responsible conduct. IBE emphasises intention rather than outcomes as a measure of morality. For example, engaging in monopoly, gambling, or trading in alcohol may bring fortune but are considered immoral endeavours. Muslims are advised to ensure 'a balance in their endeavours to ensure social well-being' and to condemn 'the evils of greed, unscrupulousness and disregard for the rights and needs of others' (Rice, 1999: 348). This is corroborated by a study in Malaysia of 144 respondents from Islamic banks in Malaysia and selected Gulf Cooperation Council countries, which reported that bank personnel perceived that their banks conform to Islamic ethical norms in their business, were concerned with their impact on society, and that ethics prevailed over profit-maximisation

(Musa et al., 2020). Research in women in business and entrepreneur roles has increased in recent years. Tlaiss (2015) cites several studies that reported women entrepreneurs themselves did not perceive Islam and its teachings as the barrier to career advancement (considering in part that Prophet Muhammad's wife pursued a career in trade), but rather the masculine, traditional interpretations of its teachings, and they also argue that the discriminatory practices against Muslim women in Muslim societies are fuelled by Muslim conservatism or cultural biases (p. 864). In their study of 30 women entrepreneurs from the UAE, Lebanon, Kuwait, and Oman, Tlaiss (2015) found women entrepreneurs embedded work and ethical values such as hard work (*amal salih*), honesty and truthfulness (*sidik* and *amanah*), fairness and justice (*haqq* and *adl*), and benevolence (*ihsaan*) in their activities – to seek well-being (*falah*) in their lives, and excellence (*itqan*) in their work and business (p. 859).

Evolution of business ethics in Islamic-centric cultures

As discussed earlier, business ethics concepts in Islamic-centric cultures derive from and rely on normative religious ethics which are primarily drawn from scriptures (such as the *Qur'an*, *Hadith*, and *Sunnah*) to reach conclusions about the overall framework of Islamic ethics (Sidani and Al Ariss, 2015). Attempts have been made to adopt a more rationalist perspective while not necessarily ignoring the traditional perspectives.

5.7 Research findings for cross-cultural effects on business ethics

In an earlier section of this chapter, we outlined Hofstede's culture dimensions theory that provides a framework to describe the effect of a society's culture on the values of its members and specifically how those values relate to behaviour. Since the 1980s, there have been many cross-cultural studies that presented the effect of Hofstede's framework in matters related to business ethics. Below are some research findings excerpted and adapted from various publications:

- Findings in the Ermasova (2021) compilation of papers:
  - American managers were more likely be loyal to their own personal beliefs than those of their employer, whereas the Korean managers were prone to tow the company line ethically, fitting with the collectivist ideal.
  - Traditional Eastern business relationships can easily turn towards bribery and corruption, but a sizable portion of the businesspeople sampled play down the risks.
  - Taiwanese culture is a mix between traditional Chinese culture and Western cultures due to its deep roots in traditional Chinese culture and its more recent exposure to Western cultures.
  - Moral foundations and Confucian ethics interacted and jointly affected managers' positions on the shareholder value model of corporate responsibility.
  - A high percentage of Americans (60 per cent) as well as Russians (67 per cent) and Slovenians (51 per cent) felt that they had to sacrifice their

personal ethics to business goals, while only 16 per cent of Turkish businesspeople felt this way. Respondents did not consider themselves as less ethical than the average person.

- Russian consumers perceived the ethical behaviour of the domestic businesses they dealt with to be higher than did consumers in Poland, Romania, and Bulgaria.
- American managers are more loyal to their own ethical beliefs, rather than to their superior's ethical beliefs, while East Asian cultures focus more on the importance of acting in the best interests of their superior in the company.
- Indian business managers find ethical decision-making to be much more difficult than American business managers do.
- Japanese managers use the concept of Kaizen, or small steps towards perfection.
- Whistle-blowing: Cultural background plays a huge role in attitudes towards whistle-blowing. The attitude towards whistle-blowing varies among different cultures significantly. In Scandinavian countries, whistle-blowing is approved of by the population and supported by government. Chinese managers are less likely to blow the whistle than their American counterparts. In contrast to the USA, Continental European countries and Russia have a more negative association with whistle-blowers. The Russian culture has the attitude that whistle-blowing is disloyalty to the collective, even treachery. Females have a higher intention for whistle-blowing than males – but only when anonymous reporting arrangements were available.

- Scholtens and Dam (2007) studied how the ethical conduct of firms might be associated with Hofstede's cultural dimensions. Their analysis of 2,700 firms in 24 countries found that the location of a firm's headquarters could be a significant factor in the communication and implementation of their code of ethics. In addition, they found that individualism and uncertainty avoidance are positively associated with firms' ethics, whereas masculinity and power distance tend to be negatively associated.
- Findings from Vitolla et al.'s (2021) study of 191 international companies in 29 countries and five continents on the impact of Hofstede's dimensions on the quality of code of ethics:

  - Companies operating in countries with high levels of power distance are more likely to provide higher quality ethical codes.
  - Individualistic societies are more likely to provide higher quality ethical codes.
  - Masculinity does not affect the quality of ethical codes. In this regard, the presence of strong masculine values, in some cases, could make the code of ethics inadequate to fight unethical behaviour, favouring the use of more rigid control tools such as surveillance, orders, and respect for the hierarchy.
  - Firms operating in societies with high levels of uncertainty avoidance are more likely to provide higher quality ethical codes.
  - Companies operating in countries with greater short-term orientation are more likely to provide higher quality ethical codes.
  - Companies operating in countries with high levels of restraint are more likely to provide higher quality ethical codes.

- Wang et al.'s (2021) study of large companies in 17 countries found that the cultural dimensions of masculinity and uncertainty avoidance are barriers to green proactivity (when corporate responses to climate change not only comply with carbon regulations but also improve carbon management and include making green investments) and a U-shape relationship exists between power distance and proactivity (for example, when power is less concentrated, managers prioritise financial issues and economic success, but when power becomes concentrated, it allows managers to pursue social objectives).

- Takeda et al. (2022) conducted a study of 476 employees in Thai, Japanese, and UK companies and found employees' degree of collectivism and ethical relativism is affected by acculturation, so that it tends to change closer to the values more prevalent in the MNCs' home cultures; the degree of change is greater when the cultural distance between MNCs' home and host nation cultures is greater.
- Halder et al. (2020), in a study of 1,929 respondents from four European countries, found cultural collectivism has a significant positive effect on green consumption values, that is, demonstration of stronger preferences for environmentally friendly products.
- Husted's (2000) study found that software piracy is significantly correlated to individualism, in addition to GNP per capita, and income inequality.
- Thanetsunthorn's (2015) study based on the corporate social responsibility (CSR) performance of 3,055 corporations from 28 countries found that corporations based in countries with higher levels of power distance, individualism, and masculinity exhibit lower levels of employee-related and community-level CSR performance.

════ Box 5.3 ════

Software piracy

Traditionally, intellectual protection has been granted to inventions and creative works through patents, trademarks, and copyrights. Now with software-driven technology, information is being treated as an asset and property. Information is seen as consisting of data that is meaningful and useful to human beings, and therefore requires intellectual property protection. Software is particularly vulnerable to illegal duplication and counterfeiting, as multiple copies can be made with minimal costs – known as 'software piracy'. It is estimated that 37 per cent of software (amounting to USD 46.3 billion) running in the world is unlicensed, and 2 out of every 5 copies of software running in the world are not paid for (www.go-globe.com/online-piracy).

Researchers have examined several different causes for this alarming spread of software piracy. One of the main findings was that it is not often seen as an ethical problem, but as an individual's evaluation of distributive fairness, comparing the ratio of outcomes to inputs. Differences in piracy rates at the country level have been shown partly due to national wealth, but also due to cultural differences. For example, the fact that the piracy rates are high in the US and Spain but low in Finland cannot be explained only by differences in national income.

Husted (2000) applied Hofstede's cultural dimensions and hypothesised that:

1 The higher the level of economic development, the lower the rate of software piracy.
2 The lower the level of income inequality (the larger the middle class), the greater the rate of software piracy.

3 The higher the power distance in a country, the higher the rate of software piracy in a country.
4 The more individualistic (less collectivistic) a society, the lower the rate of software piracy.
5 The greater the masculinity of a culture, the higher the rate of software piracy.
6 The greater the level of uncertainty avoidance in a nation, the higher the rate of software piracy.

Analysis of data from 39 countries showed support for hypotheses numbers 1, 2, and 4. No relationship was found between software piracy and power distance, uncertainty avoidance, or masculinity.

Questions

1 Go to www.hofstede-insights.com/fi/product/compare-countries and ascertain the scores for Hofstede's four cultural dimensions for countries of your choice.
2 Reflect and compare on the country scores with hypotheses 3–6 shown above. Do you agree with these hypotheses? Explain your answers.

Source: Adapted from Husted (2000)

5.8 Incorporating effects of culture on business ethics in the Comprehensive Ethical Decision-Making model

With the enormous amount of data and findings on the effects of culture on business ethics, we can now suggest ways that these can be incorporated into the ethical decision-making model that we had introduced in Chapter 4. We will use the following approaches:

1 Donaldson and Dunfee (1994, 1999) assert that 'cultural differences abound in global business activities' (p. 47), and that while Hofstede and others have shown the importance of cultural differences to business, there is a need to provide clearer specific guidance for businesses when the traditional perspectives such as utilitarianism, deontology, and virtue ethics may not help executives navigate tricky ethical issues. How do we ascertain what's right when operating under different cultural ethical norms? Their Integrative Social Contracts Theory (ISCT) describes a way for managers to balance conflicting norms and values and provides a practical guide for corporations to operate globally. Rowan (2001) further clarified that the core of ISCT is based on two types of social contract:

a Macrosocial contracts – globally acceptable fundamental principles called 'hypernorms' that may not be breached. These are generated from consistent norms such as procedural (from within individual economic communities, for example ethical codes), structural (pertaining to political and social communities), or substantive (pertaining to fundamental concepts of right and wrong).

b   Microsocial contracts – actual agreements found within individual economic communities. These represent the plurality of norms across communities in different nations and cultures with sometimes conflicting practices. Donaldson and Dunfee call this 'moral free space' where communities can develop and practise specific norms. Donald and Dunfee suggest that there's nothing wrong in acknowledging differences and each community can develop its own practices, as long as 'hypernorms' are not violated. In other words, hypernorms constitute the boundaries of 'moral free space' within which specific norms can be developed and practised. Finally, there are 'illegitimate norms' which would not be accepted in most, if not all, communities. Thus, components of the ISCT are identified as hypernorms, consistent norms, moral free space, and illegitimate norms:

- Hypernorms are fundamental principles that define the root of what is ethical for humanity. All other norms can be judged by hypernorms. They enable people to achieve basic or 'necessary' social goods such as health, education, food, clothing, and social justice. Thus, they include fundamental human rights or basic prescriptions acceptable to all religions, cultures, and organisations.
- Consistent norms are values that are culturally specific but are consistent with hypernorms and other legitimate norms such as corporations' ethical codes and value statements.
- Moral free space consists of norms that can be compatible with hypernorms but are inconsistent with other legitimate norms. They are often unique and strongly held cultural norms. Such norms can create tensions.
- Illegitimate norms are incompatible with hypernorms, such as those that violate laws and fundamental human rights.

2   Stajkovic and Luthans (1997) used a social cognitive model to suggest that national cultures affect institutional factors (such as ethics and legislation), personal factors (such as values, beliefs, moral development, and self-regulation), and organisational factors (such as code of ethics). These factors affect business ethical standards which in turn can affect business conduct, ethical or unethical, resulting in positive or negative consequences.

3   Robertson and Fadil (1999) used a culture-based consequentialist model to suggest that national cultural dimensions (such as individualism and collectivism) could affect an individual's cognitive moral development (for example, Kohlberg's CMD in Chapter 4), which in turn can affect the intensity of ethical dilemma leading to ethical behaviour.

4   Robertson et al. (2012) used a generational subculture-based model which suggests that (a) generational subculture (the notion that macro-level social, political, and economic events that occurred during a generational group's impressionable years shape a group identity), (b) national cultural values, and (c) influences from family and friends form an individual's moral philosophy, resulting in moral behaviour.

Concepts from this chapter have been incorporated in the Comprehensive Ethical Decision-Making model as shown in Figure 5.1.

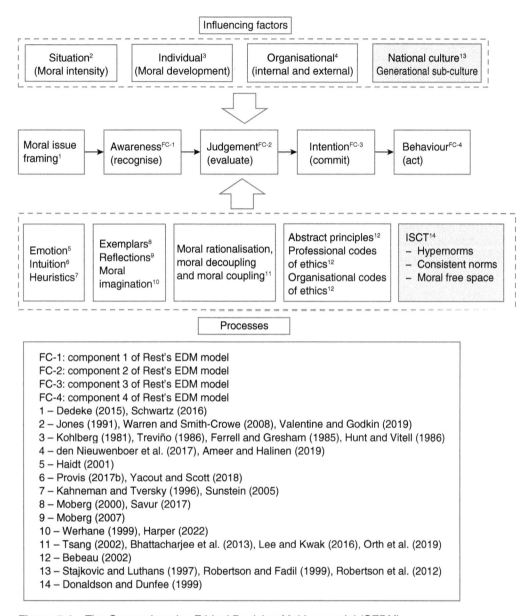

Figure 5.1 The Comprehensive Ethical Decision-Making model (CEDM)

═══════ **Summary** ═══════

- This chapter began with understanding globalisation and its rapid spread around the world. In addition to the exchange of goods, services, finance, labour, and communication that globalisation has enabled, we learned that cultural exchanges were also one of the key aspects.

(Continued)

- As a result of business being conducted across different cultures, we appreciated that business ethics can be affected by cultural differences. Here, Hofstede's five cultural dimensions and the GLOBE study are useful concepts that can inform and describe behaviour.
- Further, with the realisation that people from different cultures are embedded in varied geographical locations, which makes it difficult to categorise cultures, we adopted culture-centric differentiation which incorporates geography and religions. Five such centres were identified – Western-centric, African-centric, Confucian-centric, Indo-centric, and Islamic-centric. Of these, the Western-centric business ethics concepts have been discussed in sections of Chapters 1 to 4. Concepts of the other four centres have been elaborated in this chapter.
- We discovered that there are several concepts that seem to be similar or commonly understood in these four (African, Confucian, Indo, and Islamic) cultural centres. There were also some differences, mainly in the way the concepts are applied to business ethics. The opening case, the two mini case studies, and the two major case studies point to the various aspects of the effect of culture on business ethics.
- The Integrative Social Contracts Theory addresses the question 'How do we ascertain what's right when operating under different cultural ethical norms?' and suggests three layers of decision-making – hypernorms, consistent norms, and moral free space.
- This chapter concluded with the assertion that concepts from this chapter could be included in the Comprehensive Ethical Decision-Making model that was introduced in Chapter 4.

CASE STUDY 5.1
SIX BUSINESS SCENARIOS

Scenario One

A manager of a middle-size and state-owned company relies on his friendship with local government officials to avoid paying fines for violating pollution regulations.

Scenario Two

A sales manager for a machine-tool factory gives gifts to the procurement department of his large customers.

Scenario Three

A manager who is in charge of a procurement department in a large detergent company agreed to buy a large amount of material from his boss's brother's company.

Scenario Four

A general manager of a branch of a bank only hires his old classmates who attended college with him.

Scenario Five

A business manager in a large restaurant is visited by officials who say the manager violated an unwritten accounting regulation. The officials send the manager to jail for a week. One of the manager's employees is friends with the officials and asks the officials to let the manager pay money to avoid spending time in jail. The officials agree and the manager pays the money.

Scenario Six

A business manager develops a loyal, long-lasting relationship with his set of customers.

Questions

For each of the scenarios, reflect and discuss the following:

1 Do you think the managers in the scenarios were using *guanxi*?
2 Is this type of *guanxi* helpful or harmful to the Chinese community, the business organisation, and to the manager in the scenarios?
3 What aspects of the Chinese ethical concepts would you recommend?
4 How would you compare your findings with *Jugaad* (of India)? What aspects of the Indian ethical concepts would you recommend?
5 How would you compare your findings with *Ubuntu* (of Africa)?

Using the Case-Study Integrative Framework in Figure 0.1, discuss the following:

1 Apply the EDM process to these scenarios – use the concepts in this chapter (cultural dimensions, national cultures, and ISCT), along with concepts from previous chapters.

Source: Warren et al. (2004)

CASE STUDY 5.2
FAST FASHION ETHICAL ISSUES

Fast fashion can be defined as the design, creation, and marketing of clothing fashions based on making fashion trends quickly and cheaply. In 1960, the average American

(Continued)

adult bought fewer than 25 items of clothing each year. A household would spend about 10 per cent of its income on clothing and shoes, most of which were made in the US. But by the 1980s, a few American retailers started to outsource production due to the opening of textile mills and manufacturing plants in China and other countries in Asia and Latin America which could mass-produce inexpensive garments quickly. By 2021, the average American purchased 70 pieces of clothing each year but spent less than 3.5 per cent of their income on clothes, only 2 per cent of which were made in the US.

In order to mass-produce inexpensive garments, items are often not made ethically. In addition to textile waste, CO_2 emissions, and water pollution, a major issue is unsafe labour conditions. Factories are the so-called 'sweat-shops' where employees work in unsafe conditions, often for low wages and long hours. In many cases, children are employed. Several disasters connected with fast fashion manufacturers have cost hundreds of lives and injuries. In 2013, Rana Plaza – a building manufacturing such garments in Bangladesh – collapsed killing 1,134 people and injuring over 2,500. In 2012, a fire at a garment factory in Karachi, Pakistan killed nearly 300 people, and another fire in a garment factory in Dhaka, Bangladesh killed 112 workers.

However, the retailers are not held accountable because workers' rights in developing countries are either non-existent or not enforced. Retailers do not usually own their own factories and instead contract them out which essentially means they cannot be held accountable. In some countries, there are not enough laws to enforce a living wage, allowing brands to squeeze their factories to produce more garments with lower wage paid to workers. A recent investigation revealed that on average, a worker gets 4 per cent of the retail price of a garment. So, a USD 30 garment would generate an income of about USD 1.20 for a worker.

While it is possible that the retailers might take the view that 'when in Rome, do as the Romans do' (meaning that the rules of the country or culture where the contractor is located should be followed), there is growing awareness and pressure on the retailers to commit to more ethical responsibilities.

Questions

Using the Case-Study Integrative Framework in Figure 0.1, discuss the following:

1   Do you think the retailers, if they want to make a change, can have a say in enforcing better wage and safety conditions for such workers?
2   What do you suggest the retailers should do, considering that it might interfere with the local laws and cultural conditions?
3   Discuss and suggest ways to improve the working conditions of garment workers.
4   Apply the EDM process to these scenarios – use the concepts in this chapter (cultural dimensions, national cultures, and ISCT), along with concepts from previous chapters.

Sources:
Australian Institute (2020)
Marriott (2021)

Recommended readings

For a comprehensive view of globalisation:
Friedman, T.L. (2007), *The world is flat*, London: Allen Lane of Penguin Books, pp. 9–11 and 324–9.

For an appreciation of Hofstede's cultural dimensions and cross-cultural aspects:
Ermasova, N. (2021), 'Cross-cultural issues in business ethics: A review and research agenda', *International Journal of Cross Cultural Management*, 21(1): 95–121.
Hofstede, G., Hofstede, G.J. and Minkow, M. (2010), *Cultures and organizations: Software of the mind*, New York: McGraw Hill.
Donaldson, T. and Dunfee, T.W. (1994), 'Towards a unified conception of business ethics: Integrative Social Contracts Theory', *The Academy of Management Review*, 19(2): 252–84.

For an appreciation of African-centric business ethics:
Newenham-Kahindi, A. (2009), 'The transfer of *Ubuntu* and *Indaba* business models abroad', *International Journal of Cross Cultural Management*, 9(1): 87–108.
Adeleye, I., Luiz, J., Muthuri, J. and Amaeshi, K. (2019), 'Business ethics in Africa: The role of institutional context, social relevance, and development challenges', *Journal of Business Ethics*, 161(4): 717–29.

For an appreciation of Confucian-centric business ethics:
Provis, C. (2019), 'Business ethics, Confucianism and the different faces of ritual', *Journal of Business Ethics*, 165(2): 191–204.
Yin, J. and Quazi, A. (2016), 'Business ethics in the greater China region: Past, present, and future research', *Journal of Business Ethics*, 150(3): 815–35.
Ulusemre, T. and Fang, X. (2022), 'How do expatriate managers draw the boundaries of moral free space in the case of *guanxi*?' *Journal of Business Ethics*, 176(2): 311–24.

For an appreciation of Indo-centric business ethics:
Jain, S. (2022), 'From *Jugaad* to *Jugalbandi*: Understanding the changing nature of Indian innovation', *Asia Pacific Journal of Management*, 39(1): 1–26.
Malhotra, R. (2011), *Being different*, Noida: Harper Collins Publishers India.

For an appreciation of Islamic-centric business ethics:
Abuznaid, S.A. (2009), 'Business ethics in Islam: The glaring gap in practice', *International Journal of Islamic and Middle Eastern Finance and Management*, 2(4): 278–88.

PART II
ETHICAL ISSUES IN BUSINESS

6

TYPICAL ETHICAL ISSUES OF MANAGERS AND ORGANISATIONS

───── Learning objectives ─────

On completion of this chapter, you should be able to:

- Appreciate the range of special ethical issues that confront managers and organisations
- Examine what responsibilities managers have in the above-mentioned issues
- Appreciate the special pitfalls in these issues
- Examine how managers in organisations can manage these issues
- Reflect on how the Comprehensive Ethical Decision-Making model (CEDM) from Chapters 4 and 5 can be applied to these special ethical problems

───── Key concepts ─────

- Special ethical issues of managers and organisations
- Bribery and corruption
- Conflicts of interest
- Diversity, equity, and inclusion in the workplace
- Hiring and recruitment
- Downsizing
- Outsourcing

─Box 6.1 Opening case─

The gap between bribery laws and reality

On 17 December 1997, members of the **Organization for Economic Cooperation and Development (OECD)** signed the convention to establish legally binding standards to criminalise bribery of foreign public officials in international business transactions. In 1999, 38 OECD member countries ratified the convention and further recommendations were made in 2021. However, based on the flood of whistle-blower submissions in 2021 alleging violations, it seems that bribery of foreign officials and corruption have become worse. Enforcement of anti-bribery and anti-corruption laws depends heavily on whistle-blowers and the high-quality inside information that only they can bring. In the past two years, whistle-blowers have been awarded nearly USD 314 million.

Bribery and corruption cases observed in the last five years:

1   In 2017, Rolls-Royce, a British multinational enterprise, agreed to a settlement of around USD 1 billion in penalties for corruption allegations in Russia, Thailand, and China.
2   In 2018, Brazilian oil company Petroleo Brasileiro agreed to pay USD 1.78 billion for global bribery and bid-rigging.
3   In 2018, Credit Suisse Group AG, a global investment bank based in Switzerland, paid USD 47 million for securing business through bribery of public officials in the Asia-Pacific region.
4   In 2019, Mobile Telesystems PJSC, a Russian telecommunications firm, agreed to pay USD 850 million relating to corruption in Uzbekistan.
6   In 2020, Airbus, a global aircraft manufacturer based in Europe, agreed to pay USD 4 billion in fines for alleged bribery and corruption spanning 15 years.
7   In 2020, Novartis the Swiss-based pharmaceutical company agreed to a settlement of USD 1.3 billion for kickbacks, bribery, and price fixing.

Questions

1   If companies from non-OECD countries pay bribes, would it disadvantage companies from the OECD member countries?
2   Will it be acceptable if a company proves that getting contracts by paying bribes will create new jobs, new investments, and provide tax revenues for the government?
3   Do you think legislation and conventions (such as that introduced by the OECD mentioned above) will ever work if there's always someone ready to pay a bribe and someone ready to accept it (as shown in the six examples above)?

Source: Adapted from Kelton (2022) and OECD (2022a)

6.1 Introduction

So far in the five chapters of Part I (Introduction and Theories), we have learned key definitions such as 'ethics', 'morality', and 'business ethics', discussed the 'purpose' of business, explored the relationships between businesses and their stakeholders, explored the applications of ethical theories, concepts, and ethical decision-making models, and finally have pondered the challenges posed by cultural diversity in domestic and international settings through major religio-cultural traditions and ideologies.

Equipped with these concepts and theories, we can now embark on Part II – the practical part of this book. This part has five chapters (6 to 10) that will explore typical ethical issues of managers and organisations (and what can be done in these situations), sustainability (and ways to implement it), how businesses can operate as agents for world benefit, ethical issues in international business strategies (and how to resolve them), and finally responsible leadership (and how to enable it).

Business ethics can be viewed and comprehended at three levels (De George, 1990; Enderle, 2015) – macro (systemic), meso (organisational), and micro (individual) levels. The macro level recognises that businesses are embedded and shaped by the economic system of the society. At the meso level businesses can be conceived as 'moral actors who bear moral responsibility for their conduct and impact on people and nature' (Enderle, 2015: 731). At the micro level, the individual is the prime focus of morality engaged with theories and concepts we have discussed in earlier chapters. The three-level concept can be usefully linked to the technique of 'ethical displacement' (De George, 1990), where a solution to an ethical problem on one level may be found at another level. For example, what should a sales executive do when faced with the dilemma of either paying a bribe or losing the deal to a competitor? At the micro level, the individual may use their moral imagination to figure out a way. If a solution cannot be reached, the search for a solution can be moved to the meso (company) level which may have the required corporate culture to resolve it. If this is not achieved, the problem could be moved to the higher level of macro – an industry association or the home government or an international organisation – for a resolution (Enderle, 2015: 732).

The key actor in these three levels is the 'manager' of a business entity. Thus, managers of small, medium, and large business organisations, domestic or multinational, can face multiple challenges in managing ethics and legal compliance. The challenges can become more pronounced when there are employees and other stakeholders at various locations around the globe. Managers therefore can have tremendous influence on the behaviour of their employees, themselves, and their superiors. In addition to being responsible for their employees' behaviours, managers also serve as role models both in terms of exemplary behaviour and in an advisory capacity.

Managers would therefore be required to recognise and address a wide range of ethical issues. These can include workplace safety, child labour, cybercrimes, overbilling, privacy threats, fraud, financial irregularities involving owners, government officials, employees, customers, suppliers, competitors, media, and different cultures. Discussions on some of these issues have been spread across chapters in this book. In this chapter, we focus on some of the more typical ethical issues that managers could face on a regular basis: bribery and corruption; conflicts of interest; diversity, equity, and inclusion in the workplace; hiring and recruitment; downsizing; and outsourcing. Each of these issues has three sections: definitions and explanations, understanding the issue from research findings, and what can be done.

6.2 Bribery and corruption

Definitions and explanations

The global cost of bribery is estimated to be USD 1 trillion annually. This does not include costs resulting from non-completion and deficient completion of development projects (Peltier-Rivest, 2018; World Bank Institute, 2004). The World Bank defines corruption as 'the abuse of public office for private gain' (World Bank, 2020) and identified bribery as one of the main tools of corruption. In addition to bribes, it can include, through patronage and nepotism, the theft of state assets, and diversion of state revenues. Bribes have been commonly used to obtain government contracts, government benefits, lower taxes, and licences, speed up granting permissions, and change the outcome of legal processes. Bribery is also defined as an immoral practice that harms those most disadvantaged and involves at least two people (the giver and the taker) (Vu, 2021). Bribery activities can be a fee that firms pay to avoid hassles, disadvantages, or unfair treatment. In emerging markets, government officials can have powerful bargaining power to seek private gain. Country-level corruption and level of institutional development can also influence the act of bribery (Yim et al., 2017).

Transparency International (2022) defines corruption as 'the abuse of entrusted power for private gain'. It 'erodes trust, weakens democracy, hampers economic development and further exacerbates inequality, poverty, social division and the environmental crisis'. Corruption can happen anywhere, involve anyone, can happen with help of professional enablers including anonymous shell companies, and can adapt to changes in rules, legislation, and even technology. Some examples are public servants demanding or taking money or favours in exchange for services, politicians misusing public money or granting public jobs or contracts to their sponsors, friends, and families, and corporations bribing officials to get lucrative deals. The costs of corruption include political (freedom and rule of law), social (our participation and trust in government), environmental (a healthy and sustainable future), and economic (the opportunity to build and grow wealth).

See Box 6.2 for definitions of bribery and corruption from the United States Department of Justice and Independent Commission Against Corruption (ICAC) NSW, Australia.

So, why does corruption happen? Some say people commit minor ethical transgressions seeking to maximise material self-interest while maintaining a positive self-image. Others suggest that people engage in severe ethical transgressions either by a gradual transformation process (also called a slippery slope) or by an unexpected opportunity characterised by immediate large benefits (Köbis et al., 2017). Is it possible that a single severe act might be easier to rationalise than repeated unethical acts? To answer this, Köbis et al. (2017) examined behaviours of 855 participants across four studies and concluded that people were more likely to engage in severe corruption when this option was presented abruptly rather than gradually. A single act was easier to justify than a multistep process.

Understanding bribery and corruption from research findings

As we have described in our earlier discussions, the intensification of globalisation necessarily includes the involvement of multinational corporations (MNCs) in host countries influencing or getting influenced by local business and cultural dimensions. MNCs have been known to operate in host countries in socially irresponsible and corrupt ways – examples abound, which can be found in the various chapters of this book. Some of the questions that can be raised are:

* Do local stakeholders and government officials expect MNCs to bribe?
* Should they behave as 'Romans do when in Rome'?
* While most MNCs regard bribery and corruption as illegal and unethical, some rationalise their actions as legitimate under local institutional conditions.
* Can 'gift giving' justify gaining competitive advantage?
* Do MNC subsidiaries operating in host countries come under pressure to resort to bribery and kickbacks?

Park et al. (2021) examined foreign-owned subsidiaries operating in China and South Korea who differ in terms of institutions (both external such as government controls and judiciary, and internal such as company policies and values). South Korea had 10,580 and China had 960,000 foreign-invested firms (including 490 of the Fortune Global 500 firms) in 2018. The Corruption Perception Index (Transparency International, 2022) ranked South Korea as 32 and China 66 out of 180 countries. Data analysis of 126 and 115 executives from China and South Korea respectively revealed that:

* Strong external institutional pressures can inhibit bribery practices of subsidiaries in both China and South Korea.
* Foreign parent firms play a critical role in inhibiting bribery practices in China but not in South Korea.
* Subsidiary anti-bribery compliance can be influenced by internal values and policies in both China and South Korea.

Factors relating to bribery activities include structural factors and a country's development stage (advanced, developing, or underdeveloped). Using World Economic Forum data collected from 14,000 business executives in more than 140 countries, Ekici and Ekici (2021) identified and analysed variables that can affect bribery activities – such as public trust in politicians, favouritism in decisions of government officials, irregular payments, burden of government regulations, diversion of public funds, business costs of organised crime, reliability of police services, and intensity of local competition. Key findings from Ekici and Ekici (2021) were:

1   Globally executives believe that:

- firms making undocumented extra payments or bribes is a very common behaviour
- most problematic are diversion of public funds, favouritism in decisions of government officials, public trust in politicians, reliability of police services.

2   In advanced countries (innovation driven):

- firms making undocumented extra payments or bribes is not a common behaviour in these economies
- most problematic are the burden of government regulations, public trust in politicians, favouritism in decisions of government officials.

3   In developing countries (efficiency driven):

- firms making undocumented extra payments or bribes is a very common behaviour
- most problematic are diversion of public funds, reliability of police services, favouritism in decisions of government officials.

4   In underdeveloped countries (factor driven):

- the most common practice is irregular payments and bribes
- most problematic are public trust in politicians, favouritism in decisions of government officials, diversion of public funds, business costs of organised crime, reliability of police services, intensity of local competition.

A theory that could explain bribery and corruption

One of the most recognised and influential social theories, the Anomie theory, proposed by French sociologist Emile Durkhiem (1858–1917), suggests a condition of instability in societies or individuals, resulting from a breakdown of standards and values, or from a lack of purpose or ideals (Britannica, 2022). American sociologist Robert Merton identified one of the main causes of anomie to be lack of an acceptable means of achieving personal goals (Wickert, 2022). It is essentially a utilitarian approach (refer to Chapter 3) where goals become so important that if acceptable means of achieving them are not available to an individual, they might use unethical or illegitimate means to do so.

It is possible that people from lower social strata resort to such means because they have fewer opportunities compared to people from higher social strata. So, for example if society allows people to acquire wealth but offers inadequate means to do so, the result could cause people to violate norms.

While there are suggestions that bribery to some extent violates a 'hypernorm' (refer to Chapter 5), anomie theory suggests that 'regardless of the strength of a hypernorm, the context of a country as well as local firm conditions can create situations in which firm decision-makers see violations of hypernorms as justifiable' (Martin et al., 2007: 1402). Analysing data from 3,769 firms from 38 countries to better understand bribery practices by local firms within their cultural, national, and organisational contexts, and using measures from the GLOBE study and Hofstede Insights (2022), Martin et al. (2007) found that:

1   Country-level achievements have no effect on local firm bribery.
2   Higher country-level in-group collectivism can reduce local firm bribery activity.
3   Higher country-level humane-orientation (how people treat each other) has no effect on local firm bribery.
4   Higher country-level welfare systems can reduce local firm bribery activity.
5   Higher country-level political constraints can reduce local firm bribery activity.
6   Higher financial constraints (or obstructions to achieving critical goals) can increase local firm bribery activity.
7   Higher competitive intensity can increase local firm activity.
8   Level of GDP was a significant predictor of local firm bribery activity.

What can be done?

Attempts to mitigate or even eliminate bribery and corruption can be observed at the three levels of business ethics – macro (systemic), meso (organisational), and micro (individual) levels (see descriptions of these three levels in the introduction section of this chapter).

Macro (systemic) level

At the global level, the United Nations Conventions against Corruption is the only legally binding universal anti-corruption instrument (UNODC, 2003). The vast majority of UN member states (189 entities) have ratified this convention. At the country level, we can observe The Bribery Act 2010 of the UK (see Box 6.3). It provides comprehensive guidance and procedures which relevant commercial organisations can put into place to prevent persons associated with them from bribing. Similarly, The Prevention of Corruption Act 2018 in India contains rules for organisations and companies to form guidelines and procedures to prevent employees from providing undue advantages to public servants (PoCA, 2018).

Meso (organisational level)

Several suggestions have been forwarded for organisations to address the risk of corruption by designing and implementing prevention models that alleviate fraud motivators, reduce perceived opportunities, and improve ethics.

1   One such model has three elements (see Peltier-Rivest, 2018: 554–559 for a detailed description of these):

  • Alleviating fraud motivators: by providing psychological employee assistance programmes, fair compensation, and realistic individual performance goals.
  • Reducing perceived opportunities: through risk management programmes, targeted policies and controls, red flag analyses, and anonymous reporting programmes including whistle-blowing.
  • Improving ethics: incorporating ethical environment and governance, regular employee anti-fraud training.

2   The ISO 37001 (2016) anti-bribery management system allows organisations to prevent, detect, and address bribery by adopting anti-bribery policy, appointing a person to oversee anti-bribery compliance, and other procedures.

3   Corporate governance practices can make corruption less possible on a day-to-day basis by practising transparency, accountability, fairness, quality of records, responsibility, and integrity of information (Mahmud et al., 2022).

4   Organisations have published their own code of ethics/conduct in relation to corruption and bribery. For example, see Apple (2018), Tata Steel (2019), and BHP (2022).

Micro (individual) level

Determinants of corruption at an individual level, as found in the literature, are:

1   Age: Individuals in younger age groups (20–39 years) are more likely to bribe than older or younger individuals. People between 30 and 65 years are more likely to justify corruption.

2   Gender: Most studies show males or male-headed households to be more likely to engage in or justify bribery. However, men and women justify bribery equally.

3   Marital status: Married individuals are at higher risk of being exposed to bribery. However, some studies show married people have lower tolerance for corruption.

4   Income: Studies have mixed findings. Some show individuals with high incomes and households with higher levels of consumption to engage in bribery. Other studies have shown middle-income families more likely to bribe.

5   Education: Educated individuals are more likely to engage in bribery. Interestingly, individuals with less knowledge about how to report corruption were less likely to take bribes.

6   Type of settlement and region: Evidence is inconclusive. Some studies have shown that those living in large cities and larger communities pay more bribes. Others have shown individuals from rural areas are also more likely to bribe than those in urban areas.

See Mangafić and Veselinović (2020) for more details.

Tickner (2016) suggested that staff should confirm compliance with the code of ethics/conduct. Codes should clearly indicate what will happen when people do not comply, and that staff and contractors must declare routinely all private, personal, and financial interests relevant to decision-making. There are clear rules under various national acts that 'corporate executives should be aware of their obligations and possible retributions for bribing government officials to secure contracts, but they still indulge in corrupt practices' (Sikka and Lehman, 2015: 68). Following the well-known BAE bribery scandal, recommendations were made relating to staff training, adherence to ethical codes, enhanced role for internal audit, a register for gifts and hospitality, and linking of executive remuneration to ethical practices. Acknowledging that there are difficulties to control the supply-side of corruption (relates to what bribers such as companies do), Sikka and Lehman (2015) recommended that companies could be debarred from securing any government contracts and their executives could be personally fined. It has been suggested that the persistence of corruption indicates a failure of education at home, school, work, university, and society, necessitating an urgent need for a programme of de-schooling such that executives can recognise their contribution to social problems and their obsession with accumulation of wealth, power, and status.

It has been argued that along with legal, financial, and administrative reforms, there is a need for ethics training that emphasises character and moral reasoning. Garofalo et al. (2001) suggest the following steps for individuals:

1   Identify core virtues underlying an individual's cultural values.
2   Ask individuals to justify bribery and corruption in relation to their core virtues. This could lead to an awareness of intolerance for corruption.
3   Determine positive and negative behavioural habits that promote or detract from the desired moral climate in the organisation.
4   Develop a transformation plan to abandon negative habits.
5   The plan should include updating administrative policies, training programmes, and other regulations and procedures.
6   Individuals must now live their new habits with constant practice, and achieve their ethical goals while acknowledging mistakes.

Box 6.2

Legislation to counter corruption

Foreign Corrupt Practices Act 1977, United States Department of Justice

See FCPA (2022) and www.justice.gov/criminal-fraud/foreign-corrupt-practices-act for more details on this Act.

Key points:

- Enacted for the purpose of making it unlawful for certain classes of persons and entities to make payments to foreign government officials to assist in obtaining or retaining business.
- Prohibits any offer, payment, promise to pay, or authorisation of the payment of money or anything of value to any person:
  - while knowing that all or a portion of such money or thing of value will be offered, given or promised, directly or indirectly, to a foreign official
  - to influence the foreign official in his or her official capacity
  - induce the foreign official to do or omit to do an act in violation of his or her lawful duty
  - to secure any improper advantage in order to assist in obtaining or retaining business for or with, or directing business to, any person.
- Also applies to foreign firms and persons who cause, directly or through agents, an act in furtherance of such a corrupt payment to take place within the territory of the United States.

(Continued)

Independent Commission Against Corruption Act 1988, NSW

See ICAC (1988) and www.icac.nsw.gov.au/about-corruption/what-is-corrupt-conduct/sections-7-8-and-9-of-the-icac-act for more details on this Act.

Corrupt conduct, as defined in the Independent Commission Against Corruption Act 1988 ('the ICAC Act'), is deliberate or intentional wrongdoing, not negligence or a mistake. It has to involve or affect a NSW public official or public sector organisation. Corrupt conduct is defined as any conduct of a person, particularly a public official, that:

- constitutes dishonest actions of official functions
- constitutes a breach of public trust
- involves misuse of information or material for personal benefit or of others
- could involve a range of matters such as bribery, blackmail, fraud, theft, embezzlement, tax evasion, illegal drug dealings, illegal gambling, forgery, violence and many more – please see full list in the above-mentioned URL.

Some examples of corrupt conduct are:

- a local councillor voting in favour of a development in which the councillor has an undisclosed financial interest
- a member of the public bribing an official to pass a driver's licence test
- a former public official selling confidential information gained while working in an official capacity.

Also watch the ICAC video at: www.youtube.com/watch?v=GOLoWdcnK_o.

═══ Box 6.3 ═══

The Bribery Act 2010, UK Ministry of Justice, Principles

See Clarke (2010) and www.justice.gov.uk/downloads/legislation/bribery-act-2010-guidance.pdf for more details on this Act.

A commercial organisation should:

- Principle 1: Proportionate procedures
  Have procedures to prevent bribery by persons associated with it that are proportionate to the bribery risks it faces. They should be clear, practical, accessible, effectively implemented and enforced.

- Principle 2: Top-level commitment
  The top-level management of a commercial organisation are committed to preventing bribery and foster a culture within the organisation so that bribery is never acceptable.

- Principle 3: Risk assessment
  Assess the nature and extent of its exposure and the assessment is periodic, informed, and documented.

- Principle 4: Due diligence
  Apply due diligence procedures to mitigate identified bribery risks.

- Principle 5: Communication (including training)
  Seek to ensure that its bribery prevention policies and procedures are embedded and understood throughout the organisation and include training.

- Principle 6: Monitoring and review
  Monitor and review procedures designed to prevent bribery and make improvements where necessary.

6.3 Conflicts of interest

Definition and explanations

Conflicts of interest (CoIs) can occur in businesses and in public organisations. They arise when the personal interests of an employee conflict with the professional interests of a business. CoIs may be one of three types (Business.gov.au, 2021; Ombudsman, 2017):

- Real – where a direct conflict exists between current official duties and existing private interests. Example: where an employee deals with a complaint in which their spouse was the decision-maker.
- Apparent – where it appears or could be perceived that private interests are improperly influencing the performance of official duties whether or not that is actually the case. Example: where an employee maintains strong social and personal relationships with the area within an agency they are investigating.
- Potential – where private interests are not but could come into direct conflict with official duties. Example: an officer is known to hold views on a particular subject that could suggest he or she might not bring an open mind to the subject.

CoI in public organisations, as defined by the OECD (2003: 15) is 'a conflict between the public duty and private interests of public officials, in which public officials have private-capacity interests which could improperly influence the performance of their official duties and responsibilities'. The main causes of CoIs are financial interests, related-party business undertakings, personal relationships, and affiliations with for-profit or non-profit or political organisations.

Persons who have a conflict of interest favour their self-interest. For instance, 'medical practitioners refer their patients to other practitioners in exchange for payments (fee splitting), and when they gain secondary incomes such as from testing patients' samples in laboratories in which they hold ownership or investment interests' (Dickens and Cook, 2006: 192).

Understanding conflicts of interest from research findings

It has been observed that although CoIs have been a feature of businesses and politics almost from the beginnings of capitalism, their negative consequences have worsened in the recent past. There are numerous instances in the accounting, auditing, medicine, and law fields, and even in academic research. So, how does CoI operate at the individual level? As Moore et al. (2005:2) ask, 'how does an auditor, whose profession claims independence, end up complicit in management fraud by signing off obviously cooked books? How do physicians, who are committed to serving the interest of their patients, end up taking gifts from pharmaceutical companies, and then prescribing those companies' expensive drugs to their patients? How do academics end up selling their integrity for the fees they receive as expert witnesses?'

A content analysis for CoI in the codes of conduct of the world's top ten largest companies by market capitalisation (as identified by the World Economic Forum 2017) revealed the following areas that pertain to CoI (Dragomir, 2017):

1   Employment: there are four main aspects of CoIs in employment:

    a   Nepotism – is favouritism shown to relatives by giving them positions regardless of their competencies.

    b   Outside employment – is mostly prohibited by firms. Some companies do permit this as long as the outside employment does not involve a supplier, a competitor, or a customer. Serving on the board of directors for another firm may be an instance of CoI.

    c   Supervision of family members in the workplace because it affects relationships in the workplace and casts doubt on all decisions taken by the supervisor.

    d   A romantic relationship in the workplace can also disrupt morale, efficiency, and collaboration.

2   Contracting: this includes commercial dealings with family members or with close acquaintances. It is different from employment because resources and consequences are greater. CoIs in such relationships can involve hidden commissions (also known as 'kickbacks') by funnelling corporate funds into personal funds, and business gifts.

3   Corporate assets, products, and services: this includes hardware, software, and intellectual property, especially when a key person has left employment that could benefit a future employer (such as a competitor).

4   Insider trading: this involves using proprietary knowledge obtained during the course of their work to trade with other entities such as a supplier, business partner, or a competitor. This issue will be discussed in further detail later in this chapter.

What can be done?

In most situations, especially in small firms, there is an overlap between the company's interests and the personal interests of the employees (Dragomir, 2017). More so, when resources are shared between the company and the owners or the employees. Since it is possible that in such situations, there could be automatic ethical reasoning ('it is ok to do that' or 'it is ok to do that because I will not get caught'), it may require well-thought-out codes of conduct and ethical training to automatise the decision-making process to avoid CoIs.

Some responses that may help resolve a conflict of interest are (Dickens and Cook, 2006; Komesaroff et al., 2019):

- Avoidance of conflict of interest.
- Due disclosure (declare interests) when avoidance is not necessary or not possible.
- A clear set of tests (to assess whether declared interests are in conflict with each other) and procedures (assessment of the declared interests in a public and transparent manner and determination of appropriate responses).
- Responses:

  - For trivial CoIs or those of minor significance, a discussion to take into account the situation or for individuals to voluntarily abstain from the situation.
  - For situations with wider-ranging consequences, individuals may withdraw from the role altogether, or if the situation is more serious the individual's role could be judged to be untenable.
  - Activate the feelings of professional obligation and responsibility (also called 'social value activation'). This is in contrast to activating the risk frame. For example, doctors should put patient welfare above self-interest and auditors should put honesty above a particular client's desires.

A systematic review of 106 studies from publications and databases (Jafari Nia et al., 2022) revealed a general agreement among experts that human beings when confronted by a CoI situation find it difficult to decide in favour of the public interest, and that every person may not have the same response to CoI situations. Culturally, in societies where self-interest is common and promoted (in schools, media, and universities), people could be more inclined to put their self-interest first. From the review, Jafari Nia et al. (2022) have identified the following three strategies to manage CoIs – each through cultural, legal, and structural approaches:

1 Prevention:

- Cultural – training and activation of social values.
- Legal – declaration of interests and banning of gifts etc.
- Structural – eliminating self-dealing and re-engineering processes.

2 Confrontation:

- Cultural – official disclosure and whistle-blowing.
- Legal – avoidance.

- Structural – ensuring correctness of decisions and correcting conflicting situations.

3   Punishment:

  • Cultural – warnings and reprimanding.
  • Legal – reduction in salary or termination of employment.
  • Structural – reassignment of duties, transfer of duties, and demotion.

For a comprehensive list of guidelines and recommendations on managing CoIs see OECD (2003: 40–98).

6.4 Diversity, equity, and inclusion in the workplace

Definition and explanations

The three aspects of diversity, equity, and inclusion (DEI) are often discussed together and are sometimes used interchangeably. DEI has come into prominence due to interconnectedness from globalisation, MNC competitiveness, heterogenous and diverse groups in the workplace, rising demands, national legislation, and the policies of the International Labour Organisation (ILO).

It is further explained thus: 'diversity is being invited to the party, while inclusion is being asked to dance'. Equity, the third leg of the DEI tripod helps diversity to drive inclusion. Allowing diversity (D) without inclusion (I) presupposes a lack of equity in the workplace (Raimi et al., 2022: 2).

Definitions and practices of DEI (Raimi et al., 2022: 2; Hagman, 2021):

Diversity:

  • Diversity can be defined and practised as a workplace policy recognising, understanding, and accepting differences in employees based on their race, gender, age, class, ethnicity, physical ability, sexual orientation, spiritual practice, life experiences, political affiliations, and other social and psychological orientations.
  • Elements of diversity have been identified as (Gilshan and Chambers, 2020):
    ○ Cognitive diversity: differences in how we interpret, reason, and solve.
    ○ Identity diversity: differences in race, gender, age, ethnicity, religion, physical qualities, and sexual orientation.
    ○ Experiential diversity: socio-economic backgrounds, skills, experience etc.
  • Diversity practices are essential to promoting socially responsible actions and equitable employment outcomes.

Equity:

  • Refers to organisational actions that accommodate four dimensions: access, achievement, identity, and power.
  • Unhindered access to organisational resources for all.

- Achievement by accessing resources that support positive outcomes.
- Identity refers to how employers treat people.
- Power refers to how identities enhance or reduce the influence of people.

Inclusion:

- Refers to organisational actions that support full accommodation and participation of diverse individuals and groups.
- Can be measured by underrepresentation of diverse individuals and groups.
- Diverse individuals can still experience negative treatment through microaggressions (commonplace frequent verbal, behavioural, or environmental slights, intentional or unintentional).

Understanding workplace diversity issues from research findings

Importance of DEI can be further appreciated from Parsi (2017), who reports that:

- Minority diverse groups in the US, such as Asians, Hispanic, and multiracial groups, will hit majority status by 2044.
- Companies that have gender and ethnic diversity are, respectively, 15 per cent and 35 per cent more likely to outperform those that don't.
- Companies with higher levels of board diversity had returns that were 53 per cent higher than those with lower levels.

Age diversity

Stereotypes about what older adults can or cannot do drive age discrimination in many workplaces. This is also called 'ageism' which is defined in WHO's Global Report on Ageism (WHO, 2021). The report's survey of 83,000 people in 57 countries found that 60 per cent of respondents reported that older people were not respected in their country. The lowest levels of respect for older people were in high-income countries. While in many parts of the world mandatory retirement is legally sanctioned, there's evidence of age discrimination even in countries that have anti-age-discrimination laws (Jecker, 2022). The 'dignity as equality' argument holds that societies should respect the dignity of every person. However, in this case, discrimination can be heightened when the age factor is applied to the already discriminated groups of religious affiliation, race, physical qualities, and sexual orientation.

Effect of digitalisation on diversity in the workplace

Recruitment processes, already extensively digitised before the 2020 Covid-19 pandemic, became more automated during and after the pandemic, using artificial intelligence, analytics, machine learning, augmented reality, and virtual reality. Such technology is being applied to all stages of recruitment – from job descriptions, CV screening, scheduling interviews, first screens, online tests, and job offers, to onboarding (Kuzior et al., 2021). Within this scenario, such digitisation of HR practices has benefitted diversity and inclusion. Job seekers now look for diversity policies of future employers. Gen Z, which is entering the workforce now, puts high importance on diversity and equality. Organisations have become more aware of the importance of gender and cultural diversity among employees.

LGBTQIA+ supportive policies

Analysis from data on information from S&P's 500, Forbes' list of 200 largest privately held firms, and the Fortune 500 largest publicly traded firms found a positive relationship between individual anti-discrimination policies and firm innovation which ultimately leads to higher firm performance (Hossain et al., 2019). Using stakeholder theory (see Chapter 2) and Rawls's Theory of Justice (see Chapter 3), they argue that firms have a greater ethical imperative to foster fairness and meritocratic values, and LGBTQIA+ supportive policies form an important part of workplace diversity management. Another study of 1,014 firms found that firms with gender diverse boards are more likely to adopt LGBTQIA+ supportive policies, especially due to the effect that female directors have on corporate policies regarding the LGBTQIA+ group of internal stakeholders.

Following ethical approaches can be applied to diversity issues (LaVan and Martin, 2021):

Utilitarianism or consequentialist ethics:

- This approach would entail an analysis about the costs and benefits of strategies to mitigate workplace bullying.
- Analysis would include the self-interest of the actor and consider the impact on society.

Deontological ethics:

- This approach would consider codes of conduct, laws and regulations, principles, duties, rights, and obligations.
- It implies that employees have certain rights the way work is designed, and employers have certain obligations such as to provide psychologically safe environments.

Virtue ethics:

- This approach is about an individual's character and traits such as caring about the relations between an individual's projects and their actions.
- Beneficence (doing good) and the concept of emotional intelligence would be important aspects of this approach.

Van Dijk et al. (2012) caution that in practice, business case proponents sometimes use deontological principles (by arguing that profitability is a business imperative), and equality proponents use utilitarian principles (that diversity enhances business performance). They argue that virtue ethics is more congruent, context-sensitive, and therefore more sustainable in managing diversity.

What can be done?

One relevant place to start is with gender because (Gilshan and Chambers, 2020):

- women represent approximately 50 per cent of the population
- there's increased evidence that companies with stronger female representation at senior management and board levels perform better
- gender representation is more easily measurable and comparable than other dimensions of diversity and most companies have data to use as a starting point.

Key recommendations from the Institute of Business Ethics are available in their report (Gilshan and Chambers, 2020: 36).

Three management approaches have been suggested for ensuring contemporary and future workplaces accept and accommodate DEI practices (Raimi et al., 2022):

1 Liberal approach: Treat all individuals the same and apply the principle of neutrality on fairness and merit. Focus on the need for equal access among employees to opportunities such as services, rewards, and positions. It is based on positive action instead of affirmative action.
2 Radical approach: Favours gender quotas and other quotas as an effective tool to achieve an equitable and fair distribution of opportunities. Aim to dissolve differences between groups. Needs strong support from stakeholders such as government, employers, and employees.
3 Transformational approach: Encourage deep-level diversity in the form of values in managing relationships among diverse individuals, groups, and cultures. Mentor, sensitise, and educate organisational members on diverse backgrounds.

Finally, as suggested from the findings of Ng and Sears (2020), a CEO's words and actions alone are not sufficient for the implementation of diversity management practices. CEOs may not always support diversity actively especially when there are costs associated with it. HR managers must expect their CEOs as being committed to workplace diversity.

6.5 Hiring and recruitment

Definition and explanations

The talent recruitment process typically has four phases: sourcing (to identify and attract potential candidates to apply), screening (evaluating and ranking applicants based on skills, experience, and personality), interviewing (querying applicants with detailed questions on skills, education, prior experiences, and behaviours), and selection (to determine whether or not to offer an applicant a job) (Yam and Skorburg, 2021). Finding the right person to fit the right job and finding a competent person for each job is more critical than ever. Findings from a study (Rudman et al., 2016) suggest that employers defined competency, in addition to workplace skills, as including personal skills such as dependability, integrity, teamwork, respect, problem-solving, and decision-making. Although some employers had 'gut feelings' when hiring a new employee, most rely on a predefined and structured process to ensure a successful hire.

Understanding hiring issues from research findings

While legal compliance is essential for hiring, conforming to legal requirements alone is not sufficient to guarantee ethical hiring (Alder and Gilbert, 2006). Most nations have specific laws to ensure fairness in hiring – for example, The Fair Work Act 2009 in Australia, Employment Rights Act 1996 in the UK, Title VII of the Civil Rights Act in the USA, The Industrial Relations Code 2020 in India. A common form of legislation concerns equal employment opportunity (EEO). It is to be noted that EEO is not necessarily to encourage organisations to implement quotas, but rather to ensure that hiring decisions are made on applicants' merit and performance potential and not on their demographic characteristics, age, religion, or physical disabilities.

Following ethical approaches can be applied to hiring issues (Alder and Gilbert, 2006):

- Utilitarianism: To consider what will produce the greatest good for the company, its stakeholders, and society, a manager should hire a person who will perform the best and will accomplish the greatest good. All stakeholders including the society will benefit from it. However, the utilitarian approach will not be judged as ethical even if it produces more happiness to the hirer or the company if a person is hired based on a personal relationship (such as a brother or a sister) or a particular need (such as if the applicant has a large family).
- Deontological (duty) and rights: Using this approach, hiring should be based on the impact of that decision on individual applicants' rights. A hiring manager, by his or her position, is morally required to choose one applicant by exercising their right in a responsible manner. While all citizens have a legal right to be treated fairly, a hiring manager's duty is to go beyond the requirements of law. For example, personally ensuring that the same standards are applied to all applicants rather than leaving such processes entirely to the HR department or even to artificial intelligence.
- Fairness and justice: Using this approach, fairness is afforded to three types of organisational justice – distributive (fairness from the outcomes of organisational allocations and decisions), procedural (concerning fairness of the procedures used to make decisions and allocations), and interactional (concerning the quality of treatment applicants receive in the procedure).

When hiring new personnel, hiring managers are influenced by the concepts of moral obligation that include setting the ethical climate of a company that can result in the ultimate success of the firm, and exercising their decisions in a responsible manner. This means that managers who disregard their obligation to be ethical in hiring decisions, and fail to choose the best candidates, increase the chance of allowing bad apples into their organisations (Villegas et al., 2019).

Studies in biases and ethical decision-making in hiring in the US indicate that (Stelzner, 2022):

1   Women have a more obstructed path when pursuing a male-dominated profession.
2   Transgender applicants experience bias.
3   White Americans experience the most responses in hiring decisions when compared to other races.
4   Some studies found that Native American applicants receive the same or a higher number of responses than White Americans – possible because of recent events in the US and employers being more attuned to racial issues.

In recent times, there is increasing use of artificial intelligence (AI) in HR. It has the potential to save hours, increase efficiency, and reduce costs in recruiting. HR recruiters need not spend hours going through piles of CVs and can instead use their time for interviewing candidates. However, there are ethical challenges in this process. Can the algorithms really predict future ability, are their judgements robust, will there be discrimination, privacy issues, and account-ability? Using AI in hiring can inflict unintentional harm to human rights, including right to work, equality, free expression, and free association (Dennis and Aizenberg, 2022).

AI principles have been criticised for being vague and not actionable, and consequently not providing accountability. Without national legislation, companies may not be legally accountable for human rights infringements of their hiring algorithms, and without accountability, hiring algorithms can lead to discrimination and unequal access to employment opportunities (Yam and Skorburg, 2021).

Amazon's experiment with an AI-based recruiting process highlights one of the issues (see Box 6.4).

═══ Box 6.4 ═══

AI recruiting tool that showed bias against women

Amazon's experimental recruiting engine based on machine learning revealed that the software did not like women. The hiring tool using AI techniques gave job candidates scores ranging from one to five stars. Any applicant with five stars would get hired. But it was soon discovered that it was not rating in a gender-neutral way. That's because machine-learning models were trained to vet applicants by observing patterns in resumés submitted to the company over a ten-year period, and most were from men. So, the search engine did not select resumés which had the word 'women's' for example in 'captain of the women's chess club'. Similarly, it downgraded graduates from all-women's colleges. On the other hand, unqualified candidates were often recommended for all kinds of jobs. Finally, Amazon shut down this project.

(Continued)

Questions

Apply ethical approaches as discussed in Chapters 3 and 4 to this issue and reflect on your judgement.

- What are the ethical issues?
- Can this tool impact only gender diversity or are there other aspects that might be affected?
- Do you think AI techniques can be made fair to all in hiring?

Source: Adapted from Dastin (2018)

What can be done?

1   Literature shows that when organisations use a defined ethical hiring standard, employers are more likely to recruit and hire ethical candidates (Villegas et al., 2019). This creates the notion that managers have the responsibility of being ethical gatekeepers for their organisations.

2   Focus on means and outcomes by following the employment law of the nation, and applying utilitarian, rights, justice, fairness, and justice theories in the hiring decision-making process (Alder and Gilbert, 2006).

3   Routine use of algorithms can have a negative impact on employee–employer and applicant–employer relationships because of the difference between the values of human recruiters and the values embedded in recruitment algorithms. It is suggested that accountability gaps in AI-driven hiring systems can be framed in terms of international human rights law (Dennis and Aizenberg, 2022).

4   A human recruiter should be involved at all times during the four phases of the algorithmic hiring process. Humans, not algorithms, will know how to treat fellow humans with fairness, empathy, dignity, and respect (Yam and Skorburg, 2021).

6.6 Downsizing

Definition and explanations

Downsizing can be defined as the systematic reduction of the workforce by an employer, usually because of financial losses, cash flow issues, loss of contracts, technological changes, or international competition. Some of the ways that downsizing is done are terminating or transferring employees, voluntary buyouts, and freezing hiring. Downsizing along with restructuring, rightsizing, voluntary retirement schemes, buyouts, and layoffs are terms used for removing people from their established jobs. They are not necessarily a dismissal for individual incompetence, but rather a strategic decision by management to reduce the overall workforce (Maiya, 2011). Some examples are:

- HSBC Banking planned to slash about 35,000 jobs in 2020 in Europe and the US due to the threat to its business from the social unrest in Hong Kong and the coronavirus outbreak (www.ft.com/content/c0095f40-5203-11ea-90ad-25e377c0ee1f).
- General Motors, in a bid to avert bankruptcy, planned to cut 21,000 employees by 2010, and another 2,000 by 2011 (https://abcnews.go.com/Business/Economy/story?id=7438329&page=1). In 2019, the company targeted 4,250 salaried workers and 6,000 hourly employees for layoffs (www.cnbc.com/2019/02/01/gm-readies-to-make-4000-involuntary-layoffs-next-week.html).
- Qantas, the Australian airline, in 2020, in an effort to limit financial losses, announced it was outsourcing 2,000 ground staff on top of 6,000 job cuts (www.bbc.com/news/business-55126705).
- Car companies Mitsubishi, Ford, Toyota, and Holden downsized and then shut down their entire manufacturing operations in Australia in 2008, 2016, 2017, and 2020 respectively – in all, about 5,000 employees lost their jobs.

The effects of downsizing are (Tang and Fuller 1995; Maiya, 2011):

1 Surviving employees can experience changes in corporate loyalty, job satisfaction, and job performance.
2 Terminated employees can suffer changes in their mental health such as depression, anxiety, stress, and loss of self-esteem and identity.
3 Employees who are let go may not recover emotionally or financially.
4 Loss of long-time workers who would have served as mentors for young and inexperienced workers.
5 Older employees usually do not get new jobs or have to wait longer to get a job.

Understanding downsizing issues from research findings

The ethics of downsizing can be summarised in two issues: the moral obligation of top management to act in the best interest of the firm, and the legal obligation of the firm not to violate the rights of its employees (Hopkins and Hopkins, 1999). The first issue relates to the 'duty' of top managers to act in the interests of shareholders – consistent with Friedman's (see Chapter 2) argument that managers have a direct responsibility to the firm's owners. Based on this reasoning, decisions to downsize, with the objective of ensuring the financial stability of the firm, would be in the best interest of the firm's owners. The second issue relates to a Kantian deontological approach (see Chapter 3), that employee rights are not to be reduced. It suggests that employees are entitled to information, and their rights must not be violated during the downsizing process.

Further, Lakshman et al. (2014: 102) view the ethical dimension of a company's action with respect to downsizing as a key component of corporate social responsibility (CSR), in which companies go beyond compliance and engage in actions that can further social causes. Using a cross-cultural sample of 626 respondents from the US, Estonia, France, and

India (from different GLOBE clusters – see Chapter 5), they found that attribution of responsibility is universal and used by all four cultures to evaluate ethics and form CSR perceptions with regard to downsizing.

As we have seen above, by downsizing, firms intend to reallocate their resources efficiently in response to external changes to prepare for the future. However, the question remains whether downsizing leads firms to a successful recovery.

- Building on previous studies (which indicated that there is no evidence to suggest improvements in returns on assets, sales growth, and stock market returns), Okudaira et al. (2022) analysed data from all manufacturing plants between 2008 and 2012 with 30 or more employees in Japan. They found that employee downsizing helped plants scale down their production levels, but it did not initiate productivity gains or product innovations even years after the layoff event. More interestingly, there was an increase in the proportion of middle-aged workers, and a decline in employees in their twenties. This may explain why layoffs did not increase productivity or innovation.
- A study of 90 family and 90 non-family firms in the US (Filotheou et al., 2007) found that family firms are less likely to downsize than their non-family counterparts and that financial performance was not part of their decision process. Family firms' unwillingness to downsize could be explained based on their ingrained value systems and their stakeholder practices, because their relationship with employees is based on ethical commitments rather than financial performance alone. A similar study of 4,223 manufacturing small and medium enterprises in Spain found that family firms are less likely to downsize than non-family firms. Further, family firms engaged in R&D activities are less likely to downsize compared to non-innovative family firms (Sanchez-Bueno et al., 2020).
- Analysis from 2010 data of 4,710 publicly traded firms spanning 83 different industries including services, high technology, and manufacturing industries, but not financial firms, revealed that (Zorn et al., 2017):
  ○ downsizing firms were twice as likely to declare bankruptcy as firms that did not downsize
  ○ while downsizing enables a firm to save money in the short term, it increases the chances that the firm will declare bankruptcy in the future
  ○ financial and physical resources did not replace the downsized employees such as workers, knowledge bearers, and cultural contributors
  ○ intangible resources such as employee skills as mentioned above help reduce the likelihood of bankruptcy; for example, existing employee knowledge can be utilised to revamp processes.

What can be done?

Treat employees fairly – higher perceived fairness helps maintain higher job satisfaction and organisational commitment. Both distributive and procedural justice are important.

Communicate clearly and politely to employees – effective communication (by explaining fully why and how the downsizing will take place) between managers and employees helps determine employees' attitudes towards company downsizing. Share good and bad news, and reduce rumours.

Ethical treatment of employees – the higher the perceived ethical and moral values embraced by the company, the higher the commitment of both managers and employees (Maiya, 2011; Tang and Fuller, 1995). Other suggestions are:

1   Prior to downsizing, consider whether any positive short-term returns from downsizing will outweigh potential severe long-term consequences, as eliminating key intangible resources may limit management of negative effects.
2   Spread downsizing throughout the organisation – not just among lower-level employees.
3   Evaluate impact of downsizing with regard to the long-term interests of all key stakeholders.
4   Allow employees to leave with dignity.
5   Help those displaced find new jobs – give employees ample time to find positions elsewhere.
6   Keep employees informed about company's goals and expectations.
7   Set realistic expectations.
8   Use ceremonies to reduce anger and confusion.
9   Estimate future staffing.

6.7 Outsourcing

Definitions and explanations

Outsourcing is defined as: 'if a firm does not specialise in a certain function, it will be beneficial to transfer control of the function to a specialist organisation that will be able to offer better cost and quality' (Clott, 2004: 154). Almost any activity can be outsourced – for example, labour, accounting, sourcing of materials, finished components, maintenance of plant and machinery, cleaning, recruitment, data analysis, marketing, IT services, and even managing social media channels. Global outsourcing has become one of the defining features of the global economy because the twin pressures of globalisation and technology forces firms all over the world to aggressively look for ways to cut costs and improve productivity (Hiquet and Oh, 2019).

Further, Clott (2004) identifies pros and cons of outsourcing:

•   Arguments in favour: enables focus on core business development, cost control, access to state of the art technology, market discipline through greater transparency, and more flexibility to respond to changes in demand.
•   Arguments against: individual workers can get overworked, work in extremely challenging workplace conditions, lose health, retirement, and other benefits, and can cause ethical issues.

Outsourcing is also referred to as Business Process Outsourcing (BPO). One of the most successful BPO industries is the call centre industry where staff answer calls from companies' customers located overseas, typically located in countries such as India, China, the Philippines, and Vietnam.

A relatively recent phenomenon is crowdsourcing which is defined as 'the act of taking a job done by the employees of a company or institution and outsourcing this task to a large and undefined group of Internet users in the form of an open call for contribution' (Howe, 2008; Vander Schee, 2010). It can be used by companies to meet needs such as simple tasks like data collection and proposals, or creative tasks such as artistic design. These can be achieved either through dedicated platforms (such as IdeaStorm of Dell, Cvous, MyStarbucks Idea) or specialised platforms (such as Mechanical Turk, Innocentive).

Understanding outsourcing issues from research findings

Some of the ethical issues in international outsourcing identified are poor working conditions, child labour, and environmental pollution. While the normative view (see Chapter 3) suggests that MNCs will act responsibly because it is the ethically and morally right thing to do, MNCs should realise that outsourcing is also a matter of human rights (Hiquet and Oh, 2019). For example, the collapse of the Rana Plaza building in 2013 (ILO, 2018) killed at least 1,132 people and injured more than 2,500. These disasters, among other industrial accidents on record, highlighted the poor labour conditions faced by workers in the ready-made garment sector in Bangladesh.

The following section highlights some other key issues in outsourcing.

Legal services

Law firms have outsourced their libraries and certain back-office support services such as data processing and copying. In addition, attention has shifted from outsourcing back-office and administrative functions to outsourcing legal and law-related services themselves (Daly and Silver, 2007). Services commonly performed by paralegals and new law graduates are being outsourced, including preparation of patent applications, document review, legal research and even pieces of M&A transactions. Aside from cost savings, offshore outsourcing has the added benefit of time efficiency. For example, due to the ten-hour time difference between the US and India, a lawyer firm in the US can send assignments at the end of the day and get the work completed by next morning. Ethical issues range from unauthorised practices and enforceability of contracts to the quality of judgement that outsourced lawyers bring to their clients. Further, it has been noted that while US lawyers have been reluctant to hire foreign-trained lawyers in their domestic organisations, they feel comfortable to engage lawyers in foreign countries for cost advantages.

Crowdsourcing

Crowdsourcing's major advantages are in its relatively low cost, access to a large pool of individuals around the world, integrating non-experts into the innovation process, and offering better and less expensive solutions (Hanine and Steils, 2018). It can also improve a firm's brand image through improved visibility and generating positive word-of-mouth communication. However, crowdsourcing carries risks too: loss of control over the crowdsourcing process, long-term innovation strategy, impact on company image, hostility against the company, disclosure of key information, and negative word-of-mouth communication (also called 'crowdslapping'). Other risks are related to ethical and legal issues. The absence of clear intellectual property policy can lead to a feeling of unfairness. Another ethical issue could be the 'free work' of participants, who might experience being exploited by the company.

Accounting and preparation of income-tax returns

Accountants use outsourcing to avail expertise and to cut costs of providing services such as data processing, bookkeeping, and tax preparation. Significant ethical issues can arise when outsourcing accounting services and the preparation of income tax returns overseas. Mintz (2004) and McGee (2005) report that the hundreds and thousands of tax returns being processed overseas could have the following ethical issues:

- Whether a client is informed that tax details are being transmitted overseas electronically and that the return will be prepared by a non-resident CPA.
- Whether due care is exercised when performing such services and whether there is adequate supervision of the performance.
- Privacy of personal information and possible identity theft.

Information technologies

Outsourcing of information technology (IT) is the transfer of a company's IT functions to an outside agency – such as outsourcing payroll processing. The main benefits are economies of scale, offsetting an inefficient internal IT unit, access to higher IT professionalism, and dealing with a current lack of in-house IT project management capabilities. Ethical issues related to IT outsourcing have been identified as (Reid and Pascalev, 2002):

- Potential conflicts of interest between agents of customers and their principal, agents of vendor and their principal, and customer and vendor.
- Withholding material information.
- Disregarding and harming the interests of the employer.
- Misrepresenting facts.
- Unfair competitive advantages based on insider information.

Pharmaceutical industry and medical research

Medical research outsourcing has become a major strategy in the global pharmaceutical industry. The three forces that benefit and influence pharma companies to outsource are: the challenges of competition, the need for speed in drug development, and increasing domestic costs. Areas such as clinical research and drug testing are increasingly outsourced to lower-wage, emerging countries (Adobor, 2012). For example, in 2010, India is estimated to have earned about USD 1.5 billion from medical research outsourcing. However, critics have recognised ethical concerns and issues in this business model – such as describing destination countries as the 'guinea pigs' of the world, inadequacies in institutional and regulatory environments, and the capacity to protect vulnerable participating populations. With the involvement of multiple stakeholders (including pharma companies, sponsors, governments, and individual researchers), the critical question asked is who bears moral responsibility for the integrity of outsourced medical research. Adobor (2012: 248) suggest that 'all stakeholders may have to assume a certain degree of moral responsibility and blame in the event of ethical violations in contract research, with the larger, more visible pharmaceutical firms likely assuming a larger portion of the blame when violations become known'.

Offshoring outsourcing to emerging markets seen as tools of neo-colonial control

Several scholars have pointed to 'call-centre offshoring as a manifestation of neo-colonial control, understanding its novel forms of exploitation as colonial legacies of capitalism' (Sayed and Agndal, 2022: 283). The argument is that the transnational nature of offshoring leads to the transfer of value outside the workers' communities resulting in net outflows of resources to consuming nations at the expense of producing nations. Technology, especially the capacity of information systems, enables international clients to maintain close control over service providers. Such work settings have been variously described as 'electronic sweatshops', 'electronic panopticons', and 'panoptical wired cages' (see Sayed and Agndal, 2022: 283). Qualitative analysis of interviews with 23 individuals in the drug-discovery industry (comprised of contract research organisations and laboratory systems vendors), found the laboratory information management systems used by international pharmaceutical firms act as a neo-colonial control tool at the industry, organisational, and work practices levels.

The impact of BPO in the Philippines has been highlighted with respect to English-only policies in education (Tupas, 2018). The economic benefits of outsourcing have curtailed multilingual education by presenting the need to teach English to pupils at the earliest possible times to prepare them for life in BPO industries. Instead of using the mother tongue as the medium of instruction in the first six years of formal education (as required by law), the political compromise has been to cut it down to only the first three years. In short, 'the education system is slowly and subtly preparing students to serve the needs of a particular group of industries, and thus also (and perhaps most especially) the interests of companies and corporations' (Tupas, 2018: 84). Examples such as the expulsion in 2013 of three high school students for violating their school's English-only policy by speaking their own local language in the school premises could point to colonially induced ideologies about English that elevate English to the status of a superior language.

What can be done?

- Governance may need to be modified or redesigned to evolve from purely contract-based to relational trust-based forms or a hybrid of both.

- Relationship building and cooperation between principals/sponsors and outsourced agencies could reduce the possibilities for opportunistic behaviours. Outsourcing companies will become aware of the challenges faced by outsourced firms (Adobor, 2012).
- While individual firms can resolve their own ethical issues, collective action at the national and industry levels could provide guidelines for behaviour in this area. For example, see CPS 231 (2017) Prudential standard for outsourcing; ACSC (2022) Guidelines for procurement and outsourcing; and ICLG (2022) Technology sourcing laws and regulations USA.
- Building institutional capacity in destination countries as part of the outsourcing companies' CSR (Adobor, 2012; Hiquet and Oh, 2019).

Summary

- This chapter is the first of the five chapters in Part II (Ethical Issues in Business). Having gained an appreciation of theories and concepts in Part I of this book, we now embark on the practical aspects of business ethics. Several wide-ranging ethical issues are discussed throughout this book, but here in Chapter 6, we have focused on six issues. Each of these six issues had three sections: definitions and explanations, understanding issues from research findings, and what can be done.
- We have shown that bribery and corruption is prevalent on all three levels of business – individual, business, national (and international). While there are strong and clear laws in almost every country to prevent bribery, the practice continues to be widespread.
- We understand how conflicts of interest can present themselves under some special circumstances. They can be complex as managers may or may not realise their presence, because conflicts could be real, apparent, or potential.
- Mainly due to globalisation, managers are now increasingly made aware of the interconnected issues of diversity, equity, and inclusion. Apart from gender, race, and cultural diversity, special discussions have been included for age, digitalisation, and LGBTQIA+ issues.
- Hiring and recruitment form one of the key responsibilities of managers. Ethical issues and approaches were discussed with special emphasis on the new trend of using artificial intelligence and machine learning tools in almost all phases of recruitment from sourcing to selection.
- Downsizing was examined and understood as a process to reduce workforce numbers to achieve organisational goals. Several methods of achieving downsizing were discussed along with the ethical issues associated with them.
- Finally, outsourcing, both onshoring and offshoring, as a key component of business processes was examined. Almost every MNC today has a strategy for global outsourcing, mainly for cost and efficiency pressures. Special attention has been given to crowdsourcing, IT, the pharmaceutical industry, and the idea that offshoring can be seen as a tool of neo-colonial control.
- Case studies 6.1 and 6.2 can be analysed and reflected upon by using the CEDM model and the Case-Study Integrative Framework.

CASE STUDY 6.1

STARBUCKS CLOSED STORES NATIONWIDE FOR RACIAL-BIAS EDUCATION

On 17 April 2018, Starbucks Coffee Company announced it would be closing its more than 8,000 company-owned stores in the United States on the afternoon of 29 May 2018 to conduct racial-bias educational training geared towards preventing discrimination in their stores. The training would be provided to nearly 175,000 employees across the country and become part of the onboarding process for new employees.

Starbucks CEO Kevin Johnson said 'I've spent the last few days in Philadelphia with my leadership team listening to the community, learning what we did wrong and the steps we need to take to fix it. While this is not limited to Starbucks, we're committed to being a part of the solution. Closing our stores for racial bias training is just one step in a journey that requires dedication from every level of our company and partnerships in our local communities'.

'The company's founding values are based on humanity and inclusion', said Executive Chairman Howard Schultz, who joined Johnson and other senior Starbucks leaders in Philadelphia to meet with community leaders and Starbucks partners. 'We will learn from our mistakes and reaffirm our commitment to creating a safe and welcoming environment for every customer'.

Starbucks began a review of its training and practices to make important reforms where necessary to ensure their stores always represent their mission and values, by providing a safe and inclusive environment for their customers and employees.

The curriculum was developed with guidance from several national and local experts confronting racial bias, including Bryan Stevenson, Founder and Executive Director of the Equal Justice Initiative; Sherrilyn Ifill, President and Director-Counsel of the NAACP Legal Defense and Education Fund; Heather McGhee, President of Demos; former US Attorney General Eric Holder; and Jonathan Greenblatt, CEO of the Anti-Defamation League. Starbucks involved these experts in monitoring and reviewing the effectiveness of the measures undertaken.

The training programme was designed to address implicit bias, promote conscious inclusion, prevent discrimination, and ensure everyone inside a Starbucks store feels safe and welcome.

Once completed, the company made the educational materials available to other companies, including their licensee partners, for use with their employees and leadership.

Questions

Using the Case-Study Integrative Framework in Figure 0.1, discuss the following:

1   Apply the EDM process to these scenarios – use the concepts in this chapter (cultural dimensions, national cultures, and ISCT), along with concepts from previous chapters:

    a   Which of the three ethical approaches from Chapter 3 are applicable here?
    b   Identify key stakeholders in this incident and justify their selection.
    c   Are some of the cultural dimensions involved in this?
    d   Do you think the ISCT concept of Chapter 5 can be applied here?

2   What do you think were the factors that led to the incident at the Starbucks store?

3   Do you think this type of incident is unique or can it happen anywhere in the world? Reflect on whether or not (and if so, how) this sort of incident could happen in your country or culture or in the community that you live in.

4   Do you think racial-bias education as done by Starbucks will be enough? If not what else could be done?

Sources:
Hyken (2018a)
Hyken (2018b)
Press (2018)

CASE STUDY 6.2
OUTSOURCING IN TOURISM

Prior to the Covid-19 pandemic, travel and tourism (including its direct, indirect, and induced impacts) accounted for 1 in 4 of all new jobs created across the world, 10.3 per cent of all jobs (333 million), and 10.3 per cent of global GDP (USD 9.6 trillion). Meanwhile, international visitor spending amounted to USD 1.8 trillion in 2019 (6.8 per cent of total exports). Following a loss of almost USD 4.9 trillion in 2020 (a 50.4 per cent decline), travel and tourism's contribution to GDP increased by USD 1 trillion (a 21.7 per cent rise) in 2021.

Outsourcing in this industry takes two forms: domestic outsourcing and international offshoring.

Domestic outsourcing has seen several hotels taking decisions on internal restructuring by reducing staffing levels through outsourcing jobs in housekeeping, grounds keeping, laundry, banquets, security, food services, pool maintenance, IT, reservations, and financial services. Management of hotels have argued that such outsourcing will help reduce operational costs, staff recruitment, selection, and training.

International offshoring: In this highly competitive market, businesses have been employing state-of-the-art technology and business techniques. To ensure this, most travel and tourism business owners are outsourcing their services to countries such as India which offers a high-level talent pool, low labour costs, and excellent web connectivity. Outsourcing services include email responses, phone-based enquiries, and back-office work such as data entry, data processing, and data conversion. Other services include campaign surveys, monitoring trends, customer service, and telemarketing services.

However, outsourcing decision-makers have a moral dilemma: approve or oppose the outsourcing strategy to reduce operational costs and give the company greater flexibility to achieve expansion goals with a potentially detrimental impact on a large number of employees and organisational culture. Whether to support outsourcing of potentially thousands of front-line employees with consequences for loss of job security, seniority, and other benefits, or risk expansion plans and jeopardise future profits for their shareholders.

While many unethical actions are clear violations of laws and legislation (for example, environmental degradation, labour exploitation, sex tourism, displacement of people from their ancestral lands), others may not seem as clear (for example outsourcing, poverty tours, treating culture as a commodity).

Questions

Using the Case-Study Integrative Framework in Figure 0.1, discuss the following:

1   What are the direct and indirect impacts of outsourcing on the staff?
2   Using ethical approaches from Chapters 3 and 4, explore the ethical issues in the tourism industry.

   a   Will outsourcing as described above create the greatest benefit for the greatest number of people (utilitarian ethics approach)?
   b   Apply a deontological approach (Kantian ethics) to how the tourism industry is treating its employees.
   c   What virtues (or otherwise) can be seen in the industry's desire to outsource?
   d   Apply other applicable ethical theories and reflect on them.

3   Discuss how such management decisions affect internal and external stakeholders, including the environment.
4   How can our culture, religion, or societal values help solve this dilemma?

Sources:
Camargo (2022)
WTTC (2022)

—Recommended readings—

Ekici, A. and Ekici, S.O. (2021), 'Understanding and managing complexity through Bayesian network approach: The case of bribery in business transactions', *Journal of Business Research*, 129: 757–73.

This paper has identified the factors that have the greatest impact on bribery activities. Further, based on the countries' stage of economic development, it is further analysed in order to provide the manager and policy-maker with a more informative diagnostic tool to understand and deal with bribery activities locally and globally.

Jafari Nia, S., Abedi Jafari, H., Vakili, Y. and Ranjbar Kabutarkhani, M. (2022). 'Systematic review of conflict of interest studies in public administration', *Public Integrity*, 1–16. doi: 10.1080/10999922.2022.2068901.

This study proposes comprehensive actions to manage conflicts of interest in the public sector in terms of reviewing the existing studies and sources in this field.

LaVan, H. and Martin, W.M. (2021). 'Ethical challenges in workplace bullying and harassment: Creating ethical awareness and sensitivity'. In P. D'Cruz, E. Noronha, G. Notelaers and C. Rayner (eds), *Concepts, Approaches and Methods*, Singapore: Springer, (https://doi.org/10.1007/978-981-13-0134-6_6).

Here, we can discover mechanisms of moral disengagement as applied to bullying and harassment with specific examples. Also included are various strategies in organisations that can be used in the management of workplace bullying and harassment with the predominant ethical frameworks associated with each strategy.

Okudaira, H., Takizawa, M. and Yamanouchi, K. (2022). *Does employee downsizing work? Evidence from product innovation at manufacturing plants*, Tokyo: Research Institute of Economy, Trade and Industry.

This examines how manufacturing plants reallocated their internal resources after layoffs and whether they eventually increased their productivity or secured innovative gains. The results are interesting.

Sayed, Z. and Agndal, H. (2022). 'Offshore outsourcing of R&D to emerging markets: Information systems as tools of neo-colonial control', *Critical Perspectives on International Business*, 18(3): 281–302.

This paper analyses how information systems can serve as tools of neo-colonial control in offshore outsourcing of research and development work. It draws on critical work examining business and knowledge process outsourcing.

Stelzner, G. (2022). 'Ethics and discrimination in the hiring process: An overview of gender and race', *Minnesota Undergraduate Research & Academic Journal*, 5(4): 1–11

This paper looks into gender and racial discrimination with regard to ethical decision-making. Research includes white individuals, men, transgender people, and Native Americans.

7

SUSTAINABILITY AND THE ESG CRITERIA

─Learning objectives─

On completion of this chapter, you should be able to:

- Describe the historical developments in sustainability
- Define the concepts of sustainability and sustainability development
- Understand the planetary boundaries of the Earth's ecosystems
- Explore the three pillars of sustainability
- Understand sustainability concepts such as the IPAT equation, the SDG, and the phases of sustainability
- Understand current concepts and status of sustainable development
- Understand the ethical frameworks underpinning sustainability
- Appreciate the variety of sustainable business practices
- Understand the environmental, social, and governance (ESG) criteria
- Appreciate the future trends in sustainability

─Key concepts─

- Planetary boundaries
- Three pillars and the Triple Bottom Line
- The IPAT equation and Sustainable Development Goals
- Phase model of sustainability
- B Corp
- Greenhouse gas emissions
- Lifecycle analysis
- ESG criteria

―Box 7.1 Opening case―

Patagonia

Yvon Chouinard, an accomplished rock climber, began selling hand-made mountain climbing gear in 1957, and later in 1973 opened the first Patagonia store in Ventura near Los Angeles, California. The company expanded its products to include apparel for outdoor activities such as mountain climbing, biking, and surfing. Other related products included camping food.

The company, spearheaded by its founder Yvon Chouinard, built the Patagonia outdoor clothing brand with the clear vision to protect nature, and began initial steps to reduce their role as a corporate polluter. In the mid-1980s, they began using recycled-content paper for their catalogues. Later, with Malden Mills, they developed recycled polyester from soda bottles for use in the fleece of their jackets. They eliminated colours that used toxic metals and sulphides. In the late 1990s, they used solar-tracking skylights to reduce energy use, and carpets and partitions used recycled content. Realising that cotton, their most used fabric, contributed to environmental harm (through the use of chemicals to eliminate weeding), they decided to make their cotton sportswear 100 per cent organic by 1996. They had to persuade farmers, ginners, and spinners to make the change. In 2012, Patagonia became the first Californian company to be a 'Benefit Corporation' – also known as B Corp – a legal framework that enables mission-driven firms such as Patagonia to stay that way as they grow and change. To qualify as a B Corp, a business must have an explicit social and/or environmental mission and a legally binding responsibility towards all stakeholders.

Their steadfast mission has translated into profits donated to worthy environmental causes, LEED certified buildings, FSC certification, and 1 per cent of profits going to the Planet Organisation. In 12 years (2000 to 2012), their Common Threads Garment Recycling Program took back 45 tons of clothes for recycling from their customers and made 34 tons into new clothes. Their 2011 initiative encouraged consumers to repair and reuse their clothing rather than disposing of it. Higher quality and longer shelf life clothes were implemented. For those clothes that did wear out, Patagonia offered a free customer repair service to keep their products in use for longer.

Their Worn Wear programme – for used clothing and repairing – began small but soon became the largest garment repair facility in North America. Rips, tears, buttons, patches, and stains were taken care of in this facility. The programme even included a Worn Wear Wagon, a mobile repair truck made out of recycled materials, in which a small repair team could travel the country and repair people's Patagonian clothing for free and other brands for a fee. This programme is also supported by their 'design to be repaired' initiative.

Recently, Patagonia ran an advertisement in *The New York Times* telling people, 'Don't Buy This Jacket'. The idea was that everyone needs to consume less to lighten our environment footprint. Customers need to think twice before they buy. Patagonia felt that everything they make takes something from the planet but they can't give back. For example, each piece of Patagonia clothing 'emits several times its weight in greenhouse gases, generates at least another half garment's worth of scrap, and draws down copious amounts of freshwater now growing scarce everywhere on the planet'. They thought it would be hypocritical of them to work for environmental change without encouraging customers to think before buying.

In September 2022, Yvon Chouinard, his wife and their two adult children transferred their ownership of the company to a set of trusts and non-profit organisations. From this point forward, the profits from the company will fund efforts towards climate change and protecting wilderness areas. The company is worth USD 3 billion and its profits that will be donated could total USD 100 million each year. Mr Chouinard asserted that the planet is their largest stakeholder, and he is obliged to help it. In an interview, Mr Chouinard said 'Hopefully this will influence a new form of capitalism that doesn't end up with a few rich people and a bunch of poor people. We are going to give away the maximum amount of money to people who are actively working on saving this planet'. Big donors are increasingly making climate change a priority. In 2020 Jeff Bezos announced USD 20 billion into his Earth Fund. In 2021, Laurene Jobs, wife of Steve Jobs, allocated USD 3.5 billion to fight climate change. What's different about Chouinard's gift is that he is giving away his company and directing that the profits should be spent fighting climate change in the long term, thereby creating a new model for large-scale donations.

Sources:
Repurpose (2020)
Enrici A. (2022)
Gelles D. (2022)
Patagonia (2022a)
Patagonia (2022b)
Patagonia (2022c)
Wiki (2022l)

7.1 Introduction

Why are business leaders like Yvon Chouinard taking such drastic steps to fight climate change? What aspects of social, environmental, economic, and governance impacts can we identify in the opening case? Will others follow his lead?

These questions are linked to some of the concepts that we have discussed in earlier chapters and raise further questions, such as what are the purposes of the firm, what are their responsibilities, who are the stakeholders they are responsible to, what outcomes should we hold the firm responsible for, what are the impacts on society and on the environment from the firm's actions, and are they being addressed effectively? Collectively, these questions have generated discourses, approaches, and theories throughout most of the 20th century, and more so in the past couple of decades in the 21st century. These approaches are addressed in concepts such as 'sustainability', 'sustainable business', 'sustainable development', 'three pillars of sustainability', 'Triple Bottom Line', 'Sustainable Development Goals (SDGs)', and 'environmental, social, and governance (ESG)'. The list of topics that fall under the term 'sustainability' is wide and include plastics, water, carbon emissions, fast fashion, sustainable consumption, food, solar panels, wind energy, pollution, recycling, biodiversity, Earth ecosystems, deforestation, labour conditions, human rights, inequities, and many more.

In this chapter we explore what sustainability means, what does it mean for a business to be sustainable, how are businesses addressing it, what can governments do, what are our responsibilities as citizens and employees, and what can we expect in the future.

7.2 Historical developments in sustainability

Thoughts on sustainability (predominantly in the West) can be traced back to the late 18th and early 19th centuries when the initial idea of thinking about sustainability was based on the effect of economic activities on the environment. These effects were linked to the physical impact of the human population. Later, in the early and mid-20th century, efforts were made to scientifically understand and prove the impact of certain chemicals on human health. Rachel Carson's seminal 1962 book, *Silent Spring* (Carson, 1962), provided clear evidence of the harmful effects of improper use of the DDT chemical (a synthetic insecticide used in agriculture and to combat malaria, typhus, and other insect-borne human diseases). This led to the creation of the US Environmental Protection Agency (EPA) in 1970 and ultimately the ban of DDT in 1972 (USEPA, 2022). Thereafter, we see the idea of environmental sustainability progressing during the 1970s to 1990s, through the works of Garrett Hardin (1968) - the tragedy of the commons; Paul Elrich arguing for a dramatic reduction of population (Meadows et al., 1972) – a computer-modelled project titled 'Limits to Growth'; James Lovelock (1972) – the Gaia Hypothesis, representing Earth as a living organism; and Julian Simon (1996) – challenging the Limits to Growth theory, that humankind's ability to respond with creativity should not be underestimated.

7.3 Sustainability – definitions and explanations

The concerns about environmental sustainability voiced by these pioneers prompted the United Nations in 1983 to establish the World Commission on Environment and Development (WCED). In their report, Our Common Future (WCED, 1987), the Brundtland Commission defined sustainable development as follows: 'Sustainable development seeks to meet the needs and aspirations of the present without compromising the ability to meet those of the future' (WCED, 1987: 40).

Acknowledging that 'environment' is where we live and 'development' is what we all do to improve ourselves within that sphere, the Commission noted unprecedented pressures on the planet's land, waters, forests, and other natural resources, mostly in the developing countries. They identified links between poverty, inequality, and environmental degradation. They recommended a new era of economic growth that is forceful and at the same time socially and environmentally sustainable – thereby, for the first time, putting in place the connection between economic, social, and environmental perspectives, often known as the three pillars of sustainability (discussed further later in this chapter).

In 1992, the UN Conference on Environment and Development was held at the Earth Summit in Rio de Janeiro, and attracted government representatives and NGOs, leading to 27 principles (UNCED, 1992). One of the principles (no. 15), commonly called the Precautionary Principle, has become important in sustainability policy. It states:

> In order to protect the environment, the precautionary approach shall be widely applied by States according to their capabilities. Where there are threats of serious or irreversible damage, lack of full scientific certainty shall not be used as a reason for postponing cost-effective measures to prevent environmental degradation. (p. 3)

In 1997, the Kyoto Protocol committed states to reduce greenhouse gases (GHG) based on evidence that global warming is occurring and that human-made CO_2 emissions are driving it. It entered into force in 2005 when 192 countries signed up (although some withdrew later). In 2012, the Doha Amendment to the Kyoto Protocol was adopted for the period 2013–2020 (see Kyoto Protocol, 2022 for details).

From the 1960s the sustainability challenges spawned academic disciplines in earth sciences, environmental economics and accounting, ecological economics, environmental law, and environmental ethics. Academic journals also kept pace with research and education in these fields. Several research bodies such as the Intergovernmental Panel on Climate Change (IPCC, 2022) produce regular reports on the state of scientific, technical, and socio-economic knowledge on climate change, its impacts, and future risks, including options for reducing the rate at which climate change is taking place.

In 2004, the term ESG, short for environmental, social and governance, was coined as a process of quantifying an organisation's commitment to social and environmental factors. This formed the backbone for launch of the Principles of Responsible Investment (PRI, 2022a) at the New York Stock Exchange in 2006. The purpose of PRI is to understand the implications of ESG factors and incorporate them into investment and ownership decisions of organisations.

7.4 Sustainable development – current concepts and status

The Anthropocene Epoch and planetary boundaries

Based on major events, the time scale of Earth has been divided into timescales known as 'eons', and within eons there are 'eras', 'periods', 'epochs' and 'ages', spanning millions of years. Dinosaurs lived in the Mesozoic Era from 250 to 60 million years ago. Apes and humans gradually separated in the Miocene epoch about 10 million years ago (Wiki, 2022h). *Homo sapiens* arose and spread across continents in the Pleistocene epoch from 700 thousand to 120 thousand years ago. We are now in the Holocene Epoch which began 11,700 years ago after the major ice age. Based on recent events such as the global environmental changes, experts argue for renaming it the 'Anthropocene Epoch' – *anthro* for 'man' and *cene* for 'new' beginning with the industrial revolution in the early 1800s. The new name sends a message that humankind has caused mass extinctions of plants and animal species, polluted the oceans, and altered the atmosphere, among other lasting impacts (Stromberg, 2013). It indicates that human activity has a profound influence on the global environment leading to a high magnitude, variety, and longevity of human-induced changes (Lewis and Maslin, 2015).

Acknowledging that anthropogenic pressures on the Earth system have resulted in abrupt global environmental change, Rockström et al. (2009) proposed a new approach called the 'Planetary Boundaries' (PB) framework, consisting of nine boundaries, within which we can expect that humanity can operate safely. Crossing the boundaries and thresholds of any one or more of these PBs could spell disaster for the Earth systems and all those living in them. See Table 7.1 for the nine Earth system processes. Steffen et al. (2015) have reported that four of the nine PBs have been crossed because of human activities: climate change, biodiversity loss, land-system change, and biogeochemical flows.

Table 7.1 The nine Earth systems

	Earth system process	Indicators	Crossed: Yes/No
1	Climate change	Atmospheric CO_2 concentration	Yes
2	Rate of biodiversity loss	Extinction rate Biodiversity intactness	Yes
3	Stratosphere ozone depletion	Ozone O_3 concentration	No
4	Ocean acidification	Concentration of carbonic acid and carbonate ions	No
5	Biogeochemical flows	Phosphorous flow from fertilizers to soil and into oceans Excess nitrogen from industrial and agricultural sources	Yes
6	Land-change system	Area of forested land as a percentage of original forest cover	Yes
7	Freshwater use	Amount of blue water consumption and withdrawal from river flows	No
8	Atmospheric aerosol loading	Aerosols (haze, smoke particles, desert dust, sea salt) in the atmosphere	No
9	Introduction of novel entities – chemical pollution	Chemicals and new types of engineered materials. Three aspects: 1. Unknown disruptive effects 2. Disruptive factors not discovered until it is a problem 3. Effect not readily reversible	Unknown – needs research as there are more than 100,000 substances including nanomaterials and plastic polymers

Source: Steffen et al. (2015), 'Sustainability planetary boundaries: Guiding human development on a changing planet', *Science* (American Association for the Advancement of Science), 347 (6223): 1259855

In April 2022, Wang-Erlandsson and associates (including Steffen and Rockström), proposed a 'green water' planetary boundary. Green water, the amount of water from terrestrial precipitation, evaporation, and soil moisture, is fundamental to the Earth systems. This boundary can be represented by the percentage of ice-free land area on which root-zone moisture exists. The researchers show evidence that there is widespread deterioration indicating that the green water planetary boundary is already transgressed (Wang-Erlandsson et al., 2022). If this is confirmed, Earth would have crossed a fifth planetary boundary.

The three pillars of sustainability

The evolution and progress of the concept of sustainability over the last two centuries were crystallised when the Brundtland report from the UNCED was published in 1987 which called for a new era of economic growth that is forceful and at the same time socially and environmentally sustainable. These three factors – environment, social, and economic – became conceptualised as the three pillars of sustainable development. Purvis et al. (2019) traces the origins of this concept and notes that there appears to be no original text from which it is derived. From as early as 2001, this approach of the three pillars has been presented as a 'common view' of sustainable development. Pictorially, researchers and authors variously represent them as three circles with 'sustainability' at the centre where the three circles intersect, or as pillars that support sustainability or as three concentric circles where economy resides in society which in turn resides in the environment – as shown in Figure 7.1.

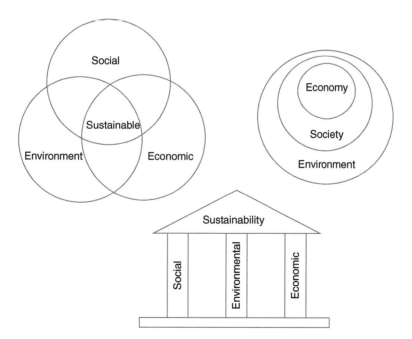

Figure 7.1 Representations of the three 'pillars' of sustainability – intersecting circles, pillars, and concentric circles

The 'social' perspective is about identifying and managing business impacts, both positive and negative, on people. The first six of the UN Global Compact's principles focus on the social dimension of corporate sustainability. Aspects include human rights, labour rights, child labour, living conditions, inequity in gender, income, education, health, justice, safety, wellness, diversity, inclusion, work-life balance, empowerment, community engagement, and more (UNGC, 2022b).

The 'environmental' perspective is about accepting the responsibility to conserve natural resources and protect global ecosystems to support health and well-being, now and in the future. Research shows that 'global emission levels are lower for countries with tighter domestic environmental regulations. One reason for this is that companies, which are the biggest contributors of carbon dioxide (CO_2) emissions, emit less CO_2 at home when domestic environmental regulations are strict. However, these companies also emit more abroad, particularly in countries with laxer environmental standards' (Ben-David et al., 2019). Therefore, new corporate efforts are needed to increase stewardship of natural resources and implement innovative solutions (UNGC, 2022c).

The 'economic' perspective is about enabling long-term economic development of a company or nation by balancing economic growth with the environmental, social, and cultural aspects of its activity.

The three pillars are also referred to as the 3 Ps – People (for social), Planet (for environment), and Profit (for economic).

Businesses can achieve sustainability through the adoption of one or more of the 17 SDGs. Discussed later in this section, 'the SDGs are intended to influence and guide not only global politics but also businesses and individuals in their actions to serve the idea of sustainable development' (Hahn, 2022: 13).

═══════ **Box 7.2** ═══════

Biogas plants: Illustrating all three pillars of sustainability

Rural areas of India traditionally used firewood and kerosene for cooking and chemical fertilisers for crops, which contributed to GHG emissions, degradation of forests, and soil and water contamination. A project implemented by an Indian NGO, SKG Sangha, changed this process through the installation of domestic biogas plants. Animal dung and kitchen wastewater are mixed in a typical biogas plant called 'digesters', where this mixture is broken down by bacteria in an oxygen-free environment in a process called anaerobic digestion, turning it into energy (gas) and valuable soil products (liquids and solids).

The project installed biogas plants (and such projects aim to empower women) in over 9,000 households. The generated gas is a renewable source of energy and is used for cooking, and the slurry of the remaining manures serves as high-quality fertiliser, replacing chemical products. The biogas installations also have positive sustainable development effects, such as alleviating workload for women and children (by eliminating the need to collect firewood) and easing health problems caused by smoke from burning firewood. The project contributes to the following ten SDGs:

1   (No poverty) – improving families' financial situation by not buying expensive fertilisers
2   (Zero hunger) – by contributing to sustainable agriculture

3   (Good health) – benefitting from better indoor air quality
4   (Quality education) – children get more time to go to school (by not collecting firewood)
5   (Gender equality) – only women are entitled to buy and own a biogas plant
7   (Affordable clean energy) – generated biogas is clean and affordable (practically free)
8   (Decent work and economic growth) – permanent jobs created, and people trained
12   (Responsible consumption and production) – contributes to sustainable waste management
13   (Climate action) – each plant avoids 6.3 tonnes of CO_2 and 3.7 tonnes of wood consumption per year
15   (Life on land) – reduced wood consumption avoids deforestation

Sources: Adapted from Biogas (2022) and EESI (2017)

The IPAT equation

To understand and reduce the complexity of the factors involved in sustainability, Meadows et al. (2005: 124–6) proposed the so-called 'IPAT equation'. The equation summarises the causes of environmental deterioration with this formula:

Impact (I) = Population (P) × Affluence (A) × Technology (T)

The impact (ecological footprint) of any nation on the planet's resources is 'related to the product of its population times its level of affluence times the damage done by the particular technology used to support that affluence' (2005: 124). Ecological footprint (EF), expressed in 'per capita' global hectares, measures the assets that a population or a product requires to produce the natural resources it consumes and to absorb its waste, especially carbon emissions (GFN, 2022). For example, the ecological footprint of Qatar is 14.3, USA 8.1, Australia 8.6, Denmark 7.7, UK 4.2, China 3.8, Brazil 2.8, and India 1.2 (GFN, 2022).

Population refers to the number of people influencing the ecological footprint. In 2022, the world's population reached 8 billion and this is likely to increase a further 4 billion or so by 2100, and each person will leave (or need) an EF through resources necessary to maintain their lifestyle. Affluence is determined by the high rate of consumption – for example, hours spent on watching the TV, driving a car, buying clothes and consumer goods – even the number of coffees we drink per day. Technological impact is essentially the energy needed to make and deliver the TV, the car, clothes, the consumer goods, and the coffees.

The equation also signifies the scope for improvement in each of the three parameters – we can reflect on the number of ways to reduce ecological footprint. Ray Anderson's (Founder of Interface – industrial carpet manufacturers) vision for Interface was to rewrite the IPAT equation by suggesting that the harmful technologies of the first industrial revolution (extracting and polluting by nature) could be replaced by the technologies of a new, sustainability-focused industrial revolution. Calling these T2 technologies, Ray moved the T from the numerator of the equation to the denominator. Thus, T2 technologies will decrease environmental impact rather than increase them (Lanier, 2019).

Sustainable Development Goals

In 2015, all 193 member states of the UN adopted a plan for achieving a better future – to end extreme poverty, fight inequality and injustice, and protect our planet by 2030. This plan comprises the 17 SDGs that define the world we want and apply to all nations (UNGC, 2022d). Figure 7.2 shows the 17 SDGs. The UNGC asserts that achieving these ambitions will take unprecedented effort by all sectors of society and business has a very important role to play in the process. This is based on the growing awareness that it is not enough for companies to focus only on short-term profits because natural disasters, social unrest, or economic disparity can damage long-term prosperity. To achieve this successfully, UNGC suggests turning global goals into local business. Guides on how a company can advance each of the SDGs are available in UNGC (2022e).

Figure 7.2 The 17 Sustainable Development Goals developed by UNGC

The phase model of sustainability

The SDGs indicated and asserted that corporations are important drivers for achieving the development goals. This means that corporations that adopt these goals to seek transition to a sustainable society can make major contributions towards this progress. Therefore, there is a need to understand the paths companies must take and to identify the stage where they are now so that they can determine how to move forward (Benn et al., 2018). Having reviewed several stages and models that have been suggested in the past few decades, Benn et al. (2018) have developed a comprehensive model that consists of six developmental phases, categorised into three waves of corporate change (see Figure 7.3) through which companies progress towards both human and ecological sustainability.

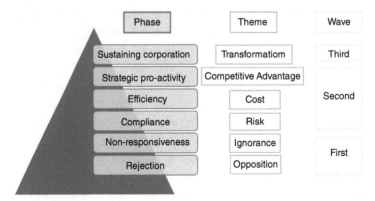

Figure 7.3 The six developmental phases, themes, and waves of corporate change

Source: Adapted from Benn et al. (2018), *Organizational change for corporate sustainability*, 4th edn. Oxon: Routledge

It is not assumed that a firm necessarily progresses through all phases step by step. It is possible an organisation may leapfrog phases or regress by abandoning previously established sustainability practices (Benn et al., 2018: 15). Phases can shift when triggered by changes such as a new CEO, stakeholder pressure, new legislation, or economic fluctuations.

Distinguishing characteristics of each phase:

First wave:

1   Rejection phase: The firm believes that employees, societal infrastructure, and natural resources are to be exploited for quick economic gain. They disregard destructive environmental impacts of their activities and expect the community to pay the costs. Sustainability pressures are actively rejected.

2   Non-responsiveness phase: Rather than active opposition, the firm suffers from ignorance or lack of awareness. For them it is 'business as usual', operating in conventional ways and not incorporating sustainability issues into their decision-making. Community issues are ignored, and environmental impacts are taken for granted.

Second wave:

3   Compliance phase: The firm focuses on reducing risk of sanctions for failing to meet minimum standards. They ensure a safe, healthy workplace and avoid environmental abuses by complying with rules and regulations. They also support charitable community programmes and see themselves as responsible corporate citizens. They are usually reactive to new government regulations and community expectations and prefer voluntary self-regulations.

4   Efficiency phase: In this phase, the firm shows a growing awareness that there are real advantages to be gained by implementing sustainable practices. The focus is on reducing costs and increasing efficiency. Thus, there will be attempts to reduce 'waste' from a production process or even think of it as a valuable resource to another firm. Such firms will be willing to incur additional expenses if it results in generating additional income.

5   Strategic proactivity phase: Sustainability becomes an important part of the firm's business strategy. The focus is on innovation. They create shared value with and for a broader set of societal stakeholders. The firm becomes a leader in sustainable business practices, an 'employer of choice', with innovative quality products that are environmentally safe and healthy.

Third wave:

6   The sustaining corporation phase: Senior executives and members of the firm have internalised the purpose of achieving a sustainable world. While pursuing economic gains, they will voluntarily go beyond by actively promoting sustainability values and practices in industry and society. They actively participate in working with governments and communities to create public policies that contribute to a more sustainable world. They cooperate with their supply chain to ensure full sustainability. Strong stakeholder engagement ensures an integrated approach to coordinate the three pillars of sustainability: economic, social, and environmental.

B Corp certification

B Corp certification began when the B Lab organisation was founded in 2006 in the US with the goal of driving change in how businesses operate, especially balancing profit and purpose. It is a private certification of for-profit companies of their social and environmental performance (B Lab, 2022). They measure a company's entire social and environmental impact. Their performance is measured in five pillars – governance, workers, community, environment, and customers (Liute and De Giacomo, 2022). To be B Corp certified, businesses need to meet high standards of verified performance, accountability, and transparency on factors such as employee benefits, charitable giving, supply chain practices, and input materials. A business must demonstrate:

- High social and environmental performance based on a risk review.
- Make a legal commitment by changing their corporate governance structure to be accountable to all stakeholders, not just shareholders.
- Exhibit transparency by allowing information about their performance to be measured against B Lab's standards.

The first 82 B Corps were certified in 2007. Businesses are expected to get re-certified every three years, thus indicating a focus on continuous improvement, leading to long-term resiliency. This process can be seen to be linked to the Sustaining Corporation Phase (the sixth phase) of the Benn et al. (2018) sustainability development progression.

Researchers have now recognised that due to its belief that a business's purpose should be larger than maximising shareholder value (it should benefit all stakeholders), 'the B Corp form has emerged in opposition to large publicly traded corporations, the dominant form of business organisation for the past century' (Kim and Schifeling, 2022). They note that the B Corp movement initially grew because of privately held small firms embracing social and environmental sustainability. These were predominantly driven by established organisations that had long nurtured their commitment to sustainability. The initial growth of B Corp was more about a social movement offering an alternative to the dominant shareholder-maximisation organisations. The pioneering members of B Corp included Patagonia (see the opening case of the chapter).

In an analysis of 68 UK-based B Corp companies engaged in two environmentally sensitive sectors – manufacturing and wholesale/retail – Liute and De Giacomo (2022) showed that:

- Companies in those two sectors tend to perform better socially than environmentally.
- Prioritising one social impact area generally leads to below-average environmental performance.
- To rule out greenwashing (defined as when green promises are not kept or are misunderstood – for example when there is a divergence between socially responsible communication and practices), B Corps should ensure certified companies display high levels of environmental performance to be able to align their 'green' claims to their performance.

Greenhouse gas emission accounting

The 2022 report from the Intergovernmental Panel for Climate Change (IPCC), the peak body responsible for reporting the state of the Earth's environment with respect to climate change, noted that 'human-induced climate change, including more frequent and intense extreme events, has caused widespread adverse impacts and related losses and damages to nature and people, beyond natural climate variability' (IPCC, 2022: 9). The report further observes that human-induced factors that cause climate change include unsustainable use of natural resources, ecosystem damage by pollutants, and exceeding the limits of atmospheric GHG. GHG are gases that trap heat in the atmosphere. These include carbon dioxide (CO_2) – mainly from burning fossil fuels; methane (CH_4) – mainly from production of fossil fuels and livestock; nitrous oxide (NO_2) – mainly from agricultural and industrial activities; and fluorinated gases – mainly from synthetic gases used in and emitted from household and industrial applications (EPA, 2022). The IPCC report asserts that emission reductions and carbon removal can reduce GHG and therefore climate-related hazards.

Corporations are therefore facing pressure from investors, advocacy groups, politicians, and the general public to reduce GHG emissions from their operations and their supply chain. Today, more than 90 per cent of S&P 500 companies publish ESG reports in some form (Perez et al., 2022), which almost always include an estimate of the company's GHG emissions. These estimates rely on an approach called the GHG Protocol.

The GHG Protocol identified three types of GHG emissions and provides guidance for measuring and reporting on them (WBCSD, 2013a; 2013b):

1 Scope 1: Direct emissions that occur directly at the company's facilities and operations – for example emissions from its production and transportation equipment.
2 Scope 2: Emissions at facilities that generate electricity bought and consumed by the company.
3 Scope 3: Emissions associated with other inputs to the company – such as from upstream operations in the company's supply chain (all suppliers) and from downstream activities by the company's customers and end-use consumers.

Scope 1 emissions are the easiest to measure as they are produced by the company and are within their control. High-emission industries include energy generation using fossil fuels, mining, metallurgical, chemical, and agribusinesses. Scope 2 are indirect emissions from electricity usage and can also be measured easily because it is possible to know and calculate GHG emissions per kWh of power used. Scope 3 are indirect emissions that are difficult to measure mainly because of lack of data availability from upstream and downstream activities. Suppliers may not have the capacity or capability to measure and report their GHG emissions and estimating emissions data from the consumers of the company's products may also introduce measurement error, bias, and manipulation. A study of the construction industry in China found that indirect emissions (Scope 2 and 3) accounted for 97 per cent of all GHG emissions, electricity usage and building materials being the two greatest contributors (Hong et al., 2015). Between 1995 and 2015, global Scopes 1, 2, and 3 emissions grew by 47 per cent,

78 per cent, and 84 per cent respectively. Globally, the industry sector emissions were high for Scopes 2 and 3, the building sector emissions were high for Scope 3, whereas the transport and energy sectors were high for Scope 1. Most of the emissions growth was in developing countries (Hertwich and Wood, 2018).

One solution to measure and report on GHG emissions more accurately was offered by Kaplan and Ramanna (2021). It suggests a process similar to estimating unit production costs – whereas financial accounting would record the monetary cost of producing a ton of material as inventory (an asset on its balance sheet), GHG units per ton of material extracted or produced can be labelled an E-liability, reflecting their environmental cost to society. So, a typical E-liability flow would be: Opening E-liabilities *plus* E-liabilities from suppliers (electricity, steel, glass, capital equipment, etc.,) *plus* E-liability produced from operations *minus* E-liabilities transferred to customers *equals* Closing E-liabilities.

7.5 Ethical frameworks for sustainability

Sustainability and sustainable businesses have all the elements of ethical business. Even though actions may take longer to materialise, ethical decision-making is seen as an important necessity. As we have seen in earlier chapters, stakeholders (narrow and broad) are increasingly expecting businesses to act responsibly towards environmental and social issues generated by businesses' actions. Businesses feel the pressure of maintaining and even enhancing their reputation by seeking to not only avoid damage to people and environments, but to proactively innovate and change their products and processes to mitigate GHG and climate change. Harder and Burford (2019) have even suggested that a fourth pillar, called 'ethical values', should be added to the traditional three pillars of sustainability (social, environmental, and economic).

In the past few decades, there have been several high-level calls for establishing a global ethical framework for sustainability. Some examples are the Earth Charter, the UN Millennium Goals, and the Sustainable Development Goals. Further to this, Nicholson and Kurucz (2019: 39) suggest that the moral theory of 'ethics of care' can help inform a deeper understanding of the ethical and moral elements of leadership for sustainability. The following ethical concepts (discussed in previous chapters) form the framework within sustainability:

1   Stakeholder theory: This theory extends a business's responsibilities from primary stakeholders to secondary or broader stakeholders. The former includes employees, customers, suppliers, investors, and local communities, while the latter includes broader society, the environment, and future generations.
2   Utilitarian ethics: This theory focuses on the consequences of one's action – so, an action is considered ethical if the outcome produces more good than harm. Therefore, it calls for balancing stakeholder interests in sustainability issues.
3   Deontological (Kantian) ethics: This theory focuses on the action itself rather than the consequences. Universal rules, principles that hold for anyone at any time, and

treating humanity as an end, not as a means, are the Kantian principles that can be unambiguously linked to sustainability issues, for both social and environmental.

4 Rights theory: This includes human rights, labour rights, natural rights, and human dignity. These rights, as declared by the UN and other jurisdictions, are entitlements that all individuals have, regardless of their membership in any state or social organisation (Wells, 2011). They include working conditions of workers around the world embodied in industry code of conduct, occupational health and safety principles, and child labour prohibition, to name a few.

5 Justice theory: This includes Rawls's principles that freedoms must be realised by everyone affected by a decision and there should be the greatest benefits for the least disadvantaged by providing equal opportunities for everyone in social, environmental, and economic issues. In particular, justice theory extends to:

   a Inter-generational justice: Duties and responsibilities that the present generation have to the past and future generations and the moral considerations that ought to be considered when thinking this through – for example the Paris Agreement of 2016–2018 mentions that there is a moral duty to protect future generations from the pollutions and responsibilities of past generations.

   b Intra-generational justice: Between different people of today's generations, to ensure justice among humans that are alive today – for example, principle 6 of the Rio declaration states that priority should be given for special situations in developing nations who are environmentally vulnerable.

6 Other ethical theories that could be applied to sustainability are virtue ethics (with an emphasis on personal character dispositions of being generous, caring, and compassionate), ethics of care (using warmth, friendliness, and trust), and discourse ethics (resolving different positions among stakeholders on sustainability issues).

7 Ethical concepts from different cultures – as discussed in Chapter 5 of this book – would also be very useful in identifying and resolving sustainability issues in local communities.

7.6 Sustainable business practices

Waves, phases, and approaches

Referring to 'The phase model of sustainability', Benn et al. (2018) suggest two approaches – incremental and transformational. They note that 'some organisations may make smaller incremental changes over time, systematically building on past successes, while others may make widespread, rapid, and quite radical alterations. Changes might focus on the business they are in, the way they do business, their structure, their corporate culture (or all of these)' (p. 25).

The incremental approach does not involve any radical changes. It includes planned, continuous, and ongoing changes that impact day-to-day operational processes, such as (Benn et al., 2018: 245):

- The way people work (job redesign and teamwork).
- Business processes (total quality management and lean systems).
- Other areas (incentive systems to align with changed goals, new relevant information systems, new or upgraded technologies to suit sustainability targets).

Benefits for the incremental approach are: developing credibility through small wins, developing capabilities in technical, operational, and human-related areas, a positive change in culture, improvements in efficiencies (for example, waste reduction), and improved organisational structure to suit the ongoing changes (see more about structure further down this section).

The transformational approach involves reinventing the organisation:

- To target a desirable sustainable future.
- To move from short-term profits to longer-term goals that include social justice and ecological improvements.
- To engage in new models and frameworks for production strategies, financing, and accounting – for example, adopting the Triple Bottom Line.

The two approaches can be applied singularly or together. Both have advantages and most successful change programmes adopt both approaches.

Types of organisational structures

In the process of change in the sustainability journey, whether the approach is incremental or transformational or both, new roles are expected to emerge in organisations – such as sustainability managers and chief sustainability officers. It is therefore important to understand how the organisational structure can impede or enable the freedom such managers have to decide what should be done in a particular sustainability decision-making situation. In any organisation's structure there is an interplay between the top-down forces of structure and the bottom-up influences of managers. Sandhu and Kulik (2019) examined data from interviews with sustainability managers and identified three organisational configurations – prospecting, orchestrating, and championing – see Table 7.2 for each configuration's implications. Their analysis showed that the championing configuration 'with semi-structured formalisation and a decentralised sustainability program provided the best conditions for managers to use their discretion to champion sustainability initiatives' (2019: 619).

Formalisation is defined as the use of explicit policies, rules, and procedures. It provides an organisation with structure and stability. Centralisation is defined as the extent to which decision-making authority is confined to higher levels of the firm's hierarchy. It can free lower-level employees from major decisions and enable them to focus on their jobs, but it can also create resentment among employees with the lack of opportunities to participate in decision-making. Decentralisation occurs when decision-making is embedded across functional areas (2019: 621 and 633).

Table 7.2   Configurations of top-down and bottom-up dynamics

Configuration	Organisation structure	Strategy type	Managerial discretion level
Prospecting	- Low Formalisation - Low Centralisation (Separate cell)	Reputational	Low
Orchestrating	- High Formalisation - High Centralisation (Corporate function)	Business Case	Moderate
Championing	- Semi-Formalisation - Decentralisation (Embedded in functions)	Long-Term and Normative	High

Source: Sandhu and Kulik (2019), compiled by author

7.7 Major areas of business for adopting sustainable practices

Accounting and finance

Professional accountants need to consider how, through their work and positions of influence, they can contribute to business resilience and influence organisations to integrate sustainability matters into organisational strategy, finance, operations, and communications (IFAC, 2015). The International Federation of Accountants (IFAC, 2015) has provided useful resources to accountants for:

- Identifying the business case at an organisational project or issue level, for example, dealing with a natural resource or energy dependency.
- Engaging the finance and accounting function such as reaching out to sustainability and operational colleagues to establish how the finance team could support them.
- Connecting sustainability to strategy, risk, and performance.
- Reducing sustainability impact of products, services, and operations, for example life-cycle analysis.
- Developing a business reporting strategy and approach, for example the GRI.
- Integrating sustainability impacts into financial reporting, for example GHG emissions reporting.
- Assuring sustainability disclosures and reporting, for example adopting ISO 14064-3 principles and guidance for making GHG assertions.

Marketing

It is recognised that there is a causal relationship between dangers to our biosphere and our unsustainable consumption practices. To explore practical solutions to make consumption practices sustainable, Haider et al. (2022) reviewed 2,289 relevant literature documents from 1976 to 2021. Their review recommends:

- That consumption sustainability be repositioned as a means of achieving a better quality of life for consumers, for example aiming for economic prosperity, environmental quality with social impact.
- Reforming the consumer mindset towards pro-social and pro-ecological choices, for example encouraging ideas of reduction, reuse, recovery, and recycling.
- Training consumers in mindful consumption practices, for example being mindful of resource extraction and waste disposal, and breaking the shopping cycle for new fashion or technology.
- Providing consumers with an infrastructure for consuming with a mindful mindset, for example encouraging sharing activities such as meals, a car, or communal laundry.
- Marketing should redefine itself as a pro-social discipline with a focus on consumer well-being, for example cleaner production practices, marketing of greener products with proper eco-labelling.
- Reshape quality of life in terms of non-financial standards, for example self-care with respect to better health, more profound social and ecological values and managing financial stability.

Production and manufacturing

The production and manufacturing systems of business are probably the most visible and impactable areas of sustainable business. The impacts of production processes on the environment and society are well documented and also discussed in several sections of this chapter. There is mounting pressure on manufacturers to account for their resource consumption and environmental footprint. Sustainable production has been defined as 'the creation of goods and services using processes and systems that are non-polluting; conserving of energy and natural resources; economically viable; safe and healthful for employees, communities and consumers; and socially and creatively rewarding for all working people' (Alayón et al., 2017: 694).

Businesses that engage in production or manufacturing operate within specific legal and regulatory environments. These include Environment Protection Acts (enacted in various countries), Building Codes, Best Practice Environmental Management, and environmental management systems. EMSs are a set of processes and practices that enable an organisation to reduce its environmental impacts and increase its operating efficiency, for example:

- ISO 14001:2015 (updated 2021) – enables an organisation to systematically manage its environmental responsibilities and achieve outcomes such as enhancing environmental performance, fulfilling compliance obligations, and achieving environmental objectives.
- The Eco-Management and Audit Scheme (EMAS, 2022) – used to evaluate, report on, and improve environmental performance. It supports organisations to find the right

tools, ensures credibility through third-party verification, and provides transparency through publicly available information.

- ISO 14005 (2019) – provides guidelines for a phased approach to establish, implement, maintain, and improve, and is an EMS that all firms can adopt.

==== **Box 7.3** ====

Sustainability initiatives: Bamboo bikes made in Ghana

After graduating with a bachelor's degree in business administration and a diploma in HRM, Bernice Dapaah ventured into entrepreneurship, partly due to the high unemployment rate in Ghana. The question she asked was 'How best can we utilise our own local raw material such as bamboo to create employment as an inclusive business model – a business that can tackle environmental issues, social and economic issues?' This led to the founding of the Ghana Bamboo Bikes Initiative (GBBI) in 2018. As the name implies, the bikes are made predominantly (about 75 to 80 per cent) of bamboo. GBBI produces mountain, road, and city bikes, as well as cargo bikes that farmers use to carry goods. The main body is bamboo while the wheels and engine are the regular ones like in other bikes. Located in Kumasi in southern Ghana, GBBI employs about 50 people, mostly women. They produce more than 1000 bikes a year and are planning to expand into electric bamboo bicycles, electric bike ambulances, and pedicabs. Ms Dapaah says that the business is not 'just an environmental symbol. We are also cultivating bamboo to feed the industry. We are also creating a space for the carbon balance. That is what we are doing. We hope to do more in the future'. To her, GBBI is more than a business; it is also about women's empowerment.

Sources:
Kuwonu (2019)
Wiki (2022f)
GBBI (2018)
UNGCCA (2018)

Suggested sustainability practices

At the operations level (compiled from various sources):

- Safe and ecologically sound products and packaging
- Managing environmental risks through supply chain initiatives
- Eliminating or reducing substances hazardous to human health and environment
- Waste and by-products: recovered, reclaimed, recycled, reduced, reused, or eliminated
- Waste management done at 'start of pipe' (changing design so that pollution is reduced or eliminated), rather than at 'end of pipe' (trapping, storing, discarding at the end of production)
- Energy and materials are acquired from renewable and sustainable sources

- Designing workplaces to minimise waste
- Eliminating or reducing chemical hazards

At the organisational level (compiled from various sources):

- Product stewardship
- Life cycle analysis
- Design for the Environment (DfE)
- Partnerships with programmes such as UNEP, UNGC
- Certification and benchmarking programmes such as the Equator Principles, Coalition for Environmentally Responsible Economies, Global Reporting Initiative, Sustainability Accounting Standards Board, Certified B Corporation (B Corp), Environmental Working Group, Fairtrade International, The Forest Stewardship Council, Global Organic Textile Standard
- Ensure security and well-being of employees
- Respect communities around workplaces and enhance economically, culturally, and physically
- Engagement with one or more of the 17 SDGs

7.8 Future trends in sustainability

1   Framework for Industry 4.0: Manufacturing has transitioned through three revolutions so far: mechanisation through water and steam power, mass production and assembly lines using electricity, and introduction and use of computers and automation. We are now in the fourth revolution in which computers are connected and communicate with one another to make decisions without human intervention (Forbes, 2018). New technologies in 4.0 include cyber-physical systems, the Internet of Things (IoT), additive manufacturing, and big data analysis. These technologies are expected to contribute to sustainability. In a recent study Jamwal et al. (2021) identified 26 enablers, predominantly in the supply chain and IT providers, for sustainability in Industry 4.0.

2   Carbon credits and its problems: Companies are pledging to become net-zero – to offset their carbon emissions using some of the processes we have discussed earlier, such as energy efficiency and renewable energy. A more recent idea is the concept of carbon credits. To offset their carbon emissions, businesses can buy carbon credits from other organisations or even nations who have net negative emissions such as generating electricity from renewable energy and rainforest nations preserving trees. However, if businesses buy 'credits from a rainforest nation agreeing to save their trees or refurbish their land, the challenge with replanting is that there is no guarantee anyone is watching to ensure success' (Silverstein, 2022).

3   Sustainability learnings from major events such as the Covid-19 pandemic: The Covid-19 pandemic (predominantly during 2020–2021) and similar world events (such events are

also called *black swan* events) exposed the limitations and fragility of global supply chain resilience and also revealed changes in social and environmental conditions. Some examples are the rise of the sharing economy, circular economy, social innovations, consumer behaviour such as reuse and recycling, supply chain localisation, and efficiency in waste management. In addition, we saw an increase in the demand for IoT and e-commerce (social distancing forced people to use online goods and services, which could increase consumerism also), and working from home with less travel reduced organisational footprints. However, research found environmental impact was higher due to individual energy consumption rather than central consumption in buildings. Localised production supported sustainable supply chains by producing only what is needed. These experiences and lessons with further research should generate understanding on how to manage and be resilient for future *black swan* events (Sarkis, 2020).

7.9 Environmental, social, and governance – history, issues, and what's next?

History

In the 1960s investors became involved in 'socially responsible investing', where investors excluded stocks or entire industries from their portfolios based on business activities such as tobacco production or involvement in the South African Apartheid regime (MSCI, 2022). Issues that were considered 'ground-breaking' in the recent past are now seen as the norm for responsible business and quickly becoming more common. These issues include employer–employee relationships, uptake of net zero targets, focus on nature-based solutions, and deeper approaches to managing diversity, equity, and inclusion. In 2004, Paul Clements-Hunt and his team created the term ESG (environmental, social, and governance) when he was working at the UN and ran the United Nations Environment Program Finance Initiative. The original idea was to have a strategy that involves measuring investment risks tied to issues such as climate change, human rights violations in supply chains and poor corporate governance, and by addressing those challenges, there were opportunities to make money – climate technologies for example (Kishan and Bloomberg, 2022). The sustainable development of the global economy and society called for the practice of the ESG principle and criteria (Li et al., 2021). Responsible investment is defined as 'a strategy and practice to incorporate environmental, social and governance (ESG) factors in investment decisions and active ownership' (PRI, 2022b).

Responding to the views of senior executives of financial institutions and other signatories of the UN Global Compact, the then UN Secretary General Kofi Annan in 2004 invited CEOs of 55 of the world's leading financial institutions to develop guidelines and recommendations on how to better integrate ESG issues in asset management – primarily by establishing the link between ESG issues and investment decisions. To make this happen, the report recommended that analysts, financial institutions, companies, investors, trustees, consultants, advisors, regulators, stock exchanges, and NGOs would all be required to contribute to create, shape, and implement ESG initiatives (UNEPFI, 2004).

Concerns

ESG ratings aim to provide an assessment of the long-term resilience of companies to ESG issues through the industry-specific evaluation of key ESG risks and opportunities. ESG soon became associated with ethical investing. Many investors now incorporate ESG factors into the investment process in addition to traditional financial analysis. ESG considerations are now prominent in one in every three dollars of global assets under management. It bloomed into a USD 40 trillion industry propelled by the financial giants of Wall Street and Europe's financial hubs, with the label now attached to everything from ETFs to loans and other financial instruments. However, Paul Clements-Hunt believes that ESG products today do little for ESG risks. Similarly, Tariq Fancy, former head of sustainability investing of BlackRock (one of the world's largest asset managers), has labelled ESG a 'dangerous placebo' and commented that ESG funds are mostly about marketing and have no real real-world impact (Ketchell, 2022; Mackintosh, 2022). Although trillions of dollars are being invested in ESG investments, Pucker and King (2022) assert that these trillions are dedicated to assuring returns for shareholders and not for delivering positive planetary impact. ESG fund selection, they say, is increasingly based on the impact of the changing world on a company's profits and losses, not the reverse. In summary, today, there is much confusion and exaggeration surrounding ESG investing due to its over-emphasis on return-on-investment.

What's next for sustainability, sustainable business, and the ESG criteria?

As we have seen earlier, ESG has received some high-profile criticism from researchers and observers who assert that there are big claims and little action. They believe that real change and progress will depend more on government regulation than corporate activity. This is because ESG data remains a challenge due to variation and inconsistency in corporate ESG reporting. To ensure comparable and comprehensive disclosures by companies, several public sector boards, councils, and foundations are being consolidated into the International Sustainability Standards Board (SustainAbility Institute, 2022).

While there are clear commitments of financial markets towards the ESG criteria within investment decisions, there are questions of how compatible ESG criteria are with corporate financial performance (CFP). Some researchers claim a positive ESG-CFP relation, others claim that results are ambiguous, inconclusive, or contradictory. Friede et al. (2015), in an analysis of more than 3,700 study results from 2,200 unique primary studies, found:

- Clear evidence for the business case for ESG investing (contrasting the existing perception of a neutral or mixed ESP-CFP performance relation).
- Positive ESG-CFP performance has been observed in emerging markets in around 70 per cent of studies and around 50 per cent of studies found a positive ESG-CFP relationship in North American markets.
- Orientation towards long-term investing should be important for investors interested in broader objectives of society.

A report on the future of ESG (SustainAbility Institute, 2022) noted it is likely that ESG functions will be further integrated deeper into business departments, private equity firms will accelerate their focus on ESG, and more businesses will link executive compensation to ESG performance.

━━━━━━━━ **Summary** ━━━━━━━━

- This chapter began with describing key events in the evolution and development of sustainability – that started in the 18th and 19th centuries, gained momentum in the early 1960s, and then rapidly evolved through the latter half of the 20th century. Today, sustainability is acknowledged as a driving force for all business activities.
- The Brundtland report was identified as the most progressive and clear definition of sustainability that acknowledges responsible development for current and future generations.
- After showing that four of the nine planetary boundaries have already been crossed, we identified the three pillars of sustainability – social, environmental, and economic – as the 'common view' of sustainability. This is also known as the Triple Bottom Line.
- We explored the IPAT equation and discussed that the Impact (I) on the environment is related to Population (P) growth multiplied by its level of Affluence (A) multiplied by the Technology (T) that is developed to support the affluence. We discovered that the UN's 17 Sustainable Development Goals can be used by businesses to turn global goals into local business.
- We discussed the phase model of sustainability, in which there are six phases through which a business could develop. At the final phase, a business can get certified as a 'B Corp' that shows achievement of high standards of performance, accountability, and transparency in sustainability.
- Greenhouse gas (GHG) emissions were defined and introduced as the single most important atmospheric cause of climate change. Three types of GHG emissions were identified – Scopes 1, 2, and 3. We discussed that most businesses measure Scopes 1 and 2, whereas Scope 3, which contains the largest amount of GHG emissions, is difficult to measure because it involves emissions from upstream and downstream activities.
- Ethical frameworks – based on ethical concepts and theories that were discussed in earlier chapters – were linked to the principles of sustainability.
- The section on sustainable business practices brought our attention to what businesses can do to make the transition to being sustainable. The incremental and transformational approaches were discussed, types of organisational structures were identified, and actions in the key areas of accounting, finance, marketing, and production were explored.
- A few key future trends in sustainability were discussed – what's required for the fourth industrial revolution, carbon credits and its problems, and learnings from major events such as the Covid-19 pandemic. The chapter concluded with discussing the ESG criteria that have become prominent in businesses moving towards sustainability.

CASE STUDY 7.1

SUSTAINABILITY COMPLEXITIES IN FOOD PRODUCTION AND CONSUMPTION

In a comprehensive report on global GHG emissions, Ritchie et al. (2020) have relied on data from the IPCC's World Resources Institute and the Climate Watch organisation. From Figure 7.4, we can see that almost three-quarters of emissions come from energy use, almost one-fifth from agriculture and land use, and the remaining 8 per cent from industry and waste. Even if we fully decarbonise our electricity supply, we would still have emissions from the other sectors. So, no single solutions will achieve net-zero emissions unless we innovate across many sectors. Of the 18.4 per cent emissions from agriculture, livestock and manure account for 5.8 per cent – this includes animals (for example, cattle and sheep) that produce GHGs when microbes in their digestive systems break down food and produce methane as a by-product. Further nitrous oxide and methane gases are also produced from decomposition of animal manures when a large number of animals are managed in a confined area (such as dairy farms, beef feedlots, swine, and poultry farms), where manure is typically

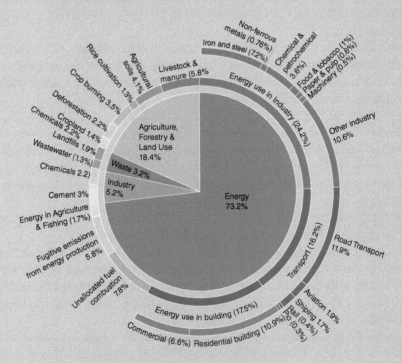

Figure 7.4 Global greenhouse gas emissions by sector

Source: 'Sector by sector: where do global greenhouse gas emissions come from?' by Hannah Ritchie. Published by Our World in Data (September 18 2020). Reproduced with permission

stored in large piles or disposed of in lagoons and other types of manure management. Of the three major types of GHG emissions (carbon dioxide, methane, and nitrous oxide), agriculture is the largest contributor to methane and nitrous oxide emissions. This means that beef and lamb tend to have a high carbon footprint.

In addition, we see that food production is responsible for approximately 26 per cent of global GHG emissions. Of this 31 per cent is from livestock and fisheries, 27 per cent from crop production, 24 per cent from land use, and 18 per cent from supply chains (Poore and Nemecek, 2018). Further, 24 per cent of food emissions come from food that is lost in supply chains or wasted by consumers. This means that food wastage is responsible for around 6 per cent of total global GHG emissions. To put this in context: 'it's around three times the global emissions from aviation. Or, if we were to put it in the context of national emissions, it would be the world's third largest emitter. Only China (21 per cent) and the United States (13 per cent) emitted more' (Ritchie et al., 2020).

Considering that the global population is expected to grow from 8 billion in 2022 to a projected 10 billion in 2050, reducing emissions in the food sector will be a great challenge, more so because food production is essential for society, we need inputs such as fertilisers, and we can't stop cattle from producing methane. Instead, it has been suggested, we need a menu of solutions such as changes to diets, food waste reduction, improvements in agricultural efficiency, and technologies that make low-carbon food alternatives.

Solutions suggested by WRI (2019) – a report sponsored by the World Bank, UNEP, UNDP, and others – include the following:

1   Raise productivity and increase efficiency of natural resource use – for example, crop yields, meat per hectare, per animal, and per kilogram of fertilisers.
2   Manage GHG emissions from manure, nitrogen fertilisers, and energy use.
3   Technological innovations in crop types, improved forms of fertilisers and additives that reduce methane emissions from cattle and rice.
4   Reduce food waste and shift diets of high meat consumers towards plant-based foods.
5   Reduce consumption of ruminant meat (cattle, sheep, and goats) – these livestock use two-thirds of global agricultural land and contribute half of agriculture's production-related emissions.

Of the above, the first three solutions are technology and operations driven and the last two involve lifestyle changes in the general population, which would be much more challenging than the first three. How do we and on what basis can we recommend people to change their diet or reduce their meat consumption? Hooper (2021) suggests the following:

1   Have the price of meat include the environmental cost of producing it.
2   Claims that excessive meat consumption can have negative health effects could be further investigated with sound evidence.
3   Reduced meat consumption could free up land that is currently used to produce grain to feed the animals. Freed-up land can be used to produce protein-rich plant food for humans.

(Continued)

4   It would make a strong argument to reduce meat consumption for the sake of the welfare of future generations (this links into the Brundtland report statement and the inter/intra-generational justice theory).

5   Animal welfare: livestock animals suffer on an industrial scale. Billions of chickens are raised in questionable and appalling conditions, millions of breeding pigs spend most of their lives in crates or in confined spaces, and millions of cattle live in concentrated animal feeding operations. Not only can an argument be made about the suffering of such animals (using ethical theories), but the enormous amount of manure-waste generated from such facilities requires liberal use of antibiotics and other pharmaceuticals to prevent the spread of infection. The possibility of leakage of such wastes into the broader community is also an issue.

6   Animals are inefficient convertors of food. The 'plant to animal conversion efficiency' (measured as the amount of plant material needed to feed an animal to get flesh or product out) is 12 per cent for chicken, 10 per cent for pork, 3 per cent for beef, 40 per cent for milk, and 22 per cent for eggs.

7   Water conservation: producing 1 kilogram of beef production needs 14,415 litres of water, sheep meat needs 10,412 litres, pork 5,988, and chicken meat 4,325 litres. Whereas rice, cabbage, potatoes, and tomatos need 2,500, 237, 287, and 214 litres of water respectively (IME, 2013).

8   Food waste also contributes to GHG emissions. The United Nations estimates globally 14 per cent of food produced is lost between harvest and retail (UN, 2022). The waste happens for different reasons in developed and developing countries. In developed countries, waste occurs at the retail and consumer end – consumers don't like 'crooked' carrots, retailers will upsell with 'three for two' offers, and the 'best before' labels can be confusing. In developing countries, waste happens at the farmers' end – crops are not fully harvested or not properly stored, and farms lack infrastructure to deliver food to the consumer.

9   Hooper (2021) suggests that a better way is to replace animal products altogether with plants. Protein content in meat products averages around 24 grams per 100 grams of meat. Protein in soya ranges from 30 to 45 grams depending on whether it is fresh or dried (Hopkins, 2019). It is estimated that soya bean plants produce 5–10 times more protein than dairy animals on the same amount of land and 15 times more than land used for meat production.

10   A final point is that people need not give up milk or cheese or even chicken or beef to make the change. Small changes such as meat-free days or no-meat-before-6pm are considered to be a great start.

Questions

Using the Case-Study Integrative Framework in Figure 0.1, reflect on the following:

1   Record the amount of different major types of food (meats, eggs, veggies, milk products, etc.) you consume in a week or month. Calculate the total GHG emissions from these foods (using data from sources mentioned in this case study or from your research). What do you conclude from this data?

2 Do you think there is a convincing argument to change food consumption habits?

3 What are the ethical issues in this case study?

4 Use the CEDM model from earlier chapters to develop your analysis, judgement, commitment, and potential actions?

5 What specific actions will you take to help mitigate agriculture-related emissions?

6 What do you think should be done locally and globally to reduce GHG emissions from agriculture, especially food-related livestock?

Sources:
Hooper (2021)
Hopkins (2019)
IEF (2013)
Poore and Nemecek (2018)
Ritchie et al. (2020)
UN (2022)
WRI (2019)

CASE STUDY 7.2
RARE EARTH METALS, BATTERIES, AND ELECTRIC VEHICLES

Some call it the 'next oil of the 21st century'. Human beings' quest for resources for energy generation has so far produced 'rare' metals such as gold, silver, copper, lead, and aluminium. But from the 1970s, we have turned our sights to the highly magnetic, catalytic, and optical properties of lesser-known clusters of rare metals found in infinitesimally small amounts in terrestrial rocks. They also happen to have the potential to contribute to a more sustainable world (Pitron, 2020). There are 17 rare earth elements (REE) ranging from atomic numbers 21, 39, and 57 to 71 in the periodic table. Other elements used in such applications are lithium and cobalt.

Reducing the consumption of non-renewable energy sources and the emissions from them has led to innovations in 'green energy' technologies such as wind turbines and electric vehicles (EVs). Wind turbines account for 4.1 per cent of electricity generation worldwide and the industry is expected to grow. Up to 600 kilograms of rare earth metals are required to operate just one wind turbine (Pozo-Gonzalo, 2021). Global sales of EVs rose by 43 per cent in 2020 as compared to 2019, and it is estimated there will be around 500 million EVs in 20 years. China dominates EV sales with around a 36 per cent share of the global market, followed by Europe (20 per cent), the US (14 per cent), and other countries (30 per cent) (Golroudbary et al., 2022).

(Continued)

The electric motors that power EVs and the generators of wind turbines use 'permanent magnets' which are manufactured using four REEs: neodymium (Nd), dysprosium (Dy), praseodymium (Pr), and terbium (Tb) (Dias et al., 2020). The batteries that power EVs use five types of minerals: lithium (Li), nickel (Ni), cobalt (Co), manganese (Mn), and graphite (a form of carbon).

As the largest supplier of REEs in the world, China satisfies over 80 per cent of the global REE demand. This has come at a huge environmental cost to China. Foreign consumption contributed to over half of the environmental costs from China's REE production, with East Asia (mainly Japan and Korea) the largest contributor to the export-induced environmental costs, followed by North America, and other countries (Zhang et al., 2022). Annual demand for REEs has doubled in the last 15 years and is expected to reach 315,000 tonnes by 2030 (Pozo-Gonzalo, 2021).

REEs, extracted through mining, have two major issues. Firstly, they are costly and inefficient because extracting a small amount requires large areas to be mined – for example, eight and half tonnes of rock need to be purified to produce one kilogram of vanadium, 16 tonnes for cerium, and around 1,200 tonnes for lutecium (Pitron, 2020: 3–4). Secondly, their production generates air pollutants, wastewater, and waste residues which can pollute surface water, ground water, farmland, and the atmosphere, causing both social and environmental harm (Zhang et al., 2022). There is evidence that an increase by 1 per cent of green energy production causes a depletion of REEs reserves by 0.18 per cent and increases GHG emissions in the exploitation phase by 0.90 per cent. It has been shown that between 2010 and 2020, the use of permanent magnets has resulted cumulatively in 32 billion tonnes CO_2-equivalent of GHG emissions globally (Golroudbary et al., 2022).

The two methods of REE mining – removing the topsoil and creating a leaching pond where chemicals are added to the extracted earth to separate the REEs – and drilling holes to insert pipes and hoses to pump chemicals into the earth both produce huge amounts of toxic waste with high risk of environmental and health hazards. Some REE ores could be laced with radioactive thorium and uranium (Nayar, 2021).

There are studies that show GHG emissions from producing EVs and fuel cell electric vehicles (FCEV, which use hydrogen cells) are equal to half of the emissions from producing internal combustion engine vehicles (ICEV, that run on petrol or diesel) (Ahmadi, 2019), and that CO_2 emissions associated with EVs over the vehicle's entire life cycle were substantially lower than those of the ICEV (Franzò and Nasca, 2021).

However, in another study, Bicer and Dincer (2018) showed that EVs and plug-in hybrid EVs result in higher toxicity, terrestrial ecotoxicity, and acidification values because of their manufacturing and maintenance phases. In contrast, hydrogen vehicles (FCEVs) yielded the most environmentally benign option.

To ensure sustainability of the REE processes, Asher (2022) suggests:

1   To guard against natural, socio-economic, and political disruptions, make the green tech supply chain (that includes REEs) sustainable by finding new sources.
2   Develop technologies that will enable replacing, reusing, and recycling REEs as much as possible.

3   Develop new technologies to make mining less environmentally destructive.

4   Redesign products such as wind turbines and EVs with a circular economy approach.

On the one hand, clean green energy is already manifesting in technologies such as wind turbines and EVs. The future seems to be heading towards electricity generation from clean renewable sources. REEs are an integral part of this process. On the other hand, there are environmental impacts in communities where REE mining occurs. It is ironic that to solve environmental problems, companies are using methods that damage the environment further (Nayar, 2021).

Questions

Using the Case-Study Integrative Framework in Figure 0.1, discuss the following:

1   What are the ethical issues in this case study? Consider the following:

   a   Who benefits from REE mining?
   b   Who experiences its negative effects?

2   If REE mining creates more environmental harm than it supposedly mitigates the climate problem, do you think there is an issue with their 'purpose'?

3   Do you think new innovations are needed to substitute REEs? Or a new way to extract REEs without the potential environmental harms?

4   Analyse the case study from the 'three pillars' approach and the IPAT equation approach. What do you conclude?

5   Since most of the REEs are sourced (currently) from Asian and African developing countries for use in products designed, produced, and consumed in developed countries, what are the ethical implications?

6   Since communities where REEs are mined also benefit from the green technology, should they just accept the social and environmental costs as a trade-off? Justify your answer.

7   Use the CEDM model from earlier chapters to develop your analysis, judgement, commitment, and potential actions.

Sources:

Ahmadi (2019)

Asher (2022)

Bicer and Dincer (2018)

Dias et al. (2020)

Franzò and Nasca (2021)

Golroudbary et al. (2022)

Nayar (2021)

Pitron (2020)

Pozo-Gonzalo (2021)

Zhang et al. (2022)

─────**─Recommended readings─**──────────────────────────

Benn, S., Edwards, M. and Williams, T. (2018), *Organizational change for corporate sustainability*, 4th edn, Abingdon: Routledge.

A trailblazing book on corporate sustainability provides new insights into how organisations can transition towards a more responsible way of conducting their business. The phase model approach makes this a core reading.

Friede, G., Busch, T. and Bassen, A. (2015), 'ESG and financial performance: Aggregated evidence from more than 2000 empirical studies', *Journal of Sustainable Finance & Investment*, 5(4): 210–33.

A study that combines 2200 individual studies that shows how the business case for ESG investing is well founded: 90 per cent of studies found a positive relationship between ESG and corporate financial performance.

Golroudbary, S.R., Makarava, I., Kraslawski, A. and Repo, E. (2022), 'Global environmental cost of using rare earth elements in green energy technologies', *The Science of the Total Environment*, 832: 155022.

This is the first global analysis of the environmental impact of using rare earth elements in green energy technologies. While there's evidence of increasing GHG emissions from this process, the article highlights the need to design and implement measures to support appropriate strategies to decarbonise green energy technologies.

Hertwich, E.G. and Wood, R. (2018), 'The growing importance of Scope 3 greenhouse gas emissions from industry', *Environmental Research Letters*, 13(10): 104013.

A good resource to understand the GHG protocol of Scope 1, 2, and 3. In focus is the unknown magnitude of Scope 2 and 3. The study also shows the growing emissions of all three scopes (especially Scope 3).

Liute, A. and De Giacomo, M.R. (2022), 'The environmental performance of UK-based B Corp companies: An analysis based on the Triple Bottom Line approach', *Business Strategy and the Environment*, 31(3): 810–27.

A good resource to understand the motion of the B Corp certification process. This study also analyses the environmental performances of 64 UK-based B Corps from the manufacturing and wholesale/retail sectors (two prominent environmentally sensitive sectors).

Purvis, B., Mao, Y. and Robinson, D. (2019), 'Three pillars of sustainability: In search of conceptual origins', *Sustainability Science*, 14: 681–95.

This article identifies the genesis and foundations of the three pillars of sustainability (social, environmental and economic) – it provides a good understanding of the concepts.

Steffen, W., Richardson, K., Rockström, J., Cornell, S., Fetzer, I., Bennett, E., Biggs, R. and de Vries, W. (2015), 'Planetary boundaries: Guiding human development on a changing planet', *Science (American Association for the Advancement of Science)*, 347(6223): 736.

This article provides a good understanding of the nine planetary boundaries and their significance in terms of the risk that crossing the boundaries could destabilise the earth systems at the planetary scale.

8

CORPORATE SOCIAL RESPONSIBILITY AND WORLD BENEFIT

On completion of this chapter, you should be able to:

- Discuss the relationship between business ethics and corporate social responsibility (CSR)
- Define and understand the concepts of CSR
- Explore the historical evolution of CSR from the 1950s to the present
- Understand how CSR can be operationalised
- Discover CSR operations in tourism, SMEs, the fashion industry, and stakeholder management
- Understand the concepts of inclusive business and the bottom of the pyramid
- Explain how businesses can be agents for world benefit
- Understand how corporate social innovation (CSI) works
- Understand the operations of social entrepreneurship

- CSR
- Bottom of the pyramid
- Business as agents of world benefit
- CSI
- Social entrepreneurship

—Box 8.1 Opening case—

Global and local social responsibility

Businesses, large and small, global and local, are realising and acknowledging that their actions must be aligned with addressing the world's pressing problems and not creating new ones. Specifically, businesses are understanding their place in society and that they need innovation and entrepreneurship to help deliver their social responsibility.

This opening case covers two organisations, a multinational company and a local SME – Microsoft Corporation and Clothing the Gaps, respectively.

Microsoft

Microsoft Corporation, best known for its products such as the Windows operating system, the Office suite, the Internet Explorer and Edge browsers, Xbox game consoles, and Surface PCs, is one of the Big Five American IT companies alongside Alphabet (Google's parent company), Amazon, Apple, and Meta (formerly Facebook).

With more than 220,000 direct employees and more than 400,000 partner organisations employing over 22 million people worldwide that include suppliers and customers of every size in every industry, Microsoft recognises that they have an enormous opportunity and responsibility to effect change through this social ecosystem.

Some notable initiatives and actions of Microsoft that highlight their social responsibilities include:

- Empowering their own employees to create an inclusive culture where everyone can thrive. During the period July 1, 2021 and June 30, 2022, Microsoft employees have completed diversity and inclusion courses, donated USD 255 million to 32,000 non-profits in 88 countries, and volunteered over 720,000 hours to causes they care about.
- Enabling access to skills for jobs in the digital economy by helping, training, and enabling learning digital skills in high schools and communities, especially for those who are historically disadvantaged because of belonging to a racial or ethnic group.
- Empowering organisations with AI and data science to help improve the health of people and communities.
- Increasing access to data for non-profits, universities, companies, and governments.
- Protecting human rights, fair immigration, and preserving cultural heritage in their supply chain and in the general population.
- Helping artisans use the internet to sell their products to the world – for example, Microsoft Airband partnered with the Avina Foundation to bring broadband access and internet training to 1,600 Pilaga Indigenous community women from the remote South American region of Gran Chaco to find a global market for their products.
- Addressing racial injustice and inequity experienced by African American communities.

In addition, Microsoft uses global standards such as the Sustainable Accounting Standards Board, UN SDGs, GRI, and the **Greenhouse Gas Protocol**. The company supports all 17 SDGs but focuses mainly on four: Goal 4 – Quality Education; Goal 8 – Decent Work and Economic Growth; Goal 13 – Climate Action; and Goal 16 – Peace, Justice, and Strong Institutions.

Clothing the Gaps

Australian Aboriginal owned and led streetwear label Clothing the Gaps operates as a social enterprise and commits a majority of its profits to the Clothing the Gaps Foundation. As an independent not-for-profit, the Clothing the Gaps Foundation is supported by not only the sales of merchandise through the label, but by donations and other independent funders. The Foundation is an independent Aboriginal-led not-for-profit run by public health practitioners.

They exist to get Aboriginal people and communities moving so that years are added to Aboriginal people's lives. Currently the life expectancy gap between Indigenous and non-Indigenous people in Australia is still too large. For the Aboriginal and Torres Strait Islander population born in 2015–2017, males can expect to live to the age of 71.6 years and females to the age of 75.6 years. This is 8.6 years lower than that of non-Indigenous males and 7.8 years lower for non-Indigenous females born in 2015–2017.

At the heart of the Clothing the Gaps Foundation lie the values of elevating, educating, advocating, and motivating people for positive change. These values are put into action by creating events, programmes, resources, and spaces to:

- *Elevate*, represent, and promote Aboriginal voices and excellence to further enable Aboriginal people to celebrate their identity and visibility in the world.
- *Educate* and start conversations with the wider Australian population about causes or issues affecting Aboriginal Australia. To promote reconciliation and welcome non-Indigenous people to learn about, celebrate, and support Aboriginal Australia.
- *Motivate* people and activate Aboriginal communities to make positive lifestyle choices and be healthier in their mind, body, and spirit through Mob Run This.
- *Advocate* and campaign for social change on issues impacting on Aboriginal people and their communities.

Acknowledging that physical activity is important because positive lifestyle habits play a key role in achieving and maintaining health and well-being, the organisation aims to increase Aboriginal physical activity participation in the following ways:

- Clothing the Gaps put on fun runs, supporting Aboriginal organisations and groups to use the event to run their own community initiatives and get moving in their own way.
- 'Mob Run This' has a double meaning, talking to not only the physical definition of getting mob active and 'running', but also the importance of having Aboriginal

(Continued)

and Torres Strait Islander people being the drivers in their own communities to deliver and create opportunities for their mob and therefore defining the need for mob to 'run this'. 'Mob' is a colloquial term identifying a group of Aboriginal people.

- 'Trad Games' that provides a unique opportunity for an activity using Traditional Aboriginal Games as the foundation for health, wellness, and human connection, including having important conversations about health and well-being. Playing Traditional Aboriginal Games enables ways to stay active, learn more about Aboriginal history, and celebrate culture whilst increasing conversations around reconciliation. These sessions are available to all kinds of groups – Aboriginal organisations and community groups, schools, kindergartens, and corporate groups.

Questions

1   Why are large companies such as Microsoft taking such global steps to showcase their social responsibility actions?
2   Why are small organisations such as the Clothing the Gaps motivated to contribute to the society that they live in?
3   Do you think these companies are doing the right things? Justify your answer.
4   Have you come across other similar companies (large and small) who exhibit such responsibilities in your communities?
5   Are there examples of businesses (large and small) who do not engage in such activities in your communities? Discuss.

Sources:
Wiki (2022j)
Microsoft (2022)
CTGF (2022)
CTG (2022)
AIHW (2022)

8.1 Introduction

What motivates large and small businesses like Microsoft and Clothing the Gaps to actively engage in socially responsible activities to ensure they are having a positive impact on their communities? Can we identify specific types of innovations and entrepreneur qualities in such engagements? Do these initiatives raise questions about the intention and authenticity of companies engaged in CSR? As we shall see in this chapter, there are diverse views – are businesses 'truly' socially responsible or do they engage in CSR only to enhance their marketing capabilities?

In earlier chapters, we have seen how and why businesses behave ethically or unethically through various theories, concepts, and cases. Specifically, in Chapter 7, we discussed the somewhat broad concepts of sustainability and ESG. Here, in Chapter 8, we proceed to show the positive actions that businesses are taking in society. There are two main sections, on corporate social responsibility (CSR), and businesses as agents of world benefit (BAWB). The second section is further sub-sectioned into corporate social innovation (CSI) and social entrepreneurship (SE).

8.2 Corporate social responsibility

Relationship between business ethics and corporate social responsibility

Do concepts in business ethics (BE) and CSR mean the same thing? For example, when we apply Freeman's normative stakeholder theory (see Chapter 2) to be one of the 'bedrocks' of BE, we suggest that businesses are 'morally' responsible to look after the interests and concerns of not just the shareholders, but also of a larger group that include customers, suppliers, employees, owners, and community. In addition, we have suggested that businesses can have a competitive advantage and also be responsible for the three pillars of sustainability, social, environment, and economy (see Chapter 7). CSR (as we shall see later) also operates on the concept that businesses are obliged to meet their responsibilities to stakeholders, specifically employees (their own and of their supply chain), the community in which they operate, and larger society. So, is CSR a subset of BE? Is CSR a means (the policies and actions) to an end (to achieve responsibilities and competitive advantages)? Would compliance with all the norms and regulations of CSR practice necessarily mean that the business entity is also following sound BE practices? Are the activities of the firm in the context of CSR and BE necessarily correlated?

BE and CSR can be evaluated for both a normative and descriptive perspective. The descriptive perspective explains or predicts the existence of a phenomenon, whereas normative perspectives explain what ought or should be done (as discussed in Chapter 3). Table 8.1 shows the relationship between BE and CSR using the above-mentioned two perspectives.

Table 8.1 Evaluation of BE and CSR from normative and descriptive perspectives

	Normative perspectives	Descriptive perspectives
Business ethics	• Relates to principles, values, and norms for organisational decision.	• Refers to codes, standards of conduct, compliance systems that typically relate to decisions that can be judged right or wrong by stakeholders such as customers. • Ethical decision-making (see Chapter 4) in organisations can impact internal and external stakeholders.

(Continued)

Table 8.1 (Continued)

	Normative perspectives	Descriptive perspectives
Corporate social responsibility	• Focuses on values and principles for fulfilling economic, legal, ethical, and philanthropic responsibilities. • CSR issues are associated with evaluations of concepts such as social issues, sustainability, consumer protection, corporate governance, and legal issues.	• Social responsibility can be legalised through laws and regulations. • CSR is associated with positive or negative impact on stakeholders. • Leaders can make decisions about how to deal with stakeholders that have CSR outcomes.

Source: Adapted from Ferrell et al. (2019), 'Business ethics, corporate social responsibility, and brand attitudes: An exploratory study', *Journal of Business Research*, 95: 491–501

One of the prominent areas where BE and CSR can be observed is customers' attitudes towards ethical products and ethical consumption. There is evidence that shows customer preference of brands promoted through social responsibility and business ethics, for example TOMS, the organisation that began donating a pair of shoes for every pair they sold and later decided to give impact grants by donating one-third of their profits (TOMS, 2022). Ethical products or brands are usually identified as doing something good for society or the consumer such as organic ingredients, vegan diet, animal welfare, or fair trade. However, a product attribute such as performance can be perceived as more important than an ethical product. In their study of 351 respondents, Ferrell et al. (2019) conclude that although CSR attitudes are important, customers value business ethics as critical behaviour in their perceptions of brand attitudes. CSR was viewed as incremental, but BE is required by establishing rules that are mandatory or essential before purchasing a brand.

Definitions of CSR

We will first need to understand what each of the words in CSR stands for. 'Corporate' refers to all forms of business organisations – large, medium, and small. 'Social' refers to human society or the welfare of a community, and encompasses states, nations, and the world. Society includes the full array of stakeholders including other living organisms such as animals, plants, and the natural environment. 'Responsibility' refers to idea that businesses should be held accountable for their actions that emanate from power, control, or management (Carroll and Brown, 2018).

Although the notion or the phenomenon of CSR is widely understood, there is uncertainty in both the corporate and academic world about the definition of CSR. A concise definition proposed by Frederick (2018: 4) is: 'CSR occurs when a business firm consciously and deliberately acts to enhance the social well-being of those whose lives are affected by the firm's economic operations'. Using three methodological approaches in defining CSR: (1) academic literature review including definitions used by business, (2) conducting interviews, and (3) theoretical reasoning that combines literature review and philosophical analysis, Dahlsrud (2008) found 37 definitions of CSR from 27 authors. Five dimensions were used to categorise the definitions: environmental, social, economic, stakeholder, and voluntariness.

Forty per cent of the definitions contained all five dimensions and 97 per cent of the definitions contained three or more dimensions.

The definition from the World Business Council for Sustainable Development had four of the above dimensions:

> [CSR is] the continuing commitment by business to behave ethically and contribute to economic development while improving the quality of life of the workforce and their families as well as of the local community and society at large.

The definition from the EU subgroup had all five of the above dimensions and elaborates further on the understanding of CSR (EU-CSR, 2011):

> CSR is the process whereby enterprises integrate social, environmental, ethical, and human rights concerns into their core strategy, operations, and integrated performance, in close collaboration with their stakeholders, with the aim of:
>
> • maximising the creation of shared value for their owners/shareholders and for their other stakeholders and society at large.
> • identifying, preventing, and mitigating their possible adverse impacts.

In a further attempt to analyse issues relating to the definitions of CSR, Orlitzky et al. (2011) have noted that a consensus seems to be emerging that CSR can be strategic (by providing benefits to the firm), altruistic (by being philanthropic), and coerced (in the form of a regulatory mechanism).

Performance of businesses can be affected by both market and non-market strategies and environments. Measurement of success in both types of strategies is corporate financial performance (CFP). Market strategies are attributed to developing new products, entering new markets (domestic and foreign), marketing tactics, and financial strategies. While these are critical for success, non-market strategies are now considered equally if not even more important. One metric that can measure non-marketing strategies is corporate social performance (CSP). CSP involves a business's principles of social responsibility, processes of social responsiveness, and policies, programmes, and outcomes (Orlitzky et al., 2003). In searching for a causal relationship between CSP and CFP (whether they are positively related) in a meta-data analysis of 52 studies with a sample size of 33,878, Orlitzky et al. (2003), found that higher CSP can result in higher CFP. Further, CSP appears to be highly correlated with accounting-based measures (such as ROA, ROE, or EPS) of CFP than with market-based indicators (such as price per share or share price appreciation).

Historical developments in CSR

At the end of the 19th century and beginning of the 20th century, social problems, emanating from the Industrial Revolution that saw a shift from an artisan work-model to mass production, forced companies to address issues such as labour rights and safety. This could be considered as the beginnings of CSR.

Some key defining moments of the evolution of CSR are shown below, compiled from Carroll (2008; Carroll and Brown, 2022), Frederick (2018), Latapí Agudelo et al. (2019), and Rodriguez-Gomez et al. (2020). CSR phases 1 to 4 were designated by Frederick (2018).

1950s to 1960s – CSR-1 phase: Corporate social stewardship

When the capitalist model of profit maximisation and market self-regulation was at its peak, negligent actions by companies violated human and labour rights. Society demanded more responsible action by companies and the United Nations set into motion a number of institutional initiatives such as the Universal Declaration of Human Rights in 1948 (UDHR). Although not legally binding, the contents of the UDHR have been elaborated and incorporated into subsequent international treaties, regional human rights instruments, and national constitutions and legal codes.

- Abrams (1951) argued that companies should make commitments beyond obtaining profits and should consider their employees, customers, and the public.
- Bowen (1953), also known as the father of CSR, in his book *Social Responsibilities of the Businessman*, defined CSR as obligations of employers related to actions that respond to the values and needs of society.
- Bowen (1953) also defined Social Responsibility as decisions and actions taken by business for reasons beyond the firm's direct economic or technical interest.

1970s – CSR-2 phase: Corporate social responsiveness

A number of social movements played a key role in introducing environmental civil rights, and women's rights issues into companies. Key social movements were the American Indian Movement, gay rights, women's liberation, equal rights amendments, environmental movements (for example, the first Earth Day and EPAs), and anti-war protests (against the Vietnam war) (Hall, 2008; Wiki, 2022c; Yeo, 2020).

- Harold Johnson in 1971 (as noted by Carroll, 1999) presented CSR as (1) driven by an enterprise responsible for its employees, suppliers, dealers, local communities, and the nation; (2) businesses carrying out social programmes to add profits to their organisation, (3) seeking multiple goals rather than only profit maximisation, (4) where strongly profit-motivated firms engage in socially responsible behaviour.
- The Committee for Economic Development suggested three concentric circles to define social responsibility: the inner circle of economic function; the intermediate circle of environmental conservation, employee relations, information, fair treatment, and safety for customers; and the outer circle of more broadly improving the social environment.
- Davis (1973) debated the case for and against social responsibilities of business. On the one hand (against) was the famous argument of Milton Friedman (more fully discussed in Chapter 2) that the only social responsibility of a business is to make

profits for its shareholders. On the other hand (for) was the idea that businesses need to go beyond the narrow economic, technical, and legal requirements, and engage in social responsibility.

- Sethi (1975) introduced the dimensions of CSP in which social responsiveness is seen as the adaptation of corporate behaviour to social needs.
- Fitch (1976) defined CSR as an attempt to solve social problems caused wholly or in part by the corporation.
- Carroll (1979) proposed that the social responsibility of business encompasses the economic, legal, ethical, and discretionary expectations.

1980s to 1990s – CSR-3 phase: Corporate/business ethics

Recognition and concerns about the impact of human actions developed by companies on society and the environment led to CSR policies to improve the image and reputation of companies.

- An empirical study by Cochran and Wood (1984) showed early signs of academic interest to ascertain whether socially responsible firms were also profitable.
- Epstein (1987) pointed out that social responsibility, responsiveness, and business ethics are closely related, with overlapping themes and concerns.
- Carroll (1991) further elaborated that total CSR (constituting four kinds of social responsibilities: economic, legal, ethical, and philanthropic), can be depicted as a pyramid – with the economic category as the base and then building upwards through the other three categories.
- In a survey of 50 academic leaders, Carroll (1994) observed that the leaders ranked CSP (that included CSR) as the fourth most important issue for research, after business ethics, international social issues, and business and society social issues.

1990s to 2000s – CSR-4 phase: Corporate/global citizenship

With rapid globalisation, the internet, and environment and ecology issues awareness, CSR became a fundamental element in companies' responses to various social needs. Initially, CSR actions were voluntary but later with institutionally driven codes of good practice CSR became integrated into business strategies as part of their core business. In a literature review, Latapí Agudelo et al. (2019: 1) showed that 'the understanding of corporate responsibility has evolved from being limited to the generation of profit to include a broader set of responsibilities to the latest belief that the main responsibility of companies should be the generation of shared value'. Porter and Kramer (2011) explained the need for creating shared value focusing on the connections between societal and economic progress. They claimed 'creating shared value' should replace CSR. Prominent thinking was in the areas of the business case for CSR, strategic CSR, implicit versus explicit CSR, and political CSR (Carroll and Brown, 2022). Business is now being seen as an agent for world benefit (discussed later in this chapter).

Operationalising CSR

The four-part definition proposed by Carroll (1979; 1999), as mentioned earlier, pointed to the operationalisation of CSR. Carroll posited that 'the social responsibility of business encompasses the economic, legal, ethical, and discretionary (philanthropic) expectations that society has of organisations at a given time' (1979: 500). Firstly, the economic component refers to society's expectation of business to produce goods and services at a profit. Secondly, society expects businesses to fulfil its economic component within the legal framework of where it operates. Thirdly, society expects businesses to follow certain kinds of behaviours and ethical norms with practices that are beyond what is required by the law. Finally, businesses are expected to engage in social roles at their discretion, not be mandated or required by law to do so (Carroll, 1999). In recent years, several researchers have suggested stakeholder engagement as a process for operationalising CSR (see Lane and Devin, 2018 for details). The following sections highlight the operationalisation of CSR in some key areas.

CSR and SME

Considering that SMEs reflect a considerable share of the global economy, it would be prudent to assume that SMEs would need to apply CSR practices into their business operations. Social entrepreneurship (discussed in a section later in this chapter) is considered as the first attempt to introduce CSR to the SME segment (Belas et al., 2021). SME social enterprises, being necessarily local community businesses, meet their social objectives through innovative approaches (social innovation is discussed in a later section). In a study of 1,585 SMEs, Belas et al. (2021) confirmed that the knowledge of the CSR concept and its implementation by entrepreneurs positively affects the perception of SMEs' sustainability. In particular, 'by adopting CSR practices and activities, SMEs may attract more customers, become more innovative, and avoid bankruptcy. These three elements together give a sense over the business sustainability in general' (p. 728).

CSR and tourism

Firms are seen to be adopting sustainable forms of tourism such as eco-tourism, green tourism, environmentally friendly travel, and alternative tourism. To reduce negative impacts, the tourism industry has increasingly adopted CSR initiatives, such as improving employees' lives, contributing to regional communities, and preserving the environment. CSR practices also include reducing waste and enhancing sustainable use of limited natural resources (Madanaguli et al., 2022). A study by Madanaguli et al. (2022) identified 669 articles on this subject. Their findings suggest that:

- CSR has become a pertinent factor in the success and growth of tourism.
- There is a need to involve key internal stakeholders such as employees, understand their roles, and their potential to increase the visibility of CSR initiatives.
- External stakeholders such as customers exhibit their willingness to participate in CSR activities and therefore should be involved.
- More research is needed involving stakeholders such as communities, ecosystems, suppliers, governments, and NGOs.

CSR and the fashion/garment industry

There is criticism that standardisation in the fashion industry, which is one of the world's largest industries, has led to unsustainable actions focusing on low-cost production at high production rates. Accusations are usually linked to its high ecological footprint resulting from 'fast fashion' and a 'throwaway culture' that involves mass production, labour abuses, and certain marketing methods. New clothes are discarded when they fall out of fashion. Every second, a truckload of textiles goes to landfill or is incinerated (Thorisdottir and Johannsdottir, 2020). Although there is awareness of sustainability issues within this industry, CSR practices seem to be lacking. Applying the micro-meso-macro framework, 'sustainable development is seen as a societal concept at the macro level, corporate sustainability is identified as a corporate concept at the meso level, and CSR is recognised as a management approach at a micro level, including systems such as ISO standards' (p. 5). To understand the relationship between sustainability and CSR in the fashion business, Thorisdottir and Johannsdottir (2020) conducted a systematic literature review of 209 academic papers that cover 16 years from 2003 to 2019. Key findings include:

- The implications of outsourcing production to countries where environmental and social standards are weak. Implications include reputational risk and poor performance that may affect their ability to gain competitive advantage.
- Problems of sweatshops related to workers' rights and labour conditions. Issues identified here were lack of training, knowledge, management commitment, lack of standards and regulations, consumer awareness, overall concern for improving brand image, and reputation of the fashion industry.
- The focus on CSR and sustainability in the fashion industry can be seen in all three levels, micro, meso, and macro, as shown in Table 8.2.

Table 8.2 Focus on CSR and sustainability in the fashion industry

Level	CSR focus	Sustainability focus
Micro (individual level including behaviours and habits of tourism consumers)	Corporations, organisations, and structure	Consumption, design, and measures
Meso (intermediate sized organisations or institutions forming structures for efficiency and knowledge)	Communication, ethics, social issues, stakeholders, and values	Entrepreneurship, pollution, and social sustainability
Macro (broad tourist patterns based on cultural or social trends, how people travel and consume)	Labour, activism, culture, human rights	Regulation, resource structures, and technology

Source: Adapted from Thorisdottir and Johannsdottir (2020), 'Corporate social responsibility influencing sustainability within the fashion industry: A systematic review', *Sustainability*, 12(21): 9167

In recent decades, multinational garment corporations have faced criticism over workers' rights violations, wage theft, gender-based violence, unsafe working conditions and dangerous levels of productivity, and infringements on freedom of association. This has resulted in sustained pressure from civil society, unions, workers, and policymakers to address these issues. One of the major issues is to pay living wages within their supply chain. Living wages provide sufficient income to cover essentials such as food, housing, and medical care, and can help prevent abuse such as forced labour. Most MNCs in this industry have made commitments to pay living wages. However, a recent investigation into whether MNCs action their commitments revealed interesting findings. LeBaron et al. (2022) studied a sample of 20 MNCs with significant influence in sourcing and retail markets across key sectors such as sportswear, fast fashion, luxury fashion, and online-only retail. They found that companies are:

- Making only modest changes and are insufficiently addressing low wages.
- Outsourcing their living-wage commitments to organisations that lack robust enforcement mechanisms.
- Diluting and distorting the definition of 'living wage', thus enabling suppliers to continue paying non-living wages.
- Making limited progress towards achieving living wages.

CSR reporting

CSR reporting is defined and understood as the measurement, disclosure, and communication of information about CSR and sustainability topics, including a firm's CSR/ESG activities, risks, and policies (Christensen et al., 2021). CSR reporting standards govern how to report and disclose such information. Firms usually include CSR information in their annual report or in a separate CSR report. It can contain a broad range of qualitative and quantitative information. CSR reports are normally certified by an auditor or an external assurance provider. The scope of the reporting is confined to the information deemed relevant for investors and/or providing information to a diverse set of stakeholders such as consumers, employees, or local communities. This can include their impacts on the environment and society such as CO_2 emissions. The Christensen et al. (2021) study on relevant academic literature in accounting, finance, economics, and management provide the following insights into CSR reporting:

- More and better CSR information can benefit capital markets and can change firm behaviour.
- Voluntary CSR reporting is similar to voluntary financial reporting.
- Mandatory CSR reporting has the potential to improve information to investors and other stakeholders and induces firms to make changes to their business operations.
- There are several implementation issues such as the CSR standards setting process, determining which information is important to whom, and enforcement of CSR standards.
- Enforcement plays a central role if a CSR reporting mandate is to have economic effects.

Developing countries have taken big steps towards engaging the private sector in social development. India amended its Companies Act 2013 to make it mandatory for companies with a net worth of INR 500 crore (USD 60 million) or more, or a turnover of INR 1,000 crore (USD 120 million) or more, or a net profit of INR 5 crore (USD 600,000) or more, to create a CSR committee. The Act mandates that at least 2 per cent of the average net profits made during the three immediately preceding financial years are spent in pursuance of the company's CSR policy (British Council, 2016; ICNL, 2022; MCA, 2022).

In African countries, there is a growing realisation that home-grown solutions are required to tackle Africa's grand challenges – rather than depending on Western investors and philanthropists (Adeleye et al., 2020). The Agenda 2063 of the African Union provides details of 20 goals and priority areas linked to the 17 SDGs. The intention is to achieve the vision of an integrated, prosperous, and peaceful Africa, driven by its own citizens, by the year 2063 (AU, 2022). At the core of this vision is self-reliance and self-sufficiency led by philanthropy and social entrepreneurship, driven by individual citizens and business organisations, and rooted in the African values of collective responsibility (see more of these concepts in Chapter 5). This is termed African mutual social responsibility, similar to the contemporary concept of CSR (Muthuri and Gilbert, 2011: 478–9).

CSR and stakeholder engagement

In a study of data from nine companies, Lane and Devin (2018) proposed a model of operationalising stakeholder engagement. Their research purpose was to determine the applicability of the general model of stakeholder engagement to the specific context of CSR. Seven of the nine organisations revealed that their CSR reports had been written to meet regulatory requirements. Six organisations mentioned responding to stakeholder concerns as the reason for developing their CSR reports. However, there was not enough detail in the information provided in the organisations' CSR reports about the process of engagement. From their research, Lane and Devin (2018) propose the following process as a model:

- Step 1: Identification and selection of stakeholders – consideration to be given to issues raised by all stakeholders, not just those of the investors and governments.
- Step 2: Securing stakeholder interest – arousing the interest of targeted stakeholders that appeals to their fears, self-interest, and ethical concerns.
- Step 3: Implementation – input strategy, method, and outcome.
- Step 4: Legitimisation of decisions and processes – achieved through assurance reports.

CSR, inclusive business, and the bottom of the pyramid

While CSR concerns itself with firms being socially responsible in a broad sense, inclusive business focuses on proactive engagement with poor people in the core operations of the business (Curtis and Bradly, 2022: 214). Additionally, it involves the poor in the value chain on business. This would include involving the poor in as many segments of the supply chain as possible – design, production, supply, logistics, wholesale and retail, and equally importantly consumption. To be called inclusive, the business has to focus on low-income countries with weak institutional environments, where the poor have no or limited access to basic services like sanitation, clean water, health, and education. Further, inclusive business should be part of the core business of a firm (and not philanthropy) and should be in the private sector that includes MNCs and SMEs alike (Curtis and Bradly, 2022: 215).

The people described above are typically referred to as the 'bottom of the pyramid' (BoP), a term proposed by Prahalad and Hart (2002) and Prahalad and Hammond (2002). From

Figure 8.1, the BoP are defined as people in Tier-4 and Tier-5 living on USD 2–10 per day and less than USD 2 per day respectively, comprising approximately 5.2 billion people or 71 per cent of the world's population. The majority of the BoP population is in China, India, and Brazil and the global market opportunity in the BoP is estimated to be around USD 5 trillion (Hammond et al., 2007: 3).

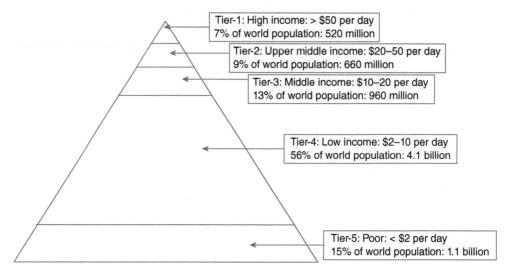

Figure 8.1   The economic pyramid showing Tiers 4 and 5 as the bottom of the pyramid

Source: Adapted from Prahalad (2005), *The Fortune at the bottom of the pyramid: Eradicating poverty through profits*, Upper Saddle River, NJ: Pearson Education Inc.

In his seminal book *The Fortune at the Bottom of the Pyramid: Eradicating Poverty through Profits*, Prahalad (2005) proposed that 'if we stop thinking of the poor as victims or as a burden and start recognising them as resilient and creative entrepreneurs and value-conscious consumers, a whole new world of opportunity will open up' (p. 1). He suggested a better approach to help the poor should involve partnering with them to innovate, achieve sustainable scenarios, actively engage the poor, and also ensure the companies serving them are profitable. Rather than ignoring the poor, ensure that they can participate in the benefits of globalisation. To cater to the BoP markets, private-sector firms would need new innovations as part of their core business. A systematic review of the literature over the last 20 years (during a surge of academic publications related to BoP) indicates a sustained and growing interest in BoP. In a study of 665 publications, Khandker (2022) found that in the first decade, BoP research focused mainly on ethics, CSR, and management, followed by marketing and strategy. The second decade saw a growing interest in innovation, international business, entrepreneurship, and small business management.

Examples of some well-known BoP initiatives:

- Project Shakti is an initiative from Hindustan Lever (HUL) in India to financially empower rural women and create livelihood opportunities for them (HUL, 2022).
- Grameen Danone Foods Ltd, a joint venture between Danone S.A., a French MNC known for dairy products, and the Grameen Group to provide nutritional yoghurt to Bangladeshi children (Rangan and Lee, 2010).
- Aravind Eye Care Clinic that has drastically reduced the cost of eye surgery through innovations and provides free services to those who cannot afford the cost (Virmani and Lepineux, 2016).

One of the first critics of the BoP concept was Karnani (2007) who argued that the capitalist approach of selling goods to the poor cannot do good to them and suggested that an alternative approach is to focus on the poor as producers and to emphasise buying from the poor – stressing that the only way to alleviate poverty is to raise the real income of the poor. Another way to alleviate poverty, according to Karnani, is to encourage employment at the BoP level. Karnani explains: 'Rather than lending USD 200 to 500 women so that each can buy a sewing machine and set up a microenterprise manufacturing garments, it might be much better to lend USD 100,000 to an entrepreneur with managerial capabilities and business acumen and help her or him to set up a garment manufacturing business employing 500 people. Now the business can exploit economies of scale, deploy specialised assets, and use modern business processes to generate value for both its owners and employees' (2007: 105). A third way is to invest in upgrading the skills and productivity of the poor to help create more employment opportunities for them.

In a similar vein, Curtis and Bradly (2022) suggest that rather than defining people in Tiers 4 and 5 as 'low-income people', they should be referred to as people deprived of basic capabilities such as education, health, nutrition, and shelter (following Amartya Sen's 'capabilities approach' discussed in this book).

What are the ethical concerns in this scenario? Davidson (2009) provided the following insights into the ethical concerns of the BoP concept:

- Appropriate products: how and who will decide what products from an MNC will be appropriate for people at the BoP? For example, cosmetic products such as eye-liner, lipstick, or blush; tobacco; or alcoholic beverages. Amounts spent by the poor on these products will reduce funds required for essentials such as food, clothing, and shelter.
- Fair pricing and packaging: it is known that price per unit for a larger pack will always be lower than for a smaller pack. Thus, although a small sachet of detergent (considered to be appropriate for the BoP market) would have a low sale price, it could be at a higher price per litre or kilogram compared to the larger pack sizes available in urban markets. A similar situation can occur for interest rates on loans to the poor.
- Advertising and promotion: honesty in advertising, especially clarity in the messaging, could disadvantage people who have no or less education. Similarly, sales promotion

tactics (using rebates, sales discounts, etc.), and creating artificial demands, although legal, may not pass ethical scrutiny.

• Distribution concerns: new distribution channels through trained rural women (as in the case of Project Shakti) could displace existing small retail outlets, street vendors, and other intermediaries.

• MNCs tend to use branded products which involves expensive advertising and promotion that could be passed on to the consumer in the higher price of the item.

• Repatriation of the 'fortune': will the seller be willing to reinvest the profits back in the BoP community or will it be repatriated to the firm's country of origin?

8.3 Businesses as agents of world benefit

It is now acknowledged that a 'revolution' is emerging all over the world with respect to the relationship between business and society. While on the one hand we are constantly informed through media about the unethical and fraudulent business actions resulting in environmental damage and corporate scandals, on the other hand we also notice businesses using their capacities to do good for society and the environment. However, as Cooperrider et al. (2012: 583) ask, 'how do we elevate and expand the positive organisation development opportunities of the former, and do so in ways that are rigorous, relevant, and value creating for business and society leadership? What does it look like, for example, when business is a force for peace and security in high conflict zones? Where are the models, especially the how-to of business, as a force for the eradication of extreme poverty? And where and how are businesses turning some of our largest global issues into business opportunities for eco-innovation and industry leading performance?'

Conceived in 2001, BAWB is an idea and a project to discover organisational innovations between business and society to create mutual value. Its goal is to identify business innovations that can transform capitalism to enable businesses to excel, people to thrive, and nature to flourish (essentially the three pillars of sustainability – as discussed in Chapter 7). Pless and Maak (2009) suggested that responsible business leaders can develop as agents of world benefit. Through their 'Project Ulysses' they asserted that a key learning objective for such leaders would be the development of a reflective moral and responsible mindset.

BAWB is thus seen as a 21st century vision. It offers new ways for people to share and engage in stories of exceptional business and social practices. The opening case and other case studies in this chapter highlight and illustrate how businesses contribute to global social good and a better life on the planet. It encompasses terms such as sustainable enterprises, natural capitalism, eco-industrial clusters, corporate social innovation, and social entrepreneurship (Cooperrider, 2017; Rimanoczy, 2014).

The BAWB project that interviewed management thinkers and top executives of global and local companies worldwide revealed three themes (Cooperrider et al., 2012):

1 Doing good for the world builds good business – when organisations' stakeholders share a clear, compelling picture of their larger role in society. By focusing on the

world around them, organisations can understand that changes never before contemplated become real and possible.

2   Any and every social, political, and environmental issue of our time can be turned into a successful business opportunity, with the right combination of social entrepreneurship, knowledge, and pragmatism.

3   'Wealth' can be redefined as more than just financial gain, to include 'well-being' for people, profits, and planet, calculated by using the 'Triple Bottom Line' measures.

As mentioned earlier BAWB involves business innovations. However, the question is, business innovations for what purpose? Will it be used without regard for socially desirable consequences (Laszlo et al., 2020)? We have also mentioned earlier that social entrepreneurship is required for turning social and environmental issues into a successful business opportunity. The following sections discuss the definition, understanding, and application of CSI and SE.

Corporate social innovation

As we have seen earlier, businesses and in particular MNCs face increased stakeholder and wider public expectations to address some of the world's pressing issues in all three pillars of sustainability – social, economic, and environmental. MNCs are addressing some of these issues innovatively through CSR programmes (such as the ones described in an earlier section of this chapter). However, Mirvis et al. (2016) have noted that there's a significant gap between stakeholder expectations and corporate social performance. Rather, innovations for the greater good are coming from social innovators, entrepreneurs, and enterprises predominantly from the non-business sectors such as individuals, communities, and NGOs.

Definition and understanding

Social innovation is defined as 'a novel solution to a social problem that is more effective, efficient, sustainable, or more than just existing solutions and for which the value created accrues primarily to society as a whole rather than private individuals' (Phills et al., 2008: 36). Firms with greater social innovation are expected to have greater social impact on society. Social innovation is considered to be one of the ways to achieve the UN's Sustainable Development Goals. Key aspects of CSI can be understood by noting the differences between CSI and traditional CSR efforts in Table 8.3.

Table 8.3   Differences between traditional CSR and CSI

Item	Aspect	Traditional CSR	CSI
1	Intent	Mostly philanthropic	Strategic investments
2	Involvement	Contributions of money and manpower	Societally relevant R&D, applying corporate assets to the challenges

(Continued)

Table 8.3 (Continued)

Item	Aspect	Traditional CSR	CSI
3	Collaboration	Contracts with NGOs or communities to deliver social services	Deeper collaboration across firm functions and external parties to co-create new ways to provide a sustainable solution to societal issues
4	Outcomes	Generate goodwill and enhance corporate reputation	In addition, CSI aims to produce new sources of revenue and generate innovative systems and corporate culture that enhances competitive advantage

Source: Adapted from Mirvis et al. (2016), 'Corporate social innovation: How firms learn to innovate for the greater good', *Journal of Business Research*, 69(11): 5014–21

Four types of knowledge and understanding are relevant for companies to be successful in CSI operations (Mirvis et al., 2016):

1 'Know-what' – Knowledge about the local conditions in their supply chain or the market they seek to enter. Usually, this knowledge is available with non-business partners who can conduct indigenous research.
2 'Know-how' – Understand how to produce and implement social innovations – especially in an unfamiliar culture and with local partners.
3 'Know-who' – Need to know local communities and customers with whom they have legitimacy and connections, and also to get access to resources that are usually beyond corporate reach.
4 'Know-why' – Understand the purpose of their organisation to engage in addressing social, environmental, and economic problems. This can boost their motivation for deeper knowledge and co-creation.

A study of 70 companies well known for CSI programmes shows that companies can choose to engage in CSI activities along two dimensions – core distance from the firm (internally or externally), and intensity of investment and impact (low USD/impact or high USD/impact). Within these dimensions, six types of partnerships have been identified (Mirvis et al., 2016; Mirvis and Googins, 2017) as shown in Table 8.4.

Table 8.4 Six forms of CSI partnerships

Distance from firm	Low USD/Impact ⟵—————————⟶		High USD/Impact
Internal (core activities)	1. Employee intrapreneurship	3. Sustainable supply chain	5. BoP or socially relevant business models
External (societal activities)	2. Social innovation engagement	4. Social entrepreneur support	6. Social enterprise partnership

Source: Adapted from Mirvis and Googins (2017), *The new business of business: Innovating for a better world*, New York: The Conference Board, GT-V2N1

Internal impact:

• Employee intrapreneurship: enables employees to propose ideas that can attract internal funding and support, including internal venture capital funding.

- Sustainable supply chain: by innovating their supply chain and securing certifications of sustainable sourcing, Fairtrade, and relevant ISO standards.
- BoP business models: helping big businesses to tap into new markets in low-income markets.

External impact:

- Social innovation engagement: enabling employees to travel to emerging markets and work with local management in small businesses or social enterprises.
- Social entrepreneur support: companies act like social venture capitalists that vet local entrepreneurs' ideas, offer financial support and guidance, and monitor progress – thus producing social impact and creating jobs.
- Social enterprise partnerships: longer-term partnering with local NGOs and social entrepreneurs to bring business solutions to social issues.

A systematic literature review of 89 academic articles on various CSI aspects and issues (Dionisio and de Vargas, 2020) revealed that:

- As society expects international corporations to be more socially responsible, it has influenced them to pursue new strategies and procedures to maintain their legitimacy and competitive advantage.
- CSI enables firms to embrace internal changes through efficient management and also external changes to establish partnerships with external stakeholders (NGOs, governments).
- Even though companies have adopted social innovations, there is still a lot of scepticism about their motivations for getting involved in social initiatives.
- There is a need to move a company into the transforming stage (see Chapter 7 for more on this) where it places CSI as a more central part of the business model.
- CSI could better improve the relationship of businesses, stakeholders, society, and communities.

Importance of local embeddedness in CSI

Local embeddedness is defined as the firm's ability to create competitive advantage based on a deep understanding of and integration with the local environment – especially so for affordable innovation in emerging markets. It is suggested that local embeddedness enhances social innovation activities by understanding local idiosyncrasies and challenges. In a study of 500 large and medium-sized companies in Ghana, Adomako and Tran (2022) showed that a firm's level of local embeddedness is positively related to social innovation orientation. Thus, local embeddedness could help the firm understand the realities of the grand challenges faced by the population in developing countries. For example, firms can partner with community-based NGOs and opinion leaders to improve the firm's ability to offer novel solutions to mitigate social problems. The study further supported the notion that local embeddedness drives social innovation which in turn influences corporate social performance.

Application of social innovation to biodiversity and ecosystem services

We may recall from Chapter 7 that some sections of the planetary biodiversity and ecosystem services are deteriorating worldwide. These systems that 'supporting and securing the needs of current and future generations, especially marginalised populations, such as indigenous people around the world, continue to deteriorate' (Ziegler et al., 2022: 2). The World Wildlife Fund's (WWF) Living Planet Report (WWF, 2022) reveals that wildlife populations have plummeted by 69 per cent, freshwater populations being hit the hardest, and stresses the links between climate change and biodiversity loss, and that our relationship with nature is broken. On 19 December 2022, at the UN COP15 conference on global biodiversity, 200 nations agreed to protect and reverse the dangerous loss to global biodiversity (COP15, 2022). The Intergovernmental Science-Policy Platform on Biodiversity and Ecosystem Services report (IPBES, 2019) portrays two faces of innovation – technological innovation that can cause continued and accelerated unsustainability and biodiversity loss, and environmentally friendly social innovation. The report suggests social innovation could become part of the solution by:

- Recognising the innovations of indigenous people and local communities.
- Recognising locally developed innovation and experimentation.
- Changes in production and consumption, especially among the affluent.
- Piloting and testing policy innovations.

Ziegler et al.'s (2022) analysis of 195 research papers on biodiversity shows that social innovation can be used to tackle drivers of biodiversity loss such as agriculture, forestry, urbanisation, aquatic pollution, and invasive species.

Social entrepreneurship

Definition and understanding

The concept of SE can be traced back to the formation of Grameen Bank by Nobel-laureate Prof Muhammad Younus in 1976 (to eradicate poverty and empower women in Bangladesh) and the establishment of the Ashoka Foundation by Bill Drayton in 1980 (to provide seed funding for entrepreneurs with a social vision) (Mair and Martí, 2006). Since SE is a relatively recent area of interest in business and management (as opposed to 'entrepreneurship' in general), researchers and commentators have approached the definition of SE in a variety of ways, most of which involve defining how broad or narrow the scope of SE might be. A broad definition of SE is a process where 'social entrepreneurs' create and develop organisations defined as 'social enterprises' (Huybrechts and Nicholls, 2012). Narrower definitions of SE include the following features (compiled from various sources):

1 Adopting a mission to create and sustain social value (not just private value).
2 Pursuing new opportunities to serve that mission by engaging in continuous innovation, adaptation, and learning.
3 Acting boldly without being limited by the resources currently at hand.

4   Decision-making characteristics of innovativeness, proactiveness, and risk-taking.

5   High sense of accountability to communities served and outcomes created.

6   Entrepreneurially virtuous behaviour to achieve a social mission.

7   Innovative, social-value-creating activity that can occur within or across the non-profit, business, or government sectors.

8   Activities and processes undertaken to discover, define, and exploit opportunities in order to enhance social wealth by creating new ventures or managing existing organisations in an innovative manner.

The following can be observed and inferred from the above list:

- Features 2, 3, and 4 are common to entrepreneurship in general business and management, whereas the other five features (1, 5, 6, 7, and 8) are distinctive for SE.
- Central focus is on social or environmental outcomes that have primacy over profit maximisation or other strategic considerations.
- Innovation can be pursued through new organisational models and processes, through new products and services, or through new thinking about, and framing of, societal challenges.
- Social entrepreneurs diffuse their socially innovative models via market-oriented action through alliances and partnerships, with the idea of reaching broader and more sustainable outcomes.

Market orientation in SE is manifested in the form of for-profit social enterprises which operate in commercial markets and generate profits to reinvest in their social mission (Alter, 2006) – as seen in the opening case 'Clothing the Gaps'. Various authors have suggested that social enterprises (unlike traditional NGOs and non-profits) have a continuous production of goods and/or services and take economic risks. The workforce can comprise volunteers and also paid workers. Alter (2006) distinguishes three core SE models based on their mission orientation:

- Embedded – where social programmes are inherent in the business activities (such as Fairtrade (2022), an organisation that aims to ensure fair prices for farmers to cover their costs when the market prices drop).
- Integrated – where social programmes overlap with business activities (such as SELCO (2022), a company rendering sustainable energy sources to rural regions of the country. This project was the first rural solar financing programme in India).
- External – where business activities are an external source of funding for social programmes (such as Basic Needs (2022), an organisation funded by venture philanthropists, which enables people with mental illness and their families to live and work successfully in their communities).

Drivers of SE

While social entrepreneurship can be found throughout history (for example, the co-operative movements and entrepreneurs providing social welfare services to their workers), some of the major drivers of SE in the 20th and 21st centuries have been:

- Major challenges such as climate change and environmental degradation; inequality and poverty; lack of access to basic healthcare, clean water, and energy, mass migration, international terrorism.
- Improved ability of people to identify and respond to social and environmental needs – mainly due to the rise of global connectedness such as via social media.
- Redefined role of the state which encourages managerial-style functioning and contracts with not-for-profits.
- Availability of new commercial revenues and partnerships between the state and business sectors.

A relevant example would be the social enterprise in events management in Adelaide, Australia called GOGO Events. It offers training and supports teams of marginalised people to create and install event programmes. Their stakeholders include a network of corporate clients, not-for-profits, and the homeless and other vulnerable people. Sarah Gun, GOGO's founder, proposed to employ homeless and disadvantaged people, including the long-term unemployed and people with mental illness, women in particular, to make and install events such as corporate dinners. Higgins-Desbiolles and Monga (2021) in their analysis of GOGO's activities note that GOGO's efforts have moved beyond CSR and suggest events businesses can help build community, create relationships of care and contribute to more sustainable futures.

As a result of the above drivers and motivators, social enterprises founded by SEs are proliferating in large numbers worldwide. A recent report estimates there are approximately 11 million social enterprises across the world (British Council, 2022). The report notes how social enterprise is one of the largest movements of our time. One of the fastest growing countries in social enterprise activity is India. It is estimated there may be as many as 2 million social enterprises currently operating in India. The survey found that 57 per cent of the social enterprises were less than five years old and the average age of the social entrepreneurs was below 44 years (British Council, 2016). Social enterprises employ 19 employees on average, and more than half create direct employment by employing disadvantaged groups. Twenty-four per cent are led by women, higher than the 8.9 per cent female-led firms in mainstream businesses. Seventy per cent work with economically disadvantaged communities, 82 per cent with women, 31 per cent with people with disabilities, and 46 per cent with children. The surveyed social enterprises have supported a total of 150 million beneficiaries over their lifetime. Research indicates the main social problems social entrepreneurs have engaged with include poverty, health, education, and unemployment. Other less-engaged-with areas are gender difference, gender discrimination, women and children rights and safety, and women's empowerment (Gupta et al., 2020).

Challenges faced by social entrepreneurs

Social entrepreneurs face multi-dimensional challenges during the entire life cycle of their organisations. Analysis of 188 research papers on SE has highlighted the following prominent challenges (Gupta et al., 2020):

- Scarcity of financial resources and resource mobility – as social enterprises produce less profit than others, they are found to be less attractive to venture capitalists and mainstream banks.

- Hybridity in the mission of social enterprises (the social mission being primary and the economic mission being secondary) complicates the situation for financiers.
- Recruiting, motivating, retaining, and training skill-based employees and volunteers.
- Impact assessment – social impact of a social enterprise is tacit and hard to measure.
- Changing socio-cultural environment and scalability dilemma.
- Institutional challenges such as wrongly understood or unknown role for social enterprises, unfavourable rules and regulations, and lack of norms of a strong role for government.
- With scarcity and depletion of resources and confronted with institutional constraints, social entrepreneurs often engage in 'social bricolage' (do-it-yourself actions using social networking).

Summary

- This chapter can be viewed as an extension of Chapter 7 (Sustainability and the ESG Criteria). However, the difference is that this chapter espouses the positive actions taken by or proposed by businesses to address the specific issues in the social context. The chapter was divided into two major areas – corporate social responsibility (CSR) and business as agents for world benefit (BAWB), which was further sub-divided into corporate social innovation (CSI) and social entrepreneurship (SE).
- The chapter began with a discussion on the relationship between business ethics (BE) and CSR by invoking the stakeholder concept that businesses are 'morally' responsible to look after the interests of their primary and secondary stakeholders, which as we know includes elements of society and the environment. The discussion elaborates on the questions: is CSR a subset of BE and is CSR a means to an end?
- The chapter then delved into the definition(s) of CSR as proposed by various entities throughout its evolution during the last hundred years or so. A researcher found 37 definitions from 27 authors. However, focusing on five key dimensions to categorise definitions, we identified a few that met the criteria of the five dimensions.
- Logically then, the chapter segued into the historical developments and the evolution of CSR. We mentioned that CSR has been around for a quite some time but took shape from the time of the Industrial Revolution. This section provided deeper insights into some key moments of CSR's evolution from the 1950s through to the 2000s.
- The next section was probably the most important one in the chapter – operationalising CSR. It highlighted how companies are implementing the CSR concept in some key areas of business – SMEs, tourism, the fashion industry, reporting of CSR, and stakeholder management. The section concluded with the concepts of 'inclusive business' and the 'bottom of the pyramid'.
- We saw that the goal of BAWB is to identify business innovations that can enable businesses to excel, people to thrive, and nature to flourish. Essentially, its motto is doing good for the world builds good business and wealth can be redefined as more than just financial gain to include the well-being of people, planet, and profits.
- We learnt from the section on CSI that it is about novel solutions to social problems and that is more effective and sustainable than existing solutions. Businesses can choose

CSI practices based on focus (internally or externally), budgets (low or high), or impacts (low or high).

- We discovered that SE is a process where social entrepreneurs develop organisations to create and sustain social values with a determination to persist until they have transformed an entire system.

CASE STUDY 8.1

CSR IN CONTROVERSIAL INDUSTRIES – SPECIFICALLY THE GAMBLING INDUSTRY

Controversial industries are defined as those that offer products and services that for reasons of decency, delicacy, morality, or even fear, evoke reactions of distaste, disgust, offence, or outrage. These could include what some call 'sinful industries' such as tobacco, gambling, alcohol, brothels, and pornography, as well as industries with environmental, social, or ethical issues such as the weapon, oil, biotech, and even cement industries. Some researchers call these 'stigmatised industries', characterised with terminology such as sin, vice, and controversy.

In such a context, questions arise:

- How can organisations in 'controversial industry sectors', which are marked by social taboos, moral debates, and political pressures, maintain reasonable, socially responsible standards?
- How do they adopt CSR-related policies and practices to meet their public legitimacy requirements?
- How is it possible for firms in these sectors to act in socially responsible ways if it produces products harmful to society or individuals?

Some industries such as the tobacco, alcohol, and fast-food industries have adopted strategic CSR communications in their programmes to improve their public image where the harmful influence of their products has garnered more social attention and criticism. Strategies adopted by companies to reduce stigmatisation include shielding and concealing firm activities (for example, online gambling), straddling both controversial and non-controversial businesses (for example, tobacco companies), and exiting the controversial industry entirely by developing multiple lines of business (for example, when Google faced ethical, political, and cultural questions when it entered China in 2010, it decided to withdraw from mainland China). Firms also adopt risk reduction strategies by engaging in CSR. Research shows that risk reduction is more significant, both economically and statistically, for companies in controversial industries compared to non-controversial industries.

The gambling industry

Despite religious and cultural objections, gambling has been part of people's lives since ancient times – in Mesopotamia the earliest six-sided dice date to about 3000 BCE; in China gambling houses were widespread in the first millennium BCE, and betting on fighting animals was common. Lotto games and dominoes (precursors of Pai Gow) appeared in China as early as the 10th century. Playing cards appeared in the 9th century CE in China. Records trace gambling in Japan back at least as far as the 14th century. Poker, the most popular US card game associated with gambling, derives from the Persian game As-Nas, dating back to the 17th century. The first known casino, the Ridotto, started operating in 1638 in Venice, Italy.

However, it emerged as a major industry only last century. This, according to some, acquired social acceptance when the gambling concept was moved from 'sin' to 'vice' to 'entertainment' with legal legitimacy. The industry now prefers the term 'gaming' with its connotation of entertainment and leisure, rather than 'gambling' which can be associated with financial loss and other social problems. In 2021, the market size of the casino and online gambling industry worldwide reached a total of USD 231 billion. The global gambling market is expected to reach USD 876 billion by 2026.

Gambling releases dopamine in the brain similar to the effects of illegal drugs that arouses a sense of happiness and satisfaction. Other 'positive' aspects of gambling could include providing an escape from everyday stress and boredom, invoking fun, random luck, and collective engagement. Economic and social benefits arising from the gambling industry include tax revenue, job creation, and sponsorship. Negative impacts of gambling include 'problem gambling' indicating an addiction to acts of gambling. This can affect not just the individual gambler, but also family, friends, and employers – for example, behavioural changes may include stealing money from them, self-harm, family break-ups, loss of employment, and even selling illegal drugs to support their gambling addiction.

CSR in the gambling industry

Research shows that the gambling industry has employed the following strategies as part of their CSR programmes:

* Communication to consumers and general public about 'gambling responsibly'.
* Operating 'responsible gambling' programmes.
* Implementing codes of practice to prevent and reduce potential harms associated with gambling.

However, critical analyses have indicated that:

* CSR programmes adopted by gambling firms have largely been oriented towards protecting financial interests.

(Continued)

- CSR initiatives emphasising economic and legal responsibilities rather than ethical and discretionary ones.
- Social impact varies considerably between countries and even between gambling venues within particular countries, depending on the level of government pressure.
- Companies devoted minimal space in their annual reports to responsible gambling problems.
- In their reports, rather than focusing on consumer protection, the focus was on employee training, codes of practice, and gambling regulation. There were very little disclosures on environmental protection.
- Organisations can adopt CSR practices as a means to legitimise their operations, signalling that they are 'not that bad at all'.

Leung and Snell (2017) conducted a study on CSR policies of gambling firms in Macao. Macao, a former Portuguese colony, became a Special Administrative Region within the People's Republic of China in 1999, has a significant number of casinos and integrated hotel resorts. It is the only place in China where it is legal to gamble in casinos. Analysis of 49 interviews comprising internal and external stakeholders revealed that CSR is:

- applied as a means to establish legitimacy
- used to attract and retain employees
- serves business interests – to reflect CSR as a business case
- used to meet institutional demands
- promoted as philanthropy – such as corporate donations and sponsorships, and employee volunteering – with the help of media
- used as sanitisation – to shift public perceptions away from negative impacts of gambling
- an attempt to reframe gambling as a freely chosen form of entertainment or leisure activity.

Questions

Using the Case-Study Integrative Framework in Figure 0.1, discuss the following:

1 Identify the key primary and secondary stakeholders of the 'controversial industries' and the gambling industry in particular.
2 Do the CSR actions taken by the 'controversial industries' go far enough?
3 Do the CSR actions taken by the gambling industry in particular go far enough? (For both these questions, explain your reasoning by applying/using the relevant concepts from this chapter.)
4 What are the ethical issues in this case study?
5 Use the CEDM model from earlier chapters to develop your analysis, judgement, commitment, and potential actions.
6 Are there any cultural issues in developing CSR programmes in the gambling industry? Explain your answer.

7   Reflect on issues, if any, from gambling or any other controversial industry, within your community and suggest what CSR actions should be implemented.

Sources:
Cai et al. (2012)
GNW (2022)
Guan, in Sio and Noronha (2022)
Lee (2022)
Leung and Snell (2017)
Lindgreen et al. (2012)
Lindorff et al. (2012)
Statista (2022)
Wiki (2022d)

CASE STUDY 8.2
JAIPUR RUGS

The Indian carpet and rug industry employs about 2 million people and exports about USD 1.8 billion every year (Sindwani, 2019). The industry had gained notoriety for employing child labour and other forms of unacceptable business practices (Bahree, 2014). However, with international pressure, domestic legislation, and community demands, there have been remarkable and visible initiatives within the industry to address these issues. One such organisation is Jaipur Rugs (JR).

NK Chaudhary founded the idea of JR in 1978, starting his business on the principles of dignity. Today, his organisation is the one of the largest manufacturers of hand-knotted rugs and he is often referred to as the 'Gandhi of the Carpet Industry'. Born in a traditional Rajasthani family in Churu, India, Chaudhary took a loan from his father to set up two looms for nine artisans and the first two identical carpets were exported.

Following his motto of 'Let goodness, fairness and most importantly love, prevail in business; profits will inevitably follow', NK Chaudhary's greatest achievement was subverting century-old practices that shunned women, artists, and the poor. In the company's early days, he removed middlemen to connect directly with tribal artisans who were considered untouchables with dignity, empathy, and respect.

(Continued)

Today, NK Chaudhary is a widely celebrated social entrepreneur and stands as an example of how profit and kindness can go together in business. JR combines the pursuit of profit with the spreading of kindness, with the aim of benefiting all the people sitting around its rugs: customers, artisans, local communities, employees, suppliers, buyers, and partners.

Headquartered in Jaipur, India and working with artisans spread across five Indian states, and through its worldwide distribution network, its rugs reach more than 60 countries around the world, from Italy to France, China, and Russia.

JR revolutionised the carpet industry by creating an entirely new business model – working directly with artisans and empowering them and their communities with a sustainable livelihood. Bringing together the 2500-years-old weaving tradition with state-of-the-art attention to sustainability and design, it is the original Indian rug, made contemporary.

CSR initiatives

JR's business model treasures peoples and the environment. Its aim is to enable everyone to reach their full potential, thereby uplifting the entire society. Following this vision, in 2004 they founded the Jaipur Rugs Foundation (JRF) with a mandate to reach out to remote rural areas and establish bonds with the village communities, so that they can start weaving rugs to improve their lives.

So far, JR has impacted 273,731 lives in 669 villages, creating 50,703 jobs and educating 5,301 people in rural areas. Around 67,046 people have been provided reliable and affordable healthcare services in communities that do not have access to these services or even the basic knowledge of how to access them. Education is offered through holistic development for children and youth and alternative education programmes to artisans in India's rural communities, with a particular focus on bridging the gender gap. They help artisan communities to learn more and access banking services, as well as government funds and welfare schemes. Skill development programmes are implemented for a range of underprivileged communities, including disabled people, to improve their living standards through carpet weaving. Each of their rugs can be traced back all the way to the person who wove it. This extreme level of traceability comes to life in the Postcard Project, an initiative that gives their customers the chance to exchange thoughts and feelings with the artisan who made their rugs.

Reducing impact on the planet includes using recycled yarn – their 'Manchaha' collection uses hand-spun leftover yarn batches, thus reducing waste and making the colour palette of rugs as unique as their design; and low-impact dyes – obtained from certified and eco-friendly raw colours.

JR maintains global standards in sustainability through:

- Child-free labour – ensuring that no child labour is involved in any process of their carpet manufacturing.
- ISO 14001: 2015 Environmental management system.
- ISO 9001:2015 Quality production standards.

- SA 8000 (2022) Social accountability.
- OEKO-TEX® Standard 100, which assures that their every component has been tested for harmful substances and is not harmful for human health.

Questions

Using the Case-Study Integrative Framework in Figure 0.1, discuss the following:

1 Identify the key primary and secondary stakeholders of (a) the carpet/rug industry in general and (b) JR. Are there any differences?
2 Do the CSR actions taken by JR go far enough to influence the attitudes and operations of other such companies in the carpet/rug industry in India and other developing nations? (For both these questions, explain your reasoning by applying/using the relevant concepts from this chapter.)
3 What are the ethical issues in this case study?
4 Use the CEDM model from earlier chapters to develop your analysis, judgement, commitment, and potential actions.
5 Are there any cultural issues in developing CSR programmes in the carpet/ rug industry? Explain your answer.
6 What would you do if you wish to purchase a rug and (a) you are not sure of the situation in which the rug was made, (b) you are aware of the socially unacceptable operations of the rug maker?

Sources:
Bahree (2014)
Jaipur Rugs (2022a)
Jaipur Rugs (2022b)
Jaipur Rugs (2022c)
Sindwani (2019)

──Recommended readings──

Cai, Y., Jo, H. and Pan, C. (2012), 'Doing well while doing bad? CSR in controversial industry sectors', *Journal of Business Ethics*, 108(4): 467–80.

The association between firm value and CSR engagement for firms in sinful industries such as tobacco, gambling, and alcohol is examined in this article.

Carroll, A.B. and Brown, J.A. (2022), 'Corporate social responsibility: A chronicle and review of concept development and refinements'. In T. Maak, N.M. Pless, M. Orlitzky and S. Sandhu (eds), *The Routledge companion to corporate social responsibility*, New York: Routledge, pp. 295–307.

This is an excellent resource to understand the definition and the evolution of CSR from the 1950s to the present – written by one of the most well-known proponents, Archie B. Carroll.

Cooperrider, D.L., Zhexembayeva, N., Trosten-Bloom, A. and Whitney, D. (2012), 'Business as agent of world benefit', *Handbook for strategic HR*, New York: HarperCollins, p. 582.

Written by one of the founders of the BAWB concept, D.L. Cooperrider, this article will provide you with an appreciation of the idea that organisational innovations are at the intersection of business and society that creates mutual value.

Dionisio, M. and de Vargas, E.R. (2020), 'Corporate social innovation: A systematic literature review', *International Business Review*, 29(2): 101641.

This article explores the definition of CSI and its relationship with MNCs, especially with new possibilities for solving social problems. Examples will help with understanding the concept even further.

Huybrechts, B. and Nicholls, A. (2012), 'Social entrepreneurship: definitions, drivers and challenges'. In C.K. Volkman, K.O. Tokarski and E.K. Wiesbaden (eds), *Social entrepreneurship and social business*, Gabler Verlag: Springer, pp. 31–48.

A comprehensive source for understanding social entrepreneurship – its meaning, what drives such entrepreneurs, its implementation, and its challenges.

Khandker, V. (2022), 'Two decades of the bottom of the pyramid research: Identifying the influencers, structure, and the evolution of the concept', *Management Review Quarterly*, 1–28. doi: 10.1007/s11301-022-00271-y.

While C.K. Prahalad's writings (there are several referred to in this chapter) are definitely worth reading, Khandker's article will provide a deeper and broader view of BoP as it analyses 665 publications on BoP published in the last couple of decades.

Mair, J. and Martí, I. (2006), 'Social entrepreneurship research: A source of explanation, prediction, and delight', *Journal of World Business*, 41(1): 36–44.

A seminal work that puts forward a view of social entrepreneurship as a process that catalyses change in a way that is not dominated by direct financial benefits for the entrepreneurs. It also shows the importance of embedding the concept within organisations.

Mirvis, P., Herrera, M.E.B., Googins, B. and Albareda, L. (2016), 'Corporate social innovation: How firms learn to innovate for the greater good', *Journal of Business Research*, 69(11): 5014–21.

A 'must-read' article on CSI. It explores how companies engage in successful social innovation and elaborates on two dimensions – focus (internal or external) and intensity of investments and impact.

Ziegler, R., Balzac-Arroyo, J., Hölsgens, R., Holzgreve, S., Lyon, F., Spangenberg, J.H. and Thapa, P.P. (2022), 'Social innovation for biodiversity: A literature review and research challenges', *Ecological Economics*, 193: 107336.

This is definitely the future of social innovation. The authors review social innovation in changing land use, exploitation of organisms, climate change, pollution, and invasive species. It reveals that local experimentation is a critical factor in tackling these issues.

9

GLOBAL STRATEGIES AND ETHICS

Learning objectives

On completion of this chapter, you should be able to:

- Appreciate the ethical challenges faced by MNEs in their global strategies
- Understand ethical issues in knowledge management
- Define liability of foreignness and its ethical issues
- Understand modern slavery and its ethical issues
- Explain the concept of international transfer pricing used by MNEs and its ethical issues
- Understand the concept of corporate governance and its ethical issues

Key concepts

- Developed country multinational enterprises and emerging country multinational enterprises
- Knowledge management
- Liability of foreignness
- Modern slavery
- International transfer pricing
- Corporate governance

─Box 9.1 Opening case─

Forced labour in medical gloves supply chain

In the Malaysian glove sector, workers frequently work 12-hour shifts, six days per week in conditions where temperatures near ovens (to heat glove-shaped moulds) can exceed 60 degrees Celsius. Packing production targets can reach 15,000 gloves per day for a single worker – equivalent to 1 pair being packed every 3 seconds. Wages are usually below AUD 2 per hour and be docked for taking too long in the bathroom or not meeting targets. The majority of workers are migrants from Nepal, Bangladesh, and Vietnam. High recruitment fees, sometimes as high as AUD 6,500, means that workers often take out high-interest loans to pay the fees and can result in having to work for free for a year to repay their recruitment debts. Other issues are overcrowding in filthy dormitories, passports being confiscated, being denied access to healthcare and other basic needs, and a lack of legal representation. One of the major importers and distributors of such gloves is Ansell Limited, an Australian MNE.

Ansell Limited began its life in 1893 in Melbourne, Australia, as a bicycle tyre manufacturing company established by Dunlop UK. In 1946, the company developed its first automated glove dipping machine. Thereafter from 1965 to 1989, Ansell developed new products, acquired industrial glove companies, and expanded production into Malaysia and the USA. From 1990 to 2002, following further acquisitions and new products, Ansell became the world's largest provider of medical, household, and industrial gloves and moved its headquarters to the USA in 1998. Between 2002 and 2019, Ansell accelerated its acquisition strategy by acquiring companies in China, Poland, Brazil, the USA, Sweden, France, Korea, Sri Lanka, and the UK.

Ansell Limited today is Australia's largest manufacturer and distributor of personal protection equipment (PPE) and in particular is the main distributor of medical gloves produced by the world's largest manufacturer of medical gloves, the Malaysian company Top Glove Corporation Bhd. With the huge increase in global demand for medical gloves during the Covid-19 pandemic, there was a three-fold increase in Top Glove's production, profits, and share prices. However, media reports alleged that the demand for gloves was met by the exploitation of Top Glove's 19,000 workers – including severe underpayment, debt bondage, overcrowding of basic accommodation, deduction of salary for accommodation and recruitment fees, and withholding of wages and identity documents such as passports. Later, Ansell, the main importer of Top Glove products into Australia, reported that it would never knowingly tolerate child, forced, or involuntary labour of any kind, under any circumstances.

Another of Ansell's suppliers, the Brightway Group, a Malaysian company that manufactures gloves for medical, industrial, and cleanroom applications, was also alleged to have breached labour laws. Ansell, which had faced similar allegations in recent years, said it was deeply concerned by reports of forced labour at Brightway. However, no action was taken to terminate the contracts. In August 2022, migrant workers at Brightway filed US lawsuits against MNEs Ansell and Kimberley-Clark, accusing them of 'knowingly profiting' from alleged use of forced labour. The lawyer representing the workers claimed that Ansell and Kimberley-Clark knew or should have known about forced labour in their disposable gloves supply chain. Both companies in their defence stated that they condemn all human rights violations, including the use of forced labour, and are committed to actively identifying and addressing violations of labour rights within their supply chain.

Earlier, in 2019, US Customs and Border Protection (CBP) had banned imports from three companies within the Brightway Group due to allegations of forced labour. Ansell's share price plunged almost 15 per cent when the US import ban was revealed, and together with Covid outbreaks in its Malaysian factories, its earnings for the first half of the year dropped by about 35 per cent.

Ansell's own factories, with investment in a new factory in India and expansion of another of its own facilities in Thailand, are not implicated in such breach of labour laws. However, it needed to utilise its Malaysian suppliers to keep up with the booming glove demand during the Covid-19 pandemic.

Ansell as a major glove purchaser also has immense power over its suppliers. Its responses are always that it is working with suppliers to make improvements. Ansell followed the advice of human rights groups and rather than walking away from suppliers with problems preferred to work with them to drive positive change through the audit process. They reiterate that if they identify suppliers who do not align with their labour standards commitment, they review potential options, including terminating the supplier relationship and finding alternative sources.

International pressure (such as the import bans by the US CBP) has led to some improvements. Some glove manufacturers have reimbursed recruitment fees and are regulating accommodation standards. A multilingual app has been introduced to allow foreign workers to report grievances. However, allegations of modern slavery remain, including those against four Australian companies – of which Ansell has attracted the greatest number of allegations.

In November 2020, Ansell issued its first Modern Slavery Statement in fulfilment of its requirements under the Australian Modern Slavery Act. The statement mentions that Ansell will uphold human rights for all. Marmo and Bandiera (2022) argue that such slavery statements, required by the **Australian Slavery Act**, position corporations and states 'within a narrative of benevolence (such as shaping a better market and a fairer supply chain) that allows for the maintenance of the status quo' (p. 67).

Questions

1 Do you think MNEs such as Ansell have a responsibility to know and regulate the activities of their supply chain?
2 What are the motivations for MNEs' inaction?
3 If the MNEs operate within the laws of their suppliers' countries, should they be held accountable for the workers' conditions?
4 Do they have the power to change the regulations of another country, especially an emerging economy?
5 Is it enough for such MNEs to provide reports and fulfil requirements under an Act?

(Continued)

6 What do you think MNEs such as Ansell should do in terms of corporate governance?
7 Are there examples of businesses (large and small) who do not engage in such activities in your communities? Discuss.
8 Read the Marmo and Bandiera (2022) article and reflect on their analysis of modern slavery.

Sources:
Ansell (2023)
AuManufacturing (2022)
Barrett (2022)
Bhutta et al. (2021)
Butler (2022)
Evans (2022)
Khadem (2019)
Marmo and Bandiera (2022)
Sinclair and Dinshaw (2022)
Terzon (2022)

9.1 Introduction

As we have seen earlier, globalisation ushered in a rapid increase in the number of multinational enterprises expanding their operations from domestic to overseas markets. Multinationals invest overseas for different reasons, including seeking markets (automotive companies entering China and India), efficiency (economies of scale and low-cost countries), knowledge (global IT companies venturing into Silicon Valley, USA and Bangalore, India), and natural resources (entering markets for minerals, oil, and gas) (Lasserre, 2018; Peng, 2022). In particular, developed country multinational enterprises (DMNEs) have been 'keenly entering, competing, and operating in developing economies since World War II' (Luo et al., 2019: 633). Analysing academic publications over 47 years from 1970 to 2016 spanning 692 articles and 21 books, Luo et al. (2019) identified five key areas in which DMNEs have engaged: (1) entering developing economies, (2) organising local activities, (3) managing alliances and joint ventures, (4) competing in dynamic environments, and (5) dealing with institutions, governments, and society. One of the key aspects of the evolution of DMNE overseas expansion strategies was that developing economies were not just a source of markets, but also of global competence and global innovation, in which the concept of reverse innovation was predominant. DMNEs became more decentralised with hubs based in key locations of emerging economies (for example Microsoft has several technical hubs for R&D in India).

In recent decades, emerging country multinational enterprises (EMNE) from the Asia-Pacific region have in some cases become leading firms in manufacturing, building materials, steel, hotels, financial services, and many more sectors (Mathews, 2006). These new players in the 21st century have managed to become MNEs, expanding from developing economies to even developed economies within a relatively short time and without the advantages of the industry leaders from developed economies. They did so by 'leapfrogging to advanced technological levels or by leveraging their way into new markets through partnerships and joint ventures' (2006: 6). In a further article, Mathews (2017) suggested that such organisations use strategies such as linkage (using collaborative partnership to gain entry), leverage resources, and learning (by repeating applications of linkage and leveraging). Some examples are Acer from Taiwan (computer hardware), Ispat from India (steel manufacturing), Tata Motors from India with Jaguar and Land Rover (automotive), Hong Leong Bank from Malaysia (banking), Lenovo from China (IT), Geely from China (automobiles), Huawei from China (telecommunications), Infosys from India (IT), and Pearl River from China (piano producer).

Whether an organisation is a DMNE or an EMNE, firms face challenges in areas of local institutional regulations, cultural, demographic, political, administrative, and ethics. This chapter discusses issues encountered by DMNEs and EMNEs in some specific areas such as knowledge management, foreign workers (including international migrants), liability of foreignness, obtaining government-controlled permits, approvals, and licences (which can entail public corruption), modern slavery, international transfer pricing (ITP), and corporate governance.

9.2 Specific issues in global strategies of DMNEs and EMNEs

Knowledge management

Knowledge management (KM) can be defined as a range of activities by individuals or by an organisation or even by an entire society that includes the process of identification, creation, acquisition, sharing, updating, and sustaining information valuable for the organisation's or society's productivity. Knowledge refers to facts or information acquired through experience, or formal and informal learning. MNEs gain competitive advantage by creating and transferring knowledge from headquarters to subsidiaries and vice versa and they often use expatriates to transfer knowledge, and such knowledge transfer is vital to subsidiary performance. In addition to expatriate competencies, the absorptive capacity of subsidiaries (the ability to recognise, assimilate, and apply the external knowledge) is also important in this process (Chang et al., 2012).

Corporate knowledge is also termed as 'intellectual property' (IP) which includes (Contractor, 2019):

1 IP formally registered with governments – such as patents, trademarks, copyrights, and brands.
2 Trade secrets not registered and kept secret – such as algorithms, software, recipes, formulae, manuals, technical procedures, customer lists which, if leaked, would give competitive advantage to rivals.

3   Unregistered and uncodified knowledge that is not written or digitalised but sits in the memory of employees or routines.

The share of the value of intangible assets, including patents, trademarks, copyrights, and special client preference rights, has significantly increased from 32 per cent in 1985 to 90 per cent in 2020 (Ocean Tomo, 2022). However, due to interactivity and cooperation within supply chains globally, there is a great likelihood of a firm's core knowledge leaking out to potential competitors. In addition, with increasing global corporate alliances (examples of recent alliances are Apple Pay and Mastercard, Toyota with Panasonic and BYD, China's electric car), companies may wish to, selectively, share information. The question, Contractor (2019) asks, is how much information should be shared without the risk of raising competition? On the other hand, due to digitalisation of corporate knowledge, confidential trade secrets (that are deliberately kept confidential) could be 'leaked' in the world of external partners, supply chain agents, and employee mobility. Fitzpatrick and Dilullo (2017) estimate that trade secrets theft costs US businesses USD 300 billion annually, mostly from current/former employees and value chain partners. Decreasing loyalty due to the inclination of companies to lay off employees when needed, and the tendencies of employees not to remain in the same job for long periods, can increase the incidences of knowledge leakage to competitors. Companies are now increasingly getting employees to sign non-compete, non-disclosure employment contracts. This situation can be further complicated with the potential conflict of knowledge ownership between those originally owning knowledge (individuals or teams) and those claiming ownership over acquired knowledge (organisations). Rechberg and Syed (2013) propose the need for a moral contract of knowledge management between organisations and individuals built on trust, fairness, and justice.

There are various situations in which issues of ethics and accountability can be seen in KM practices (Land et al., 2007):

- The motivation to increase the power of the organisation over the knowledge worker – by capturing knowledge from workers into data warehouses (making tacit knowledge explicit), thereby making the knowledge worker less valuable and ultimately made dispensable, leading to downsizing.
- Designing of data mining systems within an organisation which could be used to gather and correlate data about the activities of employees and citizens too – data such as listing citizens taking part in protest marches, creating profiles of groups of citizens, and identifying groups as threats, selling information onwards to customers whose use of the data may be unclear and unethical, and use of data working against human rights.
- IP rights raise questions around ethical behaviour for employers (unfairly exploiting knowledge of employees without providing rewards) and employees (facing the ethical dilemma of personal gain by withholding or distorting knowledge attributable to the employer).
- Questions about whether ground-breaking research such as the Human Genome Project should be patented by individuals or organisations or indeed be available freely to all humanity.

A key aspect of knowledge management is 'knowledge hiding' that usually occurs between employees and is defined as an intentional attempt to conceal or withhold knowledge that has been requested by others. In a literature review of 50 articles from 2011 to 2021, Oliveira et al. (2021) showed that the negative aspects (knowledge hoarding and hiding) lead to lack of knowledge sharing, and the positive aspects (knowledge donation and collection) lead to knowledge sharing. Factors such as mutual respect and interpersonal trust affect how an individual employee responds to a request for knowledge from a co-worker. In a survey of 436 employees in 78 teams, Men et al. (2020) found that ethical leadership was negatively related to knowledge hiding. It also highlighted the importance of an organisational climate which values employees' effort, cooperation, learning, and self-development, and where employees view knowledge hiding as a destructive behaviour.

Foreign workers

Data from the ILO (2022a) reports there are 169 million international migrant workers globally, constituting nearly 5 per cent of the global labour force. Many of them are employed by local businesses and by MNEs operating in domestic and international markets. There is a long history of exclusions, abuse, and discrimination of foreign workers, especially women, the working class, people of colour, and sexual minorities (Andrijasevic et al., 2019). The 'othering' of foreign workers has long been part of institutionalised structures and practices where employment regulations, work practices, and management were influenced by assumptions and norms about nationality, race, gender, and sexuality that had a significant impact on the lived experience of foreign workers. Andrijasevic et al. (2019: 315) contend that 'the ethical implications relate to how people are treated, the rights they are granted, the forms of discrimination they face, and the freedoms that are open to them'. This is especially pronounced when one's foreignness is on the move from post-colonial East to West, and South to North where migration from former colonies to the land of former colonisers brings the legacy of historical oppression and exploitation.

Liability of foreignness

An important strategic decision of MNEs is the mode of entry into foreign markets – where, when, and how to enter a foreign market. The challenges and success in overseas markets are primarily attributed to 'liability of foreignness' (LoF), which is the 'inherent disadvantage foreign firms experience in host countries because of their non-native status' (Peng, 2022: 143).

Asmussen and Goerzen (2013) identified three aspects of foreignness:

- Cultural distance between the MNE and the host country (for example, between Western and Eastern cultures).
- Institutional distance (regulations or lack thereof).
- Geographic or regional distance (between neighbouring countries and far-flung countries even if the far-flung regions have similar cultures and institutions).

Zhou and Guillen (2016) categorised LoF into Ownership-Specific LoF (the costs of identifying the differences in local demand and adjusting the product to suit), Location-Specific LoF (the costs of discrimination from host country governments and communities), and Internalisation-Specific LoF (the costs of managing foreign subsidiaries and risks involved in FDIs). Location-Specific LoF issues can (in addition to discrimination) include differences in ethical standards between the MNE and the host country, whether a company entering an overseas country adheres to the host country's norms, values, and meanings, and the methods used by MNEs from developing economies to overcome LoF in developed economies.

One of the challenges and liabilities when operating overseas is 'when the host country has ethical and compliance standards that are at variance (typically, lower than) those in the firm's home country' (Stening and Zhang, 2016: 3). In particular, a firm may be accountable to ethical standards in their home country that do not apply in other countries. A study involving interviews with 16 experienced and knowledgeable people in senior positions in China identified five areas where ethical issues create a LoF problem (Stening and Zhang, 2016):

1 Pollution (local firms being more willing and able to flout laws).
2 Labour (underpaid workers, and relative disregard for health and safety matters).
3 IP threat and counterfeiting.
4 Asymmetrical information availability (lack of transparency to the advantage of local firms).
5 Corruption (mostly in the form of bribery).

In order to manage the risks associated with ethical issues of LoF in China, tactics recommended by the interviewees were:

1 Financial controls: particularly in vulnerable areas such as gift giving, relationships with parties who may provide facilitation payments, invoicing, payments, receiving goods, and others.
2 Recruitment, staffing, and training: these are challenges for both local personnel and senior expatriate managers, who might need local experiences. A key issue here is the extent to which personnel should be localised. Some suggest that ethical compliance could be supported with surveillance, rewards, punishments, and other mechanisms that had personal consequences.
3 Due diligence: how such processes are undertaken in local firms, suppliers, and subcontractors.
4 Developing relationships: with key stakeholders and particularly with the government (refer to *guanxi* and other relationship process discussed in Chapter 5).
5 Organisational structure: to ensure compliance of both ethical standards and local laws, a separate compliance officer would be essential – at a senior level and reporting directly to the CEO.
6 Organisational culture: to find the right balance between control and trust. Some suggest creating an 'ethical firewall', others have suggested the culture should be one of 'trust but verify'.

LoF faced by emerging market multinationals have been defined as 'negative perceptions in host countries about these firms' willingness and ability to conduct legitimate business' (Marano et al., 2017: 386). They further suggest CSR reporting as an effective strategy to overcome such liabilities as it conveys alignment with global norms and expectations to host countries and global stakeholders.

The number of foreign initial public offerings (IPOs) in the US reached record numbers in 2021. However, not all foreign IPOs are successful in the US mainly because they are at a disadvantage relative to domestic firms due to LoF factors. In order to reduce LoF, foreign IPOs adopted strategies to achieve legitimacy such as:

- Expanding board size and having independent directors
- Adapting host capital market choice
- Adopting home country legal institutions and auditor reputation
- CSR-driven strategies (such as ESG funds)

Similarly, Pesqué-Cela et al. (2022) found that MNEs from emerging economies such as Alibaba (an e-commerce technology company from China) and Coupang (an e-commerce company from South Korea), both of whom had IPOs in 2014 and 2021 respectively, engaged with CSR-related signals prior to and continuing after the IPOs.

Box 9.2

MNEs and bottled water

Bottled water is one of the fastest-growing markets in the world. From 2001 to 2015, the total volume, in litres sold, grew from 121 to 310 billion, revenues from USD 71 billion to USD 183 billion, and per capita consumption from 20 to 43 litres. A study to measure use of widely available pre-packaged non-alcoholic water-based beverages in Australia in 2020 revealed the highest consumption was fruit juices (36.8 per cent), followed by bottled water (37.4 per cent), soda (28.9 per cent), artificially sweetened soda (18.1 per cent), sports drinks (8.1 per cent), and energy drinks (4.2 per cent).

Essentially, there are two main options for drinking water – water distributed in taps through the public network systems and water distributed in bottles sold in the market. Tap water is seen as a public good or individual right (as in SDG 6) and is not usually subjected to marketing. Bottled water on the other hand can be highly criticised especially where good quality tap water is available. Criticisms include substantially higher price relative to tap water, the commodification of nature, disrespect for the local economy and traditions, and the fact that an estimated one in three people globally do not have reliable access to potable water. Finally, all stages of the bottled water supply chain can have environmental effects – in collection, processing, packaging, transport, disposal, and even recycling. So, while tap water is usually seen as a public and cheap good, bottled water is perceived as a private, expensive, polluting, and heavily advertised commodity but one that is more potable and profitable than tap water.

In the US, by 2016, bottled water sales had overtaken 'soda' sales as the largest US beverage category. From 2019 to 2020, during the Covid-19 pandemic, sales of bottled water in

(Continued)

the US surged by 57 per cent. With consumption reaching billions of gallons per year and sales figures reaching billions of dollars, residents and environmentalists became increasingly worried about its impact. BlueTriton, earlier known as Nestle Waters North America, owns popular bottled-water brands Poland Spring and Arrowhead, and recently received a 'cease-and-desist' letter from the California State Water Resources Board alleging that during the state's historic drought, Nestle's continual water diversions depleted Strawberry Creek in the San Bernardino area, east of Los Angeles. This water diversion had led to reduced down-stream drinking water and impacted sensitive environmental resources. Further, a substantial portion of bottled water sold in developed countries comes from municipal tap water such as Coca Cola's Dasani, Pepsi's Aquafina, and Nestle's Pure Life, by purchasing, treating, and bottling municipal water before selling it at a significant price to consumers.

Exponential growth in bottled water sales can be attributed to marketing strategies based on:

- Lifestyle shifts – decline in meals consumed at home and demands for greater convenience.
- Healthy lifestyles – associated with hydration and taste preferences, representing a modern lifestyle and even being a status symbol.
- Anxieties about health risks from drinking tap water.
- Communication messages – geographic location of origin of the water, medicinal properties such as being a diuretic, liver protection, insomnia avoidance, gastronomy and digestion improvement, images of motherhood, slimming treatment, and beauty improvement.

It is important to note that in addition to the role of multinational enterprises in the bottled water industry, there are numerous 'small-scale private entrepreneurs' (Bakker, 2010: xvi) active in deliv-ering water to customers throughout developing countries. In some parts, where governments could not deliver quality potable water, WHO and UNICEF acknowledged bottled water as a suit-able source of household drinking water as long as households also had access to one other source for cooking, cleaning, and personal hygiene. As a result, local communities and social enterprises began providing water kiosks in rural areas. Studies from India and Cambodia have shown social organisations creating value for private kiosk-owners by providing marketing and technical support including grants for community-managed kiosk constructions.

A recent study by the University of Queensland in Australia (UQ, 2022), highlights the impacts of bottled water consumption using the sustainability framework (the three pillars):

- Economic impact: Tap water is approximately AUD 3 per 1000 litres compared to bottled water which is around AUD 3 per litre.
- Social impact: Bottled water can have detrimental effects on human health due to deficiencies of essential minerals such as magnesium, potassium, and calcium. It can also have concentrations of chlorine, fluoride, nitrate, and other compounds that exceed WHO guidelines. In addition, some studies have referred to health concerns related to harmful chemicals released from bottles, such as bisphenol A.
- Environmental effects: Although most bottles can be reused or recycled, bottles are produced from PET that is sourced from non-renewable fossil fuels. A large consumption of energy is required in capturing, conveying, and treating water. In addition, energy

is required in producing, cleaning, filling, sealing, labelling, refrigerating, and finally transporting to retailers and consumers. The estimated energy required for bottled water is 5.6–10.2 MJ per litre compared to 0.005 MJ per litre for tap water. While recycling of plastic bottles is being extensively pursued, it saves only one-third of the energy in the production stage and there is a limit to the number of times plastic can be recycled.

Questions

1   Make a list of risks and benefits of bottled water to society and MNEs.
2   Do you see differences in risks and benefits for people in developed and emerging countries and communities?
3   If you were a business analyst, what would you advise MNEs to do for their bottled-water business?
4   What could be done by MNEs to address SDG 6 (clean water) in regions where potable water is not available?
5   If you are in the advertising business, what would you recommend to your clients (in the bottled-water business) and to the consumers of bottled water? What would be your communication strategy?
6   Make a list of similar products (or services) – like bottled water – that are not entirely necessary (and could be avoided) and that are environmentally unsustainable. Reflect on their impacts.

Sources:

Brei (2018)
Felton (2020)
Lyne (2020)
Miller et al. (2020)
Perkins (2019)
UQ (2022)
Wellington (2020)

Obtaining government-controlled resources

MNEs entering foreign markets need to interact with local public officials to secure goods and services controlled by the state – such as 'permits, approvals, licences, utilities, customs clearances, regulatory rulings, tax concessions, judicial decisions, and procurement contracts' (Sartor and Beamish, 2020: 730). Sartor and Beamish contend that corruption can occur in both the public (government) and private (customers, suppliers, investors, and employees) domains. Public corruption can occur in these situations when government officials and bureaucrats leverage their positional power to grant such resources and even to arbitrarily modify or alter policies and regulations. This can foster uncertainty and expose MNEs to increased knowledge-based risk – that is, MNEs often find themselves lacking the knowledge and information required to navigate through the procedures with government officials. Consequently, MNEs face transaction costs that include the cost of identifying new sources of knowledge and information. Faced with the twin issues of commitment to invest in a foreign market and public corruption, responses from firms can range from outright compliance with corruption to outright avoidance of corrupt transactions. Private corruption involves trust and confidence in how transactions are executed. Research into 187 subsidiaries in 19 foreign markets by Sartor and Beamish (2020) found suitable organisational structures for MNE's foreign subsidiary investment as:

- A joint venture with a local partner when there is a higher-level of public corruption.
- A wholly owned subsidiary when there is a higher-level of private corruption.

Modern slavery

Slavery that existed for hundreds of years was abolished in most countries in the 19th and 20th centuries. However, it has gradually transformed itself into an officially approved practice and has been framed in various definitions such as bonded labour, human trafficking, forced labour, and even traditional slavery – all encompassed into the label called 'modern slavery'. While slavery based on legal ownership has been made illegal worldwide under United Nations charters (article 4 of UDHR, 2022) and in individual countries, it is now recognised as practices that involve powers attached to the right of ownership – such as forced, bonded, and child labour, as well as human trafficking and forced marriages (Crane, 2013). Stringer and Michailova (2018) contend that modern slavery is becoming globalised with a range of people and organisations including MNEs, intermediaries, and local producers playing key roles in it.

The ILO (2022b) estimates:

- There were 49.6 million people living in modern slavery in 2021, of which 27.6 million were in forced labour.
- Of the 27.6 million people in forced labour, 17.3 million are exploited in the private sector, 6.3 million in forced commercial sexual exploitation, and 3.9 million in forced labour imposed by the state.
- Women and girls account for 4.9 million of those in forced commercial sexual exploitation, and 6 million of those in forced labour in other economic sectors.
- Children account for 12 per cent of all those in forced labour. More than half of these children are in commercial sexual exploitation.

Modern slavery thus remains a viable management practice for many enterprises and as observed by Crane (2013) these organisations manage to exploit certain competitive and institutional conditions that can give rise to slavery and, further, insulate themselves from institutional pressures and even manage to sustain conditions that enable slavery to flourish. Modern slavery can be observed in supply chains of companies in high labour-intensive sectors such as:

- Food and agriculture (including rice, coffee, tea, cocoa, cotton, and fruits).
- Manufacturing (such as brickmaking, carpet weaving, clothing, leather, and fashion garments).
- The construction industry.

The management practice of modern slavery can be understood through the analysis of demand and supply. The demand is linked to the practices of MNEs seeking cheaper products in their supply chains and the supply is linked to the human supply chain that is available to be exploited due to conditions such as poverty, lack of education, unemployment, geographic isolation, cultural traditions, inequalities, religious beliefs, and ineffective regulations (Crane, 2013). MNEs through their supply chains find themselves 'entangled' with modern slavery (Van Buren III et al., 2020). They argue that while businesses face competitive pressures, they still make choices about strategies that can expose them to potential entanglement in modern slavery. Further, their actions could be designed to give them the appearance of distance from modern slavery. Recognising this, the UK Slavery Act (2015, Part 6) calls for transparency in companies' supply chains. Three types of reactions to entanglement in modern slavery have been identified (Van Buren III et al., 2020):

1 Implausible deniability: in which businesses unconvincingly deny the possibility of slavery in their supply chains – seen in cocoa bean production and denied by companies such as Nestle, Mars, and Hershey (Whoriskey and Siegel, 2019).
2 Plausible deniability: in which businesses take responsibility for conducting supplier due diligence but not for ensuring that requirements are followed up – seen in fashion brands where human rights can be monitored at first-tier suppliers but not subsequent tiers.
3 Ethical commitment: in which businesses take responsibility for complying with standards and ensuring effective remedies for any labour violations – seen in chocolate makers Jasper + Myrtle who ensure ethically sourced cocoa beans that ensure sustainability and traceability by forming a special relationship with family-run cocoa farmers in Bouganville, Papua New Guinea (Jasper and Myrtle, 2023).

However, research in this field has been slow and challenging. Caruana et al. (2021) suggest that part of the challenge in researching modern slavery relates to the difficulties of conducting empirical research on this topic. There are issues of measurement, definition, bias, and ethics, not to mention the personal safety of the researcher. Additionally, there are difficulties in obtaining appropriate data.

Although an organisation's operations may be free from slavery, exploitation can be hidden in various layers and tiers of their supply chains. Further, if we consider the consumption perspective, a country's accountability for modern slavery may extend beyond its domestic cases of human exploitation. One way to compare organisations and countries is to ascertain their 'bad labour' or 'slavery' footprints (Shilling et al., 2021). Researchers have observed that social impact displacements (such as modern slavery) typically move from developed to developing nations and have been described as 'master–servant' relationships, where the lifestyle of some countries is supported by workers in other countries (2021: 1519). Using data from 57 sectors across 140 regions of the world (that includes 120 countries), Shilling et al. (2021) showed that:

- The slavery footprint in developed countries such as North America, Western Europe, Australia, and Japan is larger than their domestic slavery mainly due to offshore production and domestic consumption.
- Conversely, countries such as India and the Democratic Republic of Congo show a decrease in the number of instances of domestic modern slavery.
- 'Importers of slavery' refers to countries that purchase products from other countries that have been produced with modern slavery. 'Exporters of slavery' are countries that use modern slavery to produce products before selling them to others for consumption. So, a country can be a net 'importer' or a net 'exporter' of modern slavery. The USA is the greatest net importer, and India and North Korea are the greatest net exporters. China, Russia, Turkey, Mexico, and Brazil are countries that are importers and exporters.

Australia introduced the Modern Slavery Act in 2018 that was widely hailed as a critical step towards tacking the global problem of modern slavery. However, key findings in a recent report by the Human Rights Law Centre (Sinclair and Dinshaw, 2022), reveal that:

- Only 23 per cent of companies fully address the mandatory reporting requirements.
- More than half (52 per cent) are failing to identify and disclose risks in their operations and supply chains – especially in garment, PPE, horticultural, and seafood industries.
- Only 27 per cent of companies could demonstrate that they are taking some form of action against modern slavery risks.
- Despite operating in high-risk sectors, only 8 per cent stated particulars of allegations or instances of modern slavery and how the company responded.
- Just 25 per cent disclosed countries of suppliers with most failing to identify suppliers beyond their Tier-1 suppliers.

What can be done?

In a study of 280 international academic papers from 1999 to 2021, Mehmood et al. (2022) reveal that modern slavery is a multilevel governance challenge that involves entities such as the states, corporations, non-state organisations (NGOs), subnational (regional and local) polities, and individuals. Each such entity can act as a governor although none can take complete control of the governance system. For example, they argue that international business and slavery are fundamentally linked by governance. Private governance involves international business practices via FDIs, IP control, market dominance exploitation, and international mobility, MNEs can therefore exert instrumental power (entails A enforcing upon B with what B does not agree) over certain actors to gain their compliance.

It is argued that modern slavery is an example of social unsustainability, and that the stakeholder theory is an appropriate theoretical lens for examining both the problem and potential solutions (Robb and Michailova, 2022). In their recent study that involved interviewing key people in various supply chains, Robb and Michailova discovered that:

- MNEs have a limited understanding of modern slavery overall, as well as the role they played in it, citing widespread ignorance and indifference.
- Combating slavery is worth the cost – due to recent public exposures, legal action, and failing to comply with modern slavery legislation. There is a business case beyond a moral imperative for MNEs to respect human rights across their supply chains.
- Greater collaboration is required between firms, suppliers, governments, NGOs, the media, and competitors to address slavery.
- The problem is too serious and complicated to address – many said they do not know where to start.

Solutions suggested in Robb and Michailova's (2022) study:

1   Establishing a structured response for mapping and prioritising risks through the supply chains.
2   Education and communication across all departments rather than just human resources, procurement, and sustainability, involving everyone from top management down. Training can include instructions for reporting suspicious activities and encouraging whistle-blowing.
3   Third-party engagement is important because MNEs may lack the expertise and reputation to address slavery. This includes involving a wide range of stakeholders many of whom may not be directly involved in the organisation.

International transfer pricing

Tax strategies deployed by MNEs include ITP which, due to its ability to provide opportunities for tax avoidance, has received public attention leading to legal disputes between MNEs and tax authorities worldwide. Hemling et al. (2022) define the phenomenon as follows:

> an MNE with a company located in a tax haven can decrease its group-level tax burden by transferring goods at artificially high prices to an affiliated company located in a high-tax jurisdiction. This increases the selling company's profit, which is subject to limited taxation, while reducing the pre-tax profit of the buying company due to the inflated cost. The net effect is a reduced tax payment for the MNE group. (p. 1)

Example: Company A purchases goods for USD 100 and sells them to its associated Company B in another country for USD 200, who in turn sells them on the open market for USD 400. Had A sold it direct, it would have made a profit of USD 300. But by routing through B, it restricted profit to USD 100 in the first country, permitting B to appropriate the balance and pay lower taxes on the remaining profit. The transaction between A and B is arranged and not governed by market forces. A profit of USD 200 is, thereby, shifted to country B. The goods are transferred on a price (transfer price) which is arbitrary or dictated (USD 200), not at the market price (USD 400) (adapted from ITI, 2023).

Emerging countries often set higher tax rates to finance economic development for two reasons: (1) to generate and increase tax revenues, and (2) due to the inability of tax author-ities to collect tax revenue. It has been argued that such higher tax rates are the main drivers for EMNEs to use investment-holding companies in the so-called tax havens to navigate around corporate taxation. In a study of a large cross-country dataset, Jones et al. (2023) found that EMNEs from weaker institutional environments are more likely to own tax haven subsidiaries. However, as they improve their institutional environment, investing in tax havens declines before increasing again when emerging countries achieve developmental stages similar to those of developed countries (p. 1).

Trade institutions such as the OECD (2022b), and most countries including the USA (IRS, 2023), India (ITI, 2023), Australia (ATO, 2023), and the UK (UK.gov, 2023), have developed policies, guidelines, and legislation to promote tax compliance. Tax authorities in many jurisdictions have pushed for a higher degree of accounting automation through enterprise resource planning (ERP) systems (for example) and most MNEs have incorporated ERP sys-tems to manage ITP transactions. However, Hemling et al. (2022) found that there was limited use of information technology for ITP management. While ITP automation was observed in workflow management (to produce documentation), in some MNEs, the actual downloading and analysis of data and the decision-making of transfer pricing was done manually, usually using spreadsheets. Others use external price-setting tools that are not integrated with the ERP system. Further, they conclude that some MNEs are sceptical that full ITP automation is realistic.

In this context, it is important to differentiate the following (adapted from various sources cited in Eden and Smith, 2022):

- Tax planning: involves strategies to minimise amount of taxes.
- Tax avoidance: tax planning where the firm takes advantage of existing legal laws to reduce its taxes.
- Tax fraud: involves deception, lying, and wilful misrepresentation of facts to gain unfair and dishonest advantage.
- Tax evasion: consists of wilful and conscious non-compliance with the law – where the firm tries to escape legal obligations by fraudulent or other illegal means.

Eden and Smith (2022) argue that ITP can be examined using two ethical lenses:

1   The tax ethics view that builds on Friedman's argument (1970) – as discussed in Chapter 2 – that the social responsibility of business is to increase its profits as long as the firm stays within the rules of the game. That means if the ITPs are legal and disclosed, MNEs are not obligated to go beyond that.

2   Moral ethics requires that MNE executives should be concerned with societal well-being, including the impacts of their transfer pricing – in particular to pay their 'fair share' of tax, especially in developing countries. In this view, ITP is seen as morally wrong because it can harm society – including loss of income tax, customs duty, depletion of natural resources, increased national debt and poverty, loss of trust in MNEs, and economic colonialism.

So, how can we explain fraudulent behaviour in white collar crimes such as those involved in ITP? Using the three components of the 'fraud triangle', Eden and Smith (2022) explain why MNEs may move from legal and ethical ITP to abusive transfer pricing:

- Component 1 – Opportunity: this comes from positions of power and the absence of controls or monitoring fraudulent behaviour – for example, absence of global rules, reluctance to share information between governments, and tax competition between governments to attract inward FDIs.
- Component 2 – Motivation: this comes in the form of pressures and incentives – for example, additional global after-tax profits and managerial bonuses.
- Component 3 – Rationalisation: this happens when MNE managers are tempted to rationalise abusive ITP on the grounds that shareholders benefit from ITP and that 'everyone is doing it'. The concept of rationalisation was discussed in Chapter 3.

Corporate governance

According to Rossouw (2009), ethics is associated with corporate governance (CG) in two different ways – the ethics of governance and the governance of ethics. Ethics of governance implies that all CG regimes have certain principles, regulations, and directives that drive the role, responsibilities, and obligations of corporations. In addition, it provides clarity of the moral responsibilities of firms in society as well as the ethical values associated with it. The 'governance of ethics' deals specifically with what corporations are expected or required to do and therefore includes 'codes of ethics, rules of conduct, ethics training of the board of directors and staff, ethics audits, and reporting on ethics performance etc.' (Rossouw, 2009: 7).

Two of the most important components of ethical context are the organisation's ethical climate and ethical culture. Kaptein (2020: 1) suggests that 'an organisation's ethical climate refers to the shared perceptions of managers and employees about what constitutes ethical and unethical behavior in the organisation. Its ethical culture are the shared perceptions of managers and employees about the conditions in the organisation for ethical behavior. In other words, ethical climate is substantive, whereas ethical culture is procedural'.

Considering and acknowledging that one of the main causes of the many high-profile CG scandals (such as Enron in 2001, BP in 2010, Volkswagen in 2015, Boeing in 2019, and others that have been discussed in this book) could be attributed to the organisational culture and more specifically the ethical culture of an organisation, Di Miceli da Silveira (2022) set out to analyse how the composition of the board of directors influences ethical culture. They found that better ethical culture could be associated with a higher proportion of independent directors, a higher proportion of female directors and older board age, whereas a decreased ethical culture was associated with a higher proportion of directors appointed by minority shareholders. Further, in a study of 362 firms in 46 different countries, Naciti (2019) found that firms with more diversity on the board and a separation between chair and CEO roles show higher sustainability performance. A higher number of independent directors led to lower sustainability performance. Of particular interest are the CG strategies of EMNEs. A broad overview of the literature indicates that 'foreign investments by emerging economy firms led to upgrade of their governance capabilities. These firms also became advocates for home country policy reforms that mandated the development of similar capabilities for local firms' (Bhaumik et al., 2019: 234).

While efforts have been made to fix what is broken in CG by regulations and other external mandates (for example the Sarbanes-Oxley Act 2002, passed in response to the Enron collapse, and the Dodd-Frank Act 2010, passed in response to the 2007–2008 financial crisis), 'these have proven insufficient for ensuring improvements in accountability, transparency, or ethical decision-making' (Steckler and Clark, 2019: 951). Focus is therefore shifting to include personal and behavioural characteristics that influence the ethical behaviour of boards of directors who, in addition to firm performance, can influence the ethical actions of the firm. One of the key personal characteristics which has attracted researchers is the relationship between 'authenticity' and boards and CG. 'Authenticity' has been understood as (adapted from various sources cited in Steckler and Clark, 2019):

- being true to oneself and also where the alignment between one's personal values and behaviours are consistent
- doing what is most congruent with deeply held values
- involving one's moral values when interacting with others
- acting on one's deeply held interior moral motivations, as opposed to taking action motivated by exterior influence
- genuine intentions to serve others
- possessing moral capacity to recognise, evaluate, and address ethical issues, the moral courage to take action, and the moral resilience to sustain ethical behaviour (similar to Rest's Four Component model of ethical decision-making discussed in Chapter 4).

Authenticity in CG is likely to exist on a continuum – that is, operative at the individual level and, by extension, collectively for the board of directors' group. As suggested by Steckler and Clark (2019), authenticity can be infused into CG in three areas:

- Selection: of board members based on the 'true to self' criteria, including strong moral values, and the courage to do the right thing.
- Cultivation: by socialisation of organisational values through 'on-boarding' and training of board members to express their personal values.
- Enactment: by involving the interaction of board responsibilities to ethical norms and practices in the discussions, deliberations, and decisions of the board.

As we have discussed in earlier chapters, artificial intelligence (AI) is now widely considered as a necessary and general solution technology for managerial, commercial, and societal problems. AI-enabled intelligent machines are increasingly being applied in areas of design, manufacturing, services, logistics, marketing, accounting and finance, banking, and many more. Recently, attention has turned to the impact of AI on decision-making by the board of directors related to CG – that is to the control and direction of the corporation. Hilb (2020) identified the following key areas of responsibility of the board of directors where AI technology could be applied:

- Co-direction: responsible for developing strategies with the top management team (TMT) – such as decisions on innovation, collaboration, optimisation, transformation, diversification, and internalisation.
- Control: to control the TMT and to fully comply with the law, accounting codes, company rules, and risk management – such as decisions on target achievement, meeting accounting standards, legal compliance, and ethical compliance.
- Coaching: to appoint and coach the TMT for effective leadership – such as decisions on executive appointments, development, compensation, and board composition.

There are new concerns about the new forms of organisational activities ensuing from expanding digital technology and networks (e.g. see Sama et al., 2022):

- While the number of digital businesses is growing, they employ a small fraction of the workforce – thereby accruing benefits to the few and thus widening the income inequality gap.
- Smaller traditional businesses get pushed out, jobs are lost, and social stability could be threatened.
- Digitalisation can translate into marginalisation and discrimination for those without equal access to technology.
- The speed of digitalisation, data analytics, and AI can add to the lack of transparency around digital business models – how they operate, whom they partner with, what their products and services are and whom they serve.

In a digital market economy, where lack of trust has eroded market values, it is essential to restore trust for the survival of the firm and for maintaining the common good. Sama et al. (2022) offer a stewardship-based model of CG as a solution to the roots of inequality and the problems facing stakeholders of digital business excesses. Stewardship is a sense of duty to both internal and external stakeholders even if the resulting action is not linked to any personal reward. Their governance model includes seven traits in the digital economy:

1   Favouring the neediest stakeholders (could be agencies, vendors, customers and/or employees) who lack access to resources – by providing them with customised tools and techniques.
2   Considering the natural environment as a stakeholder – by leveraging digital capabilities to address SDG targets.

3 Prioritising societal and spiritual good over material good – by building trust and creating technologies that improve lives.

4 Allocating limited resources fairly that benefit the marginalised – ensure data availability and promote digital democracy.

5 Correcting unfairness in the workplace and beyond – by ensuring tech tools (AI, for example) used in hiring, promotion, and contracts do not have embedded biases and algorithm flaws.

6 Exercising a long-term view – by providing leadership to preserve long-term positive social outcomes.

7 Vigilantly scanning the external environment by reducing the impact of digital information disruptions, consulting fact-checking websites.

Summary

- This chapter explores some particular challenges faced by multinational enterprises from both developed and emerging economies (DMNEs and EMNEs respectively). The special areas of interest have implications at the international, national, organisational, and individual levels. The areas discussed in this chapter are: knowledge management, liability of foreignness (LoF), government-controlled resources, modern slavery, international transfer pricing (ITP), and corporate governance (CG).

- We understood that knowledge management (KM) includes the identification, creation, acquisition, sharing, and updating of information, and importantly sustaining knowledge within the organisation. One specific area of KM is intellectual property (IP), and one specific area of interest is the 'leakage' of IP. We learnt about the ethical challenges in managing knowledge.

- The concept of LoF is critical for MNEs when entering a foreign market. We explained how the OLI strategies of most MNEs can include differences in ethical standards between MNEs and host countries. LoF was also discussed to differentiate between DMNE and EMNE experiences. Strategies used by MNEs to reduce the effects of LoF were discussed in this section. A follow-on effect of LoF is obtaining government-controlled resources such as permits, approvals, licences, utilities, customs clearances, etc. The section suggested two suitable organisational structures – joint ventures for instances of public corruption and wholly owned subsidiaries for instances of private corruption.

- The section on modern slavery began with its history and definition, and some statistics. The prevalence of modern slavery was linked to the motivations of international firms and of local governments. Suggestions and solutions were discussed.

- ITP is a unique and important area of global strategy for MNEs. We defined the ITP concept – how it works and also that it can be legal. We examined ITP using two ethical lenses: tax ethics (its fine as long as it is within the rules of the game) and moral ethics (it is not fine because it can harm society by way of not paying a fair share of taxes).

- Finally, we explored how CG is a key task for the board of directors and top management teams, which includes certain principles, regulations, and directives that drive the role, responsibilities, and obligations of corporations. Of particular interest was the need for board diversity, independent directors, and an ethical culture. History is replete with examples of failures of well-known corporations due to insufficient accountability, transparency, or ethical decision-making. We showed that one way to fix what's broken is to focus on 'authenticity' and how it can be infused into CG. There was a special mention of how artificial intelligence technology could, in the future, be applied to CG – but this will require legal and ethical considerations.

CASE STUDY 9.1
WALMART AND ITS CHALLENGES

Walmart, as the world's largest retailer and private employer, represents the global expansion of retail corporations in the 1990s that was possible due to trade liberalisation, deregulation, and privatisation. In the 1990s, the transformation of the retail industry happened due to processes such as availability of retail capital, development of information and communication technologies and new management systems like lean retailing and just-in-time production (Bank Muñoz et al., 2018: 1).

Founded by Sam Walton and James Walton in 1962 in a small town called Rogers, Arkansas, Walmart now operates 10,500 retail units under 46 banners in 24 countries and e-commerce websites. Walmart was the world's largest company by revenue in 2022 (USD 572.75 billion), according to Fortune's Global 500 2022 rankings, and also the world's largest (private) employer, with over 2.3 million employees (1.7 million in the US). As of 31 October 2022, Walmart's US operations include 5,320 units, generating over 65 per cent of its total sales. It has 5,266 units outside of the US in Latin America (4,056 units), Africa (411), Canada (402 units), and Asia (397 units).

Walmart's strategy of 'everyday low prices' spurred on a 'revolution' in retail and business practices as it sought cheaper and cheaper supply from producers around the world. Much of what's written about Walmart's business in the US focused on the effects of its vast power on communities, local small businesses, competitor retailers, labour conditions, wage levels, labour markets, unions, and suppliers. The so-called 'Walmart effect' includes 'outraged communities, about 2.2 million relatively low-paid workers, many of whom are "contingent" or part-time workers, huge discrimination lawsuits, an anti-union stance, and tremendous pressures on suppliers for efficiencies that drive sometimes already-poor human rights and labor practices even lower' (Waddock, 2022: 284).

Having saturated the rural, suburban, and exurban markets in the US, Walmart needed to move into urban and new markets globally. Early moves began in North America (Canada and Mexico) followed by Latin America (Mexico, Brazil, and Argentina), then entering Europe, and finally entering Africa (South Africa and 12

(Continued)

Sub-Saharan countries), China, and India. In each of these countries, Walmart had successes, failures, and challenges. Two major issues were observed:

- Workers shifting from a position of involvement, commitment, and motivation to one of suspicion, distrust, anger, and antagonism.
- Conflict between Walmart's 'family culture' where an employee is identified as a loyal 'collaborator', and the exploitation of cheap labour through low salaries, high turnover, high-intensity work, and large numbers of subcontracted workers.

Research indicates that Walmart needed to adapt to local institutional and regulatory circumstances:

- In Mexico, the company's strategies to construct and inculcate Walmart culture resulted in IT workers' perception of the company's promises and messages to be contradictory, meaningless, awkward, and even manipulative.
- In Brazil, the Walmart workplace culture was a key element of union struggles in the stores.
- Walmart's labour strategy to keep unions out of the shop floor across the supply chain could be part of its failure in Germany as they lacked understanding of the union model in that country.
- In spite of their opposition to unions, they had to accept them in Latin America, Africa, Asia, and Europe. These regions have laws and policies which forced Walmart to accept unions, either as a condition of entry or because of existing labour laws.
- For their supply of shrimp farming (mainly in Thailand), Walmart promotes aquaculture through voluntary codes of best practice. However, a joint venture with large shrimp producers to ensure a supply of low-cost shrimp has resulted in their subcontractors engaging in modern-day slavery through labour trafficking from neighbouring countries.
- In India's highly regulated FDI environment, Walmart in 2018 acquired 77 per cent of Flipkart, one of India's largest e-commerce companies. While Walmart expects that the deal will benefit India by providing quality and affordable goods for consumers, creating skill-oriented jobs, and generating new jobs for farmers, women entrepreneurs, and small local suppliers, online sellers fear Walmart's reputation of killing small businesses with ultra-low prices.
- In Canada, critics have identified Walmart Canada's practices of inadequate wages with few benefits, contributing to household food insecurity (HFI). In an effort to improve its image, the company entered into a partnership with Food Banks Canada with the goal of reducing HFI.
- The United Nations' Food and Agriculture Organisation (FAO) estimates that globally around 14 per cent of food produced is lost between harvest and retail, while an estimated 17 per cent of global food production is wasted. Walmart-Mexico (Walmex) has an objective to avoid generation of food waste by seeking a zero waste to landfill strategy. In spite of its sustainable waste management

policy, waste that cannot be recycled, reused, or composted (almost 27 per cent of the total waste) is disposed of in an authorised landfill site. A recent study (Carpio-Aguilar et al., 2019) has suggested Walmex should adopt a circular business model that includes processes such as reduction, donation, animal feeding, and anaerobic digestion.

In summary, from the above we can observe the challenges faced by Walmart when entering foreign markets outside of the US, and the successes, failures, and strategies adopted by the company to grow in international markets.

Questions

Using the Case-Study Integrative Framework in Figure 0.1, discuss the following:

1   Identify the key primary and secondary stakeholders of Walmart in the USA and in other countries. Are there any differences?
2   Considering Walmart's size and potential impact, do you think Walmart is addressing stakeholders' issues?
3   Are there any stakeholders whose concerns are not adequately addressed by Walmart?
4   If Walmart is playing by the 'rules of the game' (as advocated by Friedman) in each country, do they have a mandate to satisfy customers at any cost?
5   What are the ethical issues in this case study?
6   Use the CEDM model from earlier chapters to develop your analysis, judgement, commitment, and potential actions.
7   Do you think individual countries have adequate regulations to safeguard the interests of their workers and suppliers? If not, what more should they be doing?
8   Reflect on the issues faced by Walmart and suggest what actions they should be implementing which could be an exemplar for other MNE retail organisations.

Sources:
Bank Muñoz et al. (2018)
Carpio-Aguilar et al. (2019)
ET Online (2018)
FAO (2023)
Flynn (2022)
Mendly-Zambo et al. (2021)
Rincón-Moreno et al. (2018)
Saraswathy (2019)
Waddock (2022)
Walmart (2022a)
Walmart (2022b)

CASE STUDY 9.2
MNE CONTRIBUTIONS TO THE WORLD

Attaining the SDGs

The role of MNEs in attaining the SDGs is critical as it makes them drivers of change. However, because it involves multiple stakeholders, each nation state has its constraints and resources in economic, social, and environmental issues and pose enormous problems for MNEs. In particular MNEs face challenges in achieving the SDGs when operating in countries where stakeholders can bring different perspectives to the definition and potential resolution of issues. Some MNEs have performed better through their subsidiaries than others. For example, Coca Cola in India took advantage of the lack of legislation and legal requirements to maintain groundwater levels, raising concerns of water depletion leading to disagreements with local stakeholders. Unilever, on the other hand, through their Indian subsidiary HLL, empowered women of India's rural areas by encouraging them to be their salespersons, thereby improving the lives of their families. Similarly, IKEA implemented its policy on conserving energy and reducing its carbon footprint through its subsidiaries. Synergy (or lack of it) between firms can also deliver success (or failure). For example, L'Oréal's (a French firm) acquisition of Body Shop (a UK firm) did not work even though they were both from developed countries. Whereas subsequently the acquisition of Body Shop by Natura (a Brazilian firm from an emerging country) was a success as both companies were aligned to the same SDGs. Tata Motors (an Indian MNE) offered and trained marginalised communities including youths and women in eight countries – Bangladesh, Mozambique, Sudan, Tanzania, Kenya, Nigeria, Ghana, and Sri Lanka. The subsidiary of Tata Chemicals (an Indian MNE) in Kenya not only provided healthcare facilities to its employees, but also provided resources to upgrade equipment in hospitals, built schools, and gave financial support to students.

Addressing the impact of Covid-19

Covid-19 restrictions and lockdowns severely impacted travel and international business relocations including employee mobility for MNEs. The stay-at-home orders and public health measures changed the way MNEs do business globally. Lazarova et al. (2023) in their recent paper analysed the steps taken by MNEs to address key issues such as where should the work be done, what changes are needed in how the work is done, and why these changes are important considering the role of MNEs in environmental sustainability and the health and safety of employees.

- Where the global work is done has implications:

  o for MNEs in terms of changes to corporate culture – for example, cultural factors that working from home (WFH) can affect employee competence, and motivation.

  o for employees in terms of some people preferring WFH at least some of the time. For others, WFH may affect their international career aspirations.

- How the global work is being done through increased digitalisation (creating and deploying new technologies) has implications:

  o for MNEs to evolve new business models – automation and robotisation (through AI) has accelerated partly due to its capacity to substitute labour and partly due to health and safety reasons.

  o for employees, digitalisation could impact how they are managed by MNEs – for example, 'digital exhaust' (meta-data comprising logs on employees' online behaviour) can raise issues of ethics, privacy, and data protection, especially when data is interpreted, and decisions predicted by AI.

Based on the above, MNEs are now increasingly resetting changes on global work at three levels:

- Societal level – such as digitalisation, migration, global health and safety, sustainability, and restricted global mobility.
- Organisational level – such as fewer co-located employees, more remote work, restricted global mobility, and increased focus of equity, diversity, and inclusion (EDI).
- Individual level – such as emphasis on EDI, greater desire for WFH, and greater ability to change jobs.

Innovation and R&D

Considering that innovation and R&D are one of the most important competitive advantages of the 21st century, countries and companies are stimulating more innovative activities and benefitting from the outcomes. Historically, innovation and R&D activities were limited to MNEs from the 'Triad' regions (the US, Western Europe, and Japan). However, in the 21st century, we can now see MNEs having compelling reasons to do R&D work in emerging countries, particularly in China and India. The motivations for MNEs undertaking R&D activities in emerging countries are:

- Adapting products originally made in the MNE's home country to local market conditions of the host country – for example General Electric developing low-cost portable medical scanners in China and ECG machines in India.
- Carrying out R&D that could be applied to the home country because of low-cost conditions in host countries – for example pharmaceutical firms carrying out clinical trials.

(Continued)

- Carrying out R&D in host countries to learn from the innovation environment – for example 'reverse innovation': Microsoft developing products in India, and Volkswagen developing electric cars in China.
- Participating in the MNE's global network of R&D for costs, market features, and availability of knowledge and skills – for example the business process outsourcing of IBM and Microsoft in India with Wipro, TCS, and Infosys.

For mini case studies on VW in China, Motorola in Brazil, Continental AG in Mexico, Intel in Costa Rica, IBM's software development in India, Apple's R&D in China, and Adobe's R&D hub in India, see Grosse (2019). Examples of EMNEs acquiring overseas firms and R&D include Tata Motors of India acquiring Jaguar and Land Rover in the UK and Geely of China acquiring Volvo, a Swedish firm, among others.

MNEs in Africa

Africa's agro-food industry is becoming an important player in the supply chains of MNEs. The methods of entry into Africa's dynamic economies are through wholly owned subsidiaries, non-equity linkages such as franchises and licensing, and also through sales and marketing offices. Major areas in the agro-food industry are beverages with companies like Coca Cola and AB InBev, the chemicals and seeds industry with BASF, Dow Chemicals, and Bayer. The business models adopted by these MNEs link small-scale farmers into their supply chain with better planning and limiting exposure to price fluctuations in the global market. The model also ensures integrity of the product and security of supply. Foreign companies also provide seeds, fertilisers, advice on cultivation techniques, and special financial terms for greenfield suppliers. In addition to Western MNEs, there is considerable involvement from Asian businesses that goes beyond imports and exports – these companies invest directly in Africa. China has emerged as Africa's largest economic partner followed by India.

One example is a company cited by Felgenhauer and Labella (2022): Olam International. Founded by members of the Indian diaspora in Singapore, it has a presence in 24 African countries with plans to expand to all countries on the continent. It integrates entire supply chains into its strategy including sourcing, processing, and distribution of raw materials such as cocoa, sugar, beans, and nuts. Support for rice and cashew growers includes training, buying back produce, and acquiring farm equipment. Their employment generations include 5,200 growers in Nigeria, 5,500 women in cashew processing, and 3,000 employees in Mozambique.

Questions

1. Using the Case-Study Integrative Framework in Figure 0.1, discuss the following:
2. Identify the key primary and secondary stakeholders of DMNEs and EMNEs. Are there any differences?

3   Are there any stakeholders whose concerns are not adequately addressed by DMNEs in emerging countries and EMNEs in developed countries?

4   With respect to MNEs achieving SDGs, what are the ethical issues in this case study?

5   Use the CEDM model from earlier chapters to develop your analysis, judgement, commitment, and potential actions.

6   What do you think are the lessons DMNEs and EMNEs can learn from each other from their experiences?

Sources:

Felgenhauer and Labella (2022)

Grosse (2019)

Lazarova et al. (2023)

Liou and Rao-Nicholson (2021)

Majumdar (2022)

Olam (2023)

Recommended readings

Caruana, R., Crane, A., Gold, S. and LeBaron, G. (2021), 'Modern slavery in business: The sad and sorry state of a non-field', *Business and Society*, 60(2): 251–87.

A great article to understand the phenomenon of 'modern slavery'. The authors of this article explore its developments, potential drawbacks, and future deviations that might evolve within the areas of business and management.

Eden, L. and Smith, L.M. (2022), 'The ethics of transfer pricing: Insights from the fraud triangle', *Journal of Forensic and Investigative Accounting*, 14(3): 360–83.

This paper will help us understand transfer pricing in the international context. Further, it discusses the risks and benefits of transfer pricing, followed by the legality and ethics of it. An interesting discussion centres around the 'fraud triangle' (opportunity, incentive, and rationalisation).

Men, C., Fong, P.S.W., Huo, W., Zhong, J., Jia, R. and Luo, J. (2020), 'Ethical leadership and knowledge hiding: A moderated mediation model of psychological safety and mastery climate', *Journal of Business Ethics*, 166(3): 461–72.

Reading this will provide an insight into the meaning of 'knowledge hiding'. The authors use empirical analysis to show the link between ethical leadership and ethical hiding.

Pesqué-Cela, V., Li, J. and Kim, Y.K. (2022), 'Overcoming the liability of foreignness in US capital markets: The case of Alibaba and Coupang', *Asia Pacific Business Review*, 29(2): 323–49.

This paper investigates whether and how companies from emerging markets use CSR to cover the liability of foreignness when going public in the US. They suggest that such firms (in this case Alibaba and Coupang) increase their CSR activities prior to their IPO in order to signal legitimacy to investors.

Sama, L.M., Stefanidis, A. and Casselman, R.M. (2022), 'Rethinking corporate governance in the digital economy: The role of stewardship', *Business Horizons*, 65(5): 535–46.

An interesting article on how traditional governance mechanisms are ill-equipped to embrace digital technologies. The authors redefine a modern view of stewardship in a digital economy and apply its principles to a practical corporate governance model that includes truthfulness, transparency, trust, and technological equity.

Steckler, E. and Clark, C. (2019), 'Authenticity and corporate governance', *Journal of Business Ethics*, 155(4): 951–63.

Drawing on the idea that personal attributes have gained recognition as an important area of effective corporate governance, the authors of this article explore how authenticity (a personal and morally significant virtue) has the potential to influence board dynamics and decision-making – to enhance transparency and accountability.

Stening, B.W. and Zhang, M.Y. (2016), 'Ethics and the liability of foreignness: The case of China', *Journal of General Management*, 42(2): 3–16.

The concept of liability of foreignness can be understood in this reading – especially related to lack of familiarity with local cultural norms, and economic, political, and legal systems. The paper explores the challenges faced by foreign firms operating in China.

Van Buren III, H.J., Schrempf-Stirling, J. and Westermann-Behaylo, M. (2020), 'Towards ethical commitment: Avoiding MNC entanglement in modern slavery', *AIB Insights*, 20(2): 1–4.

In this article, we appreciate that MNEs are at risk of being connected (they call it 'entanglement') to modern slavery because of their strategic choices related to outsourcing. The authors highlight three types of responsibility-related reactions to entanglement in modern slavery.

10

RESPONSIBLE LEADERSHIP IN BUSINESS ETHICS

─Learning objectives─

On completion of this chapter, you should be able to:

- Appreciate the 'why' and need for responsible leadership (RL)
- Understand the definitions and the development of the RL concept within business ethics
- Explore the components of RL and roles of a responsible leader
- Understand the competencies required to be an effective responsible leader
- Get to know the latest research and applications surrounding RL
- Appreciate the future directions of RL
- Reflect on how the Comprehensive Ethical Decision-Making (CEDM) model from Chapters 4 and 5 can be applied to RL

─Key concepts─

- Responsible leadership
- Meaning of 'responsibility' in this context
- The four orientations of RL
- The ten roles model of RL
- Competency assessment of RL (CARL)
- Corporate irresponsibility
- Effect of artificial intelligence on RL

—Box 10.1 Opening case—

Chetna Sinha and the Mann Deshi Mahila Sahakari Bank

A severe drought in the Mhaswad village in the Indian state of Maharashtra reduced the population to poverty, resulting in large-scale migrations of the men to cities leaving the women to look after themselves. With restricted access to funds, women were forced to borrow from money lenders.

Chetna Sinha grew up in Mumbai, India's financial capital, where she obtained a master's degree in commerce and economics at the University of Mumbai in 1982. Upon marriage, Chetna followed her husband, a farmer, to Mhaswad. There, she witnessed the plight of rural women who were victims of the patriarchal social setup, no property rights, lack of financial independence, and fear of being disowned by husbands and family. Chetna realised that empowering women economically was the only solution, but also a major challenge.

Although subsidies from the government were necessary to improve the economic conditions of the local women, Chetna understood that the subsidies were not the solution. Instead, Chetna decided micro-credit was required because she realised that women possessed entrepreneurial potential with risk-taking abilities. However, the women did not qualify for finance due to their low income base and lack of collateral. Chetna then decided to start a rural co-operative bank for women and applied to the Reserve Bank of India (RBI) in 1994. The RBI rejected her application on the grounds that, except for her, all the group members were illiterate. This setback spurred Chetna to build capacity and ability in women by starting basic literacy classes for women. In 1997, along with her band of qualified literate members, Chetna reapplied to the RBI and was successful in obtaining a banking licence, leading to the establishment of the first rural women's bank in India – the Mann Deshi Mahila Sahakari Bank (MDMSB). Starting with an initial working capital of INR 708,000 (about USD 860) raised from 1,335 members, the bank has now reached over 310,000 women providing them with finance backing and emotional support to become successful entrepreneurs. Today, the bank has about 100,000 account holders and has loaned over USD 50 million.

Some of the key aspects of the MDMSB are:

- Doorstep banking – visiting customers regularly to provide small loans and collecting repayments.
- Customised products – such as helping women to buy goats and designing the first pension scheme for women in the informal economy.
- Non-collateral loans – women can also form a group of four to five and take a loan together.
- Privacy and financial control – in addition to accessing finance, women are supported to control their own finances and privacy through digital literacy programmes.
- Affordable finance – variety of affordable and flexible loans so that women can meet their various consumption and business needs.

Subsequently, Chetna also founded the Mann Deshi Foundation which runs financial classes where women are taught the nuances of savings, insurance, and loans. In addition to the B-schools, the foundation runs a Community Radio and a Chamber of Commerce for rural women micro entrepreneurs. In addition, the foundation runs a digital-literacy bus that visits local rural weekly markets to teach women how to benefit from cashless transactions. They regularly advocate for more inclusive finance for women by networking with the RBI, sharing their learnings and experiences.

Chetna along with six other women were invited to chair the 48th annual World Economic Forum in Davos, Switzerland in 2018. The other six women were the general-secretary of a trade union from Belgium, the director-general of **CERN**, the CEO of ENGIE France, the managing director of the IMF, the CEO of General Motors, and the Prime Minister of Norway.

Sources:
Balkawade (2016)
Wiki (2022a)
MDMSB (2022)

10.1 Introduction – why responsible leadership?

How do some leaders like Chetna Sinha act responsibly against all odds and resolve challenging issues? What separates such responsible leaders from others? What competencies are required to be a responsible leader? These are some of the key questions that drive this chapter.

The Edelman Trust Barometer publishes annual reports gauging trust levels and perceived credibility among general population towards governments, corporations, media, and non-governmental organisations (NGOs). Consider the following key points from the Edelman Trust Barometer (2022) report that analysed responses from a global sample size of more than 36,000 in 28 countries across age, gender, region, and education:

- Business becomes the only trusted institution ahead of NGOs, governments, and media.
- Business is now the only institution seen as both competent and ethical, as compared to NGOs, governments, and media.
- Trust in employers is stable or rising in 18 out of 28 countries.
- Trust in societal leaders (government leaders, religious leaders, journalists, and CEOs) declines but people are more likely to trust what is local such as people in their local community, their employer/CEO, and scientists.
- CEOs as spokespeople of and source of information about their companies is at an all time low in some countries.
- Businesses are expected to fill the void left by government in the following areas:
  – 68 per cent agree CEOs should step in, 66 per cent say CEOs should take the lead,

65 per cent say CEOs should hold themselves accountable to the public and not just to the board of directors and shareholders.
- 86 per cent expect CEOs to publicly speak out about societal challenges such as pandemic impact, job automation, societal issues, and local community issues. There is an increased likelihood of trust when businesses embrace sustainable practices, have a robust Covid-19 response, drive economic prosperity, and value long-term thinking over short-term profits.

As we have seen in our discussions in previous chapters, businesses (and therefore their leaders) are expected to not only take care of their business and direct stakeholders, but also contribute to society and the environment. Many CEOs agree that businesses should create a positive impact beyond profit, and this requires acting responsibly towards a broader set of stakeholders that includes the planet and society (Muff et al., 2022). Businesspeople and other entities such as medical and legal professionals, religious authorities, voluntary organisations, and politicians are increasingly realising the importance of upholding the dignity and rights of employees and clients, the interests of shareholders, and societal stakeholders. There is also a realisation that it is impossible to avoid involvement in ethics. But without the right leaders possessing appropriate skills, knowledge, and virtues, even the best designed ethical organisation can falter (Flynn and Werhane, 2022). The various case studies and vignettes that have been discussed in this book highlighted some positive business stories (LEGO, Taj, Cipla, Conzerv, Merck, and Starbucks) and some unethical business stories (Enron, Brent Spar, Boeing, Fast Fashion). Central to these business stories is business leadership. The unethical business stories and some recent ones such as the 2015 Volkswagen diesel emissions scandal, the 2019 opioid scandal of Purdue, and the Big Pharma marketing tactics (available as a case study in this chapter) suggest that irresponsible executive behaviour is a key reason for those scandals. In addition to the traditional descriptors used for leadership, such as transactional, transformational, servant, ethical, authentic, and spiritual leadership, the concept of responsible leadership was proposed at the beginning of the 21st century – pioneered mainly by Thomas Maak and Nicola Pless in 2006. Specifically, Waldman and Galvin (2008) propose that responsibility is missing from the established leadership descriptors mentioned above. In a nutshell, to not be responsible is to be ineffective as a leader. Responsible leadership was originally understood as 'a social, relational and ethical phenomenon, which occurs in social processes of interaction' suggesting a responsibility above and beyond traditional organisational boundaries (Maak and Pless, 2006: 99). In 2015, the annual meeting of the European Group for Organizational Studies (EGOS) had a sub-theme on responsible leadership to address social, environmental, and business implications of leadership (EGOS, 2015). The global agenda for the World Economic Forum's (WEF) 2017 meeting focused on responsive and responsible leadership (WEF, 2017).

Maak and Pless (2019) summarised the need for responsible leadership as follows:

- The state of the world in general and the lack of responsible leadership as evidenced from the various business scandals.
- The state of the business world in particular – as observed from the all-time low of trust in business leaders.

- Stakeholders expect leaders to do better and accept responsibility in areas such as human rights, distributive justice, and global warming.
- Stakeholders expect a political role from business leaders in the pursuit of global good, the fight against poverty, and as secondary agents of justice.
- In a world of contested values, responsibility lies at individual, organisational, and societal levels in the marketplace.
- Leaders cannot afford to ignore the challenges to their legitimacy.

The responsible leadership concept with reference to business ethics is relatively recent, arguably proposed and propounded in 2006 by Maak and Pless. This chapter begins with the development of the definition of responsible leadership, followed by components of and competencies needed for responsible leadership, recent research findings in responsible leadership, and future directions of responsible leadership.

10.2 Definition of and understanding responsible leadership

The term 'responsible leadership' was first used by Harvard professor George Smith in 1962 when he referred to responsible leadership that involves keeping in perspective economic and human facts inside and outside the enterprise (Maak and Pless, 2019). Considering that responsible leadership was proposed as a concept mainly due to the scandals of the past several decades, it is acknowledged that responsible leadership reflects a leadership challenge which requires leaders who care, who are morally conscious, open to the diversity of stakeholders inside and outside the firm, and who are aware of and understand the responsibilities of businesses in society.

The term 'responsibility' is defined in the Cambridge dictionary as 'something that is your job or duty to deal with' (https://dictionary.cambridge.org/dictionary/english/responsibility), and has several synonyms in the thesaurus (www.thesaurus.com/browse/responsibility) such as authority, duty, importance, obligation, power, restraint, trust, amenability, answerability, care, charge, culpability, engagement, onus, pledge, boundness, and obligatoriness. In the context of leadership, the term 'responsible' includes concepts such as appropriate ethical decision-making, accountability for one's actions, being a good citizen, and concern for others by seeking to clarify who the 'others' are. These attributes can be referred to as 'relational concepts' (Maak and Pless, 2019).

Based on Freeman's stakeholder theory (discussed in Chapter 2), Maak and Pless (2006) set an important foundation by defining responsible leadership as a social-relational and ethical phenomenon embedded in networks of stakeholders spanning multiple markets and cultures. This implies a balancing of the external pressures of stakeholders' interests with leaders' internal tensions to lead with integrity. They argued that responsible leadership is different from ethical, servant, authentic, and transformational leadership – responsible leadership focuses on social and environmental targets, sustainable value creation, and positive change. Most other leadership theories focus on followers inside the organisation, whereas responsible leadership considers stakeholders both within and outside the organisation.

Pless (2007: 438) further defined responsible leadership as a 'values-based and thorough ethical principles-driven relationship between leaders and stakeholders who are connected through a shared sense of meaning and purpose through which they raise one another to higher levels of motivation and commitment for achieving sustainable values creation and social change'. Acting on one's values can be seen as a starting point for thinking about authenticity (Freeman and Auster, 2011). Freeman and Auster assert that being authentic is an ongoing process that 'not only starts with perceived values but also involves one's history, relationships with others, and aspirations' (p. 15). But what happens when values conflict – for example between individual values and corporate values. Even though it conflicted with the company's goals, the CEO of Merck, Roy Vegelos, acted on his values when developing a drug for river blindness and making it available for sections of society free of cost (see Case Study 4.1). For Merck it was the value of profits and for Vegelos it was the value of integrity and helping an external secondary stakeholder. Freeman and Auster (2011) reiterate that creating such organisations is the work of responsible leaders and responsible leadership.

However, responsible leadership does not mean the same thing to all (Waldman and Galvin, 2008). A focus on ethics can get confused with values of religions, culture, and personal behaviour. Responsibility, on the other hand, directs attention to others to whom a leader may be responsible in terms of broad moral and legal standards, the specific concerns of others, and to be accountable for the consequences of one's actions. But there are questions of who these 'others' are and how exactly should a leader show responsibility towards them? There are two perspectives to consider: economic and stakeholder. The economic perspective suggests that a leader's responsibility begins and ends with the firm's shareholders or owners. The stakeholder perspective suggests that leaders are responsible to a broader set of stakeholders such as employees, customers, environmentalists, community, and so on (as we have discussed in Chapter 2). Waldman and Galvin (2008) indicate that both these perspectives are right. However, they argue that overall 'the stakeholder perspective may represent the more viable approach to responsible leadership' (p. 332). Thus, responsible leadership can be seen as a 'multilevel concept, encompassing individual, team, organisational, and societal levels' (Maak and Pless, 2019: 33).

Responsible leadership's importance and relevance can be further seen in the context of globalisation. International organisations may not be able to intervene in the internal affairs of sovereign nations. As a result, many global problems such as protecting human rights, enforcing labour standards, saving natural environments, or fighting corruption can remain unaddressed. Organisational leaders may attempt to address such issues through global institutions such as the UN Global Compact or the CSR-related Global Reporting Initiatives or the Social Accounting 8000 or the ISO 14001 environmental management systems (as discussed in Chapters 7 and 8). Increasingly, in order to address these challenges, research advocates a stakeholder perspective of leadership and understanding responsible leadership as a values-based ethical-principles-driven relationship between leaders and stakeholders. Voegtlin et al. (2012) suggest that responsible leaders should think of the consequences of decisions for all affected parties and engage in active stakeholder dialog by weighing and balancing differing interests (p. 12). The concepts of responsible leadership should, thus, be used as a lever to handle these globalisation challenges.

Based on data from 25 top-level business leaders and entrepreneurs from different industries and countries, Pless et al. (2012) further elaborated on differences in business focus. Some business leaders have a *narrow* focus trying to create value in either business or society. Here, the focus on business included increasing economic performance to maximise shareholder value and the focus on society included creation of social value for specific stakeholders or society. Other business leaders have a *broad* focus trying to understand and deal with the needs of multiple stakeholder groups. These differences characterised responsible leadership into four orientations (see also Table 10.1):

Narrow focus

1   Idealist
2   Traditional economist

Broad focus

3   Opportunity seeker or strategist
4   Integrator

Table 10.1   Characteristics of the four responsible leadership orientations

Factors	Idealist	Traditional economist	Opportunity seeker	Integrator
Driven by	Social agenda and humanistic values	Materialistic values: profits, shareholder value	Materialistic values and strategic orientation	Humanistic values Reconciling profit with principles
Performance focus	Social, environmental or humanitarian	Economic bottom line	Economic bottom line CSR derived from business case	Multiple bottom lines: people, planet, profits, principles
Business ventures led by	Idealists	Most profit-only businesspeople	Businesspeople responsive towards key stakeholders	Visionaries who consider social value creation as part of business purpose
Feel responsible to	Towards people Creating social value	Shareholders only	Key stakeholders	Create long-term value for stakeholders See profit as an outcome of responsible business conduct
Practise social responsibility	Always	Only: If it is legally required If it helps save costs and minimises risks If it affects profits If pushed by shareholders	Only: If it offers strategic opportunities If it has competitive advantages If it supports strategic positioning	Goal is to fulfill a higher purpose through business

Source: Adapted from Pless et al. (2012), 'Different approaches toward doing the right thing: Mapping the responsibility orientations of leaders', *Academy of Management Perspectives*, 26(4): 51–65

The responsible leadership field has enlarged considerable over the last few years with special issues in various academic journals and books and increasing interest in research (see further down this chapter for various research findings). According to Waldman and Galvin (2008), these developments bear risks of ambiguities in definitions and threaten the positioning of responsible leadership in leadership studies. Miska and Mendenhall (2018) suggested that responsible leadership can be better understood through multiple levels of analysis – the *micro level* with a focus on individuals and individual business leaders, the *meso level* with a focus on organisational context, groups, and corporate strategy, the *macro level* with a focus on institutions, culture, and society, and the *cross level* with a focus on linkages and interactions among the above three levels. However, Maak and Pless (2019) note that the current responsible leadership research has three shortcomings:

- Obsession with the leader and the traditional leader–follower dyad which emphasises an individualised rather than a socialised conceptualisation of leadership.
- Limited view of leadership work that focuses mainly on effectiveness of organisations, rather than involving internal and external entities.
- Lack of ethical intelligence that excludes moral motivation and virtues.

Agarwal and Bhal (2020) further attempted to clarify the definition of responsible leadership by stating responsible leadership as a phenomenon in which a leader aims at achieving sustainable organisational growth through the development of positive stakeholder interactions and the promotion of ethical behaviours. This assumes that leaders behave as moral people and managers, all ethical and strategic interactions take place at all leadership levels, and that responsible leadership is applicable to all employees who have leadership roles. Their study found that:

- when leaders treat stakeholders in a caring, respectful, and trustful manner, followers are likely to emulate that behaviour
- when leaders display ethical behaviours and employ disciplinary actions to correct unethical behaviours, followers also will display positive behaviours to increase a team's (and the organisation's) effectiveness
- when leaders use visible means of communication and discipline, followers will have the courage to be open about unethical issues without fear of retaliation
- when leaders go beyond self-interest to ethically achieve goals in the interest of a larger group, followers are likely to proactively raise unethical issues to promote stakeholder welfare.

10.3 Components and competencies of responsible leadership

It has been suggested that the foundations of responsible leadership should be effectively laid through childhood, in schools, and reiterated at university levels. In addition, it can be reinforced at the executive level in organisations through international service-learning programmes such as the Ulysses programme of PwC (Maak and Pless, 2019; Pless et al., 2011). This could imply that responsible leaders are made, not born, and therefore such leadership can be nurtured and developed at all levels.

To understand the notion that a leader needs to balance the external pressure of conflicting interests of stakeholders (as discussed in Chapter 2), and the internal tension to lead with integrity and ethics (as discussed in Chapters 3 and 4), a roles model was proposed by Maak and Pless (2006). Rather than focusing on traits and personality attributes, they suggest a set of ten roles that can make an effective responsible leader.

1 Visionary: *envisioning a desired future*: Having foresight, motivating through clear purpose, enabling co-creation, envisage a sustainable future.
2 Steward: *custodian of values and resources*: Protects and preserves for future generations, high ethical intelligence, accountable, responsible, leaves business, society, and planet a better place than they found it.
3 Servant: *to others*: High relational intelligence (for example, empathy), cares for both internal and external stakeholders, ensures DEI.
4 Citizen: *being an active and reflective citizen*: Cares about the well-being of communities and the larger environment, addresses and solves the world's pressing problems, active in stakeholder dialogue.
5 Change agent: *being a transforming leader*: Initiates, sells, gets support, and mobilises people for change in the organisation to align values and strategies.
6 Communicator and storyteller: *enabling meaning in times of constant change*: Exceptional in communicating and reframing challenging issues, open communication, acknowledges ability of others, uses stories to engage.
7 Networker: *weaving a web of inclusion*: Ability to connect and socialise with diverse stakeholders, building relationships, inclusive in integrating different voices.
8 Coach: *motivating and nurturing others*: Shows emotional intelligence, gives and receives constructive feedback, supports employee development, empowers others.
9 Architect: *building a responsible business*: Implements moral infrastructure (such as policies, guidelines), ethical business systems in supply chain, fosters culture of integrity.
10 Strategist: *translating vision and values into business strategy*: Evaluating impact of external developments, principled long-term perspective, ensures Triple Bottom Line performance.

In a study of 70 participants of Price Waterhouse Cooper's Ulysses project (which involved sending participants to developing countries to work in partnerships with NGOs and social entrepreneurs), Pless et al. (2011) discovered that developing responsible global business leaders required learning in six areas:

• Responsible mindset – knowledge of CSR-related issues
• Ethical literacy – moral awareness

- Cultural intelligence – general knowledge about other cultures
- Global mindset – reconciling tensions between global and local
- Self-development – self-awareness, work-life balance
- Community building – stakeholder management and interpersonal skills.

Referring to the notion that responsibility includes accountability (among other attributes as discussed previously in this chapter) around benefits for and avoiding harm to stakeholders, Pless et al. (2012) identified two dimensions: leader's motives and leader's behaviour. A responsible leader would exhibit high degrees of both dimensions. As we discussed in Chapter 2, stakeholders are classified as primary and secondary stakeholders. The duty to primary stakeholders (those that are crucial for a firm's survival) requires leaders to perform their job well by contributing to the growth of the organisation. These tasks would include structuring tasks, engaging employees, defining responsibilities, and care for employee needs. These reflect roles like the architect, coach, and strategist in the roles model of Maak and Pless (2006). However, to respond to the broader societal concerns of the secondary stakeholders (who affect or are affected by the firm, but are not engaged in the transactions with the firm nor are essential for its survival), a different role is required for leaders. Voegtlin et al. (2020) suggest three roles to ensure accountability towards both primary and secondary stakeholders:

1 Expert role:

- Accountable to primary stakeholders (shareholders, investors, supervisors, customers).
- Goals would be setting tasks and achieving performance targets.

2 Facilitator role:

- Accountable to primary stakeholders (employees).
- Goals would be motivating employees and creating a fair work environment.

3 Citizen role:

- Accountable to secondary stakeholders (NGOs, community, state, society).
- Goals would be creating long-term value for society.

Jaén et al. (2021), when examining responsible leadership in three supply chain markets at the lowest socio-economic group level, confirmed the relevance and existence of the responsible leadership roles described above. The research suggests 'tell me what your stakeholders need and expect, and I will tell you what specific roles are necessary for responsible leadership to be effective' (p. 481).

Muff and associates (Muff et al., 2022) have developed a competency assessment for responsible leadership (CARL) in which they have identified five competency dimensions for responsible leadership:

1	Stakeholder relations	3	Self-awareness	5	Change and innovation
2	Ethics and values	4	Systems understanding		

Each of the above five dimensions can be derived from three action-driven sub-competencies: knowing (knowledge), doing (skills), and being (attitudes) (Muff et al., 2022). CARL is available as an online survey (https://caresponsible leadership2030.org/) where the result is computed into a final responsible leadership score showing strengths and blind spots of an individual or a team. A recent CARL survey sample of 9,566 participants across 122 countries showed:

- Self-awareness is the central element in responsible leadership.
- Higher education leads to a better responsible leadership performance.
- Participants from the African region followed by India outperformed other participants.
- Affinity to sustainability does not mean a higher responsible leadership score.
- CEOs from sustainability-conscious organisations do not perform better.
- A leadership development course does not increase responsible leadership performance.

The traditional model of the leader is usually composed of a hero who saves the day, knows it all, is the smartest person in the room, and is often driven by power, fame, glory, or money (Joly, 2022). Today, however, people expect a different kind of leader. Hubert Joly, the Executive Chairman and ex-CEO of Best Buy, voted the most sustainable company in the US in 2019, suggests five attributes that characterise leaders who are purposeful and responsible (Joly, 2022):

- Be clear about your purpose – and how that connects to your company's purpose.
- Be clear about your role – to help others see possibilities and potential, creating energy, inspiration, and hope.
- Be clear about whom you serve – essentially all your stakeholders.
- Be driven by values – tell the truth and do what's right, and that includes honesty, respect, responsibility, fairness, and compassion.
- Be authentic – being yourself, authentic, sharing emotions and struggles when appropriate and helpful to others.

10.4 Research findings of responsible leadership in various areas

Organisational commitment and responsible leadership

Corporations and their leaders are embedded in different national systems and embrace different societal values – so responsible leadership is likely to vary across institutional and cultural contexts. A study involving 73 executives from Germany, Hong Kong, Japan, Korea, and the United States, drawing on basic data from the GLOBE study (refer to Chapter 5), found that the executives' responsibility orientations (for example, how they see their responsibility to their firm's stakeholders and wider society) varied considerably between and within Asian societies and the West (Witt and Stahl, 2016). Japanese and German executives rejected shareholder primacy, whereas the US executives expressed positive views. Japan, Korea, and Germany identified employees' well-being as a key objective, but executives in Hong Kong and the US viewed employees as an expense or a problem.

One of the key employee outcomes to perform effectively is organisational commitment behaviour, which refers to the extent to which an individual identifies with an organisation and commits to its goals (Kinicki, 2021: 55). It has been found that organisational commitment is influenced by factors such as job satisfaction, motivation, decision-making, organisational support, reward, communications, and leadership styles. There is an extensive body of literature that concerns itself with the way in which various leadership styles are related to organisational commitment. Most researchers agree that appropriate leadership fosters a high-commitment environment. Some have suggested that responsible leadership has a positive influence on employee organisational commitment (Miska and Mendenhall, 2018). In a study of a sample of full-time employed supervisors in various Australian industry sectors, Haque et al. (2019) found that:

- There was a direct relationship between responsible leadership and organisational commitment – employees who perceive higher levels of responsible leadership from their leaders are more likely to be committed to their work.
- Responsible leadership was negatively related to employee turnover intention (intent to leave) – this shows that responsible leaders' ability to develop relationships with employees can result in attracting and engaging employees, preventing turnover.

A further challenge for managerial leadership in enabling employee productivity is presenteeism, defined as being present at work but with reduced output. The cost to the Australian economy due to presenteeism is estimated to be AUD 34.1 billion (Medibank, 2011). While several studies have indicated an association between employees' perception of their manager's leadership behaviour and presenteeism, Haque et al. (2021) suggest a relationship between responsible leadership and presenteeism with the mediating role of organisational commitment and turnover intention.

Employees, as important stakeholders, also exhibit organisational commitment behaviour towards the environment (OCBE). This phenomenon refers to the environmental practices of employees within their organisations that are often not rewarded or required by the organisation's formal reward system (Han et al., 2019). Individual employees of their own accord engage in environmentally friendly practices such as saving paper, reducing energy consumption, recycling office and kitchen waste, and influencing other employees to practise green behaviour. Factors that influence OCBE include employee self-responsibility, organisational support, measures, concerns, and attitudes. In addition to this, Han et al. (2019) studied the relationship between responsible leadership and OCBE using a sample of 384 employees of different industries such as banking, insurance, medicine, teaching, and services in China. Their findings include:

- Responsible leadership has a significantly positive impact on OCBE – it strives to find a balance between society and nature, and encourages employees to show OCBE.
- Responsible leadership encourages employees to align their OCBE with their own interests, values, and goals.
- Intrinsic (for example, individual employees' values, goals, and interests) and extrinsic (for example, an environmental management system or having a reward or punishment system for environmental protection) motivations affect the role between RL and OCBE.
- The mediating role of intrinsic motivation is greater than that of extrinsic motivation.

Retaining talent with help from responsible leadership

Talent retention, specifically retaining effective employees and particularly young professionals and new managers, is viewed as a critical element in a firm's business strategy. It is recognised as a challenge in globalised dynamic emerging markets such as India, where the growth of Indian companies triggered by rapid expansion of Western companies can result in high levels of employee turnover. Further to Maak and Pless (2006), Pless (2007), and Pless and Maak's (2011) assertion that it takes responsible leadership to build businesses that benefit multiple stakeholders, it can be said if employees do not perceive the company as exhibiting responsible leadership, they will have intentions to quit. In a study of 4,352 employees from 35 firms comprised of MNCs and national firms engaged in IT, manufacturing, and the service industries, Doh et al. (2011) found that higher employee retention can be achieved by:

- high employee perception of the employer's positive stakeholder culture
- high employee perception of comprehensive and formal HR practices
- high employee perception of positive managerial support
- greater employee pride in and satisfaction with the organisation.

Reputation management

Two similar incidents from United Airlines (UA) and Delta Airlines (DA) flights highlight the effect of their CEOs' actions on their company's reputation. On 9 April 2017, a passenger on an overbooked UA flight was forcibly dragged out of the aircraft after he refused to give up his seat, suffering a concussion and loss of two front teeth. UA's CEO initially issued multiple statements and ultimately apologised. Then on 23 April 2017, a family was removed from a DA flight after they declined to give up a seat originally bought for their teenage son but which they were attempting to use for their 2-year-old son. Delta ultimately apologised and offered refunds. In both cases, the passengers received undisclosed compensation from the airlines. Using multiple sources of newspaper articles, news releases, annual reports, official websites, share prices before and after the incidents, and applying concepts of responsible leadership (especially Maak and Pless's four orientations), Varma (2021) concluded that a relationship exists between their leadership approaches and reputation as measured by variation in the share prices of United Airlines (UA) and Delta Airlines (DA). The study was focussed on the actions undertaken by the CEOs of UA and DA 'after the forceful removal of the passengers and its influence on the reputational capital as measured by the changes in the respective share prices of the airlines' (Varma, 2021: 29). Findings suggest that responsible leadership actions taken by the CEOs can explain an increase (in the 4-week period immediately after the actions) in UA share prices of almost 70 per cent and DA's share prices of 50.6 per cent.

10.5 Effects of corporate irresponsibility

Most of the world's large companies espouse social values and allocate resources to achieve social and environmental objectives. However, from the various scandals and ethical failures, it seems that some of these companies are prone to errors of judgement and wrongdoing, and are perceived to be egregious. This can be termed as corporate irresponsibility (CI). Companies are held for criminal or social negligence by relevant court rulings around the globe and are required to pay fines in the billions of dollars. But the question that remains unanswered are do these events do lasting damage to their reputation and do they really affect their sales and market value? Surdu (2022) notes that the public has a strong tendency to forget and move on. Examples include when in early 2022 Spotify was accused of offering a platform for misinformation about Covid-19. The initial dip of 12 per cent in their share prices was quickly followed by a share price rebound. Similarly, Netflix survived a recent controversy that included a British comedian's comments about the Holocaust, and Facebook bounced back after their temporary market collapse after the Cambridge Analytica scandal. However, only certain scandals, as Surdu (2022) points out, have significant negative effects on corporate reputations and performance. Examples include the ongoing negotiations of settlements in the Volkswagen emissions scandal that started in 2015, and BP's Deepwater Horizon disaster in the Gulf of Mexico in 2010 where BP is still paying fines and settling multiple lawsuits.

A study by Nardella et al. (2020) examined the relationship between CI, corporate social performance, and changes in organisational reputation. Analysis of data from 462 companies and 3,844 confirmed CI cases revealed that:

- Firms previously believed to be socially responsible are penalised by evaluators when their wrongdoings are verified by a court of law.
- Firms perceived to be least socially responsible were more likely to be penalised without their wrongdoings being established by courts.
- In CI events, evaluators penalise only certain firms in certain circumstances.
- Reputational damage occurs when highly responsible firms are perceived to be hypocritical (behaviour that suggests higher standards than the reality).

10.6 Future directions for responsible leadership

Interviews with 700 emerging leaders at the Forum of Young Global Leaders and the Global Shapers Community to find out what they think about responsible leadership (Accenture, 2020) identified the following challenges that are forcing those interviewed to redefine responsible leadership:

- Climate change – 65 per cent of CEOs agreed the need to decouple economic growth from the use of natural resources.
- Global economic fragility – 87 per cent of CEOs believed that global systems need to refocus on equitable growth.
- The Fourth Industrial Revolution – new technologies in this phase need to be managed for both their potential promise and their peril.
- The risk of leaving people behind in the workplace – while investment in emerging technologies doubled in the previous two years, only 18 per cent of organisations planned to reskill their people.
- Most CEOs say citizen trust will be critical in the next five years.
- Most emerging leaders say business models should be pursued only if they contribute to both profitable growth and societal outcomes at the same time.

While there is a need for leaders to deliver on organisational performance, continuous innovation, sustainability, and trust, a survey of 2,000 business leaders, 3,000 stakeholders, and 1,800 emerging leaders (Accenture, 2020) revealed five elements that would be needed for responsible leadership in the future:

1 Stakeholder inclusion: Safeguarding trust and positive impact for all by standing in the shoes of stakeholders when making decisions and fostering an inclusive environment where diverse individuals have a voice and feel they belong.
2 Emotion and intuition: Unlocking commitment and creativity by being truly human, showing compassion, humility, and openness.
3 Mission and purpose: Advancing common goals by inspiring a shared vision of sustainable prosperity for the organisation and its stakeholders.
4 Technology and innovation: Creating new organisational and societal value by innovating responsibly with emerging technology.
5 Intellect and insight: Finding ever-improving paths to success by embracing continuous learning and knowledge exchange.

Imagining what 'could' (instead of 'should') be done

Recognising that there exists a gap in the understanding of responsible leadership in emerging economies, Pless et al. (2022) explored a stakeholder conflict between indigenous communities in rural India and an emerging MNE headquartered in the same country. An

MNE specialising in aluminium refinery acquired land and approval from the government for a greenfield project in rural India. Protests from NGOs and indigenous people caused massive delays, a decade-long conflict, and even the death of three indigenous people. A new CEO was appointed to resolve the conflict and drive the project ahead. The new CEO identified the following challenges:

- Operations challenges – lack of infrastructure including medical facilities and schools.
- Environmental sustainability challenges – deforestation, energy consumption, greenhouse gases.
- Trust challenges – the locals' land, that was used for cultivation of food, being taken away for the project.

Using interview data, archival documents, and the concept of moral imagination (see Chapter 4), the study concluded that responsible leadership roles (as mentioned earlier in this chapter) could have been applied for resolving the situation. The roles recommended were communicator, citizen, servant, change agent, architect, coach, steward, and visionary. Specific characteristics of each of these roles were identified.

Influence of artificial intelligence on responsible leadership

As we have seen in earlier chapters, artificial intelligence (AI) is being and will be used ever increasingly in society and organisations. Business leaders are therefore expected to be responsible in using such technologies in their workplace. De Cremer (2022), however, feels that with the introduction of AI in organisations, responsible leadership is slipping. The mindset of business leaders in such circumstances could be that they feel less responsible for the decisions and actions they take in a data-driven environment simply because they now have the technology to deal with it (p. 49). Ethical algorithms or AI ethics are transforming human leadership abilities into technical competencies. Soper (2021) reported that an Amazon employee delivering packages received an automated email that he was fired because the algorithms tracking him had decided he wasn't doing his job properly. Human feedback is rare, and ratings include four categories – fantastic, great, fair, or at risk. Former company managers claim that although the company knew machines could make mistakes, it was cheaper to trust the algorithms than pay people to investigate the mistakes because drivers could be replaced easily. In a study of 239 full-time employed professionals using an online platform, Soper (2021) found that a large majority of employees felt that their jobs will become more automated in the future, will increase the pace of work, will feel more stressful, and they will be treated like a machine. De Cremer (2022) asserts that leaders do not seem to feel responsible about how to create humane working conditions, rather they prefer treating workers as data than with empathy. To genuinely lead AI adoption in a responsible way, De Cremer suggests the following:

- Avoid fostering a mindset of 'machine-first' and 'humans-second'. With so much emphasis on technology-driven services, we may lose human abilities of empathy, creativity, and imagination.
- Use AI as a tool to help leaders make better decisions – by excelling even more in their soft skills by paying more attention to how to treat their workforce.
- Two types of leadership will be necessary: purpose-driven (a concept we have discussed in Chapter 1) and inclusive (a concept we have discussed in Chapter 6) leadership.

Summary

- This chapter aimed to bring together the various concepts and applications of business ethics to propose that responsible leadership (RL) is essential for enabling effective stakeholder management, managing across cultures, sustainability, ESG, CSR, and global strategies.
- We have argued why RL is needed – primarily because of the (1) all-time low levels of trust in business leaders due to the various business scandals of recent decades, (2) pressure from stakeholders, and (3) contested values.
- Since the RL concept is relatively recent, we outlined and discussed several definitions of RL, and most definitions corresponded to the notion that RL is a social-relational and ethical phenomenon embedded in networks of stakeholders spanning multiple markets and cultures. This means balancing external stakeholder pressures with internal organisational tensions.
- We examined the four orientations that characterised RL: idealist, traditional economist, opportunity seeker or strategist, and integrator. The first two orientations are classified as 'narrow focus' of business leaders, and the last two orientations are classified as 'broad focus' of business leaders.
- To understand what makes a responsible leader effective, rather than focusing on traits of leaders, we learned that responsible leaders need to have a set of ten roles: visionary, steward, servant, citizen, change agent, communicator, networker, coach, architect, and strategist.
- From recent research, we saw that RL can influence the organisational commitment of employees, retaining talent in organisations, reputation management, and prevention of corporate irresponsibility.
- We learnt that emerging young leaders identified the challenges for responsible leaders to be: climate change, equitable growth, managing the fourth industrial revolution, reskilling people to prepare them for new technologies, regaining trust, and contributing to both profitable growth and societal outcomes.
- We discussed how the rapid introduction of artificial intelligence in almost all areas of business can make leaders less responsible for their actions because they now have (and depend on) data-driven technologies.

CASE STUDY 10.1
PURDUE PHARMA AND THE OXYCONTIN SCANDAL

Purdue Pharma, formerly Purdue Frederick Company, an American privately held pharmaceutical company, was founded in 1892 by medical doctors John Purdue Gray and George Frederick Bingham. The Purdue Frederick Company initially sold earwax removers and laxatives. Sixty years later in 1952, it was sold to two other medical doctors from the Sackler family. The present-day company was incorporated in 1991 and over the next several decades, the company focused on pain management medication, calling itself a 'pioneer in developing medications for reducing pain, a principal cause of human suffering', and started making opioid pain medications such as hydrocodone, oxycodone, and fentanyl – with brand names such as OxyContin, MS Contin, and Ryzolts. These drugs are part of a group of substances called opioids, which include opiates, which refers to drugs derived from opium, including morphine. Hydrocodone, oxycodone, and fentanyl are semi-synthetic and synthetic opioids. Because of their addictive nature, such drugs are controlled substances regulated by governments and require medical prescriptions for distribution and use.

OxyContin, containing the narcotic oxycodone, was developed to remedy moderate to severe pain. However, higher levels of the drug could cause overdose or death. Since it can cause effects similar to heroin use, such as euphoric effects, OxyContin can quickly become addictive. While it was recommended to be swallowed as whole tablets (for controlled release), abusers for rapid effects began to crush and chew, snort through the nose, or even inject the tablets by dissolving them in water.

Over the past two decades, nearly half a million Americans have died from opioid overdose. Some groups have experienced disproportionate harm from opioid use. Military veterans and older adults were particularly affected – the former due to high rates of posttraumatic stress disorder and the challenges of adjusting to civilian life, and the latter due to misuse of prescription opioids leading to subsequent use of heroin. The increased deaths have been attributed to three factors: (1) a rise in prescription opioids, (2) a rise in heroin usage, and (3) due to synthetic opioids such as fentanyl.

Purdue Pharma began an aggressive strategy to market OxyContin. Sales representatives received more bonuses for selling OxyContin than any other drugs. Special relationships were developed with pain doctors. The company initially claimed that it was unaware until years later that the drug was additive. Key Sackler family members set priorities to sell OxyContin by advocating as many prescriptions as possible. The company claimed that one dose of this so-called 'wonder drug' could relieve pain for 12 hours, which was almost twice the duration of existing drugs. So patients could potentially have a restful night. However, in practice, many patients were asking for medication before the next scheduled dose after 12 hours. Patients took other painkillers between two OxyContin doses or took OxyContin every 8 hours. However, the 12-hour relief claim was better for business. Further, Purdue misrepresented the risk of addiction to be low and trained their sales reps to advertise that the risk of addiction was less than 1 per cent. In reality, research has shown that the risk of addiction could be as high as 50 per cent. OxyContin's revenues skyrocketed from USD 48 million in 1996 to USD 1.1 billion in 2000 and USD 3 billion in 2010. This phenomenal increase in revenue could be attributed to doubling the sales force to 600 reps, spending over USD 200 million in aggressive marketing campaigns, and training their sales reps to convince general practitioners to use OxyContin for common pain conditions, along with the false claims of low risks of addiction. In addition, it was reported that Purdue provided in-kind benefits to thousands of physicians, pharmacists, and nurses by way of sponsored all-expenses paid trips to symposiums.

Later, when overdoses and deaths were exposed, executives used strategies designed to divert the blame to doctors who overprescribed, doctors who lacked training, and the abusers themselves. Not only did Purdue Pharma fail to take responsibility for its part in the opioid epidemic, it also did not take steps to reduce harm.

On 24 November 2020, Purdue Pharma pleaded guilty in the federal court in Newark, New Jersey to conspiracies to defraud the United States and violate the anti-kickback statute. In its press release, US Attorneys noted:

> Purdue admitted that it marketed and sold its dangerous opioid products to healthcare providers, even though it had reason to believe those providers were diverting them to abusers. The company lied to the Drug Enforcement Administration about steps it had taken to prevent such diversion, fraudulently increasing the amount of its products it was permitted to sell. Purdue also paid kickbacks to providers to encourage them to prescribe even more of its products.
>
> As today's plea to felony charges shows, Purdue put opioid profits ahead of people and corrupted the sacred doctor–patient relationship. We hope the company's guilty plea sends a message that the Justice Department will not allow big pharma and big tech to engage in illegal profit-generating schemes that interfere with sound medicine.

In the largest penalties ever levied against a pharmaceutical manufacturer, Purdue accepted the criminal fine of USD 3.5 billion, and an additional USD 2 billion in criminal forfeiture. A further USD 2.8 billion was provided for a civil settlement under the False Claim Act – a total of USD 8 billion. However, the amounts are largely symbolic as Purdue declared bankruptcy. The company, not individuals, pleaded guilty. Much of the profits from the sales of OxyContin were transferred to the Sackler family. Five members of the Sackler family negotiated a civil settlement to pay USD 225 million.

(Continued)

Questions

Using the Case-Study Integrative Framework in Figure 0.1, discuss the following:

1. Identify the stakeholders affected in this crisis.
2. Identify the ethical issues in this case.
3. Do you think companies should be free to market their products as they deem fit?
4. The company claimed they did nothing wrong; it was all legal; and it was a business strategy to stay ahead of competition. Discuss and justify your assessment.
5. Apply responsible leadership concepts to analyse the case. What competencies were lacking?
6. What RL roles and competencies would you recommend?

Sources:
Alonso (2021)
Chow (2019)
Dyer (2020)
US Department of Justice (2020)
Wiki (2022b)
Yakubi et al. (2022)

CASE STUDY 10.2
NOVO NORDISK

Founded in the year 1923 by August Krogh and Marie Krogh, Novo Nordisk is a Danish multinational pharmaceutical corporation headquartered in Bagsvaerd, Denmark. It has production facilities in nine countries, and affiliates in five countries. It develops, manufactures, and distributes pharmaceutical products and services, with a focus on diabetes drugs and devices. Novo Nordisk is also involved with haemostasis management, growth hormone therapy, and hormone replacement therapy. It employs more than 48,000 people globally and markets its products in 168 countries. As of April 2022, Novo Nordisk has a market cap of USD 268.69 billion.

The company was ranked 25th among the 100 Best Companies to Work For in 2010 and 72nd in 2014 by Fortune. In January 2012, Novo Nordisk was named the most sustainable company in the world by the business magazine *Corporate Knights* while spin-off company Novozymes was named fourth.

Executive management

In the late 1960s Novo Nordisk was criticised for a production method that introduced genetically engineered micro-organism enzymes that became ingredients in products such as detergents. People coming in contact with these products developed allergies and the dust had implications for employees' health. As sales fell, the company reacted with a fast response to develop dust-free enzymes. In 2001, the company was accused of giving priority to profits at the expense of less disadvantaged people in South Africa. The company reacted by engaging with NGOs and defined a new policy to develop medicines to combat diabetes in developing countries. Realising the importance of sustainability, Novo Nordisk changed its focus to health, safety, bioethics issues, and how to integrate issues of social responsibility.

Top management at Novo Nordisk made corporate values and sustainability that included stakeholder dialogue and CSR an integrated part of the company's brand. The CEO of the company believed trust to be imperative. They introduced the Novo Nordisk Way of Management to strike a balance between corporate control and decentralised decision-making. Decisions had tended to be standardised and centralised procedures and systems that led to dissatisfaction among managers in foreign subsidiaries because the systems did not always fit in with local situations and needs. The new Novo Nordisk Way of Management methodology had three elements:

- Facilitators – a team of high-profile professionals that had a blend of ages, gender, professions, and nationalities, whose task was to assess, assist and facilitate units to perform better.
- Sustainability reporting – that addressed issues recommended by the UN's Global Compact, GRI's guidelines, and the AA1000 framework. They used a Triple Bottom Line (TBL) approach in six areas – living our values, access to health, our employees, our use of animals, eco-efficiency and compliance, and economic contribution.
- Balanced scorecard – a management tool that was used for embedding and cascading the TBL throughout the organisation.

Novo Nordisk's position on intellectual property rights and patenting

The patent system is an important means for stimulating research and development. On average it takes more than ten years to develop a new medical treatment, often costing more than USD 1 billion. Exclusive rights in the form of patents are given to firms for a period of up to 20 years, enabling them to market the products to recoup the R&D investments. Novo Nordisk has a total of 1395 patents globally, out of which 642 have been granted. Of these 1395 patents, more than 49 per cent are active. European countries are where Novo Nordisk has filed the most patents, followed by the USA and Japan. These generated an annual revenue of USD 52.36 billion in the year 2021.

Recognising the need for life-saving drugs in developing countries, Novo Nordisk's position on the responsible use of intellectual property includes:

(Continued)

- Exercising IP in accordance with their corporate values – called the Novo Nordisk Way – which integrates social, environmental, and financial considerations.
- Not engaging in patenting activities nor enforcing patents in the least developed and low-income countries.
- Publicly disclosing patent status.
- Recognising that health emergencies would require exceptions to IP rights.
- Supporting principles such as patents should not be granted for cloning human beings, uses of human embryos, the formation and development of the human body, processes for modifying genetic identity of animals which can cause them harm or suffering, and other principles – see NovoNordisk (2022) for further information.

Mere compliance to the moral and legal standards of CSR is no longer sufficient for responding to the new challenges. Companies are taking on responsibilities traditionally assumed by governments by engaging in political activities via philanthropy. This means that companies assume social responsibilities that go beyond their economic roles. This phenomenon is called political corporate social responsibility (PCSR). Novo Nordisk decided to intensify their CSR engagement by assuming a politically enlarged responsibility in their leadership. Research shows that the company engaged in the following dimensions of PCSR:

1 Implementing a governance model that includes a stronger focus on processes of stakeholder management.
2 Approaching CSR by self-regulatory actions through their sustainability reporting.
3 Contributing to public good (for example, fair working conditions) that goes beyond legal liability – by working to improve human rights.
4 Identifying new ways to obtain moral legitimacy through cooperation with NGOs and other institutions in the process of global governance, especially to induce government CSR initiatives.

Questions

Using the Case-Study Integrative Framework in Figure 0.1, discuss the following:

1 Identify the components of RL in Novo Nordisk's actions.
2 Identify the relevant roles of RL that Novo Nordisk has exhibited.
3 What competencies do you think the CEO and the top management team of Novo Nordisk possessed that enabled them to demonstrate RL?

Sources:
Fiercepharma (2022)
Insights (2022)
Morsing et al. (2018)
NovoNordisk (2022)
Wiki (2022k)
Posadas et al. (2020)

Recommended readings

Doh, J.P., Stumpf, S.A. and Tymon, W.G. (2011), 'Responsible leadership helps retain talent in India', *Journal of Business Ethics*, 98(Suppl 1): 85–100.

An interesting study in the operationalisation of RL – an analysis of Indian and global organisations to show the relationship between RL and retention of employees, especially in today's fast-moving tech-driven environment.

Maak, T. and Pless, N.M. (2006), 'Responsible leadership in a stakeholder society: A relational perspective', *Journal of Business Ethics*, 66(1): 99–115.

One of the early works of Maak and Pless that describes and defines RL. In addition, this article describes in detail some of the roles of effective responsible leaders.

Miska, C. and Mendenhall, M.E. (2018), 'Responsible leadership: A mapping of extant research and future directions', *Journal of Business Ethics*, 148(1): 117–34.

This paper outlines recent developments in RL research, emphasising the transition of RL research from micro-level (individual) perspectives to multiple-level (group, organisational, national, and international) analysis.

Pless, N.M., Maak, T. and Waldman, D.A. (2012), 'Different approaches towards doing the right thing: Mapping the responsibility orientations of leaders', *Academy of Management Perspectives*, 26(4): 51–65.

A seminal paper that identified the four orientations that leaders may use to demonstrate responsibility and implement CSR – idealist, economist, opportunity seeker, and integrator.

Pless, N.M., Sengupta, A., Wheeler, M.A. and Maak, T. (2022), 'Responsible leadership and the reflective CEO: Resolving stakeholder conflict by imagining what could be done', *Journal of Business Ethics*, 180(1): 313–37.

Based on a case study, this paper focuses on what 'could' (instead of 'should') be done in understanding RL in emerging countries. They suggest using moral imagination to apply an integrative RL approach to a stakeholder conflict situation.

Waldman, D.A. and Galvin, B.M. (2008), 'Alternative perspectives of responsible leadership', *Organizational Dynamics*, 37(4): 327–41.

Here, you can read an in-depth analysis of the 'why' and the need for RL. It defines the parameters of RL, describes alternative perspectives of RL, and shows how best practices are RL.

PART III
NEW HORIZONS

11

SPIRITUALITY IN MANAGEMENT

On completion of this chapter, you should be able to:

- Understand the need for spirituality in management and business ethics
- Define and understand spirituality
- Differentiate spirituality from spiritualism and religiosity
- Understand the concepts, processes, and leadership in workplace spirituality
- Understand applications of spirituality in the workplace
- Integrate the influence of spirituality in the Comprehensive Ethical Decision-Making model

- Spirituality, spiritualism, and religiosity
- Spirituality in management
- Workplace spirituality
- Conscious capitalism
- Workplace motivations other than pay/financial reward

—Box 11.1 Opening case—

What are tech giants doing in the realm of spirituality in the workplace?

Leadership coach and strategic advisor Lisa Villeneuve reports that 'spiritual organisations truly value contribution, creativity, inclusion, and personal development, which contribute to healthy, happy, and productive employees'. She asserts that we all have the power to shape our culture within our sphere of influence, creating spaces where spirituality can thrive. A sense of purpose and connection are critical for employees to be committed and to contribute their best performance. Lisa provides examples of companies like Starbucks, Southwest Airlines, and Staples that are integrating spirituality through initiatives such as servant leadership: focusing on working in service to others for the greater good. Lisa also cites research that practices like generosity, gratitude, compassion, and **mindfulness** meditation are skills that support spirituality and well-being (Villeneuve, 2016).

Leaders of tech giants are realising that employees want new tools to solve 'age-old' problems such as stress, focus, and relationships. They are not fixing the problems with an app or a new productivity system, but by bringing in the practices of spirituality in the workplace. Twitter cofounder Evan Williams founded the 'Medium' open platform where readers find insightful thinking, and where creators can share their writing on any topic. To enable the process, he placed a room in the middle of the office where yoga and meditation could be practised (Fast Company, 2016). Another tech company that brings tech leaders and teachers together, Wisdom 2.0, addresses the challenge of not only living connected to one another through technology, but doing so in ways that are beneficial to people's well-being, effectiveness at work, and being useful to the world (Wisdom, 2023). The founder Soren Gordhamer says 'We are in the middle of a culture shift; we are no longer interested in just getting through our workday and striving towards relief at the end of our careers. It's about more quality and connection within the work-life continuum'.

In the last couple of decades, well-known multinationals (and mostly technology companies) have shown interest and embarked on programmes using spirituality practices to cope with stress and anxiety. Some of these programmes are listed below:

- Intel's Awake@Intel is an employee mindfulness training programme which consists of 90-minute weekly sessions that combine meditation, breathing, and journaling. On completion, participants have reported improved interaction with peers and direct reports, increased focus, decreased stress, and an ability to solve problems more quickly. They also reported a two-point increase in new ideas, insights, mental clarity, creativity, focus, quality of relationships, and engagement in work, leading to an overall improvement in team performance.
- Google's 'Search Inside Yourself' is a course that teaches emotional intelligence through meditation. The course follows a three-part structure – (1) focusing on training attention, (2) developing self-knowledge and self-mastery, and (3)

developing useful mental habits – that teaches emotional intelligence, boosts resilience to stress and improves mental focus. Participants have reported being calmer, more patient, better able to listen, and better at handling stress and defusing emotions.

- Aetna, an American healthcare company, has established a Mindfulness Centre at their headquarters for mindfulness and meditation training of employees with two programmes – Viniyoga Stress Reduction and Mindfulness at Work. Results show a reduction in medical claims, an increase in productivity, and a reduction in stress.

- General Mills, a US-based food company, has been offering mindfulness programmes to its employees in its Minneapolis headquarters since 2006. The courses are designed to improve employee focus, clarity, and creativity. The company also offers weekly meditation sessions and yoga classes, and it has a dedicated meditation room in every building on its campus.

Sources:
Fast Company (2016)
Schaufenbuel (2015)
Offyoga (2021)
Villeneuve (2016)
Aetna (2023)
Wisdom (2023)

11.1 Introduction

The opening case shows how large technology companies, in the last couple of decades, have taken on board programmes to deliver spirituality-related activities to their employees, and raises the question: what are the motivations for these organisations to undertake such activities and what has changed? In the wake of the scandals that have occurred over the last several decades (and possibly centuries), organisations (for-profits and not-for-profits), governments, and international bodies (the United Nations for example) have frequently introduced and incorporated guidelines, policies, rules, legislations, laws, and codes to guide us to 'do the right thing' for all stakeholders. However, as Flynn and Werhane (2022: 2) ask, 'Are the leaders of banking, commerce, business, and politics listening to and applying the prevailing ethical discourse or are they merely protecting themselves and their respective constituencies against fault and/or blame in the face of grave difficulties by tangential recourse to ethics?' They suggest an ethical leadership process model that includes the role of virtue, conscience, servant leadership, and spirituality. They note that in the Harvard Business Association's 1958 conference, spiritual values were identified as linked to the nature and strength of businesses. Every major speaker at that conference stressed the importance of more attention to spiritual values. The significance of spirituality in business was illustrated at that conference by historian Arnold J. Toynbee who pointed out that no society has ever flourished without a spiritual mission. They quote: 'spirituality means making a continuing, conscious effort to rise above these inevitable human limitations – a maximum endeavour to comprehend the ultimate values, the truth and the reality of the orderliness of the universe – and to live in accordance with this reality' (p. 5). They observe that the theme of spirituality and business constitutes a broad field, requiring ethicists and businesspeople to think holistically. Some use terms such as 'wholeness', 'integration', and 'soul of the organisation', and others discuss spirituality under the heading of leadership and to analyse the role of organisations within society.

Every chapter in this book has concepts that can be linked into the essence and meaning of spirituality: the purpose of business (Chapter 1), the importance of stakeholder management (Chapter 2), ethics (Chapter 3), ethical decision-making (Chapter 4), cultures (Chapter 5), typical ethical issues of managers (Chapter 6), sustainability (Chapter 7), CSR and business as agents of world benefit (Chapter 8), global strategic issues of MNEs (Chapter 9), and responsible leadership (Chapter 10). In particular, Chapter 5 (Business Ethics Across Cultures) discussed concepts from various religions and cultures across the globe.

This chapter introduces spirituality in management and is presented in six sections: what is spirituality – definitions and understanding; what spirituality is not – differentiating spirituality from spiritualism and religiosity; influence of spirituality on business and ethics; workplace spirituality – concepts, processes, and leadership; applications of spirituality in the workplace; and incorporating spirituality in the Comprehensive Ethical Decision-Making model (CEDM). Two case studies are available at the end of this chapter.

11.2 What is spirituality? Definitions and understanding

The word 'spiritual' has a Latin root – *spiritus* – meaning 'breath' or a life-giving principle of an entity. The life-giving action of spirit integrates different aspects of human life – physical, emotional, professional, and intellectual (Gill, 2022; Ogunyemi, 2019). Jurkiewicz and Giacalone (2004) described the role of spirituality in the workplace as a basic need for employees' personal growth due to the declining role of families, neighbourhoods, and other societal players.

Definitions

Spirituality in management is an emerging field, largely because of the realisation that spirituality is one of the defining characteristics of the human condition and can have an impact on management practices – since how we manage depends on the way we are (Ribera and Lozano, 2011). Gill (2022: 36) summarises as follows: 'Considerable progress has been made in studying the outcomes of spirituality at work, such as, for example, meaningfulness in work, sense of purpose, sense of connectedness and belonging, recognition, fulfilment, satisfaction, well-being, happiness, commitment, and organisational performance and productivity, and indeed the greater good of society'.

Dorr (2022) suggests that even though some are reluctant to use the word 'spirituality', the majority of people have some explicit or implicit vision of life which lies behind their generous or selfish actions and attitudes (p. 400). Dorr asserts that the task of 'humanising' the business world is one of the major challenges of our time. He proposes three aspects of spirituality that can provide a range of purposes and values which could be richer and more fulfilling than the ones existing in modern-day approaches to business:

1   Aspects such as respect, trust, forgiveness, love for others, our desire for personal integrity, and our concern for social and environmental justice.
2   Our search for inner peace and serenity, and a feeling of harmony and oneness with nature.
3   Our vision of the world and our sense of our own personal calling in life.

Based on their analysis of interviewing US managers and executives, Mitroff (2003) identified the following attributes to define spirituality:

* Not formal, structured, or organised   in contrast to religion
* Not denominational; it is both above and beyond denominations
* Broadly inclusive – it embraces everyone
* Universal and timeless
* The ultimate source and provider of meaning and purpose in our lives
* Expression of the awe we feel in the presence of the transcendent
* The sacredness of everything, the ordinariness of everyday life
* The deep feeling of the interconnectedness of everything
* Inner peace and calm
* Providing one with an inexhaustible source of faith and willpower

The following definitions of spritituality provide key characteristics of spirituality:

* A state of being that reflects positive feelings, behaviours, and cognitions of relationships with oneself, others, nature, and the transcendent, which provides the individual with a sense of identity, wholeness, satisfaction, joy, contentment, beauty, love, respect, positive attitudes, inner peace and harmony, and purpose and direction in life (Gomez and Fisher, 2003).
* Spirituality in the context of work organisations as the nurturing of employees' inner selves, connectedness, and community, and meaning and purpose (Houghton et al., 2016).
* Provides a feeling of belonging (Price and Hicks, 2006), orientates human beings to the needs of others through openness and cooperation (Rabell and Bastons, 2020).
* A state of well-being characterised by positive thoughts, feelings, and behaviour in one's relationships with one' s work in respect of meaning, purpose, belonging and value or worth in what we do (Gill, 2022).

Understanding spirituality

Business leaders are increasingly showing interest in understanding the process of ethical decision-making, especially in the wake of unethical decisions and moral lapses by some business leaders (many of these have been discussed in the previous chapters of this book). People therefore look for business leaders to exercise true and authentic leadership. Stakeholders expect more from businesses (Miller, 2011). For example, consumers expect more than just high-quality products and services from corporations, and employees expect more than just appropriate salaries and wages. They are increasingly concerned about societal and environmental harm. This calls for more than just 'visionary' or 'responsible' leaders in business (as we have seen some difficulties associated with responsible leadership in Chapter 10). Miller calls for a spiritual-based leadership. He asserts that 'it's too late to argue about whether spirituality belongs in the workplace', because 'our spiritual values go to work with us' (p. 187). According to Ribera and Lozano (2011: 199), spirituality can have an impact on management by the possibility of introducing spiritually enhanced values and practices in corporate cultures. However, the question is whether it makes sense to talk about spirituality in the organisational context and how to do it in a relevant way. Most organisations have the tendency to manage religious diversity in organisations by providing employees the freedom and the facilities to practice their faith. Organisations also encourage employees to celebrate and showcase their religio-cultural traditions in which all employees may be encouraged to participate. Spirituality in management on the other hand involves a certain way of doing things, a certain management style, and a certain way of treating people. It includes a commitment to certain values, and a certain organisational culture (for example, the ethical climate). Ribera and Lozano (2011) also suggest using spirituality-related criteria when making decisions (for instance, when designing workspaces or product packaging). These initiatives require courage and capabilities of employees and more specifically the management leadership – this relates to Component 4 of Rest's EDM model discussed in Chapter 4.

Spirituality is also seen as the inner source of wisdom that is reflected in values and behaviours that include empathy, compassion, humility, passion, empowerment, and love (Guillory, 2019). Spirituality can embrace believers, non-believers, and those who are unaffiliated, and can include 'meditation, prayer, Yoga, and simply treating others with dignity and respect' (p. 33).

It is to be noted that the concepts of higher purpose, stakeholders, and reflection have been discussed in Chapters 1, 2, and 4 respectively. Let us now understand the term 'meaningful' as this chapter uses this concept in a number of places – such as meaningful connection, meaningfulness in work, and meaningfulness in life. Prepositions make a difference – for example, the 'meaning of life' is different from 'meaning in life'. The former might provide the final answer to a profound secret (best left to philosophers and theologians), while the latter is about an experience. King and Hicks (2021, quoting Klinger, 1977), defined meaning in life as a pervasive quality of a person's **inner life** and is experienced both as ideas and emotions. They identified the following variables linked to the experience of meaning in life:

- Positive affect – feelings of enjoyment and pleasure are an antecedent of meaning in life.
- Social connections – as social animals, we benefit when our needs for belonging are met, so we feel that our lives matter.
- Religion and worldviews – help people experience meaning in life with guidelines for how to live and provide a sense of how the world works.
- The self – feeling a strong connection to one's self helps us to make sense of our lives: this includes a sense of purpose, identifying what one is meant to do, and authenticity.
- Mental time travel – the ability to mentally project one's self into the past and the future can enhance the feeling that life is meaningful.
- Mortality awareness – thinking about death can make some question whether their life is truly meaningful, but paradoxically, acknowledging one's demise can have the potential to lead to a more meaningful existence.

King and Hicks (2021) provide extensive empirical evidence for the above concepts. A key proponent of the concept of 'meaning in life' is Austrian psychiatrist and philosopher Viktor Frankl, a holocaust survivor, in his book *Man's Search for Meaning* (Frankl, 1959/2004), in which he concludes that finding a meaning in one's life is the prime driving force for human beings. This includes meaningfulness of events, goals, tasks, actions, and situations in the workplace that is significantly determined by personal values, beliefs, and needs.

11.3 What spirituality is not – differentiating spirituality from spiritualism and religiosity

Considering that numerous attempts have been made to define spirituality, misunderstanding of what spirituality is can hinder productive learning and application of knowledge about the essence of being human, motivation, and well-being (Gill, 2022). So, before we discuss spirituality in management, we need to understand the two fundamental misunderstandings of spirituality: (1) it has often been confused with 'spiritualism', and (2) most tend to believe that spirituality and religion are one and the same thing.

Spiritualism

Spiritualism is associated with mediums, seances, tarot cards, astrology, and the practice of communicating with the dead. Popwell (2020) traces the beginnings of spiritualism to the Victorian era (late 19th century). By 1850, groups were organised across the US and then quickly spread to Canada, England, and parts of Western Europe and became widespread because of mass media – the popular press was filled with stories that either promoted spiritualism or attempted to expose spiritualist mediums as frauds. In 1871, approximately 50,000 spiritualist publications were sold every year – in the form of books, articles in journals, news reports, and pamphlets. Famous personalities also contributed to its popularity – such as the scientist Michael Faraday, who discovered electromagnetism, but also conducted experiments to provide an explanation for the phenomenon, and Arthur Conan Doyle, author of the Sherlock Holmes mysteries and a book on the history of spiritualism, who strongly believed in the ability to communicate with the dead. Popwell (2020) thus suggests that the spiritualist movement based on spiritualism has grown rapidly as a result of the formation and development of the mass media and the associated rise of 'fake news' and misinformation.

Religiosity

Religion has been defined by French sociologist Emile Durkheim as 'a unified system of beliefs and practices relative to sacred things, that is to say, things set apart and forbidden – beliefs and practices which unite into one single moral community called a Church, all those who adhere to them' (Carls, 2022). Freedom of religion or faith is guaranteed by article 18 of the Universal Declaration of Human Rights (OHCHR, 2023). Most religions are characterised by rituals in their practice, physical gatherings, and ceremonies that can include special clothes, flowers, music, and language.

Research into the relationship between religion and spirituality has gained considerable momentum as seen from the number of publications in specific academic journals such as *Journal of Business Ethics, Journal of Management, Family Business, Journal of Religion and Spirituality in Social Work*, and journals of the Academy of Management and American Psychological Association, among others.

For some people spirituality is grounded in religion, but others claim that spirituality transcends religiousness, or even replace spirituality with a secular or humanist view. Fry (2003; 2005), a leading exponent of spiritual leadership suggests that spirituality is necessary for religion, but religion is not necessary for spirituality. This position implies that individuals can develop their personal qualities and values without being dependent on any religious or metaphysical belief systems and that workplace spirituality can be either inclusive or exclusive of religious beliefs or practices or theories. Obregon et al. (2022) contend that there seems to be a general agreement that religiosity (religious orientation or the degree to which someone is involved in religious practices) affects how a person believes and follows a particular religion which may entail sacred symbols, ritual, and prayers, whereas spirituality is seen as an individual pursuit to understand the fundamental questions of life such as the direction, its meaning, its purpose, its end, which may or may not be associated with a religious context.

One of the most widely quoted sources in spirituality and religion is Mitroff and Denton (1999). In an effort to ascertain what gave people meaning in their work and lives, and the relationship between them, they analysed interview data from high-level managers and executives from all kinds of American for-profit organisations, not-for-profits, government, and social service agencies. Key outcomes from their study include: (1) people seriously want the opportunity to realise their full potential as whole human beings both on and off the job, (2) they want to work for ethical organisations, (3) they want to do interesting work, and (4) making money is important but it is a distant fourth. Further, a significant majority differentiated strongly and sharply between religion and spirituality – religion is seen as dividing people through dogma and emphasis on formal structure, whereas spirituality is viewed as both personal and universal, perceived as tolerant, open-minded, and including everyone. Not only did everyone agree to the same definition of spirituality, but they also felt strongly that people and organisations should be 'spiritual' by following a 'higher set of ethical principles'. Further, organisations perceived as 'more spiritual' were also perceived as being more profitable, implying that spirituality gives a true and lasting competitive advantage.

11.4 Influence of spirituality on business and ethics – some key evidence

- A study by Beekun and Westerman (2012) explored the relationship between spirituality and ethics with 149 respondents comprised of semi-skilled workers, office workers, vocationally trained workers, academics, managers, and senior managers, with ages from 20 to 39 years, male and female, and years of education from 10 to 18 years, and found:
  - the intention to behave ethically was significantly related to spirituality, national culture, and influence of peers. Americans, for example, were found to be significantly less ethical than Norwegians, yet more spiritual overall.

- In another recent study of a sample of the general population of adults between the ages of 30 and 65 in the US, Anderson and Burchell (2021) showed:
  - a statistically significant relationship between spirituality and ethical decision-making (see Chapter 4 to recap EDM), suggesting that spiritual individuals demonstrate ethical judgements differently than non-spiritual individuals regardless of moral intensity (see Chapter 4)
  - that 'spiritual persons can be critical assets to the entire organisation and inherent benefits from these persons convey significant competitive advantages' (2021: 145).

- Interpreting survey data collected from 2,230 individuals, mainly from the Academy of Management and from universities in the south-western United States, Liu and Robertson (2011: 35) claim that the construct of spirituality is best captured by three correlated factors:
  - interconnection with a higher power
  - interconnection with human beings
  - interconnection with nature and all living things.

- In a systematic literature review of 52 academic journal articles on spirituality from 2001 to 2018, Obregon et al. (2022) collated the following:
  - Individuals who consider themselves spiritual demonstrate a greater propensity to consider their work significant.
  - Literature highlights the benefits and positive results of spirirtuality in performance at work on organisations.

○ Applied to business ethics, it is suggested that stakeholder management and business plans should be preceded by a spiritual commitment to future generations.

○ Indications of the effect of spirituality on organisational culture, organisational commitment, growth in organisational values and hope, loyalty to the organisation, morality, ethics, and engagement at work.

○ Spirituality has also been related to work engagement as an inherent dimension of personality.

• Evidence of 'spiritual philanthropy': philanthropy has long been the source (or even the bedrock) of corporate social responsibility activities of large organisations and of wealthy individuals. Giacomin and Jones (2022) note that the activities of most philanthropic foundations (PF) have been documented all over the world.

○ PFs in developed regions such as the US and Western Europe are based on mainly transnational activities (for example, foundations such as Rockefeller, Carnegie, Bill and Melinda Gates, Mark Zuckerberg and Priscilla Chan, Novo Nordisk, Bosch, Carlsberg, and others).

○ PFs in emerging economies such as India, China, other Asian countries, Africa, Latin Africa, and Middle Eastern countries are closely intertwined with business families operating philanthropic ventures in their country for several generations (for example, foundations such as Tata Trusts, Godrej, Shiv Nadar, Azim Premji, Heren, Dangote, and others).

○ Arguing that philanthropic foundations in emerging markets have distinct characteristics, Giacomin and Jones (2022) interviewed 70 business leaders in 18 countries in Africa, Asia, Latin America, and the Middle East. They found that 79 per cent of PFs were associated with 'spiritual philanthropy' that embodies personal or family traditions, culture, and religious values, which emphasised charitable giving and social responsibility. They also assert that, 'as business leaders in emerging markets are more directly exposed to dire social, educational and health deprivation than their counterparts in developed countries, they are less inclined towards grandiose world-making, and their foundations are more focused on delivering immediate benefits to communities in their home countries, motivated by implicit or explicit spirituality' (p. 263).

11.5 Workplace spirituality – concepts, processes, and leadership

Research interest in workplace spirituality (WPS) has focused on its positive impact on employee work attitudes such as increased job satisfaction, employee engagement, organisational commitment, reduced intention to quit, and decline in deviant behaviours. Giacalone and Jurkiewicz (2003: 13) define workplace spirituality as:

> A framework of organisational values evidenced in the culture that promotes employees' experience of transcendence through the work process, facilitating their sense of being connected in a way that provides feelings of compassion and joy.

Noting that there is an increasing need for more evidence-based empirical research into the impact of spirituality on key organisational areas, Otaye-Ebede et al. (2020) studied data collected from 366 managers and employees of a large multi-million-dollar retail chain organisation in the UK, consisting of 51 stores nationally and 676 employees. They found evidence supporting the following:

1 Workplace spirituality is positively related to ethical climate.
2 Workplace spirituality is positively related to moral judgement.
3 Workplace spirituality is positively related to prosocial motivation.
4 Aggregated ethical climate positively relates to collective employee helping behaviour and service performance.

In addition to showing the value of workplace spirituality in organisations, the research indicates how encouraging spirituality within the workplace leads to ethical decision-making among employees, thereby creating a composite ethical climate. The researchers suggest that 'since workplace spirituality is the potential influencer of ethical climate, organisations should train employees to understand the positives of workplace spirituality. Different ways to impart these values should be researched' (p. 622). In another study of responses from 223 professionals employed in the services sector of Australia, Issa and Pick (2011) found evidence that suggests the presence of spirituality, interconnectedness, optimism, and contentment were significantly associated with ethical practice in the workplace and were also factors that influence ethical climate in the workplace.

Mitroff and Denton (1999) asserted that there is an emerging and accelerating call for spirituality in the workplace – providing examples of companies as diverse as Taco Bell, Pizza Hut, BioGenenex, Aetna International, Big Six accounting's Deloitte and Touche, and law firms such as New York's Kaye, Scholer, Fierman, Hays and Haroller. Since 1999, the concept of workplace spirituality has seen a rapid increase in its study in management research – possibly after Mitroff and Denton's (and others) finding that organisations perceived as spiritual are also more profitable. The rising interest in WPS, over nearly three decades, has contributed to its legitimisation in organisation studies. It has also led to the formation of a special interest group within the Academy of Management – called Management, Spirituality, and Religion (MSR-AOM, 2023). Crossman (2018) cites several studies in the last couple of decades that suggest positive relationships between WPS and employee engagement, job involvement, commitment, performance, productivity, lower levels of absenteeism and turnover, satisfaction, and enhanced mental wellness.

Fry (2003) refers to two essential dimensions of workplace spirituality – a sense of transcendence and a need for social connection or membership. Transcendence in this context is described as having a 'calling' through one's work or being called vocationally. 'Calling' refers to how one makes a difference through service to others, and in doing so derives meaning and purpose in life. It has been used as one of the defining characteristics of a professional who, in addition to competency and mastery, also has a sense that work has some social meaning or value. They believe their chosen profession is valuable, even essential to society, and they are proud to be a member of it. Membership encompasses the cultural and social structures through which we seek to be understood and appreciated. According to Fry (2003: 703), workplace spirituality is to be understood within the context of interwoven cultural and personal values that must demonstrate their usefulness by impacting performance, turnover, productivity, and other effectiveness criteria.

Giacalone and Jurkiewicz (2003) have further identified two themes to support the assertion that spirituality in the workplace has received increased attention:

Theme 1: changes in the social and business environment in terms of instability, budget cuts, downsizing, outsourcing, technology replacing employees leading to employees' distrust of organisations they work for, compelling the employee to search for deeper meaning in work and life – for example, the search for satisfaction in the workplace beyond pay.

Theme 2: global change in values in terms of increased awareness of social and environmental sustainability, CSR, and climate change leading to employees' need for meaning in their work and the desire to make a positive impact on society.

Marques (2019) defined workplace spirituality as the awareness that interconnectedness, respect, and recognition are applicable not only to ourselves but to all those with whom we work in ways that can lead to enhanced enjoyable workplace circumstances and also to increased return on investments. The experience of performing our duties should be one that is rewarding to all involved with feelings of trust, belonging, meaning, and fulfilment. In a study of MBA students between the ages of 25 and 55 years and predominantly employed in midlevel positions in a variety of industries, the question asked was: 'How do you think your current work environment could be transformed into a more spiritual one?' Two responses were prominent: (1) 'Through daily interaction and making trust building a part of our jobs. And through listening, and then applying, in order to more fully engage the crews', and (2) 'By people helping each other out more often' (p. 15).

Workplace spirituality and spiritual leadership are also seen as a good fit for the public sector. Haensel and Garcia-Zamor's (2019) support for this notion is based on employee motivation. They cite research which shows that public sector employees attribute greater value to work that is beneficial to others and to society, to critical public sector policies, and to self-sacrifice, responsibility, and integrity. In addition, they contend that public sector employees place less emphasis on money and high income as ultimate goals in work and life. They contend that these factors and values are related to spirituality as they are related to aspects that create meaning in work by deploying creativity, emotions, and intelligence to serve the public.

11.6 Applications of spirituality in the workplace

In the 'Purpose' section of Chapter 1, we sought to answer questions such as what is the purpose of business, what is the nature of business's existence in society, what would businesses want to be known for, and are businesses making the world a better place. We outlined the process (see Figure 1.3) of defining purpose, finding the meaning of the purpose, and then formulating mission, vision, strategy, and action. Some of these ideas have been elaborated and derived from the concept of 'conscious capitalism' propounded by Mackey and Sisodia (2014). They define conscious capitalism as 'a way of thinking about capitalism and business that better reflects where we are in the human journey, the state of our world today, and the innate potential of business to have a positive impact on the world' (p. 273). Such businesses, they claim, can help billions of people to flourish, leading lives with passion, higher purpose, love, and creativity – to create a world of freedom, harmony, prosperity, and compassion. They further propose that leaders required to lead such businesses, termed as 'conscious leaders', need to have four types of capabilities:

- Analytical intelligence (IQ)
- System intelligence (SYQ)
- Emotional intelligence (EQ)
- Spiritual intelligence (SQ)

While IQ and SYQ would be a prerequisite for 'business-as-usual' needs, EQ and SQ would be required for developing relationships, stakeholder management, and an appreciation for the values and purpose of the organisation. EQ combines two characteristics – self-awareness (understanding oneself), the core of what it means to be more conscious, and empathy (understanding others), the ability to feel and understand what others are feeling.

SQ, also understood as evolving to higher levels of consciousness, involves accessing our deepest meanings, values, purposes, and higher motivations. It gives us an innate ability to distinguish right from wrong and helps us to discover our own personal higher purpose in our work and our lives. Leaders with spiritual intelligence can align their employees with their organisations' higher purposes (Danah Zohar and Ian Marshall in *Spiritual Capital*, cited in Mackey and Sisodia, 2014, p. 185). The concept and the importance of consciousness will be discussed in a section further in this chapter.

The concept of SQ (evolving to higher levels of consciousness) has been implied in some well-known theories of management and ethical decision-making:

- In his theory of human needs, Abraham Maslow proposed that human beings evolve to higher level needs from basic physiological needs to safety, to love and belonging, to esteem, and finally to self-actualisation. The final level of self-actualisation was linked to what Maslow called 'peak experiences' that include spiritual development and transcendence by describing them as the highest levels of human consciousness, behaving and relating to oneself, to significant others, to human beings in general, to other species, to nature, and to the cosmos (Papaleontious-Louca et al., 2022).
- In the cognitive moral development (CMD) theory – discussed in Chapter 4 – Lawrence Kohlberg identified several ethical levels and stages that people go through. The final stage (called universal ethical principles) is related to an individual's awareness of values and rights and is defined by the decisions of conscience (Kohlberg, 1981).

Zappala (2022) has developed four pathways to achieve SQ:

- Reflect pathway: cultivating self-awareness (knowing what one believes in and values), leading by vision and value (acting from principles and deep beliefs), and asking why (questioning and getting to the root causes of issues) – leading to understanding one's own worldview before becoming more aware of the worldview of others. Related practices include contemplative education, mindfulness, meditation, breathing techniques, reflective thinking, and visualisation.

- Connect pathway: practising holism (the ability to see larger patterns, relationships, and connections), compassion (feeling and having deep empathy), and celebration of diversity (valuing other people and unfamiliar situations). Related practices include worldview literacy, storytelling, holistic thinking, and use of ethical dilemma concepts.
- Respect pathway: a sense of vocation (feeling 'called' to serve something larger), humility (having a sense of being a player in a larger drama) – effectively becoming a servant leader. Related practices include servant leadership, service learning, gratitude, and intellectual humility.
- Express pathway: exhibiting spontaneity (living in and being responsible to the moment), reframing (standing back from a problem or a situation to see the bigger picture and context), positive use of adversity (owning and learning from mistakes), and field of independence (standing against a crowd and maintaining one's convictions). Related practices include intuitive thinking methods, studying spiritual pathfinders, arts-based practices such as poetry, music, painting, sculpture.

To assess spirituality and related concepts, MacDonald (2000), using data from two large samples of Canadian university students, provided strong evidence supporting the existence of five dimensions of spirituality:

1 Cognitive orientation towards spirituality – beliefs about the existence, validity, and relevance of spirituality for one's sense of identity and daily functioning.
2 Experiential dimension – spiritual experience and connectedness to such experiences.
3 Existential well-being – sense of meaning and purpose.
4 Paranormal beliefs – in the existence of paranormal phenomena and abilities.
5 Religiousness – intrinsic commitment to religious ideas, values, and practices.

Developing this model led to a 100-item measure to operationalise the five dimensions called the Expressions of Spirituality Inventory (ESI), and later a shorter 32-item version of the test called ESI-Revised (ESI-R). The model and measure are understood as one of the most comprehensive approaches to understanding spirituality, even though the five dimensions do not necessarily contribute to the definition of spirituality (especially due to the criticism of dimensions 4 and 5). Further, the model and the instrument 'have been used in a variety of studies and have proven useful for theory development, test validation, and empirical investigations of the relation of spirituality to personality, social, and health variables' (MacDonald et al. 2015). Studies have shown that each dimension appears to uniquely contribute to our understanding of the functionality of spirituality.

To further evaluate the reliability and validity of ESI-R, MacDonald et al. (2015) analysed data from 4,004 participants across eight countries (Canada, India, Japan, Korea, Poland, Slovakia, Uganda, and the US). Their findings include the following:

- Spirituality is viewed as a viable concept in a similar manner across cultures.
- While spirituality was found to comprise at least five dimensions, it appears to be intrinsically bound by culture and cannot be fully understood without consideration to cultural factors – meaning that while there are similarities, spirituality is not the same across cultures.

- Spirituality may not only differ in precise meaning across cultures, but also across age and sex – accounting for diversity of experience and expression.
- Existential well-being is seen as an essential characteristic linked to higher levels of spirituality.

In a recent systematic review of the extant literature of WPS that reviewed 159 conceptual and empirical articles published in more than 50 journals from 2010 to 2021, Singh and Singh (2022), grouped their findings into the following themes and classification criteria:

1   Conceptualisation of WPS at three levels:

- Individual level: WPS is an individual quest to find meaningfulness in life through work. Experiences at work enable employees to visualise work as an integral part of life.
- Group or community level: WPS improves interpersonal relationships, sense of self-worth and respect that creates a moral responsibility to perform better.
- Organisational level: WPS involves development of an organisational culture based on values such as benevolence, integrity, and humanism.

2   Religion and WPS:

- Religion is seen as a system of belief for seeking guidance from the almighty, giving credit for their survival to their faith. It is hierarchical and institutional.
- Spirituality is seen as a broader concept. It is individualistic, facilitating self-discovery, better life, and relations.
- Managers seem to prefer incorporation of spirituality in the workplace rather than promoting formal religion.

3   Antecedents and consequences of WPS:

- Analysis of the articles revealed antecedents (changes to the environment that occur immediately before a behaviour occurs) of WPS as servant leadership, work/organisational values, and life experiences.
- Consequences or outcomes of WPS have been linked to a variety of aspects such as job satisfaction, job performance, intention to quit, organisational commitment, work ethics, team effectiveness, organisational performance, sustainability, CSR, and others.

4   Literature has also referred to the 'dark side' and criticism of WPS, suggesting that:

- WPS could be used by employers to manipulate employees' spiritual needs and their inner belief system for achieving materialistic organisational goals.
- Managers may unintentionally force employees to adhere to spiritual practices that do not correspond to their beliefs or personality.
- WPS could lead to the privatisation, commodification, and commercialisation of spirituality, mainly by large corporate firms to enhance their organisational outcomes.
- WPS can be a mere control mechanism where the process is manufactured by managers for attaining operational objectives.
- If WPS values flow from top to bottom, it can lead to feelings of suppression, distress, and dissatisfaction among employees.

5   Management theories in WPS research:

- Stakeholder salience theory: as discussed in Chapter 2, stakeholder salience is impacted by three attributes: power, legitimacy, and urgency. A study by Mitchell et al. (2013) integrates the stakeholder theory in the family business to explain the impact of stakeholders' spiritual identity on the three attributes.
- Person–organisation (P–O) fit theory: defined as the degree of compatibility between individuals and their organisation which happens when there is a match between the values, knowledge, and skills of the employee and the requirements of the organisation. WPS literature has suggested strong linkages between WPS and P–O fit, where employees whose spiritual needs are fulfilled by the organisation tend to perceive their work in a greater context – by expressing their whole selves at work. WPS is seen as a strong predictor of P–O fit.

Crossman (2018) suggests that WPS can only be conceptualised in terms of the interaction between individual/personal and organisational spiritual values. Further, in addition to the notion of individual spirituality, organisations can also claim to have a spiritual identity – called organisational spiritual identity (OSI), implying that organisations can strategically engage in and foster practices of spirituality. Crossman (2018) has identified the following signifiers of OSI:

- Mission statements: also referred to as a statement of purpose (see Chapter 1 for more on purpose of business), the mission serves to illustrate organisational values, goals, self-concept, and why an organisation exists. A mission statement embodying spiritual values can suggest that the leadership intends to characterise the organisational identity in spiritual ways.
- Employee well-being services: classes in yoga, meditation, prayer, breathing, and silence before meetings for reflection are all spiritual activities that organisations encourage to enhance the well-being of employees.
- Use of spaces: physical spaces can be an indicator of OSI – such as spaces for prayer rooms, facilitating reflective environments for thinking and contemplation, provision of certain menus in canteens, and meditation rooms.
- Celebrations: to mark religious or cultural occasions such as Christmas, Eid, or Diwali, special leave for certain festivals.
- Professional development and training: some organisations provide training on spiritual matters related to diversity issues and may include spiritual leadership training.
- Paid time for service to charities, donations, and fair pricing: corporate philanthropy in the form of financial donations, paid service to charities, charging affordable prices, and donations to humanitarian programmes.

Mukherjee and Zsolnai (2022) refer to how spirituality can serve in renewing business ethics and management. They state that 'introducing spirituality in the field of business and managerial ethics creates a shift from external rule-directed behaviour towards an inner-directed, existential search for meaning. What is missing in conventional business and managerial ethics is a deep, inter-subjective intuition of the Presence of Life that guides thoughts and actions' (p. 4). Chakraborty uses the term 'consciousness ethics' to describe ethics based on the re-connection with the inner source of life. He distinguishes 'consciousness ethics' from compliance ethics and cognitive ethics (Chakraborty and Chakraborty, 2008: 40, see also Savur, 2022):

- Moral judgement, within the ethical decision-making process, is heavily influenced by a huge corpus of 'compliance ethics' (codes, legislation, etc.).
- 'Cognitive ethics' in contrast can be understood as arriving at moral judgements using intellectual concepts and theories such as utilitarianism, deontological ethics, stakeholder theory, rights, social justice, and ethics of care.
- 'Consciousness ethics' is derived from the idea that 'right consciousness' is a prerequisite to do the right thing in the right way in each and every situation – it would be specifically applicable when we know what is right but cannot act upon it or know what is wrong but cannot desist from doing it.

Zsolnai (2022) argues that a 'spiritual turn in business management is required' – that business management needs a more spiritual foundation to solve the failure of rational and materialistic management that produces large-scale ecological, social, and ethical issues (p. 63). In addition to the characterisation of responsible leadership by Maak and Pless (2019) – discussed in Chapter 10 – Zsolnai (2019) suggests there is a need for leadership to consider the interests of those stakeholders who do not have a voice and to balance the interests of stakeholders with or without power (discussed in Chapter 2). Based on Amartya Sen's (the 1998 Nobel laureate in economics) concept of social choice theory (concerned with how to translate the preferences of individuals into the preferences of a group), Zsolnai (2019) identified three classes of reason that leadership choices should satisfy:

- Ecological reason
- Reason for future generations
- Social reason

Thus, leadership actions can be considered 'reasonable' only if they satisfy the criteria of the restoration of nature, increase the freedom of future generations, and serve the well-being of society.

11.7 Incorporating spirituality in the CEDM model

Considering the discussions in this chapter on spirituality in management, we can now include spirituality in the CEDM model (last depicted in Chapters 4 and 5) as shown in Figure 11.1.

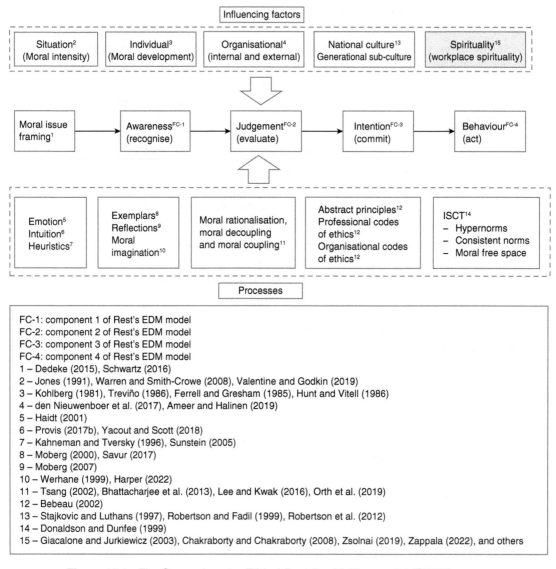

Figure 11.1 The Comprehensive Ethical Decision-Making model (CEDM)

Summary

• This chapter begins by referring to all previous ten chapters of this book suggesting that business ethics has evolved mainly due to the frequent scandals and unethical behaviour of businesses, and although concepts ranging from purpose of business (Chapter 1) to responsible leadership (Chapter 10) have been introduced, there is still a need for something more and something different. And so, this chapter introduced spirituality in management and the workplace and spiritual-based leadership as an alternative way for developing business ethics further.

- We mentioned that some people are reluctant to use the word 'spirituality', possibly due to the misunderstanding that mixes up spirituality with spiritualism, and spirituality with religion.
- We understood that spirituality in management is an emerging field and already several definitions of spirituality have been proposed by various researchers and commentators. Terms and attributes used in these definitions include interconnectedness, inner selves, calling, relationships, transcendent, meaning, purpose, openness, belonging, and a feeling of harmony and oneness with nature.
- We noted that many businesses (for example in the tech industry) have identified and implemented employee programmes to stimulate spiritual growth through the use of yoga, mindfulness, and meditation. We have referred to empirical research demonstrating correlations between spirituality and employee well-being, motivation, and improvements in overall performance.
- We discussed in detail the concepts and processes of workplace spirituality (WPS) by referring to research that has highlighted the dimensions and themes of WPS.
- The final section of this chapter suggested applications of WPS – the concept of spiritual intelligence (SQ), the four pathways and practices to achieve SQ, a way to measure and operationalise spirituality, the signifiers of organisational spiritual identity, and the concept of consciousness ethics.
- The chapter ended with showing how spirituality can be incorporated in the Comprehensive Ethical Decision-Making model.

CASE STUDY 11.1
ARAVIND EYE CARE HOSPITALS

In Chapter 8, we briefly mentioned the example of the Aravind Eye Care system in relation to social innovation and social entrepreneurship serving the people at the bottom of the pyramid. Here, we discuss in further detail the influence of spirituality on Aravind's operations and performances – how spirituality and the idea of common good motivates and drives Aravind.

In 2015, 253 million people worldwide were reported to be visually impaired – of these, 36 million were blind and 217 million had moderate to severe visual impairment. Eighty-nine per cent of visually impaired people live in low- and middle-income countries. Sixty-two per cent are in South Asia, East Asia, and South-East Asia (Ackland et al., 2017). A national survey in India conducted in 2015–2019 reported that there are an estimated 4.95 million people blind (0.36 per cent of the total population), 35 million people visually impaired (2.55 per cent), and 0.24 million blind children in India.

(Continued)

Cataracts and refractive errors such as short-sightedness remain the leading causes of blindness and visual impairment.

Realising the enormity of the situation and that the government alone could not meet the health needs of all, Dr Venkataswamy (affectionately known as Dr V), following his retirement in 1976, established the GOVEL Trust under which the Aravind Eye Hospitals were founded. Starting with an 11-bed hospital and four medical officers, Dr V saw the potential for what is today one of the largest eye care facilities in the world. Today, there are 14 Eye Hospitals, six outpatient eye examination centres, and 100 primary vision centres in South India, along with a network of community outreach centres, factories, research, and training institutes. Today, it averages over 450,000 surgeries a year, and since its inception Aravind has handled more than 65 million outpatient visits and performed 7.8 million surgeries.

The Aravind network offers three tiers of service. The first tier is the camp hospital at the bottom level of the hospital that provides free diagnosis, in addition to free transport to the city hospital, free surgery, and accommodation to people with low incomes. Aravind does not demand proof of low-income status – instead they use social norms to ensure high-income patients do not take advantage. At the second-tier of service, the patient's fee is not free, but is partially subsidised – around USD 10.30 for the surgery and extra for medicines, transportation, and food at the hospital. The third-tier service is where the patient can choose the size of the room, extra beds, air-conditioning etc. for around USD 220 for the surgery. Further, in association with another non-profit organisation, Aurolab, it manufactures intraocular lenses lowering the cost per unit to one-tenth the prevailing price.

While Aravind is seen as a large, successful, efficiently run enterprise, its foundational principles and work ethics set it apart from other healthcare organisations. Aravind is not only a business with a laudable social goal, it is inspired by the philosophy of interconnectedness of human beings and follows a management style based on compassionate care and the will to contribute to the common good. Unlike other businesses (where it is common to have opacity in sharing business practices), Aravind welcomes other eye hospitals to exchange knowledge, to learn from others and put that know-how into practice. They argue that nothing should be hidden, since the goal of all such organisations is to eradicate needless blindness and that they are all working towards a common goal. Outside India, the Lumbini Eye Institute in Nepal, as well as Muhammad Yunus' replication of the Aravind model in the form of a social business in Bangladesh – the Grameen Green Children Eye Care Hospital – illustrate Aravind's potential for spreading internationally (Virmani and Lepineux, 2016).

The Aravind venture is based on three Indian traditions of common good and takes inspiration from the Indian spiritual philosopher Sri Aurobindo.

The three Indian traditions reflecting on common good:

1   The earliest tradition is associated with Kautalya or Chanakya, political advisor to the Emperor Chandragupta Maurya (340–298 BCE). Author of the political treatise *Arthasastra*, Kautalya outlined the art of statecraft and strategies of rule for the

Emperor, emphasising the welfare and the ethics necessary for the cohesion of society.

2   The second tradition was developed by the Mauryan Emperor Ashoka when after conversion to Buddhism (around 261 BCE) he instituted a set of guidelines to meet people's economic and welfare needs. The common good implied the greatest good for the greatest number of people, further refined by the notion of *dharma* or the right action. This included a respect for life and resources, the protection of the weak and feeble or the minority religious groups.

3   The third tradition can be traced to the Gandhian ideas of *Sarvodaya* (good for all), *swadeshi* (self-sufficiency), and *swaraj* (self-rule). Thus, for Aravind, the approach to healthcare is not as a market commodity, but as an essential element of human empowerment – enhancing patients' autonomy and raising their capacity to contribute to the collective, where eye care is seen as a public good.

Aravind draws inspiration from Sri Aurobindo's notion of internal yoga that urges the evolution of human life by being more active in the world with larger vision, greater efficiency, higher creativity, and visible results. This is to be achieved through spiritual values such as love, devotion to truth, and selfless service.

Bhatnagar et al. (2020: 200) found that Dr V and Aravind 'were strongly influenced by spiritual values to actively engage in social welfare with a focus on the larger good. Guided by the spiritual philosophy of *dharma* (duty towards society) and *nishkamakarma* (righteous action with detached passion), they embarked on doing good without expectations or claiming fame and credit, rather than following the "donate and forget" kind of philanthropy'. Thus, Dr V's life highlights the significance of spirituality and a higher consciousness in transforming lives by integrating a sense of purpose in our daily work. Rather than renouncing the worldly activities or merely following rituals to seek the divine, Dr V believed that transforming the lives of others by restoring eyesight to all, irrespective of social or economic status, was an important step towards achieving this spiritual goal.

The following quote from Dr Venkataswamy appears on signs in hallways, on internal reports and communications, and on the web:

When we grow in spiritual consciousness, we identify with all that is in the world so there is no exploitation. It is ourselves we are helping. It is ourselves we are healing.

Questions

Using the Case-Study Integrative Framework in Figure 0.1, discuss the following:

1   Identify the key primary and secondary stakeholders of Aravind Eye Hospitals.

2   Are there any stakeholders whose concerns are not adequately addressed by Aravind?

3   Do you see any differences in the way Aravind satisfies the needs of stakeholders as compared to any other commercially run hospital? Discuss and reflect.

4   What do you think are the influences and effects of spirituality on the operations and performances of Aravind?

(Continued)

5   Do you think the 'Aravind way' can be applied or replicated in commercially run health organisations?
6   Do you think the 'Aravind way' can be applied or replicated in all types of industries? If not, what are the exceptions, and why?
7   How do you think the Aravind concept can be upscaled worldwide? What issues or even obstacles do you envisage?
8   Are there any similarities in your culture? If so, what?
9   What are the ethical issues in this case study. Apply the CEDM model in this chapter to develop your analysis, judgement, commitment, and potential action.

Sources:

Ackland et al. (2017)
Aravind (2023a)
Aravind (2023b)
Bhatnagar et al. (2020)
Chakrabarti (2021)
Dandona et al. (2001)
Krishnadas et al. (2022)
Mannava et al. (2022)
Virmani and Lepineux (2016)

CASE STUDY 11.2
PHIL JACKSON'S COACHING PHILOSOPHY

Phil Jackson is an American former professional basketball player, coach, and executive. He played 12 seasons in the NBA, winning the NBA championships in 1970 and 1973. He coached the Chicago Bulls from 1989 to 1998, leading them to six NBA championships. Later he coached the Los Angeles Lakers from 1999 to 2004 and again from 2005 to 2011, leading them to five NBA titles. His 11 NBA titles is an unbeaten record as a coach.

Jackson's success is attributed to strategic game-plans and a holistic approach to coaching. The strategic game-plan was based on the use of American basketball coach and innovator Tex Winter's triangle offense. The holistic approach to coaching was influenced by Eastern philosophy, which gave him the nickname 'Zen Master'.

There were several spiritual guiding forces in his life: Native American spiritual practices, Zen Buddhism (Jackson 2006), and the book *Zen and the Art of Motorcycle Maintenance* (Pirsig, 1974/1981). Phil Jackson's unique coaching philosophy was featured in episode 4 of the television series 'The Last Dance' taking the Chicago Bulls team to the next level by getting past the Detroit Pistons. His leadership philosophy was built on a foundation of meditation, mindfulness, and Buddhist ideas.

In their book *Eleven Rings: The Soul of Success*, Jackson and Delehanty (2014) reported an approach to leadership based on freedom, authenticity, and selfless teamwork. Jackson describes how he learned the secrets of mindfulness, encouraged Michael Jordan (one of the greatest players in the world) to embrace selflessness, got team players to trust one another, convinced 'ego-driven' personalities to devote themselves to something larger than themselves, and transformed teenagers into mature leaders. The 11 principles of leadership and relationships described by them are:

1   Lead from inside out – leading from the heart.
2   Bench the ego – by distributing power.
3   Let each player discover his own destiny – by getting players to think for themselves to make difficult decisions.
4   The road to freedom – to foster greater creativity and innovation.
5   Turn the mundane into the sacred – by incorporating meditation into team practices.
6   One breath, one mind – by sitting together in silence, breathing together in sync, it helped align them on a non-verbal level.
7   The key to success is compassion – a few kind, thoughtful words can have a strong transformational effect on relationships.
8   Keep your eye on the spirit – not on the scoreboard – by transcending your own limitations and helping others to transcend theirs.
9   Sometimes you have to pull out the big stick – to wake players up and raise their level of consciousness.
10 When in doubt, do nothing – on certain occasions, the best solution is to do absolutely nothing.
11 Forget the ring, we all hate losing – fixating on winning is counterproductive. It is best to create the best possible conditions for success and let go of the outcome.

Jackson said: 'What matters most is playing the game the right way and having the courage to grow, as human beings as well as basketball players. When you do that, the ring takes care of itself'. The winners of the NBA finals receive a championship ring. Thus, Jackson got players like Kobe Bryant, Shaquille O'Neal (Shaq), Scottie Pippen, and Michael Jordan to subordinate their talents to the goal of a better team. One of Jackson's practices was giving personalised books to players to read. For example, Jackson thought Shaq was being too materialistic, so he gave him Herman Hesse's book *Siddhartha*, asking him to turn in a book report. *Siddhartha* is the story of a young prince who gives up his princely life for a selfless, spiritual quest for enlightenment. Another player, John Paxton, received the book *Zen and the Art of Motorcycle Maintenance*.

(Continued)

In his book, *Sacred Hoops: Spiritual Lessons of a Hardwood Warrior*, Jackson (2006) begins by saying 'the CEO of the Chicago Bulls argued with me that people are motivated by two prime forces: greed and fear. I countered that they are motivated by their community and by love' (p. ix). Some of the key aspects of Jackson's spiritual beliefs and practices mentioned in the book are:

- Selflessness is the soul of teamwork – p. 6.
- Everything is based on mind, is led by mind, is fashioned by mind. If you speak and act with a polluted mind, suffering will follow you – from Buddha's *Dharmapada* – p. 48.
- Sitting meditation, called *zazen*, makes us immerse in action as mindfully as possible and quieten the mind – pp. 49–51.
- In Zen, the right action is the capacity to observe what's happening and act appropriately without being distracted by self-centred thoughts – p. 69.
- Zen teaching holds wisdom for anyone wanting to get the most out of a group. You cannot expect a team to perform in a way that's out of tune with its basic abilities – p. 100.
- The Lakota Sioux warriors did not perceive the self as a separate entity, isolated from the rest of the universe. A warrior did not try and stand out from his fellow band members, he strove to act bravely and honourably to help the group in whatever way he could – p. 109.
- Being completely immersed in the moment, inseparable from what we are doing. Right thoughts produce right values, right values produce right thoughts, and right thoughts produce right actions – p. 116.
- Getting the players to share their views on topics other than basketball helps build solidarity. One way they did this was to talk regularly about ethics – p. 124.

Questions

Using the Case-Study Integrative Framework in Figure 0.1, discuss the following:

1 Identify the key primary and secondary stakeholders of Phil Jackson.
2 Are there any stakeholders whose concerns are not adequately addressed by Phil Jackson?
3 Do you see any differences in the way Phil Jackson satisfies the needs of stakeholders as compared to any other business? Discuss and reflect.
4 What do you think are the influences and effects of spirituality on the operations and performances of Jackson's coaching of the Chicago Bulls and LA Lakers?
5 Do you think the 'Jackson way' can be applied or replicated in commercially run organisations? How?
6 Do you think the 'Jackson way' can be applied or replicated in all types of industries? If not, what are the exceptions, and why?
7 How do you think Jackson's philosophy can be upscaled worldwide? What issues or even obstacles do you envisage?

8   Are there any similarities in your culture? If so, what?
9   What are the ethical issues in this case study. Apply the CEDM model in this chapter to develop your analysis, judgement, commitment, and any potential actions.

Sources:
Baker (2005)
Jackson (2006)
Leadership Now (2013)
Mixon (2010)
Pirsig (1974/1981)
Sirk (2020)

Recommended readings

Dorr, D. (2022), 'Alternative business ethics: A challenge for leadership'. In G. Flynn (ed), *Leadership and business ethics*, 2nd edn, Dordrecht: Springer Nature.

The author unfolds an argument and logic progressing from the motivation for businesspeople to behave ethically, to the current 'Western' business system, to an alternative model of business operating in the street markets of Asia and Africa, to how the present system can be changed by applying concepts of spirituality.

Chakraborty, S.K. and Chakraborty, D. (2008), *Spirituality in management: Means or end?* New Delhi: Oxford University Press.

This book might be hard to access, but is well worth it. The authors focus on the idea that spirituality and management can be perceived as integrally connected.

Giacalone, R.A. and Jurkiewicz, C.L. (2003), *Handbook of workplace spirituality and organizational performance*, New York: M.E. Sharpe.

The first chapter in this book, 'The science of workplace spirituality', begins with a note that interest in this area is increasing due to widespread values shifts, increasing social anomie, and a search for meaning in personal and professional areas. What follows is a discussion of the weaknesses in the development of WPS, and then of moving towards a science of WPS.

Gill, R. (2022), 'Introduction to spirituality'. In A. Yochanan, J. Neal and W. Mayrhofer (eds), *Workplace spirituality: Making a difference*, Berlin: De Gruyter.

This book chapter will introduce you to 'spirituality' – what is it, its meaning, the misunderstandings, its links to science and religion, workplace spirituality, the dark side of spirituality, and the future trends.

Jurkiewicz, C.L. and Giacalone, R.A. (2004), 'A values framework for measuring the impact of workplace spirituality on organizational performance', *Journal of Business Ethics*, 49(2): 129–42.

A much-cited paper on how workplace spirituality might enhance organisational performance. The authors review and analyse research and introduce a values framework for WPS. This paper provided the groundwork for future researchers.

MacDonald, D.A., Friedman, H.L., Brewczynski, J., Holland, D., Salagame, K.K.K., Mohan, K.K., Gubrij, Z.O. and Cheong, H.W. (2015), 'Spirituality as a scientific construct: Testing its universality across cultures and languages', *PloS One*, 10(3), e0117701.

This analysis of data from 4004 participants from eight countries provides an insight into the measurement of spiritual constructs – quite an extensive and detailed analysis. It ends with a discussion of the meaning of the findings and directions for future research.

Marques, J. (2019), *The Routledge companion to management and workplace spirituality*, 1st edn, London: Routledge.

An extensive ensemble of 30 papers about concepts, discussions, and critiques of WPS. Marques starts off with 'Understanding the ripple effect of spiritual behavior'. Well worth it to browse through and select the paper that interests you.

Mitroff, I.I. (2003), 'Do not promote religion under the guise of spirituality', *Organization*, 10(2): 375–82.

An important resource in which the author discusses the outcomes of interviews with managers and executives from all kinds of organisations – with the primary purpose being to ascertain what gave people meaning in their work and lives, and the additional aim to explore spirituality in the workplace.

Zsolnai, L. (2022), 'Spiritual turn in business and management'. In S. Mukherjee and L. Zsolnai (eds), *Global perspectives on Indian spirituality and management*, Singapore: Springer, pp. 63–74.

The paper argues that a spiritual turn in business management is needed – using real-world examples from Europe and India that show the feasibility of the spiritually inspired business model.

12

FUTURE ISSUES AND DIRECTIONS

┌─Learning objectives─┐

On completion of this chapter, you should be able to:

- Understand the evolution of industry phases with respect to business ethics and CSR concepts
- Appreciate the views of business ethics pioneers about the future of business ethics
- Appreciate thoughts on the future of business ethics from various aspects
- Understand ethical issues in new innovations and technologies in business
- Understand the new concept of corporate digital responsibility
- Reflect on business ethics

┌─Key concepts─┐

- Future of work
- Machinewashing
- Unethical business models
- Ethics of algorithms, smart farming, blockchain, AI, robotics, and space
- Human–robot interaction
- Corporate digital responsibility

─Box 12.1 Opening case─

Vermeer's masterpiece 'Girl with a Pearl Earring'

In 1665, the Dutch painter Johannes Vermeer created a painting which became known as 'Girl with a Pearl Earring'. The oil on canvas painting is 44.5 cm high, 39 cm wide, and is signed 'IVMeer'. It depicts a European girl wearing an 'exotic dress', an 'oriental turban', and a very large pearl as an earring. The painting has been in the collection of the Mauritshuis museum in The Hague (The Netherlands) since 1902.

In February–March 2023, the painting was loaned to the Rijksmuseum in Amsterdam for display and viewing, and the Mauritshuis museum organised a competition to replace the painting during the loan period. Of the 3,500 entries, the contest's judges narrowed the field to 170 finalists, and finally five winners were chosen. The artists ranged in age from three to 94, depicting the 'girl' as a puppet, a dinosaur, and a piece of fruit. One of the five winners was Julian van Dieken's interpretation of the masterpiece. It was called 'A Girl with Glowing Earrings'. The main difference between this creation and the others were that van Dieken's was created with the AI programme Midjourney.

Midjourney is an independent research lab that produces an AI programme that generates images from natural language descriptions similar to OpenAI's DALL-E and Stable Diffusion. It was founded in mid-2022 in San Francisco, California by David Holz, with regular releases of new versions every few months – the latest version at the time of writing, 5, was released on 16 March 2023.

The AI-generated 'A Girl with Glowing Earrings' caused controversy amongst the art fraternity with people accusing the museum of 'abdicating ethical decision-making' and that it was a 'shame and an incredible insult'. Others highlighted the damaging effects of AI systems on artists and creative professionals, copyright infringements, and still others lamented the 'limited creativity of the artist'. Some question whether it should be classed as 'art' at all.

In response to criticism, the museum officials noted that the judges were impressed by van Dieken's product, and the process did not affect their decision. They ask: 'It is such a difficult question: What is art and what is not art?' They insisted that that they had not set out deliberately to make an artistic statement on AI and that they were not discussing whether AI-generated work belongs in an art museum.

In December 2022, Midjourney was used to create images in an AI-generated children's book in just one weekend. The product and the process drew criticism. One artist claimed 'the main problem... is that it was trained off of artists' work. It's our creations, our distinct styles that we created, that we did not consent to being used'. In January 2023, three artists filed a copyright infringement lawsuit against Midjourney, claiming that these companies have infringed the rights of millions of artists by training AI tools on five billion images scraped from the web without the consent of the original artists.

Sources:
AIAAIC (2023)
Al-Sibai (2023)
Enking (2023)
ET-Telecom (2023)
Straits Times (2023)
Wiki (2023a)
Wiki (2023b)

12.1 Introduction

The opening case highlights one of the issues of new technology – in this case: AI-generated art. The questions that arise are – does art need a new definition, can an AI-generated piece of art represent the creativity and skill of the 'artist', can an existing artwork (however ancient) re-generated by AI be allowed or acceptable – what are the ethical issues here?

AI-generated art is just one of innumerable outcomes from new technologies such as digital technology, AI, machine learning, robotics, virtual reality, blockchain, genomics, and space exploration. All such technologies are driven by innovators and businesses, large and small. As we have seen earlier in this book, while most business activities and innovations result in doing good for their stakeholders including society, they can also perpetuate unethical conditions and consequences.

While not published in academia, science fiction literature has several references to the ethical implications of both robots and AI. The well-known biochemistry professor and science fiction writer Isaac Asimov in the 1942 short story *Runaround* promoted the three laws of robotics, devised to protect humans from interactions with robots (Anderson, 2017; EB, 2023):

- First Law: A robot may not injure a human being or, through inaction, allow a human being to come to harm.
- Second Law: A robot must obey the orders given it by human beings except where such orders would conflict with the First Law.
- Third Law: A robot must protect its own existence as long as such protection does not conflict with the First or Second Laws.

However, enormous progress has been made in robotics since Asimov's 1942 laws. Robots are as varied as the simple robotic vacuum cleaners to the complex robots designed for a military combat environment. Given the issues stemming from the range of robotics we have today, Asimov's laws offer little more than founding principles and a much more comprehensive set of laws is required.

This chapter considers, discusses, and reflects on ethical and other related issues surrounding current and future technologies that innovators and businesses are pursuing. The chapter is structured in seven sections: evolution of industry and business ethics concepts; views from the pioneers of business ethics; thoughts on the future of business ethics; ethics and the future of work; ethical issues in technology; corporate digital responsibility; and end of book quotes and questions to ponder. Two case studies are available at the end of the chapter on space ethics and AI considerations in SDGs and emerging economies.

12.2 Evolution of industry and business ethics concepts

Humankind's evolution in innovation and production has so far been represented in five phases that has changed the way we think and work in industry. The five phases, beginning with the Industrial Revolution in the 18th century to the present, are designated as Industry 1.0, 2.0, 3.0, 4.0, and 5.0. The five phases are quite distinctive with respect to the types of energy used, the type of technology used, and the interface between industry and society in each phase. Business ethics and CSR concepts, such as the ones discussed in this book, have also evolved during the same periods. Table 12.1 shows the five industry phases placed side-by-side with concepts of business ethics and CSR that also evolved during the same time periods and can possibly provide us with some indications of the next phases of evolution in these areas. Phase 6.0 (if or when it arrives) could include new types of energy and new types of innovations. The questions for us, then, are: (1) are the current theories and concepts of business ethics adequate to deal with phase 6.0 technologies? and (2) are the current concepts of CSR or even CDR adequate to deal with phase 6.0 technologies?

Table 12.1 Periods of industry phases and concepts of business ethics and CSR

Industry phase	Period beginning	Energy/ Technology type	Typical innovations	Interface	Business ethics concepts	CSR related phases
1.0	c. 1760	Coal, steam	Machines for textiles and transportation	Faster and easier production	1785 – Deontological from Kant. 1789 – Utilitarianism from Bentham.	Beginnings of social responsibilities seen in labour rights and safety.
2.0	c. 1840	Electricity	More sophisticated machines	Cleaner production	1863 – Utilitarianism from Mill.	

Industry phase	Period beginning	Energy/ Technology type	Typical innovations	Interface	Business ethics concepts	CSR related phases
3.0	c. 1970	Electronics, IT, Internet	Automation, connectivity, cleaner energy	Reduced human input	1958 – Stages of moral development from Kohlberg. 1984 – Four components of EDM from Rest. 1984 – Stakeholder theory from Freeman.	1950–60 CSR-1 phase: corporate social stewardship. 1970s CSR-2 phase: corporate social responsiveness. 1980s–1990s CSR-3 phase; Corporate and business ethics. 1987 – the Brundtland report and the three pillars of sustainability. 1994 – Triple Bottom Line (TBL).
4.0	c. 2000	IoT, big data, cloud storage, renewable energy	Smart products, factories, precision agriculture, driverless cars, additive manufacturing	Improved energy efficiency, reduced carbon emissions, better connectivity, and flexibility, work from home	2003 – Workplace spirituality. 2006 – Responsible leadership. 2008 – Spirituality in management. 2014 – Conscious capitalism.	2004 – ESG. 2004 – Bottom of Pyramid (BoP). 2006 – B Corp. 2008-2016 – Corporate Social Innovation (CSI). 2009 – the nine planetary boundaries. 2013 – GHG emissions protocols - Scope 1,2,3. 2015 – the UN 17 Sustainable Development Goals (SDG).

(Continued)

Table 12.1 (Continued)

Industry phase	Period beginning	Energy/ Technology type	Typical innovations	Interface	Business ethics concepts	CSR related phases
5.0	c. 2017	Individualised human-machine interaction, smart materials, digital simulation, AI, machine learning, tech for energy efficiency, renewables, storage, and autonomy	Collaborative robots (Cobots), intelligent robots, synthetic pancreas, customised medical apps on phones, sustainable local production	Achieve societal goals beyond jobs and growth. Core values: sustainable, human-centric, and resilience	2021 – Corporate Digital Responsibility (CDR)	2021 – Corporate Digital Responsibility (CDR)
6.0??	Year??	New types??	New innovations??	Interfaces??	Need for revision of business ethics concepts??	Need for revision of CSR/CDR concepts??

12.3 Views from the pioneers of business ethics

Although business owners may have struggled with how business ought to be conducted for at least 3700 years, it is only in the past 40 years when academics and professionals came together, enabling 'business ethics' to emerge as an area of study. The early pioneers consisting of Kenneth Goodpaster, Norman Bowie, Joanne Ciulla, Richard De George, Thomas Donaldson, R. Edward Freeman, Daryl Koehn, Richard Nielsen, Manuel Velasquez, and Patricia Werhane have recorded at least 25 years of association with business ethics education and research (Bevan and Goodpaster, 2020). Now, the *Business and Professional Ethics Journal* editors have initiated a project aiming to capture their observations and personal memories, to address the next set of big questions and to identify prevailing themes that need to be asked and answered. These pioneers were interviewed based on a questionnaire template consisting of 13 questions. In addition to recording their goals, expectations, and contributions, the following two questions were asked (Bevan, 2021):

- What questions and issues do we still face today?
- What issues and questions will we need to address in the next 20 years?

The following are the responses from the pioneers about current and future issues for business ethics:

- Kenneth Goodpaster (2010):

  - Business ethics is a programme of applied ethics generally. What we learn in business ethics applies to medical ethics, for example, and it applies to engineering ethics: any field where there are organisations.
  - The biggest challenge now is taking seriously the notion of what humanity is and how we can get to the notion of the human good.
  - We should pursue goods that are truly good and services that truly serve humanity, and we need to take on the spirituality issue, as well as our physical needs and our emotional needs and all that we are made up of.

- R. Edward Freeman (2021):

  - Questions about what business is – in a global and multicultural sense.
  - Most of our ethical theories come from Kant and need different perspectives.
  - Closing the gap between theory and practice.
  - New technologies such as AI, autonomous cars, and data privacy.
  - To consider what kind of human beings we are going to be when our interactions are mediated by screens.
  - Simple binary distinctions like 'saints and sinners', and 'facts and values' do not help us very much.

- Joanne Ciulla (2021):

  - Bring more young people into the field.
  - Key issues – gender, ethnicity, cryptocurrencies, blockchain, AI, rating agencies, leadership.

- Manuel Velasquez (2021):

  - Suggested that when trying to think through an issue in business ethics, you should ask three questions: First, what are your options and who will be impacted by each of those options? Second, ask yourself a three-part question: which option will best contribute to the overall welfare of the people that option will affect; which option will best respect the moral rights of the people that option will affect; and which option will distribute benefits and burdens in the most just manner among the people affected? And third, weighing the answers to that three-part question, ask which option in your judgement, is the most ethical?
  - Major issue: climate change. The instinctive reaction of businesses is going to be to try to protect themselves and continue engaging in the kind of unsustainable business practices they are used to. I think the role of business ethicists is going to be to remind our business organisations that they need to turn away from their old ways of doing things and embrace new sustainable practices.

- Norman Bowie (2021):

  - Ethics should be involved in almost all thinking about business.
  - Ethical issues haven't and won't disappear.
  - What can we learn from other parts of the world? And from people who are not just like us? We have to be creative.

- Patricia Werhane (2021):

  - In the 1970s, we expected that by 2000 there would not be any problems with equal opportunity/diversity and environmental issues. But today, it is not over. But at least we are now aware of these issues.
  - Today's issues: diversity, environmental, and globalisation.

- Richard De George (2021):

  - Business ethics will continue and business has become more involved.
  - Issues: inequality, global warming, climate change.

- Richard Nielsen (2021):

  - We need practitioner-based theory building, engagement methods, ethics leadership methods, and conflict-resolution methods to solve ethical problems in the field.
  - Key issues: AI in financial trading and social media data collection, corruption in emerging countries.
  - Use four-loop action-learning method. Outcomes of individual behaviours (single-loop), value assumptions driving the individual behaviours (double-loop), organisational systems driving the assumptions that drive individual behaviours (triple-loop), and the national political-economy or culture that supports unethical organisations and individual behaviours and values (fourth-loop).

- Thomas Donaldson (2021):

  - Three convictions why business ethics will be important in the future: (1) business ethics reflects the realities of the centuries-old maturation of capitalism itself in various parts of the world, (2) law is limited in its ability to reconcile the abstract principles of higher authority with the inevitable outcomes of capitalism – legal mechanisms have difficulty reaching and ameliorating problems in key moral spaces, and (3) law and regulation lag behind technological evolution and frequently play catch-up when dealing with a new hazard.
  - The final stage in the long evolution of capitalism is to reconcile with our deeper intrinsic values and it is at this stage that business ethics reigns supreme. We are still working on the final stage of the evolution of capitalism. We have a long way to go and for this reason business ethics will not disappear.

12.4 Thoughts on future of business ethics

Some key areas of business ethics have attracted attention while considering the future of business ethics. These are (1) the intersection of law and business ethics, (2) the intersection of strategy and ethics, and (3) exploring unethical business models (Dacin et al., 2022).

The intersection of law and business ethics

In Chapter 2, we discussed the relationship between law and ethics asking questions such as 'if it is legal, must it be ethical?' and 'are illegal actions always unethical?' Recently, due to constant changes in society, the focus has been on how the goals of law can regulate business to improve individual and organisational compliance (David Hess in Dacin et al., 2022). The role of law in encouraging ethical business behaviour is constantly evolving – for example, in the tech industry, how the rights of employees and consumers can be protected (ethics) by updating policies and regulations (law). In the use of AI in employment decisions and in autonomous vehicles, employment law and product liability laws can resolve ethical issues in those industries. Laws can also play a key role in the issues of diversity, equity, and inclusion (DEI – discussed in Chapter 6).

The intersection of strategy and ethics

As discussed in earlier chapters, business creates value for stakeholders and society by providing goods and services, wages for workers, income for investors, and taxes that help to support community and government services. Businesses also give generously to charities and engage in community programmes. The creation of such values is a direct result of business strategies. At the same time, we have seen in earlier chapters that the means through which strategies are implemented may violate widely held ethical rules or codes associated with values such as honesty, fairness, equality, responsibility, justice, and freedom. Harrison (in Dacin et al., 2022) has identified questions that are important to the intersection of strategy and ethics:

* How have firm strategies changed in light of social movements associated with DEI? Do they create value for firms, stakeholders, and society?
* How do firms deal with supply chain shortages and are there any supply chain challenges that lead to unethical behaviour?
* How are firms dealing with ethical issues in developing or adopting new technologies such as AI, genetic engineering, big data, and alternative sources of energy?
* What types of strategies would be required to deal with shocks such as the pandemic and disruption due to natural disasters? Do such shocks lead firms to engage in unethical behaviours or practices?
* How do institutional, political, and societal forces vary globally leading to different strategies?

Exploring unethical business models

The negative impact of some businesses is clear, particularly if the model is one that operates outside the law – such as the sale of heroin or armed robbery, both of which could be for-profit enterprises. However, there could be some business models which are legal yet may contain elements that are inherently damaging or unsustainable – for example the tobacco business. Some jurisdictions take steps to ban such businesses – for example on 13 December 2022, the New Zealand government banned the sale of cigarettes to anyone born on or after January 2009 (BBC, 2022). There could be other such businesses with unethical business models – such as those who underpay food delivery workers or the provision of essay-cheating services to students. Killian (in Dacin et al., 2022) asks 'how do we identify such businesses'? and 'can we create a framework of unethical business models'? Killian identified seven dimensions that support a business model with an unethical core:

- Inherent harm – those that cause inherent harm to the health of consumers or to the environment – such as the tobacco industry and some forms of mining exploration respectively.
- Dependence – locking consumers or suppliers into future purchases – such as phones that do not have a standard headphone port forcing consumers to buy an adaptor or an accessory, and devices becoming redundant due to software changes.
- Facilitation – or encouraging unethical behaviour – such as essay-writing services and the dark web.
- Appropriation – privatisation or theft of common resources like water supplies, overfishing, patenting of genetic material, or even privatisation of the Moon.
- Deception – promising far beyond what can be or is delivered – such as in the field of natural medicine, beauty or diet products, and more recently the 'greenwashing' phenomenon. This can also include predatory behaviour – such as sale of products that promote unrealistic beauty standards to young women in particular.
- Exploitation – in business models ranging from the use of near-forced labour (discussed as modern slavery in an earlier chapter) to parts of the gig economy.

Such a framework would allow researchers to map the dependence of any business model on each of the dimensions and can help identify unethical business models. Having done so, aspects of business could be examined – such as design and packaging of products or services, marketing strategies, price points and availability, CSR strategies, and social impact accounting.

The *Journal of Business Ethics* recently commemorated its 40 year anniversary by inviting academics to provide a commentary on the future of business ethics (Bohm et al., 2022). Some of the key observations about the future of business ethics were:

1. The grand challenges of the 21st century, financial crisis, climate change, internet technologies, AI, and global health crisis, should be framed as grand *ethical* challenges. Jain, Kourula and Riaz (in Bohm et al., 2022: 836–40) propose that an ethical lens allows for a humble response, in which those with greater capacities take greater responsibilities and remain inclusive and cognisant of different voices and experiences.

2. Focusing on the grand challenge of environmental emergencies, and proposing the idea that business *is* nature and nature *is* business, Bohm (in Bohm et al., 2022: 840–43) argues against human–nature dualism – that is, we are all part of a self-regulating complex system with millions of nodes and feedback loops between them.

3. Continuing to focus on climate emergencies, de Bruin (in Bohm et al., 2022: 843–7), posits a scenario, 40 years from now, where business ethics will be evaluated by its ability to have helped humanity emerge from this emergency. He suggests how human

rights can take centre stage in climate change litigation, and how business ethics can enter the courtroom.

4   There is increasing evidence (as discussed in Chapters 7 and 8 in this book) that current growth-focused approaches are unsustainable and could be responsible for driving climate change, environmental degradation, and human misery. This includes increased material consumption leading to consumer demand for cheap, 'disposable', and short-lived items. Business models underpinning over-consumption are often built on exploitation, are unsustainable, and are no longer fit for purpose. Shaw, Carrington and Hassan (in Bohm et al., 2022: 847–9) therefore propose that there is an urgent need for new approaches and thinking for socially just sustainability in our current marketplace systems, and a need to revisit our understandings of growth and consumer society.

5   Cornelius (in Bohm et al., 2022: 849–52) has linked the capabilities approach (CA – of Amartya Sen, discussed in earlier chapters of this book) to global and corporate governance, arguing that CA will continue to be the foundation of human development policies, CSR, and CG.

6   Romani (in Bohm et al., 2022: 852–5) suggests that dialogue between diversity management and international management can ground future debates in business ethics.

7   Karam and Greenwood (in Bohm et al., 2022: 855–9) propose the possibility of feminist-inspired theories and methods for areas of business ethics, especially stakeholder theory, to broaden the capacity of business ethics.

12.5 Ethics and the future of work

The future of work is increasingly seen as the integration of people, technology, alternative workforces, and new ways of working. Organisations combine people and machines. In a recent survey by one of the world's largest professional services organisations, Deloitte, 85 per cent of respondents believe that the future of work raises ethical challenges, but only 27 per cent have clear policies and leaders to manage them. Respondents identified four factors that are driving the importance of ethics related to the future of work (Schwartz et al., 2020):

1   Legal and regulatory requirements – there is often a lag in laws and regulations relating to both technology and workforce issues.

2   Rapid adoption of AI in the workplace – using robots and AI, organisations can be expected to redeploy people and how will they support workers if jobs are eliminated.

3   Changes in workforce composition – 'invisible labor forces' in the gig economy and unsavoury working conditions of workers in high-tech piecework have concerns of fair pay, healthcare, and other potential benefits.

4   Pressure from external stakeholders – from customers, investors, and other external stakeholders are calling organisations to address the challenges from the future of work issues.

Respondents also indicated that most organisations were prepared to handle tech-issues such as maintenance of privacy, control of workers' data, fairness of pay, job designs, and treatment of alternative workers. Organisations were, however, not prepared for issues of automation, use of AI, and the use of algorithms. The most challenging ethical issues were identified as:

1   Reducing labour costs by extensively implementing automation and AI across the organisation and replacing workers. Data shows the automation can often disproportionately affect minorities – for example while women make up 47 per cent of the US workforce, they make up 58 per cent of the workers at risk of losing jobs to technology. One in three Hispanic women face the highest risk of job automation.

2   Using sensors and cameras to physically monitor workers in real time to observe and optimise workflows. For example, monitoring of long-distance truck drivers and monitoring in manufacturing, warehouse, and call centres.

3   Using algorithms and machine learning to vet potential candidates and make recommendations on hiring decisions.

The Deloitte report noted that some organisations are responding by creating senior executive positions with a specific focus on ethical decision-making – such as Salesforce hiring its first Chief Ethical and Humane Use Officer in 2019 to ensure emerging technologies were implemented ethically. Other organisations have given their workers access to training information, support for safer work habits, and have shown workers that the angle of cameras focus on the process and not the individual. The report also suggests that rather than reacting to ethical dilemmas as they arise, organisations should anticipate, plan for, and manage ethics as part of their strategy and mission – especially with the combination of humans, machines, and algorithms working as a team.

12.6 Ethical issues in technology

From greenwashing to machinewashing

Obradovich et al. (2019) contend that today we may be witnessing a new kind of greenwashing in the technology sector. Some scholars and observers have labelled the business ethics concept of AI ethics 'machinewashing' – derived from 'greenwashing' (defined as misleading environmental communication by companies – discussed elsewhere in this chapter). Machinewashing has been defined as a strategy that organisations adopt to engage in misleading behaviour (communication and/or action) about unethical artificial intelligence (AI) / algorithmic systems. The concept of machinewashing has only recently entered the business ethics research agenda. Seele and Schultz (2022) posit that machinewashing involves misleading information about ethical AI communicated or omitted via words, visuals, or the underlying algorithm of

AI itself. Furthermore, and going beyond greenwashing, machinewashing may be used for symbolic actions such as (covert) lobbying and prevention of stricter regulation. Examples of machinewashing cited by Seele and Schultz (2022) include:

1 Deceptive and vague terminology – ethical AI, fair AI, human-friendly AI, sustainable AI, AI to benefit everyone.
2 Inaccurate claims, meaningless claims, overstatements – 'AI is helping doctors outthink cancer, one patient at a time' – climate misinformation.
3 Mislead with visuals or graphics – robot celebrity status, digital visuals, or art.
4 Misleading by omission, selective disclosure – chatbots imitating humans and the challenges of customers to know whether they are interacting with AI or not.
5 Misleading with lobbying – tech companies lobbying governments and academia to develop policies and investment recommendations.

The problem of ethical proliferation for each technology

As we have seen earlier, the use of AI and the combination of computers and AI with robotics have ethically relevant implications for individuals, groups, and society. Sætra and Danaher (2022) argue that there is no need to create separate 'ethics of X' or 'X ethics' for each and every subtype of technology – for example computer ethics, AI ethics, data ethics, information ethics, robot ethics, and machine ethics. They suggest that although specific technologies might have specific impacts, they are often sufficiently covered and understood through already higher-level domains of ethics. The proliferation of tech ethics, they say, is problematic because:

1 The conceptual boundaries between the subfields are not well-defined. Within the sub-fields such as data ethics, big data ethics, AI ethics, digital ethics, and robot ethics, people working in AI ethics discuss the very same issues as they pertain to, for example, facial recognition technology. Privacy issues would be discussed in data ethics and digital ethics. Care and health issues would be discussed in autonomous vehicles and robots in public spaces.
2 It leads to a duplication of effort and constant reinventing the wheel, leading to similar and overlapping knowledge.
3 There is a danger that participants overlook or ignore more fundamental ethical insights and truths such as sexism, gender bias, racial injustice, and other forms of discrimination.

Sætra and Danaher (2022: 93) suggest two criteria as a way out of the predicament generated by the proliferation of ethics:

1 If the questions you address are sufficiently addressed by higher-level ethics, do not align your work with lower-level technologies.

2   If you are in fact pursuing novel questions, consider if they are general and more basic technologies and do not always rush to create a new domain-specific ethics attached to lower-level terms and technologies.

Ethical technology is about ensuring a moral relationship between technology and users. Such relationships could be in the form of respect for employees and customers, moral use of data and resources, responsible adoption of disruptive technology, and creating a culture of responsibility. Ethical issues identified by Watters (2023) are:

- Misuse of personal information such as how businesses use personal information obtained from browsing, online purchases, and participation in social media.
- Misinformation and deep fakes such as information and opinions on social media without fact checking.
- Lack of oversight and acceptance of responsibility such as when third-party technology is used, there is often confusion about where the responsibility lies, especially in the use of big data and cybersecurity concerns.
- Use of AI such as facial recognition, replacement of jobs, health tracking, and bias in AI technology.
- Autonomous technology such as self-driving cars, robotic weapons, and drones.

Consumers are increasingly interested in purchasing sustainable products. Noting that there are growing concerns that some businesses are falsely promoting their environmental or green credentials, the Australian Competition and Consumer Commission has indicated that it will analyse at least 200 business websites for misleading environmental claims across sectors such as energy, vehicles, household products, appliances, clothing, packaging, cosmetics, and food and drink packaging (Dedovic, 2022). The analysis will include monitoring for greenwashing, deceptive practices in the digital marketplace, manipulative marketing techniques, and misleading reviews and testimonials.

Application of care ethics to the future of work with robots

As discussed in Chapter 3, care ethics originated in the 1980s with Carol Gilligan challenging her supervisor Lawrence Kohlberg, where she argued that girls' concern for close relationships and how others feel when making moral decisions did not indicate immaturity (as concluded by Kohlberg) but revealed a different voice. This alternative moral theory proposed that relationships of care are the basis upon which life and flourishing arise (Ley, 2023).

Care has been defined as 'a species activity that includes everything that we do to maintain, continue, and repair our "world" so that we can live in it as well as possible. That world includes our bodies, ourselves, and our environment, all of which we seek to interweave in a complex, life-sustaining web' (Tronto and Fisher cited in Ley, 2023: 7).

The future of work with robots has a wide range of stakeholders, the three main ones being: the engineers developing technologies, the companies deploying it, and the workers using it. It is the interactions between all of these people that make the current and future robotisation work. Currently, research has focused on human–robot interactions (HRI) which examines only the relationships between humans and robots – how a robot and a person engage with each other. However, it misses the robot's indirect effects. The proposed new focus is on human–robot-systems interactions that looks at ethical concerns beyond the dyad of robots and human users. It enables identifying relationships at multiple levels – user, organisational, and societal. Beyond the immediate user level (physical and temporal), there is the organisational level where people relate to their sense of belongingness, security, and value, which can include a safe place to voice their feelings about working with robots. At the societal level, increased automation may alter how a person relates to their government, political parties, and social groups.

Ley (2023) defines the concept of 'care gaps' as those relationships not involving sufficient attentiveness, responsibility, competence, responsiveness, and solidarity. It is asserted that robots introduced or increased in a workplace can affect care gaps in three ways:

- Companies engage in 'care washing' where 'corporations try to increase their legitimacy by presenting themselves as socially responsible, while really contributing to inequality and ecological destruction' (p. 7). For example, when robots are introduced, there may be public declarations that workers will be taken care of, but employees can be left even more vulnerable than before.
- Weakening a previously existing caring relationship. For example, a manager and frontline workers may have shared a lot of face-to-face contact, and a new robot might distance the two, leaving the manager to learn about workers through data collected about workflow, rather than conversations and in-person meetings.
- When the relationships between those building a robot and those working with it are weak and therefore do not take into account workers' insights needed for technology development.

Algorithms

The following examples show how algorithms structure our lives: determining search results and ads we see online, predicting our ethnicity, predicting who might be a terrorist, what we will pay, what we read, if we can get a loan, if we have been defrauded, if we are fired, how we are recruited, and how we are sentenced and paroled. While algorithms make datasets valuable through benefits such as tailored news, better traffic predictions, more accurate weather forecasts, and car rides when and where we want them, we also hear about algorithms as unfairly biased in situations where search results are based on someone's gender, in advertisements, hiring, lending, risk assessments, etc. Martin (2019) contends that hidden behind these issues lies a tension between (1) the idea that algorithms are neutral and organic, and (2) the reality of a mix of technical and human curating (p. 836). The former suggests minimal responsibility for the developers of the algorithm where the users have no say (also called *buyer beware*) in how algorithms make decisions. Martin (2019) argues the following:

1 Developers have a responsibility for their algorithms later in use.
2 Firms are responsible and accountable for designing the role of an individual creating their algorithms.
3 Algorithms are value-laden in that they create moral consequences, reinforce or undercut ethical principles, and enable or diminish stakeholder rights and dignity.
4 Algorithms are an important factor in ethical decision-making and influence delegation of roles and responsibilities.
5 If an algorithm is designed to preclude individuals from taking responsibility within a decision, then the designer of the algorithm should be held accountable for the ethical implications of the algorithm's use.

Ethics of blockchain

A blockchain is a distributed database or ledger that is shared among various locations of a computer network. It stores information as a database electronically in digital format. The goal is to allow digital information to be recorded and distributed, but not edited, which means that ledgers and records of transactions cannot be altered, deleted, or destroyed (Tang et al., 2020). The first decentralised blockchain was conceptualised by a group of people in 2008. Since then, the blockchain file size (that contains records of all transactions that have occurred on the network) has increased from 20 GB in 2014 to around 250 GB by 2021. A typical blockchain process would be (Hayes, 2022):

1 A new transaction is entered.
2 The transaction is transmitted to a network of peer-to-peer computers scattered around the world.
3 This network of computers then solves equations to confirm the validity of the transaction.
4 Once a group of transactions are confirmed to be legitimate, they are clustered together into blocks and are 'closed'.
5 These blocks are then chained together creating a long history of all transactions that are permanent.
6 The transaction is now complete.

Blockchain technology has applications in real estate registry, data protection, luxury goods registry, document tracking, ownership authentication, healthcare records sharing, copyright management, supply chain management, and smart contracts. Fintech (financial technology) is being shaped by cryptocurrencies and other blockchain-based innovations. While there are increasing numbers of studies in the ethics of emerging technologies such as the ones discussed in this chapter (IT, computers, robotics, big data, the internet, algorithms, and AI), the ethics of blockchain has received limited attention, partly due to the lack of understanding of its processes, workings, and impacts. Tang et al. (2020) have analysed the ethics of blockchain on three levels – the technology (micro level), application (meso level), and society levels (macro level).

1   Technology (micro level):

    a   Characteristics: peer-to-peer computing, consensus algorithms, immutability, and authentication.

    b   Applications: shared ledger, secured transaction records, algorithm ensured correctness.

    c   Ethical impacts: privacy, accuracy, property, accessibility, and equality.

2   Applications (meso level):

    a   Characteristics: digital assets, digital contracts, assets exchange, bitcoin, data mining, payment.

    b   Applications: digital and physical assets, autonomous execution, efficiency, cashless payment, new investing markets, and applications in e-commerce.

    c   Ethical impacts: reduced transaction fees, simplified procedures, autonomous models, Ponzi scheme concern, volatility and speculation, tax evasion, corruption, and threats to governmental monetary policy and regulation.

3   Society, politics, economy (macro level):

    a   Characteristics: elimination of intermediaries, and central parties, decentralised trust and knowledge.

    b   Applications: autonomous applications, organisations, corporations, and society.

    c   Ethical impacts: digital democratisation (where technology becomes accessible to more people), transformation of organisations, and technological utopianism (the idea that advances in science and technology could and should bring about a utopian ideal).

Ethics of smart farming

Smart farming, a not-so-established term as yet, refers to the use of sensors, drones, weather satellites, intelligent algorithms, and robots that promises a technological 'fix' for societal issues such as provision of food for the growing world population, mitigating the environmental impact of farming, and 'fostering the safety and societal acceptability of food products by means of increased traceability and transparency' (Van der Burg et al., 2019: 1). Such technologies make more effective tasks such as irrigation, monitoring the health and location of the herd, sowing crops or milking cows, tailoring fertilisers or pesticides to plants' needs, or identifying the right time for seeding. Further, data generated from these technologies can be combined and interpreted across multiple farms in the region to provide better information to farmers. As with most new technologies, smart farming also raises ethical challenges – with questions about what would be good, right, just, and an acceptable action, and what societal goals are worth stiving for.

Analysing 44 articles from three databases on the ethical questions and reflections about the digitalisation of farms or 'smart' or 'precision' farming, Van der Burg et al. (2019) identified three interrelated themes:

1   Data ownership, accessibility, sharing and control – questions that arise are: how are data understood by different people, who owns the data, what data should be open or shared with whom, what is the meaning of fairness/equity in relation to data sharing, and how can data be protected.

2   Distribution of power – questions that arise are: what the different power-distribution is in the network in relation to the goals of smart farming, benefits to members in the network, sustainability of farms, meaning of values such as fairness, justice, transparency, and trust, and who should be involved in reflection about the goals of smart farming.

3   Impacts on human life and society – questions that arise are: does smart farming actually succeed in bringing about desirable societal goals or private company goals; how does smart farming change daily work, routines, experiences, choices, and deliberations; what are the gains and losses associated with smart farming?

Issues raised by business ethicists with regard to digital technologies:

1   Three types of unaware and often overlooked stakeholders (Trittin-Ulbrich and Martin in D'Cruz et al., 2022: 882–3):

   a   Stakeholders who are being impacted by a digital technology but are unaware of that technology being used – such as data from the job application process, social networking, and dating sites being used to train face recognition technology. Or those confronted with the results of automated decision-making without realising such technology is being applied.

   b   Digital technologies can create new 'unequal' stakeholders that interact with businesses – such as the 'gig' economy workers that often work at the whim of an algorithm, and how e-commerce platforms decide to show their products only to certain customers.

   c   Digital technologies can create new 'invisible' stakeholders – such as masses of poorly paid subcontractors in the Global South and factory workers in the delivery centres of large e-commerce retailers.

2   Revamping the notion of CSR with the exponential growth of AI and its related ethical and socio-technical issues (Du in D'Cruz et al., 2022: 884–6). Emphasising the need for CSR research in:

   a   how AI technologies can incorporate ethical and socially beneficial features
   b   how companies can develop a strategic approach to AI-related CSR
   c   how an ecosystem of businesses, government institutions, non-profits and relevant stakeholders could collectively promote long-term coexistence of machine and human intelligence.

Artificial intelligence

In a recent analysis, Chow and Perrigo (2023) state 'Tech companies are betting big on AI. Are they making the same old mistakes'? They note that while large tech companies such as Microsoft, Google, and Meta have stressed the importance of AI for years, they now seem to be prioritising speed over safety. In the rush to release tools based on AI technology, mistakes and harms from the tech companies have risen (see examples in Chow and Perrigo, 2023: 47). These analysts worry what could emerge next if this race continues to accelerate. They cite Silicon Valley's last world-changing innovation, social media, where the failures came not from connectedness, but the way tech companies monetised it through news feeds and keeping people scrolling with targeted online advertisements. They conclude with 'it is exactly this immense power that makes the current moment so electrifying – and so dangerous' (p. 48).

In an effort to guide business and innovators on the safe and ethical use of AI, the Australian Government on 16 March 2023, in a world first, launched a 'Responsible Artificial Intelligence (AI) Network' – in association with the National AI Centre and coordinated by CSIRO, Australia's national science agency (CSIRO, 2023a; 2023b; Walker, 2023). The director of the National AI Centre, Stela Solar, has asserted that 'Australian businesses have told us that understanding ethics and governance in implementing AI is lacking across organisations globally. The Responsible AI Network provides a unique offering: practical guidance and coaching from experts on law, standards, principles, governance, leadership, and technology to ensure explainability, fairness, and accountability are built into Australian AI systems' (CSIRO, 2023a).

Researchers have identified two major classifications of AI (see Bankins and Formosa, 2023). Currently we have achieved only the first, 'artificial narrow intelligence' (ANI), that is a high-functioning system that can replicate or even surpass human intelligence for a dedicated purpose – such as facial recognition, chatbots or assistants, self-driving vehicles, predictive maintenance models, and recommendation engines. The second classification is 'artificial general intelligence' (AGI) that can mimic human intelligence and behaviours with the ability to learn and apply its intelligence to solving problems. AGI is yet to be achieved because it would need the ability to discern needs, emotions, beliefs, and thought processes. There is disagreement about when, and if, AGI will ever be reached.

As with most technologies, AI generates dual effects:

- First, compared to past technologies it can undertake more cognitive tasks, expanding beyond the traditional 'blue collar' type of work in manufacturing into replacing 'white collar' types of work.
- Second, AI technology, especially that driven by machine learning, is seen to cause serious concerns around privacy, consent, and surveillance, with implications for worker autonomy, potential biases in data collection, the use of biased data, and AI-driven recruitment practices acting as information gatekeepers for human workers. Given the 'blackbox' nature of AI networks, even AI developers cannot fully understand how an AI generates its outputs.

Floridi et al. (2018) developed the AI4People framework, consisting of five ethical AI principles, with a focus on the impacts of AI on human dignity and flourishing. The five principles are:

1 Beneficence: the benefits AI can bring towards promoting human well-being and preserving human dignity in an environmentally sustainable way.
2 Non-maleficence: ensuring that AI does not harm humanity and includes not violating individuals' privacy.
3 Autonomy: giving humans back the power to decide what AI does.
4 Justice: fairly distributing the benefits and burdens from AI use and not undermining solidarity and social cohesion.
5 Explicability: ensuring that AI operates in ways that are intelligible and accountable, so that we can understand how it works and we can require someone to be responsible for its actions.

Bankins and Formosa (2023) contend that the increasing use of AI in the workplace could have implications for the experience of meaningful human work, defined as the perception that one's work has (1) worth, (2) significance, or (3) a higher purpose. They argue that these three bases are ethically important in relation to (1) Kantian (deontological) theory, (2) virtue ethics, and (3) utilitarianism respectively (see their journal article for details). They argue that the five principles of AI4People (as described above) significantly can provide benefits for employees in terms of experiencing meaningfulness in their work. (See Bankins and Formosa, 2023: 12 for details.)

12.7 Main issues and debates on the ethics of AI and robotics

Noting that technologies will usually have dual-use (as discussed earlier in this chapter), beyond 'responsible use', we also need 'responsible design'. Further, it is essential that we look at issues that arise with certain uses of AI and robotic systems which would not arise with other technologies. Muller (2020) has outlined ethical issues of human use of AI and robotics systems as follows:

1 Privacy and surveillance – mainly concerning the access to private data and data that is personally identifiable. AI increases the possibilities of intelligent data collection and analysis. The problem arises when much of the data is traded between agents, usually for a fee. With face recognition, fingerprinting, and photos becoming commonplace, the result is that 'in this vast ocean of data, there is a frighteningly compete picture of us' (Smolan, 2016 cited in Muller, 2020). One of the practical difficulties is to identify the responsible legal entity, prove the action and intent, and find a court competent enough to enforce its decision.

2   Manipulation of behaviour – deep knowledge about individuals provides the environment for 'nudges', manipulation, and deception. Advertisers and marketers can exploit behavioural biases as seen in the business models of the gambling and gaming industries – so, while physical gambling (using slot machines for example) is highly regulated, online manipulation and addiction are not. AI technologies have improved 'faking' what was once reliable evidence into unreliable evidence – such as in digital photos, sound recordings, and video.

3   Opacity of AI systems – concerns about lack of due process, accountability, community engagement, and auditing. The systems are 'opaque' to the extent that it is often impossible for the affected person to know how the system came to an output. Further, if the system uses machine learning, it will typically be opaque even to the expert – especially if the system is developed by a third party. So, if the data already involved a bias (for example, skin colour of suspects, or the gender identity of a job-seeker), then the programme will reproduce that bias in its output.

4   Bias in decision systems – in automated AI systems that rely on 'predictive analysis'. Examples of outputs are 'this restaurant matches your preferences', 'the patient in this X-ray has completed bone growth', 'application to credit card declined', 'donor organ will be given to another patient', 'bail is denied', or 'target identified and engaged'. Types of biases include the features of a person, confirmation bias where humans tend to interpret information as confirming what they already believe, and statistical bias from data that exhibits systematic errors.

5   HRI – usually seen in care robots used in healthcare for humans. In addition, using robots to lift patients or transporting materials, they can also be used in activities such as using a robotic arm to eat and giving company and comfort to patients. This issue is more critical because of the potential need of robots in ageing societies. Another area of HRI is 'sex robots', where it is argued that given the variation of human sexual preferences, humans will likely be interested in sex and companionship with robots. Questions here will be whether such devices should be manufactured and whether there should be limits in this area.

6   Automation and employment – significant gains in productivity and overall wealth from the use of AI and robotics means that fewer humans will be required for the same output. It is argued that over the years, economies adjusted and adapted to the mechanisation and automation of agriculture, and similar situations can occur in AI and robotics. However, while classical automation replaced human muscle, digital automation will replace human thought or information processing. This may mean more radical change to the labour market.

7   Autonomous systems – this includes autonomous vehicles where the classic problem is of pursuing personal interest versus the common good. An individual's accountability (of the motorist) has now shifted to the manufacturers and operators of these vehicles and to the entities responsible for taking infrastructure, policy, and legal decisions. Another area of concern is autonomous weapons. The main arguments here are that such systems support extrajudicial killings, taking responsibility away from humans.

We already have drones that search for, identify, and kill an individual human. While there could be control systems in place, such weapons might make identification and prosecution of the responsible agents more difficult.

8   Singularity – in addition to the two types of AI intelligences discussed previously, ANI and AGI, there could be in the future 'artificial super-intelligence'. Such systems could reach human level intelligence and themselves have the ability to develop AI systems. So, these super or ultra-intelligent machines could design even better machines. While the fundamental question is whether such a singularity will ever occur or be allowed to occur due to the conceivable and inherent potential risks, it would be pertinent to discuss ethical issues linked to such systems. Some of the thought processes in this area are: existential risk from super-intelligence – whether it might lead to the extinction of the human species; and how we can make sure that humans remain in control of an AI system once it is super-intelligent.

Experts doubt ethical AI design will be broadly adopted as the norm within the next decade. With the rapid unfolding of the applications of AI, experts and advocates around the world have expressed concerns about the long-term impact and implications of AI applications. The concerns are mainly about how advances in AI will affect what it means to be human, to be productive, and to exercise free will. The Pew Center and Elon University asked experts where they thought efforts to create ethical AI would stand in 2030 (Elon, 2021). The question was: 'By 2030, will most of the AI systems being used by organisations of all sorts employ ethical principles focused primarily on the public good?'

Of the 602 technology innovators, developers, business leaders, researchers, and activists who responded to this question, 68 per cent declared that ethical principles focused primarily on the public good will not be employed in most AI systems by 2030, with 32 per cent choosing the opposite option. This suggests that a majority of such experts worry that the evolution of AI to 2030 will continue to be primarily focused on optimising profits and social control. Although most accept that AI breakthroughs will improve life, they also cite the difficulty of achieving consensus about ethics.

12.8 Corporate digital responsibility

Whether it is smart devices that record data, autonomous vehicles in dangerous situations, or algorithms making recruitment decisions, AI systems, even if introduced with the best intentions, can be at risk of being exploited for unintended purposes (Lobschat et al., 2021). It is argued that designing and using digital technologies requires organisations to develop a set of norms, embedded in their culture, to govern the development and deployment of such technologies. This idea is referred to as 'corporate digital responsibility' or CDR. With increasing demands on the usability and control of data, and on the protection of personal rights, 'corporate responsibility' is shaping itself into 'corporate digital responsibility'. While CDR is not yet a standard in companies, Dorr (2021) asserts that professionals in the field of sustainable management or CR need a responsibility framework at the intersection of digitalisation, sustainability, and corporate responsibility. Mueller (2022) has noted that thus far, research on CDR is mostly conceptual in nature and needs progressive developments in practice to explore the issue empirically.

Definitions of CDR include (from various sources in Dorr, 2021):

- Voluntary corporate activities in the digital sphere that go beyond what is mandated by law today and actively help shape the digital world for the benefit of society.
- It refers on the one hand to a digital sustainability (of data and algorithms) and on the other hand to a consideration of the social, economic, and ecological effects of digital corporate actions.

Lobschat et al. (2021: 876) defines CDR as:

the set of shared values and norms guiding an organisation's operations with respect to the creation and operation of digital technology and data. It requires tech companies, individual developers and designers, and any corporate actor employing digital technologies or data processing to be aware that the code they produce or deploy, as well as data they collect and process, inherently create an ethical responsibility for them.

They identified four principal stakeholders of CDR:

- Organisations – including suppliers, partners, and companies in the value chain of digital technologies.
- Individual actors – including managers, technology designers, individual users, and also those who are excluded in the access and usage of the technology.
- Artificial and technological actors – including artificial actors such as AI that can learn to write software code itself.
- Institutional, government, and legal actors – including regulators, law enforcement, NGOs such as consumer and trade associations, and professional associations such as the Institute of Electrical and Electronic Engineers.

Summary

- This chapter focuses on future issues emanating from innovations and technologies in business. It begins with a comparison of the evolution (or progression) of the five industry phases (1.0 to 5.0), the energy type, and the innovations in each phase – interfaced with the evolution of business ethics and CSR-related concepts during the same periods. We need to contemplate on whether our current concepts of business ethics and CSR are adequate to deal with future industry phases (6.0 for example).
- We presented the views of the pioneers of business ethics – from ten academics and philosophers who pioneered business ethics about 40 years ago. They reflected on issues that we face today, and what issues they expect in the next 20 years. Most of them agree that ethical issues haven't and won't disappear, and identified issues such as new technologies, diversity, and environmental issues.

- We noted that some key areas of business ethics in the future would be the intersection of law and business ethics, the intersection of strategy and ethics, and the issue of unethical business models (rather than unethical business practices).
- We discussed specific ethical issues in the future – such as 'machinewashing' (as compared to and derived from greenwashing), whether each type of technology needs specific ethical discussions or whether there should be a higher-level domain for technology ethics, the ethics of future of work with robots, algorithms, blockchain, and smart farming, the vast areas of artificial intelligence, and space ethics (as a case study).
- We introduced the new concept of 'corporate digital responsibility', which refers to the voluntary corporate activities in the digital sphere that go beyond what is mandated – similar to the CSR concept.
- The chapter will end below with an 'end of book' section having two quotes from well-known thinkers, and a set of 12 questions will enable us to reflect on all chapters in this book and some general self-reflective questions.

CASE STUDY 12.1
SPACE ETHICS

Humans have always ventured out and explored their surroundings and beyond – for example, modern humans (*Homo sapiens)*, came out of Africa between 60,000 and 90,000 years ago (in search of sustenance), followed by the Asian and Western European expansions (in search of knowledge, profit, and settlement) – often leading to religious conversion and colonisation. These explorations were full of risks. On the positive side, there were new discoveries of all kinds, enormous growth, and increased quality of life. On the negative side there were extractive colonisation practices (resource extraction, introduction of diseases, invasive species, and destruction of indigenous people). On reflection and in hindsight, do we wish better decisions were made?

Over the centuries, humans have progressed and improved their quality of life through advances in technology – steam, electricity, electronics, computers, the internet, and now digital technologies and AI. Within the context of advances in technology, we need also need to consider the recent rapid strides in space technology and exploration. The last few decades have seen increasing collaboration between state-based organisations, such as NASA, ISRO, CNES, ESA, ROSCOSMOS, and private sector businesses such as Space X, Virgin Galactic, Blue Origin, Boeing, Orion Span, and owners of satellites. Green (2022) asserts that as with other developing technologies, 'space is the next step for ethics, and ethics is the next step for space' (p. 258). Arnould (2011) from the French agency CNES has noted that 'it is important to remember that space ethics is fundamentally and always human. It is part of the oldest dreams and myths, those same dreams which drove the human species from the lands of Africa to the territories of the sky' (p. 28). Space exploration has evolved from being a 'political status' to 'furthering science' to 'understand where we come from', to 'big business'. Questions that surface in space exploration include: is it politically and economically worth it? Is it good? – Why and for whom? Should we explore space? And can we trust ourselves to heed lessons of the past and prepare to do better in the future (better than we have done in the past)?

Acknowledging that space is an extraordinary environment, the United Nations developed a set of principles to govern the activities of states in the exploration and use of outer space (UNOOSA, 2002). These principles developed into Outer Space Treaties (OST) consisting of the following:

1   Governing the activities of states in the exploration and use of outer space including the Moon and other celestial bodies.
2   Rescue of astronauts, return of astronauts and return of objects launched into outer space.
3   International liability for damage caused by space objects.
4   Registration of objects launched into outer space.
5   Governing the activities of states on the Moon and other celestial objects.

Observing that because of the special nature of space activities – their expense, their danger, their public visibility, and their unique challenges and opportunities – Arnould (2020) observes that space and ethical reflections must go together.

Following are some specific space ethics issues:

- Space debris – linked to sustainability, responsible leadership, and intergenerational justice.
- Military use of space – linked to article IV of OST, dual-use, and regulation and deterrence.
- Protecting Earth from asteroids – linked to responsibility to protect Earth, consequences of inaction, and motivation.
- Search for Extra-Terrestrial Life (ETL) – linked to ethical consideration of ETL, our behaviour towards ETL, ETLs' rights, and ethical approaches.
- Responsible exploration – linked to 'contaminated' astronauts, human quarantine issues, and the precautionary principle.
- Commercial, private, and new nations – linked to ensuring ethics in corporations' power, tourism, and mining.
- Long voyages to planets and stars – linked to ethics of reproduction, conception, health issues, end-of-life issues, human evolution, and ethical decision-making.
- Human settlements on the Moon, Mars and beyond – justifying settlements, environmental ethics (including destruction from resource extraction), governance issues, and spreading life to the universe.

Further, there are fundamental (both scientific and philosophical) questions:

- Does life exist beyond Earth?
- Do we have definitions of 'life'?

(Continued)

- What is / should be the destiny of life in the universe?
- How hard should we look for life?
- How should we behave when we encounter life elsewhere?
- Should 'contaminated' astronauts be allowed to return to Earth?

Questions

Using the Case-Study Integrative Framework in Figure 0.1, discuss the following:

1. Identify the key primary and secondary stakeholders of space exploration.
2. Are there any stakeholders whose concerns are not adequately addressed?
3. Do you think ethical theories and concepts discussed in earlier chapters can be applied or replicated in space exploration?
4. Of all the topics on business ethics in this book, which do you think are the most relevant to new technologies in general and space ethics in particular and why? Which are the least important and why?
5. Of all of the ethical tools and concepts discussed in this book, which do you find to be the most useful to discuss ethical issues in new technologies and space in particular and why? Which do you find the least useful and why?
6. Can we rely on our reflections on the past and prepare to do better in the future (better than we have done in the past)?
7. Do you think concepts discussed in this book need to be revisited for new technologies? Why and how?
8. What are the ethical issues in this case study? Apply the CEDM model in this chapter to develop your analysis, judgement, commitment, and potential actions.

Sources:
Arnould (2011)
Arnould (2020)
Green (2022)

CASE STUDY 12.2

AI CONSIDERATIONS IN SDGS AND EMERGING ECONOMIES

The consultancy firm Oxford Insights, in their recent report (Oxford Insights 2021), ranked the preparedness of 160 countries to score governments on their readiness to implement AI in the delivery of public services. Their approach was based on three pillars: (1) the government pillar (vision, governance, ethics, digital capacity, adaptability), (2) the technology sector pillar (competition, size, innovation capacity, human capital), and (3) the data and infrastructure pillar (data availability, data representativeness, infrastructure). The US was ranked first, followed by Singapore and the UK. Nordic countries ranked high in the index. East Asian countries made up one-quarter of the top 20 ranked countries. The lowest ranked regions included Sub-Saharan Africa, Central Asia, and some regions of South Asia.

Recent research by Alonso et al. (2020) found that new technology risks widening the gap between rich and poor countries by shifting more investment to advanced economies where automation is already established. They identified that the threat to developing countries comes from replacing rather than complementing their labour force, which has traditionally provided an advantage to less developed countries. They found that (1) the gap in per capita GDP between advanced and developing economies widens where robots easily substitute workers, and (2) higher real wages appear to be associated with higher use of robots in manufacturing. They further observe that the advantage of having a growing youth population in developing countries could be considerably reduced by the increasing use of robots in developed countries, and suggest that policymakers in emerging countries should act to mitigate such risks.

AI is expected to affect global productivity, equality and inclusion, environmental outcomes, and other areas in both the short and long term, with potential impacts of both positive and negative impacts on sustainable development. Vinuesa et al. (2020) assessed the extent to which AI might impact all 17 SDGs and found that positive impacts far outweigh negative impacts on SDGs, as shown below:

Positive impacts from AI-based technology:

- Society-related SDGs: 82 per cent of targets within the nine society-related SDGs – for instance in SDG 1 (no poverty), SDG 4 (quality education), SDG 6 (clean water and sanitation), SDG 7 (clean energy), and SDG 11 (sustainable cities).
- Economic-related SDGs: 70 per cent of targets within the five economic-related SDGs – for instance in SDG 8 (decent work), SDG 9 (innovation and infrastructure), SDG 10 (reduced inequalities), SDG 12 (responsible consumption and production), and SDG 17 (partnerships).
- Environment-related SDGs: 93 per cent of targets within the three environment-related SDGs – for instance in SDG 13 (climate action), SDG 14 (life below water), and SDG 15 (life on land).

Negative impacts from AI-based technology:

- Society-related SDGs: 38 per cent of targets – for instance AI may trigger inequalities that may act as inhibitors on SDGs 1, 4, and 5.
- Economic-related targets: 33 per cent of targets – for instance AI may trigger inequalities that may act as inhibitors on SDGs 8, 9, and 10.
- Environment-related SDGs: 30 per cent of targets – for instance efforts to achieve SDG 13 on climate change action could be undermined by the high energy needs of AI applications, especially if non-carbon-neutral energy sources are used.

(Continued)

Areas where AI can transform developing countries (Eliacik, 2022):

- Emergency response and disaster relief – predictive models allow first responders to automatically assess activity and movement using a wide range of data sources such as social media, online discussion forums, news sources etc. – as used after the 2015 earthquake in Nepal. AI can also create digital maps of the area to identify which places need most assistance.
- Agriculture – smart agriculture to monitor crops, forecast when to plant and harvest, and efficient use of pesticides. Microsoft, in association with the International Crop Research Institute for the Semi-Arid Tropics, created the AI Sowing App which pinpoints the best time to plant seeds, prepare land, and use fertiliser. It also has a function that finds the moisture adequacy index, both in real time and into the future.
- Health – making precise diagnoses, providing treatment options, and forecasting disease epidemics – examples include using drones in Rwanda to deliver blood and medical supplies to hospitals and clinics.
- Education and tutoring – can improve the way people work, learn, and educate, especially in developing countries' schools where there could be a lack of qualified instructors and other tools in addition to children having to travel long distances. Two large learning platforms in Africa – Dapito and Eneza Education – help students to study remotely. Eneza Education gives lessons and assessments to over 860,000 subscribers.

Questions

Using the Case-Study Integrative Framework in Figure 0.1, discuss the following:

1 Identify the key primary and secondary stakeholders of AI technologies and applications.
2 Are there any stakeholders whose concerns are not adequately addressed?
3 Do you think ethical theories and concepts discussed in earlier chapters can be applied in AI technologies?
4 In relation to developing economies, of all topics in business ethics in this book, which do you think are the most relevant to AI in particular and why? Which are the least important and why?
5 In relation to developing economies, of all of the ethical tools and concepts discussed in this book, which do you find to be the most useful to discuss ethical issues in AI in particular and why? Which do you find the least useful and why?
6 Can we rely on our reflections of the past and prepare to do better in the future (better than we have done in the past)?
7 Do you think concepts discussed in this book need to be revisited for new technologies such as AI? Why and how?
8 What are the ethical issues in this case study? Apply the CEDM model in this chapter to develop your analysis, judgement, commitment, and potential actions.

Sources:
Alonso et al. (2020)
Chatterjee and Dethlefs (2022)
Eliacik (2022)
Jordan (2020)
Oxford Insights (2021)
Vinuesa et al. (2020)

End of the book

Quotes to ponder upon

Edward O. Wilson (in Rhodes, 2021: 109) – a renowned biologist, naturalist, ecologist, and entomologist:

> Once we solve our largest problems, control population, limit global warming, increase average human prosperity up to the level of the west, clean up the environment, stop driving one species after another to extinction, then we come to a more subtle limit. We realise that we are pure biological organisms, no different from other biological organisms, and have no particular purpose in the world except to reproduce our kind. That psychological or spiritual crisis, that deflation of human pretensions, will follow as certainly as have the previous deflations: the Earth is not the centre of the universe, that we have evolved through natural selection, and not as a separate creation, that we are not purely rational but driven by emotional processes.

Jonas Salk (1992: 18) – developer of one of the first successful polio vaccines:

> Those who have preceded have left a rich heritage upon which to build the future. From the various cultures, lessons will be learned and incorporated with the ideals of our ancestors. They will be passed on as our vision of a world in which understanding, goodwill, and friendship will be appreciated by their presence, rather than by their actualisation.
>
> It will be necessary to rebuild many bridges, and build new ones among nations, cultures, religions, humanistic and scientific disciplines. We need to find ways and means for competing cooperatively in the search for a civilised way to reduce human and material wastage. As already suggested, we have more knowledge than we have as yet applied. We now need the will. This is the challenge for an epoch in which convergence, synthesis, bridge-building, and friendship become synonymous with

understanding in all its forms as the way to reciprocal well-being. If we are to be good ancestors, transmitting the possibility of a better life and the joy of living, we have work to do now. The first step is to open ourselves to the as yet unrealised possibilities that exist in humankind. Only in the future will it be known whether or not we have been wise ancestors. However, now is the time to accept the challenge.

Questions to ponder upon

1   Of all the topics on business ethics in this book, which do you think are the most important and why? Which are the least important and why?

2   Of all of the ethical tools and concepts discussed in this book, which do you find to be the most useful and why? Which do you find the least useful and why?

3   Take a business ethics case study from outside of this book and apply an ethical tool or concept from this book to it. What can you learn by this application?

4   Reflect on: What is your purpose in life? What gives your life meaning? Does this purpose or meaning relate to business? Why do you think this? How do you know?

5   Everyone has their own tendencies to view ethics in particular ways, and it is beneficial to know our own tendencies and blind spots. Of the ethical concepts discussed in this chapter, which are you most familiar with? Which are you most likely to use when thinking about or discussing ethics? Which are you least familiar with? Which are you least likely to use when thinking about or discussing ethics? Why?

6   Building on question 5, once you have considered this about yourself, can you see how this might lead to agreements and disagreements with others on ethical issues? What ways might there be to use this knowledge to enhance or reduce disagreements between people?

7   With regard to business ethics, how might these ethical concepts affect how business ethics is considered in particular contexts, such as in a classroom, at a corporation, or in a governance meeting? How might these ethical concepts affect discussions across cultures (both for good and for bad)?

8   Why should people be ethical? (Note: this can be construed as asking 'why should people follow "should" statements?').

Recommended readings

Bankins, S. and Formosa, P. (2023), 'The ethical implications of artificial intelligence (AI) for meaningful work', *Journal of Business Ethics*. doi: 10.1007/s10551-023-05339-7.

Some AI tech replaces work, some help us to tend machines, and some can amplify human skills. This paper helps us understand the ways in which AI technologies can enhance or diminish employees' experiences of meaningful work.

Bohm S., Carrington M., et al. (2022), 'Ethics at the centre of global and local challenges: Thoughts on the future of business ethics', *Journal of Business Ethics*, 180(3): 835–61.

The seven commentaries in this paper address the grand challenges in today's globalised world – such as financial crisis, climate change, internet technologies, AI, and global health crisis – by placing business ethics at their centre.

Dorr, S. (2021), *Corporate digital responsibility: Managing corporate responsibility and sustainability in the digital age*, Bonn: Springer.

This book provides practical, quick-to-implement analysis, aids, and examples of how to identify and implement corporate digital responsibility. It explains what characterises CDS, why it makes sense to think about it together with sustainability, and what mistakes can be made.

Floridi, L., Cowls, J., Beltrametti, M. et al. (2018), 'AI4People – an ethical framework for a good AI society: Opportunities, risks, principles, and recommendations', *Minds and Machines*, 28: 689–707.

The AI4People was set up to steer AI towards the good of society, everyone in it, and the environment we share. This article reports on the findings of AI4People by introducing the core opportunities and risks of AI for society, presents five ethical principles, and offers 20 concrete recommendations to support good AI.

Green, B.P. (2022), *Space ethics*, Lanham, MD: Rowman and Littlefield.

This book looks at the exploration and use of space through an ethical lens, and provides insights into specific questions. It also investigates the various human ethical resources available for such examinations.

Vinuesa, R., Azizpour, H., Leite, I. et al. (2020), 'The role of artificial intelligence in achieving the Sustainable Development Goals', *Nature Communications*, 11: 233.

This paper assesses the effect of AI on the achievement of the Sustainable Development Goals. The authors found that AI can enable the accomplishment of 134 targets across all 17 goals, but it may also inhibit 59 targets. They suggest regulatory insight and oversight for AI-based technologies to enable sustainable development.

GLOSSARY

Affirmative action   Also known as 'positive action' involves policies and practices that promote the opportunities of defined minority groups to give them equal access to that of the majority population.

AIDS   Acquired immunodeficiency syndrome is the last stage of HIV infection and occurs when the body's immune system is badly damaged because of the HIV virus.

AI-enabled algorithmic management   Set of instructions or programming that enables machines to operate independent of direct human intervention, but within constraints, to achieve a goal or solve a problem.

Alternative tourism   A term for all forms of travels opposed to mass tourism with special attention to economic, social, cultural, and environmental considerations.

Altruistic   Selfless concern for the well-being of others.

American Indian Movement   Founded in Minneapolis, Minnesota in 1968, it addressed systemic issues of poverty, discrimination, and police brutality against Native Americans.

Anomie   Lack of the usual social or ethical standards in an individual or group.

Anthropocene Epoch   An unofficial unit of geologic time dating from the commencement of significant human impact on Earth's geology and ecosystems, including climate change.

Australian Slavery Act   Identifies conduct that would constitute slavery and slavery-like offences, human trafficking, and child labour, whether or not the conduct took place in Australia.

BAE   A British multinational arms, security, and aerospace company based in London, England.

Beneficence   An act of charity, mercy, and kindness linked to doing good to others including moral obligations.

Biogas   A mixture of gases such as methane, carbon diocese, and hydrogen sulphide, produced from raw materials such as agricultural waste, manure, municipal waste, food waste etc.

Brundtland Commission   A sub-organisation of the UN, founded in 1983, headed by Gro Harlem Brundtland, former Prime Minister of Norway, which aimed to unite countries in the pursuit of sustainable development.

Business Process Outsourcing (BPO)   A method of subcontracting various business-related operations to third-party vendors – usually referred to as offshore outsourcing.

Categorical Imperative   Proposed by philosopher Immanuel Kant – denotes an absolute and unconditional, requirement that must be obeyed in all circumstances no matter what the consequences.

CERN   The European Organization for Nuclear Research, known as CERN, located in Geneva, is an intergovernmental organisation that operates the largest particle physics laboratory in the world.

Classical economics   Originating in Great Britain in the 18th to 19th century, it is a theory of market economies of self-regulating systems driven by laws of production and exchange – its main proponents were Adam Smith, David Ricardo, John Stuart Mill, Thomas Malthus, and John-Baptiste Say, among others.

Code of conduct   A set of rules outlining the norms, rules, and responsibilities or proper practices for an individual or an organisation.

Code of ethics   An organisation's ethical guides, principles, and best practices for honesty, integrity, and professionalism that members of an organisation are expected to uphold.

Cognitive   Relating to being conscious; thinking, reasoning, remembering, imagining, and using language.

Colonisation   The act of sending settlers to establish political control over a place.

Cybersecurity   The protection of computer systems and networks from attack by malicious actors that may result in unauthorised information disclosure, theft of, or damage to hardware, software, or data, as well as protection from the disruption or misdirection of the services these provide.

Danone   A French multinational food-products company based in Paris focusing on dairy products, plant-based products, water, and early life nutrition, among others.

Data mining   Process of extracting and discovering patterns in large datasets involving machine learning and statistics.

Data warehouses   A data management system designed to enable and support business intelligence activities.

Deforestation   Occurs when humans remove or thin forests for timber or to use the land for crops, grazing, extraction of materials, or property development.

Demography   A statistical study of populations especially of human beings – such as births, deaths, income, disease, and the changing structure of human populations.

Deontology   States that actions are good or bad according to a clear set of rules and duty.

Design for Environment   A design approach to reduce the overall environmental impact of a product, process, or service.

Digital democracy   Process to empower marginalised communities to use technology.

Discourse   Written or spoken communication or debate (dictionary meaning).

Downsize   To reduce organisational size by eliminating staff positions, usually done to cut costs and stabilise finances. It is more permanent and intentional than layoffs.

Downstream operations   When materials flow away from the organisations to customers, such as with finished products.

Due diligence   The investigation or exercise of care that a reasonable business or person is normally expected to take before entering into an agreement or contract with another party.

Earth Summit   A UN conference held in Rio de Janeiro, Brazil in 1992 for member states to cooperate together internationally on development issues after the Cold War.

Eco-industrial clusters   Geographic concentrations of interconnected industries in a specialised field that coordinate to share resources efficiently.

Empirical evidence   Is an important part of scientific research in which information is obtained through observation, analysis, and documentation.

Energy management system   An ongoing process of identifying, planning, and implementing improvements in the way an organisation uses energy.

Enlightenment   The Age of Enlightenment was an intellectual and philosophical movement in Europe in the 17th and 18th centuries. Prominent philosophers included Francis Bacon, René Descartes, David Hume, Immanuel Kant, Gottfried Leibniz, John Locke, Jean-Jacques Rousseau, Adam Smith, and Voltaire. Three main ideas that dominated this period were deism, liberalism, and republicanism.

Enron   Formerly one of largest energy companies in the US, employing over 20,600 staff and with revenues of USD 101 billion in 2000, and named as 'America's most innovative company', Enron crashed in 2001 due to systematic and creatively planned accounting fraud.

Epicurus   An ancient Greek philosopher (341 to 270 BCE) who taught that all humans should seek to attain peace in which the person is completely free from pain or suffering.

Ethical absolutism   The existence of moral principles, values, and rules as true. Regardless of culture and religion, moral principles are applicable eternally and universally.

Ethical consumption   The practice of buying ethically made products that protects the environment and local people, while boycotting products that exploit children, are tested on animals, or damage the environment.

Ethical egoism   Holds that every person acts only from self-interest, focused only on maximising individual pleasure.

Ethical relativism   Moral principles are relative to the factors and circumstances in different contexts and there are not intrinsically right and wrong actions.

Ethics   The role of ethics is to study morality using ethical theories, through observations and analysis, and if necessary, remedy any unjustifiable behavioural norms.

Expatriate   A person who lives outside their native country.

Facial recognition technology   A technology capable of matching a human face from a digital image or a video frame against a database of faces. Such a system is typically employed to authenticate users through ID verification services, and works by pinpointing and measuring facial features from a given image.

Fast fashion   The business model of designing and mass-producing fashion clothing at a low cost and bringing them to retail stores quickly, while the demand is at its highest. It leverages trend replication and at times uses low-quality materials to bring inexpensive styles to the end consumer.

Fiduciary relationship   A relationship in which one party places special trust, confidence, and reliance in another who has the duty to act for the benefit of the party – for example a lawyer and a client.

Fortune 500   Annual list published by the Fortune magazine that ranks 500 of the largest US corporations by total revenue.

Free-riding   When those who benefit from resources, public goods, and common resources do not pay for them or under-pay.

Gen Z   The generation of people born between 1995 and 2012.

Gig economy   Where individuals can connect (usually through mobile apps or websites) to provide services with consumers.

Golden rule   Treat others as you would want others to treat you.

Great Australian Bight   A large open bay off the central and western portions of the southern coastline of two Australian states – South Australia and Western Australia.

Greenhouse Gas Protocol   Provides standards and tools that help track progress towards climate goals.

Greenwashing   A form of advertising or marketing spin in which green PR and green marketing are deceptively used to persuade the public that an organisation's products, aims, and policies are environmentally friendly.

Guanxi   Originating in China, the literal meaning is 'one must pass the gate to get connected to networks', and is understood as special interpersonal relationships between individuals.

Heuristics   Are probability judgements used to estimate the likelihood of reaching a decision, for example, trying to guess a price based on past trends or guessing the population of a city.

HIV   Human immunodeficiency virus, which attacks the body's immune system. If not treated, can lead to AIDS. With no current effective cure, it can be controlled with proper medical care.

Human Genome Project   A global project to generate the first sequence of the human genome (a complete set of genetic information).

Hypothesis A supposition, proposition, or proposed explanation made on the basis of limited evidence as a starting point for further investigations.

Indaba Originating from the Zulu and Xhosa peoples of South Africa it is a traditional social structure of handling and resolving any debate or conflict that may arise in a group.

Industrial Revolution The transition of manufacturing processes from hand production to machines that occurred in Great Britain, Europe, and the US from around 1760 to 1840.

Industry 4.0 Also called the Fourth Industrial Revolution, it represents the rapid change to technology, industries, and societal processes in the 21st century and includes artificial intelligence, gene-editing, and advanced robotics.

Informed consent When someone has been given adequate information to enable the person to make an informed decision.

Inner life One's private space of emotions, thoughts, values, practices, hopes, and reflection that nurtures one's spirit and sense of well-being.

Intellectual property Refers to creations of the mind that includes inventions, literary and artistic works, designs, symbols, names, and images used in business. Various types include patents, copyrights, and trademarks.

Intermittent Occurring at irregular intervals, not continuous or steady.

Internet of Things Describes physical objects with sensors, processing ability, software, and other technologies that connect and exchange data with other devices and systems over the internet or other communications networks. Examples of where the Internet of Things is used: smart homes, security systems, cameras, and in healthcare systems.

Intuitive level Having the ability to understand or know something without any direct evidence or reasoning process.

Jugaad An Indian term referring to creative improvisation and making things happen in ways that are frugal, flexible, and inclusive.

Karl Marx A German philosopher (1818–1883) and also an economist, historian, sociologist, and a revolutionary, whose enormously influential books *The Communist Manifesto* and *Das Kapital* proposed the theory that human societies develop through class conflict – between the ruling class (bourgeoise) and the working class (proletariat).

Kgotla Originating from Botswana, it is a public meeting, community council, or traditional law court.

Kinship altruism A behaviour that benefits a relative's chances of survival or reproduction at some cost to one's own chances of survival – for example, a parent risking their own life to protect and care for their offspring.

Kyoto Protocol Adopted in Kyoto, Japan in 1997 that commits state parties to reducing greenhouse gas emissions.

Leviathan   Introduced by Thomas Hobbes in 1651, it is a concept that refers to a state with a strong central government that maintains order and stability at all costs.

Life cycle analysis   A methodology for assessing environmental impacts at all stages of the life cycle of a product, process, or service.

Magnitude   The size or extent of something.

Mahatma Gandhi   An Indian anti-colonist nationalist and political ethicist, who employed non-violent resistance to lead the successful campaign for India's independence from British rule in 1947.

Mandate   An authority or official order to do something such as carry out a policy.

Market self-regulation   A process where members of an industry, trade, or sector of the economy monitor their own adherence to legal, ethical, or safety standards, rather than have an outside, independent agency such as a third-party entity or governmental regulator monitor and enforce those standards.

Mindfulness   A mental state where we focus on the present, without judging or being distracted. It is a significant element of Hindu and Buddhist traditions and is based on Zen, Vipassana, and Tibetan meditation techniques. It can reduce stress, depression, and anxiety.

Monopoly   Occurs in a market with an absence of competition.

Moral dilemma   A situation where there's a conflict of having moral reasons to do each of two actions, but only one action is possible.

Moral injunctions   Injunction means an authoritative warning or order. Moral injunctions can be directed at individuals and also at a larger social and political community. For example, they could be rules to not do something even when it's the right thing to do.

Moral judgement   Refers to a decision, a process, an activity, or capacity to evaluate something or someone in terms of moral standards. Evaluation could be good or bad, or right or wrong.

Morality   Behavioural rules about activities that are considered right and wrong, that are accepted by society at a particular time in that society's history.

Morally minimum mandatory duties   A set of principles upheld as indispensable for moral conduct. Complying with the law but going no further is also termed the moral minimum.

Multiculturalism   The presence of, or support for, several distinct cultural or ethnic groups within a society.

Natural rights   Rights that are not dependent on the laws or customs of any particular culture or government, and so are universal, fundamental, and inalienable.

Neo-colonial control   Takes the form of economic imperialism, globalisation, cultural imperialism, and conditional aid to influence and control a developing country – usually by a former colonial master. Previous forms of colonial control were direct military control or indirect political control.

New World   A term used to mean the majority of Earth's western hemisphere, specifically the continents of North and South America.

Old World   A term originating in Europe c. 1596, after Europeans became aware of the existence of the Americas. The Old World is composed of the continents of Africa, Asia, and Europe.

Operationalisation   Turning abstract concepts into measurable observations.

Organization for Economic Cooperation and Development (OECD)   An intergovernmental organisation, founded in 1961, to stimulate economic progress and world trade. It has 38 member countries and is based in Paris, France.

Othering   Labelling and defining a person as a subaltern native, as someone who belongs to a socially subordinate category.

Outsource   A business practice where an organisation hires a third party to create goods or perform services that were traditionally performed in-house. Outsourcing can be onshoring (domestic) or offshoring (international). It is usually done to cut operating costs.

Oxymoron   A figure of speech in which contradictory terms appear in sequence – for example, old news, deafening silence, organised chaos.

Panopticon   A disciplinary concept brought to life in the form of a central observation tower placed within a circle of prison cells. From the tower, a guard can see every cell and inmate, but the inmates can't see into the tower. Prisoners will never know whether or not they are being watched.

Paranormal   Implies that the scientific explanation of the world around us is normal and anything that is above, beyond, or contrary to that is para.

Portmanteau   A word that blends two other words, for example motel or brunch.

Probability   How likely it is that something is going to happen.

Process flow diagram   A type of flowchart that illustrates the relationships between major components.

Product liability   An area of law where manufacturers, distributors, suppliers, retailers, and others who make products available to the public are held responsible for the injuries those products cause.

Product stewardship   Shared responsibility to manage environmental impacts of products and materials at different stages of production, use, and disposal.

Proportionality   Any relationship that is always the same ratio, usually for the same denominator.

Proximity   Nearness in space, time, or relationship.

Qur'an   The central religious text of Islam, containing revelations from God.

Rationalist   Rationalism is the view that regards reason as the main source and test of knowledge.

Reciprocity   The social norm or practice of exchanging things with others usually responding to a positive action with another positive action.

Referent groups   Formal or informal groups against which consumers compare themselves, typically to understand social norms.

Reformation   A religious reform movement in Europe in the 1500s that resulted in a new branch of Christianity called Protestantism.

Religiousness   The quality of believing strongly in a particular religion and obeying its laws and practices.

Renaissance   A French word meaning 'rebirth', renaissance is referred to as the revival of European art and literature during the 14th to 16th centuries.

Renqing   A Chinese word meaning reciprocity by continuously exchanging favours with others.

Resource-based view   A managerial framework view that a firm's sustained competitive advantage is based on its valuable, rare, inimitable, and non-substitutable resources.

Return on investment (ROI)   Is a ratio between net income and investment – a high ROI refers to higher gains from an investment.

Reverse innovation   Refers to innovations developed in and for developing markets that were later successfully adapted and adopted in developed markets.

S&P 500   A stock market index that tracks the stock performance of 500 of the largest companies listed in the stock exchanges in the US.

Santhal   An ethnic group of eastern India.

Self-awareness   The experience of one's own personality or individuality, not to be confused with consciousness. While consciousness is being aware of one's environment and body and lifestyle, self-awareness is the recognition of that awareness. Self-awareness is how an individual experiences and understands their own character, feelings, motives, and desires.

Sentient   The capacity to perceive, and experience feelings and sensations.

Service-learning   An educational approach that combines learning objectives with community service in order to provide a pragmatic, progressive learning experience while meeting societal needs.

Shared value   A business concept designed to create solutions to social and environmental problems. Also known as the link between competitive advantage and corporate social responsibility.

Shareholder   Any person, company, or institution that owns shares in a company's stock. They usually receive dividend payments and/or capital gains (or losses).

Social-relational   Interpersonal relationship between two or more individuals within and/or between groups.

Societal infrastructure   Consists of facilities, spaces, services, and networks that support the quality of life and well-being of communities.

South Australia   A state in the southern central part of Australia.

Stakeholder   Any person, group, or organisation that has a stake or vested interest in the decision-making and activities of an organisation. See Chapter 2 for further details.

Statutes   A formal written legislative authority that governs the legal entities of a city, state or a country – typically comprised of commands, prohibitions, and policies.

Stockholder   See **shareholder** and **stakeholder**.

Sunnah   The traditions and practices of the Islamic prophet Muhammad that constitute a model for Muslims to follow.

Tariff meters   Devices that measure electric energy for billing purposes.

Teleological   Relating to the explanation for something in terms of the purpose or end they serve rather than the cause.

Telos   A term used by the Greek philosopher Aristotle for the final cause of an entity, or the end goal. Teleology is the study of objects regarding their aims, purposes, or intentions.

Temporal immediacy   Relating to time, when something is likely to happen.

Transactional   Exchange or interaction between people or businesses that involves activities such as buying or selling and recording such data.

Transparency International   A non-profit organisation founded in 1993 in Berlin, Germany, whose purpose is to combat global corruption. It publishes the Corruption Perceptions Index for each country.

Trickle down   An economics term that refers to the idea that wealth from the top should trickle down to those at the bottom.

Triple Bottom Line   An accounting framework, claimed to have been coined by John Elkington in 1994, that in addition to the traditional 'profit' bottom line, adds two more bottom lines, social and environmental concerns.

Ubuntu   An African philosophy that emphasises 'being self through others'. It is expressed as 'I am because of who we all are'. Originating from South Africa, with equivalent terms in other African languages, it can refer to words such as humanity, common sense, and generosity, and is basically a relational concept with interdependence and interconnectedness as the main features.

UN Global Compact   A UN agreement to get businesses and firms worldwide to adopt sustainable and socially responsible policies.

Unconscious bias   An unfair belief about a group of people that you are not aware of and that affects your behaviour and decisions. It is often interpreted as the first impression and intuitions we have when interacting with other people. Unconscious bias can manifest in many ways, such as how we judge and evaluate others, or how we act towards members of different groups.

Upanishads   Late-Vedic and post-Vedic Sanskrit texts attributed to the central religious concepts of Hinduism.

Upstream operations   When materials flow into the organisation, such as raw materials.

Utilitarianism (or consequentialism)   States that the rightness of an action can be judged only by its consequences.

Utility   Something being useful, profitable, or beneficial.

Vedas   A large body of religious texts, composed in Sanskrit, consisting of four texts, originating in ancient India from c. 1500–900 BCE.

Venture capitalists   Firms or funds that provide capital for start-ups, early-stage, and emerging companies that have been deemed to have high growth potential.

Wall Street   A street in the financial district of Manhattan, New York, which is a figure of speech for the financial markets of the US as a whole.

Wasta   A practice in Arab societies, it is a social network, interpersonal connections rooted in a family, tribe, and extended relationships, where people use personal relationships to gain favour.

Whistle-blowing   An act of a whistle-blower (for example an employee), with inside knowledge of an organisation, who reports misconduct, dishonest, or illegal activity that may have occurred within that organisation.

World Bank   An international financial institution, established in 1944 with headquarters in Washington DC, USA, that provides loans and grants to governments for capital projects.

World Economic Forum   An international non-governmental organisation, founded in 1971, headquartered in Switzerland, with a mission to improve the state of the world by engaging world leaders. Its annual meeting is held in Davos, Switzerland.

Zinc plating   Electrodeposition of a thin coating of zinc metal on the surface of another metal to prevent rusting.

REFERENCES

AA1000 (2022), AA1000 Assurance Standard, (www.accountability.org/standards/aa1000-assurance-standard/).

ABA (2021), Banking code of practice, (www.ausbanking.org.au/wp-content/uploads/2021/10/2021-5-Oct-Banking-Code-WEB.pdf).

ABLIS (2014), Competition and consumer (franchising) regulation, (www.legislation.gov.au/Details/F2022C00463/Download).

Abosag, I. (2015), 'The antecedents and consequence of Et-Moone B2B relationships', *Industrial Marketing Management*, 51: 150–7.

Abrams, F.W. (1951), 'Management's responsibilities in a complex world', *Harvard Business Review*, 29(3): 29–34.

Abuznaid, S.A. (2009), 'Business ethics in Islam: The glaring gap in practice', *International Journal of Islamic and Middle Eastern Finance and Management*, 2(4): 278–88.

Accenture (2020), Redefining responsible leadership, (www.accenture.com/us-en/insights/consulting/responsible-leadership?c=acn_glb_responsiblebusiyoutube_11108624&n=smc_0120).

Ackland, P., Resnikoff, S. and Bourne, R. (2017), 'World blindness and visual impairment: Despite many successes, the problem is growing', *Community Eye Health*, 30(100): 71–3.

ACSC (2022), Guidelines for procurement and outsourcing, Australian Signals Directorate, (www.cyber.gov.au/acsc/view-all-content/advice/guidelines-procurement-and-outsourcing).

Adeleye, I., Luiz, J., Muthuri, J. and Amaeshi, K. (2020), 'Business ethics in Africa: The role of institutional context, social relevance, and development challenges', *Journal of Business Ethics*, 161(4): 717–29.

Adewale, A. (2019), 'A model of virtuous leadership in Africa: Case study of a Nigerian firm', *Journal of Business Ethics*, 161(4): 749–62.

Adobor, H. (2012), 'Ethical issues in outsourcing: The case of contract medical research and the global pharmaceutical industry', *Journal of Business Ethics*, 105(2): 239–55.

Adomako, S. and Tran, M.D. (2022), 'Local embeddedness, and corporate social performance: The mediating role of social innovation orientation', *Corporate Social Responsibility and Environmental Management*, 29(2): 329–38.

Aetna (2023), Mindfulness and meditation, (www.aetnainternational.com/en/about-us/explore/fit-for-duty-corporate-wellness/mindfulness-meditation-9-stress-management-strategies-for-the-workplace.html).

Agarwal, S. and Bhal, K.T. (2020), 'A multidimensional measure of responsible leadership: Integrating strategy and ethics', *Group & Organization Management*, 45(5): 637–73.

Ahmadi, P. (2019), 'Environmental impacts and behavioral drivers of deep decarbonization for transportation through electric vehicles', *Journal of Cleaner Production*, 225: 1209–19.

Ahn, H. (2008), 'Junzi as a tragic person: A self psychological interpretation of the analects', *Pastoral Psychology*, 57(1/2): 101–13.

AIAAIC (2023), Vermeer 'Girl with a Pearl Earring' AI facsimile, (www.aiaaic.org/aiaaic-repository/ai-and-algorithmic-incidents-and-controversies/vermeer-girl-with-a-pearl-earring-ai-facsimile).

AIHW (2022), Deaths in Australia, (www.aihw.gov.au/reports/life-expectancy-death/deaths-in-australia/contents/life-expectancy).

Alayón, C., Säfsten, K. and Johansson, G. (2017), 'Conceptual sustainable production principles in practice: Do they reflect what companies do?' *Journal of Cleaner Production*, 141: 693–701.

Alder, G. and Gilbert, J. (2006), 'Achieving ethics and fairness in hiring: Going beyond the law', *Journal of Business Ethics*, 68(4): 449–64.

Alenezi, M., Hassan, S., Abdelrahim, Y. and Albadry, O. (2022), '*Wasta* and favoritism: The case of Kuwait'. In B. Alareeni and A. Hamdan (eds), *Explore Business, Technology Opportunities and Challenges After the Covid-19 Pandemic* (vol. 495), Cham: Springer.

Algumzi, A.A. (2017), 'The impact of Islamic culture on business ethics: Saudi Arabia and the practice of *wasta*', Thesis for PhD, Lancaster University School of Management.

Alonso, C., Kotjari, S. and Rehman, S. (2020), How artificial intelligence could widen the gap between rich and poor nations, (www.imf.org/en/Blogs/Articles/2020/12/02/blog-how-artificial-intelligence-could-widen-the-gap-between-rich-and-poor-nations).

Alonso, J.S. (2021), 'Purdue Pharma deceptive research misconduct', *Voices in Bioethics*, 7, (https://journals.library.columbia.edu/index.php/bioethics/article/view/7786).

Ali, A.J. and Al-Owaihan, A. (2008), 'Islamic work ethic: a critical review', *Cross Cultural Management*, 15(1): 5-19.

Al-Sibai, N. (2023), Lazy artists use AI to rip off famous Dutch painting for museum exhibition, (https://futurism.com/the-byte/artists-ai-vermeer-girl-pearl-earring).

Alter, S.K. (2006), 'Social enterprise models and their mission and money relationships'. In A. Nicholls (ed), *Social entrepreneurship: New models of sustainable social change*, Oxford: Oxford University Press.

Ameer, I. and Halinen, A. (2019), 'Moving beyond ethical decision-making: A practice-based view to study unethical sales behavior', *Journal of Personal Selling & Sales Management*, 39(2): 103–22.

Ananthram, S. and Chan, C. (2021), 'Institutions and frugal innovation: The case of Jugaad', *Asia Pacific Journal of Management*, 38: 1031–60.

Anderson, D.R. (2005), *Corporate survival: The critical importance of sustainability risk management*, Lincoln, NE: iUniverse.

Anderson, M.R. (2017), After 75 years, Isaac Asimov's Three Laws of Robotics need updating, (https://theconversation.com/after-75-years-isaac-asimovs-three-laws-of-robotics-need-updating-74501).

Anderson, S.E. and Burchell, J.M. (2021), 'The effects of spirituality and moral intensity on ethical business decisions: A cross-sectional study', *Journal of Business Ethics*, 168(1): 137–49.

Andrijasevic, R., Rhodes, C. and Yu, K.-H. (2019), 'Foreign workers: On the other side of gendered, racial, political and ethical borders', *Organization*, 26(3): 313–20.

Ansell (2023), Ansell's history, (www.ansell.com/us/en/about-us/our-history).

Apple (2018), Apple anti-corruption policy, (https://s2.q4cdn.com/470004039/files/doc_downloads/gov_docs/Anti-Corruption_Policy.pdf).

Aravind (2023a), Dr Govindappa Venkataswamy, (https://aravind.org/our-founder/).

Aravind (2023b), Our story, (https://aravind.org/our-story/).

Aristotle (350 BCE/2000), *Nicomachean ethics*, R. Crisp (ed), Cambridge: Cambridge University Press.

Arnold, D.G., Audi, R., and Zwolinski, M. (2010), 'Recent work in ethical theory and its implications for business ethics', *Business Ethics Quarterly*, 20(4): 559–81.

Arnould, J. (2011), *Brief history of space ethics: Icarus' second chance*, Wien: Springer-Verlag.

Arnould, J. (2020), *Ethics manual for the space odyssey*, Adelaide: ATF Press.

Asher, C. (2022), Climate-positive, high-tech metals are polluting Earth, but solutions await, (https://news.mongabay.com/2022/03/climate-positive-high-tech-metals-are-polluting-earth-but-solutions-await/).

Asmussen, C.G. and Goerzen, A. (2013), 'Unpacking dimensions of foreignness: Firm-specific capabilities and international dispersion in regional, cultural, and institutional space', *Global Strategy Journal*, 3(2): 127–49.

ATO (2023), International transfer pricing, (www.ato.gov.au/Business/International-tax-for-business/In-detail/Transfer-pricing/International-transfer-pricing---introduction-to-concepts-and-risk-assessment).

AU (2022), Agenda 2063: The Africa we want, (https://au.int/en/agenda2063/overview).

AuManufacturing (2022), Ansell responds to forced labour allegations against a supplier, (www.aumanufacturing.com.au/ansell-responds-to-forced-labour-allegations-against-a-supplier).

Australian Institute (2020), What is fast fashion? Everything to know, (https://australianstyleinstitute.com.au/shopping-habits-say-fast-fashion-ethics-sustainability/).

Automation (2009), Schneider Electric acquires Conzerv in India, (www.automation.com/en-us/articles/2009-2/schneider-electric-acquires-conzerv-in-india).

B Lab (2022), How did the B Corp movement start, (www.bcorporation.net/en-us/faqs/how-did-b-corp-movement-start).

Bahree, M. (2014), Your beautiful Indian rug was probably made by child labor, (www.forbes.com/sites/meghabahree/2014/02/05/your-beautiful-indian-rug-was-probably-made-by-child-labor/?sh=5a33801674a0).

Baker, E. (2005), 'Sacred hoops: *Spiritual Lessons of a Hardwood Warrior*, by Phil Jackson', (https://digitalcommons.lmu.edu/cgi/viewcontent.cgi?article=1291&context=ce).

Bakker, K.J. (2010), *Privatizing water governance failure and the world's urban water crisis*, New York: Cornell University Press.

Balkawade, M. (2016), 'A case study of the Mann Deshi Mahila Sahakari Bank (MDMSB): A model of financial capability through social entrepreneurship', *IRA-International Journal of Management & Social Studies*, 3(2): 282–98.

Banaji, M.R., Bazerman, M.H. and Chugh, D. (2003), 'How (un)ethical are you?' *Harvard Business Review*, 81(12): 56–64.

Bank Muñoz, C., Kenny, B. and Stecher, A. (2018), 'Situating Walmart in a global context: Workplace culture, labor organizing, and supply chains'. In K. Bank Munoz, B. Kenny and A. Stecher, (eds), *Walmart in the Global South*, Austin, TX: University of Texas Press.

Bankins, S. and Formosa, P. (2023), 'The ethical implications of artificial intelligence (AI) for meaningful work', *Journal of Business Ethics*, (https://doi.org/10.1007/s10551-023-05339-7).

Barnes, M., Brannelly, T., Ward, L. and Ward, N. (2015), 'Introduction: The critical significance of care'. In M. Barnes, T. Brannelly, L. Ward and N. Ward (eds), *Ethics of care – Critical advances in international perspective*, Bristol: Policy Press.

Barney, I. (2003), 'Engaging stakeholders: Lessons from Orissa', *The Journal of Corporate Citizenship*, 10: 51–63.

Barrett, C. (2022), Ansell accused of 'knowingly profiting' from forced labour at Malaysian glove supplier, (www.smh.com.au/world/asia/ansell-accused-of-knowingly-profiting-from-forced-labour-at-malaysian-glove-supplier-20220810-p5b8se.html).

Basic Needs (2022), About the organisation, (https://skoll.org/organization/basicneeds/).

Bauman, Z. (1993), *Postmodern ethics*, Oxford: Blackwell.

Bauman, Z. (1998), 'What prospects of morality in times of uncertainty?' *Theory, Culture & Society*, 15(1): 11–22.

Baumhart, R.C. (1961), 'How ethical are businessmen?' *Harvard Business Review*, 39(4): 176.

Bazerman, M.H. and Tenbrunsel, A.E. (2011), 'Ethical breakdowns – Good people often let bad things happen', *Harvard Business Review*, 89(4): 58–65.

BBC (2022), New Zealand passes legislation banning cigarettes for future generations, (www.bbc.com/news/world-asia-63954862).

Bebeau, M.J. (2002), 'The defining issues test and the four component model: Contributions to professional education', *Journal of Moral Education*, 31(3): 271–95.

Bebeau, M.J. and Thoma, S.J. (1999), 'Intermediate concepts and the connection to moral education', *Educational Psychology Review*, 11(4): 343–60.

Beekun, R.I. (1996), *Islamic business ethics*, Herndon, VA: International Institute of Islamic Thought.

Beekun, R.I. and Westerman, J.W. (2012), 'Spirituality and national culture as antecedents to ethical decision-making: A comparison between the United States and Norway', *Journal of Business Ethics*, 110(1): 33–44.

Beekun, R.I., Guo, J., Westerman, J. and Westerman, J. (2019), 'Effects of Confucian values and national culture on business ethics in China: An empirical examination'. In C. Cobanoglu, M. Cavusoglu and A. Corbaci (eds), *Global Conference on Business and Economics (GLOBE 2019)*, Istanbul: USF M3 Publishing.

Belas, J., Çera, G., Dvorský, J. and Čepel, M. (2021), 'Corporate social responsibility and sustainability issues of small- and medium-sized enterprises', *Corporate Social Responsibility and Environmental Management*, 28(2): 721–30.

Ben-David, I., Kleimeier, S., and Viehs, M. (2019), Research: When environmental regulations are tighter at home, companies emit more abroad, (https://hbr.org/2019/02/research-when-environmental-regulations-are-tighter-at-home-companies-emit-more-abroad).

Benn, S., Edwards, M. and Williams, T. (2018), *Organizational change for corporate sustainability*, 4th edn, Abingdon: Routledge.

Berger, R. (2015), 'The transformation of Chinese business ethics in line with its emergence as a global economic leader', *Journal of Chinese Economic and Foreign Trade Studies*, 8(2): 106–22.

Berger, R. and Herstein, R. (2013), 'The evolution of business ethics in India', *International Journal of Social Economics*, 41(11): 1073–86.

Bero, L. (2016), Essays on health: How food companies can sneak bias into scientific research, (https://theconversation.com/essays-on-health-how-food-companies-can-sneak-bias-into-scientific-research-65873).

Bevan, D. (2021), 'A polyphony of pioneers', *Business and Professional Ethics Journal*, 40(3): 271–82.

Bevan, D. and Goodpaster, K.E. (2020), 'The business ethics pioneers project', *Business and Professional Ethics Journal*, 39(3): 271–85.

Bhatnagar, N., Sharma, P. and Ramachandran, K. (2020), 'Religion and business families' philanthropic practices', in A. De Massis and N. Kammerlander (eds), *Handbook of qualitative research methods for family business*, Cheltenham: Edward Elgar Publishing, (https://doi.org/10.4337/9781788116459.00016).

Bhattacharjee, A., Berman, J.Z. and Reed, A. II (2013), 'Tip of the hat, wag of the finger: How moral decoupling enables consumers to admire and admonish', *Journal of Consumer Research*, 39(6): 1167–84.

Bhaumik, S., Driffield, N., Gaur, A., Mickiewicz, T. and Vaaler, P. (2019), 'Corporate governance and MNE strategies in emerging economies', *Journal of World Business*, 54(4): 234–43.

BHP (2022), Our code: Your guide to living, our charter values every day, (www.bhp.com/about/operating-ethically/our-code/work-with-integrity/manage-corruption-risks).

Bhutta, M., Bostock, B., Brown, J.A., Day, E., Hughes, A., Hurst, R., Trautrims, A. and Trueba, M. (2021), Forced labour in the Malaysian medical gloves supply chain before and during the COVID-19 pandemic: Evidence, scale and solutions, (https://eprints.ncl.ac.uk/file_store/production/279369/4E4283A6-CAF0-4CC0-81B3-71319D17A108.pdf).

Bicer, Y. and Dincer, I. (2018), 'Life cycle environmental impact assessments and comparisons of alternative fuels for clean vehicles', *Resources, Conservation and Recycling*, 132: 141–57.

Biogas (2022), Biogas plants for 9000 families in India, (www.myclimate.org/information/carbon-offset-projects/detail-carbon-offset-projects/india-biogas-7149/).

Bissing-Olson, M., Fielding, K., and Iyer, A. (2016). 'Experiences of pride, not guilt, predict pro-environmental behavior when pro-environmental descriptive norms are more positive', *Journal of Environmental Psychology*, 45: 145–53.

Blasi, A. (1990), 'Kohlberg's theory and moral motivation', *New Directions for Child Development*, 47: 51–7.

Blodgett, M.S. (2011), 'Substantive ethics: Integrating law and ethics in corporate ethic programs', *Journal of Business Ethics*, 99(1): 39–48.

Blount, S. and Leinward, P. (2019), 'Why are we here?' *Harvard Business Review*, November–December: 132–9.

Boatright, J.R. (1995), 'Aristotle meets Wall Street: The case for virtue ethics in business', *Business Ethics Quarterly*, 5(2): 353–9.

Boatright, J.R. (2003), *Ethics and the conduct of business*, 4th edn, Upper Saddle River, NJ: Pearson Education International.

Boeing (2022), Boeing's mission and values statements, (www.boeing.com/principles/values.page).

Bohm, S., Carrington, M., Cornelius, N., de Bruin, B., Greenwood, M., Hassan, L., Jain, T., Karam, C., Kourula, A., Romani, L., Riaz, S. and Shaw, D. (2022), 'Ethics at the centre of global and local challenges: Thoughts on the future of business ethics', *Journal of Business Ethics*, 180(3): 835–61.

Bolton, S.C., Kim, R.C.-h. and O'Gorman, K.D. (2011), 'Corporate social responsibility as a dynamic internal organisational process: A case study', *Journal of Business Ethics*, 101(1): 61–74.

Borgerson, J.L. (2007), 'On the harmony of feminist ethics and business ethics', *Business and Society Review*, 112(4): 477–509.

Borgerson, J.L. (2018), *Caring and power in female leadership: A philosophical approach*, Newcastle upon Tyne: Cambridge Scholars Publishing UK.

Bowen, H.R. (1953), *Social responsibilities of the businessman*, New York: Harper and Row.

Bowie, N. (2021), 'Business ethics pioneers: Norman Bowie', *Business & Professional Ethics Journal*, 40(3), 283–94.

Brand Finance (2015), LEGO overtakes Ferrari as the world's most powerful brand, (https://brandfinance.com/press-releases/lego-overtakes-ferrari-as-the-worlds-most-powerful-brand).

Brei, V.A. (2018), 'How is a bottled water market created?' *Wiley Interdisciplinary Reviews: Water*, 5(1). doi: 10.1002/wat2.1220.

Brenner, S.N. and Molander, E.A. (1977), 'Is the ethics of business changing?' *Harvard Business Review*, 55(1): 57–71.

Bris, A. (2021), 'Danone's CEO has been ousted for being progressive – blame society not activist shareholders', (https://theconversation.com/danones-ceo-has-been-ousted-for-being-progressive-blame-society-not-activist-shareholders-157383).

Britannica (2022), Anomie, (www.britannica.com/topic/anomie).

British Council (2016), The state of social enterprise in India, (www.britishcouncil.org/sites/default/files/bc-report-ch4-india-digital_0.pdf).

British Council (2022), More in common: The global state of social enterprise, (www.britishcouncil.org/sites/default/files/more_in_common_global_state_of_social_enterprise.pdf).

BRT (2019), How CEOs put principles into practice, Business RoundTable, (https://opportunity.businessroundtable.org/ourcommitment/).

Buchanan, M. (2002), 'Wealth happens', *Harvard Business Review*, April, (https://hbr.org/2002/04/wealth-happens).

Business.gov.au (2021), Employees and conflict of interest, Australian Government: Business, (https://business.gov.au/people/employees/employees-and-conflicts-of-interest#:~:text=Examples per cent20of per cent20conflicts per cent20of per cent20interest, being per cent20considered per cent20for per cent20a per cent20job).

Butler, B. (2022), US bans imports of disposable gloves from Ansell supplier in Malaysia over allegations of forced labour, (www.smh.com.au/world/asia/ansell-accused-of-knowingly-profiting-from-forced-labour-at-malaysian-glove-supplier-20220810-p5b8se.html).

Cai, Y., Jo, H. and Pan, C. (2012), 'Doing well while doing bad? CSR in controversial industry sectors', *Journal of Business Ethics*, 108(4): 467–80.

Camargo, B.A. (2022), 'The expansion of MexHospitality: Exploring the ethical implications of hospitality outsourcing'. In M. Sigala, A. Yeark, R. Presbury, M. Fang and K.A. Smith (eds), *Case based research in tourism, travel, hospitality and events*, Singapore: Springer.

Carls, P. (2022), Émile Durkheim (1858—1917), (https://iep.utm.edu/emile-durkheim/).

Carpio-Aguilar, J.C., Rincón-Moreno, J. and Franco-García, M-L. (2019), Potential of carbon footprint reduction within retailers: Food waste at Walmart in Mexico'. In N. Yakovleva, R. Frei, and S. Rama Murthy (eds), *Sustainable development goals and sustainable supply chains in the post-global economy*, Cham: Springer International Publishing.

Carroll, A.B. (1979), 'A three-dimensional conceptual model of corporate social performance', *The Academy of Management Review*, 4(4): 497–504.

Carroll, A.B. (1991), 'The pyramid of corporate social responsibility: Towards the moral management of organizational stakeholders', *Business Horizons*, 34(4): 39–48.

Carroll, A.B. (1994), 'Social issues in management research', *Business & Society*, 33(1): 5–29.

Carroll, A.B. (1999), 'Corporate social responsibility', *Business & Society*, 38(3): 268–95.

Carroll, A.B. (2008), 'A history of corporate social responsibility'. In A. Crane, D. Matten, A. McWilliams, J. Moon and D.S. Siegel (eds), *The Oxford handbook of corporate social responsibility*, Oxford: Oxford University Press.

Carroll, A.B. (2010), 'Reflections on the business ethics field and *Business Ethics Quarterly*', *Business Ethics Quarterly*, 20(4): 715–17.

Carroll, A.B. and Brown, J.A. (2018), 'Corporate social responsibility: A review of current concepts, research, and issues'. In J. Webber and D.M. Wasieleski (eds), *Corporate Social Responsibility* (vol. 2). Bingley: Emerald Publishing.

Carroll, A.B. and Brown, J.A. (2022), 'Corporate social responsibility: A chronicle and review of concept development and refinements'. In T. Maak, N.M. Pless, M. Orlitzky and S. Sandhu (eds), *The Routledge companion to corporate social responsibility*, New York: Routledge.

Carson, R. (1962), *Silent spring*, Boston: Houghton Miffin Company.

Caruana, R., Crane, A., Gold, S. and LeBaron, G. (2021), 'Modern slavery in business: The sad and sorry state of a non-field', *Business and Society*, 60(2): 251–87.

Cavusgil, E. (2007), 'Merck and Vioxx: An examination of an ethical decision-making model', *Journal of Business Ethics*, 76(4): 451–61.

Chakrabarti, B. (2021), 'Scaling compassion, blurring boundaries: Partners and cooperation in aravind eye care system'. In Y. Okada and S. Stanislawski, (eds), *Institutional interconnections and cross-boundary cooperation in inclusive business*, Bingley: Emerald Publishing Limited.

Chakraborty, S.K. and Chakraborty, D. (2008), *Spirituality in management: Means or end?* New Delhi: Oxford University Press.

Chang, Y.-Y., Gong, Y. and Peng, M.W. (2012), 'Expatriate knowledge transfer, subsidiary absorptive capacity, and subsidiary performance', *The Academy of Management Journal*, 55(4): 927–48.

Chatterjee, J. and Dethlefs, N. (2022), Developing countries are left behind in the AI race – and that's a problem for all of us, (https://theconversation.com/developing-countries-are-being-left-behind-in-the-ai-race-and-thats-a-problem-for-all-of-us-180218).

Chen, A., Treviño, L.K. and Humphrey, S.E. (2020), 'Ethical champions, emotions, framing, and team ethical decision making', *American Psychological Association*, 105(3): 245–73.

Chen, M.S. and Eweje, G. (2020), 'Establishing ethical *guanxi* (interpersonal relationships) through Confucian virtues of *xinyong* (trust), *lijie* (empathy) and *ren* (humanity)', *Corporate Governance (Bradford)*, 20(1): 1–15.

Chen, X. (2021), *The essentials of Habermas*, Cham: Springer Nature.

Chow, A.R. and Perrigo, B. (2023), 'The AI arms race is changing everything: Tech companies are betting big on AI. Are they making the same old mistakes?' *TIME*, 26 February / 6 March: 45–8.

Chow, R. (2019), 'Purdue Pharma and OxyContin – a commercial success but public health disaster', *Harvard Public Health Review*, 25 (Fall/Spring), (www.jstor.org/stable/pdf/45345199.pdf?refreqid=excelsior%3A45a1f3f333b2586abaae3cdf6be32781&ab_segments=&origin=&initiator=&acceptTC=1).

Christensen, H.B., Hail, L. and Leuz, C. (2021) 'Mandatory CSR and sustainability reporting: Economic analysis and literature review', *Review of Accounting Studies*, 26: 1176–248.

Cioffi, J. (1997), 'Heuristics, servants to intuition, in clinical decision-making', *Journal of Advanced Nursing*, 26(1): 203–8.

Ciulla, J.B. (2011), 'Is business ethics getter better? A historical perspective', *Business Ethics Quarterly*, 21(2): 335–43.

Ciulla, J.B. (2021), 'Business ethics pioneers: Joanne B. Ciulla', *Business & Professional Ethics Journal*, 40(3), 295–307.

Clarke, A.D. (2006), 'SMEs and corporate governance: Politics, resources and trickle-down effects', Corporate Law Teachers Association Conference, Brisbane, 5–7 February.

Clarke, K. (2010), The Bribery Act 2010, Ministry of Justice UK, (www.justice.gov.uk/downloads/legislation/bribery-act-2010-guidance.pdf).

Clott, C.B. (2004), 'Perspectives on global outsourcing and the changing nature of work', *Business and Society Review*, 109(2): 153–70.

CNN (2021), Mumbai terror attacks fast facts, (https://edition.cnn.com/2013/09/18/world/asia/mumbai-terror-attacks/index.html).

Cochran, P.L. and Wood, R.A. (1984), 'Corporate social responsibility and financial performance', *Academy of Management Journal*, 27(1): 42–56.

Cohan, J.A. (2002), '"I didn't know" and "I was only doing my job": Has corporate governance careened out of control? A case study of Enron's information myopia', *Journal of Business Ethics*, 40: 275–99.

Cohen, A.B. (2009), 'Many forms of culture', *American Psychologist*, 64(3): 194–204.

Cohen, A.B. (2010), 'Just how many different forms of culture are there?' *American Psychologist*, 65(1): 59–61.

Cohen, S. (1996), 'Who are the stakeholders? What difference does it make?' *Business & Professional Ethics Journal*, 15(2): 3–18.

Cohen, S. (1999), 'Good ethics is good business – revisited', *Business & Professional Ethics Journal*, 18(2): 57–68.

Comparably (n.d.), LEGO Group mission, vision & values, (www.comparably.com/companies/lego-group/mission).

Compton, K. (2021), 'Vioxx lawsuits'. In K. Connolly (ed.), *Drug watch, from 14 cited research articles*, (www.drugwatch.com/vioxx/lawsuits/).

Cone, C.L. (2012), Good purpose 2012, (www.purpose.edelman.com).

Consultancy (2021), KPMG installs Richard Boele as first ever Chief Purpose Officer, (www.consultancy.com.au/news/4289/kpmg-installs-richard-boele-as-first-ever-chief-purpose-officer).

Contractor, F.J. (2019), 'Can a firm find the balance between openness and secrecy? Towards a theory of an optimum level of disclosure', *Journal of International Business Studies*, 50: 261–74.

Cooperrider, D. (2017), 'Business as an agent of world benefit: Why do good things happen to good companies?' *AI Practitioner*, 19(2): 67–75.

Cooperrider, D.L., Zhexembayeva, N., Trosten-Bloom, A. and Whitney, D. (2012), 'Business as agent of world benefit'. In J. Vogelsang, M. Townsend, M. Mihahan, D. Jamieson, J. Vogel, A. Viets, C. Royal, L. Valek (eds). *Handbook for Strategic HR*, New York: AMACOM (HarperCollins Leadership).

COP15 (2022), UN biodiversity conference COP 15, (www.unep.org/un-biodiversity-conference-cop-15).

Cote, R. (2021), 'Ethical perspective: Ethics in the pharmaceutical industry: Vioxx recall', *Journal of Leadership, Accountability and Ethics*, 18(1): 11–22.

CPS 231 (2017), Prudential standard CPS 231 outsourcing, Australian Government, (www.apra.gov.au/sites/default/files/Prudential-Standard-CPS-231-Outsourcing- per cent28July-2017 per cent29.pdf).

Craft, J.L. (2013), 'A review of the empirical ethical decision-making literature: 2004–2011', *Journal of Business Ethics*, 117(2): 221–59.

Crane, A. (2013), 'Modern slavery as a management practice: Exploring the conditions and capabilities for human exploitation', *The Academy of Management Review*, 38(1): 49–69.

Crossman, J.E. (2018), 'Internal auditing of organizational spiritual identity (OSI)'. In S. Dhiman, G.E. Roberts and J.E. Crossman (eds), *The Palgrave handbook of workplace spirituality and fulfillment*, Cham: Palgrave Macmillan.

CSIRO (2023a), Australia announces world first responsible AI network to uplift industry, (www.csiro.au/news/News-releases/2023/Australia-announces-world-first-responsible-AI-Network-to-uplift-industry).

CSIRO (2023b), National Artificial Intelligence Centre, (www.csiro.au/naic).

CTG (2022), Clothing the Gaps, (www.clothingthegaps.com.au/).

CTGF (2022), Clothing the Gaps – Foundation, (www.clothingthegapsfoundation.org.au/).

Curtis, S. and Bradly, A. (2022), 'Inclusive business – A private-sector approach to poverty alleviation in developing economies'. In T. Maak, N.M. Pless, M. Orlitzky and S. Sandhu (eds), *The Routledge companion to corporate social responsibility*, New York: Routledge.

Dacin, M.T., Harrison, J.S., Hess, D., Killian, S. and Roloff, J. (2022), 'Business versus ethics? Thoughts on the future of business ethics', *Journal of Business Ethics*, 180(3), 863–77.

Dahlsrud, A. (2008), 'How corporate social responsibility is defined: An analysis of 37 definitions', *Corporate Social Responsibility and Environmental Management*, 15(1): 1–13.

Daly, M.C. and Silver, C. (2007), 'Flattening the world of legal services? The ethical and liability minefields of offshoring legal and law-related services', *Georgetown Journal of International Law*, 38(3): 401–47.

Dandona, L., Dandona, R. and John, R.K. (2001), Estimation of blindness in India from 2000 through 2020: Implications for the blindness control policy, (https://pubmed.ncbi.nlm.nih.gov/11804362/).

Dane, E. and Pratt, M. (2007), 'Exploring intuition and its role in managerial decision making', *Academy of Management Review*, 32(1): 33–54.

Danley, J.R. (2005), 'Polishing the Pinto: Legal liability, moral blame, and risk', *Business Ethics Quarterly*, 15(2): 205–36.

Dastin, J. (2018), Amazon scraps secret AI recruiting tool that showed bias against women, (www.reuters.com/article/us-amazon-com-jobs-automation-insight-idUSKCN1MK08G).

Davis, K. (1973), 'The case for and against business assumption of social responsibilities', *Academy of Management Journal*, 16(2): 312–22.

Davidson, K. (2009), 'Ethical concerns at the bottom of the pyramid: Where CSR meets BOP', *Journal of International Business Ethics*, 2(1): 22-32.

Dawson, S. (2001), 'Ethics in Australian small business', *Business & Professional Ethics Journal*, 20(1): 25–36.

D'Cruz, P., Du, S., Noronha, E., Parboteeah, K.P., Trittin-Ulbrich, H. and Whelan, G. (2022). 'Technology, megatrends and work: Thoughts on the future of business ethics', *Journal of Business Ethics*, 180(3): 879–902.

De Cremer, D. (2022), 'With AI entering organizations, responsible leadership may slip', *AI and Ethics*, 2(1): 49–51.

De George, R.T. (1990), 'Using the techniques of ethical analysis in corporate practice'. In G. Enderle, B. Almond and A. Argandoña (eds.), *People in corporations: Ethical responsibilities and corporate effectiveness*, Dordrecht: Kluwer Academic Publishers.

De George, R.T. (2010), *Business Ethics*, 7th edn, Upper Saddle River, NJ: Prentice Hall.

De George, R.T. (2015), A history of business ethics, Markula Center for Applied Ethics, University of Santa Clara, (www.scu.edu/ethics/focus-areas/business-ethics/resources/a-history-of-business-ethics/).

De George, R.T. (2021), 'Business ethics pioneers: Richard T. De George', *Business & Professional Ethics Journal*, 40(3): 309–19.

Dedeke, A. (2015), 'A cognitive-intuitionist model of moral judgment', *Journal of Business Ethics*, 126(3): 437–57.

Dedovic, A. (2022), ACCC cracks down on greenwashing, fake online reviews, (www.businessnewsaustralia.com/articles/accc-cracks-down-on-greenwashing--fake-online-reviews.html).

den Nieuwenboer, N.A., da Cunha, J.V. and Treviño, L.K. (2017), 'Middle managers and corruptive routine translation: The social production of deceptive performance', *Organization Science*, 28(5): 781–803.

Dennis, M. and Aizenberg, E. (2022), 'The ethics of AI in human resources', *Ethics and Information Technology*, 24: 25.

Deshpande, R. (2012), The ordinary heroes of the Taj Hotel: Rohit Deshpande at TEDxNewEngland, (www.youtube.com/watch?v=vQGz1YRqBPw).

deVries, P. (1986), 'The discovery of excellence: The assets of exemplars in business ethics', *Journal of Business Ethics*, 5(3): 193–201.

Di Lorenzo, D. (2007), 'Business ethics: Law as a determinant of business conduct', *Journal of Business Ethics*, 71(3): 275–99.

Di Miceli da Silveira, A. (2022), 'Corporate governance and ethical culture: Do boards matter?' *Review of Managerial Science*, 16(4): 1085–116.

Dias, A.P., Bobba, S., Carrara, S. and Plazzotta, B. (2020), The role of rare earth elements in wind energy and electric mobility, EU JRC Science for Policy Report, (www.jrc122671_the_role_of_rare_earth_elements_in_wind_energy_and_electric_mobility_2%20(1).pdf).

Dickens, B.M. and Cook, R.J. (2006), 'Conflict of interest: Legal and ethical aspects', *International Journal of Gynaecology and Obstetrics*, 92(2): 192–7.

Dionisio, M. and de Vargas, E.R. (2020), 'Corporate social innovation: A systematic literature review', *International Business Review*, 29(2): 101641.

Doh, J.P., Stumpf, S.A. and Tymon, W.G. (2011), 'Responsible leadership helps retain talent in India', *Journal of Business Ethics*, 98(Suppl 1): 85–100.

Donaldson, T. (1991), 'Rights in the global market'. In R.P. Nielsen (ed), *The politics of ethics* (The Ruffin series in business ethics), Oxford: Oxford University Press, (https://doi.org/10.5840/ruffinoup199128).

Donaldson, T. (2021), 'Business ethics pioneers: Thomas Donaldson', *Business & Professional Ethics Journal*, 40(3): 321–7.

Donaldson, T. and Dunfee, T.W. (1994), 'Towards a unified conception of business ethics: Integrative Social Contracts Theory', *The Academy of Management Review*, 19(2): 252–84.

Donaldson, T. and Dunfee, T.W. (1999), 'When ethics travel: The promise and peril of global business ethics', *California Management Review*, 41(4): 45–63.

Donaldson, T. and Preston, L.E. (1995), 'The stakeholder theory of the corporation: Concepts, evidence, and implications', *Academy of Management Review*, 20(1): 65–91.

Dorr, D. (2022), 'Alternative business ethics: A challenge for leadership'. In G. Flynn (ed), *Leadership and Business Ethics*, 2nd edn, Dordrecht: Springer Nature.

Dorr, S. (2021), *Corporate digital responsibility: Managing corporate responsibility and sustainability in the digital age*, Bonn: Springer.

Dragomir, V.D. (2017), 'Conflicts of interest in business: A review of the concept', *Accounting and Management Information Systems*, 16(4): 472–89.

Duignan, B. (2020), Postmodernism, *Encyclopedia Britannica*, (www.britannica.com/topic/postmodernism-philosophy).

Dunfee, T.W. (1996), 'On the synergistic, interdependent relationship of business ethics and law', *American Business Law Journal*, 34(2): 317–25.

Durkheim, E. (1912/1964), *The elementary forms of the religious life,* Project Gutenberg, London: George Allen and Unwin Ltd.

Dyer, O. (2020), 'Purdue Pharma to plead guilty and pay USD 8.3bn over opioid marketing', *BMJ*, 371: m4103.

EB (2023), Three laws of robotics, (www.britannica.com/topic/Three-Laws-of-Robotics).

Edelman (2022), Edelman Trust Barometer 2022, (www.edelman.com/sites/g/files/aatuss191/files/2022-01/2022 per cent20Edelman per cent20Trust per cent20Barometer per cent20FINAL_Jan25.pdf).

Eden, L. and Smith, L.M. (2022), 'The ethics of transfer pricing: Insights from the fraud triangle', *Journal of Forensic and Investigative Accounting*, 14(3): 360–83.

EESI (2017), Fact sheet – Biogas: Converting waste to energy, (www.eesi.org/papers/view/fact-sheet-biogasconverting-waste-to-energy).

EGOS (2015), Responsible leadership: Addressing social, environmental and business implications of leadership, (www.egos.org/jart/prj3/egos/main.jart?rel=de&reserve-mode=active&content-id=1392376003637&subtheme_id=1368705987343).

Ekici, A. and Ekici, Ş.O. (2021), 'Understanding and managing complexity through Bayesian network approach: The case of bribery in business transactions', *Journal of Business Research*, 129: 757–73.

Eliacik, E. (2022), How could AI transform developing countries? (https://dataconomy.com/2022/06/artificial-intelligence-in-developing-countries/).

Elon (2021), Survey XII: What is the future of ethical AI design? (www.elon.edu/u/imagining/surveys/xii-2021/ethical-ai-design-2030/).

EMAS (2022), Eco-management and audit scheme, (https://ec.europa.eu/environment/emas/index_en.htm).

Enderle, G. (2004), 'Global competition and corporate responsibilities of small and medium-sized enterprises', *Business Ethics: A European Review*, 13(1): 50–63.

Enderle, G. (2015), 'Exploring and conceptualizing international business ethics', *Journal of Business Ethics*, 127(4): 723–35.

Enking, M. (2023), Thousands of artists reimagine Vermeer's 'Girl with a Pearl Earring', (www.smithsonianmag.com/smart-news/girl-with-a-pearl-earring-vermeer-artificial-intelligence-mauritshuis-180981767/).

Enrici, A. (2022), Patagonia's founder has given his company away to fight climate change and advance conservation: 5 questions answered, (https://theconversation.com/patagonias-founder-has-given-his-company-away-to-fight-climate-change-and-advance-conservation-5-questions-answered-190827).

EPA (2022), Overview of greenhouse gases, (www.epa.gov/ghgemissions/overview-greenhouse-gases).

Epstein, E.M. (1987), 'The corporate social policy process: Beyond business ethics, corporate social responsibility, and corporate social responsiveness', *California Management Review*, 29(3): 99–114.

Erblich, T. (2019), 'Purpose and ethics: How companies are redefining business, communities and society', (www.linkedin.com/pulse/purpose-ethics-how-companies-redefining-business-society-tim-erblich/).

Ermasova, N. (2021), 'Cross-cultural issues in business ethics: A review and research agenda', *International Journal of Cross Cultural Management*, 21(1): 95–121.

Escadas, M., Jalali, M.S. and Farhangmehr, M. (2019), 'Why bad feelings predict good behaviours: The role of positive and negative anticipated emotions on consumer ethical decision making', *Business Ethics: A European Review*, 28(4): 529–45.

ET Online (2018), What Walmart's Flipkart acquisition means for India, consumers and its arch-rival Amazon, (https://economictimes.indiatimes.com/industry/services/retail/softbank-ceo-confirms-walmart-flipkart-deal/articleshow/64093437.cms).

ET-Telecom (2023), Girl with AI earrings sparks Dutch art controversy, (https://telecom.economictimes.indiatimes.com/news/girl-with-ai-earrings-sparks-dutch-art-controversy/98543707?redirect=1).

EU-CSR (2011), Corporate social responsibility, (https://ec.europa.eu/info/sites/default/files/recommendations-subgroup-corporate-social-responsibility_en.pdf).

Evans, S. (2022), Ansell shares tumble as medical glove demand softens, (www.afr.com/companies/healthcare-and-fitness/ansell-shares-tumble-as-medical-glove-demand-softens-20220131-p59shy).

Fairtrade (2022), How Fairtrade works, (www.fairtrade.net/about/how-fairtrade-works).

FAO (2023), Technical platform on the measurement and reduction of food loss and waste, (www.fao.org/platform-food-loss-waste/flw-events/international-day-food-loss-and-waste/en).

Fast Company (2016), The future of work: How Google and Twitter train their employees to be more mindful, (www.fastcompany.com/3055974/how-google-and-twitter-train-their-employees-to-be-more-mindful).

FCPA (2022), Foreign Corrupt Practices Act 1977 amended 1998, US Department of Justice, (www.justice.gov/criminal-fraud/foreign-corrupt-practices-act).

Felgenhauer, K. and Labella, P. (2022), Big players in African fields, (www.oecd.org/dev/41301739.pdf).

Felton, R. (2020), How Coke and Pepsi make millions from bottling tap water, as residents face shutoffs, (www.consumerreports.org/bottled-water/how-coke-and-pepsi-make-millions-from-bottling-tap-water-as-residents-face-shutoffs/).

Ferrell, O.C. and Gresham, L.G. (1985), 'A contingency framework for understanding ethical decision making in marketing', *Journal of Marketing*, 49(3): 87–96.

Ferrell, O.C., Gresham, L.G. and Fraedrich, J.P. (1989), 'A synthesis of ethical decision models for marketing', *Journal of Macromarketing*, 9(2): 55–64.

Ferrell, O.C., Harrison, D.E., Ferrell, L. and Hair, J.F. (2019), 'Business ethics, corporate social responsibility, and brand attitudes: An exploratory study', *Journal of Business Research*, 95: 491–501.

Fiercepharma (2022), Novo Nordisk leads pharma pack breaking into Reputation Institute's corporate responsibility ranking, (www.fiercepharma.com/marketing/novo-nordisk-leads-pharma-pack-breaking-into-ri-s-corporate-responsibility-study-ranks).

Filotheou, A., Kassinis, G. and Stavrou, E. (2007), 'Downsizing and stakeholder orientation among the Fortune 500: Does family ownership matter?' *Journal of Business Ethics*, 72(2): 149–62.

Fire in the Blood – HIV AIDS drugs and big pharma (2020), (www.youtube.com/watch?v=uMsseS_Lqs0).

Fire in the Blood – trailer (2013), (www.youtube.com/watch?v=eVf2UUu_w4o).

Fisher, C. and Lovell, A. (2009), *Business ethics and values: Individual, corporate and international perspectives*, 3rd edn, Harlow: Pearson Education Ltd.

Fitch, H.G. (1976), 'Achieving corporate social responsibility', *The Academy of Management Review*, 1(1): 38–46.

Fitzpatrick, W.M. and Dilullo, S.A. (2017), 'Protecting trade secrets: Legal challenges and liabilities for organizations', *Competition Forum*, 15(1): 208–33.

Flash of Genius (2010), (www.youtube.com/watch?v=ab2ej-c5XSY).

Floridi, L. and Craig, E. (1998), 'Egoism and altruism', *Routledge encyclopedia of philosophy*, Abingdon: Routledge.

Floridi, L., Cowls, J., Beltrametti, M., Chatila, R., Chazerand, P., Dignum, V., Luetge, C., Madelin, R., Pagallo, U., Rossi, F., Schafer, B., Valcke, P. and Vayena, E. (2018), 'AI4People – An ethical framework for a good AI society: Opportunities, risks, principles, and recommendations', *Minds and Machines*, 28: 689–707.

Flynn, G. (2022), *Leadership and business ethics*, 2nd edn, Dordrecht: Springer Nature.

Flynn, G. and Werhane, P.H. (2022), 'A framework for leadership and ethics on business and society'. In G. Flynn (ed), *Leadership and business ethics*, 2nd edn, Dordrecht: Springer-Verlag.

Fobosi, S.C. (2020), South Africa's minibus taxi industry has been marginalised for too long: This must change, (https://theconversation.com/south-africas-minibus-taxi-industry-has-been-marginalised-for-too-long-this-must-change-142060).

Forbes (2018), What is Industry 4.0? (www.forbes.com/sites/bernardmarr/2018/09/02/what-is-industry-4-0-heres-a-super-easy-explanation-for-anyone/?sh=2b9c0a239788).

Frankl, V.E. (1959/2004), *Man's search for meaning*, London: Penguin.

Franzò, S. and Nasca, A. (2021), 'The environmental impact of electric vehicles: A novel life cycle-based evaluation framework and its applications to multi-country scenarios', *Journal of Cleaner Production*, 315: 128005.

Frederick, W.C. (2018), 'Corporate social responsibility: From founders to Millennials'. In J. Webber and D.M. Wasieleski (eds), *Corporate social responsibility* (vol. 2), Bingley: Emerald Publishing.

Freeman, R.E. (2005), 'A stakeholder theory of the modern corporation', *Perspectives in business ethics*, McGraw-Hill, Boston.

Freeman, R.E. (2021), 'Business ethics pioneers: R. Edward Freeman', *Business & Professional Ethics Journal*, 40(3), 329–35.

Freeman, R.E. and Auster, E.R. (2011), 'Values, authenticity, and responsible leadership', *Journal of Business Ethics*, 98(Suppl 1): 15–23

Freeman, R.E., Dmytriyev, S.D. and Phillips, R.A. (2021), 'Stakeholder theory and the resource-based view of the firm', *Journal of Management*, 47(7): 1757–70.

Freeman, R.E., Harrison, J.S. and Wicks, A.C. (2007), *Managing for stakeholders: Survival, reputation, and success*, New Haven, CT: Yale University Press.

Freeman, R.E., Martin, K.E. and Parmar, B.L. (2020), *The power of and – Responsible business without trade-offs*, New York: Columbia University Press.

French, W. and Weiss, A. (2000), 'An ethics of care or an ethics of justice', *Journal of Business Ethics*, 27(1/2): 125–36.

Friede, G., Busch, T. and Bassen, A. (2015), 'ESG and financial performance: Aggregated evidence from more than 2000 empirical studies', *Journal of Sustainable Finance & Investment*, 5(4): 210–33.

Friedman, M. (1970), 'The social responsibility of business is to increase profits', *The New York Times Magazine*, 13 September. (www.nytimes.com/1970/09/13/archives/a-friedman-doctrine-the-social-responsibility-of-business-is-to.html).

Friedman, T.L. (2007), *The world is flat*, London: Allen Lane of Penguin Books.

Fritzsche, D.J. (2000), 'Ethical climates and the ethical dimension of decision making', *Journal of Business Ethics*, 24(2): 125–40.

Fry, L.W. (2003), 'Towards a theory of spiritual leadership', *The Leadership Quarterly*, 14(6): 693–727.

Fry, L.W. (2005), 'Towards a theory of ethical and spiritual well-being, and corporate social responsibility through spiritual leadership'. In R.A. Giacalone and C.L. Jurkiewicz (eds), *Positive psychology in business ethics and corporate responsibility*, Charlotte, NC: Information Age Publishing.

Frynas, J.G. (2005), 'The false developmental promise of corporate social responsibility: Evidence from multinational companies', *International Affairs*, 81(3): 581–98.

Fuller, T. and Tian, Y. (2006), 'Social and symbolic capital and responsible entrepreneurship: An empirical investigation of SME narratives', *Journal of Business Ethics*, 67(3): 287–304.

Garofalo, C., Geuras, D., Lynch, T.D. and Lynch, C.E. (2001), 'Applying virtue ethics to the challenge of corruption', *Innovation Journal*, 6(2): 1–12.

Gates, D. (2020), 'Boeing whistle-blower alleges systemic problems with 737 MAX', *Seattle Times*, 18 June, (www.seattletimes.com/business/boeing-aerospace/boeing-whistleblower-alleges-systemic-problems-with-737-max).

GBBI (2018), Ghana's eco-friendly bamboo bikes, (www.youtube.com/watch?v=8YHH-Iq-0ac).

Gelles, D. (2022), Billionaire no more: Patagonia founder gives away the company, (www.nytimes.com/2022/09/14/climate/patagonia-climate-philanthropy-chouinard.html).

GFN (2022), Ecological footprint, (www.footprintnetwork.org/our-work/ecological-footprint/) and (https://data.footprintnetwork.org/#/).

Giacalone, R.A. and Jurkiewicz, C.L. (2003), *Handbook of workplace spirituality and organizational performance*, New York: M.E. Sharpe.

Giacomin, V. and Jones, G. (2022), 'Drivers of philanthropic foundations in emerging markets: Family, values and spirituality', *Journal of Business Ethics*, 180(1): 263–82.

Gigerenzer, G. (2008), 'Why heuristics work', *Perspectives on Psychological Science*, 3(1): 20–9.

Gigerenzer, G. and Goldstein, D.G. (1996), 'Reasoning the fast and frugal way: Models of bounded rationality', *Psychological Review*, 103(4): 650–69.

Gill, R. (2022), 'Introduction to spirituality'. In Y. Altman, J. Neal and W. Mayrhofer, (eds), *Workplace spirituality: Making a difference*, Berlin: De Gruyter.

Gilshan, D. and Chambers, M. (2020), *The ethics of diversity*, London: Institute of Business Ethics.

Gioia, D.A. (1992), 'Pinto fires and personal ethics: A script analysis of missed opportunities', *Journal of Business Ethics*, 11(5–6): 379–89.

GNW (2022), Global gambling market to reach USD876 billion by 2026, (www.globenewswire.com/news-release/2022/06/09/2459937/0/en/Global-Gambling-Market-to-Reach-876-Billion-by-2026.html).

Godwin, L.N. (2015), 'Examining the impact of moral imagination on organizational decision', *Business & Society*, 54(2): 254–78.

Golroudbary, S.R., Makarava, I., Kraslawski, A. and Repo, E. (2022), 'Global environmental cost of using rare earth elements in green energy technologies', *The Science of the Total Environment*, 832: 155022.

Gomez, R. and Fisher, J.W. (2003), 'Domains of spiritual well-being and development and validation of the spiritual well-being questionnaire', *Personality and Individual Differences*, 35(8): 1975–91.

Goodpaster, K.E. (1991), 'Business ethics and stakeholder analysis', *Business Ethics Quarterly*, 1(1): 53–73.

Goodpaster, K.E. (2010), 'Business ethics: Two moral provisos', *Business Ethics Quarterly*, 20(4): 740–2.

Graafland, J. van de, Ven, B. and Stoffele, N. (2003), 'Strategies and instruments for organising CSR by small and large businesses in Netherlands', *Journal of Business Ethics*, 47(1): 45–60.

Graness, A. (2018), 'The "libertarian paradigm" of Severino Elias Ngoenha'. In R. Oelofsen (ed), *An African path to a global future* (Cultural heritage and contemporary change series, vol. II), Washington: African Philosophical Studies.

Grant, B. (2009), 'Merck published fake journal', *The Scientist*, (www.the-scientist.com/the-nutshell/merck-published-fake-journal-44190).

Gray, M. (2010), 'Postmodern ethic'. In M. Gray and S.A. Webb (eds), *Ethics and Value Perspectives in Social Work*, London: Palgrave.

Green, B.P. (2022), *Space ethics*, Lanham, MD: Rowman and Littlefield.

Green, R.M. (1993), 'Business ethics as a postmodern phenomenon', *Business Ethics Quarterly*, 3(3): 219–25.

Greene, J.D., Nystrom, L.E., Engell, A.D., Darley, J.M. and Cohen, J.D. (2004), 'The neural bases of cognitive conflict and control in moral judgment', *Neuron*, 44(2): 389–400.

Greene, J.D., Sommerville, R.B., Nystrom, L.E., Darley, J.M. and Cohen, J.D. (2001). 'An fMRI investigation of emotional engagement in moral judgement', *Science*, 293: 2105–8.

Greenpeace (2022), About us, Greenpeace International, (www.greenpeace.org/international/tag/about-us/).

GRI (2022), Global Reporting Initiative, Amsterdam, The Netherlands, (www.globalreporting.org).

Grosse, R. (2019), 'Innovation by MNEs in emerging markets', *Transnational Corporations*, 26(3): 1–31.

Guan, J., in Sio, S.H. and Noronha, C. (2022), 'Value co-creation through corporate social responsibility in a typical controversial industry: Evidence from Macao', *Journal of Global Scholars of Marketing Science*, 32(1): 36–53.

Guillory, W.A. (2019), 'Managing spirituality from a personal perspective'. In J. Marques (ed), *The Routledge companion to management and workplace spirituality*, 1st edn, London: Routledge.

Gupta, B. (2006), '"Bhagavad Gita" as duty and virtue ethics', *Journal of Religious Ethics*, 34: 373–95.

Gupta, P., Chauhan, S., Paul, J. and Jaiswal, M.P. (2020), 'Social entrepreneurship research: A review and future research agenda', *Journal of Business Research*, 113: 209–29.

Gustafson, A. (2000), 'Making sense of postmodern business ethics', *Business Ethics Quarterly*, 10(3): 645–58.

Guzak, J.R. and Hargrove, M.B. (2011), 'The role of intuition in ethical decision making'. In M. Sinclair (ed), *Handbook of intuition research*, Cheltenham: Edward Elgar Publishing.

Habbe, A.H., Kusumawati, A., Alimuddin, R.Y. and Muda, I. (2020), 'Cognitive moral development, organizational situation and ethical decision making in business and accounting', *International Journal of Financial Research*, 11(5): 93–104.

Habermas, J. (1993). *Justification and application*, Cambridge, MA: The MIT Press.

Haensel, K. and Garcia-Zamor, J-C. (2019), 'A theoretical approach to spiritual leadership in public organizations'. In J. Marques (ed), *The Routledge companion to management and workplace spirituality*, 1st ed, London: Routledge.

Hagman, J.E. (2021), 'The eighth characteristic for successful calculus programs: Diversity, equity, & inclusion practices', *PRIMUS: Problems, Resources, and Issues in Mathematics Undergraduate Studies*, 31(1): 70–90.

Hahn, R. (2022), *Sustainability management*, Fellbach: Rudiger Hahn.

Haider, M., Shannon, R. and Moschis, G.P. (2022), 'Sustainable consumption research and the role of marketing: A review of the literature (1976–2021)', *Sustainability*, 14(7): 3999.

Haidt, J. (2001), 'The emotional dog and its rational tail: A social intuitionalist approach to moral judgement', *Psychological Review*, 108(4): 814–34.

Haidt, J. (2010), 'Moral psychology must not be based on faith and hope: Commentary on Narvaez', *Perspectives on Psychological Science*, 5(2): 182–4.

Haidt, J. (2012), *The righteous mind*, New York: Pantheon Books.

Halder, P., Hansen, E.N., Kangas, J. and Laukkanen, T. (2020), 'How national culture and ethics matter in consumers' green consumption values', *Journal of Cleaner Production*, 265: 121754.

Hall, S. (2008), 'Protest movements in the 1970s: The long 1960s', *Journal of Contemporary History*, 43(4): 655–72.

Hamilton, J., Knouse, S. and Hill, V. (2009), 'Google in China: A manager-friendly heuristic model for resolving cross-cultural ethical conflicts', *Journal of Business Ethics*, 86(2): 143–57.

Hammond, A.L., Kramer, W.J., Katz, R.S., Tran, J.T. and Walker, C. (2007), The next 4 billion: Market size and business strategy at the base of the pyramid, (https://files.wri.org/d8/s3fs-public/pdf/n4b_full_text_lowrez.pdf).

Han, Z., Wang, Q. and Yan, X. (2019), 'How responsible leadership motivates employees to engage in organizational citizenship behavior for the environment: A double-mediation model', *Sustainability*, 11(3): 605–18.

Handy, C. (2002), 'What's a business for?', *Harvard Business Review*, 80(12): 49–132.

Hanine, S. and Steils, N. (2018), 'Crowdsourcing : A double-edged sword outsourcing strategy', *Positive and Negative Aspects of Outsourcing*. doi: https://doi.org/10.5772/INTECHOPEN.74531.

Hannah, S.T., Avolio, B.J. and May, D.R. (2011), 'Moral maturation and moral conation: A capacity approach to explaining moral thought and action', *Academy of Management Review*, 36(4): 663–85.

Haque, A., Fernando, M. and Caputi, P. (2019), 'The relationship between responsible leadership and organisational commitment and the mediating effect of employee turnover intentions: An empirical study with Australian employees', *Journal of Business Ethics*, 156(3): 759–74.

Haque, A., Fernando, M. and Caputi, P. (2021), 'Responsible leadership and employee outcomes: A systematic literature review, integration and propositions', *Asia-Pacific Journal of Business Administration*, 13(3): 383–408.

Harder, M. and Burford, G. (2019), 'Sustainability and business ethics'. In M. Harder and G. Burford (eds), *Measuring intangible values*, 1st edn, London: Routledge.

Hardin, G. (1968), 'The tragedy of the commons', *Science New Series*, 162(3859): 1243-48.

Hare, R. (1991), 'The philosophical basis for psychiatric ethics'. In S. Bloch and P. Chodoff (eds), *Psychiatric ethics*, 2nd edn, Oxford: Oxford University Press.

Harper, P.T. (2022), 'Moral imagination and the strivings for moral progress: A reflection on Richard Rorty'. In G. Flynn (ed), *Leadership and business ethics*, Dordrecht: Springer.

Harris, H. (2013), 'Courage as a management virtue'. In H. Harris, G. Wijesinghe and S. McKenzie (eds), *The heart of the good institution*, Dordrecht: Springer.

Harris, H., Wijesinghe, G. and McKenzie, S. (eds) (2013), *The heart of the good institution*, Dordrecht: Springer.

Harrison, F.E. (1981), *The managerial decision-making process*, 2nd edn, Boston, MA: Houghton Mifflin.

Harrison, F.E. (1993), 'Interdisciplinary models of decision making', *Management Decision*, 31(3): 27–33.

Hart, H.L.A. (1958), 'Positivism and the separation of law and morals', *Harvard Law Review*, 71(4): 593–621.

Hartman, E.M. (2006), 'Can we teach character? An Aristotelian answer', *Academy of Management Learning & Education*, 5(1): 68–81.

Hartman, L.P. (1998), *Perspectives in business ethics*, 1st edn, Chicago, IL: McGraw-Hill.

Hassi, A. and Storti, G. (2012), 'Globalization and culture: The three H scenarios'. In H. Cuadra-Montiel (ed), *Globalization – approaches to diversity*, London: IntechOpen.

Hattangady, H. and Sen, A. (2019), *Lift off*, Chennai: Westland Publications.

Hayes, A. (2022), Blockchain facts: What is it, how it works, and how it can be used, (www.investopedia.com/terms/b/blockchain.asp).

Hayibor, S. and Wasieleski, D.M. (2009), 'Effects of the use of the availability heuristic on ethical decision-making in organisations', *Journal of Business Ethics*, 81(1): 151–65.

Hemling, L., Plesner Rossing, J.C. and Hoffjan, A. (2022), 'The use of information technology for international transfer pricing in multinational enterprises', *International Journal of Accounting Information Systems*, 44: 100546.

Hernando, Y., Colwell, K. and Wright, B.D. (2016), 'Doing well while fighting river blindness: The alignment of a corporate drug donation programme with responsibilities to shareholders', *Tropical Medicine & International Health*, 21(10): 1304–10.

Hertwich, E.G. and Wood, R. (2018), 'The growing importance of Scope 3 greenhouse gas emissions from industry', *Environmental Research Letters*, 13(10): 104013.

Higgins-Desbiolles, F. and Monga, M. (2021), 'Transformative change through events business: A feminist ethic of care analysis of building the purpose economy', *Journal of Sustainable Tourism*, 29(11–12): 1989–2007.

Hilb, M. (2020), 'Towards artificial governance? The role of artificial intelligence in shaping the future of corporate governance', *Journal of Management and Governance*, 24(4): 851–70.

Hiquet, R. and Oh, W.Y. (2019), 'Ethics issues in outsourcing to emerging markets: Theoretical perspectives and practices'. In O. Osuji, F.N. Ngwu and D. Jamali (eds), *Corporate social responsibility in developing and emerging markets*, Cambridge: Cambridge University Press.

Höffe, O. and den Haan, J. (2013), *John Rawls: A theory of justice*, O. Höffe (ed), Joost den Haan (trans.), Boston, MA: Brill, Leiden.

Hofstede, G. (1980), *Cultural consequences: International differences in work related values*, London: Sage.

Hofstede, G., Hofstede, G.J. and Minkow, M. (2010), *Cultures and organizations: Software of the mind*, New York: McGraw Hill.

Hofstede Insights (2022), Intercultural management, (www.hofstede-insights.com/models/national-culture/).

Hong, J., Shen, G.Q., Feng, Y., Lau, W.S. and Mao, C. (2015), 'Greenhouse gas emissions during the construction phase of a building: A case study in China', *Journal of Cleaner Production*, 103: 249–59.

Hooper, R. (2021), *How to spend a trillion dollars: Saving the world and solving the biggest mysteries in science*, London: Profile Books.

Hopkins (2019), Protein content of common foods, (www.hopkinsmedicine.org/bariatrics/_documents/nutrition_protein_content_common_foods.pdf).

Hopkins, W.E. and Hopkins, S.A. (1999), 'The ethics of downsizing: Perceptions of rights and responsibilities', *Journal of Business Ethics*, 18(2): 145–56.

Hossain, M., Atif, M., Ahmed, A. and Mia, L. (2019), 'Do LGBT workplace diversity policies create value for firms?' *Journal of Business Ethics*, 167(4): 775–91.

Houghton, J.D., Neck, C.P. and Krishnakumar, S. (2016), 'The what, why, and how of spirituality in the workplace revisited: A 14-year update and extension', *Journal of Management, Spirituality and Religion*, 13(3): 177–205.

House, R.J., Hanges, P.J., Javidan, M., Dorfman, P.W. and Gupta, V. (eds.) (2004) *Culture, leadership, and organizations: The GLOBE study of 62 societies*, Thousand Oaks, CA: Sage.

Howe, J. (2008), *Crowdsourcing: Why the power of the crowd is driving the future of business*, New York: Crown Business.

Huff, C. and Frey, W. (2005), 'Moral pedagogy and practical ethics', *Science and Engineering Ethics*, 11(3): 389–408.

HUL (2022), Enhancing livelihoods through Project Shakti, (www.hul.co.in/planet-and-society/case-studies/enhancing-livelihoods-through-project-shakti/).

Hunt, S.D. and Vitell, S. (1986), 'A general theory of marketing ethics', *Journal of Macromarketing*, 6(1): 5–16.

Husted, B.W. (2000), 'The impact of national culture on software piracy', *Journal of Business Ethics*, 26(3): 197–211.

Huybrechts, B. and Nicholls, A. (2012), 'Social entrepreneurship: Definitions, drivers and challenges'. In C.K. Volkman, K.O. Tokarski and K. Ernst (eds), *Social entrepreneurship and social business*, Wiesbaden: Springer Gabler Verlag.

Hyken, S. (2018a), Starbucks closes 8,000 stores for Racial Bias Training – is it enough? (www.forbes.com/sites/shephyken/2018/06/01/starbucks-closes-8000-stores-for-racial-bias-training-is-it-enough/?sh=25e0ddad2831).

Hyken, S. (2018b), Starbucks gets an A in crisis management, (www.forbes.com/sites/shephyken/2018/05/10/starbucks-gets-an-a-in-crisis-management/?sh=45f36cdc7998).

ICAC (1988), Independent Commission Against Corruption, NSW Australia, (www.icac.nsw.gov.au/about-corruption/what-is-corrupt-conduct/sections-7-8-and-9-of-the-icac-act).

ICLG (2022), Technology sourcing laws and regulations USA, (https://iclg.com/practice-areas/technology-sourcing-laws-and-regulations/usa).

ICNL (2022), FAQ: Corporate social responsibility in India, (www.icnl.org/wp-content/uploads/India-FAQ-3---Corporate-Social-Responsibility-FINAL.pdf).

IEF (2013), Club of Rome and ARC launch of ValuesQuest, (https://iefworld.org/node/658).

IFAC (2015), Accounting for sustainability – from sustainability to business resilience, (www.ifac.org/system/files/publications/files/IFACJ3441_Accounting_for_sustainability_FINALWEB.pdf).

ILO (2018), The Rana Plaza accident and its aftermath, (www.ilo.org/global/topics/geip/WCMS_614394/lang--en/index.htm).

ILO (2022a), Statistics on migrant workers, (https://ilostat.ilo.org/topics/labour-migration/).

ILO (2022b), Forced labour, modern slavery and human trafficking, (www.ilo.org/global/topics/forced-labour/lang--en/index.htm).

IME (2013), Global Food: Waste not, Want not, (www.imeche.org/docs/default-source/default-document-library/global-food---waste-not-want-not.pdf?sfvrsn=b3adce12_0).

Insights (2022), Novo Nordisk – key insights and patents, (https://insights.greyb.com/novo-nordisk-patents/).

IPBES (2019), Summary for policymakers of the global assessment report on biodiversity and ecosystem services of the Intergovernmental Science-Policy Platform on Biodiversity and Ecosystem Services, Bonn: IPBES Secretariat.

IPCC (2022), The Intergovernmental Panel on Climate Change, (www.ipcc.ch/).

IRS (2023), Transfer pricing, (www.irs.gov/businesses/international-businesses/transfer-pricing).

ISO 14001:2015 (updated 2021), Environmental management systems – requirements with guidance for use, (www.iso.org/standard/60857.html).

ISO 14005 (2019), Environmental management systems – guidelines for a flexible approach to phased implementation, (www.iso.org/standard/72333.html).

ISO 37001 (2016), Anti-bribery management systems, Geneva: International organization for standardization, (www.iso.org/files/live/sites/isoorg/files/store/en/PUB100396.pdf).

ISO 9001 (2015). What does ISO mean? Understanding ISO, (https://isoglobal.com.au/what-is-iso/).

Issa, T. and Pick, D. (2011), 'An interpretive mixed-methods analysis of ethics, spirituality and aesthetics in the Australian services sector', *Business Ethics*, 20(1), 45–58.

ITI (2023), Transfer pricing law in India, (https://incometaxindia.gov.in/pages/international-taxation/transfer-pricing.aspx).

Jackson, P. (2006), *Sacred hoops: Spiritual lessons of a hardwood warrior*, New York: Hyperion.

Jackson, P. and Delehanty, H. (2014), *Eleven rings: The soul of success*, London: Penguin Books.

Jaén, M.H., Reficco, E. and Berger, G. (2021), 'Does integrity matter in BOP ventures? The role of responsible leadership in inclusive supply chains', *Journal of Business Ethics*, 173(3): 467–88.

Jafari Nia, S., Abedi Jafari, H., Vakili, Y. and Ranjbar Kabutarkhani, M. (2022). 'Systematic review of conflict of interest studies in public administration'. *Public Integrity*, 1–16. doi: 10.1080/10999922.2022.2068901.

Jain, S. (2022), 'From *Jugaad* to *Jugalbandi*: Understanding the changing nature of Indian innovation', *Asia Pacific Journal of Management*, 39(1): 1–26.

Jaipur Rugs (2022a), About our founder, (www.jaipurrugs.com/au/about/our-founder).

Jaipur Rugs (2022b), About our company, (www.jaipurrugs.com/au/about/company).

Jaipur Rugs (2022c), About sustainability, (www.jaipurrugs.com/au/sustainability).

Jalsenjak, B. (2019), 'Ethical absolutism v ethical relativism'. In S. Idowu, R. Schmidpeter, N. Capaldi, L. Zu, M. Del Baldo and R. Abreu (eds), *Encyclopedia of sustainable management*, Cham: Springer, (https://doi.org/10.1007/978-3-030-02006-4_116-1).

Jamwal, A., Agrawal, R., Sharma, M., Kumar, V. and Kumar, S. (2021), 'Developing a sustainability framework for Industry 4.0', *Procedia CIRP*, 98: 430–35.

Jasper and Myrtle (2023), Nunu chocolate, (https://jasperandmyrtle.com.au/nunu-chocolate-from-bougainville/).

Jauregui, B. (2014), 'Provisional agency in India: *Jugaad* and legitimation of corruption', *Journal of the American Ethnology Society*, 41(1): 76–91.

Jecker, N.S. (2022), 'The dignity of work: An ethical argument against mandatory retirement', *Journal of Social Philosophy*, 54(2): 152–68.

Johnson, G., Scholes, K. and Whittington, R. (2005), *Exploring corporate strategy*, 7th edn, Harlow: Prentice Hall.

Joly, H. (2021), 'Creating a meaningful corporate purpose', *Harvard Business Review*, October, (https://hbr.org/2021/10/creating-a-meaningful-corporate-purpose).

Joly, H. (2022), 5 principles of purposeful leadership, *Harvard Business Review*, (https://hbr.org/2022/04/5-principles-of-purposeful-leadership).

Jones, C., Temouri, Y., Kirollos, K. and Du, J. (2023), 'Tax havens and emerging market multinationals: The role of property rights protection and economic freedom', *Journal of Business Research*, 155: 113373.

Jones, T.M. (1991), 'Ethical decision making by individuals in organisations: An issue-contingent model', *Academy of Management Review*, 16(2): 366–95.

Jones, T.M., Felps, W. and Bigley, G.A. (2007), 'Ethical theory and stakeholder-related decisions: The role of stakeholder culture', *Academy of Management Review*, 32(1): 137–55.

Jordan, N. (2020), Artificial intelligence is helping developing countries, (https://borgenproject.org/artificial-intelligence-is-helping-developing-countries/).

Joseph, C. and Haidt, J. (2007), 'The moral mind: How 5 sets of innate moral intuitions guide the development of many culture-specific virtues, and perhaps even modules'. In P. Carruthers, S. Laurence and S. Stich (eds), *The innate mind* (vol. 3), New York: Oxford University Press.

Jurberg, A. (2020), 11 celebrity endorsements gone wrong, (https://bettermarketing.pub/11-celebrity-endorsements-gone-wrong-dfa3dc24ff93).

Jurkiewicz, C.L. and Giacalone, R.A. (2004), 'A values framework for measuring the impact of workplace spirituality on organizational performance', *Journal of Business Ethics*, 49(2): 129–42.

Kahneman, D. (2011), *Thinking, fast and slow*, London: Penguin Books Ltd.

Kahneman, D. and Tversky, A. (1996), 'On the reality of cognitive illusions', *Psychological Review*, 103(3): 582–91.

Kaler, J. (2000), 'Reasons to be ethical: Self interest and ethical business', *Journal of Business Ethics*, 27(1/2): 161–73.

Kaplan, R.S. and Ramanna, K. (2021), 'Accounting for climate change', *Harvard Business Review*, November–December: 120–31.

Kaptein, M. (2020), 'Ethical climate and ethical culture'. In D.C. Poff and A.C. Michalos, (eds), *Encyclopedia of business and professional ethics*, Cham: Springer.

Karnani, A. (2007), 'The mirage of marketing to the bottom of the pyramid: How the private sector can help alleviate poverty', *California Management Review*, 49(4): 90–111.

Kayange, G.M. (2018), 'Rediscovering individual-based values in *Ubuntu* virtue ethics: Transforming corporate entities in post-colonial Africa'. In R. Oelofsen (ed), *An African path to a Global future* (Cultural heritage and contemporary change series, vol. II), Washington: African Philosophical Studies.

Kelemen, M. and Peltonen, T. (2001), 'Ethics, morality and the subject: The contribution of Zygmunt Bauman and Michel Faucault to "postmodern" business ethics', *Scandinavian Journal of Management*, 17: 151–66.

Keller, V. (2015), 'The business case for purpose', *Harvard Business Review – Analytical Services Report*: 1–15.

Kelton, E. (2022), 'Significant resolutions' of foreign bribery cases expected this year, (www.forbes.com/sites/erikakelton/2022/02/10/significant-resolutions-of-foreign-bribery-cases-expected-after-big-drop-in-2021/?sh=3019b86369e9).

Ketchell, M. (2022), Sustainable investment: Is it worth the hype? Here's what you need to know, (https://theconversation.com/sustainable-investment-is-it-worth-the-hype-heres-what-you-need-to-know-182533).

Khadem, N. (2019), Australia: Ansell says investigation into alleged Top Glove labour abuses underway, (www.business-humanrights.org/en/latest-news/australia-ansell-says-investigation-into-alleged-top-glove-labour-abuses-is-underway/).

Khandker, V. (2022), 'Two decades of the bottom of the pyramid research: Identifying the influencers, structure, and the evolution of the concept', *Management Review Quarterly*, 1–28. doi: 10.1007/s11301-022-00271-y.

Killian, L.J. (2021), 'Habermas and discourse ethics'. In E.Z. Taylor and P.F. Williams (eds), *The Routledge handbook of accounting ethics*, Abingdon: Routledge.

Kim, S. and Schifeling, T. (2022), 'Good Corp, Bad Corp, and the rise of B Corps: How market incumbents' diverse responses reinvigorate challengers', *Administrative Science Quarterly*, 67(3): 674-720.

King, L.A. and Hicks, J.A. (2021), 'The science of meaning in life', *Annual Review of Psychology*, 72(1): 561–84.

Kinicki, A. (2021), *Organizational behavior*, 3rd edn, New York: McGraw-Hill.

Kishan, S. and Bloomberg (2022), 'It's a whirligig': ESG pioneer expects shakeout for funds hyped by 'fairy dust', (https://fortune.com/2022/03/20/whirligig-esg-pioneer-expects-shakeout-for-funds-hyped-by-fairy-dust-russia-paul-clements-hunt-hairobi-blended-capital-group/).

Kitchener, K.S. (1984), 'Intuition, critical evaluation and ethical principles: The foundation for ethical decisions in counseling psychology', *The Counseling Psychologist*, 12(3): 43–55.

Klein, G. (2015). 'A naturalistic decision-making perspective on studying intuitive decision making', *Journal of Applied Research in Memory and Cognition*, 4(3): 164–8.

Ko, C., Ma, J., English, A.S. and Haney, M.H. (2017). 'How ethical leadership cultivates healthy guanxi to enhance OCB in China', *Journal of Human Resources*, 55(4): 408-29.

Köbis, N.C., van Prooijen, J., Righetti, F. and Van Lange, P.A. (2017), 'The road to bribery and corruption: Slippery slope or steep cliff?' *Psychological Science*, 28(3): 297–306.

Kohlberg, L. (1981), *The philosophy of moral development*, San Francisco, CA: Harper and Row.

Komesaroff, P.A., Kerridge, I. and Lipworth, W. (2019), 'Conflicts of interest: New thinking, new processes', *Internal Medicine Journal*, 49(5): 574–7.

KPMG (2014), 'The business codes of the Fortune Global 200: What the largest companies in the world say and do', (www.ethicsmanagement.info/content/The%20Business%20 codes%20of%20the%20Fortune%20Global%20200.pdf).

KPMG (2022), 'Richard Boele', (https://home.kpmg/au/en/home/contacts/b/richard-boele.html).

Krishnadas, R., Ravindran, R.D. and Nemperumalsamy, P. (2022), 'Dr. Govindappa Venkataswamy: Reimagining eye care in the third world – From provincial to planetary', *Indian Journal of Ophthalmology*, 70(5): 1450–52.

Kroeber, A.L., and Kluckhohn, C.K. (1952). *Culture: A critical review of concepts and definitions*, Cambridge, MA: Harvard University Press.

Kuwonu, F. (2019), Young Africans create green businesses, (www.un.org/africarenewal/ magazine/august-november-2019/young-africans-create-green-businesses).

Kuzior, A., Kettler, K. and Rąb, Ł. (2021), 'Digitalization of work and human resources processes as a way to create a sustainable and ethical organization', *Energies*, 15(1): 172.

Kyoto Protocol (2022), What is the Kyoto Protocol?, (https://unfccc.int/kyoto_protocol).

Lakshman, C., Ramaswami, A., Alas, R., Kabongo, J.F. and Rajendran Pandian, J. (2014), 'Ethics trumps culture? A cross-national study of business leader responsibility for downsizing and CSR perceptions', *Journal of Business Ethics*, 125(1): 101–19.

Lakwo, T., Oguttu, D., Ukety, T., Post, R. and Bakajika, D. (2020), 'Onchocerciasis elimination: Progress and challenges', *Research and Reports in Tropical Medicine*, 11: 81–95.

Land, F., Amjad, U. and Nolas, S.M. (2007), 'The ethics of knowledge management', *International Journal of Knowledge Management*, 3(1): 1–9.

Landes, D.S. (1998), *The wealth and poverty of nations: Why some are so rich and some so poor*, New York: W.W. Norton & Company.

Lane, A.B. and Devin, B. (2018), 'Operationalizing stakeholder engagement in CSR: A process approach', *Corporate Social Responsibility and Environmental Management*, 25(3): 267–80.

Lanier, J.A. (2019), Man without numbers, (www.raycandersonfoundation.org/articles/math-without-the-numbers).

Lasserre, P. (2018), *Global strategic management*, 4th edn, London: Palgrave Macmillan.

Laszlo, C., Cooperrider, D. and Fry, R. (2020), 'Global challenges as opportunity to transform business for good', *Sustainability*, 12(19): 8053.

Latapí Agudelo, M.A., Jóhannsdóttir, L. and Davídsdóttir, B. (2019), 'A literature review of the history and evolution of corporate social responsibility', *International Journal of Corporate Social Responsibility*, 4(1): 1–23.

LaVan, H. and Martin, W.M. (2021). 'Ethical challenges in workplace bullying and harassment: Creating ethical awareness and sensitivity'. In P. D'Cruz, E. Noronha,

G. Notelaers and C. Rayner (eds), *Concepts, Approaches and Methods*, Singapore: Springer, (https://doi.org/10.1007/978-981-13-0134-6_6).

Lawrenz, J. (2021), 'Confucius, Aristotle, and the Golden Mean: A diptych on ethical virtues', *The European Legacy*, 26(2): 149–69.

Lazarova, M., Caligiuri, P., Collings, D.G. and De Cieri, H. (2023), 'Global work in a rapidly changing world: Implications for MNEs and individuals', *Journal of World Business*, 58(1): 101365.

Leadership Now (2013), Phil Jackson's 11 principles of mindful leadership, (www.leadershipnow.com/leadingblog/2013/06/phil_jacksons_11_principles_of.html).

Leavy, B. (2021), 'Interview Hubert Joly: The new capitalism formula – purpose first, people at the centre, then profits', *Strategy & Leadership*, 49(3): 11–17.

LeBaron, G., Edwards, R., Hunt, T., Sempéré, C. and Kyritsis, P. (2022), 'The ineffectiveness of CSR: Understanding garment company commitments to living wages in global supply chains', *New Political Economy*, 27(1): 99–115.

Lebron, C.J. (2019), 'Without the loving strains of commitment'. In D. Satz and A. Lever (eds), *Ideas that matter: Democracy, justice, rights*, Oxford: Oxford Scholarship Online. doi: 10.1093/oso/9780190904951.001.0001.

Ledoux, K. (2015), 'Understanding compassion fatigue: Understanding compassion', *Journal of Advanced Nursing*, 71(19): 2041–50.

Lee, J.M., Paik, Y., Vance, C., Li, D., and Groves, K. (2022), 'The evolution of business ethics in China and the United States: Convergence, divergence, or crossvergence?' *Management and Organization Review*, 18(4): 658–85.

Lee, J.S. and Kwak, D.H. (2016). 'Consumers' responses to public figures' transgression: Moral reasoning strategies and implications for endorsed brands', *Journal of Business Ethics*, 137(1): 101–13.

Lee, T.H. (2022), 'CSR communication in stigmatized industries'. In A. O'Connor (ed), *The Routledge handbook of corporate social responsibility communication*, New York: Routledge.

LEGO (n.d.a), LEGO Group to invest up to US$400 million over three years to accelerate sustainability efforts, (www.lego.com/en/us/aboutus/news/2020/september/sustainability).

LEGO (n.d.b), LEGO history – About us, (www.lego.com/en/us/aboutus/lego-group/the-lego-group-history).

LEGO (2022), Find a LEGO store (www.lego.com/en-us/stores/directory).

Lehnert, K., Park, Y., and Singh, N. (2015), 'Research note and review of the empirical ethical decision-making literature: Boundary conditions and extensions', *Journal of Business Ethics*, 129(1): 195–219.

Lehrer, J. (2009), *How we decide*, Boston, MA: Houghton Mifflin Harcourt.

Lepak, D.P. and Colakoglu, S. (2006), 'Ethics and strategic human resource management'. In J.R. Deckop (ed), *Human resource management ethics*, Greenwich, CT: Information Age Publishing.

Leung, T.C.H. and Snell, R.S. (2017), 'Attraction or distraction? Corporate social responsibility in Macao's gambling industry', *Journal of Business Ethics*, 145(3): 637–58.

Lewis, S.L. and Maslin, M.A. (2015), 'Defining the Anthropocene', *Nature*, 519: 171–80.

Ley, M. (2023), 'Care ethics and the future of work: A different voice', *Philosophy and Technology*, 36(1): 7.

Li, T., Wang, K., Sueyoshi, T. and Wang, D.D. (2021), 'ESG: Research progress and future prospects', *Sustainability*, 13(21): 1–28.

Lindgreen, A., Maon, F., Reast, J. and Yani-De-Soriano, M. (2012), 'Corporate social responsibility in controversial industry sectors', *Journal of Business Ethics*, 110(4): 393–5.

Lindorff, M., Prior Jonson, E. and McGuire, L. (2012), 'Strategic corporate social responsibility in controversial industry sectors: The social value of harm minimisation', *Journal of Business Ethics*, 110(4): 457–67.

Linehan, C. and O'Brien, E. (2017), 'From tell-tale signs to irreconcilable struggles: The value of emotion in exploring the ethical dilemmas of human resource professionals', *Journal of Business Ethics*, 141(4): 763–77.

Liou, R.S. and Rao-Nicholson, R. (2021), 'Multinational enterprises and Sustainable Development Goals: A foreign subsidiary perspective on tackling wicked problems', *Journal of International Business Policy*, 4(1): 136–51.

Liu, C.H. and Robertson, P.J. (2011), 'Spirituality in the workplace: Theory and measurement', *Journal of Management Inquiry*, 20(1), 35–50.

Liute, A. and De Giacomo, M.R. (2022), 'The environmental performance of UK-based B Corp companies: An analysis based on the Triple Bottom Line approach', *Business Strategy and the Environment*, 31(3): 810–27.

Livnat, I. and Villa Braslavsky, P. (2020), 'Who takes care of "care"?' *Gender, Work, and Organization*, 27(2): 270–77.

Lobschat, L., Mueller, B., Eggers, F., Brandimarte, L., Diefenbach, S., Kroschke, M. and Wirtz, J. (2021), 'Corporate digital responsibility', *Journal of Business Research*, 122: 875–88.

Lopez Jimenez, D., Dittmar, E.C., Vargas, P. and Jenny, P. (2020), 'Self-regulation of sexist digital advertising: From ethics to law', *Journal of Business Ethics*, 171(4): 709–18.

Lovelock, J.E. (1972), 'Gaia as seen through the atmosphere', *Atmospheric Environment*, 6(8): 578-80.

Luo, Y., Zhang, H. and Bu, J. (2019), 'Developed country MNEs investing in developing economies', *Journal of International Business Studies*, 50(4): 633–67.

Lyne, I. (2020), 'Bottling water differently, and sustaining the water commons? Social innovation through water service franchising in Cambodia', *Water Alternatives*, 13(3): 731–51.

Maak, T. and Pless, N.M. (2006), 'Responsible leadership in a stakeholder society: A relational perspective', *Journal of Business Ethics*, 66(1): 99–115.

Maak, T. and Pless, N.M. (2019), 'Responsible leadership: Reconciling people, purpose, and profit'. In S. Kempster, T. Maak and K. Parry (eds), *Good dividends: Responsible leadership of business purpose*, London: Routledge.

MacDonald, D.A. (2000), 'Spirituality: Description, measurement, and relation to the five factor model of personality', *Journal of Personality*, 68(1): 153–97.

MacDonald, D.A., Friedman, H.L., Brewczynski, J., Holland, D., Salagame, K.K.K., Mohan, K.K., Gubrij, Z.O. and Cheong, H.W. (2015), 'Spirituality as a scientific construct: Testing its universality across cultures and languages', *PloS One*, 10(3): e0117701.

MacIntyre, A. (2007), *After virtue*, 3rd edn, Notre Dame, IN: University of Notre Dame Press.

Mackey, J. and Sisodia, R. (2014), *Conscious capitalism*, Boston, MA: Harvard Business School Publishing.

Mackintosh, J. (2022), Why the sustainable investment craze is flawed, (www.wsj.com/articles/why-the-sustainable-investment-craze-is-flawed-11642865789).

Madanaguli, A., Srivastava, S., Ferraris, A. and Dhir, A. (2022), 'Corporate social responsibility and sustainability in the tourism sector: A systematic literature review and future outlook', *Sustainable Development*, 30(3): 447–61.

Mahmud, N.M., Mohamed, I.S. and Arshad, R. (2022), 'The supply-side of corruption: A review of scenario, causes and prevention measure', *Journal of Financial Crime*, 29(1): 34–44.

Mair, J. and Martí, I. (2006), 'Social entrepreneurship research: A source of explanation, prediction, and delight', *Journal of World Business*, 41(1): 36–44.

Maitland, I. (2010), 'A theory of ethical business cycle', *Business Ethics Quarterly*, 20(4): 749–50.

Maiya, U. (2011), 'Critical issues in downsizing in India', *Review of Management*, 1(2), (www. researchgate.net/publication/344689841_Critical_Issues_in_Downsizing_in_India).

Majumdar, R. (2022), India woos Africa with trade, tech, investment, (www.dw.com/en/india-woos-africa-with-trade-tech-and-investment/a-62770071).

Malagueno, R., Pillalamarri, S., Jose Rezende, A. and Botelho da Costa, M. (2020), 'The effects of length of service and ethical ideologies on moral development and behavioral intentions: A study among Brazilian public sector tax auditors', *Journal of Applied Accounting Research*, 21(4): 589–613.

Malhotra, R. (2011), *Being different*, Noida: Harper Collins Publishers.

Malnight, T.W., Buche, I. and Dhanaraj, C. (2019), 'Put purpose at the core of your strategy', *Harvard Business Review*, September–October: 70–79.

Mangafić, J. and Veselinović, L. (2020), 'The determinants of corruption at the individual level: Evidence from Bosnia-Herzegovina', *Economic Research – Ekonomska Istraživanja*, 33(1): 2670–91.

Mannava, S., Borah, R.R. and Shamanna, B.R. (2022), 'Current estimates of the economic burden of blindness and visual impairment in India: A cost of illness study', *Indian Journal of Ophthalmology*, 70(6): 2141–5.

Manzano, J.A.F. (2021), 'We the peoples: A Rawlsian perspective of international justice', *Journal of Leadership, Accountability and Ethics*, 18(3): 122–32.

Marano, V., Tashman, P. and Kostova, T. (2017), 'Escaping the iron cage: Liabilities of origin and CSR reporting of emerging market multinational enterprises', *Journal of International Business Studies*, 48(3): 386–408.

Marmo, M. and Bandiera, R. (2022), 'Modern slavery as the new moral asset for the production and reproduction of state-corporate harm', *Journal of White Collar and Corporate Crime*, 3(2): 64–75.

Marques, J. (2010), 'Towards greater consciousness in the 21st century workplace: How Buddhist practices fit in', *Journal of Business Ethics*, 92(2): 211–25.

Marques, J. (2019), *The Routledge companion to management and workplace spirituality*, 1st edn, London: Routledge.

Marriott, H. (2021), The truth about fast fashion: Can you tell how ethical your clothing is by its price? (www.theguardian.com/fashion/2021/jul/29/the-truth-about-fast-fashion-can-you-tell-how-ethical-your-clothing-is-by-its-price).

Martin, G. (1998), 'Why should business be ethical?' *Business & Professional Ethics Journal*, 17(4): 39–60.

Martin, K. (2019), 'Ethical implications and accountability of algorithms', *Journal of Business Ethics*, 160: 835–50.

Martin, K.D., Cullen, J.B., Johnson, J.L. and Parboteeah, K.P. (2007), 'Deciding to bribe: A cross-level analysis of firm and home country influences on bribery activity', *Academy of Management Journal*, 50(6): 1401–22.

Mathews, J.A. (2006), 'Dragon multinationals: New players in the 21st century globalization', *Asia Pacific Journal of Management*, 23(1): 5–27.

Mathews, J.A. (2017), 'Dragon multinationals powered by linkage, leverage and learning: A review and development', *Asia Pacific Journal of Management*, 34(4): 769–75.

Matten, D. and Crane, A. (2005), 'Corporate citizenship: Towards an extended theoretical conceptualization', *Academy of Management Review*, 30(1): 166–79.

Matteson, M. and Metivier, C. (2023) Case: The Ford Pinto, (https://philosophia.uncg.edu/phi361-matteson/module-1-why-does-business-need-ethics/case-the-ford-pinto/).

MCA (2022), HAQ on CSR cell, Ministry of Corporate Affairs, Government of India, (www.mca.gov.in/MinistryV2/faq+on+csr+cell.html).

McGee, R.W. (2005), Ethical issues in outsourcing accounting and tax services, (https://papers.ssrn.com/sol3/papers.cfm?abstract_id=648766).

MDMSB (2022), Mann Deshi Sahakari Bank, (https://manndeshibank.com/).

MEA (2022), Part III Fundamental Rights, (www.mea.gov.in/Images/pdf1/Part3.pdf)

Meadows, D., Randers, J. and Meadows, D. (2005), *Limits to growth: The 30-year update*, London: Earthscan.

Meadows, D.H., Meadows, D.L., Randers, J. amd BehrensIII, W.W. (1972), *The limits to growth: A report for the Club of Rome's project on the predicament of mankind*, New York: Universe Books.

Medibank (2011), Sick at work: The cost of presenteeism to your business and the economy, (www.medibank.com.au/content/dam/client/documents/pdfs/sick_at_work.pdf).

Mehmood, W., Ahmad, A., Aman-Ullah, A. and Mohd-Rashid, R. (2022), 'Modern slavery: A literature review using bibliometric analysis and the nexus of governance', *Journal of Public Affairs*. doi: 10.1002/pa.2832.

Men, C., Fong, P.S.W., Huo, W., Zhong, J., Jia, R. and Luo, J. (2020), 'Ethical leadership and knowledge hiding: A moderated mediation model of psychological safety and mastery climate', *Journal of Business Ethics*, 166(3): 461–72.

Mendly-Zambo, Z., Raphael, D. and Taman, A. (2021), 'Take the money and run: How food banks became complicit with Walmart Canada's hunger producing employment practices', *Critical Public Health*, 33(1): 60–71.

Menghaney, L. (2013), 'How India brought cheap HIV drugs to Africa', *BMJ*, 347(5): 4439-f7013.

Microsoft (2022), Achieving more – 2022 impact summary, (https://query.prod.cms.rt.microsoft.com/cms/api/am/binary/RE5b9S0).

Mill, J.S. (1863). Chapter 2: What utilitarianism is, (www.utilitarianism.net/books/utilitarianism-john-stuart-mill/2).

Miller, C., Ettridge, K., Wakefield, M., Pettigrew, S., Coveney, J., Roder, D., Durkin, S., Wittert, G., Martin, J. and Dono, J. (2020), 'Consumption of sugar-sweetened beverages, juice, artificially-sweetened soda and bottled water: An Australian population study', *Nutrients*, 12(3): 817.

Miller, W.C. (2011), 'Spiritual-based leadership'. In L. Zsolnai (ed), *Spirituality and ethics in management*, New York: Springer.

Mintz, S. (2004), 'The ethical dilemmas of outsourcing', *The CPA Journal*, 74(3): 6–9.

Mirvis, P. and Googins, B. (2017), *The new business of business: Innovating for a better world*, New York: The Conference Board, GT-V2N1.

Mirvis, P., Herrera, M.E.B., Googins, B. and Albareda, L. (2016), 'Corporate social innovation: How firms learn to innovate for the greater good', *Journal of Business Research*, 69(11): 5014–21.

Miska, C. and Mendenhall, M.E. (2018), 'Responsible leadership: A mapping of extant research and future directions', *Journal of Business Ethics*, 148(1): 117–34.

Mitchell, R.K., Agle, B.R. and Wood, D.J. (1997), 'Towards a theory of stakeholder identification and salience: Defining the principle of who and what really counts', *Academy of Management Review*, 22(4): 853–86.

Mitchell, R.K., Robinson, R.E., Marin, A., Lee, J.H. and Randolph, A.F. (2013), 'Spiritual identity, stakeholder attributes, and family business workplace spirituality stakeholder salience', *Journal of Management, Spirituality & Religion*, 10(3): 215-52.

Mitroff, I.I. (2003), 'Do not promote religion under the guise of spirituality', *Organization*, 10(2): 375–82.

Mitroff, I.I. and Denton, E.A. (1999), *A spiritual audit of corporate America: A hard look at spirituality, religion, and values in the workplace*, San Francisco, CA: Jossey-Bass Publishers.

Mixon, P. (2010), Los Angeles Lakers' Phil Jackson: The real secret behind the zen, (https://bleacherreport.com/articles/538530-los-angeles-lakers-phil-jackson-the-real-secret-behind-the-zen).

Moberg, D. and Seabright, M. (2000), 'The development of moral imagination', *Business Ethics Quarterly*, 10: 845–84.

Moberg, D.J. (2000), 'Role models and moral exemplars: How do employees acquire virtues by observing others?' *Business Ethics Quarterly*, 10(3): 675–96.

Moberg, D.J. (2007), 'Practical wisdom and business ethics – Presidential address to the Society of Business Ethics Atlanta, August 2006', *Business Ethics Quarterly*, 17(3): 535–61.

Moberg, D.J. and Calkins, M. (2001), 'Reflection in business ethics: Insights from St. Ignatius' spiritual exercises', *Journal of Business Ethics*, 33(3): 257–70.

Moore, D.A., Loewenstein, G., Cain, D.M., Bazerman, M.H. (2005), 'Introduction'. In *Conflicts of interest: Challenges and solutions in business, law, medicine, and public policy*, Cambridge: Cambridge University Press.

Moore, G. (2013), 'Re-imagining the morality of management'. In H. Harris, G. Wijesinghe and S. McKenzie (eds), *The heart of the good institution*, Dordrecht: Springer.

Morsing, M., Oswald, D. and Stormer, S. (2018), 'The ongoing dynamics of integrating sustainability into business practice: The case of Novo Nordisk A/S'. In G.G. Lenssen and N.C. Smith (eds), *Managing sustainable business*, Dordrecht: Springer.

Moss, T. (2021), LEGO builds on its position as world's no.1 toy maker, (www.wsj.com/articles/lego-builds-on-its-position-as-worlds-no-1-toy-maker-11632843755).

Moumakwa, P.C. (2011), The Botswana Kgotla system: A mechanism for traditional conflict resolution in modern Botswana – case study of the Kanye Kgotla. Tromsø: Faculty of Humanities, University of Tromsø.

MSCI (2022), The evolution of ESG investing, (www.msci.com/esg-101-what-is-esg/evolution-of-esg-investing).

MSR-AOM (2023), Management, Spirirtuality & Religion, (https://msr.aom.org/home).

Mueller, B. (2022), 'Corporate digital responsibility', *Business and Information Systems Engineering*, 64(5), 689–700.

Muff, K., Delacoste, C. and Dyllick, T. (2022, 'Responsible leadership competencies in leaders around the world: Assessing stakeholder engagement, ethics and values, systems thinking and innovation competencies in leaders around the world', *Corporate Social Responsibility and Environmental Management*, 29(1): 273–92.

Mukherjee, S. and Zsolnai, L. (2022), *Global perspectives on Indian spirituality and management*, Singapore: Springer.

Muller, V.C. (2020), Ethics of artificial intelligence and robotics, (https://plato.stanford.edu/entries/ethics-ai/?utm_source=summari).

Musa, M.A., Sukor, M.E.A., Ismail, M.N. and Elias, M.R.F. (2020), 'Islamic business ethics and practices of Islamic banks', *Journal of Islamic Accounting and Business Research*, 11(5): 1009–31.

Muthuri, J.N. and Gilbert, V. (2011), 'An institutional analysis of corporate social responsibility in Kenya', *Journal of Business Ethics*, 98(3): 467–83.

Naciti, V. (2019), 'Corporate governance and board of directors: The effect of a board composition on firm sustainability performance', *Journal of Cleaner Production*, 237: 117727.

Nadler, S. and Shapiro, L. (2021), *When bad thinking happens to good people: How philosophy can save us from ourselves*, Princeton, NJ: Princeton University Press.

Nardella, G., Brammer, S. and Surdu, I. (2020), 'Shame on who? The effects of corporate irresponsibility and social performance on organizational reputation', *British Journal of Management*, 31(1): 5–23.

Narvaez, D. (2010), 'Moral complexity: The fatal attraction of truthiness and the importance of mature moral functioning', *Perspectives on Psychological Science*, 5(2): 163–81.

Narvaez, D. and Lapsley, D.K. (2009), 'Moral identity, moral functioning, and the development of character'. In B.H. Ross, D. Bartels, C. Bauman, L. Skitka and D.L. Medin (eds), *The psychology of learning and motivation*, vol. 50, Burlington, VT: Academic Press.

Nathanson, S. (2022), 'Act and rule utilitarianism'. In J. Fieser and B. Dowden (eds), *Internet encyclopedia of philosophy*, (https://iep.utm.edu/util-a-r/#H2).

Naude, P. (2019), 'Decolonising knowledge: Can *Ubuntu* ethics save US from coloniality?' *Journal of Business Ethics*, 159(1): 23–37.

Nayar, J. (2021), Not so green technology, (https://hir.harvard.edu/not-so-green-technology-the-complicated-legacy-of-rare-earth-mining/).

NBES (2022), The 2021 national business ethics survey, Ethics Resource Center, (www.ethics.org/global-business-ethics-survey/).

Newenham-Kahindi, A. (2009), 'The transfer of *Ubuntu* and *Indaba* business models abroad', *International Journal of Cross Cultural Management*, 9(1): 87–108.

New York Times (2020), How Boeing's responsibility in a deadly crash 'got buried', (www.nytimes.com/2020/01/20/business/boeing-737-accidents.html).

Ng, E.S. and Sears, G.J. (2020), 'Walking the talk on diversity: CEO beliefs, moral values, and the implementation of workplace diversity practices', *Journal of Business Ethics*, 164(3): 437–50.

Nicholson, J. and Kurucz, E. (2019), 'Relational leadership for sustainability: Building an ethical framework from the moral theory of ethics of care', *Journal of Business Ethics*, 156(1): 25–43.

Nicolaides, A. (2009), 'Business ethics in Africa', *Journal of Contemporary Management*, 6: 490–501.

Nielsen, R. (2021), 'Business ethics pioneers: Richard Nielsen', *Business & Professional Ethics Journal*, 40(3), 337–49.

NovoNordisk (2022), Our position on intellectual property and patenting, (www.novonordisk.com/sustainable-business/access-and-affordability/intellectual-property-rights-and-patenting-position.html).

NPR (2011), Heroes of the Taj Hotel: Why they risked their lives, (www.npr.org/2011/12/23/144184623/mumbai-terror-attacks-the-heroes-of-the-taj-hotel).

Nussbaum, M. (2001), *Upheavals of thought: The intelligence of emotions*, New York: Cambridge University Press.

Nzelibe, C.O. (1986), 'The evolution of African management thought', *International Studies of Management and Organization*, 16(2): 6–16.

O'Boyle, E.J. (2002), 'An ethical decision-making process for computing professionals', *Ethics and Information Technology*, 4(4): 267–77.

Obradovich, N., Powers, W., Cebrian, M. and Rahwan, I. (2019), Beware corporate 'machinewashing' of AI, MIT Media Labs via the *Boston Globe*, (www.media.mit.edu/articles/beware-corporate-machinewashing-of-ai/).

Obregon, S.L., Lopes, L.F.D., Kaczam, F., da Veiga, C.P. and da Silva, W.V. (2022), 'Religiosity, spirituality and work: A systematic literature review and research directions', *Journal of Business Ethics*, 179(2): 573–95.

Ocean Tomo (2022), Intangible asset market value study, (www.oceantomo.com/intangible-asset-market-value-study/).

OECD (2003), *Managing conflict of interest in the public service: OECD guidelines and country experiences*, Paris: OECD, (www.oecd.org/gov/ethics/48994419.pdf).

OECD (2011), OECD guidelines for multinational enterprises, (www.oecd.org/daf/inv/mne/48004323.pdf).

OECD (2022a), Anti-bribery convention, (www.oecd.org/corruption/oecdantibriberyconvention.htm).

OECD (2022b), Transfer pricing, (www.oecd.org/tax/transfer-pricing/oecd-transfer-pricing-guidelines-for-multinational-enterprises-and-tax-administrations-20769717.htm).

O'Fallon, M.J. and Butterfield, K.D. (2005), 'A review of the empirical ethical decision-making literature 1996–2003', *Journal of Business Ethics*, 59(4): 375–413.

Offyoga (2021), Why companies like Intel, Aetna and Google are investing in employee mindfulness training programs, (www.offyoga.com/blog/2021/1/6/why-companies-invest-in-mindfulness-training-programs).

Ogunyemi, K. (2019), 'Spirituality, Responsibility, and Integrity'. In J. Marques (ed), *The Routledge companion to management and workplace Spirituality*, New York: Routledge.

OHCHR (2022), Countries (www.ohchr.org/en/countries).

OHCHR (2023), International standards – Special rapporteur on freedom of religion or belief, (www.ohchr.org/en/special-procedures/sr-religion-or-belief/international-standards).

Okudaira, H., Takizawa, M. and Yamanouchi, K. (2022), *Does employee downsizing work? Evidence from product innovation at manufacturing plants*, Tokyo: Research Institute of Economy, Trade and Industry (RIETI).

Olam (2023), We are imagining global agriculture, (www.olamgroup.com/).

Oliveira, M., Curado, C. and Garcia, P.S. (2021), 'Knowledge hiding and knowledge hoarding: A systematic literature review', *Knowledge and Process Management*, 28(3): 277–94.

Ombudsman (2017), Conflict of interest guidelines, Office of the Commonwealth Ombudsman, (www.ombudsman.gov.au/__data/assets/pdf_file/0030/29919/Conflict-of-Interest-Guidelines-September-2017.pdf).

Orlitzky, M., Schmidt, F.L. and Rynes, S.L. (2003), 'Corporate social and financial performance: A meta-analysis', *Organization Studies*, 24(3): 403–41.

Orlitzky, M., Siegel, D.S. and Waldman, D.A. (2011), 'Strategic corporate social responsibility and environmental sustainability', *Business & Society*, 50(1): 6–27.

Ortega-Liston, R. (2006), 'Public servants as moral exemplars for business, law, higher education managed health care and the citizenry', *Journal of Public Management and Social Policy*, 12(1): 77–82.

Orth, U.R., Hoffmann, S. and Nickel, K. (2019). 'Moral decoupling feels good and makes buying counterfeits easy', *Journal of Business Research*, 98: 117–25.

Otaye-Ebede, L., Shaffakat, S. and Foster, S. (2020), 'A multilevel model examining the relationships between workplace spirituality, ethical climate and outcomes: A social cognitive theory perspective', *Journal of Business Ethics*, 166(3): 611–26.

Oxford Insights (2021), Government AI readiness index 2021, (https://static1.squarespace.com/static/58b2e92c1e5b6c828058484e/t/61ead0752e7529590e98d35f/1642778757117/Government_AI_Readiness_21.pdf).

Paine, L.S. (1994), 'Law, ethics, and managerial judgment', *The Journal of Legal Studies Education*, 12(2): 153–70.

Palazzo, G.S. and Scherer, A.G. (2006), 'Corporate legitimacy as deliberation: A communicative framework', *Journal of Business Ethics*, 66(1): 71–88.

Papaleontiou-Louca, E., Esmailnia, S. and Thoma, N. (2022), 'A critical review of Maslow's theory of spirituality', *Journal of Spirituality in Mental Health*, 24(4): 327–43.

Pardales, M.J. (2002), 'So, how did you arrive at that decision? Connecting moral imagination and moral judgement', *Journal of Moral Education*, 31(4): 423–37.

Park, B.I., Hong, S.J. and Xiao, S.S. (2021), 'Institutional pressure and MNC compliance to prevent bribery: Empirical examinations in South Korea and China', *Asian Business & Management*, 21: 623–56.

Parsi, N. (2017), Workplace diversity and inclusivity gets innovative, (www.shrm.org/hr-today/news/hr-magazine/0217/pages/disrupting-diversity-in-the-workplace.aspx).

Patagonia (2022a), Don't buy this jacket, (www.patagonia.com/stories/dont-buy-this-jacket-black-friday-and-the-new-york-times/story-18615.html).

Patagonia (2022b), Worn wear, (www.patagonia.com.au/pages/wornwear).

Patagonia (2022c), Company history, (www.patagonia.com/company-history/ retrieved).

Peltier-Rivest, D. (2018), 'A model for preventing corruption', *Journal of Financial Crime*, 25(2): 545–61.

Peng, M.W. (2022), *Global strategy*, 5th edn, Boston, MA: Cengage.

Perez, L., Hunt, V., Samandari, H., Nutall, R. and Biniek, K. (2022), Does ESG really matter – and why? (www.mckinsey.com/capabilities/sustainability/our-insights/does-esg-really-matter-and-why).

Perkins, T. (2019), The fight to stop Nestle from taking America's water to sell in plastic bottles, (www.theguardian.com/environment/2019/oct/29/the-fight-over-water-how-nestle-dries-up-us-creeks-to-sell-water-in-plastic-bottles).

Pesqué-Cela, V., Li, J. and Kim, Y.K. (2022), 'Overcoming the liability of foreignness in US capital markets: The case of Alibaba and Coupang', *Asia Pacific Business Review*, 29(2): 323–49.

PEW (2015), World population by income, (www.pewresearch.org/global/interactives/global-population-by-income/).

Philippe, D. and Durand, R. (2011), 'The impact of norm-conforming behaviours on firm reputation', *Strategic Management Journal*, 32: 969–93.

Phillips, R. (1997), 'Stakeholder theory and a principle of fairness', *Business Ethics Quarterly*, 7(1): 51–66.

Phillips, R., Freeman, R.E. and Wicks, A.C. (2003), 'What stakeholder theory is not', *Business Ethics Quarterly*, 13(4): 479–502.

Phills, J.A., Deiglmeier, K. and Miller, D.T. (2008), 'Rediscovering social innovation', *Stanford Social Innovation Review*, 6(4): 34–43.

Pirsig, R.M. (1974/1981), *Zen and the art of motorcycle maintenance*, London: Corgi.

Pitron, G. (2020), *The rare metals war: The dark side of clean energy and digital technologies*, Melbourne: Scribe Publications.

Pizarro, D.A. and Bloom, P. (2003), 'The intelligence of the moral intuitions: A comment on Haidt (2001)', *Psychological Review*, 110(1): 193–6.

Pless, N.M. (2007), 'Understanding responsible leadership: Role identity and motivational drivers', *Journal of Business Ethics*, 74(4): 437–56.

Pless, N.M. and Maak, T. (2009), 'Responsible leaders as agents of world benefit', *Journal of Business Ethics*, 85(1): 3-13.

Pless, N.M. and Maak, T. (2011), 'Responsible leadership: Pathways to the future', *Journal of Business Ethics*, 98(suppl 1): 59–71.

Pless, N.M., Maak, T. and Stahl, G.K. (2011), 'Developing responsible global leaders through international service-learning programs', *Academy of Management Learning & Education*, 10(2): 237–60.

Pless, N.M., Maak, T. and Waldman, D.A. (2012), 'Different approaches towards doing the right thing: Mapping the responsibility orientations of leaders', *Academy of Management Perspectives*, 26(4): 51–65.

Pless, N.M., Sengupta, A., Wheeler, M.A. and Maak, T. (2022), 'Responsible leadership and the reflective CEO: Resolving stakeholder conflict by imagining what could be done', *Journal of Business Ethics*, 180(1): 313–37.

PoCA (2018), The Prevention of Corruption (Amendment) Act, 2018, Ministry of Law and Justice, India, (www.egazette.nic.in/WriteReadData/2018/187644.pdf).

Poore, J. and Nemecek, T. (2018), 'Reducing food's environmental impacts through producers and consumers', *Science*, 360(6392): 987–92.

Popwell, K. (2020), 'Spiritualism and the resurgence of fake news'. In K. Dalkir and R. Katz (eds), *Navigating fake news, alternative facts, and misinformation in a post-truth world*, Pennsylvania: IGI Global, (DOI: 10.4018/978-1-7998-2543-2).

Porter, M.E. and Kramer, M.R. (2011), 'Creating shared value: How to reinvent capitalism and unleash a wave of innovation and growth', *Harvard Business Review*, 89: 62–77.

Posadas, S.C., Tarquinio, L. and Rea, M.A. (2020), 'Political corporate social responsibility and the role of companies: Evidence from Novo Nordisk'. In V. Mauerhofer, D. Rupo and L. Tarquino (eds), *Sustainability and law*, Cham: Springer International Publishing.

Potts, N. (2011), 'Marx and the crisis', *Capital & Class*, 35(3): 455–73.

Pozo-Gonzalo, C. (2021), Demand for rare-earth metals is skyrocketing, so we're creating a safer, cleaner way to recover them from old phones and laptops, (https://theconversation.com/demand-for-rare-earth-metals-is-skyrocketing-so-were-creating-a-safer-cleaner-way-to-recover-them-from-old-phones-and-laptops-141360).

Prabhu, J. and Jain, S. (2015), 'Innovation and entrepreneurship in India: Understanding *Jugaad*', *Asia Pacific Journal of Management*, 32: 843–68.

Prahalad, C.K. (2005), *The fortune at the bottom of the pyramid: Eradicating poverty through profits*, Upper Saddle River, NJ: Pearson Education Inc.

Prahalad, C.K. and Hammond, A. (2002), 'Serving the world's poor, profitably', *Harvard Business Review*, 80(9), 48–124.

Prahalad, C.K. and Hart, S. (2002), 'The fortune at the bottom of the pyramid', *Strategy + Business*, 26(2), (www.strategy-business.com/article/11518).

Pratt, S. and Tolkach, D. (2022), 'Ethical-decision making of "flights to nowhere" passengers in the COVID-19 and climate change era', *Current Issues in Tourism*, 26(5): 735–51.

Press (2018), Starbucks to close stores nationwide for racial bias education, (https://stories.starbucks.com/press/2018/starbucks-to-close-stores-nationwide-for-racial-bias-education-may-29/).

PRI (2022a), ESG – a brief history of its development, (https://carbon-view.com/esg-a-brief-history-of-its-development-part-1/).

PRI (2022b), What is responsible investment? (www.unpri.org/an-introduction-to-responsible-investment/what-is-responsible-investment/4780.article).

Price, T.L. and Hicks, D.A. (2006), 'A framework for a general theory of leadership ethics', In G.R. Goethals and G.L. Sorenson (eds), *The quest for a general theory of leadership*, Cheltenham, UK: Edward Elgar Publishing.

Provis, C. (2013), 'Judgement, virtue and social practice'. In H. Harris, G. Wijesinghe and S. McKenzie (eds), *The heart of the good institution*, Dordrecht: Springer.

Provis, C. (2017a), 'Confucianism, virtue, and wisdom', in A.J.G. Sison, G.R. Beabout and I. Ferrero (eds), *Handbook of virtue ethics in business and management*, Dordrecht: Springer.

Provis, C. (2017b), 'Intuition, analysis and reflection in business ethics', *Journal of Business Ethics*, 140(1): 5–15.

Provis C. (2017c), 'Modern business and the doctrine of the mean', *Research in Ethical Issues in Organizations*, 18: 115–30.

Provis, C. (2019), 'Business ethics, Confucianism and the different faces of ritual', *Journal of Business Ethics*, 165(2): 191–204.

Pucker, K.P. and King, A. (2022), ESG investing isn't designed to save the planet, (https://hbr.org/2022/08/esg-investing-isnt-designed-to-save-the-planet).

Pullen, A. and Vachhani, S.J. (2020), 'Feminist ethics and women leaders: From difference to intercorporeality', *Journal of Business Ethics*, 173(2): 233–43.

Purvis, B., Mao, Y. and Robinson, D. (2019), 'Three pillars of sustainability: In search of conceptual origins', *Sustainability Science*, 14: 681–95.

Rabell, B.M. and Bastons, M. (2020), 'Spirituality as reinforcement of people-focused work: A philosophical foundation', *Journal of Management, Spirituality & Religion*, 17(5): 403–18.

Rachels, J. (1993), *Elements of moral philosophy*, 2nd edn, New York: McGraw-Hill.

Rahim, A.B.A. (2013), 'Understanding Islamic ethics and its significance on the character building', *International Journal of Social Science and Humanity*, 3(6): 508–13.

Raimi, L., Tariq, M.U. and Kah, J.M. (2022), 'Diversity, equity, and inclusion as the future workplace ethics: Theoretical review'. In L. Raimi and J.M.L. Kah (eds), *Mainstreaming diversity, equity, and inclusion as future workplace ethics*, Pennsylvania: IGI Global.

Rainforest (2022), For business, Rainforest Alliance, (www.rainforest-alliance.org/for-business/).

Ramanujan, A.K. (1989), 'Is there an Indian way of thinking? An informal essay', *Contributions to Indian Sociology*, 23(1): 41–58.

Rangan, V.K. and Lee, K. (2010), Grameen Danone Foods Ltd., a social business, (www.hbs.edu/faculty/Pages/item.aspx?num=39376).

Rawls, J. (1971), *A theory of justice*, Cambridge, MA: Harvard University Press.

Rawls, J. (2001), *Justice as fairness: A restatement*, Erin Kelly (ed), Cambridge, MA: Harvard University Press.

Razzetti, G. (2019), Mapping Zappos' fun, weird culture, (www.fearlessculture.design/blog-posts/zappos-culture-design-canvas).

Rechberg, I. and Syed, J. (2013), 'Ethical issues in knowledge management: Conflict of knowledge ownership', *Journal of Knowledge Management*, 17(6): 828–47.

Reference (2020), What was Enron's mission statement? (www.reference.com/business-finance/enron-s-mission-statement-c6696fde36f55fbe).

Reid, R.C. and Pascalev, M. (2002), 'Strategic and ethical issues in outsourcing information technologies'. In G. Dhillon (ed), *Social Responsibility in the Information Age: Issues and Controversies,* Pennsylvania: IGI Global.

Repurpose (2020), 3 business sustainability case studies and why they worked, (https://repurpose.global/blog/post/3-sustainability-initiatives-and-why-they-worked).

Rest, J.R. (1979), *Development in judging moral issues*, Minneapolis, MN: University of Minnesota Press.

Rest, J.R. (1984), 'Research on moral development: Implications for training counseling psychologists', *The Counseling Psychologist*, 12(3): 19–29.

Rest, J.R. (1986), Moral development: Advances in research and theory, New York: Praeger.

Rest, J.R. (1994), 'Background: Theory and research'. In J.R. Rest and D. Narvaez (eds), *Moral development in the professions*, Hillsdale, NJ: Erlbaum.

Rest, J.R. and Narvaez, D. (eds) (1994), *Moral development in the professions: Psychology and applied ethics*, Hillsdale, NJ: Lawrence Erlbaum Associates.

Reynolds, S.J. (2006), 'A neurocognitive model of the ethical decision-making process: Implications for study and practice', *Journal of Applied Psychology*, 91(4): 737–48.

Rezkalla, P. (2022), Aren't right and wrong just matters of opinion? On moral relativism and subjectivism, (https://press.rebus.community/intro-to-phil-ethics/chapter/arent-right-and-wrong-just-matters-of-opinion-on-moral-relativism-and-subjectivism/).

Rhodes, R. (2021), 'Energy and longevity', *The New Philosopher*, 32: 104–9.

Ribera, R. and Lozano, J.M. (2011), 'The impact of spirituality in management'. In L. Zsolnai (ed), *Spirituality and ethics in management*, New York: Springer.

Rice, G. (1999), 'Islamic ethics and the implications for business', *Journal of Business Ethics*, 18(4): 345–58.

Rimanoczy, I. (2014), Business as agent for world benefit? (www.huffpost.com/entry/business-as-agent-for-wor_b_6048086).

Rincón-Moreno, J., Franco-García, M-L., Carpio-Aguilar, J.C. and Hernández-Sarabia, M. (2018), 'Share, optimise, closed-loop for food waste (SOL4FoodWaste): The case of Walmart–Mexico'. In M.L. Franco-García, J. Aguilar and H. Bressers (eds), *Towards Zero Waste*, Cham: Springer International Publishing.

Ritchie, H., Roser, M. and Rosado, P. (2020), CO_2 and greenhouse gas emissions, (https://ourworldindata.org/co2-and-other-greenhouse-gas-emissions).

Robb, B. and Michailova, S. (2022), 'Multinational enterprises' narratives about and approaches to modern slavery: An exploratory study', *Review of International Business and Strategy*, 33(2). doi: 10.1108/RIBS-10-2021-0128.

Robbins, S.P., Millett, B., Cacioppe, R. and Waters-Marsh, T. (2001), *Organisational behaviour*, 3rd edn, Frenchs Forrest, NSW: Prentice Hall.

Robertson, C. and Fadil, P.A. (1999), 'Ethical decision making in multinational organizations: A culture-based model', *Journal of Business Ethics*, 19(4): 385–92.

Robertson, C.J., Ralston, D.A. and Crittenden, W.F. (2012), 'The relationship between cultural values and moral philosophy: A generational subculture theory approach', *AMS Review*, 2(2–4): 99–107.

Robison, P. and Newkirk, M. (2019), Relationship between Boeing, FAA safety regulators under scrutiny, (www.insurancejournal.com/news/national/2019/03/25/521514.htm).

Rockström, J., Steffen, W., Noone, K., et al. (2009), 'Planetary boundaries: Exploring the safe operating space for humanity', *Ecology and Society*, 14(2): 32.

Rodriguez-Gomez, S., Arco-Castro, M.L., Lopez-Perez, M.V. and Rodríguez-Ariza, L. (2020), 'Where does CSR come from and where does it go? A review of the state of the art', *Administrative Sciences*, 10(3): 60.

Rogers, G.A.J. (2021), John Locke, *Encyclopedia Britannica*, (www.britannica.com/biography/John-Locke).

Rohner, U. (2017), Credit Suisse Global Wealth Report 2017, (www.credit-suisse.com/media/assets/corporate/docs/about-us/research/publications/global-wealth-report-2017-en.pdf).

Ross, B., Rhee, J., Hill, A.M., Chuchmach, M., and Katersky, A. (2014), Toyota to Pay $1.2B for hiding deadly 'unintended acceleration', (https://abcnews.go.com/Blotter/toyota-pay-12b-hiding-deadly-unintended-acceleration/story?id=22972214).

Rossouw, G.J. (1997), 'Business ethics in South Africa', *Journal of Business Ethics*, 16(14): 1539–47.

Rossouw, G.J. (2009), 'The ethics of corporate governance', *International Journal of Law and Management*, 51(1): 5–9.

Rowan, J.R. (2001), 'How binding the ties? Business ethics as integrative social contracts – ties that bind: A social contracts approach to business ethics, Thomas Donaldson and Thomas W. Dunfee Boston: Harvard Business School Press, 1999', *Business Ethics Quarterly*, 11(2): 379–90.

Rudman, W., Hart-Hester, S., Richey, J. and Jackson, K. (2016), 'Hiring for competency: Hiring to not fail vs. hiring to succeed', *Perspectives in Health Information Management*, Summer: 1–6.

SA8000 (2022), SA8000 standard, social accountability international, New York, (https://sa-intl.org/programs/sa8000/).

Sætra, H.S. and Danaher, J. (2022), 'To each technology its own ethics: The problem of ethical proliferation', *Philosophy and Technology*, 35(4): 93.

Salk, J. (1992). 'Are we being good ancestors?', *World Affairs: The Journal of International Issues*, 1(2): 16-18.

Saltzstein, H.D. and Kasachkoff, T. (2004), 'Haidt's moral intuitionist theory: A psychological and philosophical critique', *Review of General Psychology*, 8(4): 273–82.

Sama, L.M., Stefanidis, A. and Casselman, R.M. (2022), 'Rethinking corporate governance in the digital economy: The role of stewardship', *Business Horizons*, 65(5): 535–46.

Sanchez-Bueno, M.J., Muñoz-Bullón, F. and Galan, J.I. (2020), 'Socially responsible downsizing: Comparing family and non-family firm', *Business Ethics*, 29(1): 35–55.

Sandhu, S. and Kulik, C.T. (2019), 'Shaping and being shaped: How organizational structure and managerial discretion co-evolve in new managerial roles', *Administrative Science Quarterly*, 64(3): 619–58.

Saraswathy, B. (2019), 'The Flipkart-Walmart deal in India: A look into competition and other related issues', *Antitrust Bulletin*, 64(1): 136–47.

Sarkis, J. (2020), 'Supply chain sustainability: Learning from the COVID-19 pandemic', *International Journal of Operations & Production Management*, 41(1): 63–73.

Sartor, M.A. and Beamish, P.W. (2020), 'Private sector corruption, public sector corruption and the organizational structure of foreign subsidiaries', *Journal of Business Ethics*, 167(4): 725–44.

Savur, S. (2013), 'Theorising ethical decision-making process for research in small and medium enterprises (SMEs) in Australia'. In H. Harris and M. Schwartz (eds), *Ethics, values and civil society* (*Research in Ethical Issues in Organizations*, vol. 9), Bingley: Emerald Publishing.

Savur, S. (2017), 'Role of exemplars in ethical decision-making in small and medium enterprises (SMEs)', Responsible leadership and ethical decision-making (*Research in Ethical Issues in Organizations*, vol. 17), Leeds: Emerald Publishing, pp. 21–35.

Savur, S. (2022), 'Ethical decision-making – Synthesizing S.K. Chakraborty's classification of ethics with levels of moral judgement and the four-component model'. In S. Mukherjee and L. Zsolnai (eds), *Global perspectives on Indian spirituality and management*, Singapore: Springer.

Savur, S., Provis, C. and Harris, H. (2018). 'Ethical decision-making in Australian SMEs: A field study', *Small Enterprise Research*, 25(2): 114–36.

Sayed, Z. and Agndal, H. (2022), 'Offshore outsourcing of R&D to emerging markets: Information systems as tools of neo-colonial control', *Critical Perspectives on International Business*, 18(3): 281–302.

Scales, D. (2020), The problem with brand purpose, Forbes Agency Council, (www.forbes.com/sites/forbesagencycouncil/2020/05/05/the-problem-with-brand-purpose/?sh=13dbb6146b9b).

Schaufenbuel, K. (2015), Why Google, Target, and General Mills are investing in mindfulness, (https://hbr.org/2015/12/why-google-target-and-general-mills-are-investing-in-mindfulness).

Scherer, A.G. and Palazzo, G.S. (2008), 'Globalization and corporate social responsibility'. In A. Crane, D. Matten, A. McWilliams, J. Moon and D.S. Siegel (eds), *The Oxford handbook of corporate social responsibility*, New York: Oxford University Press.

Scherer, A.G., Palazzo, G.S. and Matten, D. (2009), 'Introduction to the special issue: Globalization as a challenge for business responsibilities', *Business Ethics Quarterly*, 19(3): 327–47.

Scholtens, B. and Dam, L. (2007), 'Cultural values and international differences in business ethics', *Journal of Business Ethics*, 75(3): 273–84.

Schur, M. (2022), *How to be perfect: The correct answer to every moral question*, London: Quercus Editions Ltd.

Schwartz, J., Denny, B., Mallon, D., Van Durme, Y., Yam, R. and Poynton, S. (2020), Ethics and the future of work, (www2.deloitte.com/us/en/insights/focus/human-capital-trends/2020/ethical-implications-of-ai.html).

Schwartz, M.S. (2004), 'Effective corporate codes of ethics: Perceptions of code users', *Journal of Business Ethics*, 55(4): 323–43.

Schwartz, M.S. (2016). 'Ethical decision-making theory: An integrated approach', *Journal of Business Ethics*, 139(4): 755–76.

Seabrook, J. (1993), The flash of genius, in annals of invention, *The New Yorker*, 11 January, (www.newyorker.com/magazine/1993/01/11/the-flash-of-genius).

Seele, P. and Schultz, M.D. (2022), 'From greenwashing to machinewashing: A model and future directions derived from reasoning by analogy', *Journal of Business Ethics*, 178(4): 1063–89.

Segal, T. (2021), Enron scandal: The fall of a Wall Street darling, (www.investopedia.com/updates/enron-scandal-summary/).

SELCO (2022), Selco-India, (https://selco-india.com/who-we-are/).

Sethi, S.P. (1975), 'Dimensions of corporate social performance: An analytic framework', *California Management Review*, 17(3): 58–64.

Shah, A.K. and Oppenheimer, D.M. (2008), 'Heuristics made easy: An effort-reduction framework', *Psychological Bulletin*, 134(2): 207–22.

Shapiro, S.B. and Reiff, J. (1993), 'A framework for reflective inquiry on practice: Beyond intuition and experience', *Psychological Reports*, 73(3): 1379–94.

Shaw, W.H. and Barry, V. (2010), *Moral issues in business*, 11th edn, Belmont, CA: Wadsworth.

Shell (2022), Brent Spar dossier, (www.shell.co.uk/sustainability/decommissioning/brent-spar-dossier.html).

Shepherd, D.A., Parida, V. and Wincent, J. (2020), 'The surprising duality of *Jugaad*: Low firm growth and high inclusive growth', *Journal of Management Studies*, 57(1): 87–128.

Shilling, H., Wiedmann, T. and Malik, A. (2021), 'Modern slavery footprints in global supply chains', *Journal of Industrial Ecology*, 25(6): 1518–28.

Sidani, Y. and Al Ariss, A. (2015), 'New conceptual foundations for Islamic business ethics: The contributions of Abu-Hamid Al-Ghazali', *Journal of Business Ethics*, 129(4): 847–57.

Sikka, P. and Lehman, G. (2015), 'The supply-side of corruption and limits to preventing corruption within government procurement and constructing ethical subjects', *Critical Perspectives on Accounting*, 28: 62–70.

Silverstein, K. (2022), Not all carbon credits are created equal: Here's what companies must know, (www.forbes.com/sites/kensilverstein/2022/06/22/not-all-carbon-credits-are-created-equal-heres-what-companies-must-know/?sh=6b9c80b15328).

Simola, S. (2003), 'Ethics of justice and care in corporate crisis management', *Journal of Business Ethics*, 46(4): 351–61.

Simon, J.L. (1996), *The ultimate resource 2*, Princeton: Princeton University Press.

Sims, R.L. and Keon, T.L. (1999), 'Determinants of ethical decision making: The relationship of the perceived organizational environment', *Journal of Business Ethics*, 19(4): 393–401.

Sinclair, A. and Dinshaw, F. (2022), HRLC – paper promises? Evaluating the early impact of Australia's Modern Slavery Act, (www.hrlc.org.au/reports/2022/2/3/paper-promises-evaluating-the-early-impact-of-australias-modern-slavery-act).

Sindwani, P. (2019), India's carpet industry which employs 2 million people and exports USD 1.8 billion every year has stagnated in the last five years, (www.businessinsider.in/policy/economy/news/indias-carpet-industry-which-employs-2-million-people-and-exports-1-8-billion-every-year-has-stagnated-in-the-last-five-years/articleshow/71550028.cms).

Sinek, S. (2013), People don't buy what you do, people buy why you do it, (www.youtube.com/watch?v=UedER61oUy4).

Singer, P. (2021), Ethics philosophy, *Britannica*, www.britannica.com/topic/ethics-philosophy.

Singh, J.J., Garg, N., Govind, R., and Vitell, S.J. (2018). 'Anger strays, fear refrains: The differential effect of negative emotions on consumers' ethical judgments', *Journal of Business Ethics*, 151(1): 235–48.

Singh, R.K. and Singh, S. (2022), 'Spirituality in the workplace: A systematic review', *Management Decision*, 60(5), 1296–325.

Sirk, C. (2020), Zen and the art of winning: Phil Jackman's team leadership, (https://crm.org/articles/zen-and-the-art-of-winning-phil-jacksons-team-leadership retrieved).

Sisodia, R., Wolfe, D. and Sheth, J. (2014), *Firms of endearment*, 2nd edn, Upper Saddle River NJ: Pearson Education.

Sivarajan, R., Varma, S.M. and Reshmi (2021), 'To *Jugaad* or not? How Mumbai's gig workers thrive against psychological contract discrepancies', *South Asian Journal of Human Resources*, 8(3): 103–32.

Smith, P.B., Torres, C., Leong, C-H., Budhwar, P., Achoui, M., and Lebedeva, N. (2012), 'Are indigenous approaches to achieving influence in business organizations distinctive? A comparative study of *guanxi, wasta, jeitinho, svyazi* and pulling strings', *International Journal of Human Resource Management*, 23(2): 333–48.

Solomon, R.C. (1992), *Ethics and excellence: Cooperation and integrity in business*, Oxford: Oxford University Press.

Sonenshein, S. (2007), 'The role of construction, intuition, and justification in responding to ethical issues at work: The sensemaking-intuition model', *The Academy of Management Review*, 32(4): 1022–40.

Soper, S. (2021), 'Fired by bot at Amazon: "It's you against the machine"', *Bloomberg*, 28 June, (www.bloomberg.com/news/features/2021-06-28/fired-by-bot-amazon-turns-to-machine-managers-and-workers-are-losing-out).

Sprotzer, I. and Goldberg, I.V. (1992), 'Fetal protection: Law, ethics and corporate policy', *Journal of Business Ethics*, 11(10): 731–5.

Stajkovic, A.D. and Luthans, F. (1997), 'Business ethics across cultures: A social cognitive model', *Journal of World Business*, 32(1): 17–34.

Stanford (2022a), Kant's moral philosophy, *Stanford encyclopedia of philosophy*, (https://plato.stanford.edu/entries/kant-moral/).

Stanford (2022b), Isaish Berlin, *Stanford encyclopedia of philosophy*, (https://plato.stanford.edu/entries/berlin/#BerlDefiValuPlur).

Starvish, M. (2013), LEGO, (https://hbswk.hbs.edu/item/hbs-cases-lego).

Statista (2022), Casinos worldwide – statistics & facts, (www.statista.com/topics/1053/casinos/#topicOverview).

Steckler, E. and Clark, C. (2019), 'Authenticity and corporate governance', *Journal of Business Ethics*, 155(4): 951–63.

Steffen, W., Richardson, K., Rockström, J., et al. (2015), 'Sustainability planetary boundaries: Guiding human development on a changing planet', *Science*, 347(6223): 1259855.

Stelzner, G. (2022), 'Ethics and discrimination in the hiring process: An overview of gender and race', *Minnesota Undergraduate Research & Academic Journal*, 5(4): 1–11.

Stening, B.W. and Zhang, M.Y. (2016), 'Ethics and the liability of foreignness: The case of China', *Journal of General Management*, 42(2): 3–16.

Stensota, H.O. (2015), 'Public ethics of care – a general public ethics', *Ethics and Social Welfare*, 9(2): 183–200.

Stephens Balakrishnan, M. (2011), 'Protecting from brand burn during times of crisis: Mumbai 26/11: A case of the Taj Mahal Palace and Tower Hotel', *Management Research Review*, 34(12): 1309–34.

Stewart, K., Felicetti, L. and Kuehn, S. (1996), 'The attitudes of business majors towards the teaching of business ethics', *Journal of Business Ethics*, 15(8): 913–18.

Straits Times (2023), Girl with AI earrings, standing in for Vermeer masterpiece, sparks Dutch art controversy, (www.straitstimes.com/world/europe/girl-with-ai-earrings-standing-in-for-vermeer-masterpiece-sparks-dutch-art-controversy).

Stringer, C. and Michailova, S. (2018), 'Why modern slavery thrives in multinational corporations' global value chains', *Multinational Business Review*, 26(3): 194–206.

Stromberg, J. (2013), What is the Anthropocene and are we in it?, (www.smithsonianmag.com/science-nature/what-is-the-anthropocene-and-are-we-in-it-164801414/).

Sunstein, C.R. (2005), 'Moral heuristics', *Behavioral and Brain Sciences*, 8(4): 531–73.

Surdu, I. (2022), Why big firms are rarely toppled by corporate scandals – new research, (https://theconversation.com/why-big-firms-are-rarely-toppled-by-corporate-scandals-new-research-176270).

SustainAbility (2007), Raising our game, can we sustain globalization? (www.sustentabilidad.uai.edu.ar/pdf/sde/Raising_Our_Game.pdf).

SustainAbility Institute (2022), What's next for sustainable business: 2022 trends report, (www.sustainability.com/globalassets/sustainability.com/thinking/pdfs/2022/esi-sustainability-trends-report-2022-2.pdf).

Takeda, S., Secchi, D. and Bray, J. (2022), 'Ethics-related value acculturation: The case of Thai employees working at UK and Japanese MNCs in Thailand', *Cross Cultural & Strategic Management*, 29(4): 846–69. doi: 10.1108/CCSM-10-2020-0204.

Tang, T.L. and Fuller, T.M. (1995), 'Corporate downsizing: What managers can do to lessen the negative effects of layoffs', *S.A.M. Advanced Management Journal*, 60(4): 12–15.

Tang, Y., Xiong, J., Becerril-Arreola, R. and Iyer, L. (2020), 'Ethics of blockchain', *Information Technology and People*, 33(2): 602–32.

Tata Steel (2019), Anti-bribery and anti-corruption policy of Tata Steel Limited, (www.tatasteel.com/media/11802/1-abac-policy_final.pdf).

Taylor, H. (2003), 'Stemming the tide of river blindness: The early years of ivermectin', *The Medical Journal of Australia*, 179(11/12): 617–19.

Taylor, M. and Soliman, H.T. (2020), Equinor has abandoned oil-drilling plans in the Great Australian Bight – so what's next? (https://theconversation.com/equinor-has-abandoned-oil-drilling-plans-in-the-great-australian-bight-so-whats-next-132435).

Teather, D. (2005), Nike lists abuses at Aisan factories (www.theguardian.com/business/2005/apr/14/ethicalbusiness.money).

Tenbrunsel, A.E. and Smith-Crowe, K. (2008), '13 ethical decision making: Where we've been and where we're going', *The Academy of Management Annals*, 2(1), 545–607.

Terzon, E. (2022), Ansell accused of 'knowingly profiting' off the labour of slaves: Shuvo is one of them, (www.abc.net.au/news/2022-08-24/ansell-slave-labour-brightway/101362990).

Thanetsunthorn, N. (2015), 'The impact of national culture on corporate social responsibility: Evidence from cross-regional comparison', *Asian Journal of Business Ethics*, 4(1): 35–56.

There We Go – Lifting 25,000 tonnes in 9 seconds: Brent Bravo Lift (2019), (www.youtube.com/watch?v=D5xXmEHPFp8&t=706s).

Thoma, S.J. (2002), 'An overview of the Minnesota approach to research in moral development', *Journal of Moral Education*, 31(3): 225–45.

Thorbecke, C. (2022). 'Oxfam report says Australian billionaires and world's richest men have doubled wealth during pandemic', *ABC News*, (www.abc.net.au/news/2022-01-17/oxfam-report-covid-pandemic-billionaires-increase-fortune/100760968).

Thorisdottir, T.S. and Johannsdottir, L. (2020), 'Corporate social responsibility influencing sustainability within the fashion industry: A systematic review', *Sustainability*, 12(21): 9167.

Tickner, P. (2016), *Fraud and corruption in public services*, London: Routledge.

Tlaiss, H.A. (2015), 'How Islamic business ethics impact women entrepreneurs: Insights from four Arab Middle Eastern countries', *Journal of Business Ethics*, 129(4): 859–77.

TOMS (2022), Impact, (www.toms.com/us/impact.html).

Torrey Project (2019), Ethics + stakeholder focus = greater long-run shareholder profits, (www.torreyproject.org/post/ethics-stakeholder-focus-greater-long-run-shareholder-profits).

Transparency International (2022), What is corruption? (www.transparency.org/en/what-is-corruption).

Transparency International, (2021), Corruption perceptions index 2021, (www.transparency.org/en/cpi/2021).

Treadgold, J. (2022), Abhilash Mudaliar – What is the role of business & finance in society? (https://johntreadgold.com/goodfuturepodcast/abhilash-mudaliar-role-of-business-in-society/).

Treviño, L.K. (1986), 'Ethical decision making in organisations: A person–situation interactionist model', *Academy of Management Review*, 11(3): 601–17.

Treviño, L.K. and Nelson, K.A. (2014), *Managing business ethics: Straight talk about how to do it right*, 6th edn, Hoboken, NJ: John Wiley.

Trinca, H. (2021a), 'Giving gets a whole new look', *The Weekend Australian*, 30–31 October: 44.

Trinca, H. (2021b), 'The problem with purpose', *The Weekend Australian*, 4–5 September: 44.

Tsang, J. (2002), 'Moral rationalization and the integration of situational factors and psychological processes in immoral behavior', *Review of General Psychology*, 6(1): 25–50.

Tupas, R. (2018), '5 inequalities of multilingualism: Outsourcing, neoliberalism and languages-in-education'. In C.S.K. Chua (ed), *Un(intended) language planning in a globalising world: Multiple levels of players at work*, Berlin: Mouton de Gruyter.

Tversky, A. and Kahneman, D. (1973), 'Availability: A heuristic for judging frequency and probability', *Cognitive Psychology*, 5(2): 207–32.

UDHR (2022), Universal declaration of human rights, (www.un.org/en/about-us/universal-declaration-of-human-rights).

UK.gov (2023), Transfer pricing, (www.gov.uk/government/consultations/draft-regulations-the-transfer-pricing-records-regulations-2023).

UK Slavery Act (2015), Part 6 – Transparency in supply chains, (www.legislation.gov.uk/ukpga/2015/30/part/6/enacted).

Ulusemre, T., and Fang, X. (2022), 'How do expatriate managers draw the boundaries of moral free space in the case of *guanxi*?' *Journal of Business Ethics*, 176(2): 311–24.

UN (2022), Stop food loss and waste, for the people, for the planet, (www.un.org/en/observances/end-food-waste-day).

UN Office on Drugs and Crime and SA Department of Public Service and Administration (2003), Country corruption assessment report: South Africa, (www.westerncape.gov.za/text/2004/4/sacorruptionassessmentreport2003.pdf).

UNCED (1992), The Rio declaration on environment and development: 27 principles, (www.iau-hesd.net/sites/default/files/documents/rio_e.pdf).

UNEPFI (2004), Who cares wins: Connecting financial markets to a changing world, (www.unepfi.org/fileadmin/events/2004/stocks/who_cares_wins_global_compact_2004.pdf).

UNGC (2022a), The ten principles of UN global impact, United Nations Global Impact, (https://unglobalcompact.org/).

UNGC (2022b), Social sustainability, (www.unglobalcompact.org/what-is-gc/our-work/social).

UNGC (2022c), Environment, (www.unglobalcompact.org/what-is-gc/our-work/environment).

UNGC (2022d), Sustainable Development Goals (SDG), (www.unglobalcompact.org/sdgs/about).

UNGC (2022e), How your company can advance each of the SDGs, (www.unglobalcompact.org/sdgs/17-global-goals).

UNGCCA (2018), UN global climate action awards: The bamboo bikes, Ghana, (https://unfccc.int/climate-action/momentum-for-change/women-for-results/ghana-bamboo-bikes-initiative).

UNHRC (2022), United Nations Human Rights Council, (www.ohchr.org/en/hrbodies/hrc/home).

UNODC (2003), United Nations convention against corruption, UNODC, Vienna, (www.unodc.org/unodc/en/corruption/uncac.html).

UNOOSA (2002). United Nations Treaties and Principles on Outer Space, (www.unoosa.org/pdf/publications/STSPACE11E.pdf).

UQ (2022), The real cost of bottled water, (https://sustainability.uq.edu.au/projects/recycling-and-waste-minimisation/real-cost-bottled-water).

Urban Institute (2017), Nine charts about wealth inequality in America (updated), (https://apps.urban.org/features/wealth-inequality-charts/).

US Department of Justice (DoJ) (2020), Opioid manufacturer Purdue Pharma pleads guilty to fraud and kickback conspiracies, Press Release Number 20-1282, (www.justice.gov/opa/pr/opioid-manufacturer-purdue-pharma-pleads-guilty-fraud-and-kickback-conspiracies).

US Department of Justice (DoJ) (2021), Verdict and settlement with Boeing, (www.justice.gov/opa/pr/boeing-charged-737-max-fraud-conspiracy-and-agrees-pay-over-25-billion).

USEPA (2022), DDT – a brief history and status, (www.epa.gov/ingredients-used-pesticide-products/ddt-brief-history-and-status).

Valentine, S. and Godkin, L. (2019), 'Moral intensity, ethical decision making, and whistleblowing intention', *Journal of Business Research*, 98: 277–88.

Van Buren, H.J. III, Schrempf-Stirling, J. and Westermann-Behaylo, M. (2020), 'Towards ethical commitment: Avoiding MNC entanglement in modern slavery', *AIB Insights*, 20(2): 1–4.

Van der Burg, S., Bogaardt, M.-J. and Wolfert, S. (2019), 'Ethics of smart farming: Current questions and directions for responsible innovation towards the future', *NJAS – Wageningen Journal of Life Sciences*, 90–1(1): 1–10.

Van Dijk, H., van Engen, M. and Paauwe, J. (2012), 'Reframing the business case for diversity: A values and virtues perspective', *Journal of Business Ethics*, 111(1): 73–84.

Van Wyk, I. and Venter, P. (2022), 'Perspectives on business ethics in South African small and medium enterprises', *African Journal of Business Ethics*, 16(1): 81–104.

Vander Schee, B.A. (2010), 'Crowdsourcing: Why the power of the crowd is driving the future of business', *Human Resource Management International Digest*, 18(3): 1–4.

Varma, T.M. (2021), 'Responsible leadership and reputation management during a crisis: The cases of Delta and United Airlines', *Journal of Business Ethics*, 173(1): 29–45.

Velasquez, M. (2021). 'Business ethics pioneers: Manuel Velasquez', *Business & Professional Ethics Journal*, 40(3): 351–7.

Velasquez, M., Andre, C., Shamks, T. and Meyer, M.J. (2022), *Ethical relativism*, Markkula Centre of Applied Ethics, Santa Clara University.

Velez-Calle, A., Robledo-Ardila, C. and Rodriguez-Rios, J.D. (2015), 'On the influence of interpersonal relations on business practices in Latin America: A comparison with the Chinese *guanxi* and the Arab *wasta*', *Thunderbird International Business Review*, 57(4): 281–93.

Vidaver-Cohen, D. (1997), 'Moral imagination in organizational problem-solving: An institutional perspective', *Business Ethics Quarterly*, 7(4): 1–26.

Villegas, S., Lloyd, R.A., Tritt, A. and Vengrouskie, E.F. (2019), 'Human resources as ethical gatekeepers: Hiring ethics and employee selection', *Journal of Leadership, Accountability and Ethics*, 16(2): 80–88.

Villeneuve, L. (2016), Spirituality: Google and Starbucks are doing it. What about you? (www.linkedin.com/pulse/spirituality-google-starbucks-doing-what-you-lisa-watson/).

Vinuesa, R., Azizpour, H., Leite, I., Balaam, M., Dignum, V., Domisch, S., Felländer, A., Langhans, S.D., Tegmark, M. and Nerini, F.F. (2020), 'The role of artificial intelligence in achieving the Sustainable Development Goals', *Nature Communications*, 11: 233.

Virmani, A. and Lepineux, F. (2016), 'Aravind eye care system as transformational entrepreneurship: Spiritual roots, multi-dimensional impact', *Philosophy of Management*, 15(1): 83–94.

Vitolla, F., Raimo, N., Rubino, M. and Garegnani, G.M. (2021), 'Do cultural differences impact ethical issues? Exploring the relationship between national culture and quality of code of ethics', *Journal of International Management*, 27(1): 100823.

Voegtlin, C., Frisch, C., Walther, A. and Schwab, P. (2020), 'Theoretical development and empirical examination of a three-roles model of responsible leadership', *Journal of Business Ethics*, 167(3): 411–31.

Voegtlin, C., Patzer, M. and Scherer, A.G. (2012), 'Responsible leadership in global business: A new approach to leadership and its multi-level outcomes', *Journal of Business Ethics*, 105(1): 1–16.

Vu, M.C. (2021), 'Tensions and struggles in tackling bribery at the firm level: Perspectives from Buddhist-enacted organizational leaders', *Journal of Business Ethics*, 168(3): 517–37.

Waddock, S. (2022), 'Corporate responsibility: The dark-side paradoxes of success'. In G. Flynn (ed), *Leadership and business ethics*, 2nd edn, Dordrecht: Springer Nature.

Wakelin-Theron, N. and Ukpere, W.I. (2021), 'Exploring the impact of COVID-19 on the taxi industry in the City of Johannesburg', *Harvard Deusto Business Research*, X(2), 272–94.

Waldman, D.A. and Galvin, B.M. (2008), 'Alternative perspectives of responsible leadership', *Organizational Dynamics*, 37(4): 327–41.

Walker, J. (2023), 'How to implant ethics into artificial intelligence', *The Weekend Australian*, 18–19 March: 24.

Walker, L.J. (2002), 'The model and the measure: An appraisal of the Minnesota approach to moral development', *Journal of Moral Education*, 31(3): 353–67.

Wall Street Journal video on B737 Max – what happened? (2020), (www.youtube.com/watch?v=0jTN0JD4I5M).

Walmart (2022a), How many people work at Walmart? (https://corporate.walmart.com/askwalmart/how-many-people-work-at-walmart).

Walmart (2022b), Unit counts by country, October 31, 2022, (https://s201.q4cdn.com/262069030/files/doc_downloads/2022/FY2023-Q3-Unit-Count-Market-Summary-for-IR.pdf).

Walsh, J. (1987), 'Merck donates drug for river blindness', *Science*, 238(4827): 610.

Wang, H., Guo, T. and Tang, Q. (2021), 'The effect of national culture on corporate green proactivity', *Journal of Business Research*, 131: 140–50.

Wang, W. and Wertheimer, A.I. (2022), 'History, status, and politicization of the FDA', *Research in Social and Administration Pharmacy*, 18(5): 2811–16.

Wang-Erlandsson, L., Tobian, A., van der Ent, R.J. et al. (2022), 'A planetary boundary for green water', *Nature Reviews: Earth & Environment*, 3: 380–92.

Warren, D.E., Dunfee, T.W. and Li, N. (2004), 'Social exchange in China: The double-edged sword of *guanxi*', *Journal of Business Ethics*, 55(4): 355–72.

Warren, D.E. and Smith-Crowe, K. (2008), 'Deciding what's right: The role of external sanctions and embarrassment in shaping moral judgments in the workplace', *Research in Organizational Behavior*, 28: 81-105.

Waterford, J. (2021), Bob Hawke was a giant, for all his flaws, (www.canberratimes.com.au/story/6128108/bob-hawke-was-a-giant-for-all-his-flaws/).

Watters, A. (2023), 5 ethical issues in technology to watch for in 2023, (https://connect.comptia.org/blog/ethical-issues-in-technology).

WBCSD (2013a), Greenhouse gas protocol – FAQs, (https://ghgprotocol.org/sites/default/files/standards_supporting/FAQ.pdf).

WBCSD (2013b), Technical guidance for calculating Scope 3 emissions (version 1.0), (https://ghgprotocol.org/sites/default/files/standards/Scope3_Calculation_Guidance_0.pdf).

WCED (1987), Our common future, (https://sustainabledevelopment.un.org/content/documents/5987our-common-future.pdf).

Weaver, G.R. (2004), 'Ethics and employees: Making the connection', *The Academy of Management Executive*, 18(2): 121–5.

Weber, J. and Elm, D.R. (2018), 'Exploring and comparing cognitive moral reasoning of Millennials and across multiple generations', *Business and Society Review*, 123(3): 415–58.

WEF (2017), Overview, (WEF_AM17_Overview.pdf).

Welldon, E. (2012), 'Joining the resistance', *British Journal of Psychotherapy*, 28(4): 545–8.

Wellington, A. (2020), 'Contextualizing a human rights perspective for water ethics: From exploitation to empowerment and beyond'. In I.L. Stefanovic and Z. Adeel (eds), *Ethical water stewardship*, Cham: Springer International Publishing, (https://doi.org/10.1007/978-3-030-49540-4_3).

Wells, G. (2011), *Sustainability in Australian business: Fundamental principles and practice*, Milton: John Wiley and Sons Australia.

Werhane, P.H. (1998), 'Moral imagination and the search for ethical decision-making in management'. In D.J. Bevan, R.W. Wolfe and P.H. Werhane (eds), *Systems thinking and moral imagination (Issues in business ethics*, vol. 48), Cham: Springer, (https://doi.org/10.1007/978-3-319-89797-4_5).

Werhane, P.H. (1999), *Moral imagination and management decision-making*, New York: Oxford University Press.

Werhane, P.H. (2002), 'Moral imagination and systems thinking', *Journal of Business Ethics*, 38(1): 33–42.

Werhane, P.H. (2021), 'Business ethics pioneers: Patricia Werhane', *Business & Professional Ethics Journal*, 40(3), 359–66.

Westwood, P.A. (2020), 'The role of the sense of justice in Rawls' theory', *Revista de Filosofia Aurora*, 32(56): 542–57.

Weyler, R. (2016), Brent Spar: The sea is not a dustbin, (www.greenpeace.org/international/story/47744/brent-spar-the-sea-is-not-a-dustbin/).

WHO (2021), *Global report on ageism*, Geneva: World Health Organization, (www.who.int/teams/social-determinants-of-health/demographic-change-and-healthy-ageing/combatting-ageism/global-report-on-ageism).

WHO (2022), Onchocerciasis – key facts, (www.who.int/news-room/fact-sheets/detail/onchocerciasis).

Whoriskey, P. and Siegel, R. (2019), Cocoa's child laborers: Mars, Nestle and Hershey pledged nearly two decades ago to stop using cocoa harvested by children, (www.washingtonpost.com/graphics/2019/business/hershey-nestle-mars-chocolate-child-labor-west-africa/).

Wickert, C (2022), Anomie theory (Merton), (https://soztheo.de/theories-of-crime/anomie-strain-theories/anomie-theory-merton/?lang=en#:~:text=Merton's%20anomie%20theory%20is%20that,innovation%2C%20and%2For%20conformity).

Wiki (n.d.a), Brent Spar, (https://en.wikipedia.org/wiki/Brent_Spar).

Wiki (n.d.b), LEGO, (https://en.wikipedia.org/wiki/Lego).

Wiki (2022a), Chetna Sinha, (https://en.wikipedia.org/wiki/Chetna_Sinha).

Wiki (2022b), Purdue Pharma, (https://en.wikipedia.org/wiki/Purdue_Pharma).

Wiki (2022c), 1970s, (https://en.wikipedia.org/wiki/1970s#Society).

Wiki (2022d), Gambling, (https://en.wikipedia.org/wiki/Gambling).

Wiki (2022e), Cipla, (https://en.wikipedia.org/wiki/Cipla).

Wiki (2022f), Bernice Dapaah, (https://en.wikipedia.org/wiki/Bernice_Dapaah retrieved).

Wiki (2022g), Enron scandal, (https://en.wikipedia.org/wiki/Enron_scandal).

Wiki (2022h), Geologic time (https://en.wikipedia.org/wiki/Geologic_time_scale#Divisions_of_geologic_time).

Wiki (2022i), HIV/AIDS in Africa, (https://en.wikipedia.org/wiki/HIV/AIDS_in_Africa).

Wiki (2022j), About Microsoft, (https://en.wikipedia.org/wiki/Microsoft).

Wiki (2022k), Novo Nordisk, (https://en.wikipedia.org/wiki/Novo_Nordisk).

Wiki (2022l), Patagonia Inc, (https://en.wikipedia.org/wiki/Patagonia,_Inc).

Wiki (2022m), Zappos, (https://en.wikipedia.org/wiki/Zappos).

Wiki (2023a), Girl with a Pearl Earring, (https://en.wikipedia.org/wiki/Girl_with_a_Pearl_Earring).

Wiki (2023b), Midjourney, (https://en.wikipedia.org/wiki/Midjourney).

Wisdom (2023), Wisdom 2.0, (www.wisdom2summit.com/about).

Witt, M.A. and Stahl, G.K. (2016), 'Foundations of responsible leadership: Asian versus Western executive responsibility orientations towards key stakeholders', *Journal of Business Ethics*, 136(3): 623–38.

Woermann, M. (2011), 'In corporations we trust? A critique of contractarian-based corporate social responsibility models', *African Journal of Business Ethics*, 5(1): 26–35.

Woermann, M. and Engelbrecht, S. (2019), 'The *Ubuntu* challenge to business: From stakeholders to relationships', *Journal of Business Ethics*, 157(1): 27–44.

World Bank (2020), Anticorruption fact sheet, (www.worldbank.org/en/news/factsheet/2020/02/19/anticorruption-fact-sheet#:~:text=Corruption%E2%80%94the%20abuse%20of%20public,affected%20by%20fragility%20and%20conflict).

World Bank Institute (2004), The costs of corruption, (http://web.worldbank.org/archive/website00818/WEB/MEDIAMEN.HTM).

WRI (2019), Creating a sustainable future: A menu of solutions to feed nearly 10 billion people by 2050, (www.wri.org/research/creating-sustainable-food-future).

WTTC (2022), Economic impact reports, World Travel and Tourism Council, (https://wttc.org/research/economic-impact).

WWF (2022), Living planet report 2022, (https://wwflpr.awsassets.panda.org/downloads/lpr_2022_full_report.pdf).

Yacout, O.M. and Scott, V. (2018), 'Ethical consumer decision-making: The role of need for cognition and affective responses', *Business Ethics: A European Review*, 27(2): 178–94.

Yakubi, H., Gac, B. and Apollonio, D.E. (2022), 'Marketing opioids to veterans and older adults: A content analysis of internal industry documents released from State of Oklahoma v. Purdue Pharma LP, et al.', *Journal of Health Politics, Policy and Law*, 47(4): 453–72.

Yam, J. and Skorburg, J.A. (2021), 'From human resources to human rights: Impact assessments for hiring algorithms', *Ethics and Information Technology*, 23: 611–23.

Yeo, S. (2020), How the largest environmental movement in history was born, (www.bbc.com/future/article/20200420-earth-day-2020-how-an-environmental-movement-was-born).

Yim, H.R., Lu, J. and Choi, S. (2017), 'Different role of lobbying and bribery on the firm performance in emerging markets', *Multinational Business Review*, 25(3), 222–38.

Yuan, L., Chia, R. and Gosling, J. (2023), 'Confucian virtue ethics and ethical leadership in modern China', *Journal of Business Ethics*, 182(1): 119–33.

Zappala, G. (2022), 'A meaningful participatory model of conscious leadership: Cultivating spiritual intelligence for conscious capitalism'. In M. Dion and M. Pava (eds), *The spirit of conscious capitalism: Contributions of world religions and spiritualities*, Cham: Springer Nature.

Zappos.com (2022), Zappos, (www.zappos.com/about).

Zhang, M., Hartley, J.L., AL-Husan, F.B., and ALHussan, F.B. (2021), 'Informal interorganizational business relationships and customer loyalty: Comparing *guanxi, yongo,* and *wasta*', *International Business Review*, 30(3): 101805.

Zhang, T., Zhang, P., Peng, K., Feng, K., Fang, P., Chen, W., Zhang, N., Wang, P. and Li, J. (2022), 'Allocating environmental costs of China's rare earth production to global consumption', *The Science of the Total Environment*, 831: 154934.

Zhou, N. and Guillen, M.F. (2016), 'Categorizing the liability of foreignness: Ownership, location, and internalization-specific dimensions', *Global Strategy Journal*, 6(4): 309–29.

Ziegler, R., Balzac-Arroyo, J., Hölsgens, R., Holzgreve, S., Lyon, F., Spangenberg, J.H. and Thapa, P.P. (2022), 'Social innovation for biodiversity: A literature review and research challenges', *Ecological Economics*, 193: 107336.

Zorn, M.L., Norman, P., Butler, F.C. and Bhussar, M. (2017), 'If you think downsizing might save your company, think again', *Harvard Business Review*, 26 April, (https://hbr.org/2017/04/if-you-think-downsizing-might-save-your-company-think-again).

Zsolnai, L. (2019), 'Responsible leadership and reasonable action'. In M. Chatterji and L. Zsolnai (eds), *Ethical leadership: Indian and European spiritual approaches*, London: Palgrave Macmillan.

Zsolnai, L. (2022), 'Spiritual turn in business and management'. In S. Mukherjee and L. Zsolnai (eds), *Global perspectives on Indian spirituality and management*, Singapore: Springer.

Zyglidopoulos, S.C. (2002), 'The social and environmental responsibilities of multinationals: Evidence from the Brent Spar case', *Journal of Business Ethics*, 36(1/2): 141–51.

INDEX

Page numbers in *italics* refer to tables, those in **bold** indicate boxes.